PUBLICATIONS

OF THE

NAVY RECORDS SOCIETY

Vol. 171

THE POSTWAR FLEET
VOLUME 1, 1944–1950

The Navy Records Society was established in 1893 for the purpose of printing unpublished manuscripts and rare works of naval interest. The Society is open to all who are interested in naval history, and any person wishing to become a member should either complete the online application form on the Society's website, www.navyrecords.org.uk, or apply to the Hon. Secretary, email address honsec@navyrecords.org.uk.

Subscriptions should be sent to the Membership Secretary, 19 Montrose Close, Whitehill, Bordon, Hants, GU35 9RG.

Members are advised that the Annual General Meeting of The Navy Records Society takes place in London on a Wednesday in July. Members should consult the Society's website, www.navyrecords.org.uk, for more details.

THE POSTWAR FLEET

VOLUME 1, 1944–1950

Edited by

CAPTAIN JEREMY STOCKER, MA, Ph.D, RNR

PUBLISHED BY BOYDELL & BREWER
FOR THE NAVY RECORDS SOCIETY
2024

First published 2024

A Navy Records Society publication
Published by Boydell & Brewer Ltd
P0 Box 9, Woodbridge, Suffolk IP12 3DF, UK
and Boydell & Brewer Inc.
668 Mt Hope Avenue, Rochester, NY 14620–2731, USA
website: www.boydellandbrewer.com

ISBN 978-1-739-29641-4

A CIP catalogue record for this book is available from the British Library

Printed and bound in Great Britain by
TJ Books Limited, Padstow, Cornwall

THE COUNCIL
OF THE NAVY RECORDS SOCIETY
2023–24

PRESIDENT

Vice Admiral SIR ADRIAN JOHNS, K.C.B., C.B.E., K.St.J., A.D.C.

VICE PRESIDENTS

V. PRESTON, M.A., Ph.D.
C.S. BECK, M.A., Ph.D.
Professor R. HARDING, M.A., Ph.D., F.R.Hist.S.
P.B. HELLAWELL, M.A., Ph.D.

COUNCILLORS

Professor A.D. LAMBERT, M.A., Ph.D., F.R.Hist.S.
M. WILCOX, M.A., Ph.D.
L. HALEWOOD, B.A., M.A.
E. JONES, M.A., Ph.D.
Professor J. BEELER, A.B., M.A., M.L.I.S., Ph.D., F.R.Hist.S.
J. DANCY, M.A., D.Phil.
C. LAMBERT, B.A., M.A., Ph.D.
M. SCHOTTE, A.B., M.A., Ph.D.
Professor E. CHARTERS, M.A., D.Phil., F.R.Hist.S.
N. BLAKE, M.A.
M. DUFFY, M.A., Ph.D., F.R.Hist.S.
Professor C.M. BELL, M.A., Ph.D.
T. DOUGALL, M.A., Ph.D.
M. CRUMPLIN, F.R.C.S., F.R.Hist.S., F.I.N.S., F.H.S.
A. BOND, M.A.
L.-J. GILES, B.A., Res.M., A.F.H.E.A.
M. WILLIS, B.A., M.A.
N. BLACK, M.A., Ph.D.
Capt. K. ROWLANDS, Ph.D., R.N.
B. REDDING, M.A., Ph.D.
B. PAPPALARDO, B.A.
M. HEASLIP, M.A., Ph.D., F.R.Hist.S.

HON. SECRETARY, A. PLUMBLY, B.A., M.A., A.C.A.

HON. TREASURER, P. NORTHCOTT, M.A.

GENERAL EDITOR, B. JONES, M.Phil., Ph.D.

MEMBERSHIP SECRETARY, Mrs. J. GOULD

ONLINE EDITOR, S. WILLIS, M.A., Ph.D., F.R.Hist.S

SOCIAL SECRETARY, Ms. K. JAMIESON

CONTENTS

ACKNOWLEDGEMENTS

I am grateful to the Publications Committee of the Navy Records Society for commissioning this volume, and to the General Editor Dr Ben Jones for his guidance. The staff of the National Archives at Kew are unfailingly knowledgeable and helpful, making every visit a pleasure. I am also in the debt of Stephen Prince and Edward Hampshire of the Naval Historical Branch in Portsmouth who kindly gave me access to some material, mainly for background, not held at Kew. Commander Alastair Wilson RN helped with some of the biographical details.

Crown copyright material from the National Archives has been reproduced by kind permission of the Stationery Office.

My inspiration for editing this volume was the late Professor Eric Grove's seminal work *Vanguard to Trident: British Naval Policy since World War II*. Eric was my PhD supervisor, my mentor and my friend. This volume is dedicated to his memory.

LIST OF ABBREVIATIONS

A/A	Anti-Aircraft
A & As	Alterations & Additions
ACNS	Assistant Chief of Naval Staff
ACNS(W)	ACNS (Weapons)
ACS	Aircraft Carrier Squadron
A/D	Air Direction
Adm	Admiral
AFD	Admiralty Floating Dock
AFO	Admiralty Fleet Order
AIO	Action Information Organisation
AoF	Admiral of the Fleet
APW	Armistice and Post War (Committee)
ARY	Admiralty Repair Yard
ASR	Air-Sea Rescue
A/S	Anti-Submarine
AU	All-up
AVA	A.V. Alexander
BB	Battleship
BD	Boom Defence
BPF	British Pacific Fleet
BYMS	British Yard Class Minesweeper
CA	Heavy Cruiser
CAG	Carrier Air Group
Capt	Captain
CAS	Chief of the Air Staff
CF	Coastal Forces
CIGS	Chief of the Imperial General Staff
CL	Light Cruiser
CoS	Chiefs of Staff
CTC	Commando Training Centre
CTE	Commando Training Establishment
CV	Aircraft Carrier
CVE	Escort Aircraft Carrier
CVL	Light Aircraft Carrier

DACR	Director of Airfields and Carrier Requirements
DAWT	Director of Air Warfare and Flying Training
DCNP	Deputy Chief of Naval Personnel
DD	Destroyer
DEMS	Defensively Equipped Merchant Ship
DLT	Deck Landing Training
DNC	Director of Naval Construction
DNAW	Director of Naval Air Warfare
DNOR	Director of Operational Requirements
DofD	Director of Dockyards
DofM	Director of Manning
DofP	Director of Plans
DPC	Defence Production Committee
DPS	Director of Personal Services
DTSD	Directorate of Tactical and Staff Duties
D/U	Date Uncertain
EI	East Indies
EinC	Engineer in Chief
EVT	Education and Vocational Training
FADE	Fleet Air Direction Escort
FBC	Future Building Committee
FBD	Fast Battery Drive
FC	Full Commission
FES	Far East Station
FO	Flag Officer
FOCRF	Flag Officer Commanding Reserve Fleet
FOMA	Flag Officer Malaya and Admiral Superintendent
FOSM	Flag Officer Submarines
FOSNI	Flag Officer Scotland & Northern Ireland
FOTS	Flag Officer Training Squadron
FP	Fishery Protection
FRU	Fleet Requirements Unit
HA	High Angle
HDML	Harbour Defence Motor Launch
HE	High Explosive
HO	Hostilities Only
HSTS	High Speed Target Ship
HTP	High Test Peroxide
JIC	Joint Intelligence Committee
JPS	Joint Planning Staff
JTWC	Joint Technical Warfare Committee
JWPS	Joint War Production Staff

IE	Initial Equipment (aircraft)
L of C	Lines of Communication
LA	Low Angle
LC	Landing Craft
LCA	Landing Craft Assault
LCG(L)	Landing Craft Gun (Large)
LCP(L)	Landing Craft Personnel (Large)
LCM	Landing Craft Mechanised
LCS(R)	Landing Craft Support (Rocket)
LCT(R)	Landing Craft Tank (Rocket)
LSD	Landing Ship Dock
LSI	Landing Ship Infantry
LST	Landing Ship Tank
M	Military Branch
MAP	Ministry of Aircraft Production
MFV	Motor Fishing Vessel
MGB	Motor Gun Boat
ML	Motor Launch
MMS	Motor Minesweeper
MOLCAB	Mobile Landing Craft Advanced Base
MONAB	Mobile Naval Air Base
MP	Manpower
MRS	Medium Range System
M/S	Minesweeper
MTB	Motor Torpedo Boat
MWT	Ministry of War Transport
NAAFI	Navy, Army, Air Force Institute
ND	Navigation & Direction
NLO	Naval Liaison Officer
NMM	National Maritime Museum
NS	National Service
OBB	Old Battleship
OBC	Old Battlecruiser
PG	Persian Gulf
PPO	Principal Personnel Officers
PR	Photo Reconnaissance
QF	Quick Firing
RA	Rear Admiral
RAN	Royal Australian Navy
RAPWI	Recovery Allied Prisoners of War and Internees
RCN	Royal Canadian Navy
RDU	Receipt & Despatch Unit

RIN	Royal Indian Navy
RML	Rescue Motor Launch
RNC	Royal Naval College
RNEC	Royal Naval Engineering College
RNTF	Royal Navy Torpedo Facility
RNZN	Royal New Zealand Navy
RRF	Revised Restricted Fleet
SACSEA	Supreme Allied Command, South East Asia
SDPC	Ship Design Policy Committee
SEAC	South East Asia Command
S/M	Submarine
SMBA	Special Military Branch Acquaint
SO	Senior Officer
TNA	The National Archives
TS	Transmitting Station
VAD	Voluntary Aid Detachment
VCNS	Vice Chief of Naval Staff
VE	Victory in Europe
VJ	Victory over Japan
W/T	Wireless Transmitter

KEY PERSONALITIES

Prime Minister		
10 May 1940	– 26 July 1945	Winston Churchill
26 July 1945	– 26 October 1951	Clement Attlee
Minister of Defence		
10 May 1940	– 26 July 1945	Winston Churchill
26 July 1946	– 20 December 1946	Clement Attlee
20 December 1946	– 28 February 1950	A.V. Alexander
28 February 1950	– 26 October 1951	Emanuel Shinwell
First Lord of the Admiralty		
11 May 1940	– 25 May 1945	A.V. Alexander
25 May 1945	– 26 July 1945	Brendan Bracken
3 August 1945	– 4 October 1946	A.V. Alexander
4 October 1946	– 24 May 1951	1st Viscount Hall
Parliamentary Secretary to the Admiralty		
3 April 1940	– 26 July 1945	Victor Warrender, 1st Baron Bruntisfield
26 July 1946	– 2 March 1950	John Dugdale
2 March 1950	– 26 October 1951	James Callaghan
First Sea Lord		
15 October 1943	– 24 May 1946	Admiral of the Fleet Sir Andrew Cunningham
24 May 1946	– 29 September 1948	Admiral of the Fleet Sir John Cunningham
29 September 1948	– 20 December 1951	Admiral of the Fleet the Lord Fraser of North Cape
Deputy First Sea Lord		
29 July 1942	– 26 May 1946	Admiral Sir Charles Kennedy-Purvis

Controller of the Navy

1 May 1942	– 24 September 1945	Admiral Sir Frederic Wake-Walker
1 December 1945	– 7 June 1949	Admiral Sir Charles Daniel
7 June 1949	– March 1953	Admiral Sir Michael Denny

Vice Chief of Naval Staff

8 June 1943	– 1 October 1945	Vice Admiral Sir Edward Neville Syfret
1 October 1945	– 13 October 1947	Vice Admiral Sir Rhoderick McGrigor
13 October 1947	– 30 November1949	Vice Admiral Sir John Edelsten
30 November 1949	– 7 October 1951	Vice Admiral Sir George Creasy

Director of Plans

6 March 1942	– 1 April 1944	Captain Charles Lambe RN
1 April 1944	– 9 January 1946	Captain Guy Grantham RN
9 January 1946	– January 1948	Captain John Stevens RN
January 1948	– 13 January 1950	Captain Thomas Brownrigg RN
14 January 1950	– April 1952	Captain R. Dymock Watson RN

Note: Some handover dates are inexact, as individuals were sometimes left to make their own arrangements.

GENERAL INTRODUCTION

The Royal Navy fleet that 'fought' much of the Cold War against the Soviet Union was largely the result of decisions made during, and immediately after, the Second World War. The flagship of the fleet that fought in the South Atlantic against Argentina in 1982, HMS *Hermes*, had been ordered in 1943 with war against Japan in mind.

> In 1945 the Royal Navy faced poverty, but it enjoyed a considerable wartime windfall in the shape of numerous new warships, particularly carriers, cruisers, destroyers and frigates. Its misfortune was that these ships had been designed very tightly in a weight-critical world.[1]

This 'windfall' comprised nearly 9,000 ships of all types, and a manpower strength of 790,000 officers and men, plus a further 74,000 women.[2] But much of this fleet was war-torn and facing rapid obsolescence. Even recently completed ships were somewhat outdated in the face of increasing submarine speeds, the greater potency of air attack and the as-yet little understood implications of atomic warfare.

The strategic situation was somewhat similar to that of 1919 after the previous world war. Britain faced near-bankruptcy, uncertain future relations with its wartime allies, and almost immediate demobilisation and retrenchment. It was not until the latter part of the period considered in this book that the Navy had any real basis on which to plan for the future as the Cold War crystallised, the nature of future requirements gradually became clearer and the feasible scale of provision for defence was established.

Until at least the end of 1943 the focus of British naval planning was, naturally, war against Germany and, increasingly, Japan. Defeat of the latter remained the priority right up to its surrender. But from early 1944 increasing attention was given to the size and shape of the postwar fleet, though other than reference to pre-war requirements there was little to guide Admiralty planners or the Government.

[1] Norman Friedman, 'Electronics and the Royal Navy' in Richard Harding (ed.), *The Royal Navy 1930–2000: Innovation and Defence* (Abingdon, 2005), p. 247.

[2] Desmond Wettern *The Decline of British Seapower* (London, 1982), p. 1.

Once peace returned the Admiralty had to face the twin, but irreconcilable, requirements of retrenchment and the emerging threat posed by Britain's wartime ally, the Soviet Union.

> After the defeat of the Axis, only two other Great Powers would remain; war with one of them was unthinkable, but with the other a conflict could not be ruled out.[1]

In the short term, the Navy also had to deal with a host of immediate postwar tasks, such as mine clearance and repatriation of prisoners of war. Beyond that, Britain and its navy still had huge, world-wide imperial commitments.

The years immediately after the end of the Second World War therefore saw some of the greatest and most rapid changes in the Service's history. Much of it was driven by short-term imperatives rather than longer-term strategic requirements. This volume deals with this period of rapid change and postwar adaptation. It begins in early 1944 when the War was still to be won but postwar requirements were starting to influence fleet planning. It concludes in mid-1950 when the outbreak of the Korean War in the Far East brought about a substantial re-think and an ambitious rearmament programme.

The volume is divided into four parts:

Part I covers the last 19 months of the War. During this period the defeat of Germany by mid-1945 seemed increasingly certain, especially after Allied forces became securely lodged ashore after D-Day. By this time the war at sea against Germany had largely been won already. The surrender of Japan just three months after Germany was not, however, foreseen until it actually happened. As late as July 1945 the War Cabinet and the Chiefs of Staff expected the war in the Far East to last well into 1946. The defeat of Japan would require a large-scale invasion of the Japanese Home Islands, to which Britain intended to contribute three Army divisions and a huge, largely carrier-based, fleet. Fleet planning during this period was therefore based on the imminent end of the war in Europe and the Atlantic but continuing operations in the Pacific, though with a growing eye on postwar (ie post-Far East war) requirements.

Part II deals with the immediate postwar period of retrenchment. The sudden end of the war against Japan occasioned by the use of atomic bombs against Hiroshima and Nagasaki in August 1945 brought about a rapid re-evaluation of the future fleet. The full scale of Britain's economic crisis was soon apparent to the recently elected Labour Government under

[1] Julian Lewis, *Changing Direction: British Military Planning for Post-war Strategic Defence, 1942–47* (London, 1988), p. 107.

Churchill's wartime deputy, Clement Attlee. There was therefore an urgent need to save money spent on the armed forces and, perhaps even more urgent, to release manpower for the rebuilding of the civilian economy.

Part III outlines the first attempts to devise a long-term plan for the future. It was sometimes referred to as the 'Nine-Year Plan' as it was intended to produce a modern fleet by 1957. This was the date which for planning purposes was assumed to be when war with the Soviet Union might become likely. There was, however, no single plan but rather a planning timescale. This planning period coincided with the full onset of the Cold War but also a renewed economic crisis which, from the outset, brought about the deferral of plans almost as soon as they were made.

Part IV has at its heart efforts to reconcile strategic requirements with economic constraints, resulting in the 'Revised Restricted Fleet'. This was still the basis of long-term fleet planning when the Cold War became, in part, hot. The outbreak of the Korean War in June 1950 was soon to overturn all the previous planning assumptions and bring about a substantial, if short-lived, rearmament programme. The start of a new war in the Far East marks the end of the period considered in this volume.

* * *

Documents are arranged in broadly chronological order, except where a number of documents relate to a single issue. For example, where a memorandum is followed by minutes of meetings at which the subject of the memorandum was discussed and decisions taken, the documents are kept together in order to improve the flow of the narrative. This may overlap chronologically with documents concerned with a different topic, which are presented either before or after those grouped together.

Most documents in this volume included their own title, including the large number of memoranda and minutes. In this case the original title is included together with the original document reference and its National Archives reference. Where the original did not contain a title, the subject of the document or the sender and recipient are indicated in *italics*. Many of the most important documents are very long and, with a summary, conclusions, annexes, appendices and recommendations, somewhat repetitive. Key extracts rather than the full text have therefore been selected to convey the essential points. Where text has been omitted, this is shown by … Similarly, several tables many of which set out the future size and shape of the Fleet as then planned have been simplified to include only those columns containing the pertinent details. For example, shipyard job numbers have been omitted.

The majority of documents originate in the Cabinet (or War Cabinet), The Defence Committee of the Cabinet, the Chiefs of Staff Committee, the Board of Admiralty and the Joint Planning Staff. The Admiralty's Director of Plans (a member of the Joint Planners) features heavily. In most cases these formal documents were the outcome of extensive preliminary staff work and earlier drafts. Space only permits the inclusion of the 'final' product, noting that in almost all cases this 'final' document was soon overtaken by a fresh round of discussions, decisions and a new 'final' document. The reader will be struck by how soon confident assumptions and firm decisions became outdated and, in effect, discarded.

* * *

The document selection begins with the Blue List (List of Ships Building) from January 1944, which summarises the huge 1942 and 1943 New Construction Programmes. Though neither Programme was ever completed, ships ordered in these years formed the basis of much of the postwar fleet. It is, in effect, an opening stocktake. The selection concludes with the Pink List of 6 June 1950, which gives a statement of the composition and disposition of the Fleet just prior to the start of the Korean War. It includes a list of ships building, production of a separate Blue List having ceased in March 1946. This Pink List provides a closing statement for the volume.

PART I

WARTIME PLANNING FOR THE POSTWAR FLEET, JANUARY 1944 – AUGUST 1945

The 'Blue List' (List of Ships Building) of January 1944 [1] provides a useful stocktake of the Navy's future plans at the point where serious consideration was starting to be given to the size and shape, not just of the fleet that would fight Japan in the Far East, but of the postwar Fleet. It includes the huge 1942 and 1943 building programmes and as-yet incomplete construction from earlier programmes. Of note, no battleships or cruisers had been ordered since 1941, types that had hitherto been the mainstay of the Fleet. This was because priority had been accorded to aircraft carriers, escorts and landing ships, both because they were more pressing requirements and because they could be completed more quickly.

Part V of the Blue List is especially useful as it summarises building programmes since 1939 as well as the future dates for completion of ships still under construction. During 1944 the Admiralty expected to commission 17 carriers, 51 destroyers, 129 smaller escorts, 36 submarines and 38 minesweepers, but just 3 cruisers (one of which was immediately transferred to the Royal Canadian Navy). The figures for 1945 were similar, except that there were to be very few additional sloops, frigates and corvettes as by then the focus would firmly be on operations against Japan for which there was little requirement for convoy escorts.

At the beginning of 1944 the Director of Plans (DofP), Captain Charles Lambe, was working on that year's building programme [2–5] looking as far ahead as 1949 for the future strength of the RN and making assumptions about the likely loss-rate of ships whilst hostilities continued. He drew attention to the dislocation to existing plans already being caused by the construction of landing vessels (which were ordered under supplementary construction programmes, not the annual programmes). A paper for the Future Building Committee noted the need to rationalise the number of different gun types in service [6].

The 1944 Construction Programme [7] was approved by the Cabinet in May [8]. A new start was to be made on building battleships and cruisers, though at the cost of deferring large carriers already authorised. A stated postwar requirement for 12 battleships seems to be have been based on little more than this being the pre-war number (excluding battlecruisers), and this was not the last time that, given huge uncertainty about the future, pre-1939 figures for ships and manpower were taken as a starting-point. The needs of the war against Japan were reflected in the numbers of large destroyers and submarines [22 and 20, respectively], while new large gun-armed ships (battleships and cruisers) which took longer to build were to meet postwar requirements.

At the same time that the 1944 Programme was approved, the Admiralty Board considered a paper on the postwar Fleet [9, 10]. The paper's emphasis on control of sea communications reflected experience in

Atlantic and Mediterranean waters more than imminent operations against the shore in Normandy and, later, the Far East. It argued for that perennial objective, a 'balanced fleet' comprising all existing elements. It claimed to be based on wartime experience but didn't refer to any specific analysis. The statement that 'The basis of the strength of the Fleet is the battleship' certainly did not reflect recent experience nor the requirement for carriers and long-range submarines for the war against Japan. In arguing the deterrent value of a strong fleet, the paper was on firmer ground. Including ships in reserve and refit, the postwar requirement (including Dominion navies) was for 12 battleships, 24 carriers, 50 cruisers (again, the pre-war number), over 300 destroyers and escorts, and 86 submarines.

This fleet would require 170,000 officers and men, a substantial *increase* over the pre-war total as it now included the entire Fleet Air Arm. The financial cost and manpower requirement of this huge force was set out by the Controller [11], together with what today would be called a 'drum-beat' of future construction. The Director of Plans noted that the proposed Fleet would require more men than hitherto assumed [12].

After the successful Normandy landings, although victory over Germany was confidently expected sometime in 1945, the war against Japan was anticipated to last until at least 1946 or possibly 1947. Accordingly, the Chiefs of Staff had to consider the requirements of post-conflict reconstruction and re-building the peacetime economy at home while prosecuting the war in the Far East. Releasing manpower for the former whilst meeting the needs of the latter presented a major planning task [13, 14].

These early attempts to fashion the postwar Navy, like many others to follow, never came to fruition. Each plan, whether formally approved or not, was soon overtaken by events, changing assumptions and, increasingly, financial realities.

In August DofP (by now Captain Guy Grantham) produced an interesting paper on small cruisers, highlighting a substantial postwar shortage of numbers [15]. Though his ideas were not taken up [16], proposals for ships in the 5,000–7,000 ton range have been a persistent theme right up to the present day.

The Board had to consider the priority to be accorded warship construction against the needs of the Mercantile Marine [17]. It was decided to press on with all warships which could be completed by the end of 1946, both for the war against Japan and for the postwar Fleet. Vessels that could not be completed by then would take second priority to merchant construction.

By the end of 1944 attention was turning to the ability of existing carriers, in service and under construction, to operate the new, heavier aircraft soon to enter service [18]. The size and capacity of aircraft lifts was a particular concern and it was apparent that most ships, either recently completed or soon to complete, would already need modification. That the Navy was acquiring aircraft that its new carriers could not operate is striking, and prompted a discussion on the size of future fleet carriers [21]. Consideration was also given to postwar aircraft requirements, assuming that the war with Japan would be over by the end of 1946 [19, 20]. A total of 800 carrier-borne types would be required, plus over 200 shore-based support aircraft. Front-line types would be replaced every two years, perhaps reflecting wartime practice but wholly unrealistic under peacetime conditions and financial limitations.

At the start of 1945 attention returned to manpower requirements after the defeat of Germany but with war against Japan still in progress [22]. Continued pressure to reduce Service manpower, even while fighting was still taking place in the Far East, meant that the Navy's requirement was now stated to be 665,000 though this was not as large a reduction as that sought by the Prime Minister. The Fleet Air Arm and its carriers would account for over 200,000 men alone. Discussion of manpower numbers (there would be many more in the next few years) inevitably led to estimates of the size and shape of the Fleet itself. The British Pacific Fleet alone would still comprise four battleships, 16 cruisers, 19 carriers, 48 destroyers, 53 escorts and 40 submarines plus, for the first time in the RN's history, a substantial Fleet 'Train'. Other ships were required for postwar duties at home, in the Mediterranean and elsewhere. 'Fleet and Auxiliary' naval bases would be required almost everywhere between Scotland and Australia – a total of 41 dockyards and other bases. This was a 'postwar' (Europe) but 'wartime' (Far East) fleet in transition.

In February it was time to consider the 1945 Construction Programme [23]. DofP's proposal tried to balance the need for merchant ship construction with the Navy's need for modern units in the postwar fleet, especially as many large units had been deferred in favour of more immediate requirements. In the light of expected losses in the Far East, Grantham urged the laying-down of *Lion*-class battleships and *Gibraltar*-class fleet carriers in order to maintain the strength of the postwar fleet. For the first time a large list of cancellations was included in his paper, principally submarines and landing craft. There was also mention of a new design of escort to be built in both anti-submarine and anti-aircraft versions, which would eventually lead to the Types 12, 41 and 61 classes of frigates in the1950s.

The following month DofP undertook a useful stocktake of efforts so far to plan the postwar Fleet [24]. He set out a number of questions that would need to be addressed in the years to come. By 1950, the end-date for this volume, few of them had been satisfactorily resolved.

By the time the Cabinet considered the 1945 Programme in June [35] it had been scaled back considerably. Germany had surrendered and it was apparent that the war against Japan would be prosecuted only by ships already in commission or under construction and in fact existing programmes were also to be reduced. It is worth emphasising, however, that each year's construction programme only included new ships to be authorised (and perhaps not even ordered) during the year in question. At any one time the list of ships actually under construction would be very much greater, consisting of vessels ordered under several preceding construction programmes. So, for example, in 1945 just £5 million was to be accounted for by '1945' ships and £145 million by ships from earlier programmes.

Having previously considered the future of cruisers and carriers, in April DofP turned his attention to battleships [25]. He came to a similar conclusion to that he had reached earlier in relation to cruisers – that numbers were more important than the size of individual ships. His argument in favour of 'quick hitting and manoeuvrability' rather than protection was an echo, probably unconsciously, of Jackie Fisher's advocacy of the battlecruiser 40 years earlier. The matter was taken further the following month by the report of the Battleship Committee set up under Rear Admiral Servaes to examine the best size and armament for future ships [26]. Their conclusion was similar to Grantham's – that size needed to be kept under control (the existing Staff Requirement could have resulted in a ship as large as 72,000 tons) – but that the answer was a trade-off between armament and protection. In reality, no new battleships were built after *Vanguard* was commissioned soon after the end of the War and existing ships saw little postwar service.

In April and May 1945, the Plans Division produced a seminal document on the postwar Navy [27, 28]. It was a back-to-first-principles paper which identified a number of basic assumptions about the postwar world and the Navy's roles in both peace and war. Its aim was to provide a basis for all postwar planning but reads as much as a piece of advocacy, which perhaps was its other purpose. The emphasis was again on the control of sea communications and all the fleet elements required to achieve it. The need for a large Reserve, of both ships and personnel, was clearly stated.

A few days after the surrender of Germany, the Treasury Permanent Secretary issued instructions to all Government departments to rescind or restrict wartime financial delegations [29]. This was a timely foretaste of the financial constraints that were soon to dominate defence planning. Also of increasing importance was the need to limit the manpower demands of the Services in order to release men for the civilian economy, even while the war with Japan continued [30–33]. A postwar requirement of 170,000 for the Navy was re-stated, noting that the number of long-service (ie Regular) personnel was now below the pre-war total of 133,000.

Planning for the postwar Fleet was not confined to numbers and types of ships, manpower and money. Technical developments and the future of warfare also figured, notably in a major report by an 'ad hoc' committee chaired by Sir Henry Tizard, later the Ministry of Defence's Chief Scientific Advisor.[1] Established in November 1944, the Joint Technical Warfare Committee reported in June 1945 [34]. A matter of weeks before Hiroshima Tizard speculated about the future of atomic energy. In relation to war at sea, the Tizard Report forecast longer-range, faster aircraft and submarines, and re-emphasised the importance of protected convoys. The future potential of guided missiles was noted. But overall, and of course with the benefit of hindsight, it was a somewhat conservative view of likely changes over the next 20 years – essentially more, but better or more alarming, of the same.

In June and July, the Admiralty considered the future of the submarine force [36, 37], still dominated by the needs of the war against Japan but with reference to peacetime requirements. This was a stocktake and rationalisation exercise, in which older or damaged boats would be discarded and some new construction suspended, possibly to be cancelled later.

Following the dropping of the atomic bombs on Hiroshima and Nagasaki, Japan announced its surrender on 15 August. 'It was an abrupt and unexpected event.'[2] This overturned all previous assumptions about the likely timescale for the end of the war in the Far East, and with it the basis on which fleet planning had been taking place.

[1] For a good discussion of the Joint Techical Wafare Committee and the Tizard Report, see Lewis, *Changing* Direction, Chapter 5.

[2] George Moore, *Building for Victory: The Warship Building Programmes of the Royal Navy 1939–1945* (Gravesend, 2003), p. 122.

1. *Blue List, 7 January 1944*

[NHB] 11 January 1944

PART I
SHIPS BUILDING FOR THE ROYAL NAVY[1]

Type and Class	Year of Com-pletion	Month of Completion	Name	Where Building	Remarks
Battleships	–	Suspended	Lion	Tyne	
Lion Class	–	Suspended	Temeraire	Birkenhead	
	–	Suspended	Conqueror	Clyde	
	–	Suspended	Thunderer	Clyde	
Vanguard Class	1945	December	Vanguard	Clyde	42,300 tons 8 – 15″, 16 – 5.25″
Aircraft Carriers					
Fleet Class	1944	30 March	Implacable	Clyde	23,000 tons 16 – 4.5″
Ark Royal Class	1946	March	Audacious	Belfast	
	1946	October	Ark Royal	Birkenhead	31,600 tons
	1947	May	Eagle	Newcastle	8 twin 4.5″
	–	–	Africa	Clyde	
Gibraltar Class	1948	February	Gibraltar	Newcastle	
	–	–	Malta	Clyde	
	–	–	New Zealand	Birkenhead	
Colossus Class	1944	August	Colossus	Newcastle	
	1944	October	Glory	Belfast	
	1944	December	Vengeance	Tyne	
	1944	December	Venerable	Birkenhead	
	1945	January	Edgar	Newcastle	
	1945	March	Mars	Barrow	
	1945	March	Warrior	Belfast	
	1945	May	Theseus	Clyde	
	1945	June	Triumph	Barrow	14,000 tons
	1945	June	Ocean	Clyde	
	1945	August	Majestic	Barrow	
	1945	August	Magnificent	Belfast	
	1945	August	Terrible	Plymouth	
	1945	November	Hercules	Newcastle	
	1945	November	Powerful	Belfast	
	1946	January	Leviathan	Tyne	
Light Fleet Carriers	1946	July	Elephant	Barrow	
	1946	August	Albion	Tyne	
	1946	November	Monmouth	Clyde	
	1947	January	Polyphemus	Devonport	
	1947	February	Bulwark	Belfast	

[1] Some details have been omitted or simplified. Only Parts I & V are reproduced.

	1947	April	Arrogant	Tyne	
	1947	September	Centaur	Belfast	
	1947	December	Hermes	Birkenhead	
Escort Carriers					
British (Audacity Class)	1944	9 February	Campania	Belfast	15,000 tons
American (Smiter Class)	1943	9 Dec	Begum	Tacoma	
	1943	2 Dec	Empress	Tacoma	
	1943	2 Dec	Shah	Tacoma	
	1943	18 Dec	Nabob	Tacoma	
	1943	31 Dec	Premier	Tacoma	
	1944	15 Jan	Speaker	Tacoma	
	1944	29 Jan	Arbiter	Tacoma	
	1944	31 Jan	Queen	Tacoma	
	1944	15 Feb	Ruler	Tacoma	
	1944	14 Mar	Rajah	Tacoma	
	1944	30 Mar	Puncher	Tacoma	
	1944	30 Mar	Smiter	Tacoma	
	1944	31 Mar	Trouncer	Tacoma	
	1944	15 May	Reaper	Tacoma	
	1944	15 Jun	Ranee	Tacoma	
	1944	30 Jun	Thane	Tacoma	
Cruisers					
Minotaur Class (Modified Fiji)	1944	End Mar	Swiftsure	Newcastle	8,000 tons
	1944	Early Sep	Minotaur	Belfast	9 – 6″
	1945	Jul	Bellerophon	Clyde	10 – 4″
Tiger Class (Improved Fiji)	1944	Mid Oct	Superb	Tyne	
	–	D/U	Defence	Clyde	8,000 tons
		Aug	Blake	Clyde	9 – 6″
		Sep	Hawke	Portsmouth	10 – 4″
		Deferred	Tiger	Newcastle	
Fast Minelayers					
Abdiel Class	1944	31 Jan	Apollo	Tyne	2,650 tons 4 – 4″
Destroyers					
Saumarez Class	1944	March	Shark	Clyde	1,710 tons, 4 – 4″
Troubridge Class	1944	10 Jan	Terpsichore	Dumbarton	1,710 tons, 4 – 4″
Ulster Class	1943	20 Dec	Urania	Barrow	1,710 tons, 4 – 4″
	1944	31 Jan	Ursa	Southampton	
	1944	21 Feb	Undaunted	Birkenhead	
Valentine Class	1944	17 Feb	Valentine	Clyde	1,710 tons, 4 – 4″
	1944	14 Feb	Vixen	Cowes	
	1944	End April	Volage	Cowes	
Wager Class	1944	31 Jan	Wakeful	Clyde	
	1944	Feb	Wizard	Barrow	
	1944	End Feb	Wager	Clyde	1,710 tons, 4 – 4″
	1944	April	Whelp	Tyne	
	1944	April	Wessex	Clyde	

	1944	May	Wrangler	Barrow	
	1944	June	Whirlwind	Tyne	
Zambesi Class	1944	Early April	Myngs	Tyne	
	1944	Early May	Zephyr	Tyne	
	1944	End May	Zambesi	Birkenhead	
	1944	June	Zealous	Birkenhead	1,730 tons
	1944	June	Zest	Southampton	4 – 4.5″
	1944	July	Zodiac	Southampton	1 – 4″
	1944	Aug	Zebra	Dumbarton	
	1944	Oct	Zenith	Dumbarton	
Caesar Class	1944	Early April	Caprice	Clyde	
	1944	Early May	Cassandra	Clyde	
	1944	June	Cambrian	Greenock	1,710 or
	1944	Early July	Caesar	Clyde	1,730 tons
	1944	July	Cavalier	Cowes	4 – 4.5″
	1944	Aug	Cavendish	Clyde	1 – 4″
	1944	Oct	Carysfort	Cowes	
	1944	Nov	Carron	Clyde	
Chequers Class	1944	June	Chevron	Clyde	
	1944	Sep	Cheviot	Clyde	
	1944	Oct	Chaplet	Southampton	
	1944	Dec	Charity	Southampton	1,710 or
	1945	March	Chequers	Clyde	1,730 tons
	1945	April	Childers	Dumbarton	4.5″
	1945	June	Chivalrous	Dumbarton	
	1945	Early June	Chieftain	Greenock	
Cossack Class	1944	June	Cockade	Clyde	
	1944	Sept	Comet	Clyde	
	1944	Sept	Cossack	Tyne	
	1944	Dec	Constance	Tyne	1,710 or
	1944	End Dec	Contest	Cowes	1,730 tons
	1945	Feb	Consort	Clyde	4.5″
	1945	Feb	Comus	Southampton	
	1945	April	Corso	Southampton	
Crescent Class	1944	Nov	Croziers	Clyde	
	1944	Early Dec	Crescent	Clyde	
	1945	Jan	Crusader	Clyde	
	1945	Jan	Crystal	Clyde	1,710 or
	1945	March	Craccher	Cowes	1,730 tons
	1945	End May	Creole	Cowes	4.5″
	1945	Early Oct	Cretan	Clyde	
	1946	End Jan	Crown	Clyde	
1943 Design Weapon Class	1945	June	Battleaxe	Glasgow	
	1945	End Aug	Tomahawk	Cowes	
	1945	Sept	Broadsword	Glasgow	
	1945	Nov	Sword	Cowes	
	1945	Nov	Crossbow	Southampton	
	1945	Dec	Cutlass	Glasgow	
	1946	End Jan	Musket	Cowes	
	1946	Jan	Rifle	Dumbarton	
	1946	Feb	Culverin	Southampton	
	1946	Feb	Dagger	Glasgow	
	1946	April	Spear	Dumbarton	
	1946	April	Howitzer	Southampton	
	1946	June	Longbow	Southampton	

	–	–	Halberd	Greenock	
	–	–	Claymore	Greenock	
	–	–	Carronade	Greenock	
	–	–	Dirk	Greenock	
	–	–	Grenade	Greenock	
	–	–	Poniard	Greenock	
Battle Class	1944	April	Barfleur	Tyne	
	1944	End June	Armada	Tyne	
	1944	July	Trafalgar	Tyne	
	1944	Aug	Camperdown	Clyde	
	1944	End Aug	Solebay	Tyne	
	1944	Sept	Hogue	Birkenhead	
	1944	Oct	Finnisterre	Clyde	
	1944	End Oct	Saintes	Tyne	
	1944	Nov	Lagos	Birkenhead	
	1944	Dec	St. Kitts	Tyne	
	1945	Jan	Cadiz	Clyde	
	1945	Jan	Gravelines	Birkenhead	
	1945	March	St. James	Clyde	
	1945	March	Aisne	Newcastle	
	1945	March	Agincourt	Tyne	
	1945	March	Barrosa	Clyde	
	1945	March	Sluys	Birkenhead	
	1945	April	Gabbard	Tyne	2,315 or 2,325 tons 4.5″
	1945	May	Albuera	Newcastle	
	1945	May	Vigo	Clyde	
	1945	May	Alamein	Tyne	
	1945	June	Dunkirk	Clyde	
	1945	June	Namur	Birkenhead	
	1945	July	Belleisle	Clyde	
	1945	July	Corunna	Tyne	
	1945	Aug	Jutland	Tyne	
	1945	Aug	Navarino	Birkenhead	
	1945	Sept	Matapan	Clyde	
	1945	Sept	Malplaquet	Clyde	
	1945	Oct	Mons	Tyne	
	1945	Oct	San Domingo	Birkenhead	
	1945	End Oct	Oudenarde	Tyne	
	1945	Nov	Omdurman	Clyde	
	1945	Dec	Somme	Birkenhead	
	1945	Dec	Poitiers	Tyne	
	1946	Jan	River Plate	Tyne	
New Design	1946	Jan	Vimiera	Birkenhead	
	1946	Feb	Waterloo	Clyde	
	1946	March	St. Lucia	Clyde	
	1946	April	Trincomalee	Clyde	
	1946	June	Ypres	Clyde	
	1946		Talavera	Clyde	
Submarines					
"U" Class	1943 on	Dec on	36 boats (8 unnamed)	Barrow (15) Newcastle (21)	545 tons 1 – 3″ gun 4 21″ tubes

"S" Class	1944 – 1945	Jan – April	21 boats	Chatham (1) Clyde (6) Birkenhead (14) Barrow (13) Chatham (3)	715 tons 1 – 3″ gun 7 21″ tubes
"T" Class	1943 – 1945	Oct – April	24 boats	Devonport (4) Portsmouth (4) Barrow (20) Birkenhead (11) Chatham (2) Clyde (3)	1,090 tons 1 – 4″ gun 11 21″ tubes
"A" Class	1945 – 1946	April on	46 boats	Devonport (2) Portsmouth (2) Walker (6)	1,090 tons 1 – 4″ gun 9 21″ tubes
Sloops					
Modified Black Swan Class	1944 – 1946	Feb on	14 ships Plus 3 'projected'	Bowling (1) Chatham (4) Clyde (1) Dumbarton (6) Southamp. (2)	1,375 tons 6 – 4″
Frigates					
River Class	1943 – 1944	Dec on	13 ships	Various	1,365 tons 1 – 4″
Loch Class (British)	1944 – 1945	Feb – Jan	59 ships	Various	
Captain Class	1943 – 1944	Dec – Feb	23 ships	Massachusetts	1,600 tons 3 – 3″
Frigates Maritime Commission	1943 – 1944	Nov – Mar	20 ships	Providence RI	2,318 tons 3 – 3″
Corvettes					
Flower Class	1944	Jan – Mar	3 ships	Clyde	900 tons 1 – 4″
Castle Class	1943 – 1944	Dec – Oct	27 ships	Various	1,010 tons 1 – 4″
Minesweepers					
Algerine Class	1943 on	Nov on	67 ships	21 in UK 46 in Canada	850 tons 1 – 4″

PART V
SUMMARY OF SHIPS BUILT AND BUILDING FOR THE ROYAL NAVY AT HOME AND ABROAD

Class of Ship	No Building at the Outbreak of War	No. Laid Down since the Outbreak of War	Total of II and III	No. Completed to Date	No. yet to Complete	No. Lost during War (New Ships from IV)
Battleships	7	3	10	5	1 (4 suspended)	1
Aircraft Carriers	6	31	37	5	32	0
Escort Carriers	–	42	42	25	17	3
Monitors	–	2	2	2	0	0
Cruisers	19	16	35	27	8	6
Fast Minelayers	4	2	6	5	1	2
Destroyers	52	245	297	181	116	34
Submarines	12	227	239	112	127	36
Sloops	4	29	33	19	14	1
Frigates	–	207	207	91	115	0
Corvettes	3	183	186	152	34	18
Gunboats	3	0	3	3	0	1
Depot Ships	3	1	4	4	0	1
Minesweepers	10	188	198	126	72	6
Trawlers	18	218	236	202	34	19

YEARLY COMPLETION OF SHIPS FOR THE ROYAL NAVY

Type and Class	1943	1944	1945	1946	1947	1948	Date uncertain	Suspend -ed
Battleships								
Lion Class	–	–	–	–	–	–	–	4
Vanguard Class	–	–	1	–	–	–	–	–
Aircraft Carriers								
Fleet Class	–	1	–	–	–	–	–	–
Ark Royal Class	–	–	–	2	1	–	1	–
Gibraltar Class	–	–	–	–	–	1	2	–
Light Fleet Class	–	–	–	3	5	–	–	–
Colossus Class	–	4	11	1	–	–	–	–

Escort Carriers								
Audacity Class	–	1	–	–	–	–	–	–
Smiter Class	5	11	–	–	–	–	–	–
Cruisers								
Minotaur Class	–	2	1	–	–	–	–	–
Tiger Class	–	1	3	–	–	–	1	–
Fast Minelayers								
Abdiel Class	–	1	–	–	–	–	–	–
Destroyers								
Saumarez Class	–	1	–	–	–	–	–	–
Troubridge Class	–	1	–	–	–	–	–	–
Ulster Class	1	2	–	–	–	–	–	–
Valentine Class	–	3	–	–	–	–	–	–
Wager Class	–	7	–	–	–	–	–	–
Zambesi Class	–	8	–	–	–	–	–	–
Caesar Class	–	8	–	–	–	–	–	–
Chequers Class	–	4	4	–	–	–	–	–
Cossack Class	–	5	3	–	–	–	–	–
Crescent Class	–	2	5	1	–	–	–	–
Weapon Class	–	–	6	7	–	–	6	–
Battle Class	–	10	25	7	–	–	–	–
Submarines								
U Class	1	11	–	–	–	–	24	–
S Class	–	15	6	–	–	–	–	–
T Class	5	10	4	–	–	–	5	–
A Class	–	–	24	7	–	–	15	–
Sloops								
Modified Black Swan	–	8	3	–	–	–	3	–
Frigates								
River Class	1	11	–	–	–	–	1	–
Loch Class	–	58	1	–	–	–	–	–
Captains	12	11	–	–	–	–	–	–
Maritime Commission	8	12	–	–	–	–	–	–
Corvettes								
Flower Class	–	3	–	–	–	–	–	–
Castle Class	1	26	–	–	–	–	–	–
Minesweepers								
Algerine Class	2	12	7	–	–	–	–	–
Canadian Algerine	–	21	–	–	–	–	25	–
American AM & BAM	–	5	–	–	–	–	–	–
Trawlers								
Isles Class	1	21	8	–	–	–	1	–
Military Class	–	3	–	–	–	–	–	–

2. *Memorandum by Director of Plans*

[ADM 205/36] [undated: Dec 1943 or Jan 1944]

FUTURE BUILDING COMMITTEE
1944 NEW CONSTRUCTION PROGRAMME

Review of Fleet Strength

In Appendix A, DofP has endeavoured to show the estimated strength of the British Fleet at the beginning of each year allowing for new construction already laid down or approved to be laid down … From the table it can be seen that the maximum strength of the Fleet based on present programmes is not likely to exceed the following:–

		January 1944	January 1947	January 1949
Fleet Carriers		5	7	13
Light Fleet Carriers		–	18	24
Escort Carriers		25	38	38
Battleships and Battlecruisers		10	11	11
Cruisers:-[1]	Heavy	10	10	10
	Medium	20	27	27
	Light	14	15	15
Destroyers		96	202	202
Submarines		74	185	185

2. Applying the average British annual loss rate these figures become:–

Fleet Carriers		5	3	6–7
Light Fleet Carriers*		–	14	16
Escort Carriers		25	35	33
Battleships and Battlecruisers		10	6	3–4
Cruisers:–	Heavy	10	6	4
	Medium	20	19–20	14–15
	Light	14	10	6–7
Destroyers		96	139	97
Submarines		74	125	85

* An arbitrary loss rate has been applied

NOTES:–

a) The actual operational strength, after allowing for damage repair, periodical refit and modernisation etc, would in general be not more than two-thirds of the totals shown above.

b) No allowance has been shown above for obsolescence and it must be pointed out that whilst the Carrier force is composed of modern ships,

[1] Definitions of Heavy, Medium and Light Cruisers are in WP(44)245, Doc. No. 7.

by 1947 the operational value of the following Battleships and Cruisers, if they have not become casualties, will be seriously impaired by age:–

NELSONs	(2)	20 years' service
QEs and RENOWN	(4)	32 years' service
LONDONs	(10)	19 years' service

3.

a) The construction of the following ships is suspended:–

4 Battleships
4 Cruisers, 8″
1 Cruiser (Fiji), 6″

b) The following ships have been approved in the 1941 and 1942 programmes but have not yet been ordered:–

3 Sloops

Proposals for 1944 New Construction Programme

It is customary to balance the proposals for any programme with the slips and facilities that are expected to become available within the 'programme' year (ie September 1944 to September 1945).

Due to the present overloaded state in the shipyards, resulting from supplementary programmes such as those for Transport Ferries and LCT, it is not yet possible to give any clear indication of the facilities that will become available.

It is therefore intended to point out the 'weak spots' in our future fleet strength and propose what might be the minimum programme required to meet new requirements and dangerous deficiencies:–

Aircraft Carriers

In 1942 and 1943 we embarked on programmes for the construction of:–

6 Fleet Carriers
24 Light Fleet Carriers
3 Escort Carriers

The need for these ships was justified, but the labour and facilities available for their construction within the forecast time are insufficient. It was estimated that the time to build would be 3½ years for Fleet carriers and 2½ years for Light Fleets. With the facilities available these periods are likely to be extended to 4 to 5 years and 2½ to 3 years respectively, if the full programmes are continued.

It is proposed that the AFRICA (repeat ARK ROYAL) and the 3 GIBRALTAR class Fleet Carriers, all of the 1943 programme, be suspended. The Light Fleet programme should be fully manned up with the labour released so as to maintain their dates of completion, if by this means we could ensure the earlier delivery of the full Light Fleet carrier programme essential to our participation in the Pacific War.

Battleships

The KING GEORGE V class took 4 years and 7 months to build. The VANGUARD, due to enter service in the latter half of 1945, is at present the only Battleship under construction.

The LION, TEMERAIRE, CONQUEROR and THUNDERER remain suspended from previous programmes.

Nine to twelve months would be required to prepare the plans and order the materials before laying down a Battleship approved in this programme and the earliest date of completion would therefore be late 1949 or early 1950.

It is clear from the forecast of our Fleet strength that we may have only 6 effective Battleships by the beginning of 1947, with the possibility of a further reduction to this number if the war in the Pacific should drag on beyond that date.

Viewing the balanced Fleet of the future (1947 and after), DofP considers that 6 is the minimum acceptable strength. Further, the replacement of the overage QEs cannot be delayed indefinitely.

Whatever place may ultimately be assigned to the Carrier in the hierarchy of sea power, it cannot usurp the essential function of the battleship. The SCHARNHORST action proved this, if proof was necessary. Nothing can alter the fact that at the end of the Japanese war the Americans will have many battleships, but the maritime British Empire will have very few and the Russians may be just starting to build. Unless, therefore, we make a start now rebuilding the Battle Fleet we shall in a few years have sold ourselves body and soul to countries who are likely enough to be potentially hostile. After the experience of the last twenty years, this is surely unthinkable.

Weighing the strategical arguments against the overload in the shipyards, DofP proposes that we should ask for the reinstatement of 2 LIONs at a priority which would allow the preliminary work to be progressed and berths reserved for their laying down.

Cruisers

In January 1947 it is estimated that we shall have 36 cruisers as against 44 at the present time. This reduction in strength was forecast, but in the 1943 programme it had to be accepted in order to build up our Carrier force.

Any Cruisers approved in the 1944 programme cannot complete until late in 1947. In order to maintain the balance of our forces in 1947 and to provide 'front line' replacements for the large proportion of old and battle-scarred Cruisers, DofP proposes that we should ask for approval to build 5 new Cruisers in this programme. This is no more than the annual loss rate experienced in the past four years of war.

Aircraft Maintenance

To maintain the efficiency of the aircraft in our carriers in the Pacific and Indian Ocean areas where this cannot be done from shore-based aerodromes, it is essential to provide the carrier force with Aircraft Maintenance ships. Draft specifications indicate that these ships will be about 17,000 tons displacement. It has been estimated that they are likely to take some 17 to 20 months to build, though this is considered by DNC to be an underestimate.

As these ships will be required at the earliest possible date their laying down will depend on how soon the specifications and designs can be completed.

It is proposed to include 2 of these ships in the 1944 programme and, as soon as sufficient information is available, that consideration should be given to a temporary suspension of 2 of the 1943 Light Fleet Carriers, if it should prove otherwise impossible to build these ships in a reasonable time. This consideration cannot be given if an arbitrary cut in the 1943 Light Fleet Carrier programme is ordered by the Prime Minister.

Fast Fleet Oilers

To provide the necessary mobility, Fast tankers are required to operate with the Fleet. We have already asked for the assignment or loan of such ships from the US Navy, who have built tankers to meet this requirement, but a polite refusal has indicated that they have only sufficient to meet their own needs.

These ships will also be required at as an early date as possible. It is proposed to ask for the construction of 2 Fast Tankers.

Destroyers

The continual demand throughout the war for more destroyers to operate with the Fleet and carry out the many tasks assigned to these ships is sufficient background to ask for the maximum number that can be laid down in the 1944 programme. These should complete in the second half of 1946 and first half of 1947.

It is proposed to ask for the construction of about 14 Battle class and 9 Weapons which it is believed will be the maximum constructional capacity. This may well be less when the full effect of the Transport Ferry programme on other construction is assessed.

Submarines

Our deficiency lies in long range submarines. On present programmes the construction of long-range A class submarines is limited to a total of 46. Estimated losses must be deducted from this number.

It is therefore proposed to ask for the construction of the maximum number of A class submarines which it is believed will amount to a total of about 20. These would be expected to complete in the latter half of 1946 and through 1947.

Escort Vessels

a) Frigates and Corvettes

It is not proposed to ask for the construction of any further Frigates or Corvettes.

b) Sloops

It is proposed to ask for the construction of one sloop of the Modified Black Swan class in addition to the 3 still remaining to be ordered as approved in the 1941 and 1942 programmes. It is considered most desirable to continue the construction of this class of ship, which affords most valuable AA protection in escort work.

Fleet Minesweepers

No further vessels of this type are at present required.

Small Vessel Construction

Covering:– A/S and A/S M/S Trawlers
Motor Minesweepers
Boom defence vessels
Boom gate vessels
Cable ships
Salvage vessels
Wreck dispersal vessels
Ocean going tugs

Present programmes should cover our requirements in these types of vessels, notwithstanding heavy losses resulting from special operations. It is not therefore intended to ask for construction of any of these types in the present programme. Any unlikely heavy losses will be made good, as and when they occur, in supplementary programmes.

Coastal Force Craft

These craft are at present under consideration in relation to the rationalisation of manpower and no clear estimate as to our future requirement can yet be made.

Fleet Attendant Tankers

Some 20 of our Fleet Attendant Tankers have been in service for 25 years. The gradual replacement of those tankers, approved by the Board in 1938, has been delayed due to the general scarcity of berths to meet all our wartime needs. While the commercial type of oiler can be used for Admiralty freighting purposes, special types are required for Fleet Attendance duties, with good manoeuvrability and capable of carrying in bulk furnace fuel, diesel oil and two grades of petrol.

With a special view to meeting our requirements when the Fleet is operating in Eastern waters, it is proposed to ask for the construction of:–

6 vessels of 1,500 tons (cargo capacity), 11 knots
6 vessels of 3,000 tons (cargo capacity), 13 knots

3. *Minutes of First Sea Lord's Meeting*

[ADM 205/36] 13 January 1944

1944 NEW CONSTRUCTION PROGRAMME

The First Sea Lord called a meeting … to discuss the 1944 New Construction Programme, Director of Plans' memorandum being used as a basis for discussion.

2. The following were present:–

Deputy First Sea Lord
Controller
Fifth Sea Lord
VCNS
ACNS(W)
DofP [*and others*]

3. General agreement with the Director of Plans' memorandum was expressed. The First Sea Lord said that if we thought only of wartime considerations, we were likely to be left with an inadequate postwar navy. It was very desirable that the Cabinet should lay down a policy on which to base our plans for a postwar navy. We would certainly require a navy after the war adequate to carry out our duties as a first-class maritime power. DofP was requested to include something to this effect when re-drafting his memorandum.[1]

4. In the subsequent discussion on the memorandum the following decisions were reached:–

(a) Battleships

Of the four battleships which remain suspended from previous programmes, it was decided to ask for two of them now to be proceeded with. ACNS(W) was requested to review the matter of main and secondary gun armament and forward his proposals.

(b) Aircraft Carriers

It was decided to postpone the building of two of the fleet carriers in the 1943 programme and to leave it to the Controller to proceed with the other two when he was satisfied that this would not interfere with the building of light fleets. It was thought unlikely

[1] The final draft of this memorandum, dated 19 Feb 1945, is reproduced as Doc. No. 23.

that we should be allowed to build more than four of the light fleets approved in the 1943 programme. It was decided, however, to make certain of obtaining eventually eight of these light fleets by putting the balance left over into the 1944 programme.

(c) Cruisers
It was decided to ask approval to build five new cruisers, the type of cruiser depending on what gun armament would be likely to be available. It was, however, decided that the cruisers should mount 6″ guns and that they should have a satisfactory HA armament.

(d) Aircraft Maintenance Ships
The Controller pointed out that the only way to get aircraft maintenance ships in time to satisfy our Pacific requirements was either to convert two of the 1942 light fleets now completing or to convert escort carriers. The Fifth Sea Lord was asked to examine this question and to forward his views as to how best the requirement could be met.

(e) Fast Fleet Oilers
The Controller stated that in normal circumstances our tanker tonnage is included in the merchant ship-building quota. He was asked to endeavour to arrange … to build fast fleet oilers in lieu of other tankers. The importance of this type of vessel was stressed and it was agreed that the Controller should aim at providing four of them.

(f) Destroyers
It was decided to ask for 24 destroyers. The type of destroyer and the proportion between large and medium types was left undecided. The First Sea Lord wished attention specially directed to providing the medium type with a heavier main armament than is present being considered for the 'Weapon' class.

(g) Submarines
It was decided to ask for 20 'A' class submarines. This was felt to be wise in view of the present high rate of sinkings. The rate at which these submarines would be built would be reviewed in the light of the war trend.

(h) Escort Vessels
It was decided not to ask for the construction of any further frigates or corvettes.

(i) Sloops
It was considered most desirable to continue the construction of this class of ship and the Controller was asked to consider whether we could increase the present proposal to construct one sloop.

(j) Fleet Minesweepers
It was agreed not to ask for the construction of any further vessels of this type.

(k) Small Vessel Construction
It was decided not to ask for the construction of any of these vessels in the present programme.

(l) Coastal Force Craft.
It was noted that the question of constructing more of these craft is at present under consideration.

(m) Fleet Attendant Tankers.
DofP was asked to reconsider the size, speed and number of this type of ship required.

...

4. *Director of Plans to First Sea Lord*[1]

[ADM 205/36] 27 January 1944

POST WAR FLEET

Copy to:– VCNS, DFSL

I understand you have been asked to have a preliminary talk with the Prime Minister about this.

2. The subject will inevitably be broached in the 1944 Building Programme paper, which the DFSL has agreed shall be taken by the Future Building Committee at their weekly meeting on Monday 7 February. That paper cannot be ready before then, because some of its essential components are to be discussed by the Committee tomorrow, e.g. the 5.25-inch cruiser v. the improved BELFAST, the armament of the new destroyers, 14″, 15″ or 16″ guns for the new LIONs etc.

3. But the outline of the 1944 Programme was submitted to you at your meeting on 13 January and had your provisional approval. The final paper will therefore be something on these lines:–

a) The 1944 Programme will only mature in time for the latter part of the war against Japan.
b) For this, a certain specified Fleet can be forecast, but in carriers the sky's the limit.
c) What survives of the 1944 Programme will become the basis in modern ships of the postwar Fleet.
d) For the strength of the postwar Fleet the paper can only make an arbitrary estimate. Anything we forecast can be shot down by

[1] Signed by Capt R.K. Dickson, Deputy Director of Plans.

"collective security" arguments and is little use until the major political questions are settled. But we shall put in for a reasonably balanced Fleet, based on modern ideas about aircraft carriers and divisional lifts. This will assume that at the Peace Conference we do not subscribe to the League of Nations, resurrected under another name. It will also assume that, for the present, we do not contemplate building against the USA, but that the British Empire must be prepared to defend itself at sea against any other combination of Powers.

4. I suggest it should be put to the Prime Minister, in words of one syllable, that unless we make a start rebuilding the Battle Fleet now, we shall sell ourselves body and soul to the Americans the moment this war is over. Further, we may sell ourselves to the Russians too. They are our nearest and most dangerous neighbours. There is nothing to prevent them building a Battle Fleet, but they well hesitate to do so if they see from the beginning that we intend to keep ahead of them, and in fact have made a start. Everything earlier than the KING GEORGES will be obsolete after the war and anyway they may all be sunk. The Russians know this and are using their present opportunity to supply themselves with the cream of our technical experience.

5. No one knows better than the Prime Minister that:–

a) the Covenant of the League of Nations stands today as the most conspicuous monument to human folly in the history of the world, and why;
b) that force is the ultimate and inevitable arbiter of human affairs;
c) and therefore that, without a first-class Navy, a maritime Empire will have no bargaining power in a world which has learnt the lessons of 1919–1939.

Surely his political instinct will tell him that the experience of the ordinary Englishman in 1940 will demand that his rulers come down to earth this time?

5. *Plans Division Memorandum*

[ADM 1/17036] 19 February 1944

Future Building Committee
1944 New Construction Programme
INTRODUCTION

We have now reached the stage when we can look with confidence into the future, and although it may not be possible accurately to predict the end of hostilities, we can make reasonable assumptions as to the probable duration of the war for the purposes of planning our future naval strengths.

2. We have therefore assumed that any ships in our naval programmes that can complete before the end of 1947 should be regarded as having a possible influence on the outcome of the war. Those completing subsequent to 1947 have been regarded as part of what we consider necessary to ensure that the British Empire will be backed by a modern and balanced Navy, essential to her position as a First-Class Maritime Power in the postwar world.

3. We have made the further assumption that the manpower both for the Navy and for the facilities at present available to the shipbuilding industry will be increased rather than reduced subsequent to the defeat of Germany.

4. The 1943 New Construction programme has been gravely upset. Orders for LCT have had to be placed with warship building firms and we have had to embark on a large programme of LST; this has completely disorganised the programme as originally planned. The preparation of the Fleet Train has also to be met and a number of our older ships must be refitted and re-equipped to make them suitable for an intensified Naval and Air war in the Far East.

5. All these commitments throw a heavy load on the Shipbuilding industry and the full effect of the additional programmes referred to in para. 4 above cannot yet be accurately forecast. The following programme therefore shows adjustments to existing programmes as well as proposals for the construction of further units to bring our Fleet up to the required strength.

6. The need which we stressed in the 1942 and 1943 Programmes for the construction of a large number of Aircraft Carriers is still as urgent as ever and due consideration has been given to this in the following proposals. ...[1]

Aircraft Maintenance Ships

26. We have given much study to the problem of maintaining the aircraft to be carried by the large number of Aircraft Carriers due to enter service during the next 3 years, and after. In order to keep up an efficient frontline strength in aircraft and avoid undue wastage, maintenance facilities will be required at all advanced bases.

To provide such facilities on shore would require a vast organisation of equipment, personnel, and shipping to continually transport them to the forward areas as the advances develop. Having due regard

[1]Paragraphs 7–25 & 28 provide the draft for much of WP(44)245 (Doc. No. 7) and are therefore not reproduced here.

to both the mobility of the Fleet and the economy of effort necessary in the Eastern Theatre of operations we consider it necessary to provide Aircraft Maintenance ships to service the fully assembled aircraft. We further contemplate that these ships will constitute a permanent addition to the Fleet.

27. To provide some of these ships at the earliest possible date we therefore intend to complete 2 of the Light Fleet Carriers approved in the 1942 programme as Aircraft Maintenance Ships.[1]

...

Other Vessels

29. It is anticipated that existing approved programmes will cover our own needs in the types of vessels shown below, notwithstanding heavy losses … in the future.

Fleet Minesweepers
A/S, M/S and A/S M/S Trawlers
Motor Minesweepers
Boom Defence Vessels
Boom Gate Vessels
Small Cable Ships (Loop Layers)
Salvage Vessels
Wreck Dispersal Vessels
Ocean Going Tugs

30. It is not therefore proposed to ask for any more of these vessels in this programme. Approval will be sought in supplementary programmes to make good any unduly heavy losses if and when these should occur.

Fast Fleet Tankers and Small Fleet Attendant Oilers

31. It is customary for the Admiralty requirements for tanker tonnage to be provided out of Merchant Shipbuilding facilities. Special types, however, are required to serve the Fleet, possessing higher speeds and better manoeuvrability than the commercial types now under construction in the merchant ship programme. It takes longer to build such vessels and their construction will result in a slight loss to the overall tanker tonnage output for the year.

32. To provide the Fleet with the mobility that is necessary when operating at great distances from our bases fast tankers capable of operating at a speed of 20 knots are considered necessary.

[1] The *Colossus*-class light fleet carriers originally named *Edgar* and *Mars* were completed the following year as the maintenance carriers *Perseus* and *Pioneer.*

33. We therefore ask for approval that 2 Fast Tankers of 13,000-ton capacity, 20 knots speed, and of special design should be built as part of the Merchant Ship Programme at an early date.
34. The anticipated expansion of the Fleet and the opening up of bases in the Far East make it necessary to supplement our numbers and replace some of our small Fleet Attendant Tankers, some of which are now over 25 years old and incapable of ocean passage.
35. We ask for approval for the following Fleet Attendant Tankers, of special design, to be built as part of the Merchant Ship Programme as soon as possible:–

6 vessels of 1,500 capacity and speed of 11 knots
6 vessels of 3,000-ton capacity and speed of 14 knots.

6. *Future Building Committee Memorandum*

[ADM 116/5151] 21 March 1944

FB(44)12 POST WAR FLEET
Memorandum by ACNS(W)

Gun design and production with our existing resources is a lengthy business and we should therefore consider now whether any different type of gun and mounting is required. The fewer types we have in service the better.
2. The armament and general chacteristics of the Post War Fleet are more or less settled:–

Battleships	– 16″ guns HA/LA 5.25″ or 4.5″, still to be decided
Fleet and Light Fleet Carriers	– 4.5″ HA/LA
Large Cruisers	– 6″ LA and it is hoped 4.5″ HA/LA
Large Destroyers	– 4.5″ HA/LA

3. It is now for consideration whether we shall need
   (a) small cruisers
   (b) small destroyers and if so, what are their functions.
4. As regards small cruisers, there are three choices:
   (a) 5.25″ cruisers with four turrets of about 8,000 tons.
   (b) LA 6″ cruiser with 4″ HA of about the same size as the 5.25″ cruiser …
   (c) 4.5″ cruiser of about 6,000 tons …

5. As regards small destroyers, if these are required, it is suggested that their principal duty would be A/A and A/A escorts to the Fleet, but they would be called upon for a more offensive role in attacks on enemy convoys, inshore work and against E-boats. The choice of gun armament would seem to be between the 4″ twin and 4.5″ single.

7. *War Cabinet Memorandum*

[CAB 66/49] 1 May 1944

WP(44)245 NEW CONSTRUCTION PROGRAMME 1944
by First Lord of the Admiralty

The war has now reached the stage when we can reasonably claim to foresee that within a more or less short space of time the main naval effort will be directed against Japan. Indeed, we can now begin to look beyond the war against Japan, and so far as concerns naval construction we *must* look beyond it, for ships must now be ordered longer than ever in advance of the commencement of work, since the time needed to assemble materials has become progressively longer as general production planning has grown more complex. The programme set out below, therefore, takes account, firstly, of our estimated needs for finishing the war in the Far East, and, secondly, of those ships which will have to be ordered, though not necessarily laid down, in the coming financial year if we are to make a timely start in providing a balanced and up-to-date postwar Fleet. In drawing up these proposals it has been assumed, as there seems to be good reason for assuming, that after the defeat of Germany reductions in other war industries will make available increased supplies of manpower for providing the requirements of the Fleet.

2. The 1943 New Construction Programme has been gravely upset. Orders for LCTs have had to be placed with warship-building firms and we have had to embark on a large programme of LSTs; this has disorganised the programme as originally planned. The preparation of the Fleet Train has also to be fitted in and a number of our older ships must be refitted and re-equipped to make them suitable for an intensified Naval and Air war in the Far East.

Outline of Programme

3. The 1944 programme is as follows:–

Redesign the 4 "Lion" class battleships and proceed with the production of 6 Triple 16-inch Turrets of revised design.

5 6-inch Cruisers.
22 Fleet destroyers.
20 Submarines.

5 Sloops (including 3 authorised in previous programmes).
32 Small type MTBs
Miscellaneous small craft.
Landing ships and craft are dealt with in paragraph 23 below.

Aircraft Carriers

4. In the 1943 Programme the Cabinet approved the construction of four Fleet Carriers, *Malta, New Zealand, Africa* and *Gibraltar.* The plan for building these ships has been thrown out and delayed for the reasons given in paragraph 2 above. A still further interruption will occur if a follow-up programme of LSTs, has to be carried through in the United Kingdom. It would, in any case, not be possible to build all these four ships without prejudicing capacity which will be necessary for the proposed Battleships. The first two of these Fleet Carriers will not be laid down until some date in the first half of 1945 and it is proposed to postpone the laying-down of the other two in order to leave the way clear for laying down two Battleships as soon as the state of the design works enables this to be done.

5. Of the eight Light Fleet Carriers included in the 1943 Programme (which will be larger and faster than those of the 1942 Programme and Supplementary Programme) only four are at present being actively progressed. The need for a large number of aircraft carriers is, however, still great and on this ground, there is every reason for building the remaining four of these vessels. It must be recognised, however, that forthcoming operations may result in such heavy losses in cruisers that additional cruiser construction, over and above that proposed in this paper, may have to take priority even over the building of more aircraft carriers, important though these are. If this possibility is realised, I would submit revised proposals to the War Cabinet at the appropriate time. Otherwise, the full programme of Light Fleet Carriers approved in 1943 will be executed.

Battleships

6. The *Vanguard*, due to enter service in 1946, is at present the only battleship under construction. Every effort will be made to accelerate her completion.

The *Lion, Temeraire, Conqueror* and *Thunderer* remain suspended from previous programmes.

7. In present circumstances a battleship takes several years to construct from the date of keel laying. Eighteen months must be allowed before keel laying to settle, in the light of the most recent experience, the detailed design both of the turrets and of the ship, and to progress the work on the turrets.

I estimate that by 1950 our effective battleship strength will be reduced to those surviving out of:–

4 *KGVs*
1 *Vanguard*
2 Modernised *Nelsons*

8. We are unlikely to come through unscathed in the Pacific war. On the other hand, the Admiralty consider that we should ultimately need 12 Capital ships if our postwar Navy is to be a well-balanced Fleet. It is desirable, therefore, to proceed now with the preliminary work to allow us to reinstate the Battleship programme in the near future.

9. I therefore ask for approval to revise the design of the ships and the turrets and to proceed with the construction of 6 – 16-inch turrets to the new design, to enable us to lay down the *Lion* and *Temeraire* with the ships of the 1945 Programme.

Cruisers

10. In the 1942 and 1943 Programmes I called attention to the need for Aircraft Carriers and stated that, in order to provide the necessary air component of the Fleet, I was prepared to forgo the construction of Cruisers. Accordingly, no Cruisers were included in the 1943 Programme and we also cancelled Cruisers outstanding from previous programmes.

11. Our new construction in Cruisers as it now stands is confined to the completion of 3 in 1944, 3 in 1945 and one in 1946; a total addition of 7 ships to our present strength.

12. The modern Cruiser takes some 3 years to build; and assuming that facilities cannot be made available until 1945, it is necessary to review our Cruiser strength of 1948. Our effective strength in Cruisers at that date will amount to those that survive out of the following:–

Heavy Cruisers (8-inch)	10
Medium Cruisers (6-inch and over 6,000 tons displacement)	27
Light Cruisers (6-inch and under, less than 6,000 tons displacement)	14

Of these, the 8-inch cruisers will be over age, having seen some 20 years' service and in the Medium Cruiser Class those surviving out of the 5 *Leander*s will have seen 14 to 17 years' service. The losses experienced so far average about 5 Cruisers a year, so that, if this can be taken as an indication of what we may expect in the future years of war, the strength shown above may be reduced by some 20 Cruisers.

13. Whatever the future losses may prove to be, the Admiralty consider that we can no longer forgo the construction of cruisers required by 1948 to replace the older ships and maintain the surface striking-power of the Fleet.

14. In the 1943 Programme the Admiralty were inclined to favour a cruiser with 5.25-inch guns, to the exclusion, for the time being, of the 6-inch-gun cruiser. Further experience and investigation of the design problems involved, however, show that the greater need, for the present

at least, is for a 6-inch gun. I therefore include 5 6-inch Cruisers in this programme. I expect that the necessary facilities will become available to lay down and commence work on these ships in the second and third quarters of 1945.

Since these 5 cruisers will only replace one year's wastage at the rate hitherto experienced, additional cruiser construction may be needed if we experience unusually heavy losses this year *(vide* paragraph 5).

Destroyers

15. As in the past, our destroyers will be required to play a prominent part in all future operations. The casualty rate is always high and, in consequence, the build-up of strength is slow. I propose to continue our policy of the past by including in this programme as many Destroyers as our capacity allows.

16. Facilities should become available for the construction of 14 Battle Class and 8 Weapon Class destroyers; the last of these would be laid down in the Autumn of 1945. I ask for these 22 destroyers.

Submarines

17. Our deficiency lies in submarines possessing the long range required for Far Eastern operations. As stated in the 1943 Programme, we have developed a new design, the 'A' Class, which is suitable for this purpose and embodies all the modern equipment developed as a result of experience throughout the War. The existing programmes include a total of 46 'A' Class submarines. Submarine losses have averaged 20 a year over the past four years and this experience must be taken into account in settling the further provision to be made.

18. The 'A' Class submarine takes on the average somewhat over twelve months to build, so that any now approved may be expected to enter service during 1946.

I include 20 'A' Class submarines in this Programme. We have cancelled orders, approved in previous programmes, for 10 'U' Class submarines, since these do not have the long range now required

Sloops

19. During the last two years we have cut down the construction of Sloops in order to use the capacity for Frigates and Corvettes, which can be produced more quickly. In view of the present favourable trend of the U-boat war, we have already cancelled 56 of the Corvettes (including 36 from Canada) and 61 of the Frigates approved in previous programmes.

20. Unlike the Frigate and Corvette, which are essentially anti-submarine vessels, and nothing more, the Sloop provides good AA protection, by virtue of her 6 4-inch guns on three twin mountings, as well as fulfilling all the requirements of an anti-submarine vessel. These ships are designed

to operate in an independent role all over the world. They possess good endurance and a reasonable turn of speed …

21. I ask for approval to order 5 Sloops of the Modified Black Swan Class, of which 3 can be reinstated from programmes approved by the War Cabinet in 1941 and 1942.

Coastal Forces

22. The Admiralty do not expect to need to place any further orders to supplement the strength of our coastal forces. Formal approval is, however, sought for the construction of 32 small MTBs to provide for wastage and already ordered with Treasury sanction, to ensure continuity of production.

Landing Craft and Ships

23. We are continuing to build all those types of landing craft required for forthcoming operations (I have therefore included provision in the Programme for such numbers as will, broadly speaking, absorb capacity for a further twelve months), but I should propose to review the situation as soon as the outlook is reasonably clear and make a more specific submission to the Cabinet then. The details of the interim provision are set out in Table I of the Annex to this paper.

The construction of further LSTs when the ships already authorised complete has been the subject of discussion by the Defence Committee. The follow-up programme required is 78; 36 to replace wastage and 42 to increase the assault lift from three to four divisions. The construction of further LSTs in the United Kingdom could only be at heavy cost in merchant and warship building, and no final decision has been taken. 36 further LSTs could, however, be built in the Dominions without interfering with the present warship and merchant ship programmes. These would replace wastage and, as I consider that it is desirable that we should be able to replace our own wastage from our own sources, I ask authority to place orders in the Dominions for these further 36 LSTs.

Small Craft

24. As usual I seek approval for the large number of miscellaneous small craft required for the servicing of the Fleet and all the other maritime activities in which we have to engage.

Ships of previous Programmes cancelled

25. As mentioned in paragraphs 18 and 19 above, we have cancelled orders, approved in previous Programmes, for 10 'U' Class Submarines, 56 Corvettes and 61 Frigates. In addition, it is not now intended to proceed with the following ships authorised in 1943 and earlier Programmes, but not ordered:–

16 Small MTBs.
10 Steam Gun Boats.

4 Boom Defence Vessels.
6 Fleet Minesweepers.

Other Vessels

26. My colleagues will observe that there are a large number of warship categories not represented in this programme. This is because the Admiralty hope that programmes already approved will meet our need in these types. If, however, losses should prove so heavy as to falsify this expectation, I shall seek approval for the necessary replacements in a later supplementary programme.

27. Statements are appended showing the estimated cost of this programme separately and in conjunction with previous programmes.

TABLE I – NEW CONSTRUCTION PROGRAMME – 1944

Estimate of Expenditure by Financial Years

–	1944	1945	1946	1947	1948	Total
	£	£	£	£	£	£
5 – 6-inch Gun Cruisers	–	4,800,000	6,250,000	6,500,000	1,450,000	19,000,000
22 Fleet Destroyers	1,250,000	13,500,000	6,770,000	–	–	21,520,000
20 Submarines (A Class)	600,000	5,000,000	3,100,000	–	–	8,700,000
2 Sloops	85,000	425,000	425,000	85,000	–	1,020,000
32 Motor Torpedo Boats	605,000	371,000	–	–	–	976,000
36 LSTs	3,550,000	7,000,000	3,652,000	–	–	14,202,000
180 Landing Craft Tank	6,250,000	7,000,000	596,000	–	–	13,846,000
84 LC(Gun) or LC Support (R)	1,800,000	3,200,000	–	–	–	5,000,000
600 LCA	500,000	800,000	260,000	–	–	1,560,000
60 LCS (Medium)	300,000	60,000	–	–	–	360,000
250 LC Mech.	650,000	600,000	–	–	–	1,250,000
Small Craft and Motor Boats	2,988,000	2,783,000	181,000	–	–	5,952,000
	18,578,000	45,539,000	21,234,000	6,585,000	1,450,000	93,386,000

TABLE II – ESTIMATED EXPENDITURE ON NEW CONSTRUCTION BY FINANCIAL YEARS

–	1944	1945	1946	1947	1948	1949	1950
	£,000	£,000	£,000	£,000	£,000	£,000	£,000
Programmes prior to 1943 Prog.	78,000	37,000	11,600	3,750	2,500	600	400
1943 Prog and Additions	65,500	55,800	38,000	14,800	6,200	500	–
1944 Programme	18,578	45,539	21,234	6,585	1,450	–	–
	162,078	138,339	70,834	25,135	10,150	1,100	400

8. *Extract of Conclusions of War Cabinet*

[ADM 229/34] 18 May 1944

WM(44)65th NAVAL CONSTRUCTION PROGRAMME

The War Cabinet had before them a Memorandum by the First Lord of the Admiralty on the new Construction Programme 1944 (WP(44)245). The 1944 Programme was as follows:–

Redesign the 4 'Lion' class battleships and proceed with the production of 6 Triple 16-inch turrets of revised design.

5 6-inch Cruisers
22 Fleet Destroyers
20 Submarines
5 Sloops (including 3 authorised in previous programmes)
32 Small MTBs
Miscellaneous small craft

In addition, the programme included provision for such numbers of landing ships and craft as would, broadly speaking, absorb capacity for a further 12 months. But the position would be reviewed and a more specific submission would be made to the War Cabinet as soon as the outlook was reasonably clear.

Authority was asked to place orders in the Dominions for a further 36 LSTs. No final decision has been taken about the construction of further LSTs in this county when those already authorised had been completed …

The War Cabinet's conclusions were as follows:–

(1) The New Construction Programme 1944 proposed by the First Lord of the Admiralty was approved.
(2) The completion of the LSTs under construction in this country should be accorded the highest priority.

…

9. *Memorandum for the Board*

[ADM 205/41] 15 May 1944

B.374 THE EMPIRE'S POST-WAR FLEET

The attached memorandum … [is] in relation to an enquiry by the Prime Minister as to the Admiralty policy on the composition of the postwar Fleet …

PRINCIPLES OF IMPERIAL DEFENCE

1. The basis of Imperial Defence is the control of sea communications. Without this control members of the British Commonwealth become disconnected units each one too weak for defence against a first-class

power. With assured sea communications the whole strength of the Empire can be brought to bear in any part of the world with the greatest economy and effect.

2. Sea Power, exercised by a proper proportion of surface forces, carrier-borne and shore-based air forces, is the means by which sea communications are controlled.

3. A healthy and adequate Merchant Navy is an essential element of Sea Power.

4. Strategically placed bases, well-protected, are essential for the successful exercise of sea-power, both in the defence of sea communications and in the domination of those which a potential enemy might wish to use.

CONSTITUENTS OF THE FLEET

5. War experience has shown that the essential constituents of any Fleet are Battleships, Aircraft Carriers, Cruisers and Destroyers, supported by a Fleet Train, and supplemented by an adequate force of shore-based aircraft.

6. A battleship cannot operate within range of carrier-borne or shore-based aircraft, without the protection and striking power afforded by naval aircraft. To avoid undesirable limitation in the freedom of movement of the Battle Fleet, the aircraft must accompany the force in carriers.

7. Battleships and Aircraft Carriers are complementary, and the enthusiast for one arm or the other must not be allowed to upset the balance. This war has proved the necessity of battleships and no scientific development is in sight which might render them obsolete. The Aircraft Carrier is needed to provide both a powerful striking force which can be wielded outside gun range, and fighter protection for the whole force. These large and necessarily few units must have with them Cruisers and Destroyers.

8. All these indispensible units of the Fleet have many duties as shown in the following paragraphs.

DETAILED FUNCTIONS OF FLEET UNITS

9. A. Battleships

The basis of the strength of the Fleet is the Battleship. Besides providing support for all classes of ships, the Battleship is the most powerful unit for destroying the enemy's surface forces once they are brought to gun action. A heavier broadside than the enemy is still a very telling weapon in a Naval action.

B. Aircraft Carriers

The main functions of Aircraft Carriers are to provide:–

(a) A long-range weapon of offence.

(b) Fighter protection for the Fleet and for amphibious assaults.

(c) Reconnaissance.
(d) Defence against submarine attack in conjunction with surface A/S vessels.
(e) Means for attack and defence of Trade.

C. Cruisers

The Cruiser is an important component of the Fleet. Included among more important duties are:–

(a) Support of destroyer striking forces.
(b) Attack and defence of Trade.
(c) Reconnaissance.
(d) A/A gun support of Aircraft Carriers.
(e) Protection of the Fleet, by drawing off and attacking enemy light surface forces.
(f) Independent operations.

D. Destroyers

There is no limit to the duties which Destroyers may be called upon to perform. These duties include:–

(a) Day and night striking forces.
(b) Fleet anti-submarine and anti-aircraft screen.
(c) Raiding operations.
(d) Protection of convoys.

E. Fleet Train

To [e]nsure full mobility the Fleet must be accompanied by certain facilities of supply and maintenance to supplement the capacity of such bases as may exist in the operational area.

OTHER NAVAL FORCES

10. There are certain other types of ships which, though not forming part of a composite Naval force, are essential to Naval warfare. They can be briefly stated as follows:–

SUBMARINES

11. It must now be accepted that attack against merchant ships carrying essential supplies and war materials will always be the inevitable result of total warfare. Submarines are needed to enforce blockade in waters close to the enemy's shore where surface vessels are unable to operate, and for special reconnaissance operations.

ANCILLIARY CRAFT

12. Minesweepers, Minelayers, Convoy Escorts and Coastal Craft whose names indicate their functions are required.

AMPHIBIOUS FORCES

13. The technique of the seaborne assault must be developed and landing ships and craft are necessary in peace-time for research and training.

FORMATION OF AN OPERATIONAL FORCE OR COMPOSITE SQUADRON

14. Whereas a battleship can carry out its functions when operating singly, aircraft carriers must work in pairs in order to obtain full operational efficiency. The smallest efficient tactical unit is therefore 1 Battleship and 2 Carriers with the necessary attached Cruisers (3) and Destroyers (9).

15. Experience has shown that 4 Carriers is the maximum number that can be operated simultaneously as one unit. If flexibility and handiness are taken into account, it follows that a composite squadron should consist of not more than:–

 2 Battleships
 4 Aircraft Carriers
 6 Cruisers
 with not less than 18 Destroyers.

and a squadron of this size must be supported by a train of:–

 1 Heavy Repair Ship
 1 Fast Tanker
 1 Destroyer Depot Ship
 1 Aircraft Repair Ship

16. When desired such a composite squadron can be split into two Divisions, without impeding operational flexibility or tactical training. In such an event the disposition of the Fleet Train would depend on the circumstances attending the operational requirements.

POLITICAL ASSUMPTIONS IN DETERMINING THE EMPIRE'S NAVAL STRENGTH

17. Without knowledge of the strength of the postwar Navies of other nations, the task of fitting proposals for the Empire's Naval Strength into any clear-cut strategical picture is extremely difficult. The Admiralty can, in fact, only determine what minimum Naval forces would be needed at the outbreak of a war, to maintain the Empire's sea communications while the strength of the Fleet is being expanded. Should there be indications, at any time, that other powers are embarking upon disproportionate building programmes, these minimum forces would have to be reviewed.

18. No system of world security that is designed after the war can succeed unless the leading nations of the world are adequately armed. The members of the British Empire will together form one of the leading nations, and sea power will be an essential component of its armed strength.

19. A strong Empire Fleet is a deterrent, and a weak Fleet an encouragement, to Foreign Powers to attempt an armaments race.

STRENGTH AND DISPOSITION OF THE NAVY

20. With the foregoing political assumptions in mind, the proposed strength of the Navy, which is shown in the ensuing paragraphs, is based on the following requirements and duties:–

(a) Support of the Empire's policy and interests.
(b) Ability to control sea communications at all times, assuming that America will never be hostile.
(c) Rapid concentration of force in any vital area in the event of peace being threatened.
(d) Training, and the resulting ability to expand rapidly in time of war.
(e) Research and development of tactical practice, new weapons and appliances.
(f) Showing the flag.

21. As Empire interests and shipping will be scattered over every ocean and sea, a considerable fleet will be required to carry out the duties mentioned above. The strength of forces to be based in each area is dependent upon the extent of local Empire interest and the need for training and local defence.

22. The forces estimated to be necessary in peace are shown in the table below. The proportion of the fleet in reserve or in dockyard hands at any time would depend on the circumstances. It will not be possible to form and train squadrons for the aircraft carriers in reserve in the time taken to mobilise the ships. provision must therefore be made for reserve aircraft squadrons to be adequately training in peace time on modern types of aircraft which must be available for them on outbreak of war. These reserve squadrons should be formed on the lines of the RAF Volunteer Reserve squadrons in prewar days.

SHIPBUILDING RESOURCES

23. An efficient and prosperous shipbuilding industry is essential for the maintenance of sea power and can only be kept alive by a steady building programme based on the replacement and modernisation of out of date warships and merchant ships.

24. THE STRENGTH OF THE EMPIRE'S NAVY

Station	Battleships	Aircraft Carriers	Cruisers	Destroyers	Escorts A/A & A/S	Submarines	Minesweepersrs	Coastal Forces	S/M Depot Ships	Dest. Depot Ships	Heavy Repair Ships	Aircraft Repair Ships	Fast Tankers
ATLANTIC													
HOME WATERS	3	4	6	27	8	20	8	16	1		1	1	1
CANADA &		1	3										
WEST INDIES													
SOUTH AFRICA		1	3		4		2						
MEDITERRANEAN	2	2	6	18	6	8	2	8		1	1	1	1
FAR EAST													
INDIAN OCEAN		1	3		6								
AUS, NZ & EI	1	2	6	9	6	8	4	8	1	1	1	1	1
CHINA & PACIFIC		1	6	9	6					1			
TOTAL IN FULL COMMISSION	6	12	33	63	36	36	16	32	2	3	3	3	3
IN RESERVE (some modernising)	6	12	17	63	154	50	104		2	2	1	1	1
GRAND TOTAL	12	24	50	126	190	86	120	32	4	5	4	4	4

25. With the above dispositions composite squadrons could be readily formed, for reinforcing one part of the world at the expense of another. Some Reserves of the smaller classes of ships could be stationed abroad.

LANDING SHIPS AND CRAFT

26. Landing ships and craft would be kept in reserve in the different parts of the world where army training is needed. They would be commissioned for short periods to fit in with the training programme. A nucleus would be kept in permanent commission in Home Waters for scientific research and tactical development.

OFFICERS AND MEN

27. A sufficient drafting margin should be kept so that no man is called upon to do more than alternate two-year commission abroad. The total number for the proposed Fleet would be in the order of 170,000 inclusive of all Empire contingents,

The strength of the fleet at the outbreak of the present war was 138,000. This included the Dominion and RIN figures totalling 9,000 approximately while the strength of the Fleet Air Arm (RN and RAF) only accounted for 4,200 of the total.

As an example of the increase of complement resulting from added equipment and AA guns, it is of interest that the war complement of the ILLUSTRIOUS in 1939 with 33 aircraft embarked was 1,220. By April 1944, with 48 aircraft embarked, it is now 1,710.

The new proposed figure includes the necessary drafting margin and a considerable increase in Fleet Air Arm personnel.

THE DOMINIONS

28. It is to be hoped that the Dominions will continue to contribute to the Empire's Naval strength to the greatest extent possible.

10. *Board Minute*

[ADM 167/120] 19 May 1944

The Empire's Post-War Fleet

3954. The Board considered … a memorandum by the First Sea Lord on the composition of the Empire's postwar Fleet.

The forces estimated to be necessary in peace comprisede:–

12	Battleships	32	Coastal Forces
24	Aircraft Carriers	4	Submarine Depot Ship
50	Cruisers	5	Destroyer Depot Ships
126	Destroyers	4	Heavy Repair Ships
190	Escorts (A/A and A/S) and Sloops	4	Aircraft Repair Ships
86	Submarines	4	Fast Tankers
120	Minesweepers		

The total personnel required for the proposed Fleet was estimated to be of the order of 170,000 inclusive of Empire contingents.

The Board took note of the memorandum.

11. *Memorandum by Controller*

[ADM 116/5052] 9 June 1944

NACON 41 POST WAR FLEET

Revised estimates have been made both to cover a different composition of the fleet and to bring the cost within certain specified limits.

2. The fleet to be built and maintained is set out below, the numbers in Reserve being shown separately.

Class	Total Number	In Reserve	Balance
Battleships	12	6	6
Fleet Carriers	8	4	4
Light Fleet Carriers	16	8	8
Heavy Cruisers	30	10	20
Light Cruisers	20	7	13
Depot Ships & Tankers	21	7	14
Fleet Destroyers	128	64	64

'U' Submarines	29	17	12
'A' Submarines	57	33	24
Minesweepers	120	104	16
Escorts (Sloops)	190	160	30
Landing Ships	80	60	20
Landing Craft	800	600	200
Mosquito Craft	80	40	40

3. … To bring the costs within the limits suggested it has been found necessary to spread the construction over a longer period and to keep some ships in service slightly longer than assumed in previous papers. Our proposal is that the larger vessels ie Cruisers and above, with Depot Ships, should remain active for a period of 20 years, with a further period of 5 years in reserve. The smaller ships should have a total life of 20 years, 5 of these being in Reserve, whilst Landing and Mosquito Craft have been assumed to have a total life of 10 years …

5. … If the idea, put forward in previous papers, of a "Gross Reproduction Rate" were to be adopted the constant labour force would be 17,500 and the ships to be laid down would be approximately:

Battleships	1 every second year
Fleet Carriers	1 every third year
Light Fleet Carriers	3 every two years
Heavy Cruisers	6 every five years
Light Cruisers	4 every five years
Depot Ships	1 each year
Fleet Destroyers	6 each year
'U' Submarines	3 every 2 years
'A' Submarines	3 each year
Minesweepers	6 each year
Escorts (Sloops)	10 each year
Landing ships	4 each year
Landing Craft	80 each year
Mosquito Craft	8 each year

…

7. Turning now to the problem of labour other then in the shipyards … the manpower required would be:

I	Shipyard and Engine Shop Workers	24,500
	Guns, Mountings, Armour & Ammunition	28,000
		52,500
II	Dockyard Labour, Repairs & Refits	40,000
	Victualling & Stores, Building, Establishments	18,000

	Miscellaneous Contract Labour		45,000
			103,000
III	Naval Personnel:	Active	120,000
	Reserve		140,000
			260,000

…

10. The average total annual expenditure over the years 1947/71 is £153M, which is roughly equivalent to £108M at pre-war price …

12. *Plans Division Memorandum*

[ADM 116/5052] 11 September 1944

PD.0154/1944 *Director of Plans Remarks on Controller's Paper NACON 41 – "The Post War Fleet"*

The strength of the Fleet to be kept in reserve and in full commission during peace has been based in NACON 41 upon that given in the paper "The Empire's Post-War Fleet", issued from the First Sea Lord's Office on 4 May 1944, which was noted by the Board; but no action has been taken to authorise the acceptance of that paper as a basis for planning generally.

2. It appears that the number of men required to man such a fleet amounts to considerably more than the Vote A proposals hitherto accepted by the Board for peacetime planning … 220,000 as opposed to the First Sea Lord's figure of 170,000 of which 130,000 is expected to be the UK commitment and 40,000 is expected to be the Empire contribution.

3. Since it is most unlikely that we shall receive for a considerable time any firm guidance from the War Cabinet either upon the strength of the postwar fleet to be allowed, or upon the manpower we may expect to be allocated to the Navy in peacetime, any planning must be done with the clear acceptance that its basis may be undermined completely by subsequent decisions.

4. The "Empire's Post-War Fleet" paper was the result of the Naval Staff having to cut down its requirements for the postwar fleet to meet the requirements of a manpower direction from Board level. These reduced requirements represent what is probably less than a base minimum …

…

11. Since we are planning the maintenance of a Navy in peace it seems reasonable to accept our experience in wartime as a guide to the age limit for scrapping ships. From this experience it is considered that the replacement cycle proposed [in NACON 41] could be accepted, assuming

that our refitting policy allows each ship to remain adequately modernised throughout the span of her useful life …
13. It is also considered that the replacement cycle for coastal craft and landing ships and craft requires further study … the need for experiment and research rather than numbers should take pride of place during the immediate postwar period.
…
15. What is required in DofP's opinion is a building programme which will maintain the strength of the Fleet in the most up to date types for the longest period of years and at the same time develop an industry so firmly established that in peace it cannot flag and disintegrate and which in war can be expanded from a solid basis …
16. … DofP would prefer to forego for a year or so the achievement of our full naval strength in modern ships, if in exchange we could achieve a new construction policy resulting in a regular output.
17. Such a modification of the programme would have other advantages. It is clear that many of the developments of this war are still in their infancy … These improvements should not have to wait for years before being incorporated in new construction …
SUMMARY
21. DofP agrees that for present planning of our postwar naval shipbuilding industry we should accept the size of the Fleet as laid down in "The Empire's Post-War Fleet", dated 4 May 1944.
22. It is also agreed that the replacement age of ships should be as proposed provided full allowance is made in money, labour and material for keeping ships thoroughly modernised.
23. While the object should be to attain the full strength of the Fleet in modern ships as quickly as possible, this should be not done in such a way that in the period 1955–65 we shall have very few new ships coming forward …

13. *Chiefs of Staff Committee Memorandum*

[CAB 80/85] 7 July 1944

COS(44)597(O) *Also WP(44)380*
MANPOWER ONE YEAR AFTER THE DEFEAT OF GERMANY

In accordance with the instructions of the War Cabinet we have examined the effect of limiting the Services *one year after the European War*, to 3,000,000 man and women. We have taken no account of those short-term commitments which are likely to be completed during the year immediately following Germany's defeat.

ANNEX I
NAVAL MANPOWER

1. A statement of the forces, other than Dominion ships, required for the Japanese war plus naval commitments in other theatres, is given in Appendix I. These figures make no allowance for casualties in ships except in the case of submarines. A reduction of 20,000 officers and men has, however, been made in manpower requirements in anticipation that casualties in ships will be suffered. Dominion ships and ships on loan and manned by Dominions are given in Appendix II.

2. The ships fully manned are sufficient only to provide for one strong cover or striking force in addition to those required to support one major amphibious operation, and for the security of sea communications. A possible distribution of forces is given in Appendix III. Those tentatively allocated to the support of amphibious operations would be required in whatever area we were developing operations. It will be seen that even allowing for the full use of Dominion forces we have no surplus.

3. For European waters, naval forces are assessed on a minimum basis and in the event of an emergency reliance is placed on the timely diversion of ships working up, on passage, or from the Indian Ocean. The forces for Europe amount to no more than –

Home, North Sea and Baltic	*Mediterranean*
1 Battleship	4 Cruisers
5 Cruisers	8 Destroyers
16 Destroyers	

4. It has been assumed that it will be practicable to close all temporary bases at Home, in the Mediterranean and in the Atlantic. Only permanent naval bases, those required for training and development, and bases for mine clearance will be maintained, and these will be on a reduced scale of complement.

5. The savings which have thus been effected by reductions in bases, in anti-submarine escorts and defensive measures in the West, have, however, been largely absorbed in the expansion in the FAA, in aircraft carriers for their role in the Far Eastern war, in the provision of the Fleet Train and the development of new bases in the Eastern theatre.

6. The maintenance personnel for the fleet in the Far East has been assessed at its lowest figure and cannot be reduced. As an example, the Special Repair Ratings (Dockyard) allowed only an amount to the equivalent of one-third of the requirement of Chatham Dockyard. Whereas in the European Theatre the full and well-established naval and civil maintenance resources were available, in the Eastern Theatre maintenance facilities are largely non-existent and must be improvised and maintained by the Navy alone both for the Fleet and Amphibious Forces.

7. The amphibious forces have been calculated for a three divisional lift.
8. On the above basis, naval manpower requirements for the year 1945 are estimated to be 760,000 men and 60,000 women. Of the 820,000 personnel mentioned approximately:–

35.5% are required for the Fleet set out in Appendix I, landing ships and support Fleet Train, other than aircraft carriers and aircraft maintenance and repair ships.
29.6% are required for FAA aircraft carriers, aircraft maintenance ships and air stations.
7 % for Combined Operations personnel, landing craft crews etc.
7.3% for Royal Marines, including Special Service forces.
2.9% DEMS, including men at present provided by the army.
16.5% for naval bases and base defences, Boom Defence and Special Heavy Repair Parties. Operational bases and port parties. Admiralty etc,
1.2% for Coastal Forces.

APPENDIX I TO ANNEX I

Strength of Fleet for 1945

(This strength is that attained up to 31 December 1945, plus ships completing early 1946 for which provision must be made in 1945.)

(1)	Total (2)	No. in Care and Maintenance (3)	No. with 3/5/crews (see Note 1) (4)	No. with Full Crew (5)
Battleships & Battlecruisers	15	5	3	7
Fleet Carriers	7	...	2	5
Light Fleet Carriers	14	...	3	11
Escort Carriers	39	...	13	26*
8-in Cruisers	8	...	2	6
6-in Cruisers	24	4	4	16
Light Cruisers	23	8	6	9
A.A. Cruisers	4	...	1	3
Fleet Destroyers	154	...	38	116
Submarines	160	...	110 (see Note II)	50
Fighter Direction Ships	3	...	...	3
Minelayers	5	...	2	3
Monitors, Large	3	...	1	2
Escorts, S/M and A/A	567	200	97	270
Minesweepers	832	...	207	625 (Note III)

*Three of these CVE may be required as aircraft ferries

Notes

I – The ships shown in column (4) are those refitting, training, working up, on passage etc. ...

II – Submarines in column (4) to have full crews. To maintain one submarine in the Eastern theatre, one additional submarine is needed to cover refit, working up, time on passage. Forty submarines are necessary for A/S and S/M training. An allowance of 20 crews is required to meet estimated total losses.

III – The possibility of reducing the number of minesweepers has been carefully considered. The saving in manpower would be small (6,000 for 150 vessels) and it would result in a delay of six to twelve months in clearing mines. This would probably affect the resumption of fishing and trade.

APPENDIX II TO ANNEX I

Dominion-owned and Dominion-manned Ships

	RAN	RNZN	RCN	RIN	Total	Estimated No. Fully Manned (see Note I)
Escort Carriers	...	...	2	...	2	2
8-in Cruisers	2	...	...	...	2	
6-in Cruisers	1	2	2	...	5	6
Old Cruisers	1	...	...	...	1	
A/A Ship	...	...	1	...	1	...
Fleet Destroyers	9	...	7	...	16	12
Escorts	16	2	202 (Note II)	10	120	90

NOTES

I – About ¾ of the total strength is considered as being fully manned, ie the same basis as for RN.

II – A proportion of the Flower class corvettes, of which there are more than 100 in the RCN, will probably be paid off as many of them have seen four hard years in the Atlantic. The figures in the last two columns have therefore been arbitrarily adjusted.

APPENDIX III TO ANNEX I

Possible Distribution of Naval Forces at 1 January 1946

All fully-manned ships, including Dominion ships, are shown. No allowance has been made for casualties. Ships refitting, working up and on passage are omitted, but a deduction from the figures in the table must be made for local refits.

	Europe	SE Asia (Note I)	Pacific (Note II) Striking Force	Pacific (Note II) Amphibious Operations and Theatre Duties	Total Appendices I and II
BB / OBB / OBC	1	2	2	...	7
CV	...	1	4	...	5
CVL	...	1	4*		11* (Note III)
CVE	...	6	...	19 (Note IV)	25
CA / CL	9	6	8	17	40
DD	24	16	36	52	128

NOTES

I – In the event of an emergency in Europe, this force might have to provide reinforcements.

II – If we adopt a Bay of Bengal strategy, the forces shown for the support of amphibious operations, and part of the carrier striking force, would have to be transferred to that theatre.

III – It is unlikely that more than a maximum of 8 will be operationally available before April 1946.

IV – This includes relief carriers for assaults, A/S escort carriers and theatre ferrying.

14. *Joint Planning Staff Memorandum*

[CAB 84/65] 25 August 1944

JP(44)226(O) MANPOWER ONE YEAR AFTER THE DEFEAT OF GERMANY – REDUCTION OF SERVICE REQUIREMENTS

Note by the Secretary

1. It will be remembered that the Chiefs of Staff Committee has presented to the War Cabinet its requirements for manpower one year after the defeat of Germany in COS(44)597(O), which has been reproduced as WP(44)380. The estimate of their requirements amounted to 3,404,500 men and women.

2. After discussion by the War Cabinet the Prime Minister issued a directive, entitled WP(44)431 stating that the service requirements must be revised so as to effect savings of 700,000 on this figure. The relative paragraphs are reproduced as Annex I.

...

ANNEX I
EXTRACT FROM WP(44)431

7. We are given to understand that the total supply of labour will fall short by 1¾ millions of the total of the various civil and military requirements which have been framed. It would be impossible at this stage to settle exactly how this deficit is to be met, but it is clear at any rate that military requirements must be cut. For the present I should like to see the effect worked out of a cut of 1,100,000 on Service and munitions requirements.

...

10. In the military field, it would be sufficient, for our immediate purpose, if we say that plans should be based on a cut in the total Service manpower of 700,000 – leaving 400,000 to be found by reductions in the output of munitions. ... I should like to see the effect of these cuts worked out on the following broad lines:–

Royal Navy

11. Having regard to the overpowering Naval force which will be available for the war against Japan, I consider that the Navy should bear a cut of at least 200,000 men. The principles on which this should be worked out are:–

(a) That only ships of the highest quality should be retained in active service.

(b) That there can be some reduction in the Fleet Air Arm in view of the overwhelming air effort which will be concentrated against Japan.

Above all, however, intense efforts should be made to reduce the Navy ashore all over the world, which is out of proportion to the size of the Fleet which will engage the enemy.

...

15. *Future Building Committee Memorandum*

[ADM 205/36] 28 August 1944

FB(44)17 Revised *Memorandum by Directorate of Tactical and Staff Duties and Director of Plans*

The Case for the Small Cruiser as a Unit of the Fleet of the Future

1. Introduction

...'Small Cruiser' is used to denote a ship of the following broad characteristics:–

6/7,000 tons	6 – 5.25″ HA/LA guns in three twin turrets, two forward and one aft.
Endurance 4,500 miles at 20 knots (Comparable to Battle Class)	Torpedo tubes and close-range weapons
Speed 30/32 knots	Good radar and communications
Good subdivision	Splinter protection

2. Cruiser Functions

   The main functions required of Cruisers in the future would appear to be:–

   1. Fleet work
   2. Inshore operations
   3. Support of Carriers in Task forces

3. Small v Large Cruiser

   The advantages of each type are as follows:–

Small Cruiser	Large Cruiser
(i) Presents a smaller target	(i) Greater hitting power
(ii) More manoeuvrable and greater possibility of evading bombs or torpedoes	(ii) Greater endurance and sea-keeping qualities
(iii) Can be operated in waters where a large Cruiser would not be risked (eg East Coast 1940, Crete 1941, Bay of Biscay 1944)	(iii) Better protection
(iv) Can be built in larger numbers for a given expenditure of money or capacity	

…

7. Summary

   It is considered that Small Cruisers will be required for:–

   (i) Offensive strikes in enemy coastal waters
   (ii) Accompanying Destroyers to provide them with the facilities which they lack
   (iii) Backing Destroyer torpedo attacks
   (iv) Making torpedo attacks by night or in bad visibility
   (v) Minor bombardments

   They will also be required for carrying out the following Defensive functions:–

(vi) Defence of Carriers against air attack
(vii) Holding off surface attack whilst Carrier disengages
(viii) Strengthening AA fire power of the Screen against torpedo carrying or missile directing aircraft
(ix) Support of escort carriers

8. Conclusion

The need for large, ocean going Cruisers is not questioned, either now or for the future; but it is submitted that this war has also proved the values of the small, handy Cruiser with power to hit and the capacity to defend herself. The need for such ships is shown particularly by the growth of Destroyers into ships of 3,000 tons. The 'Battle' class destroyers are virtually cruisers, but even their size and elaborate equipment does not give them the power to perform adequately the functions given in the preceding paragraph. An intermediate type between destroyers and the large cruiser is therefore required.

9. Recommendation

That there will be a demand for numbers of Cruisers is certain – a far greater demand than we can hope to meet with valuable and heavy ships of 15,000 tons. For this reason alone, apart from the arguments for the small Cruiser per se, it is considered that future building programmes should make provision for Cruisers of 6/7,000 tons.

16. *Future Building Committee Minutes*

[ADM 205/36] 29 August 1944

FB(44)10th Meeting SMALL CRUISERS

…

The Committee had before them FB(44)17, The Case for the Small Cruiser as a Unit of the Fleet of the Future.

2. The Chairman[1] referred to previous discussions on the subject and to the Board decision against building small cruisers at present. This had been brought to a head by a recent enquiry from the Australians, when it had been decided … that the present Admiralty policy was not to build any warship between the large Battle Class Destroyer and the 15,000-ton cruiser. He had been asked, however, to give consideration to the question of long-term policy.

3. In a discussion on general principles the following points were made:–

(i) It would not be possible to mount two triple 6″ turrets in a ship of less than 8,500 tons, while the addition of the necessary secondary

[1] Deputy First Sea Lord.

armament would put the tonnage up to 9,000 tons as a minimum. Six-inch guns are out of the question with a displacement of 7,000 tons.

(ii) The supreme advantage of the small cruiser is for use in dangerous and inshore waters where the 15,000-ton cruiser would be too valuable to risk. This has been borne out by experience in the present war.

(iii) The small cruiser will be required as Leader for a Destroyer striking force. Owing to the increased complexity of radar and fighter direction etc it is becoming more and more necessary for this purpose which even the Battle Class Destroyer cannot adequately meet.

4. It was agreed that if a small cruiser is eventually authorised the principle should be to limit the displacement to 7,000 tons and the main armament to three 5.25″ turrets … Standards of amenities should tend towards the characteristics of a large destroyer rather than of a cruiser …

17. *Board Minute*

[ADM 167/120] 22 November 1944

Shipbuilding Policy during the remainder of the War

3983. … At the First Lord's request, the Controller … had had under consideration the policy to be followed from the present time until the cessation of hostilities with Japan. An important object was to release capacity for building high class merchant ships and thus assist in the rapid recovery of the British Mercantile Marine while at the same time not detracting from the effective Naval strength which could be brought to bear on the enemy so long as the war against Japan continued.

The policy proposed was that work on warships should be pressed on in the case of every ship which can be completed in time to fight in the Far East by 31 December 1946. This would mean in the case of cruisers and above, ships completing by 30 June 1946, and in the case of destroyers and below, ships completing by 1 September 1946. For the rest, it was not proposed that any ships (except three destroyers) should be cancelled. It was, however, intended that merchant ships should take precedence of them. In some cases, it might prove desirable to press on with a warship already laid down, in order to clear the slip for merchant work. In general, however, work on these ships would be treated as a stand-by job.

The First Sea Lord considered that work should be pressed on in the case of every ship which can be completed by the end of 1946. Even so, he emphasised that the policy which was proposed, though it might not affect the war fleet, would have a very large effect on the strength of the postwar fleet.

The Board took note of the memorandum and approved the policy which was proposed, subject to the modification that work would be pressed on in the case of all ships which can be completed by 31 December 1946. The First Lord said that when the Board approved the New Construction Programme 1945 for submission to the War Cabinet, they would need to take full account of the effect of this policy on the postwar fleet and to consider what report they should make to the War Cabinet on the retardation or deferment of ships or the 1944 and earlier programmes.

18. *DACR*[1] *to Fifth Sea Lord*[2]

[ADM 1/17395] 4 December 1944

The following information has been prepared and is submitted with reference to your memorandum (not to DofP) dated 30 November 1944 about a meeting Head of Air is arranging with regard to the production of the O5/43, the Sea Hornet and the N.22/43 in 1947.

2. From data of new aircraft received from CNR, DACR has studied the weights and dimensions as regards carriers in service, including COLOSSUS Class. All later carriers were designed for, and will be able to operate, all the new types.

3. The following figures are relevant to this study:–

(a) CARRIERS

	Lifts		Hangar Height	Arrester Gear	Remarks
	Dimensions	Designed Load			
COLOSSUS	45 x 34	lb 15,000*	17′6″	lb 15,500⁺	*20,000 overload – very slowly ⁺Some overload may be permissible after trials
IMPLACABLE	45x33(F) 45x22(A)	20,000	14′0″	20,000	

[1]Capt E.O.F. Price RN.
[2]RA Sir Thomas Troubridge.

INDOMITABLE	45x33(F) 45x22(A)	14,000	14′0″ (U) 16′0″ (L)	15,500 18,000 @80 kts	* With 3 1/8″ centre span
ILLUSTRIOUS	45 x 22	14,000	16′0″	20,000 @50kts*	

(b) AIRCRAFT

Type	Weight (AU)	Length	Span (F)	Height (Folded)
S.11/43 B/R (Twin)[1]	21,000	45′	20′	14′9″
O.5/43 T.D/B[2]	20,000	44′11″	20′	15′6″
N.11/44 L.R.F.[3]	18,000	39′7″	10′ (approx.)	15′7″
N.5/44 F. (Twin)[4]	15,600	37′	27′6″	13′9″
N.22/43 F.[5]	11,170	34′	18′6″	15′9″

4. It will be seen from the above that:–

(a) COLOSSUS can carry N.22/43.
N.5/44 if overloads on lifts and arrester gear allowed.
N.11/44 if overloads on lifts and arrester gear allowed.

cannot carry S.11/43. Too heavy and length critical.
O.5/43. Too heavy and length critical.

(b) IMPLACABLE can carry N.5/44. (Upper hangar only as span is 27′6″).

cannot carry remainder – all too high for hangars (14′). Lengths of S.11/43 and O.5/43 are critical on lifts.

(c) INDOMITABLE can carry N.22/43 (Lower hangar only).
N.5/44 (upper hangar only as span is 27′6″ and with overload on lift).

cannot carry S.11/43. Too heavy, too long for lifts. Upper hangar too low.

[1] Shorts Sturgeon.
[2] Fairey Spearfish.
[3] Westland Wyvern.
[4] de Havilland Sea Hornet.
[5] Hawker Sea Fury.

O.5/43. Ditto
N.11/44. Too heavy for lifts.

(d) ILLUSTRIOUS can carry N.22/43.

cannot carry S.11/43. Too heavy and length critical.
O.5/43. Ditto.
N.11/44. Too heavy for lifts.
N.5/44. Span 27′6″. Too wide for lifts.

5. In cases where the aircraft length is the same as that of the lift, sufficient clearance may be obtained by pushing the rudder of the aircraft over if the travel is sufficient.

6. DNC is being asked to investigate the possibility of increasing the load capacities of the lifts to an acceptable operational standard (full speed) to take the aircraft in the various cases set out above.

19. *Minutes of Fifth Sea Lord's Meeting*

[ADM 1/17395] 13 December 1944

A.02086/44 Post-War requirements of Naval Aircraft

The 5th Sea Lord held a meeting at Rex House on 7 December to consider the requirements of aircraft for the Naval Air Arm in the immediate post war years.

2. The primary purpose of the meeting was to determine, as a guide to the Ministry of Aircraft Production for production planning, the peak outputs of the new types of Naval aircraft, such as the O.5/43, the Sea Hornet and the N.22/43, in 1947/8 on the assumption that the war with Japan would be over by the end of 1946 …

It was agreed to assume for the purpose stated:–

(i) that the postwar first line strength would be 500 carrier-borne aircraft, with provision for an additional 300 aircraft for RNVR training with Squadrons on a cadre basis;
(ii) that of these, 700 would be of the latest types and the remaining 100 older types such as Barracuda and Seafire;
(iii) that there would be no drop in the target war strength of 1600 during the first six months following the end of hostilities;
(iv) that American types of aircraft would then drop out of the first line, automatically reducing it to approximately 800;
(v) that the 700 mentioned in (ii) above would comprise approximately 385 fighter aircraft, 300 strike aircraft and 15 Amphibians.

NOTE:– … DAWT had tentatively proposed that the makeup of the Fighter strength of 385 and the Strike strength of 300 might be as below.

It was evident, however, from DACR's memorandum of 4 December … in which he shows that existing Fleet and Light Fleet Carriers will not be able to operate all the new types of aircraft, that it would be necessary for DAWT to review this make up in collaboration with DACR, consulting DofP on the present intentions with regard to the new construction programme of Fleet and Light Fleet Carriers.

Fighters

~ N.22/43	120 (rising to about 160 in the first half of 1948)
* N.5/44 or ø N.11/44	120 (" " " ")
Seafire	85 (reducing to nil)
Night Firefly	60
Total	385

~ N.22/43 = Sea Fury (single engined fighter)
* N.5/44 = Sea Hornet (twin engined fighter)
ø N.11/44 = Westland Fighter Bomber

Strike

O.5/43	100 – 120
Sea Mosquito or S.11/43	100
Firebrand	100 – 80 (might be replaced in 1948 by the N.44/44)
Total	300

Amphibia

Sea Otter or replacement	
S.14/44 (late S.12/40)	15

It was further agreed that, as a measure of insurance against the war with Japan continuing for longer than now forecast, peak rates of output of Naval aircraft in 1947/48 should be assessed on (a) the basis of war requirements and (b) a peacetime basis. It was to be assumed that Lend/Lease would continue throughout the period of the Japanese war.

Training and Ancillary Aircraft

I. Operational Types

It was agreed that the requirements of First Line types of aircraft for the Training Services in peace time could not be determined arbitrarily but should be calculated.

II. Basic Training and communications aircraft

Action as for First Line types.

III. Fleet Requirements Units

DGD's peace time requirements were stated as follows:–

Target towing aircraft		92
Silent Co-operation	(a) Twins	49
	(b) DB	31
	(c) Fighter	35
'Shepherd' aircraft		31 (+31 'Sheep')
	Total	238

… the assessment was based on one aircraft averaging one hour's flying per day per annum.

5th Sea Lord expressed the view that a strength of 236 aircraft for Fleet practices under peace conditions was much too high, especially in relation to a carrier-borne strength limited to 800 aircraft. The aircraft, shore facilities and manpower required for the FRU services would, under present arrangements, have to come out of the quota available for the Naval Air Arm proper and he thought that the requirements should be reviewed in the light of budgetary possibilities after the war …

Policy of re-equipping

It was agreed

(i) that the aim should be to re-equip First Line Squadrons with new types or much improved marks of existing types every two years; that the re-equipping should be spread over the two years so that Squadrons using a certain type should be completely re-equipped with the new or better type at the end of two years, viz:– when a still newer type was first beginning to come in;

(ii) that the effect of such a policy on the requirements of spares must be borne in mind;

(iii) that development should be progressed to the fullest possible extent by a bold prototype programme;

(iv) that for aircraft which showed distinct promise on the completion of the prototype stage, there might first be a pre-production run sufficient to provide, say, two squadrons to obtain tactical experience.

Peace-time provisioning

(i) Reserves

Mention was made of the importance of creating a war potential and devoting the limited funds available in peace time to this end and not building up large reserves of aircraft in current service. It was agreed that it was most desirable that reserves of aircraft should be kept as low as possible and account taken of the fact that there would be a better return from repair in peace time.

(ii) Wastage

5th Sea Lord said that there must be no loophole for criticism of the allowance for wastage and that our figure must be supported by firm statistical data.

A figure of 5% per month was mentioned as the pre-war allowance made for First Line wastage but this has since been found incorrect, the actual figure being 20% per annum.

20. *Minute by Head of Air Branch*

[ADM 1/17395] 5 February 1945

DAWT's forecast of a first line strength of 600 IE aircraft was given to CNR some considerable time ago to assist … in making a preliminary survey of the position of the aircraft industry in the immediate postwar years. The estimate was purely speculative but was based on the best information available at the time.

2. In a paper on the Empire postwar Fleet (PD/L/0.52/44), of which the Board took note in May 1944,[1] allowance was made for 12 aircraft carriers in full commission and a further 12 in reserve or modernising.

3. Last November, the Naval Staff suggested that as a tentative basis for planning requirements of aircraft, it should be assumed that the 12 carriers in commission would comprise:–

3 Fleet Carriers each with 60 aircraft	=	180
9 Light Fleet Carriers each with 36 aircraft	=	324
Total (say)		500

Provision of first line squadrons at full strength for the 12 carriers in reserve or modernising is not contemplated. To provide for them to be equipped with reasonable speed in emergency, some voluntary system of RNVR training with squadrons on a cadre basis is intended. It has been provisionally estimated that such a scheme might require an IE of 300 aircraft.

4. On the foregoing assumption, therefore, the first line strength of aircraft in the immediate postwar years would be 500 IE, backed by auxiliary training units with an IE of 300 – a total of 800 IE.

5. The Naval Staff have tentatively suggested that of this total 700 IE should be of the latest types of aircraft (made up of about 385 fighters, 300 strike and 15 amphibians) and the remaining 100 IE of older types such as Barracuda and Seafire.

[1]Board Memorandum B.374 and Board Minutes, 19 May 1944, reproduced as Docs Nos 9 & 10.

6. Submitted for information. It is emphasised that at this stage all these figures can be little more than intelligent guesses; that the Admiralty are not in any way committed to them and that they have not the sanction of higher authority. Some such figures are, however, necessary to enable preliminary steps to be taken in connection with long-term planning. They will be subject to review as the postwar picture comes more clearly into focus.[1]

21. *Minutes of Sea Lords' Meeting*

[ADM 205/51] 28 February 1945

OPTIMUM SIZE OF THE FLEET CARRIER

Papers prepared by the 5th Sea Lord and the Director of Navigation respectively on the optimum size of the Fleet Carrier were discussed. There were three alternative designs:– X, XI and Y. Of these the X type was the largest and the design had already been prepared. The XI type was not quite so large and its dimensions coincided very closely with the maximum advocated by the Director of Navigation. The Y type was a smaller type of a size comparable with the new ARK ROYAL.

The following points were made in discussion:–

(a) The large carrier was required so that a long-range strike could be flown off if required … the X design could carry 90 aircraft as against 83 of the XI. Both types could dock in 9 ports in the British Empire.
(b) ACNS(F) put forward the case for having more smaller carriers instead of a few large ones. He considered that the maintenance of such big ships and their handling in harbours would present considerable difficulties.
(c) The 5th Sea Lord said he regarded the large carrier as a good insurance, in view of the fact that the future designs of aircraft were so uncertain … The First Sea Lord agreed with this view.
(d) ACNS(W) said that … if the decision was going with the large carrier, he preferred the X type of which the design was already prepared.
(e) First Sea Lord said that he considered the 50 extra feet of the X type might well prove a distinct disadvantage in restricted harbours such as Malta, Gibraltar etc.

After further discussion it was decided to adopt the XI design.[2]

[1]Minute seen by Fifth Sea Lord and First Lord of the Admiralty, latter minuted 'concur' on 18 Feb.

[2]This became the *Malta* design. Details of all three designs are in FB(45)2 Appendix A dated 17 Jan 1945, also in ADM 205/51. XI would have displaced 56,850 tons. See also David Hobbs, *British Aircraft Carriers*, Chapter 22.

22. *Joint Planning Staff Memorandum*

[CAB 84/65] 3 January 1945

JP(44)226 (Final) MANPOWER ONE YEAR
AFTER THE DEFEAT OF GERMANY:
REDUCTION OF SERVICE REQUIREMENTS

In accordance with instructions, we have reviewed, in the light of changes in our probable commitments, the previous estimate[1] that 3,404,500 men and women would be required by the three fighting services one year after the defeat of Germany.

2. We have taken into account the effect on our commitments of the following:–

(a) A Directive[2] by the Prime Minister which proposed that the Services should make an examination of the effects of the following cuts:–

Navy	200,000
Army	300,000
Air Force	200,000
Total	700,000

(b) Certain rulings given at two meetings of the Armistice and Post-War Committee …

(c) Strategy decisions taken at "Octagon" …[3]

Strategic Requirements

3. The commitments which have to be met by the armed forces one year after the end of the European War are:–

(a) The security of the United Kingdom.
(b) The prosecution of the war against Japan.
(c) The provision of certain forces of occupation in Europe.
(d) The security of our Imperial lines of communication, of India and of our position in the Middle East.

…

[1] COS(44)597(O), Doc No. 13.
[2] WP(44)431, an extract is reproduced in Doc. No. 14 as an enclosure to JP(44)226(O).
[3] The second Quebec Conference, in Sept 1944.

6. Analysis of the effort of the three Services is broadly as follows:–

Navy

Surface and S/M Forces	268,220
Naval Air Forces	200,210
Naval Assault Forces	103,930
Depots, new entry and technical training establishments	45,240
Recruits	14,000
Naval Personnel replacing civilians	33,400
	665,000

…

ANNEX I
NAVAL MANPOWER REQUIREMENT ONE YEAR AFTER THE DEFEAT OF GERMANY

The Naval manpower requirements for the period of one year after the defeat of Germany have been re-examined on the following basis:–

(a) The strategy agreed at "Octagon" will be implemented in full.

(b) The Dominion Navies will man such naval forces as are given in paragraph 13.

(c) Only the most modern ships will be kept in full commission.

(d) The Naval Air Arm will be reduced to a strength of 1,600 first line aircraft from 2,500.

2. Naval commitments on the above assumptions are:–

(a) The deployment in the Pacific of a self-supporting British Fleet.

(b) The deployment in the Indian Ocean of assault forces capable of lifting 3 divisions with the necessary supporting naval forces.

(c) The security of British sea communications.

(d) The provision of naval forces to support British interests and meet British responsibilities in the Mediterranean and in European waters.

(e) The provision of naval control commissions in Germany and other enemy countries.

(f) The provision of a mine clearance force in European waters.

3. To implement the above commitments, naval forces with their air components have been provided in Tables I and II below.

TABLE I

Strength of Fleet Manned by Royal Navy (ie excluding Dominion Fleets) for 1945

	Ships in reserve with reduced crews	Ships for training and with special crews	Ships with full complements		
			Europe	East Indies	Pacific
Battleships	4	–	1*	2	4
Cruisers	7	3	10	6	16
Fleet Destroyers	53	–	24	18	48
Submarines	73	26	–		40
Large Monitors	–	–	–	3	–
Fast Minelayers	–	–	–	–	3
Escorts	169	–	–	107	53
Fleet Carriers	–	–	–	–	6
Light Fleet Carriers	–	–	–	–	10
Escort Carriers	8	3	–	13	6
Fleet Minesweepers	38	–	75	48	–
Minor Sweeping Vessels	52	–	210	70	8

* To have 3/5 complement.

TABLE II

Deployment of Naval Aircraft

	United Kingdom & Med.	East Indies	Pacific	Total
Fighter Aircraft	170+	350	550	1,070
Striking Aircraft	130+	60	340	530
Communication Aircraft	170	60	70	300
Fleet Requirement Aircraft	120	90	90	300
Training Aircraft	1,080	—	—	1,080
Total	1,670	560	1,050	3,280

+ Allocated to carriers working up and on passage.

A detailed statement of the deployment of naval forces and of the principal bases and establishments to maintain these forces, is given in Appendices A and B.

4. For a given manpower, the size of the fleet which can be deployed is dependent on the base facilities available in the area of operations and the degree to which it must be self-supporting. The repair and maintenance of ships is normally a civil responsibility, carried out by Dockyards, Storing Yards and Ship Repair Yards. The requirement of repair and maintenance ships is then small.

The Indian Ocean and Pacific theatres are comparatively undeveloped in these respects and this has necessitated the provision of a large Fleet Train, which has proved a heavy drain on manpower.

5. In the result, to obtain a proper balance between the Fleet and the resources to support it, the Fleet has been reduced as under:–

	820,000 Fleet	Reduced Fleet
Battleships	10	7
Fleet Carriers	7	6
Light Fleet Carriers	14	10
Escort Carriers	39	19
Cruisers	47	32
Fleet Destroyers	154	90
Escorts	367	160
Submarines	50	40
First Line Aircraft	2,500	1,600

Dominion ships are not included. The smaller number of Fleet and Light Fleet carriers shown is due to delay in completion.

Naval Air Forces

6. The large programme of aircraft carrier construction approved in 1941 and 1942 is now coming forward, and the expansion of naval air forces will reach the new ceiling of 1,600 first line aircraft in 1945. This will provide the aircraft required for all the modern Fleet and Light Fleet carriers, the assault carrier force (CVE) and a small anti-submarine Escort Carrier Force. As further Light Fleet carriers are completed, corresponding escort carriers will be paid off or relegated to ferrying duties.

The greatest importance is attached to the deployment in the Pacific of the largest number of aircraft carriers within our means, whilst providing for the air support of assault operations in South-East Asia Command.

Assault Forces

7. The Admiralty recognise the essential nature of, and the great part to be played, by these forces in the implementation of our strategy, but would draw attention to the heavy cost in naval manpower. The Assault Forces require large supply and maintenance organisations on shore. They are investigating every possible means to reduce this cost by new methods and organisations without impairing the high standard of results required.

Bases and Shore Training Organisations

8. Naval bases and shore establishments have been the subject of special scrutiny in the past twelve months. The Admiralty have adopted the following policy for the period after the defeat of Germany:–

(a) To close in the United Kingdom, Atlantic and Mediterranean all bases other than Dockyard ports, essential mine clearance and working-up bases;

(b) To establish and maintain only such bases as are necessary for the Fleet and Assault Forces in the Indian Ocean and for the Fleet in the Pacific;

(c) To reduce Dockyard and working-up bases at (a) in the Mediterranean and Atlantic to a peace-time footing, depots at home by 25 per cent of present establishments and to maintain training establishments and working-up bases as necessary to conform to requirements; the whole will be subject to periodical review.

This policy has already been implemented at home and in the Mediterranean so far as permissible before the defeat of Germany.

9. The Eastern theatre is seriously deficient in naval and commercial ship repair and maintenance establishments. Australian facilities are barely sufficient for meeting repair and supply needs of the Australian Navy. There is no alternative to the provision by the Admiralty of additional maintenance facilities for the Pacific Fleet.

The Admiralty wish to lay special stress on the inflatory effect on naval manpower figures, and particularly the number serving on shore, which results from the undertaking by the Navy of civil responsibilities in this respect.

Ancilliary Naval Services

10. The employment of Merchant Ships in active theatres, and particularly when participating is assault operations, will require the provision of Naval personnel to man the armament of defensively equipped Merchant Ships. Only ships east of Calcutta, north of Australia and in the South-West, Central and North-West Pacific area will be fully equipped in this respect.

11. Coastal Forces in the Far East will be confined to ML and HDML types which can be used for many purposes and are economical to maintain. In Europe and the Mediterranean, a small number of all types will be available for river, coastal work and for instructional and development purposes.

Mine Clearance Forces

12. Considerable reduction will be made in the Minesweeping Forces. Older ships will be paid off and flotillas will consist only of modern types of vessel. It is estimated that a period of at least two years after the defeat of Germany will be required to complete mine clearance in European waters.

Dominion and Colonial Contributions

13. The contribution of Dominion ships and Dominion-manned British ships is expected to be as under:–

Class	*RAN*	*RNZN*	*RCN*	*RIN*	*SANF*
Cruisers	3	2	2	–	–
Fleet Destroyers	9	–	13	–	–
Escorts	16	2	50	22	6
Fleet Minesweepers	52	–	–	20	–
AA Ships	–	–	1	–	–

14. The Canadian contribution, whose composition is not yet settled, is limited by the Canadian Government's decisions that –

(a) RCN forces are only to be employed in the Pacific.

(b) The total seagoing personnel is not to exceed 13,000 officers and ratings.

15. The Australian Government have stated their inability to provide any Dockyard repair personnel to meet our needs, but will provide 3,600 men for supply duties.

16. All ship repair facilities in New Zealand are being made available. Additional manpower for naval purposes is unlikely to be available.

…

Reductions in Manpower

19. The deployment of personnel is set out in Appendix C. After allowing for the possible employment of Italian labour, Dominion and Colonial assistance in ME, the total manpower required from the United Kingdom will be 631,000 (578,600 men and 53,000 women) for the Fleet and Fleet Establishments and 33,400 (32,400 men and 1,000 women) for Civil Establishments, to be manned by uniformed personnel. Of these:–

268,200 are for naval surface and S/M forces.

200,210 are for Naval Air Forces, including the personnel for aircraft carriers and supporting train.

103,930 are for Naval Assault Forces.

45,240 are for service in depots, new entry and technical training establishments for RN, RM and WRNS personnel …

33,400 are for civilian services.

14,000 are recruits.

…

APPENDIX A
STRENGTH AND DISPOSITION OF FLEET MANNED BY THE ROYAL NAVY ONE YEAR AFTER THE DEFEAT OF GERMANY

Deployment of Naval Forces

Item	Pacific	East Indies Station, SEAC	Mediterranean and Other Stations	United Kingdom and North-West Europe
1. Fleet Units, Escort Forces, Fleet Repair 7 Maintenance Ships. (Naval Air Units NOT included)	4 Battleships 16 Cruisers 48 Destroyers 3 Fast Minelayers 53 Escorts 12 'X' Craft	2 Battleships 6 Cruisers 18 Destroyers 3 Monitors 3 Gunboats 107 Escorts 2 Fighter Direction Ships	6 Cruisers 16 Destroyers 1 Gunboat	1 Battleship (reduced complement) 4 Cruisers 8 Destroyers 2 Training Cruisers 1 Cruiser (Gunnery & D.R.E.) 1 Controlled Minelayer (Training)
	3 Destroyer Depot Ships 11 Fleet Repair Ships 2 Accommodation Ships 2 Armament Maintenance Ships 1 Seaward Defence Ship 1 Local Craft Maintenance Ship 1 Fleet Amenities Ship 4 Escort Maintenance Ship 2 Submarine Depot Ships 1 'X' Craft Depot Ship 2 Fast Tankers 2 Net Layers 2 Fleet Tugs	1 Destroyer Depot Ship 2 Fleet Repair Ships 2 Accommodation Ships 1 Fleet Amenities Ship 4 Escort Maintenance Ships 1 Submarine Depot Ship 1 Net Layer 1 Fleet Tug	1 Destroyer depot Ship 1 Fleet Tug	2 Submarine Depot Ships 2 Fleet Tugs *Reserve Fleet* 4 Battleships 7 Cruisers 53 Fleet Destroyers 1 Destroyer Depot Ship 6 Controlled Minelayers 8 Escort Carriers 73 Submarines 169 Escorts 90 Minesweepers 72 Coastal Craft

	40 Submarines			
		26 Submarines for submarine & anti-submarine training		
	← 6 cable ships, 5 surveying ships, 91 boom working vessels, 8 mooring vessels, 6 boom carriers, 2 gate vessels, 20 rescue tugs, 6 salvage ships, 18 wreck disposal craft →			
2. Naval Air Units	6 Fleet Carriers 7 Light Fleet Carriers 6 Escort Carriers 3 Aircraft Repair Ships 3 Aircraft Engine Repair Ships 3 Aircraft Component Repair Ships 2 Naval Air Target Vessels	13 Escort Carriers 2 Naval Air Target Vessels	8 Light Fleet Carriers working up for the Pacific Fleet	3 Escort Carriers (training) 18 Naval Air Target Vessels
3. Assault Fleet		18 LSI(L), 6 LSI(M), 1 LSI(S) 3 LSI(H), 3 LSH(L), 6 LSH(S) 4 LSF, 144 LST, 7 LSD, 8 LSE, 6 LST (training), 3 LST Maintenance ships, 3 SOBG Ships, Landing & Support craft for 3 Naval Assault Forces	1 LSI(L), 1 LSI(S), 2 LST } Training	1 LSI(H), 2 LST } Training plus major landing ships and craft (C&M, new production and craft in transit)
4. Coastal Forces	24 HDML	68 ML, 78 HDML, 4 support	12 ML	24 MTB, 12 ML, 12 HDML
5. Minesweeping	1 M/S Depot Ship 8 BYMS	48 Fleet Minesweepers 44 BYMS, 14 Motor M/S 12 Dan Trawlers 1 M/S Depot Ship	Forces allocated from UK mine clearance force	75 Fleet Minesweepers, 88 BYMS 104 Motor Minesweepers 18 Dan Trawlers

APPENDIX B

FACILITIES REQUIRED ASHORE TO OPERATE AND MAINTAIN THE FLEET SHOWN IN APPENDIX A

Item	Pacific	East Indies Station, SEAC	Mediterranean and Other Stations	United Kingdom and North-West Europe
Fleet and Auxiliary Bases	Melbourne – RN GHQ Sydney – Main Fleet Base Brisbane – Fleet Base Darwin – Advanced Fleet Base Fremantle – Submarine Base Townsville } Minor Repair Cairns } Bases	Aden } Main Fleet & Colombo } Repair Bases Durban } Kilindini } Trincomalee } Abadan } Escort & Bahrein } small repair Basra } bases Bombay } Diego Suarez } Karachi } Madras } Mauritius } Massawa } Seychelles } Addu Atoll – fuelling base Palk Bay – convoy assembly	Gibraltar } Dockyard Malta } Ports Alexandria – Reduced Fleet Base Taranto – Repair Base Capetown – Minor Repair Base Simonstown – Dockyard Port Falkland Islands – W/T Station Bermuda – Dockyard Port	Devonport } Dockyards, Portsmouth } Naval & RM Chatham } Depots, Sheerness } Training & Rosyth } Technical Establishments Scapa } Working-up Portland } bases Clyde } Tobermory – A/S Working-up base
Naval Air Units	13 Mobile Naval Air Bases 2 Transportable Air Maintenance Yards 2 Receipt & Despatch Units	6 Naval Air Stations 4 Aircraft Repair & Storage Depots	4 Naval Air Stations	26 First-line and Training Naval Air Stations 28 RDU, Repair & Maintenance Yards and/or Storage Depots, Training Schools and other small commitments
Assault Bases		Bombay } C.T.C. Cocanada }	Kabret – C.T.C.	Inveraray – C.T.C.

Coastal Force Bases	Advanced Fleet Base	Cochin Mandapan } Landing craft Vizagapatam Calcutta Karachi } LST Bases Madras 6 mobile Landing Craft Bases	Malta	HMS *Hornet*, Gosport
Minesweeping Bases	As required	Chittagong Cochin As required	Cyprus Haifa	Dover, Harwich, Lowestoft, Grimsby, Immingham, Hartlepool, Newcastle, Aultbea, Liverpool, Swansea

23. *Memorandum for the Board*[1]

[ADM 167/125] 19 February 1945

B.403 1945 New Construction Programme

Introduction

Although the Naval war against Germany has now reached the last stage, new ships are required for the war in the Far East to build up our forces for the final assaults. Following this primary requirement, consideration must be given to the strength of the Post War Fleet. Side by side with these Naval requirements stand the needs of the Mercantile Marine whose rapid recovery during the early postwar years is so essential in the economic interests of the country. To meet these needs a strong and efficient shipbuilding industry is essential, and due consideration must be given to this industry in the preparation of our future plans.

2. A preliminary study has been made of the problem concerned with the reconstruction of the Mercantile Marine (mainly in high class Merchant Ships), and the long-term postwar prospects of the British shipbuilding industry. There are as yet many unknown factors but best estimates indicate that a minimum total of 5 million tons of Merchant Ships, rising to a possible 10 million tons if all conditions conspire favourably, must be built in the immediate postwar years. Making allowance for Naval construction already envisaged for the Japanese war this programme might be expected to extend over a period of 3 to 5 years after the end of the European war.

3. When the replacement programmes for the Merchant Navy and the Royal Navy have been completed the demand in the shipyards is likely to require a reduction in capacity of the order of 40%, which will call for a decline in labour force to about 100,000.

4. The Shipyards will thus be compelled either to turn over to other work or to discharge the men to other employment. In either case if mass unemployment is to be avoided the changeover must be effected gradually. To do this it is clearly necessary to have long term ship construction programmes, with sufficient flexibility to allow for warship building to be most active in periods when Merchant shipbuilding is low, and vice versa assuming that consideration of defence etc permit this course.

5. In considering these matters the Board of Admiralty have reviewed the present naval shipbuilding programme and the proposed new programme has the following objects in view:–

[1]Prepared by DofP, also for the Future Building Committee. The policy set out in this memorandum was approved by the Board on 23 Feb (Board Minute 3998).

(a) To press on with the construction of all ships at present ordered that can be completed in time to take an effective part in the war against Japan. This includes all ships that can be completed by the end of 1946.
(b) To go slow and in some cases defer the construction of the majority of the ships that cannot in any case be completed by the end of 1946. This will release shipyard capacity for merchant ship construction in those yards which have during the war years been employed mainly on warships.
(c) Those warships in (b) above to be built at a rate and in sequence with the merchant shipbuilding programme, so as to assist in minimising the violent fluctuations of the shipbuilding industry that so nearly led to disaster between the wars and to allow for any reduction in shipyard capacity ultimately found to be necessary to be achieved by gradual steps.

6. It should, however, be appreciated that the construction of many ships in the Naval programme, especially Aircraft Carriers and Cruisers, though badly needed, has already been delayed in order to build special types of Naval ships and craft yet more urgently needed to meet the changing aspects of war. Further deferment of such construction must inevitably lead to a reduction in strength and efficiency of the Fleet in the early postwar years, as it will mean a delay in the replacement of battle damage[d] and of over-age ships of the Fleet.

7. Owing to the fact that future merchant ship construction is dependent on the orders placed by a considerable number of shipowning companies it is impossible to plan a Joint naval and merchant building programme for *any* substantial period in advance, although this would be the ideal arrangement from the point of view of production …

9. The only satisfactory means of overcoming these difficulties is to have a longer term Naval plan than has previously been the custom, sufficiently flexible to absorb specialised labour as it becomes surplus to merchant ship construction owing to fluctuations in demand; this conservation of labour would, in turn, permit of the acceleration of either Naval or Merchant programmes, as necessary.

10. Finally, it is of equal importance that the marine engineering and ordnance industries should be kept running in parallel to the capacity for ship construction. Sufficient strengthening of the Scientific Staff with the necessary financial support for research and development will also be required to ensure that the ships included in the proposals that follow are ahead of those of other nations both in design and methods of construction.

OUTLINE OF PROGRAMMES

11. Cancellations. The following cancellations have already been made during 1944:–

42	Submarines	(1942/44 Programmes)
9	Fleet Minesweepers (1943 Programme)	
2	Salvage Vessels (1943 Programme)	
5	Boom Vessels (1943 Programme)	
2	Cable Ships (Transferred to Trinity House)	
54	Coastal Craft (Some turned over to Army and Air Ministry)	
3	Destroyers (1943 Weapon class)	
3	MMS (1943 Programme)	
5	LCS(M) (1943 Programme)	
59	LCS(M) (1944 Programme)	
230	LCA	"
44	LCG(M)	"

12. It is now proposed to cancel the following:–

1 Destroyer Depot Ship (1942 Programme)
2 MTB Carrier Ships (1942 Programme)
1 Fleet Repair Ship (1942 Programme)
2 Sloops (1944 Programme)

13. New Construction. The following proposals cover new construction which cannot according to present plans complete before the end of 1946.

Battleships		
LION and TEMERAIRE	1938 Programme. Suspended.	Proceed with construction so as to complete not later than 1952.
CONQUEROR and THUNDERER	1939 Programme. Suspended	To remain deferred.
Aircraft Carriers		
3 ARK ROYALs (Fleet)	1942 Programme	Construction to continue.
4 GIBRALTARs (Fleet)	1943 Programme (2 deferred in 1944 Prog.)	Construction of 2 to be deferred.
4 HERMES (Light Fleet)	1943 Programme	Construction to continue.
4 HERMES (Light Fleet)	1943 Programme	Construction to be deferred.
Cruisers		
1 TIGER Class	1941 Programme (later suspended)	Build in slow time so as to complete not later than 1950. The ship of the 1941 programme to be built to the 1944 design.
5 Heavy Cruisers	1944 Programme	
Destroyers		
14 BATTLE Class	1944 Programme	To be built so as to complete 1947/9 inclusive
4 WEAPON Class	1943 Programme	
4 WEAPON Class	1944 Programme	

Submarines		
8 A Class 3 Improved A 1 Experimental type	1943 Programme 1943 Programme	To be built in slow time
Surveying Ships		
5 Special Surveying Ships	1943 Programme	3 to be built at normal pace. 2 to be laid down and built as convenient – to complete not later than 1950

…

14. Battleships – Resulting from the approval given to our proposals in the 1944 Programme, the design work on the LION and TEMERAIRE has been progressed. The design work on their 6–16″ turrets has begun, but construction has not started. We now estimate that it will be possible to lay down these ships in 1946. The time under construction of the KGVs varied from 4 years to 5 years and 7 months. The construction of the LIONs is likely to take longer, and we estimate the earliest date by which these two could be completed would be by the end of 1950. By that date our effective battleship strength (maximum shown in brackets below) will depend on casualties of the Japanese war; the age of those ships that survive will be as follows:–

	(2)	NELSONs	over 23 years
	(4)	KGVs	8 to 10 years
	(1)	VANGUARD	5 years
Total	(7)		

15. The KGVs and the VANGUARD will be in the forefront of the battle in the Pacific, and casualties amongst these, our newest battleships, may considerably reduce the effective strength of the Battle Fleet. It is therefore of primary importance the LION and TEMERAIRE should be laid down at the earliest date. In view of the age of our Battle Fleet their completion should not be delayed beyond the end of 1952. We ask for approval to proceed accordingly.

We further propose that the CONQUEROR and THUNDERER should remain deferred for the time being, but that we should proceed with the construction of the 6 – 16″ turrets in continuation of those for the first two ships of the class. It is not possible to proceed with the construction of 12 turrets concurrently, as insufficient gun mount pits are available, but it is important to undertake the orders as a smooth programme, thus assisting the ordnance trade.

16. Aircraft Carriers – The developments in the design of carrier-borne aircraft, which may be expected to take place in the postwar years, have been closely studies. It is concluded that there is a need for a small number of large carriers capable of operating heavily loaded long-range aircraft,

and we therefore propose to proceed with the construction of two aircraft carriers of the GIBRALTAR class.

17. By the end of the Japanese war the 14 COLOSSUS class Light Fleet Carriers of the 1942 Programme, constructed as an emergency measure and therefore subject to limited requirements, will have been completed and our Carrier fleet will then consist of those that survive the war out of:–

Fleet Carriers:–	3	ILLUSTRUOUS Class
	1	INDOMITABLE Class
	2	IMPLACABLE Class
Light Fleet Carriers:–	14	COLOSSUS Class

18. All of these carriers will be equipped with various light types of aircraft such as the Barracuda, Seafire and the American Hellcat, Corsair and Avenger. At the end of 1946 and during 1947 the modern, heavy, long range strike aircraft, which cannot be operated by any of these carriers, will begin to come into service; these are the long range reconnaissance bomber (S.11/43), the long range 2-seater torpedo bomber (05/43) and the single-seat torpedo fighter (N.11/44).[1]

19. It may, therefore, be necessary for these carriers to be equipped primarily with fighter aircraft whilst the HERMES Class (Light Fleet Carriers of the 1943 Programme), the ARK ROYAL Class (Fleet Carriers of the 1942 Programme) and the GIBRALTARs (Fleet Carriers of the 1943 Programme) will operate the new long range strike aircraft for which they were designed. The ILLUSTRIOUS and IMPLACABLE classes would require extensive reconstruction to enable them to operate the long-range strike types.

20. It is therefore apparent, in view of the losses we may expect in the war against Japan, and the need to provide the Fleet with a minimum force of modern strike aircraft, that the construction of the two GIBRALTARs, the three ARK ROYALs and the first 4 of the HERMES class must be proceeded with.

21. While it is desirable that these ships should be completed as early as possible their dates of completion may be affected by the requirements of Merchant Shipbuilding.

In order to free the greatest possible capacity for Merchant shipbuilding, if this be required, without jeopardising the essential requirements of the Fleet in postwar years, the following programme of completion would be acceptable:–

ARK ROYAL Class	1 in 1947
	1 in 1948
	1 in 1949

[1] The Sturgeon, Spearfish and Wyvern, respectively.

HERMES Class	2 in 1947
	1 in 1948
	1 in 1949
GIBRALTAR Class	1 in 1950 or as soon after as possible, depending on the requirements of Merchant shipbuilding. 1 one year later.

Our Aircraft Carrier fleet would then be in 1950, without allowing for casualties –

Class	No.	Completed	Age in 1950
ILLUSTRIOUS	3	1940/41	9 – 10 years
INDOMITABLE	1	1941	9 years
IMPLACABLE	2	1944	6 "
COLOSSUS	14	1945/46	4 – 5 years
ARK ROYAL	3	1947/49	1 – 3 "
HERMES	4	1947/49	1 – 3 "
Total	27	Average Age	4.7 years

Of these only 7 (the ARK ROYAL and HERMES classes) will be able to operate the long-range aircraft, and 18 will be Light Fleet Carriers.

22. We therefore propose to defer the laying down of 2 of the very large carriers of the GIBRALTAR class (Fleet Carriers of the 1943 Programme) and the last 4 of the Light Fleet Carriers of the HERMES class until we have gained experience in the operation of the earlier Light Fleets and the situation in the shipyards becomes easier. In the meantime, we shall keep the design of these carriers continuously under review so that their construction could be started with very little delay, should the need arise.

23. Cruisers – In our last programme we drew attention to the fact that the effective strength of our cruisers was becoming seriously impaired by over-age and that we could not therefore afford to continue the construction of Aircraft Carriers to the almost total exclusion of cruisers. The reconstruction of the older cruisers to carry modern weapons and equipment is no longer practicable.

The age of our Cruiser Fleet in 1950 will be:–

Class	No.	Completed	Age in 1950
8″ Cruisers	10	1928/30	20–23 years
LEANDER	5	1933/36	15 – 17 "
ARETHUSA	2	1935/36	14 – 15 "
SOUTHAMPTON	6	1937/39	11 – 13 "
FIJI and UGANDA	9	1940/43	7 – 10 "
DIDO and SCYLLA	11	1940/43	7 – 10 "
SWIFTSURE	2	1943	7 years
TIGER	5	1944/46	4 – 6 years
Total	50	Average Age	12.5 years

24. The total number of cruisers (50) does not make any allowance for casualties during the next two years of war. As already remarked, only the most modern of these will form part of the British Pacific Fleet and it will therefore be amongst these that our losses will occur.
25. The 5 cruisers approved in the 1944 Programme could be laid down late in 1945 and early 1946 and under normal conditions would take about 3½ years to build. We propose, however, to lay these down as they can best be fitted in with the Merchant ship programme provided their completion is not delayed beyond the year 1950. We ask approval to proceed accordingly, and for the one remaining ship of the TIGER class, approved in the 1941 Programme but not yet laid down, to be built to the 1944 design. These cruisers will be powerful ships with a main armament of twelve six-inch guns of new design, a secondary armament of twelve 4.5-inch guns and reasonably armoured.
26. Destroyers – It is proposed that in shipyards where Merchant ships might be built, destroyers that could not be completed by the end of 1946 should be slowed down as necessary to permit the construction of Merchant Ships. By this arrangement we shall have all the destroyers considered necessary for the Japanese war, and provide for a steady replacement after the war of about one Flotilla per year. Our Flotillas should thus be kept up to date without over-burdening the country financially in any one year and will provide the destroyer building shipyards and more particularly the specialist yards with a steady flow of destroyer work.
27. Submarines – It will be seen from paragraph 5 that we have already made drastic reductions in the Submarine programme. The bulk of the remainder of the submarines under construction will complete by about mid-1946 whilst the construction of a few, about 8 in all, will be slowed down in order to assist the shipyards towards a gradual rather than a sudden closing down of this kind of work.

It is most necessary, however, to continue the progress that is now being made in the design and construction of submarines. To enable this to be done, approval is sought to include in this programme 4 submarines, 3 of which will be built to an improved A class design and the other a new and experimental type in which it is hoped to develop revolutionary improvements in underwater performance.
28. Surveying Ships – As soon as Mine Clearance permits, it will be necessary to embark on an extensive programme of surveying, embodying accurate charting of the many wrecks around our coasts, the complete re-survey of all esturial waters and extensive work overseas in all areas normally used by British shipping. For this work 20 ships will be required. At present there are four available (2 Minesweeper design, 1 converted

yacht and 1 vessel built for but never used by the Ministry of Agriculture and Fisheries).

29. While it is realised that it will be necessary to accept conversions as Naval vessels released from operations become available, these are never fully satisfactory and a proportion of specially constructed ships are needed for this most essential work.

We therefore ask approval to build 5 Surveying Ships of about 1,400 tons, to provide one in each of the areas – Home, Mediterranean, West Indies, Africa and New Zealand waters. It is proposed to lay down 3 of these ships as soon as possible and the remaining 2 as convenient so as to complete not later than 1950.

30. Escort Vessels – It is proposed to design a new type of Escort Vessel of about 1,400 tons and with a speed of about 25 knots. The hull will be of standard construction, which will lend itself to mass production, as a protype for rapid expansion in war. A proportion will be finished as A/S vessels and a proportion as A/A ships.

31. Fast Fleet Oilers – The need for these ships has been foreseen for some time, and the mobility of the Fleet in the Pacific at the present time is restricted as there are none available. They are required to be capable of 20 knots and able to oil at sea three ships at a time …

24. *Memorandum by Director of Plans*

[ADM 205/53] 5 March 1945

PD/OL.046/45. STATE OF PLANNING FOR THE POST-WAR FLEET

…

On 4 May 1944 a memorandum was issued by the First Sea Lord's Office headed "The Empire's Post-War Fleet"[1] [It] … enunciates briefly the principles of Imperial defence, the constituents of the Fleet, detailed functions of Fleet units, the formation of the Operational Force … and made numerical proposals for the strength og the Empire's postwar Navy …

The total number of officers and men required to man this Fleet was stated to be "in the order of 170,000, inclusive of all Empire contingents". The memorandum was sent to the Prime Minister.

The Board 'took note' of it on 19 May and directed that an office memo for planning purposes should be issued accordingly.

[1]Reproduced as Doc. No. 9.

On 8 June 1944 … DPS stated that something in the order of 220,000 men would be required to man and maintain this Fleet.

DofP therefore put forward a revised draft Office Memornadum giving a total of 220,000 personnel, of which the RN contribution would be 170,000. Board Minutes from 1 August owards discussed these discrepancies. In consequence:

(a) The Prime Minister was told by the First Sea Lord (8 August) that the estimated Empire total Vote A would be 220,000, including an RN contribution of 170,000.
(b) The issue of an Office Memorandum has been shelved, and it was agreed to raise this issue again in January 1945.

The above broadly summarises the position as it stands today, and this memorandum is written to call attention to the necessity for a further examination and the need for reaching an early decision on postwar Naval requirements …

Reasons for reaching an early decision are:

(i) To provide a clear Admiralty policy, backed by sound arguments … With the approaching end of the war it will be increasingly necessary to justify … the necessity for all the money spent on the Navy.
(ii) To give a sound basis for the production of the annual Shipbuilding Programme, for deciding upon the correct types of ship to build and for postwar planning and reconstruction. Some of the latter problems are now urgent.
(iii) To enable future manning, maintenance, supply and training requirements to be forecast, including naval aircraft and the assault fleet.
(iv) To decide upon what state Imperial Naval and Naval Air Arm bases are to be maintained.

…

At the end of the war, we shall have a Navy which has been developed to meet the requirements of naval warfare in it latest known form. It will represent the experience of over six years of war and it is therefore sound that no major alterations should be made to its structure until the value of such alterations should be established … to ensure keeping up to date, adequate sums must be spent on Research and Development.

…

It is suggested that when the Admiralty view is called for by the Cabinet or any inter-Service body, the Admiralty should be ready with an agreed case approved by the Board as Admiralty policy. It is known that the other Ministries are preparing such cases, and the Admiralty cannot afford to fall behind in this matter, though it is realised that the Admiralty policy may in the long run have to be modified in the light of Cabinet decisions.

A suggested list of some of the problems concerning the structure of the postwar navy is attached at Annex …

ANNEX

(1) What will be the functions and rersponsibilities of the Navy in the years following the defeat of Japan?

(2) What should be the balanced composition and structure of the Navy which it will be necessary to have, including naval aircraft, landing ships and craft, Fleet Train and seagoing ships necessary for training reserves and new entries?

(3) Is it practicable to establish a long term warship building policy?

(4) What will be our world-wide naval base requirements and how are these to be organised? To what extent should our base commitments abroad be semi-permanent or mobile organisations? The composition of the Fleet Train will depend on [this].

(5) What is to be the Admiralty policy in regard to control, supply of and training of shore-based aircraft employed on control of sea communications?

(6) What is to be the system of manning the Navy, including the provision of adequate reserves and the training organisation?

(7) What is to be the Admiralty policy with regard to the Merchant Navy? The question of subsidising ship owners in the construction of new Merchant ships convertible to Escort Carriers, assault shipping etc is relevant.

25. *Minute by Director of Plans*

[ADM 1/18659] 23 April 1945

BATTLESHIPS

I am not clear in my own mind what form of battleship we should now build. We want balanced fighting groups of battleships and aircraft carriers, capable of striking hard by day or night in any state of weather. If we have a large number of carriers … the few modern battleships we now have and the two or three of the largest size which we might build, would probably be quite inadequate to meet our needs for forming balanced groups or fighting units.[1]

[1] In Feb 1945 the Director Naval Construction had identified a minimum displacement of 67,000 tons for a battleship to meet the then current Staff Requirement. Letter to ACNS(W) in ADM 1/18659 (not reproduced).

2. I think a battleship need only be the most powerful unit afloat if she is to engage in single combat with the champion fighting ship of the enemy's fleet. My point is made by the handling by the Germans of their fleet units in this war. They undoubtedly had the most powerful ship afloat in the BISMARCK, and yet they lost her by using her as a single unit. All their other major losses at sea have been caused in a similar way – GRAF SPEE, SCHARNHORST, for example.

3. The multi-gun battleship was, in my mind, produced to increase the rate of hitting; director firing was also a means to this end. With modern radar, accurate calibration of guns, shell and propellants to give consistent ranging, is it really necessary to build ships with so very many guns? By doing so, we let ourselves in for large targets, huge costs and difficulties in berthing and docking. Because we are going to build a few carriers of the largest size that is no reason why battleships should necessarily be equally massive. The very large carrier is of greatest value as a means for the development of aircraft with higher performance than those in normal use. Normal practice does not require such a very large ship for the operation of aircraft, and I am not convinced that the huge battleship is necessary for hard hitting with guns.

4. We are not contemplating building a more powerful fleet than the United States, and I see no reason for trying to out-build them in individual classes of ship, unless it can be proved as essential to the well-being of the future of the British Empire.

5. To sum up, our requirements will be met by the small battleship to form an essential part of a composite unit, consisting of aircraft carriers, battleships, cruisers, destroyers, etc. Her main function will be to fight when the aircraft carriers cannot function effectively, ie at night, in bad weather, or in poor visibility. In these conditions size is not necessarily an advantage; the emphasis should be rather on quick hitting and manoeuvrability, to which should be added habitability and ease of maintenance. I would rather have two ships with 6 – 16″ guns each than one much larger ship with 9 – 16″ guns, massive side armour, very long endurance, and every known complication of control.

26. *Report by Battleship Committee*[1]

[ADM 1/17251] 1 May 1945

M.058985/45

TERMS OF REFERENCE

To provide an appreciation of the best size and armament for the modern battleship, taking into account the following factors and allowing for other relevant considerations such as cost, complement and docking facilities.

(a) A battleship designed to meet the present Staff Requirements cannot be kept under a standard tonnage of 56,000 tons and a length of 930 feet. Such a ship is thought by many to be too big. The size results largely from attempting to meet Staff Requirements for:–
  (i) Main armament,
  (ii) Protection above and under water.

(b) In view of the advances in accuracy and effectiveness of main armament, as a result of recent developments, it is arguable that the main armament can be reduced and yet be efficient for its purpose.

(c) 100% protection is not possible even in a ship of this size and it is arguable that the degree of protection given by meeting Staff Requirements is not worth the price paid in increased size and that a reduced degree of protection should be accepted. This applies particularly to under side protection.

FUNCTION OF THE BATTLESHIP

1. In May 1944 the Sea Lords agreed that "The basis of the strength of the Fleet is the battleship. Besides providing support for all classes of ship the battleship is the most powerful unit for destroying the enemy's surface forces once they are brought to action. A heavier broadside than the enemy is still a very telling weapon in a naval action." We are of the opinion that this definition holds good today and our review is formulated accordingly.

2. The method by which the battleship fulfills its functions is by providing the surface and anti-aircraft gun support in a balanced force working as a tactical unit. Hitting power is therefore of primary importance in battleship design.

3. In preparing this appreciation we have assumed that the gun remains the primary weapon for providing fire power from surface craft.

[1] RA R.M. Servaes & Capt E.G.A. Clifford.

FOREIGN NAVIES

4. In determining our building programme an important consideration is the size of the navy or combination of navies we may have to meet. The countries likely to maintain battleships in the postwar period are America, Russia and France.

5. Although war against the United States of America may be discounted the American building programme affects us in two ways, namely –

(a) Other foreign nations are likely to follow the American lead in regard to size and armament if her ships are bigger than our own.

(b) We expect to fight in alliance with America and it is desirable therefore that our ships should have similar characteristics to those of her navy.

6. Particulars of the latest American battleships of the IOWA Class are given in paragraph 42. The MONTANA Class, whose construction has been suspended, are designed to mount twelve 16″ guns on a deep displacement of 70,780 tons.

7. An appreciation by the Director of Naval Intelligence regarding battleship construction by Russia and France is attached (Appendix A).[1] Broadly speaking, the conclusions are that Russia will embark on an ambitious building programme but that it is too early to determine what France will do.

8. In 1937 Russia laid down two battleships, each of 44,000 tons, mounting nine 16-inch guns and just before the war France built the RICHELIEU and JEAN BART of 35,000 tons, mounting eight 15-inch guns.

9. We consider that there is no reason why Russia and France should not build capital ships of large size when they can commence rebuilding.

SIZE OF THE BATTLESHIP

10. The requisite fire power in a balanced force may be mounted in a few large ships or in a greater number of smaller ones.

11. Battleships must be able to move rapidly in time of war from one theatre of operations to another and their size must take available harbour, docking, repair facilities, and the navigability of the Suez and Panama Canals into account. The importance of strategical mobility increases when there are a limited number of ships available.

12. Unless enormous and costly improvements to harbours and docks etc are made, which are most unlikely in the foreseeable future, we consider that the maximum size of the Battleship should not greatly exceed the following dimensions:–

[1] Not reproduced.

Length	..	..	..	850 feet
Beam	..	..	..	115 feet
Draught	..	..	..	34 feet

Standard Displacement of the order of 44,000 tons

…

14. Other factors in favour of the smaller ship are:–
   (a) A larger number of small ships will provide greater security and more strategical and tactical flexibility.
   (b) There would be a great disinclination to risk a very large and valuable ship, whose loss or temporary immobilisation for refit or repair would have a disproportionate effect on our total strength.

COST AND COMPLEMENT

15. The very approximate cost of the 1945 LION class battleship (Design B) mounting nine 16-inch guns on a standard displacement of 59,000 tons would be £13¼ millions.

16. A smaller ship, mounting six 16-inch guns with a standard displacement of about 45,000 tons would cost approximately £10¾ millions.

17. The cost of a ship mounting six 16-inch guns with a standard displacement of only 35,000 tons would be approximately £9 millions.

18. To mount, for example, eighteen 16-inch guns in two large ships would therefore cost £26½ millions; to mount a similar number of guns in three small ships would cost £32¼ millions.

19. The complement for the nine-gun ship would be approximately 2,000 men and for the smaller ship ships 1,850 men … assum[ing] that the same AA armament would be mounted in each ship.

20. From the above it will be seen that 4,000 men would be required to man two nine-gun ships and 5,550 to man three smaller ones. A larger number of small ships would therefore cost more in men and money that a smaller number of large ones, although in peace time a saving could be effected by keeping one of the smaller ships in reserve.

MANOEUVRABILITY

21. The battleship should be sufficiently handy to be able to manoeuvre with the aircraft carriers and should be able to take avoiding action against the straight running torpedo and against shell fire during the flight of the projectile. The advent of homing weapons and radio-controlled missiles, however, will make this quality less efficacious as a means of escaping damage and improved manoeuvrability will thus afford no justification for reducing protection.

EFFECT OF MODERN DEVELOPMENTS

22. We do not consider that the main armament can be reduced merely because modern developments have increased its accuracy and effectiveness. The size of the main armament is determined in relation to that of

the potential enemy and it is only reasonable to assume that his technical efficiency and methods will be equal to our own.

23. In our opinion the effect of modern developments will be to increase the range at which actions will normally be fought and to make the chance of a night encounter at short range exceedingly remote.

24. We have also been given to understand that the contest between radar and radar counter-measures is fairly even and it may well be that we shall on occasions still have to rely on visual methods of control.

MAIN ARMAMENT

25. We have considered various alternative armaments of 16-inch, 15-inch and 14-inch guns with a view to reducing the size of the ship. We understand that a saving of not more than 3,000 tons can be effected by mounting three 15-inch triple turrets instead of three 16-inch, whilst a further saving of 2,000 tons can be made if the calibre is reduced to 14-inch.

26. The comparative rates for causing damage of those three armaments are 1.27, 1.00 and 0.75, respectively.

27. We consider the additional weight for the 16-inch gun is worth the increased damage effect obtained, moreover the moral effect on the enemy of 16-inch fire, together with the fact that ships of foreign Powers will probably mount this gun, must be taken into account. There is the further consideration that much design work has already been done on the 16-inch triple turrets and a change now would involve a delay of at least a year if the calibre were to be altered, or about nine months if the design were to be changed from triple to twin mountings. We therefore recommend that the 16-inch gun should comprise the main armament.

28. On the data before us we consider that not more than six 16-inch guns can be mounted in a balanced ship unless it is to become prohibitive in size. Moreover, we consider six guns to be the minimum number to ensure a sufficient rate of hitting and efficient control, allowing for damage and breakdowns.

29. In a nine-gun triple turret ship there can be no argument as to the disposition of the turrets, but in a six gun ship the best alternatives seem to lie between two triple turrets mounted forward and three twin turrets, two forward and one aft.

30. The twin turret arrangement would require a slightly larger ship, but would have the advantage that one heavy underwater hit could not put the whole of the main armament out of action, as might occur with a hit near the bulkhead between the magazines of the two triple turrets mounted forward. A ship, however, which has sustained major damage of this nature could take little further part in the battle even if she had an after turret left capable of firing.

31. Two triple turrets mounted forward would have the advantages of providing improved 'A' arcs and would also free the after part of the ship from blast, thus allowing a better lay out for the secondary and A.A. armaments. Moreover, experience in this war indicates that the after guns normally fire a considerably fewer number of rounds in action. The arguments between the two different arrangements are very evenly balanced but on the whole, we think the greater advantage lies with the two triple turrets forward.

SECONDARY ARMAMENT

32. A secondary armament of 4.5″ HA/LA guns, 40mm AA guns and light close-range weapons of the order proposed in the Staff Requirements for the 1945 LION class battleship is recommended. This is based on the ability to engage up to 6 separate aircraft targets. Should, however, considerations of length and weight make a reduction necessary the number of 4.5″ turrets should be reduced from twelve to ten.

SPEED AND ENDURANCE

33. The battleship must have sufficient speed to operate with the aircraft carriers. The full speed of the carriers is governed more by the fact that they must be able to fly off modern aircraft in a flat calm than on tactical considerations. We consider that a speed of two to three knots less than that of the fastest aircraft carrier can be accepted for the battleship. This should give the designed speed of the battleship in the region of twenty-nine knots deep.

34. The minimum endurance should be 6,000 miles at twenty knots but greater endurance is desirable if it can be provided. A high economical speed has obvious advantages.

PROTECTION

35. The protection of a ship naturally falls under two main headings:–

Under Water

36. Under water protection is the most important factor. Damage above the water line will impair the fighting efficiency of the ship and possibly put her temporarily out of action; damage below the water line will very often entail a complete loss …

Above Water

40. The development of rocket projectiles and heavy armour piercing bombs makes it impossible to provide full protection for the magazines and machinery spaces except at a prohibitive cost in weight of armour …

44. To reduce the size of the 1945 LION to the limits desired, while retaining nine 16-inch guns, would result in the ship having entirely inadequate protection. Bearing in mind the limited number of ships that can be provided, their cost and time to build, we do not recommend that this should be done.

45. The only practicable way of substantially reducing the size is to reduce the main armament from nine to six guns.

CONCLUSIONS AND RECOMMENDATIONS

46. We recommend that a ship should be designed with the following broad characteristics, the size being kept as small as possible and in any case within the limits given in paragraph 12 above:–

Main Armament	Six 16-inch guns in two triple turrets mounted forward.
Secondary Armament	Twenty-four or twenty 4.5″ HA/LA in twin turrets.
Protection:–	Magazines. 12½ belt – 6″ deck. Machinery Spaces. 11½ belt – 4″ deck.
Under Water	Protection and sub division to be arranged to withstand without immobilisation up to two severe under water explosions, near misses from heavy bombs and hits from 'Uncle Tom' type weapons.
Speed	Minimum 29 knots (Deep and clean).
Endurance	As much as possible – minimum 6,000 miles at 20 knots.

47. We believe that a ship embodying the above characteristics provides a fair balance between mobility, fire power and protection. Her displacement can be only very approximately stated but we understand it would not exceed 45,000 tons.

27. *Note by First Sea Lord*

[ADM 205/51] 24 April 1945

STATE OF PLANNING FOR THE POST WAR FLEET
With reference to the minutes of the Sea Lords' meeting of 13 March 1945 the attached paper is a draft prepared by the Director of Plans[1] in reply to question 1:–
"What will be the functions and responsibilities of the Navy in the years following the defeat of Japan?"

2. It is intended to consider this paper at a Sea Lords' meeting to be held early in May. It is further intended that the paper in its finally approved form should be issued to all departments within the Admiralty on a top-secret basis as a background for postwar planning …

[1]The final version of the Director of Plans's paper is PD/OL.0133/45, reproduced as Doc. No. 28.

3. I attach considerable importance to this paper, which contains some controversial questions. These need resolving so that planning for the future can proceed.

28. *Plans Division Memorandum*

[ADM 167/125] 29 May 1945

PD/OL.0133/45 THE POST-WAR NAVY AND
THE POLICY GOVERNING ITS COMPOSITION

I. The Basis of Imperial Defence

The basis of Imperial Defence is the control of sea communications. Without this control the countries of the British Commonwealth become disconnected units, each one too weak for defence against a first-class power. With assured sea communications the whole strength of the Empire can be brought to bear in any part of the world with the greatest economy and effect. Equally important is the defence of the United Kingdom base.

Sea Power, exercised by a proper proportion of surface forces, carrier-borne and shore-based aircraft and supported by submarines, auxiliary units, strategically placed bases and a sound administration, is the means by which sea communications are controlled. Naval forces alone cannot control sea communications; they require the co-operation of air forces and also must rely on the Army and Air Force for the holding or gaining of base areas necessary for the conduct of sea operations. The inter-dependence of the three fighting Services is the basis of Imperial Strategy and a correct balance between the Services must be established.

II. Basic Assumptions

(a) Though Germany and Japan will be completely disarmed for a period, it is not certain that they will be prevented from becoming a threat to world peace in the foreseeable future. Human memory is notoriously short and the possibility of a resurgent Germany and Japan must be taken into account.

(b) War against the United States of America is unthinkable. In any future war, it is to be hoped that the United States of America will again be allied to the British Empire. From past experience it is unlikely that America will take part in the early stages of a war, and the Empire may be faced once more with "holding the ring" alone.

(c) The success of a World Security Organisation must not be assumed. In the present stage of international understanding, it would be unwise to rely entirely on a World Security Organisation. Whether this materialises or not, strong forces of all arms must be maintained if the British Empire is to retain the status of a first-class power. Sea power will be an essential component of the Empire's armed strength.

(d) Owing to its strategic mobility, the Navy may be the first arm to be employed in many areas of the world, should it be necessary to resort to force or bring pressure to bear to keep the peace. In any world security organisation, it will probably be the Navies and Air Forces which will provide the Empire's most effective contribution.

III. Functions of the Navy in Peace

(a) To keep the peace and support British Policy; to safeguard British world-wide interests and to demonstrate to other nations of the world that the Empire is in a position to contribute its full share to international security.

(b) To ensure both the necessary readiness if war breaks out and the co-ordinated strength so as to deter any nation which may be tempted to resort to war.

For the Navy these will involve intensive training in full co-operation with the other Services. The Fleet must be kept fully efficient and adequate reserves of men built up for manning ships in reserve and new construction. Peace-time limitations of finance and manpower, even with full Dominion co-operation, will clearly prohibit the keeping in commission of more than a small proportion of the wartime Fleet. The problem is therefore to decide the correct proportion between the components of the Navy so that it can be expanded to its wartime strength with as little delay as possible, from the size necessary for its peacetime functions.

British interests are world-wide and will require the stationing of ships in all parts of the world. Besides exerting British influence and rendering assistance to British nationals, in case of civil disorder or other calamities, the Navy has an important role in 'showing the flag'. This latter function should result in greatly expanded exports, without which it is certain that the country's finances will be unable to support a large Navy except when at war.

IV. Role of the Navy in War

The role of the Navy in war is to play its full part in the control of sea communications. This may be divided into:–

(a) Destruction of the Armed Forces of the Enemy

The early destruction of an enemy's sea and air forces is the most certain and economical method of protecting the Empire's sea communications. This will also afford freedom of action for the forces of all Arms which is necessary for ultimate victory.

(b) Defence of Imperial Sea Communications
Protection must be provided to merchant shipping in all threatened areas against surface, air and under water attack. Whilst the main cargoes of food, war equipment and raw materials are carried in ships, protection must continue to be afforded by surface ships, supported by carrier-borne and shore-based aircraft.

(c) Attack on Enemy Communications
The destruction of the enemy's naval forces and the defence of the Empire's trade routes will, in general, cut the enemy's sea communications. Additional measures will, however, be required to stop the enemy's coastal trade.

(d) Co-operation with the other Services in amphibious operations
The Navy is required to transport overseas and land the Armies in assault operations. Besides the provision and manning of specialised shipping for this purpose, the Fleet has to protect the assault convoys and to cover and support landing operations. It is true to say that no enemy can be finally defeated until the armed strength of the Empire has been convoyed by sea and brought to bear in the industrial heart of the enemy's country.

V. Composition of the Navy

Without knowledge of the strength of the postwar Navies of other nations, the task of fitting proposals for the Empire's Naval strength into any clear-cut strategical picture is extremely difficult. The Admiralty can, in fact, only determine what minimal naval forces would be needed at the outbreak of a war to maintain the Empire's sea communications, whilst the strength of the Fleet is being expanded. Should there be indications at any time that other powers are undertaking a disproportionate building programme, these minimum forces would have to be revised.

The modern Navy in war must contain or control the following components:–

(a) Fighting units to counter the enemy's heavy surface forces. These must include a proper proportion of capital ships, aircraft carriers, cruisers and destroyers, organised in composite fighting squadrons or groups.
(b) Escort squadrons for the direct protection of shipping. These squadrons will comprise AA Cruisers, Light Carriers and Escorts in proportions varying with the tactical developments of the future.
(c) Shore-based aircraft for reconnaissance, striking and defence.
(d) Minesweeping forces for clearing shipping routes and harbour approaches.

(e) Fast Minelayers, submarines and coastal craft to attack the enemy's communications and coastal traffic.
(f) An amphibious lift and supporting forces for overseas operations.
(g) Adequate naval and air bases, facilities for establishing and defending advanced operating bases and an appropriate shore organisation to support them.
(h) A Fleet Train organisation for the support of the Fleet in operational areas over long periods.

Whilst navies are required to fight in all parts of the world, in all conditions of climate and weather, by day and night, they will continue to comprise units of all these classes. None has yet been rendered obsolete by scientific development, though their characteristics and relative numbers will undoubtably change as new weapons and tactics are evolved.

The strength of forces required for countering an enemy surface fleet depends on the number of heavy ships that a potential enemy possesses. On the other hand, trade protection forces depend on the number of merchant ships at sea at any one time and the length of the sea routes threatened rather than on the actual scale of the threat. In the same way can be calculated the minesweeping effort required to keep clear the Channels and approach routes to the ports that will enable that trade.

Requirements for training and development in peacetime will necessitate the retention in commission of a proper proportion of all the components of the Navy.

VI. Scientific Research

It is of the greatest importance that the Navy should keep ahead of those of other nations in the application of science to both offensive and defensive weapons. This will need continuous research and development on a large scale and the allocation of the necessary resources.

VII. Shipbuilding Resources

An efficient and prosperous shipbuilding industry is essential for the maintenance of sea power. This will not be achieved unless a steady building programme is maintained, based on the replacement and modernisation of out of date warships and merchant ships. As the smaller units of the Navy can be built a great deal more rapidly than battleships, aircraft carriers and cruisers, the balance of the various components of the Navy in peacetime must be adjusted accordingly. Therefore, there must necessarily be a preponderance of the major units in being; the number in full commission or reserve will be dependent on the Empire's international relations, world-wide British interests and the requirements of training.

In order to meet the needs of rapid expansion on the outbreak of war, especially as regards escorts for trade, it will be essential to establish a special organisation for this purpose in peace. This will involve the selection of firms, the preparation and issue of detailed and up to date drawings and instructions and also the holding of stocks of the necessary materials. In no other way can the rapid construction of ships be achieved. Similar arrangements will be required for naval aircraft.

VIII. Dominion Navies

It is evident that the Dominions are taking an increasing interest in their Navies and it is desirable that they should be given every encouragement and assistance to bear their full share of the burden of Imperial Defence in Peace as well as in War. The Dominions should be encouraged to develop base facilities to accord with Empire strategic requirements. In addition, it is desirable that they maintain their shipbuilding and munitions industries. For these, a steady programme of construction would be necessary. They could also build certain components on an economic basis, if orders from the United Kingdom were added to their own requirements.

Although it would be desirable for individual Dominion Governments to maintain naval forces of all types required to meet their own particular needs, this is not considered of major importance provided their squadrons and flotillas from part of the Empire Navy as a whole.

The policy of exchange between the Royal Navy and the Dominion Navies, both of ships and personnel should be greatly extended and opportunities to take part in staff and administrative duties provided, in order to widen the experience and common doctrine as a foundation for close co-operation in war.

IX. Empire Bases

To retain the mobility, of which the Navy alone of the three Services is capable, and the ability to operate in all parts of the world, a base organisation corresponding to the strength of the Fleet in war is required. Adequate provision can be made under three headings:–

(a) The Main Base, comprising full docking, repair, storage, training and manning facilities, situated in a rear area reasonably free from enemy attack and backed by a developed industry and if possible, a white population.
Such bases will be essential in the United Kingdom, can and should be fully developed in Australia, South Africa and Canada.

(b) The Secondary Base, forward of the Main Base and comprising docking, naval air and repair facilities already established for naval and commercial purposes in areas which may not necessarily be defensible in time of war, but where additional facilities such as floating docks and temporary storage and training facilities can be provided.

Some bases will not warrant large scale development for purely naval purposes. Others which have special peacetime functions will be developed accordingly.

(c) The Advanced Operational Base, which may be established in any convenient area near the scene of naval operations, where a good anchorage and potential air strip sites exist. For this purpose, the bulk of the facilities will be afloat in ships of the Fleet Train, but portable defence and constructional equipment will also be required. This organisation will be developed from the existing practice in the Pacific.

X. Manning and Conscription

It is of primary importance that the best and most economical use should be made of every officer and man in the postwar Navy. Modern navies require a high proportion of technical and administrative personnel. Conscription may well be a part of our postwar defence policy.

These considerations suggest that the Navy requires in peace a hard core of senior ratings, technicians and administrative personnel trained and organised so that their potential capabilities are dully employed. These should be supplemented by lower categories similarly trained and organised. In addition, adequate naval reserves of specialist and non-technical categories must be available on mobilisation. The provision of reserves of flying crews needs special attention in view of the length of training required and the high rate of turnover.

Conscription ensures a wide choice of personnel of varying educational and technical experience to meet particular needs, and should provide a reserve of partially trained men far larger and of better potential value than the Navy has possessed before.

If conscription is retained after the war ends, it will be no less necessary than formerly to ensure that service in the Navy is attractive and therefore largely first choice amongst men called up. This can be achieved if men in their year's training are made to feel that they are part of the Navy and are encouraged to work for commissions in the Reserve. There is the added advantage that ships, whose lower ratings are largely conscripts, will be manned on the same basis as in war. This should be of direct advantage to the officers and men of the long service categories serving with them.

The effects of (a) the high proportion of technical ratings necessary in the Fleet; (b) the requirements of bases and the specialised components of the modern navy; and (c) the possible perpetuation of conscription will react on the future size of Vote "A" and ultimately of the Fleet to be maintained.

The aim should be to simplify equipment and maintenance so that with the greater potential of reserves, the Fleet can be more easily and economically provided in peace and the Navy mobilised for war more rapidly.

XI. The Merchant Navy and Trade

A healthy Merchant Navy is an essential element of Sea Power, and a well-equipped merchant fleet will be an important element in the recovery of British overseas trade. An efficient and well-found deep-sea fishing industry will provide a ready reserve of vessels of great operational value and trained seamen to man them. It will be necessary for the Admiralty to take steps to ensure that the construction of shipping embraces the essential needs of war. The principal features of concern to the Admiralty are those of speed, self-defence and ease of conversion to certain specialised roles. Compromise will be necessary to avoid undue reduction in commercial efficiency, but the important object of increasing the minimum speed of merchant ships should be possible of achievement.

For economic reasons it will not be practicable to include merchant ships in peace-time convoy exercises with the Fleet, but Merchant Navy officers should be kept abreast of developments in the defence of Trade and tactical methods practised with units of the Fleet Train.

XII. Summary of Admiralty Policy

(a) Sufficient forces will be kept in commission to safeguard British world-wide interests and to maintain training and development for war. Each component which will form part of the Fleet in war will be included so that long service officers and men are ready for an immediate expansion of the Fleet when an emergency arises.

(b) In addition to ships in full commission, an adequate number will be maintained in reserve to meet immediate needs at the beginning of a war. As the larger ships of the Fleet take longer to build than smaller, simpler types, a relatively high proportion of ships of the reserve will be of the larger categories.

(c) A steady programme of building and reconstruction will be maintained based on the replacement and modernisation of out of date ships. Special steps will be taken to ensure the rapid construction of the smaller and simpler types of ships, such as escorts, to meet the needs of rapid expansion on the outbreak of war.

(d) Every encouragement and assistance will be given to Dominion Governments to build up modern Fleets and Base facilities and to maintain their shipbuilding and munition industries. The exchange of ships and personnel will be greatly expanded.

(e) Full co-operation with the Army and the RAF will continue. Inter-Service training will necessitate the provision of shore-based aircraft for sea reconnaissance, striking and defence. It will also involve the provision of an assault lift and the manpower for all those functions of amphibious operations which are necessarily the duty of the Seaman.

(f) Main bases for the Fleet will be maintained in the United Kingdom and the Dominions. Secondary bases and facilities to meet peacetime requirements will be provided in British overseas possessions. Facilities for establishing advanced operating bases will be retained. This will be covered by the Fleet Train and an appropriate nucleus shore organisation to support it.

(g) Long service personnel, consisting of officers, senior technical and administrative ratings, may be supplemented by conscript entries. For all classes service in the Navy must be attractive, so that adequate reserves of specialist and non-technical categories may be available on mobilisation. The aim will be to simplify equipment and maintenance, so that the Fleets can be more easily and economically manned in peace and the Navy more rapidly mobilised for war.

(h) The merchant fleet will be an important element in the recovery of British overseas trade; a modern deep-sea fishing fleet provides a valuable reserve of seamen and vessels. All practicable steps will be taken to ensure that the construction of shipping embraces the essential needs for war. Facilities will be provided for Merchant Navy officers to keep abreast of developments in the defence of trade.

(i) It is of primary importance to keep ahead of other countries in the application of science to both offensive and defensive weapons. To this end, scientific research and development will be continued on a large scale and the necessary resources will be allocated.

29. *Treasury Letter to all Departments*[1]

[ADM 167/125] 14 May 1945

TC No.9/45 Control of Expenditure after the Defeat of Germany

1. I am directed by the Lords Commissioners of His Majesty's Treasury to state that during the last few years, when the nation's resources have

[1]Signed by Sir Edward Bridges, Cabinet Secretary and Permanent Secretary to the Treasury.

all been devoted to the prosecution of the war, the main instrument for ensuring that those resources were used in accordance with Government policy has been the system of allocation of manpower and material between competing war purposes. The end of hostilities in Europe calls for a review of the position and for the issue of fresh instructions to Departments.

2. For some considerable time to come, pressure on the nation's resources will remain intense. More particularly, while the war against Japan lasts, it will only be possible to meet the more vital of the other competing demands – housing, the repair of war damage, the rebuilding of civil industry including, in particular, the export trade, and other civil purposes. The first essential, therefore, is to increase to the utmost the total volume of resources available for these purposes by the speedy winding-up of all services rendered unnecessary by the end of the war in Europe. In the second place, regard must be had to the total means available, before deciding that services suspended or contracted during the war can be resumed or expanded or that new services can be instituted. In the third place, the present burden of war taxation must be reduced as soon as possible; but this cannot be done unless the present level of expenditure, which is not far short of double the proceeds of taxation even at its present high level, is substantially reduced as quickly as possible.

3. In furtherance of this policy, I am to inform you that the following measures will be taken:–

(a) Service and Supply Expenditure. The size and character of the Forces to be deployed in the Far East will be settled by directives issued by the Prime Minister and Minister of Defence.

The existing delegations from the Treasury of financial authority will continue so far as they relate to immediate operational needs. It will be for consideration, between officers of the Treasury and of the Department concerned, how far existing delegations for other purposes should be withdrawn or reduced. The Service and Supply Departments should for their part consider how far their delegations to subordinate authorities should now be restricted.

The programme of the Supply Departments will be governed by what is necessary to meet the needs of the Forces in the field. The Treasury will make such proposals for stricter control as are compatible with conditions from time to time.

(b) All services administered by civil Departments in support of active operations or of passive defence in connection with the war in Europe are to be brought to an end as soon as possible …

(c) General. No Department should automatically resume or expand services which have been suspended or contracted at the beginning of, or in the course of, the war. Treasury authority must be sought in each case and also, or course, for the institution of new services.

(d) Establishment matters. The general principles set out in the preceding paragraphs apply equally in the field of establishments. Savings in manpower are urgently necessary over the whole field of Government employment (including Service and Supply Departments) and all Departments are asked to ensure that reductions in services are followed without delay by reductions in their staffs …

30. *War Cabinet Memorandum*

[ADM 167/125] 16 May 1945

WP(45)307 THE NAVY'S MANPOWER REQUIREMENTS FOR THE PERIOD 1 JUNE TO 31 DECEMBER 1945

Memorandum by First Lord of the Admiralty

Commencing on the 18 June 1945 the Navy in common with the other two Services will begin to reduce its overall strength and men and women will be released in accordance with the Re-allocation Plan. The releases will be at a slow rate initially as a considerable amount of re-deployment of the Navy's personnel is necessary. Many of the escort vessels hitherto employed in home waters are destined for the East and their crews must be reformed with men who are not due for release till later. Some of the redundant escort vessels have to be prepared for reserve while others must be destored prior to being laid up or scrapped. This process will take time and will involve many changes in personnel. We are also considerably in arrears with our requirements for officers and ratings on the East Indies and Pacific Stations, and we still have substantial commitments for supplying the Armies of Occupation. Until all these requirements have been met, and the operating and maintenance bases in home waters have been paid off, only a limited number of men will become available to relieve those who are due for release in the early Age and Service Groups.

2. It is understood that in the period of 18 months following the cessation of hostilities in Europe the Army will be reducing its strength by about 50 per cent and will be releasing a million and a half men, and that the War Office intend to do this by releasing a definite number of Age and Service Groups throughout all branches and categories. Owing to the requirements for naval warfare in the Pacific, the reduction which can be made in the strength of the Navy will be relatively very much less, and further it will be quite impossible to release an equal number of Age and Service Groups throughout the various branches of the Navy. This is provided for in the

Re-allocation Plan. In some of the bigger branches such as the Seaman branch, owing to the fortuitous distribution of the Age and Service Groups it is likely that we will be able to go further than the Army, but in many of the other branches it will be extremely difficult to release even the earlier groups. The position with regard to officers will be even more difficult.

Numbers which may be released from the Navy

3. During the next 12 months, it is estimated that, after allowing for wastage and for other factors, the Royal Navy will be able to release about 167,000 men and 20,000 women, without replacement, when reducing to the minimum strength required for the Japanese campaign as at present planned. For the reasons given in paragraph 1, releases will initially be at a relatively slow rate but it is expected that about 90,000 men will be released by the end of 1945.

New allocations required to make good deficiencies

4. Despite the fact that the Navy will be reducing its strength, new allocations of manpower in the period 1 June to 31 December 1945 will be essential. The principal reason is that the composition of the personnel of the Navy required for the Japanese war is very different from what it has been while our main forces have been deployed in Home Waters and in the Atlantic and Mediterranean. When operating in these areas, the support and maintenance of the fleet and of its attendant craft, and the construction of airfields and of accommodation on shore for personnel and for stores have been carried out largely by civilian labour provided by the dockyards and shipyards and by civilian constructional services. These civilians cannot be moved to the East except as members of a uniformed service and so they become a charge against Vote A. It will, therefore, be necessary to recruit a number of skilled men and technicians who cannot be found by any process of remustering and retraining within the Navy.

5. Apart from these men, the Naval Air Arm has not yet reached its peak of expansion and requires further entries, while in other branches, such as Radio Mechanics, Engine-room and Electrical Artificers and Mechanics, Royal Marine Engineers etc, the additional equipment now provided and the special conditions of the war in the Pacific call for expansion.

6. Another reason is that in several branches of the Navy other than the Seaman, Stoker, and Royal Marines, there are considerable shortages and, furthermore, a high proportion of the men now serving are in the Age and Service Groups due for early release, some 17,000 of them being men over 50 in age and Service Group 1. Unless, therefore, new entries are provided few, if any, releases can take place in certain branches and the Military Needs Clause will have to be invoked to a greater extent than is desirable for the wellbeing of the Navy, particularly as the men who would

be retained would be those with long records of service in the Royal Navy in peace and war.

7. This situation was foreseen and throughout the last year or more endeavour has been made to strengthen these branches by remustering and retraining suitable men from other branches. It has not, however, been possible to retire a proper balance by these methods and the repeated cuts applied to the Navy's manpower allocations in the last 18 months have not allowed sufficient entries to be made. New entries are, therefore, essential now for the express purpose of restoring the balance.

8. For the above reasons it is necessary to ask for a minimum new allocation for the Royal Navy of 40,000 men for the period 1 June to 31 December 1945. This is over and above the transfer of the balance of the 17,000 men from the RAF which was approved to take place after the German war when the allocations for the first half of 1944 were decided at the end of 1943.

...

Summary of New Allocations required for the Royal Navy for the period 1 June to 31 December 1945

	New Allocations	Transfers from RAF
MEN –		
(a) To make good deficiencies	40,000	17,200
(b) Replacement of Class B releases	16,000	–
(c) Replacement of wastage Replacement of battle casualties Replacement of men of low medical category unfit service overseas To facilitate redeployment To accelerate releases in Class A	Nil	–
TOTAL, Men	56,000	17,200 (ii)
WOMEN –		
(d) WRNS	3,000	–
(e) VADs	450	–
(f) Nurses	300	–

Tentative Balance Sheet – June to December 1945

New allocations to make good deficiencies	40,000
New allocations as Class B replacement	16,000
Total Entries	56,000

Estimated releases, Class A	90,000
Estimated releases, Class B	9,000
Total releases	99,000
Benefit to Industry	43,000

31. *Chiefs of Staff Committee Memorandum*

[ADM 116/5658] 5 June 1945

COS(45)373(O) PROVISIONAL PERSONNEL REQUIREMENTS FOR THE POSTWAR NAVY

Memorandum by the First Sea Lord

The arguments used by the Chief of the Air Staff in COS(45)321(0) and by the Chief of the Imperial General Staff in C0S(45)367(0) with regard to the necessity for establishing provisional minimum figures for the post war strengths of the Royal Air Force and of the Army are equally applicable to the Navy.

2. As is the case in the other two Services the number of officers and ratings of the Royal Navy whose regular engagements are still current is considerably below the pre-war figure of 133,000.

3. It is considered essential to establish some minimum figure for planning purposes. The response to the call for volunteers for transfer has been so far disappointing, due in large measure to our inability to give any indication of post war manning figures, and, consequently, conditions of service. Numbers of trained and suitable officers and men will be lost to the Royal Navy unless we can offer them some indication of this nature.

4. Apart from questions of personnel, many other postwar problems cannot be planned until a reasonably firm indication can be given of the minimum strength of the Navy. This applies particularly to our requirements for training establishments, for naval air stations and for the rebuilding of those naval barracks and other Admiralty properties which have been damaged by enemy action.

5. Until a worldwide survey of the forces required to safeguard the interests of the British Empire and to implement our obligations under the World Security Organisation has been made on an inter-Service basis, it is only possible to estimate roughly the number of officers and ratings who will be required for the Navy in peace

6. The size of the post war Navy has been under examination for some months, and it is estimated that, excluding such assistance as may be forthcoming from the Dominions and Colonies, the minimum number of long service officers and ratings required will be of the order of 170,000.

7. The reasons for this increase over the pre-war figure of about 133,000 (which did not include the Fleet Air Arm) include:–

(a) The technical and scientific developments and the increased weight of air attack have brought about a considerable increase in the complements of ships, notably to man the radar warning equipment and the large number of anti-aircraft weapons which are now so essential.

(b) It will be necessary to maintain nucleus organisations for forces such as minesweeping and coastal forces which are now an integral part of the Fleet and also a nucleus organisation to maintain the mobility of the Fleet, ie the Fleet Train.

(c) Inter-Service co-operation must continue and so the post war Navy must include a nucleus of amphibious forces both for training and for development.

(d) Carrier-borne air forces are fundamental to sea warfare and an integral part of the Royal Navy. A large proportion of the Navy's manpower must be devoted to this end. Besides the requirements of ship-borne aircraft, naval airfields must be maintained for flying training, and the accommodation of disembarked aircraft.

8. The necessity for all those increases and for these additional activities have been proved during the war, and it will be necessary to maintain organisations in peace to train personnel and to provide scope for technical progress.

9. I therefore ask the Chiefs of Staff to record it as their provisional view that the post war needs of British security will require a Navy of not less than 170,000 long service officers and ratings exclusive of such assistance as may be forthcoming from the Dominions.

32. *Chiefs of Staff Committee Memorandum*

[CAB 80/96] 22 July 1945

COS(45)484(O) MANPOWER IN THE SECOND HALF OF 1945

Memorandum by the Admiralty

ACCELERATION OF RELEASE OF MEN AND WOMEN

At the 173rd Meeting of the Chiefs of Staff Committee, the Chief of the Air Staff represented that the share of the increased release of men which had been imposed on the Royal Air Force by the Chancellor of the Exchequer was unduly heavy. The Chiefs of Staff therefore invited the Service Departments to prepare statements showing the effect of progressive additional cuts of 10,000, 20,000 and 30,000 men, and so on, over and above the numbers recommended by the Chancellor.

2. In their Memorandum the Chiefs of Staff referred to "cuts" but it is desired to point out that these are not, in fact, "cuts", but increased releases in 1945.

* COS 176th Mtg. Minute 1.

EFFECT OF 20,000 INCREASE IN MANPOWER RELEASES

3. The original figure for 1945 releases by the Navy was 90,000. The Chancellor, in CP(45)72, has proposed an increase to 110,000. It should be administratively possible to achieve this increase, but it will inevitably retard the build-up of forces in the East Indies and Pacific as already approved, particularly in regard to the 2nd and 3rd Assault Forces, destroyers, escorts and aircraft carriers, with their attendant support.

* COS(45)310(O).

EFFECT OF FURTHER INCREASE IN MANPOWER RELEASE IN 1945

4. If the Royal Navy are required to increase still further the numbers of releases in 1945, the only method of so doing within the pledged Reallocation Plan, would be to bring forward into 1945 the release of age and service group No. 27, which contains over 20,000 ratings and Royal Marines other ranks. It is not possible without enquiry to all Stations to state definitely the whereabouts of all men in this age and service group, but it is estimated that at least 65 per cent of them are now serving abroad. To release them this year it would be necessary to find reliefs and send them out by October 1945. This would undoubtedly jeopardise considerably the efficiency of the Fleets which will be engaged at that time in the execution of planned operations. Further, the necessity for sending reliefs out for these men would entail retarding still more the reinforcements to the Far East referred to in paragraph 3 and as the ratings concerned would be largely in the higher and more skilled grades, would seriously affect the operational efficiency of Fleets whose personnel have already been diluted to a very high degree. The provision of the necessary personnel shipping would also present difficulty.

5. To release ratings of age and service group No. 27 who may be in home waters whilst retaining those who are abroad would contribute little and would break the pledge given in the Reallocation Plan and would render it increasingly difficult to keep the necessary administrative machinery moving at home.

6. It is not considered, therefore, that the Royal Navy can effect any further releases in 1945 over and above the 20,000, making a total of 110,000 men already recommended by the Chancellor of the Exchequer. This is 72 per cent of the total net reduction of men to be effected in running down to the numbers required …

WOMAN POWER

7. It has been recommended that the releases in 1945 shall be increased from 15,000 by a further 7,000. The WRNS are particularly integrated in the administrative machine for effecting releases. For example, women comprise 88 per cent of the clerical staff, 79 per cent of the cooking and catering and 97 per cent of L/T communications in naval administration in the UK. They could not be removed without relief or the machinery would break down. In any case, time would be required to train men (even if they were available) for this work, which is in a large degree specialised. The use of men for this purpose would delay the release of men …

8. No assurance can, therefore, be given that more than 15,000 women can be released in 1945 and it will certainly be impracticable to increase the figure beyond 22,000 which would represent 77 per cent of the net reduction of women to be effected in running down to the numbers required …

9. If the Navy reach the figures for release recommended by the Chancellor, they will by the end of 1945 have reduced 73 per cent of the net reduction required to be made …

10. The Royal Navy, when fully re-deployed, will have some 62 per cent of its total forces in the Eastern Theatre and these circumstances make an increased speed of release a more difficult problem than if the majority of the personnel were still in European waters.

33. *Second Sea Lord*[1] *to First Lord's Private Office*

[ADM 116/5658] 9 August 1945

In connection with the First Lord's meeting on Friday 10 August to discuss the postwar personnel requirements of the three Services, I would suggest that points to which his attention might be drawn are:–

(a) The requirement for the Post War Fleet was put at 220,000 inclusive of Dominion and Colonial contingents. The figure of 170,000 exclusive of Dominion and Colonial assistance assumes therefore a strength of 50,000 for the Dominions etc. Navies. The 1939 strength of the Dominion and Indian Navies was 9,000.

(b) It might be inferred from paragraph 4(c) of the memorandum[2] that the figure of 170,000 makes some allowance for conscripts who will be an effective addition to the strength of the Navy. I do not think that it does,

[1] Adm (later AoF) Sir Algernon Willis.

[2] COS(45)154 (not reproduced), which deals largely with a common tri-service basis for calculating manpower requirements.

or that it would be right that it should; but it is desirable that it should be clear whether it does or not.

(c) It is stated in paragraph 4(c) of the memorandum that the Navy estimate the average proportion of conscripts who will be an effective addition to the strength of the Navy to be one third or less. I think that this estimate needs to be examined:– I should doubt whether any substantial number of conscripts under training would in fact be effective.

(d) I presume that the figure of 170,000 does include provision for the new functions of the Royal Marines, but I think that the First Lord may wish to confirm that it does.

(e) Until the Committee which is considering the pay code for the postwar Services has made a great deal more progress, I do not think that any useful announcement could be made about the conditions of service which can be offered to hostilities personnel who volunteer for regular service.

34. *Chiefs of Staff Committee Memorandum*

[CAB 80/94] 16 June 1945

COS(45)402(O) FUTURE DEVELOPMENT IN WEAPONS AND METHODS OF WAR

Report by Sir Henry Tizard's "Ad Hoc" Committee[1]

Introduction

We have interpreted our terms of reference as an invitation to predict, as best we can, advances in the science and technology of weapons during the next ten or twenty years, and their effect on the tactics and strategy of warfare. We have not attempted to deal exhaustively with the normal development of existing weapons and already known methods, but have confined ourselves mainly to the consideration of those which might, in our judgment, change the pattern of defence of this country and the Empire, and our power to wage offensive war.

…

Main Conclusions

4. We summarise here the main conclusions which, in our view, should seriously be taken into account in future decisions of strategy and tactics:–

(a) Although we have had no official information, we must point out that the practical achievement of the release of atomic energy is likely to bring about an industrial revolution and have an immense

[1] The Tizard Report was later revised in the light of the development of atomic weapons. TWC(46)15 (revise) in DEFE 2/1252 (not reproduced).

influence on technology in peace and war. If atomic energy can be released explosively, the character of war, the size and composition of military forces, and the scope of armament production will be completely changed. The storage in peace of a suitable number of atomic bombs would give an immense advantage to an aggressor willing to use them in an attack without warning. We foresee no other possible developments of equal significance. Our subsequent conclusions would have to be modified once atomic energy can be employed either as a source of heat or in the form of a bomb …

(g) No adequate proportion of our essentials imports is likely to be carried by air within the next twenty years. Foreseeable developments in the range and speed of only slightly sub-sonic aircraft and of submarines and torpedoes will give decisive advantage to a properly equipped enemy attacking our convoys, until carrier-operated supersonic aircraft and methods of nullifying torpedo attack are evolved. We believe that these defensive measures are technically feasible, though we cannot forecast when they will be achieved. Fast ships sailing alone will not enjoy the immunity they have had in this war …

(i) Foreseeable developments in bombardment by aircraft and pilotless weapons are likely to force our main naval bases further from those of the enemy. Increasing value will attach not only to the base facilities but to the industrial potential of the major Dominions

…

PART II.

WAR AT SEA.

25. … there is little reason to suppose that within twenty years air transport will be able to carry more than a small proportion of the necessary imports and exports in war-time. We shall continue to depend on merchant ships and they may be subject to a variety and viciousness of attack far beyond that experienced in this war. The defence of sea communications and the strength of the Royal Navy, reinforced but not replaced by aircraft, will remain the supreme necessity.

The Threat to our Sea Communications

26. Within twenty years an enemy may have at his disposal:–

(a) Reconnaissance aircraft of maximum speed up to 600mph at great heights and cruising speed of 500 mph, able to cross from Europe to North America and back without refuelling and equipped with radar to enable them to detect any surface ship within a radius of 200 miles.

(b) Large forces of attack aircraft, of the same order of performance as the reconnaissance aircraft, but of similar range, fitted with blind attack equipment and probably also with weapons capable of being guided or of homing, on to the target.

(c) Ocean-going submarines capable of long range and high speed under water, eg with a submerged range of at least 200 miles at 20 knots, in addition to a normal long surface range. Diving depth may increase to 1,000 feet or more, though possibly not in combination with very high speed. Radio navigational aids when submerged are to be expected. The performance of submarines can thus be greatly improved even without the use of atomic energy; but if it proves possible to use atomic energy for their propulsion, the underwater range will be unlimited for all practical purposes.

(d) Torpedoes carrying at least 1,000 lbs HE capable of a range of over 10 miles at 60 knots, or a duration of five hours and range of 100 miles at 20 knots. Submarines could then deliver an effective attack by 'browning' a convoy with torpedoes that would crisscross the track of a convoy until they approached a ship close enough to home on it. We estimate that a chance of a hit under these conditions would be very much higher than at present unless effective counter-measures against homing torpedoes can be evolved.

27. One must not underrate the enemy's difficulties, even if he is equipped with all these formidable weapons; but it is wise to prepare for the worst, though not to fall into the error of being so pessimistic that nothing seems worth trying.

28. We should assume, for instance, that it will be impossible for a convoy, or a large single ship, to cross the Atlantic without being located and shadowed by enemy aircraft operating from Europe. We must thus assume combined aircraft and submarine attacks on Transatlantic convoys similar, but much larger in scale than any that have occurred in this war. Since we must assume the submarine will be fitted with radio navigational aids effective when submerged, the homing of submarines on to convoys will be greatly facilitated.

29. The first conclusion that we draw from this is that large, fast ships, sailing alone, will not enjoy the immunity that they have had in this war, for they will certainly be attacked when far away from sufficient fighter protection, by destructive forces of long-range aircraft. It follows that all goods and troops will have to be transported in strongly-protected convoys.

Protection of our Sea Communications against Air Attack

30. Now as to the nature of the protection. It is inconceivable that continuous fighter cover provided by land-based aircraft will be sufficient, except possibly within 500 miles from land. Even then it will involve an uneconomic use of aircraft. The cardinal point to remember is that it will be possible to inflict crippling losses on an attacking force of aircraft without a great superiority in fighter speed and rate of climb. Attacking aircraft, flying or capable of flying at a speed well above that of sound must themselves be attacked by fighters capable of flying at a speed well above that of sound and these will necessarily be aircraft of relatively small endurance. It is estimated for example that a fighter aircraft flying at 1,000 mph will not have an endurance, at that speed, of much more than half an hour. We can imagine fighter aircraft of this type coming into service within twenty-five years. What is much more difficult to imagine is the evolution of aircraft flying steadily within plus or minus 10 per cent of the speed of sound, or say between 600 and 800 mph … we shall want the greatest attainable excess of fighter speed in order to intercept and attack within the available time.

31. It follows that to secure protection from the kind of attack from the air that must be envisaged in the future, convoys must be escorted by carriers from which a large number of supersonic speed fighter aircraft can be operated. Though there should be little difficulty in the unassisted take-off of supersonic fighters from the decks of moderate-sized carriers owing to their very high thrust/weight ratio, assisted take-off is likely to become universal for carrier operations before the supersonic fighter materialises. The crucial problem is thus that of landing. The development of such aircraft and the necessary landing technique is a matter of the highest importance. The methods of detection of approaching aircraft and of interception and attack by fighters (probably with rockets fitted with proximity fuses) require working out and constant practice …

32. It is assumed, of course, that the convoys will be provided, as at present, with powerful defence against submarines by surface vessels faster than the submarine and by carrier and land-based aircraft. In addition, special ships for high angle anti-aircraft weapons will be needed. Thus, the convoy escort force of the future will be of formidable size and strength and the total requirement in ships, aircraft and men for the defence of our trade will amount to a formidable commitment even if the largest possible convoys are employed. Indeed, it follows that there will be just as much need for a surface navy in the future as in the past, but it will be different in the size, number and nature of the component ships. We cannot foresee a time when a Navy will no longer be needed for the

protection of overseas trade. We return later to a consideration of the right type of warships to meet the changing conditions

33. Much interest is now being taken in this country and in the United States in the development of various forms of pilotless guided or homing antiaircraft projectiles for the defence of ships against air attack. We agree that experimental work on these lines is important, but we do not think that too much faith should be put on them. To deal successfully with a heavy air attack many such projectiles would have to be in the air at the same time on their way to the target, and the problem of sufficiently accurate control under these conditions would appear to us to be extremely difficult.

34. It is not yet possible to estimate how guided anti-aircraft missiles are likely to compare with anti-aircraft fire of the conventional but improved types. The former will no doubt prove to be more deadly individually, particularly against jinking targets. On the other hand, the latter gain much a much higher rate of fire. But whichever type, or combination of types, is found to be best, we would emphasise that fighter and AA defence are essentially complementary. The presence of fighters compels attacking aircraft into formation, and this multiplies by a large factor the effectiveness of each round of AA fire, the more so since it is difficult for a formation to take effective avoiding action.

35. To sum up this part of our argument, we have faith in carrier-borne supersonic fighter aircraft supplemented by AA of guided or conventional type as an adequate defence in the future against air attack by land-based aircraft operating over 500 miles from our own land bases. Our definition of adequate defence is that the enemy will incur at least 20 per cent losses and the attack will not be pressed home with sufficient firmness to cause compensating loss to our own ships. If, however, suicide attacks, for instance by air launched piloted bombs, become a normal method of warfare, then the provision of an adequate defence of our convoys may prove difficult.

Protection of our Communications against Submarines

36. We must now consider defence against the submarine of the future. We must be prepared eventually to counter the development of enemy submarines capable of prolonged high submerged speed. If atomic energy is used for their propulsion it may be possible to locate them by radio-active methods, but we are not hopeful about this, and must exclude it for the present as a possibility. We think that the best counter measures will be found in a combination of the following developments and tactics:–

(a) By the development by ourselves also of very high-performance submarines. These are required not only for experiment and training, which is essential, but for use in war, among other things, for blockading enemy bases, for detecting and attacking submerged enemy submarines and on their way to and from their hunting grounds and possibly also in the actual defence of convoys.

(b) By the development of suitable fighter aircraft and methods of interception so as to cause a high rate of casualty to reconnaissance machines. This involves interception at great distances from the convoy eg 200 miles.

(c) We must provide adequate anti-submarine air cover from carriers of the area surrounding a convoy. Concurrently detecting devices of the radar type can, and must be, greatly improved particularly against Schnorkelling submarines. We attach great importance to the improvement of devices of the sonobuoy type, that are dropped from aircraft and which then can detect and locate submarines by hydrophone or asdic; such devices may be needed in large numbers.

(d) We have some confidence that the homing torpedo may prove a very important weapon against submarines. The basic scientific problems involved in the design of such torpedoes to be used from aircraft and surface ships against fast and deep submarines need careful study.

(e) Methods can be developed for detecting and destroying approaching torpedoes.
We can visualize detecting devices which will automatically operate counter attack, just as modern radar, with predictors, can be used for the automatic control of AA fire. Hydrophone detection, though capable of improvement, has serious limitations and it goes without saying that every attempt must be made to find other means …

37. All the above countermeasures find their application against small submarines working inshore and in narrow waters. There is no doubt that devices to distinguish wrecks from submarines in comparatively shallow waters can be greatly improved by normal processes of development, as can also electrical and other detection systems operated from shore.

38. The great increase in the speed of submarines will influence developments in these ways:–

(a) It must not be expected that a small increase in the speed of merchant ships will have such a useful effect as in this war and it may well be quite out of the question to secure a convoy speed comparable to that of a submerged submarine. On the other hand, it may happen in the end that atomic energy will make possible the economic development of merchant ships of high speed …

(b) There will be a serious difficulty in providing A/S escorts with an adequate margin of speed in rough weather. Secondly, there is a danger that the size and power of the necessary escort vessel will make it so large that the provisioning of adequate numbers may prove very difficult. It is in this connection that high-performance submarines may play a valuable role in counter-attacking the submarines attacking a convoy.

39. We do not attach much importance to the defensive value of bombing attack with present types of explosives and incendiaries on manufacturing districts and submarine bases, partly for the reason, as explained in Part III that we do not think that strategic bombing, as practised in this war, will be sustained in a future war in the face of a well-developed and coordinated defence, and partly for the reason that submarine bases can be made almost impregnable to aircraft attack.

Mining

40. It is probable that sea-mines will be extensively used in any future war, if only because of the considerable economic effort required to sweep them when many different types are used. It is also certain that 'unsweepable' types will be further developed – or more precisely, types which require expendable ships for their successful removal. These types will either cause many casualties or will require a prodigious fleet of expendable sweepers. It must be emphasised that it is false to assume that every weapon necessarily has a counter-measure which is economical enough to be practicable, and for this reason a full study of the implications of the 'unsweepable' mine should be made. It is certainly possible to develop navigational aids whereby ships could be restricted to very narrow channels under all conditions of weather and we consider this a matter of major importance. We are less confident of the improvement of methods of locating mines.

Radio and Radar

41. We anticipate that in a future war, as in this last, a radio and radar battle will proceed, in which new devices are matched by counter-measures, and these by counter-counter-measures. It is impossible to prophesy in this field, but certain conclusions can be drawn. As each device is introduced its countermeasure must be produced too. Adequate research, development and production capacity must be earmarked for the unpredictable demands of counter-measures against enemy devices. Radar transmissions from ships may in many cases prove hazardous through weapons homing on to them; thus, a ship's radar may have to be transferred to aircraft in radio or television communication with the ship. Communications between ships and eventually between aircraft will be by 'flash' methods. Much technical effort will be needed to allow interception and direction finding on these transmissions.

Composition of Naval Forces

42. We now turn to the probable effect of future technical developments on the composition of the Royal Navy. We assume that it will be impossible to operate heavy surface forces without carrier support in any area where heavy enemy air activity is expected.

43. The aircraft carrier is at present essential, both for the protection of trade and for offensive action against the enemy fleet. Its size will depend on the development of aircraft; obviously, it must be kept as small as possible. Since assisted take-off will be used, the future design and use of carriers will depend essentially on the solution of the landing problem.

44. The problem of how the operation of carriers and heavy surface forces are likely to be related in the future is one of great complexity. Though no conclusions of universal application can be drawn from the Pacific war, owing particularly to the prevalent good weather, it is significant that so far, no battle fleet consisting of aircraft carriers and supporting surface craft has been in action at gun range with a battle fleet of similar composition. All such actions have been fought at aircraft range and by day. Experience in the Pacific confirms the view that the destruction of the enemy's air force is the decisive event in such a naval battle and that the fleets are unlikely often to close enough for surface action to be required to gain a strategically decisive victory. As far as we can foresee, the trends of technical development are such as to make probable that such fleet battles are likely in the future also to be decided at aircraft range, even in bad weather or at night.

45. If the fighter and AA defences of a fleet both by day and night improve sufficiently to make an attack on a fleet relatively ineffective, it does not follow necessarily that the fleets will close to gun range. A more likely result is a longer drawn-out air battle, on the outcome of which the outcome of the whole action will depend.

46. The battleship and cruiser, as they exist today, are certain to change in character and size. Battleships have gradually become bigger and bigger because only thus could they carry bigger and longer-range guns. It is not only the threat of air attack that has changed the situation; the advent of the rocket creates a revolution. We must now assume that in future the surface battle will be joined when the masts of one fleet can be detected from the masts of the other – in other words, at horizon distance, which may be taken as approximately 30 miles. Rocket-propelled projectiles, effective at this range, or well over, could be fired from ships much smaller than a modern 'battleship'. We do not think that it will be feasible to provide armour sufficient to protect a ship from serious damage if hit; speed and manoeuvrability will be more important than armour. The problem is therefore how small to make the capital ship. It must be large enough to

carry a substantial main armament, batteries of anti-aircraft guns, and the instruments to control the AA fire and the flight of the rocket projectiles. It must also be large enough to have the necessary endurance and seaworthiness in the worst weather. Our view is that the aim should be to reduce the size of the capital ship as much as possible. Numbers count, particularly by multiplying the targets for the enemy's fire, and so it is surely better, for instance, to have 4 capital ships of 10,000 tons in place of one of 40,000 tons, assuming the total number of weapons to be the same. This is not a matter on which we can give a precise opinion, but we feel that in future success will go to the fleet that carries its weapons in a large number of units, has the most accurate radar equipment, and causes, by tactical handling and the use of scientific devices, the maximum confusion to the enemy radar. It should be noted that, although we are sceptical about the effective use of guided projectiles against heavy air attack, we believe that their use against surface ships will be perfectly feasible, as the relative speed of the target is so low, and it will not be necessary to cause abrupt changes in the flight path of the projectile.

47. Naval craft for amphibious operations have played a substantial part in this war and it is probable that they will do so in another. Considerable further development in the design of these craft must be expected. This is particularly so since the general design of landing craft was largely extemporised during this war.

48. We have nothing to say about destroyers and the smaller vessels of the fleet, including coastal forces, except that there is nothing yet to indicate that they will not be needed in twenty years' time for much the same purposes as they are needed today and therefore need continuous development.

The Role of the Navy

49. It may be that the improvement of long-range bombers and rockets will force us to seek the main supply and repair base of the fleet in, for example, Canada rather than in this country, thus continuing a movement to the rear which started over fifty years ago. By the same token, it would then be true that no European enemy could hope to have a sufficiently secure naval base for surface vessels from the north of Norway to the south of Spain, so we should have little to fear from an enemy fleet attacking, or supporting a landing on our coasts, provided we maintain a land-based air force highly trained for attack on ships. Nevertheless all, we repeat, turns on the production of very high-speed fighters, technically superior to the enemy's. If our hopes in this direction are falsified in ten years' time, the whole position will have to be reviewed, for sea communications to the United Kingdom will, in that event, be most seriously in danger in war against a European Power.

50. It will be seen that there are great dangers ahead. These may be assumed by some to support the extreme view that the supreme importance of the Navy is giving way to that of the Air. We wish to record our view that though this may happen in the distant future, it will not be in our life-time. The need is no longer to concentrate mainly on the defeat of surface forces by surface forces, but primarily to counter the threat from the air and from under the water. Most thought should therefore be given to the defeat of the air and submarine menace and to participation in combined operations. The Navy alone is no longer our sure defence and the scientific development that we foresee forces us to the conclusion that the air and sea war are indivisible …

35. *Cabinet Memorandum*

[CAB 66/67] 29 June 1945

CP(45)54 THE NEW CONSTRUCTION PROGRAMME 1945
Memorandum by First Lord of the Admiralty

1. The New Construction Programme which my predecessor placed before the War Cabinet in 1944 took account, first, of our estimated needs for finishing the war in the Far East, and, second, of ships required to make a start towards providing a balanced and up-to-date postwar Fleet.

2. This year the main concern of the Navy remains the build-up for the Far Eastern war, and I propose to press on with the construction of all ships on order which it is expected will complete before the assumed date of the end of the Japanese war.

3. Construction of ships for the postwar fleet must continue unless we are to find ourselves after the war seriously deficient in important classes. This construction may, however, proceed in a more leisurely manner and I aim, by adjustments in the rate of building or approved programmes, to make available shipyard capacity for reconstruction of the Merchant Navy in a number of Yards which have, during the war years, been employed mainly on warship building. If the demand for merchant ships lags, warship construction may be speeded up.

4. In this connection, it is pertinent to observe that if we are to secure more stable conditions in the shipbuilding industry after the war, and to maintain an adequate labour force, it will be necessary for the Admiralty to take a long-term view of our Naval building programmes. The problems involved are under examination in the Admiralty, who are deeply concerned in the future wellbeing of the industry. The turnover from wartime activity to peace involves obvious difficulties:– in particular we must provide for the rapid building of merchant ships of types urgently

needed for the re-establishment of the Merchant Navy, and must avoid a too rapid falling off in production when the urgent merchant ship orders are fulfilled. What in effect I propose is to use the Naval orders for postwar delivery as a cushion to absorb so far as possible the shocks of transition.

5. The main provision for the Japanese war and for the essential nucleus of the postwar Fleet has been made in earlier programmes. In view of the manpower situation and the demands of reconstruction, I do not wish to seek authority for more than the base minimum under both these categories and the 1945 New Construction programme is, therefore, a very modest one. Indeed, changes in the war situation have made it unnecessary to proceed with a considerable number of ships of approved programmes. A list of the cancellations during 1944 is in an Appendix.

6. Since the 1944 New Construction Programme was approved, the following additions have been made, Treasury sanction having been obtained for the expenditure involved in each case:–

30 Landing Craft (LCM(1)).
22 Floating Docks
And a number of miscellaneous small craft.

Outline of Programme

7. The 1945 programme is as follows:–

Preliminary work on *Lion* and *Temeraire.*
1 Experimental Type Submarine.
4 Escort Vessels.
5 Surveying Ships.
1 Cruiser dock, 2 LST docks and 22 small floating docks.
A number of miscellaneous small craft.

Battleships

8. Last year approval was given to revise the design of the *Lion* and *Temeraire* and to proceed with the construction of six 16″ turrets to enable the *Lion* and *Temeraire* to be laid down with the ships of the 1945 programme if possible. Design work on the ships and turrets has accordingly begun.

9. Only our newest battleships are being sent to the Pacific and in view of the possibility of casualties among them and the age of the rest of our battle fleet, I consider that we can delay no longer steps to maintain our effective strength in Capital Units. I therefore feel justified in asking tor Cabinet approval to place orders as necessary to enable *Lion* and *Temeraire* to be laid down as early as possible. I hope this will be in 1946, but in any case, I regard it as important that their completion should not be delayed beyond the end of 1952.

10. I propose that *Conqueror* and *Thunderer* should remain deferred for the time being.

Aircraft Carriers

11. I do not propose any additions to programmes already authorised. The hope which my predecessor expressed last year that it might be possible to execute the full Programme of Light Fleet Carriers approved in 1943 has not, however, been realised and I am afraid that the second four Carriers must be deferred for the time being.

Cruisers

12. The only change in authorised programmes which I propose is the building of the remaining ship of the 'Tiger' Class approved in the 1941 programme to the 1944 design. I shall aim at ensuring the completion of this ship and the cruisers of the 1944 programme by 1950.

Destroyers

13. Present arrangements should provide us with all the destroyers considered necessary for the Japanese war and with sufficient replacements to carry us over the immediate postwar years.

Submarines

14. The advance of the Americans in the Pacific has shortened Japanese communications and reduced the opportunities of, and accordingly the demand for, submarines. It has, therefore, been found possible to cancel 37 'A' Class Submarines, 20 from the 1943 programme, 17 from the 1944 programme, and two 'T' Class Submarines from the 1942 programme. I propose to build the remaining three Submarines of the 1944 programme to an improved 'A' Class design.

I consider it imperative that we should exert ourselves to catch up with recent revolutionary German developments as soon as possible and I accordingly seek approval for the construction of one submarine of new and experimental type in which it is hoped to develop improvements in underwater performance.

Escort Vessels

15. I ask approval to proceed with the design of four escort vessels of a new type, each of about 1,400 tons and with a speed of about 25 knots. These ships are largely for experimental purposes; two will be finished as A/S vessels and two as A/A ships.

Floating Docks

16. My proposals provide for the construction of one Cruiser dock in Canada, two docks for landing ships and twenty-two docks for small craft. All these docks are required for the repair of ships taking part in the war in the Far East.

Surveying Ships

17. As soon as Mine Clearance permits, it will be necessary to embark on an extensive programme of Surveying embodying accurate charting of the many wrecks around our coasts the complete re-survey of all Estuarial

Waters and extensive work overseas in all areas normally used by British shipping. I therefore ask approval to build five surveying ships of about 1,400 tons, to provide one in each of the areas – Home, Mediterranean, West Indies, Africa, and New Zealand waters. I propose to lay down three of these ships as soon as possible, and the remaining two as convenient so as to complete not later than 1950.

Small Craft

18. I seek approval in the normal way for the large number of miscellaneous small craft required to serve the Fleet and to carry out various other necessary duties.

19. Statements are appended showing the cancellations during 1944, and the estimated cost of this programme separately and in conjunction with previous programmes.

APPENDIX

LIST OF CANCELLATIONS DURING 1944

No.	*Description*	*Programme Year*
3	Destroyers	1943
2	Loch Class Frigates	1943
2	Submarines (T Class)	1942
20	Submarines (A Class)	1943
17	Submarines (A Class)	1944
2	Sloops	1944
9	Fleet Minesweepers	1943
3	Motor Minesweepers	1943
*56	Coastal Craft	Various
7	Boom Defence Vessels	1943
2	MTB Carrier Ships	1943
347	Landing Craft (LCS(M), LCG(M), LCA and LCS)	1943 and 1944
2	Salvage Vessels	1943
1	Repair Ship	1942
†2	Cable Ships	1943
2	Destroyer Depot Ships	1942

* A number of these have been transferred to the War Office and RAF.

† One transferred to Trinity House.

TABLE I
NEW CONSTRUCTION PROGRAMME 1945
Estimate of Expenditure by Financial Year

Vessels	1945	1946	1947	1948	1949	1950	1951	1952	Total
	£	£	£	£	£	£	£	£	£
1 Experimental Type S/M	20,000	130,000	120,000	42,000	–	–	–	–	312,000
4 Escort Vessels	260,000	1,000,000	1,100,000	340,000	–	–	–	–	2,700,000
5 Surveying Ships	90,000	400,000	340,000	250,000	250,000	120,000	–	–	1,450,000
2 6,000-ton Floating Docks for LSTs	600,000	350,000	–	–	–	–	–	–	950,000
1 Cruiser Floating Dock	600,000	400,000	–	–	–	–	–	–	1,000,000
22 300-ton Concrete FDs	1,920,000	100,000	–	–	–	–	–	–	2,020,000
Small craft & Motor Boats	1,300,000	760,000	–	–	–	–	–	–	2,060,000
Total	4,790,000	3,140,000	1,560,000	632,000	250,000	120,000	–	–	10,492,000
NEW DESIGN BATTLESHIPS									
Lion and *Temeraire* (b) (New design)	250,000(a)	2,5000,000	4,000,000	4,500,000	4,5000,000	4,000,000	3,500,000	3,250,000	26,500,000
Grand Total	5,040,000	5,640,000	5,560,000	5,132,000	4,750,000	4,120,000	3,500,000	3,250,000	36,992,000

NOTES:– (a) Includes a small amount of expenditure on design of turrets in 1944.
(b) The battleships, which were actually sanctioned as part of the 1938 Programme, will be built to a new design and it has been thought Convenient to tabulate the cost with the new 1945 programme rather than as a carry-over from earlier Programmes (Table II).

TABLE II

Estimated Expenditure on New Construction (All Programmes) by Financial Year

Programme	1945	1946	1947	1948	1949	1950	1951	1952
	£	£	£	£	£	£	£	£
Programmes prior to 1943 Programme (excluding *Lion* and *Temeraire)*	40,500,000	13,850,000	6,350,000	1,220,000	400,000	–	–	–
1943 Programme	65,500,000	21,500,000	9,400,000	4,050,000	3,050,000	470,000	–	–
1944 Programme	39,180,000	17,900,000	9,050,000	4,500,000	830,000	100,000	–	–
1945 Programme (including *Lion* and *Temeraire)*	5,040,000	5,640,000	5,560,000	5,132,000	4,750,000	4,120,000	3,500,000	3,250,000
	150,220,000	58,890,000	29,360,000	14,902,000	9,030,000	4,690,000	3,500,000	3,250,000

NOTES:– (1) The above calculation are framed on the basis of certain supplies being received under Lend/Lease from United States. In so far as such supplies are not
Received, the figures would be proportionately increased.

(2) No provision is made in the Table for expenditure on the two battleships *Conqueror* and *Thunderer* (ex 1939 Programme) which are deferred for the time being.

36. *Admiral (Submarines)*[1] *to Secretary of the Admiralty*

[ADM 1/19610] 21 June 1945

929/SM.0320 FUTURE STRENGTH OF THE SUBMARINE FLEET

Be pleased to lay before Their Lordships these my proposals for implementing the policy laid down in Admiralty Message 172315 June …

2. The required submarine strength is dependent upon –
   (a) Number of submarines required in the Far East.
   (b) Number of submarines required for A/S and submarines training.
   (c) Size of the postwar submarine fleet.
   (d) Progress and state of submarines under construction.

3. With reference to paragraph 2(a) above, owing to the time spent refitting, working up and on passage both ways, it requires 60 submarines to maintain 30 in the Eastern Theatre. To this must be added new construction submarines for which crews have to be provided before the older submarines can be relieved on the station and be reduced to reserve. Thus, the number of submarines for which manning provision has now to be made is in excess of 60 but will be reduced to 60 when new construction is completed and as older submarines are placed in reserve. Similarly, if the number of submarines in the Eastern Theatre is later reduced, a further saving in manpower will be effected.

4. With reference to paragraph 2(b) above, Admiralty Message 020100 June … fixed the number of British submarines required for A/S training at 20 and … Admiralty Letter M.057912/44 of 7 October 1944 laid down 6 as the number required for submarine training.

5. With reference to paragraph 2(c) above, it is understood that the total peacetime submarine strength (in full commission and reserve) may be approximately 90.

6. The state of new construction submarines is dealt with more fully in paragraph 7 below and in Appendix III, but it is considered that, in view of the advanced state of many submarines now under construction, provision should be made for a submarine strength slightly in excess of 90 to allow for losses and action damage, and that this total should be made up of modern submarines, the necessary reductions to achieve the desired total being effected by –
   (a) Determining a date beyond which the building of new construction submarines should be suspended.
   (b) Scrapping certain old or damaged submarines.

[1]RA (later AoF Sir) George Creasy.

(c) Placing other surplus submarines in reserve pending their disposal to allies or scrapping.

7. With reference to paragraph 6(a) above, it is suggested that the construction of any submarines which are not due to complete by 31 March 1946, should be suspended. This will entail suspending 3 Ts and 14 As (for details see Appendix I).

8. It is proposed to scrap 15 old and damaged submarines as shown in Appendix II.

9. Details and service of the maximum total number of submarines which it is proposed to retain now in full commission and in reserve with reduced complement, is shown in Appendix III. 94 full commission, 18 reserve.

10. By 31 March 1946, if the proposal in paragraph 7 above is approved, the number of submarines in full commission will be reduced to 86, with 26 in reserve. The number in full commission will be further reduced should later reviews of the submarine situation show that a fewer number of operational submarines will be required in the Far East. The number of submarines in reserve will be reduced by scrapping or disposal to Allies.

11. It is understood that U Class submarines are to be allocated to the Chinese. It is requested that the number of U Class to be allocated to French, Norwegians, Danes or any other nationalities may be communicated at an early date.

12. Manpower provision must also be made for supervision of captured U-boats as long as this commitment holds and also for manning certain U-boats for the extensive trials required by Admiralty Departments. A manning forecast for 31 March 1946 based on the above proposals is contained in Appendix IV.

Appendix I

New Construction Submarines the building of which it is considered should be suspended[1,2]

'T' Class	'A' Class
3	14

Appendix II

Old and damaged submarines which it is proposed to scrap[1]

'T' Class	'S' Class	'U' Class
9	5	1

[1]In the interests of space, named lists are not reproduced.

[2]In the event, five named boats in Appendix I were completed in 1945–47 and served well into the 1960s.

Appendix III

Submarines including new construction which will be required for operations[1]

(a) OPERATIONAL

'A' Class	'T' Class	'S' Class
11	24	33

TOTAL – 68, but see paragraphs 3 and 10 of covering letter.
13 of the above are not yet in commission

(b) SUBMARINE TRAINING in full commission[1]

TOTAL – 6

(c) A/S TRAINING[1]

Far East 6 Canada 4 UK 10

TOTAL – 20

(d) Submarines in immediate reserve pending decisions as to disposal

'U' Class

17 (reduced complement)[1]

…

(e) DEPOT SHIPS REQUIRED

Eastern Theatre

ADAMANT MAIDSTONE WOLFE

United Kingdom

FORTH	Third Submarine Flotilla, working up submarines ex refit and new construction for Far East.
CYCLOPS	Seventh Submarine Flotilla for A/S training flotilla.
TITANIA	as accommodation ships at Blockhouse …

Appendix IV

Submarine Manpower forecast for 31 March 1946

Number	Type	Crew Required	Spare Crew	Total
OPERATIONAL				
11	A	622	161	783
22	T	1243	312	1555
27	S	1175	298	1473
60 Total				
SUBMARINE AND A/S TRAINING				
1	A	56	10	66
1	T	56	9	65
6	S	258	43	301
18	U	594	132	726
26 Total				

RESERVE				
3	T	56	9	65
6	S	86	14	100
17	U	187	31	218
26 Total				
MISCELLANEOUS				
4	XE Craft	4	–	4
Depot Ship & Base S/M rating		140		140
Liaison personnel		12		12
			TOTAL	5508
			20% Drafting Margin	1102
			GRAND TOTAL	6610

37. *Minute by Head of Military Branch*

[ADM 1/19610] 19 July 1945

M.059119/45

In the light of the decision that fewer submarines are required for operations in the Far East, FOSM has reviewed his entire submarine position … He points out that while 60 submarines are required to maintain 30 in the Eastern Theatre, manning provision must be made for something over 60 until new construction is completed and older submarines are placed in reserve.

2. … all 11 'A' Class, 24 'T' Class and 33 'S' Class, a total of 68 vessels including new construction will be required for operations.

3. It has already been decided that 6 submarines are required for submarine training …

4. … 20 submarines are earmarked for A/S training in accordance with Admiralty instructions …

5. The number of submarines at present in reserve pending a decision as to disposal is 17 …

6. FOSM proposes that as a result of the above allocations, the following steps should now be taken:–

(i) A decision should be made that beyond a certain date the building of new construction submarines should be suspended.

(ii) Certain submarines, including damaged vessels, should be scrapped.

(iii) Other surplus submarines should be placed in reserve pending their disposal to Allies or scrapping.

7. With reference to sub-paragraph 6(i), it is suggested that the construction of any submarines not due to complete by 31st March 1946 should be suspended. This includes 3 'T's and 14 'A's … The question whether those selected for suspension should be cancelled can be considered later …

PART II

POSTWAR RETRENCHMENT, AUGUST 1945 – MARCH 1947

The early and entirely unexpected end of the war against Japan overturned many previous planning assumptions. In one sense, the Naval Staff's task was made much easier as they no longer had to prepare for operations expected to last well into 1946. Nor did planning the future fleet need to allow for the expected high loss-rate of ships. This was particularly significant as only the most modern units were being deployed to the Far East and it would therefore have been those that were lost rather than older ships whose remaining service life was limited anyway. But to complicate matters, the Admiralty now had to accelerate demobilisation of personnel, as well as bring forward plans for the size and shape of the postwar Fleet. They also had to take account of the atom bomb, which would require a revision of the Tizard Report.[1]

The wider context for postwar planning was dire. The Government's economic advisor John Maynard Keynes spoke of a 'financial Dunkirk'. Not only was the country almost bankrupt, but its economy was still on a war footing.[2] Defence spending accounted for 18 per cent of gross national product.[3]

> The Services and the Government approached the question from opposite directions; the former assessed the threat and the minimum forces required at the outbreak of war; the latter surveyed the shattered state of the country's finances and laid down expenditure ceilings which made nonsense of the Service demands.[4]

Work started almost immediately to review existing refit and construction plans [38–40, 42]. Other tasks included acceleration of the process of demobilisation and the re-establishment of a peacetime manning structure [41]. The Admiralty understood from the outset that a continuation of conscription was useful for the Navy only as a source of war reservists. In peacetime, conscripts were actually a drain on training resources.

An early study considered the future of naval bases [43]. It retained a distinctly 'imperial' approach and proposed a worldwide network of over 30 overseas bases plus those in the United Kingdom itself. The vulnerability of the latter to air attack meant making the maximum use of bases in the Dominions. The proposed plan may not have been as overly ambitious as, in retrospect, it appears. The scale of manpower reductions

[1] Lewis, *Changing Direction*, p. 245.

[2] John Bew, *Citizen Clem: A Biography of Attlee* (London, 2016), p. 368.

[3] Bew, *Citizen Clem*, p. 412.

[4] Undated paper, *Future Composition of the Navy and the Relevant Estimates*. Naval Historical Branch.

required and, later, decolonisation were not yet clear and a continuation of prewar global responsibilities was taken for granted.

For the moment, the Admiralty had to deal with immediate postwar responsibilities (though these were much less than for the Army), the release of 'hostilities only' personnel for the civilian economy and the disposition of the active fleet itself. For 1946 [44] it was proposed to maintain active Fleets at Home, in the Mediterranean and the Pacific and smaller squadrons in the East Indies, the West Indies and the South Atlantic plus a huge Reserve Fleet, also at home. It would mean keeping in full commission a total of four battleships, 10 carriers, 29 cruisers, 64 destroyers, 76 escorts and 46 submarines. Of note, the responsibilities that the Navy and the other Services had to discharge and for which they required these forces were determined by the Chiefs of Staff themselves. As yet, there was no higher political direction. This fleet would still require approximately 400,000 men, almost a year after the end of hostilities [45].

In the longer-term, the Navy wanted the 170,000 longer-service officers and men previously identified, plus another 10,000 to train conscripts [46]. The Cabinet's Defence Committee, chaired by the Prime Minister, considered the three Services' requirements in October [47]. Attlee himself pointed out that the United States would in future have responsibility for the Pacific, and that the Chancellor would take a view on the finance available. It was clear that the Services were not going to get all that they asked for.

A Plans Division paper in September [48] set out in detail the peacetime fleet to be maintained in the longer term, making its own assumptions about what this fleet was required to do. With due acknowledgment of uncertainty about the future and the worldwide nature of Britain's responsibilities, but also the absence of a serious opponent at sea, the proposal for over 200 ships in full commission looks as optimistic as the short-term plan for 1946. In the event of a major war, the Fleet on mobilisation would comprise over 500 ships, including 32 carriers and 1,300 aircraft. But it was at least a first attempt to shape the postwar Navy.

The Director of Naval Construction (DNC) summarised the existing building programme in a paper for the Admiralty [49]. It included 30 big ships – battleships, cruisers and carriers – and 150 destroyers and below, with outline costings to 1951. Allowing for a small number of cancellations, the rest were still needed to maintain the big fleet being planned and would cost, on average, £34 million per year [50]. The First Lord, A.V. Alexander, doubted this sum would be available and wanted to plan on half that amount being spent [51]. He emphasised that until strategic requirements became clearer finance 'would play an unusually important part', a foretaste of the challenges to come. As financial realities became clearer, decisions were soon taken on an extensive list of cancellations [52]. Six carriers, a cruiser, 24 destroyers and 12 submarines were amongst those to go from the building programme. This was matched by a similarly large programme of sale and scrapping of existing ships [53], mainly obsolete vessels and wartime emergency construction.

The Chiefs of Staff, supported by their respective Directors of Plans, were faced by an insoluble problem in trying to plan the size of the postwar forces [54]. They could not determine political requirements, the future availability of manpower or the likely financial settlement. But what they did not do, which in retrospect seems like a missed opportunity, is conduct an audit of what was available and the maximum forces that could be sustained from that within a range of manpower and financial 'envelopes' (to use a modern term).

There was a comprehensive review of all Admiralty 'production' (what today we would call the equipment programme) [55, 56]. Further cancellations had already taken place and more would be necessary. Other ships would be delayed in order to save money in the short term. The immediate result was a revised 1945 Construction Programme [57–59] which now comprised just one submarine and four escorts, all experimental types, plus smaller craft. By now the list of cancellations from the 1941–44 Programmes included 6 carriers, a cruiser, 27 destroyers and over 50 submarines and work on the new battleships had ceased.

A further review of the submarine force took place in December [60, 61] which now assumed a peacetime strength of 85, allowing for more disposals and transfers to other navies. Further cancellations of all types of ships, and the financial savings that would result, were also considered the same month [62–64]. Most notable was the cancellation of the large carrier *Eagle*, already a quarter complete (the name was subsequently reallocated to her sister-ship *Audacious*). Several smaller carriers, which soon proved to be inadequate, were retained though none ever saw service in the RN. The loss of *Eagle* meant the Navy never attained an adequate number of carriers able to operate the most modern aircraft in significant numbers, as orders for the remaining pair of even larger *Malta*-class were cancelled at the same time.

In January 1946 the Joint Planning Staff (headed by the three Service Directors of Plans) looked at commitments out to 1951 [65]. Still without higher political direction other than the need to release manpower and save money, they assumed no major war during the period but a range of peacetime commitments and the need to provide a nucleus for expansion and preparation for war. In the RN's case, this meant the ability to grow within three years to 645,000 personnel.

The Chiefs of Staff, as directed by the Prime Minister, revised their previous report [44] on the size of the forces for 1946 [66, 67] and looked further ahead to 1947 [68]. The Navy's main task was the protection of British interests abroad and at sea. With reductions in the Pacific Fleet and transfers of several ships from the active to the Reserve Fleet, the manpower total now came down to 375,000 at 30 June 1946. The report for March the following year noted, again, the continuing political uncertainty. The proposed fleet in commission would comprise four battleships, 12 carriers, 17 cruisers, 48 destroyers, 38 escorts, 45 submarines and 40 fleet minesweepers distributed between the various Fleets and Squadrons, plus a larger force in the Reserve Fleet. It would require 225,000 personnel (about 16 per cent of the Forces' total number).

The three Services had been directed to re-examine their longer-term manpower proposals submitted the previous September [46]. A revised memorandum went to the Defence Committee in January [69]. The most pressing issues were to establish the future strengths of the respective Services and the terms and conditions of service of Regular personnel, which had not been updated since 1939. The Admiralty stuck to its requirement of 180,000, including 10,000 to train conscripts if a permanent National Service was introduced. But it suggested a one-fifth reduction to 144,000 as a minimum for planning purposes, pending a full review (not yet forthcoming) of defence commitments. In subsequent discussions by the Defence Committee [70] it emerged that the Navy still had 190,000 men East of Suez. The Prime Minister suggested a figure for the RN of 175,000 in total (ie including conscripts) by the end of the year and directed the Service Departments to examine the consequences of such a figure, which was provisionally approved. DofP pointed out that in Regular terms this was almost the same as the 144,000 the Admiralty had suggested, and that it would not require much, if any, reduction in the size of the Fleet though it would require some re-disposition of ships [71].

To get to these numbers by the end of 1946 meant releasing a staggering half a million men and women from the Navy during the year [72]. This was achievable, though at risk to certain manpower categories and would require further re-dispositions, reducing overseas commitments especially in the Pacific. It assumed there was no risk of a major emergency in the following two to three years [73]. This the Prime Minister agreed [74]. Manpower was to prove 'the most chronic postwar naval problem'.[1]

[1]Eric Grove, *Vanguard to Trident: British Naval Policy since World War II* (London, 1987), p. 19.

In the meantime, the Planners produced a report on naval assault forces, assuming peacetime training needs and a brigade lift requirement [75]. It would require over 10,000 men just to man the necessary craft, a larger number than the brigade itself would comprise.

The pressure to reduce spending by cutting back on equipment purchases continued [76, 77]. But the construction programme still included a battleship, 15 carriers and four cruisers, plus over 100 smaller vessels. Between January 1946 and March 1947, the Navy expected to take delivery of over 1,000 aircraft. There was therefore to be no 1946 Construction Programme (ie no additional ships were to be requested or authorised) [78]. The downward pressure on manpower also continued, with a reduced target strength of 200,000 instead of 230,000, and by the end of 1946 rather than March the following year [79, 80] – 'The [financial] picture for 1946 is grim'.

The Service ministries and the Chiefs of Staff still didn't have overall political and strategic direction from the Cabinet, other than the ever-increasing demands that they save money and manpower. But they did now get updated technical advice on the 'Nature of Future Wars' from the Joint Technical Warfare Committee [81]. Their report re-emphasised the Navy's role in securing sea communications, but in the light of recent developments. The atomic bomb was considered important, not at sea itself, but against ports. At sea, faster submarines, mining and air attack would be the main threats, including guided missiles. The demise of the battleship was foreshadowed and the paper argued for the maximum number of smaller surface units.

At the end of March 1946, the Admiralty published the last-ever Blue List (List of Ships Building) [82]. Henceforth, the construction programme was included in the Pink List. The list of ships under construction was, despite the cancellations of the previous year and the increasing demands for economy, still an impressive legacy from the wartime programmes. It included a battleship (*Vanguard*, which was about to commission), 13 carriers, 9 cruisers (not all of them laid down), 32 destroyers and 14 submarines. It was notable how many completion dates were 'uncertain'.

Soon after publication of the final Blue List a fresh review of submarine dispositions was completed [83]; 45 submarines and 5 depot ships were retained in commission plus a further 28 boats in reserve.

A further review of postwar manpower and commitments in May [84] brought the Navy's manpower total after December 1947 down to 182,000, including WRNS and conscripts. The active Fleet would still include 4 battleships, 9 carriers, 23 cruisers, 130 destroyers and escorts and 45 submarines though a significant proportion would have reduced complements for training and trials duties. Ships' service lives were being extended in order to maintain the size of the Fleet at reduced cost [85].

In June 1946 the existing *Neptune*-class design for a 6″ cruiser authorised under the 1944 Programme was cancelled and a more modern *Minotaur* design with new twin turrets was substituted [86]. It was never built.

The financial pressure on the Admiralty was maintained into July 1946 with further arbitrary budget and manpower cuts [87]. The Prime Minister continued to interrogate the Admiralty about its manpower requirement, noting that it was still substantially higher than before the War when the German, Italian and Japanese navies were all potential enemies. In response, the Naval Staff produced a lengthy justification for their needs with a detailed comparison between 1938 and 1947 [88].

In September Plans Division produced a ten-year plan [89] of replacements in order to maintain the already proposed Post War Fleet [48]. The hoped-for fleet was still huge and though in the short term it could be met from existing units and extant building programmes, new construction from about 1949 would be required, including battleships and carriers. The paper also summarised those ships that had so far been cancelled, comprising two battleships, five fleet carriers, four light fleet carriers, a cruiser, 47 destroyers, 54 submarines and hundreds of smaller craft.

The Admiralty had briefly considered the implications of peacetime conscription [41] soon after the end of the War and was to come back to the topic repeatedly in the following years. A tri-service working party on the matter reported to the Defence Committee in October [90, 91]. The Navy thought it could man the fleet in peacetime (170,000 total) solely with volunteers, but the number of reserves required for mobilisation (210,000) would require compulsory service. It was agreed that the call-up period would be 18 months, followed by 5½ years reserve liability.

The Defence Committee also considered the size of the armed forces out to March 1948 [92, 93]. This major report by the Chiefs of Staff again had to provide its own strategic guidance, with the First Sea Lord cautioning against the introduction of a new 'ten-year rule' [94]. The Navy had to meet three requirements: to train for war, to protect British interests abroad and to provide a nucleus for expansion for war. The discussion of manpower requirements inevitably led to yet another statement on the planned fleet itself (the eighth since August 1945), divided into three categories – Training and Experimental, 'Police' Forces (ie peacetime commitments) and a Reserve Fleet. On mobilisation, this would produce a fleet comprising six battleships, 30 carriers, 33 cruisers, 127 destroyers, 328 escorts and 95 submarines, *in addition* to the ships to be provided by the Dominions: six carriers, seven cruisers, 90 destroyers and 53 escorts.

There is an obvious air of unreality to such a list, and there was no mention of at whom such a fleet would be directed in war (the Soviet Union was the only possible candidate) or how it would be employed. This huge fleet required, in peacetime, 220,000 men and women (including trainees). However, existing manpower limitations would restrict the Navy to 178,000 which in turn would allow a fleet in commission at the end of 1947 consisting of two battleships, six carriers, 13 cruisers, 55 destroyers and escorts and 17 submarines. This total starts to look more familiar – these are the sorts of numbers the Navy was operating well into the 1960s, although with more escorts and submarines at the expense of battleships and cruisers.

At the beginning of 1947 a review of production and research and development [95] was another attempt to limit spending. Construction of ships authorised during the War and not subsequently cancelled was continued, together with a modest programme of repair but little by way of modernisation. But the urgent need to replace obsolete types meant that for 1947–8 the Admiralty still intended to acquire over 400 combat aircraft, including the first Sea Vampire jets. The search for economies led to a wider review of the Defence Estimates for 1947–48 [96, 97]. The Services' 'pain and grief' statements were matched by the Chancellor's insistence that financial and manpower economies had to be found. For perhaps the first time, the size of the Soviet Navy was mentioned in relation to the size of the RN.

In February Plans Division discussed a 1947 Construction Programme [98]. Ships previously authorised but on which work had not yet commenced were regarded as now cancelled. Plans for the Post War Fleet outlined in September 1945 [48] and the associated programme of replacements [89] had been suspended as a consequence of 'stringent economy'. But some programme of replacements could not be put off, and it was proposed to include in the new programme six cruisers, three escorts, two submarines and several smaller units. Several of these already had Treasury approval – in the case of one of the cruisers as far back as 1941. The submarines and escorts would be of new 'experimental' designs.

The following month the Principal Personnel Officers' Committee (Second Sea Lord being the RN's representative) reported on the manpower position for the following year (1948) [99]. The effects of demobilisation of large numbers of men were still being felt, and the Navy was, like the other Services, 'unbalanced'. By March 1948 there would be 189,000 personnel serving in the Navy, including Royal Marines, WRNS, conscripts and Locally-Entered Personnel (LEPs) overseas.

38. *Notes on Controller's Monthly Meeting by the Deputy Controller*[1]

[ADM 116/5342] 22 August 1945

1. Revised Priorities:

Consequent on the general ceasefire the broad general policy for priorities … has been drawn up and will be issued shortly for general guidance …

2. Refit and Repair Programme:

The following decisions regarding ships under and due for refit or repair were taken:–

(A) Battleships

(i) VALIANT	To go on as already arranged.
(ii) RENOWN	Due four months' refit in October 1945. Pending clarification of future of this ship … to be suspended.
(iii) QUEEN ELIZABETH	No preparatory work to be undertaken.
(iv) RODNEY and NELSON	Preparatory work to be held in abeyance pending decision as to future of these ships.

(B) Aircraft Carriers

(i) ILLUSTRIOUS	It has been approved to extend refit to allow full Modernisation … new lifts, modified funnel uptakes etc. …
(ii) CVEs	Future policy regarding refits requires clarification …

(C) Cruisers

(i) SHEFFIELD, KENYA and MAURITIUS	refits … to proceed as already arranged.
(ii) AUSTRALIA	Navy Board considering future of this ship, and possible curtailment of present refit …
(iii) NEWCASTLE	Now in Tyne … for modifications … after refit in USA …
(iv) LEANDER	Due to be taken in hand, after refit in USA …
(v) SCYLLA	Future of this ship requires to be clarified …

(D) Destroyers

Refits and A & As require review. As a general policy only those Fleet Destroyers of 'Q' and later classes should be considered

[1] RA Sir Charles Simeon.

for full refits … refits of RN HUNTs Types II, III and IV … to continue …

(E) Submarines

Pending clarification of future submarine fleet, normal refits to continue.

(F) Frigates and Minesweepers

The two frigates being fitted out as generating stations to go on … All minesweeping craft likewise.

(G) General

The broad refit and repair policy should be to withdraw HM Ships from contractors' yards and revert to the use of the Royal Dockyards for all refits of warships, as soon as practicable. This implies the weeding out of all unessential work, especially on ships which will probably be scrapped or disposed of in order to make room in the Royal Yards for more important units which will be required in the postwar Fleet …

3. Conversion Programme …[1]

4. New Construction

(A) Battleships

VANGUARD To be completed … final inspection 3.1.46 …

(B) Aircraft Carriers

Fleet Carriers. At present ARK ROYAL, AUDACIOUS, EAGLE, MALTA and NEW ZEALAND are nominated as part of the postwar fleet …

1942 Light Fleets. All COLOSSUS class are nominated a part of postwar fleet. Ships under construction to proceed …

1943 Light Fleets. The four ships of the HERMES class are nominated as part of the postwar fleet … to proceed …

(C) Cruisers

TIGER, DEFENCE, SUPERB, BLAKE and HAWKE are all nominated for postwar fleet. SUPERB to complete according to previous programme. Remainder to proceed …

(D) Destroyers

CHEQUERS, COSSACK and CRESCENT Classes to complete …

BATTLEAXE Class (16 ships) under consideration to convert to Fast Escorts during building. Alternative is to stop. Meantime ships proceed …

GALLANT Class (8 ships) to complete …

[1] Not reproduced. Deals mainly with amphibious and support vessels.

TRAFALGAR and ARMADA Classes to complete …
1st Flotilla of DARING Class – do –
AGINCOURT, MONS and JUTLAND Classes, and 2nd Flotilla of the DARING Class under consideration to cancel 24 out of 32 of these ships. …

(E) Submarines
Under consideration to cancel THOR, TIARA, AGGRESSOR, ASGARD and ADEPT. Final decision … will be taken when postwar fleet is settled.

(F) Sloops
Number of sloops to be completed depends on requirements of postwar fleet, which may be influenced by conversion of BATTLEAXE Class …

(G) Minesweepers
To complete …

(H) Frigates
All are nominated for postwar fleet, and to proceed …

…

39. *Minutes of Fifth Sea Lord's Meeting*

[ADM 1/17477] 24 August 1945

POST WAR NAVAL AIR POLICY

The Fifth Sea Lord[1] said that recent developments made it necessary to reach early agreement on postwar Naval Air requirements. Many important factors still remained unknown, but it had been tentatively suggested by the First Sea Lord that a peacetime [strength] of 500, backed by a potential First Line reserve of 200/300, to be manned by the RNVR and mobilised in emergency, could be supported by some 60,000 of the total peacetime strength of the Royal Navy, which was likely to be from 170,000 to 200,000 Officers and Ratings …

The minimum figure [approximately 77,000 required for 500 aircraft], which was about 44% of the probable total peacetime strength of the Royal Navy, made allowance for one MONAB and for FRU and ancilliary aircraft and the crews of ten aircraft carriers in commission … about 24 air stations would be required at home and 10 overseas …

[1] RA T.H. Troubridge.

40. *Mottershead*[1] *to First Lord of the Admiralty*

[ADM 116/5342] 28 August 1945

The position on the 1945 and earlier Building Programmes, following your meeting with the First Sea Lord, Controller, Vice Controller and Deputy Controller on 13 August appears to be as follows:–

New Construction Programme 1945

No reconsideration of this appears to have been initiated in the Department. Clearly, the paper as circulated on 29 June requires revision.[2] For example, it states that the main concern of the Navy this year remains the build-up for the Far Eastern War and that it is proposed to press on with the building of all ships which were then expected to complete before the assumed date of the end of the Japanese War (November 1946). The Programme also contains proposals for the construction of docks, all required for the repair of ships taking part in the war in the Far East.

Apart from the revisions required on these points the Programme may require a more radical revision. The original paper stated that in view of the possibility of casualties among the battleships sent to the Pacific and the age of the rest of the Battle Fleet, it was not considered that we could long delay steps to maintain our effective strength in capital units. The Cabinet were therefore asked to approve the placing of orders to enable LION and TEMERAIRE to be laid down as early as possible. Does this proposal still hold?…

It will be necessary … to present the Programme to the Cabinet and I suggest therefore that you might ask the First Sea Lord to initiate the necessary revision of the Cabinet memorandum of 29 June …

Ships already building, refitting, converting etc

The Deputy Controller held a meeting on 22 August to revise the arrangements for ships already building, refitting or converting … I understand that the Naval Staff will now consider these recommendations, but I think … firm proposals [should] be submitted to the Board as soon as possible. These proposals should cover every kind of ship, vessel and craft … There is no indication in the report, or on the official papers, of any revision of programme following the end of the Japanese War.

There will probably be a tendency for the Department to say that it is impossible to make firm proposals in advance of the consideration by the Chiefs of Staff of our postwar defence commitments and a decision of the Cabinet upon them. Would it not be possible to direct that, in general,

[1] F.W. Mottershead, First Lord's Private Secretary.

[2] CP(45)54, reproduced as Doc. No. 35.

work on ships building, which would not form part of the Post-War Fleet as at present contemplated, should be stopped? It has already been agreed that work on Naval ships generally should be put on low priority wherever possible …

41. *Note for First Lord*

[ADM 116/5658] 29 August 1945

Meeting with Secretaries of State for War and Air[1]

PERSONNEL REQUIREMENTS FOR POST-WAR FORCES

I EFFECT OF ATOMIC BOMB ON PROBLEM

1. Atomic bomb warfare will clearly have far-reaching effect on the postwar defence forces of the country …

2. It is, however, not possible at present to gauge this factor and urgency of making plans to ensure continuance of the forces during the immediate future (made more pressing by collapse of Japan with resultant probable increase in speed of demobilisation) is reason for placing some proposals before Cabinet …

II NAVY'S REQUIREMENT

3. Calculated on a postwar fleet … requiring 220,000 officers and men. Estimated that the Dominions and Colonies might provide 50,000 of these, leaving UK contribution as 170,000.

4. No account taken of conscription after the war. Navy's requirement in conscripts (based on war reserve requirements, conscripts being wholly non-effective personnel in peace so far as Navy is concerned) is 35,000. Training staffs for this body will require additional 10,000 men in regular force.

5. Navy's total manpower bid is therefore:–

Regular engagements	180,000	
Conscripts	35,000	per annum
Total	215,000	

III EFFECT OF WORLD SECURITY PLANS

6. Whilst ultimately the World Security plan might lead to a scaling down of forces throughout the world, initially the plan would depend for its success on the major states in the organisation having effective forces to play their part …

[1] The three Service Ministers met on 29 Aug (Minutes in ADM 116/5658) and agreed to jointly submit a paper to the Cabinet – CP(45)161, reproduced as Doc. No. 46.

IV CONDITIONS OF SERVICE

7. No success is likely to attend efforts to attract men on hostilities only engagements to transfer to permanent service, until postwar conditions of service (of which pay is the most important) are settled. The most optimistic forecast of a date by which a new pay code could be fully ready for publication is December 1945 for men and June 1946 for officers. If it is suggested that this factor makes it unnecessary to determine the numbers to be allowed for the postwar forces, the reply is that the Vote A numbers are an essential preliminary for planning for the organisation of the forces, organisation of the various branches etc, eg distribution of the naval numbers as between ships, air, Royal Marines and especially those branches which have been introduced during the war …

42. *Minute by Director of Plans*

[ADM 1/19610] 2 September 1945

SUBMARINES

The proposals for scrapping surplus submarines, which were submitted to the Board in M.059119/45, were made before the end of the Japanese war. In order to reduce the submarine fleet to its proposed peacetime strength, these proposals now require amplification.

2. It has been proposed in the Plans Division paper 'The Composition of the Post War Fleet' that the submarine strength should ultimately be 85, of which approximately half would be in reserve. If this is approved, the 85 would be composed of 12 'A' Class, 27 'T' Class, 37 'S' Class and 9 'U' Class.

3. The present state of submarines in commission, in reserve and building is:–

	'A'	'S'	'T'	'U'	Minelayer
In Commission	2	37	29	24	1
In Reserve	–	2	3	12	–
Building	24	41	6	–	–
Total	26	41	38	36	1

4. To reduce these numbers to the proposed peacetime figures given in paragraph 2 above, the following action is proposed …

'A' Class	To cancel construction of 14 submarines.
'S' Class	To scrap 4 out of 5 old or damaged submarines.
Minelayer	To scrap RORQUAL.
'T' Class	To cancel the construction of 2 submarines. To scrap 9 old or battle-damaged submarines.

'U' Class — The following firm or tentative requests for 'U' Class submarines are under consideration:–

China	2
Greece	2
Norway	2
Denmark up to	6
Turkey	2
Total	14 maximum

The British post war requirement is 9 'U' Class and it is therefore proposed that 13 'U' Class should be scrapped now …

43. *Plans Division Memorandum*

[ADM 205/50] 5 September 1945

PD 0139/45

ORGANISATION AND REQUIREMENT
OF POST WAR NAVAL BASES

The Board has taken note of the paper 'The Post War Navy and the Policy Governing its Composition' (PD/OL 0119/45)[1] which includes the principles of the Naval Base Policy. This policy is there defined as follows:–

> "To retain the mobility, of which the Navy alone is capable, and the ability to operate in all parts of the world, a base organisation corresponding to the strength of the Fleet in war is required."

This organisation is considered in greater detail in the following paper.

BRITISH EMPIRE RESPONSIBILITY

2. The security and defence of the British Empire as a whole depends upon an agreed Imperial policy. The increasingly vulnerable position of the United Kingdom Base makes the importance of Naval Bases in the Dominions and Colonies proportionately greater.

3. It is undesirable to spend large sums on the construction of bases in all parts of the world or in areas where the facilities provided may never be used. If the following recommendations are accepted, it is considered that the essential needs of the Fleets of the Empire can be met both adequately and in the most economical way.

4. All expenditure on base installations should be incurred in British possessions, and every encouragement should be given to the Dominions

[1] Updated as PD/OL.0133/45 and reproduced as Doc. No. 28.

and Colonies to contribute to the defence of the Empire as a whole, by maintaining and where possible expanding the facilities already in being.

DISPOSITION OF BASES

5. In the past a number of Naval Bases were created covering areas of strategic importance and from which it was possible for Naval forces to exercise control at relatively short distances.

6. It is no less desirable now that base facilities should be as near the probable areas of operation as possible – it is, however, less practicable. This is due to the development of new long-range weapons of attack.

THE EFFECT OF WEAPON DEVELOPMENT ON THE DISPOSITION OF BASES

7. Two of the results of the increasing range and destructiveness of weapons are:–

(i) The security of sea communications becomes even more important. For example, the destruction to industrial plants caused by air attacks on Britain in 1940/41 made it more than ever necessary to secure the sea communications of the United Kingdom.

(ii) In 1940/41 alternative repair bases across the Atlantic were brought into use when the English South Coast yards were no longer able to carry on with large scale repairs.

CLASSIFICATION OF BASES

8. Bearing in mind the factors stated above, it is proposed that Naval bases should be divided into three main classes, depending on the function they fulfil. These may be stated as:–

a) Main Naval Bases
b) Operational Naval Bases
c) Advanced Naval Bases

REQUIREMENTS OF BASES

9. Main Naval Bases

Main Naval Bases should provide all the facilities to support a Fleet of all type of ships, including full docking, refitting, storage, manning, training and shore air facilities for Carrier Groups. They should be situated so far as possible in a rear area free from sustained enemy attack. Main base areas should be defensible and be backed by a developed industry and a white population.

10. Main Naval Bases are also required in the United Kingdom in peace. Owing to recent developments in weapons it is all the more necessary that the facilities provided should be widely dispersed if possible …

13. Operational Naval Bases

These should be established nearer likely operational areas than their respective Main Naval Bases. They will in general be exercise bases in peace and operational bases in war. They should be able to maintain the Fleet in the operational area for long periods without return to a Main Base. They should have certain permanent facilities but, above all, they should be planned to be capable of considerable expansion and rapid defence on the threat of war …

14. Advanced Naval Bases

The function of the Advanced Naval Base is to provide facilities for replenishment and rest between operations. They may be established in any convenient area, near the scene of naval operations, where a good anchorage and potential air strip sites exist. Where the nature of the war or the distances involved demand it, the bulk of the facilities and supplies would be afloat in the Fleet Support Ships but portable defence and constructional equipment would also be required …

15. The Fleet Support Ships ('Fleet Train')

… The Fleet may … have to be maintained for long periods at a great distance from its main base. Moreover, once an operation has been launched ships may have to carry out continuous operations for several weeks on end within striking distance of their objective and well ahead of the nearest advanced naval base …

17. The Fleet Support Ships will be required to carry and establish the additional facilities required at Operational and Advanced Naval Bases. It will necessarily therefore consist of special ships, craft and personnel organised and trained to provide and handle specialised facilities … As the foregoing will be required in war, a nucleus should be maintained in peace.

…

24. Selection of Bases

In this paper it is only possible to deal by name with the proposed Main Naval Bases, most of the proposed Operational Naval Bases and some examples of Advanced Naval Bases. The use of bases in Allied territory and of ports under the control of the World Security Organisation may also be available.

25. The following establishment of bases shows how the various areas, oceans and seas are covered by the proposed base organisation.

MAIN NAVAL BASES

United Kingdom Bases	
Malta	(in peace and possibly in war)
Halifax with St John, NB	East coast of Canada
Esquimalt with Vancouver	West coast of Canada
Durban with Capetown	South Africa
Sydney	Australia

PROBABLE OPERATIONAL NAVAL BASES

Atlantic and Home Waters	Mediterranean	Indian Ocean	Pacific
United Kingdom	Malta (in war)	Kilindini	Singapore
Bermuda	Gibraltar	Trincomalee with Colombo	Brisbane
St Johns NF	Alexandria	Auckland	
Simonstown		Bombay	Hong Kong
Freetown		Karachi	
		Fremantle	
		Aden	

EXAMPLES OF ADVANCED NAVAL BASES

Jamaica	Haifa	Andaman Is.	Port Darwin
Trinidad	Cyprus	Addu Atoll	Brunei
Bathurst	Port Sudan	Masirah Is.	Manus
		Bahrein	
		Mauritius	

44. *Chiefs of Staff Memorandum*

[CAB 80/97] 6 September 1945

COS(45)565(O) MANPOWER REQUIREMENTS AT 30 JUNE 1946[1]

The Chiefs of Staff have approved the attached report on the size and deployment of the Armed Forces which will be required on 30 June 1946, as a basis for calculation of manpower requirements by the Service Ministries and Supply Departments.

SIZE AND DEPLOYMENT OF THE ARMED FORCES ON 30TH JUNE 1946[2]

…

Navy

In addition to the Navy's world-wide commitments in support of British interests and for the maintenance of security there will be large requirements for ships to back occupational forces and for the protection of British nationals and property in the Far East. There will also be a

[1]Based on an earlier paper by the Joint Planning Staff, JP(45)205(Final) 2 Sept 1945 in CAB 84/74.

[2]This report was considered by the Defence Committee of the Cabinet on 14 Sept (DO(45) 6th Meeting Item 1). The Committee 'Invited the Service Departments … to pay regard to … possible economies …'

heavy commitment for the transport of men and supplies which it will be difficult to meet with the depleted world shipping and emergency requirements will, where practicable, have to be met by the Royal Navy. It will be important to complete mine clearance, salvage and disposal of wrecks as soon as possible to facilitate shipping movement and to maintain Ocean Air Sea Rescue, Survey and Fishery Protection organisations …

APPENDIX I

BRITISH NAVAL FORCES REQUIRED ON 30 JUNE 1946

The following are the main British Naval Units required on 30 June 1946. We have assumed that Australian, New Zealand and Canadian Naval forces will meet commitments in their home waters and that the Royal Indian Navy will make available ships of the AA sloop, modern ocean escort and minesweeper classes for service outside Indian waters if required.

Home Fleet	Reserve Fleet
1 Battleship	6 Battleships
2 Fleet Carriers	2 Fleet Carriers
4 Cruisers	15 Other Carriers (including one for DLT and one for experimental purposes)
3 Cruisers (Cadets training, experiments and trials)	16 Cruisers
16 Destroyers	32 Destroyers
24 Escorts	100 Escorts
30 Submarines	40 Submarines

Note: – From the ships shown in Reserve, 4 Cruisers, together with the necessary number of aircraft carriers to lift 4,000 officers and men, will be required for movement of Naval personnel.

Mediterranean Fleet	East Indies Squadron
2 Light Fleet Carriers	2 Light Fleet Carriers
5 Cruisers	6 Cruisers
16 Destroyers	8 Destroyers
8 Escorts	20 Escorts
8 Submarines	

British Pacific Fleet

3 Battleships
2 Fleet Carriers
2 Light Fleet Carriers
7 Cruisers
24 Destroyers
16 Escorts
[x]5 Gun Boats
8 Submarines

[x] To be in reserve until required.

South America and West Indies Squadron	South Atlantic Squadron
2 Cruisers	2 Cruisers
4 Escorts	4 Escorts

Other Commitments

Clearance Forces

Mine clearance forces, cable and surveying ships, Boom Defence vessels, Salvage ships and wreck disposal craft to be retained to clear sea communications with the minimum delay.

Assault Shipping and Craft

There will be widespread requirements for movement or personnel, vehicles and stores for occupational and rehabilitation purposes. It is estimated that all LSI(L) and LST(3) already available or due for completion in the near future will be fully occupied throughout 1946. Major landing craft will also be required, but it is not proposed that further flotillas or replacements be sent to the Far East.

Coastal Forces

Requirements for coastal forces will be limited to a nucleus in commission for trials and training and a flotilla in the Mediterranean to meet emergency calls.

Fleet Auxiliaries and Mobile Repair Facilities

A reduced number of fleet auxiliaries and mobile repair facilities will be required to maintain East Indies and British Pacific Fleets pending decision on postwar base policy and during reconstructions of shore facilities.

45. *Cabinet Memorandum*

[CAB 129/2] 14 September 1945

CP(45)170 NAVAL MANPOWER REQUIREMENTS IN JUNE 1946 AND PROGRAMME OF RELEASES TO THAT DATE

Memorandum by The First Lord of the Admiralty

Proposed strength of the Navy in June 1946

It is estimated that to carry out the tasks envisaged by the Chiefs of Staff in COS(45)565(O) the Navy will require in June 1946 a strength of approximately 400,000 men and 15,000 women. The relative proportions of men and women are subject to revision. These figures *do not* include the number of recruits who will be under training on that date as the intake for the first half of 1946 has not yet been decided. In any case these new recruits are ‘ineffectives’.

2. The strength of the Navy on 31 May 1945 before the start of releases under the Re-allocation Plan, was 772,000 men and 73,500 women (a total of 845,500), so that the net reduction in strength between that date and the 30 June 1946, assuming the proportions in paragraph 1, will be of the order of 372,000 men and 58,500 women (total 430,500). With the further speed up in the rate of releases now planned, it is estimated that the strength of the Navy on 31 December 1945 will be 642,000 men and 55,500 women (total 697,500), a net reduction since 31 May 1945, after allowing for new entries, of 130,000 men and 18,000 women (total 148,000).
3. By June 1946 the Navy, therefore, has to reduce its strength by 51 per cent of the May 1945 figure. Just over one-third of this reduction will be effected by December 1945, despite considerable new intake in the second half of this year.
4. *Releases in 1945* – The target given to the Navy for the number of releases in Class A to be effected between the 18th June and 31 December 1945 (MP(45) 8th Meeting), was:–

Men	110,000
Women	15,000
Total	125,000

Up to the end of August the releases and discharges reported to the Admiralty, excluding Class B, were 28,600 men and 8,950 women. Steps have been taken to speed up Class A releases still further during 1945, and if these are successful the target will be substantially exceeded … it is hoped that between 18 June, when releases started, and 31 December 1945 the numbers released, excluding Class B, will reach:–

Men	140,000
Women	18,000
Total	158,000

If this can be achieved the Navy will have exceeded its target of Class A releases by 30,000 men and 3,000 women (total 33,000) …
6. This is a considerable speed-up in the rate of releases for which we were planning as recently as July. Our original figure for the numbers of men to be released in Class A up to the end of 1945 was 90,000. In August this figure was increased to 110,000 and under the arrangements now being made the planned figure is 149,500, of which it is hoped to accomplish 140,000, an increase of 55 per cent on the original figure.
7. *Releases in 1946* – Appendix attached[1] shows the proposed time-table of releases to effect the necessary run-down in numbers by June 1946 …

[1] In the interests of space, the Appendix is not reproduced. The overall picture is adequately represented in the main body of the Memorandum.

the Admiralty aim to reach a peak of over 8,600 releases of men per week in January 1946 …

8. *Release of women in 1946* – To reach the reduced strength of 15,000 WRNS by June 1946 a new reduction of 40,500 will be required from the estimated strength as at 31 December 1945, and a programme of releases is being arranged accordingly …

9. *Manpower expended in Maintaining Surplus War Equipment* – At their meeting on 6 September 1945, the Chiefs of Staff made reference to the manpower which was now being devoted to the maintenance of surplus war equipment and to the economies which might be possible when decisions had been reached regarding the disposal of this equipment. So far as the Navy is concerned this would apply generally to surplus war material and stores, including aircraft and particularly to those ships which are now being maintained in reserve either in the case of lease-lend ships until a decision is reached if and when they are to be returned to America, or in other instances whether the ships are to be purchased from us by other Nations. In any case this is an interim commitment for which no manning provision has been made in the June 1946 figures.

10. *Allocation of New Entries for the Second Half of 1945* – The Navy was allocated 47,000 men … but … it is unlikely that more than about 30,000 can be absorbed …

46. *Cabinet Memorandum*

[CAB 129/2] 8 September 1945

CP(45)161 PROVISIONAL REQUIREMENTS FOR THE POST-WAR ARMED FORCES

Memorandum by The First Lord of the Admiralty and the Secretaries of State For War and Air

The accelerated process of demobilisation has brought the Services face to face with the urgent problem of retaining on regular engagements a sufficient number of officers and other ranks – particularly experienced NCOs – to man the postwar Navy, Army and Air Force on a permanent basis.

2. At present, appointments to permanent commissions, the grant of substantive promotion to officers and NCO, and offers of re-engagement are limited in all three Services to the 1939 peace establishment.

3. It is clear that decisions cannot yet be taken on the strength and composition of the sea, land and air forces which are to be maintained permanently in peace. But time is pressing and the Services must be given interim decisions as a basis for immediate action. Officers and

men of first-rate quality are daily accepting release because they can be told nothing definite about their postwar prospects in the Services. This is a matter of special difficulty in new branches which have been formed since the war and in which the numbers of permanent officers and men are negligible …

4. The Principal Personnel Officers of the Services have accordingly reviewed the position and have submitted the annexed report giving an estimate of provisional requirements to serve as a basis for immediate action. Their recommendations have been endorsed by the Chiefs of Staff (COS Conclusions of 186th Meeting (a) Item 16).

5. We therefore ask the approval of the Cabinet for the following provisional figures for the three Services, without prejudice to the ultimate strength and composition of the Services …:–

Navy	170,000
Army	275,000
RAF	200,000

6. These figures are founded upon different bases for each Service:–

(a) For the Royal Navy they represent the estimated minimum postwar requirement of long-service officers and ratings, and presuppose that a substantial part of the burden of providing for the Naval Defence of the Empire will be undertaken by the Dominions and Colonies. In the event of compulsory national service being retained, an additional 10,000 will be required to provide the necessary administrative services and training facilities …

7. The question of conditions of service is closely allied with that of numbers, and it is of the utmost importance that we should be in a position to promulgate firm conditions of service in the postwar Forces at the earliest possible moment. A review of Service pay and pensions is now being carried out by an Interdepartmental Committee under Treasury auspices, whose recommendations are expected before the end of the year. The Service Departments will have to have their plans cut and dried before then so that the incentive anticipated from the announcement of the new pay code may not be lost; for this purpose, they must know the numbers within which recruitment on regular engagements can proceed. The plans involve a great deal of complex calculation and an early decision on the provisional figures is essential.

8. We therefore ask the Cabinet to approve the figures given in paragraph 5 above as a basis for immediate action, on the understanding that the ultimate size of the three Services would remain to be determined.

ANNEX
PROVISIONAL PERSONNEL REQUIREMENTS FOR POST-WAR FORCES

Introduction

1. At their 146th (45) meeting on the 7th June, 1945, the Chiefs of Stall gave consideration to three papers put forward respectively by the Admiralty, War Office and Air Ministry in which each had sought to give an estimate of its immediate requirements in postwar Regular personnel with a view (without prejudice to any ultimate decisions about our strategic requirement and the consequent strength of our armed forces as a whole and of their component services) to providing figures up to which each Service might be permitted to recruit personnel on a provisional basis, so that irreplaceable trained men now in the Services, who might be attracted to remain, would not be lost to the Services through uncertainty over their prospects …

Navy Estimate

7. From preliminary appreciations of the numbers and types of ships and naval aircraft which will be required to fulfil the Royal Navy's world-wide commitments in peace, it is estimated that a minimum of 170,000 long-service officers and ratings will be required, excluding any assistance by the Dominions and Colonies.

This estimate is an increase of 37,000 over the 1939 figure of 133,000. The principal reasons for this are:–

(a) The technical and scientific developments and the increased weight of air attack have brought about a considerable increase in the complements of ships, notably to man the radar warning equipment and the large number of anti-aircraft weapons which are now so essential.

(b) It will be necessary to maintain nucleus organisations for forces such as mine-sweeping and coastal forces which are now an integral part of the Fleet and also a nucleus organisation to maintain the mobility of the Fleet, ie the Fleet Train.

(c) Inter-Service co-operation must continue and so the postwar Navy must include a nucleus of amphibious forces both for training and for development.

(d) Carrier-borne air forces are fundamental to sea warfare and an integral part of the Royal Navy. A large proportion of the Navy's manpower must be devoted to this end. Besides the requirements of ship-borne aircraft, naval airfields must be maintained for flying training and the accommodation of disembarked aircraft.

The necessity for all these increases and for these additional activities has been proved during the war, and it will be necessary to maintain organisations in peace to train personnel and to provide scope for technical progress.

If conscription is continued into the peace years a further number of long service officers and ratings will be required to train and administer the conscripts …

Conclusion

11. Accordingly, for the reasons set out above, we put forward our separate proposals in a joint paper and seek authority to use these proposals as a temporary basis upon which to retain in the Services those who are willing, if some prospect is afforded to them, to stay on upon Regular engagements. Although we are fully conscious of their limitations, these provisional proposals are of an urgent character if we are not soon to lose, as the release scheme operates, the valuable trained men whom we wish to retain as the nucleus of the postwar forces and who, if they are now offered good prospects and some security of tenure, would be glad to remain. Finally, we desire to emphasise as strongly as possible that any approval which may be given to the present proposals applies only to what is in the nature of a token instalment, for the limited purpose set out above, and is entirely without prejudice to the ultimate size of the three Services, to be determined when postwar strategic requirements have been settled.

47. *Defence Committee Minutes*

[CAB 69/7] 5 October 1945

DO(45) 7th Meeting

1. PROVISIONAL REQUIREMENTS FOR POST-WAR ARMED FORCES – CP(45)161

The Committee had before them a memorandum by the First Lord of the Admiralty and the Secretaries of State for War and Air containing their proposals with regard to the provisional requirements for the postwar Armed Forces …

The Prime Minister said that every effort should be made to avoid accepting a high figure now and of being faced in the future with having to cut down that figure … [he] said that the present estimate seemed to him to be high in view of our financial abilities …

The Prime Minister drew attention to the financial implications of producing more expensive weapons, which appeared to require more personnel who would have to be more highly paid than previously. It would be necessary to see what forces this country could afford on those terms …

[He] pointed out that a decision was being requested on the whole matter before the postwar situation was properly examined and before the matter had been discussed with the Dominions and Colonies. The present estimates appeared to be high under the circumstances.

The First Lord of the Admiralty said that he appreciated that the Cabinet could not now give a decision on the ultimate strength of the Armed Forces, but he felt that something must be done in the near future if many good men were not to be lost. The figures now under consideration were provisional ones which were without prejudice to the ultimate strength and composition of the Services, but they would serve as a most useful basis for the personnel staffs to work on in determining how many vacancies to offer in the regular Forces …

The Prime Minister said that before the war we had had to be prepared for war with Germany and Japan who were strongly armed. The armed forces of those countries had been destroyed. It was our policy now to work in unison with other big powers and therefore we should not require such strong Armed Forces as before. He asked where the danger now lay.

The First Lord of the Admiralty said that it had been found in the past that the British Navy was always called upon to bear the first brunt of the war and he considered that we should always have sufficient naval forces to maintain world-wide security. The naval estimate was the result of preliminary but very careful examination of the minimum naval forces which would be required. This estimate had been worked out on the assumption that we should only have 4 battleships in commission as compared with 15 before the war. The number of aircraft carriers remained the same, although in addition it was proposed to have 10 light fleet carriers. The number of cruisers and destroyers had been reduced. It was proposed also to maintain sufficient assault lift for one Brigade for use as required in an emergency.

The Prime Minister said that we had kept the seas open for the last 100 years. America now proposed to take over the responsibility for the Pacific and part of the Atlantic. Our estimates should take this fact into account.

The First Lord of the Admiralty said that it was generally hoped that the World Organisation for Security would prove adequate. There was, however, a certain level below which we could not afford to fall. It was always possible to reduce our naval forces but it took some considerable time to build them up again. Any reduction below this minimum would tend to increase any potential danger and we should therefore have to accept the fact that a certain premium would have to be paid for safety …

The Prime Minister said that no decision could be made on the provisional estimates in their present form. It would, in any case, be necessary to obtain a Cabinet decision on the matter. Before such a decision could be taken it would be necessary for the Chancellor of the Exchequer to go into the question of finance. What was required was an estimate of the minimum cadre required by the Armed Forces showing officers and other ranks separately in the various arms and an estimate of the cost in round figures of the maintenance of such forces.

THE COMMITTEE:–

> Invited the Service Departments to resubmit their estimates of requirements in the form of a report for consideration by the Cabinet showing the minimum regular cadre of officers and other ranks in the various arms which were required to [be] maintain[ed] in the postwar Armed Forces, together with an estimate of the financial commitment involved.

48. *Plans Division Memorandum*

[ADM 1/17300] 12 September 1945

PD.0140/45 COMPOSITION OF THE POST-WAR NAVY

The policy governing the composition of the Post-War Navy has been set out in PD/OL.0133/45.[1] The problems to be resolved in this paper are therefore:–

(a) The number of ships in commission and their distribution in peace.

(b) The size of the Fleet available on the outbreak of war and hence the size of the Reserve Fleet.

PART I

THE NAVY IN PEACE

2. In peace the Navy has three main functions:–

(i) Training for war.

(ii) Safeguarding British life and property.

(iii) Furthering British policy and interest abroad.

3. Training for War. This aspect of the problem will be greatly affected by whether conscription is retained and the length of the period of call-up. For the purpose of this paper, it is assumed that conscripts will continue to be drafted into the Navy for, at least, some years; it may well be difficult to make provision for balanced reserves without conscription.

4. Two of the immediate effects of conscription will be an increase in the number of short training establishments required and in the amount of instruction it will be necessary to give ratings afloat.

[1] Reproduced as Doc. No. 28.

5. Over and above the training of the individual, tactical training of the Fleet as a whole and development of new methods of sea warfare will be required; this will involve co-operation with the other Services. Tactical and material trials and experiments will be needed. These requirements can only be met by the retention of two main fleets, since the concentration of all tactical training into one fleet would abolish competition and mean that all problems would be approached from one angle only. If foreign service is not to assume unacceptable proportions, one fleet should be based on the United Kingdom and the other abroad, preferably in the Mediterranean.

The battleship is still the only ship that can strike the heaviest blow, keep on striking then under any conditions of geographical position, weather or light and until it is proved that Battleships have outlived their usefulness, it is considered that they must continue, in small numbers, to form part of the Main Fleets.

6. Safeguarding British life and property. British interests are world-wide and the inherent mobility of the Navy makes it still an effective and economical instrument for settling minor troubles or disputes. The mere existence of a strong Navy is a considerable influence for peace and quiet, and the presence of H.M. ships at ports will often prevent unrest; the universal popularity of the bluejacket is also a national asset. In the postwar years minor disturbances of many kinds may be expected in all parts of the world, and our naval dispositions should provide for ships to reach possible areas of disturbance before trouble can spread or get out of hand.

7. Furthering of British policy and interests abroad. 'Trade follows the flag'. This proved very true between 1919 and 1939 during which period it was found necessary, for economic reasons, to revive the South American Squadron. If we wish to regain, let alone improve, our pre-war standard of living, our export trade will need re-establishing and greatly increasing. Without this we shall be unable to maintain armed forces commensurate with our territorial possessions and responsibilities. 'Showing the flag' by HM Ships is one of the best ways of fostering British trade and at the same time guarding British lives and property.

TRAINING AND MORALE

8. Only a Service with contented personnel will attract volunteers of the right type. Most young men enjoy travel and are interested in seeing other countries if conscription is approved, as many as possible of the men called up should have a glimpse of sea service outside Home Waters. On the other hand, there are strong arguments for. arranging that the average service on foreign stations does not exceed service in UK or Home Waters.

9. The large numbers of men who will be undergoing elementary training and the need for building up reserves in all categories will necessitate training in all classes of ships, vessels and naval establishments.

ALLOCATION OF SHIPS TO DIFFERENT STATIONS

10. It is considered therefore that, in the main, our object will be best achieved by disposing the battleships, large carriers, destroyers and submarines in Home Waters and in the Mediterranean. Cruisers and escorts are required on all Stations. Carriers will normally be restricted to those areas where Naval Air Stations are available and weather conditions suitable for flying training; and this will limit the foreign stations on which they can be based. The disposition of Assault Forces will depend on requirements of the other Services, but it seems probable that an assault lift for 1 brigade will be able to cover in turn Home Waters, the Mediterranean and possibly India.

THE DOMINIONS

11. Every encouragement should be given to the Dominions to bear their share of Imperial defence. The number of ships and personnel contributed by them to the Empire Navy will affect the numbers which it is necessary for the United Kingdom to provide. The decision however as to what ships can and will be maintained by the Dominions must remain a matter for their own Governments.

12. It is hoped they will maintain forces for the purpose of controlling the sea communications in their own areas, but these forces may not always be adequate. Moreover, a rigid adherence to their respective areas would not provide adequate training or lead to the development of a common Empire naval doctrine; interchange of personnel, staffs and forces between the Royal and Dominion Navies should therefore continue.

THE SIZE OF THE POST-WAR NAVY IN COMMISSION

13. The proportion of the Navy to be kept in commission in peace may be said to depend on the training commitment, which is fairly constant, and on the international situation which will vary. Financial stringency will limit the Navy to a size which will barely meet the training commitment and cover possible international obligation, including the provision of World Security measures.

14. It is estimated that to retain the status of a first-class naval power, meet our training commitment, ensure an adequate standard of efficiency, provide flexibility and contented personnel and allow for experiments, trials and development, the Empire will need, in peace, a fleet in commission of the following order:–

4 Battleships
4 Fleet Carriers
10 Light Carriers

32 Cruisers
64 Destroyers
45 Submarines
60 Escorts
An assault lift for one brigade.

together with the necessary Fleet auxiliaries, ancillary craft and bases. Ships likely to be maintained by the Dominions are included in the above. The aircraft first line strength would be about 500. Allowance has been made for training carriers and cruisers (see appendix to Annex I); it will also be necessary to keep in commission some additional assault craft for basic training, trials and development.

The ships in reserve are shown in PART III.

MANNING THE FLEET

15. If allowance is made for a Dominion contribution of some 30,000 officers and men, it is estimated that the Royal Navy will need to provide some 170,000 long service officers and men to man this peacetime Fleet and to maintain ships in reserve. This figure does not include conscripts. If efficiency is not to suffer unduly and the necessary training is to be achieved, it is estimated that the number of conscripts in the Royal Navy should not exceed 20 per cent of the long service total. The length of time for which a conscript remains fitted for immediate employment in emergency can only be determined by experience, which is not yet available. For the present, however, it would seem prudent not to put the figure higher than 7 years. With the assistance of long service reservists this should make provision for the manning of the fleet on mobilisation.

PART II

THE FLEET REQUIRED ON THE OUTBREAK OF WAR

16. Though Germany and Japan are to be completely disarmed and it may be assumed that the United Nations Organisation will ensure that they remain so, there still exist in Europe and Asia potential disturbers of the peace. Although war with the USA is unthinkable, and their support may be confidently expected, Great Britain and the Dominions may well find themselves unsupported by allies initially in a situation which leads to hostilities on a major scale.

17. It is essential therefore to have immediately available at the outbreak of war strong Empire Naval forces, quite apart from the requirements of the World Security Organisation.

18. Although there is little doubt that the Empire could, if desired, outbuild any two nations (USA excluded), it were better to maintain an adequate margin of strength and thus discourage competition, than cut to the bone and subsequently be forced into a building race, with its attendant interruption of trade, reconstruction and improvement in civilian

standards of life. A strong fleet and a steady replacement programme will avoid the necessity to expand rapidly at some future date in conditions necessarily expensive and unsatisfactory.

19. The ability of potential enemies to produce submarines and aircraft quickly and secretly is an additional and very good reason for retaining strong forces. The views recently put forward by Sir Henry Tizard indicate the probability of these weapons constituting the major threat to sea communications in any future war.[1]

FORCES NEEDED FOR THE CONTROL OF SEA COMMUNICATIONS

20. Home Waters and the Atlantic. This area is of the first importance to Great Britain. Any prolonged interruption of our communications would be a wound from which there might no recovery. All types of warships will be required; heavy units sufficient to destroy similar enemy forces, escorts and carriers for the protection of trade and military convoys; coastal forces for inshore operations; submarines for reconnaissance and operations in waters not under our full control; minesweeping and minelaying forces; amphibious forces for limited operations on enemy territory. In many of these activities the co-operation of the other Services will be necessary.

As far as Amphibious Forces are concerned, it is unlikely that sufficient Army forces will be available to undertake major landing operations in the early stages of hostilities. Adequate Amphibious forces for such minor operations as may be necessary during this period should be available from those required for peacetime development and training.

21. Minesweepers to keep open the approaches to essential harbours and to preserve freedom of action of the fleets will be required in considerable numbers. Boom Vessels, Gate Vessels, Netlayers, etc. will be needed. Minelayers, Monitors, and Gunboats, also have important duties to perform. All forces will require maintenance ships and harbour craft of all types for their effective support. Though a large number of coastal units may not be available in the initial stages, provision for rapid expansion should be made.

OTHER NAVAL FORCES

22. In addition to the forces needed in the Atlantic and Home Waters for the protection of shipping, on which the continuous supply and well-being of the United Kingdom depend, squadrons and flotillas will be required to ensure the movement of Armies, supplies and food between the Dominions, Colonies, outlying garrisons and areas of active operations.

For these duties, it is probable that Carriers, Cruisers and smaller vessels will be necessary. Much, however, depends on such unpredictable

[1] COS(45)402(O), reproduced as Doc. No. 34.

factors as the disposition of ships by an enemy and the course of operations and a balanced and mobile reserve of all types of ship will be needed if our world-wide communications by sea are to be maintained and protected.

SUMMARY OF FORCES NEEDED

23. It is apparent therefore that Heavy Forces may be needed in European Waters and in the East and Lighter Forces in all areas of naval activity, with a preponderance in the Atlantic. It is visualised that the composition of Heavy Units will be dictated by tactical considerations, though their characteristics are unlikely to vary greatly. The Lighter Forces will, however, differ considerably as between one area and another and according to the duties for which they are required. Whilst the Heavy Forces must be comparable to the potential opposition, certain light forces can be computed on an absolute basis. For instance, experience has shown that a minimum of 10 escort groups are required for the North Atlantic route alone, whilst some 50 vessels are required for the coastal convoys of the British Isles.

FORCES AVAILABLE

24. It is estimated that should a major war break out in the early postwar period, the Empire will be capable of mobilizing a fleet of modern ships of the order of:–

10 Battleships
9 Fleet Carriers
23 Light Carriers
43 Cruisers
144 Destroyers
220 Escorts
85 Submarines

with an appropriate backing of ancillary vessels, coastal and amphibious forces. The Carriers will be capable of operating a first-line strength of about 1300 aircraft. Crews for the full number of ships shown will not be available immediately on the outbreak of war.

WAR RESERVE

25. Besides meeting our offensive and defensive needs in the early days of war we must allow for increased Naval Commitments which will as always arise as war progresses. Additional light craft and even cruisers can be built with reasonable speed and certain types of merchant vessels can be converted to war purposes. Battleships and Heavy Carriers, however, take several years to build and a reserve must therefore be retained as an insurance against additional commitments and the hazards of war.

MANPOWER

26. It is estimated that some 500,000 officers and men will be required to man the Navy in the opening stages of war and that this figure may

rise to 600,000 within 18 months. If the effective Dominion contribution is assumed as 60,000 officers and men, it follows that our target for mobilisation should be about 400,000 long service personnel or trained reservists, with a further intake of 140,000 for training during the subsequent 18 months.

PART III
RESERVE FLEET

27. In peace, there will be a Reserve Fleet of the order of:–

6 Battleships
5 Fleet Carriers
13 Other Carriers
11 Cruisers
80 Destroyers
160 Escorts
40 S/Ms

The majority of these ships already form part of the Fleet, the remainder are well advanced in their construction.

28. As the Reserve Fleet, which will include modern units, may be required immediately on the outbreak of war, it should be kept fully efficient and up to date. It is possible that a system of rotation between the Active and Reserve Fleets whereby ships and vessels alternate between the two will be found to be the best method of keeping all units efficient.

29. The following detailed statements are attached:–

Annex I	Proposed Dispositions in Peace
Appendix to Annex I	Tabular Statement of Proposed Dispositions
Annex II	Tabular Statement showing ships of the Navy, numbers in full commission and reserve, Support Fleet and ancilliary units.

ANNEX I
PROPOSED DISPOSITIONS IN PEACE

Home Waters. A main Fleet, consisting of 2 Battleships, 2 Fleet Carriers, 2 Light Carriers, a Cruiser Squadron, 3 Destroyer Flotillas, an Escort Group and on S/M Flotilla. In addition, Light Carriers, Cruisers, Destroyers, Escorts and S/Ms will be required for development, trials and special training.

Foreign Waters – Preferably Mediterranean. Similar to the Home Fleet but without the special training, development and trials components. It is possible that the number of Carriers may have to be restricted by the airfield accommodation available.

West Atlantic. A force of Cruisers and Escorts permanently on the Station with periodical visits by Carriers and heavy forces from home waters.

Africa. A force of Cruisers and Escorts.

East Indies. A force of a Light Carrier, Cruisers, Escorts.
Pacific. A force of a Light Carrier, Cruisers, Escorts and Submarines.
Australia, New Zealand and Canada. Forces as decided by the Dominion Governments concerned. It is hoped that these forces will comprise Light Carriers, Cruisers, Destroyers and Escorts.

APPENDIX TO ANNEX I
PROPOSED DISPOSITIONS OF MAIN UNITS IN PEACE

	Home	Med.	West Atlantic	Africa	E.I.	Pacific	Australia & N.Z.	Canada	Total
Battleships	2	2	–	–	–	–	–	–	4
Fleet Carriers	2	2	–	–	–	–	–	–	4
Light Carriers	2+2*	2	–	–	1	1	1	1	10
Cruisers	5+3⁺	5	4	2	4	4	3	2	30
Destroyers	24	24	–	–	–	–	8	8	64
Escorts	16ᴼ	8	4	4	4	8	8	8	60
Submarines	25ᴼ	10	–	–	–	10	–	–	45

* DLT, Training and Development
⁺ For experiments and trials and cadets training
ᴼ Includes provision for A/S training

ANNEX II
COMPOSITION OF EMPIRE NAVY IN PEACE

Item	Full Commission	Reserve	Total
Battleships	4	6	10
Cruisers	32	11	43
Destroyers	64	80	144
Escorts	60	160	220
Minelayers	–	3	3
Monitors	–	2	2
Fleet Minesweepers	16	16	32
Other Minesweepers	–	48	48
Gunboats	–	5	5
Surveying Ships	7	–	7
Submarines	45	40	85
Destroyer Depot Ships	2	1	3
Sub. Depot Ships	3	1	4
Fleet Oilers	5	5	10
Fleet Repair Ships	3	2	5
Fleet Tugs	12	–	12
Escort Main. Ships	1	3	4
Net Layers	1	1	2
Seaward Defence Ship	–	1	1
Fleet Carriers	4	5	9
Other Carriers	10	13	23
Aircraft Repair Ships	3	4	7
Note:– An Aircraft First Line Strength of 500 is assumed			
Coastal Forces	24	20	44

Boom Defence Vessels	–	70	70
Cable Ships	6	–	6
Harbour Craft		2	
Carrying Ships	–	14	14
Salvage Vessels	4	2	6

Landing Ships and Craft will also be required to lift one Brigade and for experimental and training duties. The exact composition remains to be decided.

49. *DNC Memorandum*

[ADM 1/19096] 10 October 1945

10852/45

PRESENT AND FUTURE NAVAL BUILDING PROGRAMMES[1]

The attached paper on the financial and labour aspects of existing and future naval construction programmes has been drawn up in order that a long-term plan may be devised and the necessary adjustments to the present building programme determined and applied.

2. The latter is a matter of urgency as without it, departments are neither able to reorganise their production to meet future requirements, nor shut down on unproductive expenditure.

3. Action so far has been confined to suspending certain ships in anticipation of possible eventual cancellation. We should now go forward and settle these cancellations and deferments.

4. In the attached paper an attempt has been made to draw up a long-term plan for naval construction in light of the requirements of the postwar fleet, as set out in PD.0140/45 of 12 September 1945 with the subsequent replacements necessary over a term of years. This broad plan also takes into account from consideration of past experience and probable future developments in the fields of availability of money and labour the material realities of the situation with which we may expect to be faced in post war years.

5. The immediate problem is to obtain approval to modify the existing new construction programme as set out in paragraph 15 of this paper.

6. The determination of the general long-term plan is also a matter of some urgency as it affects a variety of activities waiting for guidance as to the future. Such as for example the armour and large gun mounting industry.

[1] This Memorandum was sent to the First Lord of the Admiralty, Deputy First Sea Lord, VCNS, the Secretary to the Admiralty Board and the Director of Plans, amongst others.

FINANCIAL AND LABOUR ASPECTS OF EXISTING AND FUTURE NAVAL CONSTRUCTION PROGRAMMES

PRESENT PROGRAMME

At present we have the following ships building, ordered, or due to be ordered from previous approved programmes up to and including the 1944 programme:–

Battleship	1	
Large Fleet Aircraft Carriers	5	(See note 1)
Light Fleet Aircraft Carriers	13	
Cruisers	11	(See note 2)
Destroyers	90	
Submarines	30	
Sloops	10	
Minesweepers	1	
Frigates	20	

Note 1 Includes two MALTA Class Large Carriers (XI design) of the 1943 programme under design and provisionally ordered.

Note 2 Includes six heavy cruisers under design but not yet ordered.

Note 3 The two large aircraft carriers Africa and Gibraltar and four Hermes Class of the 1943 Programme ordered, but subsequently suspended, have properly been omitted from the above.

PRESENT PROPOSED MODIFICATIONS TO PROGRAMME

2. It has at present been proposed … that of the above the following should be cancelled:–

Destroyers	13
Submarines	12
Sloops	5

and in addition, the following suspended:–

Destroyers	8
Frigates	5

PRESENT PROGRAMME IN RELATION TO POST WAR FLEET

3. The total number of ships remaining in the building programme, after reduction by the total numbers in paragraph 2, assuming that the suspension in fact become cancellations, is a considerable proportion of the number of ships proposed to form the post war Fleet as set out in PD.0140/45. These proportions are as follows:–

Type of Ship	Number proposed for post war Fleet vide Annex II to PD.0140/45	Number of ships remaining in present building programme	Percentage of post war Fleet
HEAVY SHIPS:–			
Battleships Large Fleet Carriers	19	6	32%
MEDIUM SHIPS:–			
Cruisers Other Carriers	66	24	36%
LIGHT SHIPS:–			
Destroyers	144	69	47%
Escorts	220	20	9%
SUBMARINES:–			
All Classes	85	18	21%

We are thus at present proposing to build about 1/3 of the post war fleet except in the case of escorts which are mostly already in existence.

COST OF PRESENT PROGRAMME

4. The completion of this large programme, allowing for the reductions already proposed as in paragraph 2, calls for the expenditure of approximately £150,000,000. Of this sum about £40,000.000 will fall due by the end of this financial year, leaving a liability of the order of £110,000,000 to fall on the estimates of ensuing financial years. After making allowance for the extension of completion dates due to low priorities and similar factors it is estimated that this liability for £110,000,000 will fall on each succeeding financial year as follows:–

Financial Year	Annual Charge for ships ordered and building	Additional Charge for two MALTA Class Carriers	Additional Charge for six large Cruisers	Total annual liability
	£ m	£ m	£ m	£ m
1946	41.0	–	1.0	42.0
1947	20.0	4.0	5.0	29.0
1948	9.0	4.0	5.0	18.0
1949	2.0	4.0	5.0	11.0
1950		4.0	4.0	8.0
1951		2.0		
	72.0	18.0	20.0	110.0

COST OF PROJECTED 1945 PROGRAMME

5. If the projected 1945 programme of:–

Battleships	2
Submarines	4
Escort Vessels	4
Surveying Ships	5

is proceeded with then a further total liability of approximately £30,000,000 will occur and be spread over roughly the same period, the maximum being in about 1949–51.

COST OF PRESENT PROGRAMME IN RELATION TO WAR

6. The liabilities for new construction charges set out in paragraph 4 above do not look formidable against the background of the inflated expenditure of the war years, where the expenditure on new construction has been:–

Year	Expenditure on Battleships, Carriers, Cruisers, Destroyers, Submarines, Sloops, Frigates, Corvettes and Minesweepers	Expenditure on all other types of craft, depot ships, floating docks etc	Total expenditure
	£ m	£ m	£ m
1939	41.3	8.8	50.1
1940	50.4	30.3	80.7
1941	59.3	30.6	89.9
1942	63.1	45.1	113.2
1943	79.4	44.5	123.9
1944	77.0	56.3	133.3 est.
1945	50.1	41.1	91.1 est.

…

50. *Principal Assistant Secretary, Admiralty to Under Secretary (London)*

[ADM 1/17300] 22 October 1945

POST-WAR FLEET

A statement (Appendix A) is enclosed giving £34,000,000 as the average annual cost of new construction need to maintain a postwar navy of the size detailed in the staff memorandum PD.0140/45 …

APPENDIX A
ANNUAL COST OF NEW CONSTRUCTION TO KEEP IN BEING POST-WAR FLEET INDICATED IN STAFF MEMORANDUM PD.0140/45

Class	Life of Vessel Years	Total estimated cost Votes 8 & 9	Annual replacement cost per unit	Number In Comm.	In reserve	Total annual replacement cost
Battleship	26	13,250,000	510,000	4	6	5,100,000
Cruisers	25	3,800,000	152,000	32	11	6,536,000
Destroyers:–						
Weapons	22	900,000	41,000	32	40	
Battles		1,150,000	52,000	32	40	6,696,000
Escorts:–						
25 A/A Sloops		510,000	23,200			580,000
111 Loch, River & Bay Frigates	22	275,000	12,500	60	160	1,387,500
23 Castle		163,000	14,100			324,300
61 Hunt		500,000	22,700			1,382,700
Minelayers	22	1,000,000	45,400	–	3	136,200
Monitors	25	1,000,000	40,000	–	2	80,000
Fleet Minesweepers						
Other mine-sweepers (MMS)	25	250,000	10,000	16	16	320,000
Gunboats	20	40,000	2,000	–	48	96,000
Surveying Ships	30	100,000	3,300	–	5	16,500
Submarines	22	500,000	22,700	7	–	159,000
Destroyer Depot Ships	16	435,000	27,000	45	40	2,295,000
Submarine Depot Ships	30	2,000,000	66,700	2	1	200,000
Fleet Oilers	30	2,000,000	66,700	3	1	267,000
Fleet Repair Ships	30	500,000	16,700	5	5	167,000
Fleet Tugs	30	2,500,000	83,300	3	2	416,500
Escort Mainten-ance Ships	30	120,000	4,000	12	–	48,000
Net Layers	30	500,000	16,700	1	3	67,000
Seaward Defence Ships	30	400,000	13,300	1	1	26,500
Fleet Carriers	30	250,000	8,300	–	1	8,300
Other Carriers	24	10,000,000	417,000	4	5	3,753,000
Aircraft Mainten-ance, Component Repair & Engine Repair Ships	20	2,750,000	137,500	10	13	3,162,000
Coastal Forces	30	500,000	16,700	3	4	117,000
B.D. Vessels	10	50,000	5,000	24	20	220,000
Cable Ships	30	90,000	3,000	–	70	210,000
Harbour Craft Carrying Ships	30	175,000	5,800	6	–	35,000
Maintenance Ships	30	250,000	8,300	–	2	16,500
for Harbour Craft	30	200,000	6,600	–	12	81,000
Salvage Vessels	30	350,000	11,700	–	2	
Landing Craft	30	200,000	6,700	4	2	46,000
	various					50,000
					TOTAL	34,000,000

51. *Loose Minute by First Lord of the Admiralty*

[ADM 1/17300] 26 October 1945

I agree that the memorandum PD.0140/45 should be circulated to the Board for discussion at a meeting …

The resources which will be made available to the Services during the next few years will inevitably depend upon the progress of the general financial position and in particular upon the rate at which the present annual rate of accumulation of debt can be reduced. It is true that a figure of £500 million a year has been mentioned as the possible total annual expenditure on the Services. I incline to believe that this figure will prove to have been optimistic. In any event we must expect a drive to keep down expenditure on the Services, and on the Navy in particular.

With these considerations in mind, I think we should work out what fleet could be provided on the assumption that the annual sum spent on new construction was about half that contemplated in this paper, that is to say about £17 million, and what might be the approximate corresponding size of Vote A. In making this calculation I suggest that the lives of the ships should be assumed to be a little longer than the figures given on this paper. Account should also be taken, if it has not been taken already, of possible reductions in the present costs of shipbuilding and equipment resulting from the cessation of overtime and other wartime increases.

I do not suggest that these calculations should be made in great detail at the present stage, but only sufficiently to enable the Board to have a broad picture of the fleet which might be provided on the hypothesis I have mentioned when they consider PD.0140/45.

I recognise that the hypothesis itself is somewhat arbitrary. But the hypothesis on which the fleet put forward in PD.0140/45 is based is itself necessarily arbitrary, and until the strategic and international requirements on which the size of the fleet must ultimately be based are clearer finance will inevitably play an unusually important part in determining its size.

52. *DNC Memorandum*

[ADM 1/19096] 16 October 1945

10873/45

NEW CONSTRUCTION PROGRAMME
Suspensions & Cancellations

Provisional decisions have been taken as to the future of the present new construction programme. These decisions are subject to approval by the Board which it is anticipated will be given shortly.

2. The ships following will be CANCELLED:–

AIRCRAFT CARRIERS

(a) AFRICA and GIBRALTAR.

(b) Last four of the 1943 Light Fleets, namely HERMES,[1] ARROGANT, MONMOUTH and POLYPHEMUS.

CRUISERS

(c) HAWKE

DESTROYERS

(d) All eight ships of the JUTLAND Class.

(e) Six ships of the MONS Class, namely MONS, OUDENARDE, NAMUR, NAVARINO, OMDURMAN and SAN DOMINGO.

(f) Two ships of the AGINCOURT Class, namely ALBUERA and BELLISLE.

(g) Two ships of the BATTLEAXE Class, namely CLAYMORE and SWORD.

(h) Six ships of the CUTLASS Class namely DAGGER, DIRK, SPEAR, HOWITZER, LONGBOW and MUSKET.

SUBMARINES

(i) The twelve "A" Class already suspended.

SLOOPS

(j) Five MODIFIED BLACK SWAN Class.

FRIGATES

(k) Five BAY Class.

(l) Two BAY class … may be completed.

3. The remainder of the present programme will be completed, but portions of it will be deferred as follows:–

(a) The laying down and completion of the two remaining Fleet Carriers of the 1943 programme, namely MALTA and NEW ZEALAND will be deferred one year.

(b) The second flotilla of the DARING Class will be deferred one year …

(c) The construction of the six large 6 inch Cruisers of the 1944 programme, not yet ordered, will proceed but probably at a slower rate …

4. The present programme amended as above will occupy the building and financial capacity available for the next few years; thereafter, it is the intention, so far as practicable, to start a steady annual fleet replacement programme. The scope and form of this programme is now under

[1]The name HERMES was subsequently re-allocated to the ship previously called ELEPHANT.

consideration. In this connection, it is not now the intention to proceed with the construction of the two Battleships previously projected for the 1945 programme, nor is it likely that such ships will be included in any new programme during the next few years. The order for the LION and TEMERAIRE, which has stood suspended for many years, will now be finally cancelled.

5. The above is promulgated for information of departments who should now take action to revise and modify their production programmes accordingly in anticipation of final approval. Official cancellation of ships concerned with the firms should not, however, be taken until formally approved by the Board …[1]

53. *Defence Committee Memorandum*

[CAB 69/7] 24 October 1945

DO(45)22 SALE AND SCRAPPING OF WARSHIPS

Memorandum By The First Lord Of The Admiralty

Now that active operations have ended, I seek the approval of the Cabinet to the following policy with regard to the disposal of warships:–

(a) In so far as there is a reasonable ready market for them, either at home or abroad, the Admiralty should sell, in consultation with the Treasury where necessary, as many as possible of the warships and craft surplus to our probable postwar needs.

(b) In the cruiser category, in which most of our ships are obsolete, we should realise all the possible sales although we shall not in any event have as many under-age cruisers as we shall need postwar. Only cruisers completed before September 1939 would be sold or transferred, except to the Dominions or India.

(c) Vessel and craft surplus to probable postwar needs for which no ready market can be foreseen should be scrapped. The type or condition of many vessels would clearly preclude sale; in other cases, I would propose to interpret "ready market" as a good prospect of sale within, say, two years of paying off …

2. Table A, appended hereto, shows *inter alia*:–

(i) The numbers of vessels in each main category at present in the Royal Navy after discounting lend-lease vessels which the United

[1] Distribution List not reproduced. It included VCNS and the First Lord's Private Office. This list of cancellations and deferrals had in fact already been approved by the First Lord of the Admiralty on 15 Oct – Loose Minute by F.W. Mottershead, First Lord's Private Secretary dated 18 Oct, also in ADM 1/19096.

States are entitled to have back, and requisitioned vessels which must be returned to owners.

(ii) The bids so far received from possible purchasers at home and abroad, together with certain commitments already entered into for the transfer of vessels on terms other than sale. This information, so far as concerns overseas bids and commitments, is elaborated in Table B.

(iii) The approximate *maximum* numbers for which I at present seek approval to scrap.

(iv) The numbers remaining after these various processes have been completed if all the present bids turn into effective purchases.

Possible Sales

3. … discussions are proceeding with European Allies concerning their postwar naval requirements. Dominions, India and perhaps on a very small scale the Colonies may wish to acquire a few of our warships. There are also possibilities of selling warships to Portugal, Eire and certain South and Central American States. In addition, we have commitments to Turkey, Egypt and Persia for the replacement of ships taken over, or in the case of Persia, sunk during the war. With the approval of the late Prime Minister substantial commitments have been undertaken for the rehabilitation of the Chinese Navy.

4. Some requirements notified by Foreign Governments have been for quasi-commercial purposes (eg the French have already taken a number of landing craft for inland water transport). It is difficult, however, to gauge the commercial market either at home or abroad … the Admiralty fully appreciate the immediate financial advantage of selling as many surplus warships as possible and also the long-term advantages of building up good will abroad for our shipbuilding industry, I feel bound to point out that, in practice, the total of sales realised may not be very large.

Maintenance

5. Vessels retained for possible sale will need to be maintained and we have also to care for lend-lease vessels. The Navy seems likely to continue to suffer from an acute shortage of officers and men qualified for this duty. We therefore have to strike a balance between the need for maintenance and the shortage or personnel. In the result, it has been necessary to lay up large numbers of ships and craft, surplus to immediate needs, on mud berths without any maintenance … these vessels will deteriorate and many of them will soon be fit only for the scrapping yard … The vessels at present in maintained reserve and unmaintained reserve are shown respectively in Columns D and E of Table A.

Sales

6. We have yet to determine the size and composition of the postwar fleet; but so far as can be foreseen we should be able, except for cruisers … to realise all the likely sales and to scrap all the vessels which I propose to scrap without reducing the remaining serviceable ships below the numbers required post-war.

7. Special considerations apply to cruisers. Allowing for those which it will be uneconomical to repair or refit for service in the Royal Navy and discounting vessels over 20 years old, we now have only 34. The obvious deduction is that none of these should be sold at all. Of these 34 cruisers only 22 will have been completed since the outbreak of war and I would readily agree that none of these should be transferred, except to Empire Navies. The rest, however, are not up to date and even at large expense could not be made really modern. Accordingly, if the cruiser force of the fleet is to be made adequate in numbers and individual efficiency, some replacement building is inevitable. This being so, and given the financial, commercial and political advantages of meeting demands from foreign countries for second-hand British cruisers, I feel that the right policy is to reap those advantages and to accept the corollary that, in so doing, the amount of cruiser replacement building will be somewhat increased.[1]

8. Undoubtably, the moment for achieving the maximum of success for a policy of disposal abroad is the present when so many countries are beginning to plan their defence programmes afresh and when their own shipyards are, in general, unlikely to be in production for some time. It is accordingly important that negotiations for sale should be brought to conclusion in the shortest possible time. For this reason, I hope that the Cabinet will agree:–

- (i) that this factor should be borne in mind in settling prices. (Another factor favouring the acceptance of relatively low prices is brought out in the following paragraph on scrapping);
- (ii) that I should have general discretion to dispose, under the conditions set out above, of warships and craft of the category of destroyer and below, on the understanding that I should report my decisions for covering approval at intervals. For ships above the category of destroyer, I will seek the prior approval of the Cabinet in each case …

[1] Somewhat surprisingly, within weeks of this statement the new cruiser *Hawke*, on which work had already started in Portsmouth Dockyard, was cancelled.

Scrapping

9. I have explained above why it will not be possible to dispose of very large numbers of redundant war vessels as going concerns, and Column G in Table A indicates broadly the maximum numbers in each case for which I seek approval to break up … It must, however, be remembered that the capacity of the breaking-up yards of the country is limited and labour is short. It will be, therefore, a long process covering some years … I should welcome early guidance on this point, since it would then become not merely cheaper … but also simpler, to scuttle in deep water those vessels which would be available for scrapping in excess of the need for scrap metal. Moreover, the scuttling of surplus vessels would provide a means for disposing of some small part of the surplus ammunition which inevitably exists as a result of the unexpectedly early termination of the Japanese war and the storage of which is an acute problem in all theatres.

[Extract from DO(45) 11th Meeting, 29 October 1945 Item 4 [CAB 69/7]:–

THE COMMITTEE:–

(a) Approved the policy as set out above.
(b) Agreed that, as a general principle, there should be no scuttling of surplus vessels, all of which should be converted to scrap.]

TABLE A

A	B	C	D	E	F	G	H
Category and numbers now available to RN *less* land/lease & requisitioned vessels and on loan to Allies	Numbers already approved for scrapping since 1 Jan 45	Numbers already sold since 30th Sep 39	Numbers of "A" in Maintained Reserve	Numbers of "A" in Reserve without maintenance	Bids received and commitments to be met out of "D" or from vessels in commission	Approx maximum number to be scrapped (+ and in "F" where sale is not realised) and including "B"	Numbers remaining after deducting "F" & "G" including balance of vessels in maintained reserve and new construction not yet completed
Battleships (including Renown, 4 used as training & accommodation ships and 8 which will never become effective fighting ships) 14	2	–	3	4	–	12 5	10 (allows for 1 new construction)
Aircraft Carriers (4 could							9 (including 3 new construction)
never be effective) 10	–	–	–	4	–	4	18 (including 13 new construction)
Light Fleet Carriers 5	–	–	–	–	–	–	4
Escort Carriers 5	–	–	–	–	1	–	
Cruisers							
8-inch 9	–	–	–	–	–	–	} 48 (including 3 new construction)
Under 8-inch 14	–	–	3	10	6	7	
Under 6-inch 30	–	–	–	–	–	–	
Fleet Destroyers 97	2	Holland 6	2	3	29	4	64 + 77 new construction
Escort Destroyers 148	30	–	8	74	4	91	58

Sloops								
A.A.	28	–	–	1	11	–	–	27
A.S.	19	2	–	6	–	2	18	
Frigates	77	2	Holland 1	15	2	11 Rivers	–	74 (including 8 new construction)
Corvettes	125	–	Holland 1	31	69	50 Flowers	48	32
Submarines	118	–	Holland 3	17	6	8	25	85
Minesweepers	418	–	–	18	9	12	300	106
Fast Minelayers	3	–	–	–	–	–	–	3
Landing Ships	2	–	–	1	–	–	3	–
Major Landing Craft	867	75	157	449	–	200	567	100
Minor Landing Craft	2,845	99	9	1,596	–	As yet no indication	1,899 (less sales)	446

TABLE B
Bids received and commitments to be met out of Column D in Table A

Category of Ship	Country Bidding	Number of Ships Required
Aircraft Carriers, CVE	Holland	1
Cruisers	China	1 (on loan)
Fleet Destroyers	Holland	1
Escort Destroyers	Norway	1
Sloops	Turkey	2 (on credit terms)
Frigates	Chile	1 (nebulous)
Corvettes	Turkey	12 (including 10 on credit)
Submarines	France	15 (very nebulous)
Minesweepers	Norway	2
	Greece	2
	China	1 (on loan)
	France	1
	Venezuela	1 (nebulous)
	Egypt	1
	Denmark	2 (Rivers)
	India	9 (Rivers)
	Portugal	1
	Greece	6
	Denmark	2
	Eire	6 All Flowers
	China	2 (on loan)
	Chinese Maritime Customs	2
	Persia	4
	Turkey	2
	Norway	2
	Greece	2
	China	2 (on loan)
	S. Africa	8
	Turkey	4

[*Plus numerous minor vessels*]

54. *Chiefs of Staff Minutes*

[CAB 79/41] 1 November 1945

COS(45) 264th Meeting SIZE OF POST-WAR ARMED FORCES

… When the question of preparing a forecast of defence requirements for the period 1946–50 had been discussed with the Directors of Plans … serious doubt had been expressed as to whether the Joint Planning Staff would in fact be able to produce estimates of any value; one of the main difficulties being to decide on what political assumptions our military requirements should be based.

… Assuming that the period of conscript service was fixed at two years … the conscript element in the armed forces would probably not exceed 400,000 … the number of recruits likely to be forthcoming would not support regular forces much in excess of 500,000 …

The Directors of Plans explained that they were approaching the problem from two directions. First, they were trying to estimate what forces would be required over a period, on the assumption that the political situation developed along certain lines … The second line of approach was to try and estimate the minimum forces required to provide a nucleus for rapid expansion in the event of war …

THE COMMITTEE:

… emphasis[ed] the difficulties of submitting a forecast of defence requirements over a period of five years …

55. *Defence Committee Memorandum*

[CAB 69/7] 5 November 1945

DO(45)28 ADMIRALTY PRODUCTION FOR THE PERIOD 1 OCTOBER 1945 – 31 DECEMBER 1946

MEMORANDUM BY THE FIRST LORD OF THE ADMIRALTY

Introduction

The Admiralty have been asked (Prime Minister's Personal Minute M.92/45 of 2 October 1945) to provide for the Defence Committee a paper stating the dimensions of the production programme planned to the end of 1946. The occasion for this request was the reduction of 300,000 men and women in the labour force engaged in the munition industries at the end of 1945 which was being examined by the Joint War Production Staff. The Joint War Production Staff reported to the Manpower Committee of the Cabinet on 8 October 1945 MP(45)44. The paragraphs of this report concerning the Admiralty labour force are as follows:–

"6. The Admiralty labour force to be employed on the 31 December 1945 was previously estimated at 600,000. This force was comprised as follows:–

Shipbuilding, ship repair and ancilliary services (including 60,000 in dockyards)	390,000
Administrative staff for shipyards etc	55,000
Other commitments and maintenance, manufacturing Components, torpedoes etc	155,000
	600,000

7. The merchant shipbuilding and repair programme is of such priority that it should not be reduced. Shipyards are also engaged in certain urgent naval repair work and the conversion of ships for the transport of personnel. Furthermore, in order to accelerate merchant ship construction, it is necessary to proceed with work on certain naval ships so that berths can be cleared for new merchant ships. It follows, therefore, that almost the whole of any reduction in the labour force must come out of the figure of 155,000 quoted in the above table. Bearing in mind the reductions which have already been made, the Admiralty consider that they can aim as a target for the end of December at a reduction of 10,000 in the ancilliary services for shipyards and of 50,000 under the heading 'other commitments and maintenance'. If these cuts are achieved, their labour force at that date will be down to 540,000. Further reductions would have immediate repercussions on the construction of merchant vessels."

2. There are certain immediate difficulties in providing the Defence Committee with a true picture of the Admiralty's production programme planned to the end of 1946.

3. The main difficulty is that no proposals for a postwar Fleet as a target at which production should be aimed have yet received the approval of the Cabinet. Discussions are proceeding and I hope at an early date to place a paper before the Cabinet …

APPENDIX 3 [simplified]

SUMMARY OF SHIPS, UNDER CLASSES, UNDER CONSTRUCTION OR DUE TO BE ORDERED ON THE 15 AUGUST 1945 AND THOSE CANCELLED OR COMPLETED AND THOSE REMAINING UNDER CONSTRUCTION OR TO BE ORDERED

Class of Vessels	Under construction on 15.8.45 and due to be ordered	Since Cancelled	Since Completed	Remaining under construction 17th October 1945				To be ordered
				In an advanced stage of construction		Not in an advanced stage of construction, but required for the postwar fleet		
	Nos.	Nos.	Nos.	Programme	Nos.	Programme	Nos.	Nos.
Battleship	1	–	–	1940	1	–	–	–
Large Aircraft Carriers	7	2	–	1940 (1) 1942 (2)	3	1943	2	–
Light Aircraft Carriers	18	4	–	1942 (10) 1943 (4)	14	–	–	–
Cruisers	11	1	–	1941 (3) 1942 (1)	4	–	–	6
Destroyers	97	24	7	1942 (26) 1943 (16)	42	1944	24	–
Submarines	35	12	1	1941 (2) 1942 (17)	19	–	–	3
Sloops	10	5	1	1940 (2) 1941 (2)	4	–	–	–
Minesweepers	2	–	1	1943	1	–	–	–
Frigates	23	7	14	1943	12	–	–	–
Transport Ferries	22	10	7	1943	5	–	–	–
Boom Vessels	2	–	–	1943	2	–	–	–
Landing Craft	607	489	66	–	82	–	–	–
[plus numerous minor vessels]								

APPENDIX 7
NAVAL AIRCRAFT
Production Programme October 1945 to December 1946

	Fighter Aircraft				Strike Aircraft						
	Seafire	Seafang	Sea Fury	Sea Hornet	Firefly	Firebrand	Sea Mosquito	Barracuda	Spearfish	Sturgeon	Amphibian Sea Otter
1945 –											
October	52	1	–	–	45	14	2	25	–	–	6
November	49	1	–	–	43	12	5	20	–	–	8
December	40	3	–	–	36	9	5	8	–	–	8
1946 –											
January	36	5	1	–	28	8	5	9	–	–	8
February	33	8	2	–	26	8	5	10	–	–	5
March	36	12	3	–	26	8	5	10	–	–	4
April	30	15	3	–	26	8	5	8	–	–	4
May	30	15	4	–	26	8	5	7	1	–	4
June	30	15	6	–	26	8	5	5	2	1	4
July	28	15	8	1	20	6	5	3	3	1	4
August	26	12	8	2	24	8	5	–	5	2	3
September	28	15	12	3	25	8	5	–	5	3	3
October	24	15	14	5	25	8	5	–	8	4	3
November	23	15	16	6	24	8	5	–	8	5	3
December	18	14	18	8	22	8	5	–	8	5	2
Total	483	161	95	25	422	72	72	105	38	21	69
	Fighters:– 764				Strike:– 787						Amphibian:– 69 (non-combat)

56. *Defence Committee Minutes*

[CAB 69/7] 7 November 1945

DO(45) 13th Meeting

1. ADMIRALTY PRODUCTION FOR THE PERIOD 1ST OCTOBER 1945 TO 31ST DECEMBER 1946 (DO(45)28)

The Committee had before them a Memorandum by the First Lord of the Admiralty setting out the dimensions of the Admiralty production programme planned up to the end of 1946 (DO(45)28).

Mr Alexander, Introducing the Memorandum, said that the Admiralty had started last November to study the cuts that might be made in their programme when the war ended. The result was that they had been able to cancel programmes to the value of £24½ million between 15 August and 15 October, and had ordered the cancellation of a further programme worth £96 million on 15 October. About £16 million had been previously spent on these programmes, so that the net saving was about £100 million. On receipt of the Prime Minister's Minute of 2 October, the programmes had again been scrutinized, and as a result the Admiralty hoped to reduce expenditure in the 15 months covered by the Paper from £234 million to £199 million, of which probably as much as £100 million would be spent in the period covered by the recent vote of credit, ie before 31 March 1946. He would like to draw attention to the fact that this allowed for a reduction of £8 million in the Fleet Air Arm programme, though exactly how this reduction would be achieved had not yet been worked out. If it was achieved, it would mean a further cut in labour and aircraft production below the figures shown in the Appendices to the Paper …

It was suggested that larger cuts should be made in the construction programme, not only on financial grounds, but also in order to release fitting-out labour, and particularly electricians … In reply, it was pointed out that the remaining construction programme had been very carefully examined, and as far as possible an economic balance had been struck between the necessity for keeping a balanced labour force and cushioning the change-over to merchant shipbuilding, and the need for reducing labour. The figures for labour employed were rapidly decreasing. For example, the numbers employed on new Naval work two years ago were 64,000, whereas last week they were 34,000. A good deal of the remaining construction would be undertaken very slowly, and it was only hoped to start two of the six new cruisers during the period under review.

Mr Alexander pointed out that there was as yet no overall strategic plan for the postwar period, and final Admiralty commitments could not thus be assessed. One could not yet tell whether it would be safe to bank entirely on the success of the World Organisation, but in any case we ought never to allow ourselves to be left in the situation we found ourselves in in 1940, when we were so dangerously weak at sea that we only Just managed to scrape through.

Lord Cunningham pointed out that we now only had 43 cruisers, including all the old ones, whereas we had started the war with 62. We could not afford to stop all progress and our equipment must at all times be kept up to date.

Mr Bevin[1] said that there was a natural tendency on the part of Governments and Chancellors of the Exchequer to seize the opportunity in peacetime of driving the Services down so low that they could not recover. He was against cutting the armed forces down below the danger limit. On the other hand, ho felt strongly that drastic economy in 1946 would be not only in the national interest, but also in the interest of the Services themselves, who would thus avoid accumulating a lot of equipment which would become rapidly out of date. He would much rather see greatly reduced programmes in 1946 and 1947, accompanied by very active research and a complete overhaul of our defence requirements, with the intention of a more liberal expenditure in 1948 and later years. In this way the economy of the country would be benefitted in the immediate future, and the Services would reap the benefit in the shape of really up to date weapons.

Mr Dalton[2] said he entirely agreed with this policy. He wanted to see a sharp fall in expenditure now, which could be followed by a rise at a later date. He welcomed the present Paper as the first detailed statement of a Service programme. The period it covered contained most of the next financial year, which would be a year for which estimates would have to be presented to Parliament. He would therefore like to have the figures in the programme examined in detail by the Treasury and the Admiralty, with the object of seeing what further reductions could be made.

The Prime Minister, summing up the discussion, said that it was clear that no decision could be taken on the programme at the present meeting. The details should be examined as proposed by the Chancellor of the Exchequer.

THE COMMITTEE:–

Took note of the Memorandum, and invited the Chancellor of the Exchequer and the First Lord of the Admiralty to arrange for it to be examined in detail in the light of the discussion which had taken place, with a view to a revised programme being brought before the Committee in due course.

[1]Foreign Secretary.
[2]Chancellor of the Exchequer.

57. *Board Memorandum*

[ADM 167/124] 5 November 1945

B.434 NEW CONSTRUCTION (REVISED) PROGRAMME 1945[1]

Memorandum by the First Lord of the Admiralty

My predecessor in the last Government placed before the Cabinet on 29 June of this year a Memorandum giving details of the proposed New Construction Programme 1945 (CP(45)54)[2] which was based on the need for the Navy to build up for the Far Eastern war.

2. With the end of the Japanese war, the basis of the New Construction Programme 1945 has changed and it is now necessary for the shipyards to give first priority to Merchant Ship construction. I therefore put forward certain revised proposals for which I ask the approval of my colleagues. The basis of these proposals is:–

(a) To proceed at normal speed with such vessels as may be required for the immediate replacement of a few deficiencies of outstanding importance;

(b) To proceed slowly with, or to defer, the construction of those vessels which, though needed for the postwar Navy, may be used as a cushion to absorb the shocks of the fluctuations in the Shipbuilding Industry. A Warship Building Programme with sufficient flexibility can be used to even out the slumps and booms of Merchant Shipbuilding production.

3. A further advantage of a long-term Naval Building Programme is that it will also give time to enable advantage to be taken of research into the lessons of the war.

OUTLINE OF PROGRAMME

4. In substitution for the programme outlined in paragraph 7 of CP(45)54 I propose that the 1945 Programme should now be as follows:–

1 Experimental Type Submarine
4 Escort Vessels
5 Surveying Ships
6 Small Floating Docks
A number of miscellaneous small craft.

The last two items were added since the 1944 New Construction Programme was approved; Treasury sanction having been obtained in each case.

[1]This memorandum was presented to the Cabinet as CP(45)291 on 27 Nov 1945 (CAB 129/2).

[2]Reproduced as Doc. No. 35.

BATTLESHIPS

5. The preliminary work on the "LION" and "TEMERAIRE" has ceased.

AIRCRAFT CARRIERS

6. I have cancelled two of the Large Fleet Carriers and four of the Light Fleet Carriers of the 1943 Programme.[1]

CRUISERS

7. I propose that 6 Cruisers of previously authorised programmes should be laid down, two immediately and the remainder over a longer period so that they can best be fitted in with the Merchant Shipbuilding programme.[2] I ask approval to proceed with one turret of new design 6-inch mountings in advance of construction, to be fitted in one of the above Cruisers of the 1944 Programme.

DESTROYERS

8. I have cancelled a further 24 Destroyers of the 1943 Programme[3] on the understanding that certain replacements should be made in the future on a long-term basis which will supply the Shipyards with a steady flow of work.

SUBMARINES

9. As a further reduction, I have cancelled a further ten 'A' Class and two 'T' Class Submarines of the 1943 and 1944 Programmes. To keep abreast of the progress that is being made in the design and construction of Submarines, I propose that the 1945 Programme should include one Submarine of a new and experimental type.

ESCORT VESSELS

10. I also ask approval to proceed with the design of four Escort Vessels of a new type, each of about 1,400 tons and with a speed of 25 knots. These are largely experimental vessels; two will be A/S vessels and two A/A ships.

FLOATING DOCKS

11. One Cruiser dock being constructed in Canada and two docks for landing ships have been cancelled, together with 16 of the 22 Docks for small craft. The remaining six had progressed so far that it was more economical to complete them.

SURVEYING SHIPS

12. I ask approval to build two surveying ships of about 1,400 tons. These ships are to carry out the essential work of Surveying, embodying the accurate charting of the many wrecks around our coasts, the complete re-survey of all Estuarial Waters and extensive work overseas in all areas normally used by British shipping.

[1] *Malta* and *Hermes* classes, respectively.

[2] *Neptune* class. None were ever laid down.

[3] Battle and Weapon classes.

SMALL CRAFT

13. I ask approval in the normal way for the miscellaneous small craft required to serve the Fleet and other various duties.

14. Amended statements are appended showing the cancellations in 1944 and up to the end of October 1945 and the estimated cost of this Programme separately and in conjunction with previous Programmes.

LIST OF CANCELLATIONS DURING 1944 AND IN 1945 UP TO 30.10.45

No.	*Description*	*Programme Year*
1	Cruiser	1942
2	Large Fleet Carriers	1943
4	Light Fleet Carriers	1943
27	Destroyers	1943
4	Submarines ("T" Class)	1942
30	Submarines ("A" Class)	1943
17	Submarines ("A" Class)	1944
7	Frigates	1943
3	Sloops	1941
2	Sloops	1942
2	Sloops	1944
9	Fleet Minesweepers	1943
3	Motor Minesweepers	1943
(a) 265	Coastal Craft	Various
10	Boom Defence Vessels	1943
55	Transport Ferries	1943
2	M.T.B. Carrier Ships	1943
965	Landing Craft (LCS(M), LCG(M), LCA, LCT, LCS)	1942–44
2	Salvage Vessels	1943
1	Repair Ship	1942
(b) 2	Cable Ships	1943
2	Destroyer Depot Ships	1942
16	300-ton Concrete Floating Docks	1945 *(c)*
2	6,000-ton Floating Docks	1945 *(c)*
1	15,000-ton Floating Dock	1945 *(c)*
4	Accommodation Arks	1945 *(c)*
	Miscellaneous small craft and Motor Boats	

(a) A number of these have been transferred to War Office and RAF.

(b) One transferred to Trinity House.

(c) Approved in advance of approval to 1945 programme.

…

58. *Anonymous Loose Minute*

[ADM 1/17797] 23 November 1945

New Construction (Revised) Programme 1945

The 1945 programme as now revised and reduced is of very small dimensions. The only items in this programme which can be properly classed as new additions to the fighting fleet are the two 'prototype' escort vessels (one A/A and the other A/S) and one experimental-type submarine. The two surveying ships will go towards meeting a very heavy demand for the resumption of surveying as soon as mine clearance permits. The small craft are mainly motor boats for new construction ships or earlier programmes. The inclusion of six small floating docks is a formality, since they are now completed. They were ordered with Treasury sanction in advance of the 1945 programme to meet urgent war needs. Other floating docks, accommodation arks and small craft ordered under similar circumstances have been cancelled.

2. As is clear from Table 2 of the Cabinet Paper[1] the bulk of the continuing expenditure on new construction is for vessels approved in earlier programmes. Big cuts in this expenditure have already been made by cancellations. They include 447 ships and craft in the financial year 1944, with a resultant saving, allowing for expenditure on work actually carried out when vessels were cancelled, of approximately £30,000,000. Further cancellations of nearly 1,000 ships and craft have been made since 1 April 1945 with a saving of about £80,000,000. Following upon recent discussions in the Defence Committee of the Admiralty production programme the rump of the New Construction Programme is being reviewed in conjunction with the Treasury.

3. The attached table shows the state of advancement of the ships from earlier programmes on which work is proceeding. Most of these (71 of a total of 125 ordered) have already been launched.

4. Carriers account for a very substantial part of the work now in progress. Large carriers capable of operating heavily loaded long-range aircraft are considered essential for the postwar fleet and work is therefore proceeding on the three Ark Royal class carriers. Light Fleet carriers (of which 9 are launched but not completed and 4 laid down but not launched) are also needed. It is envisaged that there should be 23 Light Fleet Carriers in the Post War Fleet, but with construction as at present the strength by 1950 will only be 18 and the balance will have to be found from 5

[1] CP(45)291, reproduced as B.434 as Doc. No. 57.

existing British CVEs until such time as they can be replaced by further new construction.

5. Six cruisers and three submarines authorised in earlier programmes but not yet laid down are being retained. Our cruiser strength is being impaired by over-age. The average age in 1950 will be 12½ years:– ten 8-inch cruisers out of a total strength of 47 cruisers will then be over 20 years old. These figures take account of 2 cruisers which we propose to sell to the Dutch and the Chinese respectively, but no account of any other possible sales to foreign powers. There is therefore a strong case for proceeding with the construction of modern cruisers. Two will be laid down immediately and the others as best they can be fitted with the merchant shipbuilding programme. The submarine programme has already been drastically reduced by cancellations. It is however very important to continue progress in design and construction and three A Class submarines from the 1944 Programme which have not yet been ordered will accordingly be retained and built to an improved design.

NAVAL NEW CONSTRUCTION (excluding 1945 Programme)

Class	LAUNCHED but not completed	LAID DOWN but not launched	ORDERED not laid down	AUTHORISED not yet ordered
Battleship	1 to complete April '46.			
Fleet Carriers		3 (2 to launch early '46)	2	
Lt Flt Carriers	9 (3 to complete early '46. Remainder not until end '46 at earliest).	4		
Cruisers	2 (Will not complete until end '46 at earliest).	1 (due to launch Dec '45)	1 (suspended)	5
Destroyers	31 (18 to complete within 3 months. Remainder by mid '46).	11 (5 due to launch shortly)	23	
Sloops	2 to complete by mid '46.	2 (to launch Dec '45 & Feb '46)		
Submarines	12 (4 almost complete. 8 probably by mid '46).	7 (2 due to launch shortly)		3
Frigates	14 (8 to complete within 3 months. 6 (or 4 if 2 are cancelled by mid '46).			
TOTALS	71 (33 by Mar '46 30 " Jun '46 8 " end '46 or early '47)	28 (of which 12 are due to launch during next 3 months.)	26	8

59. *Cabinet Conclusions*

[CAB 128/2] 27 November 1945

CM(45) 56th Meeting

1. The Cabinet had before them a memorandum by the First Lord of the Admiralty (CP(45)291) submitting revised proposals for the New Construction Programme 1945.

The First Lord of the Admiralty explained that his predecessor had submitted in June a New Construction Programme (CP(45)54) based on the needs of the Navy for the war in the Far East. This programme had been drastically revised, in the light of the new situation created by the end of the Japanese war; and a new programme was now submitted which was based on the following principles:– (i) to proceed at normal speed with vessels required for the immediate replacement of outstandingly important deficiencies; and (ii) to proceed slowly with, or to defer, the construction of vessels which, though needed for the postwar Navy, could be used as a cushion to absorb the shocks of the fluctuations in the shipbuilding industry. The cost of the revised programme would be only £3 million, as compared with a cost of £10 million for the earlier programme.

Points in discussion were:–

(a) Special attention was drawn to the statement summarised at (ii) above. It was most important, from the point of view of the Government's employment policy, that full weight should be given to the possibility of varying warship building in order to even out the slumps and booms of merchant shipbuilding.

(b) Would it be possible for the Admiralty to submit to the Cabinet corresponding information about prospective naval construction by other countries?

The First Lord of the Admiralty undertook to make enquiries on this point.

(c) *The Prime Minister* said that, as part of a review of production programmes for all three Services, the Defence Committee were already considering how much naval construction should be carried out in the immediate future; and he therefore suggested that the specific points dealt with in paragraphs 5–14 of CP(45)291 should be remitted to the Defence Committee.

The Cabinet:–

(1) Approved the revised proposals for the New Construction Programme 1945, as follows:–

1 experimental-type submarine.

2 escort vessels.

2 surveying ships.
6 small floating docks.
A number of miscellaneous small craft.

(2) Agreed that the points raised in paragraphs 5–14 of CP(45)291 should be considered by the Defence Committee.

60. *Admiral (Submarines)*[1] *to Secretary of the Admiralty*

[ADM 1/18578] 4 December 1945

1733/SM.320 FUTURE STATE OF THE SUBMARINE FLEET[2]

Be pleased to lay before Their Lordships the following remarks and proposals regarding the future state of the Submarine Fleet, with particular reference to the disposition of submarines and submarine depot ships, the scrapping of further 'U' Class submarines and the situation regarding submarines in reserve. My remarks are based on the assumption that the peace time strength of the Submarine Fleet will be stabilised at 85 submarines.

2. There are at present 103 submarines in commission or under construction and these are made up as follows:–

Class	In full commission or to commission shortly	In immediate reserve	Under construction	Total
'A'	4	–	12	16
'T'	27	Nil	Nil	27
'S'	14	23	Nil	37
'U'	3	20	Nil	23
			Total:–	103

Note:– 27 submarines approved to be scrapped by Admiralty Letter M.08543/45 of 27 November 1945 are not included in the above figures.

3. The total number of submarines in full commission and under construction (up to and including 1943 programme) is 103, is 18 in excess of the assumed peace time allowed strength of 85 and it is intended that as the 12 remaining new construction 'A' Class come forward, so a similar number of 'U' Class now in immediate reserve, be placed in Category 'C' reserve and berthed on mud flats pending their scrapping. This will leave

[1] RA G. Creasy.

[2] With minor amendments (including a reduction in submarine numbers from 85 to 82), these proposals were approved on 27 Feb 1946. Loose Minute in ADM 1/18578.

6 'U' Class to be kept in immediate reserve pending disposal to allies, it being understood [that four] may be turned over to the Norwegians and two more to the Chinese.[1]

4. On completion of all 16 'A' Class the proposed disposition of submarines is as follows, based on the assumption that 5 depot ships will be available:–

		Full Commission	Imm. Reserve
China Flotilla	HMS ADAMANT	8 'A' Class	–
Med. "	HMS FORTH	8 'T' Class	–
Home Fleet	HMS MAIDSTONE	8 'T' Class	–
A/S Flotilla Portland	HMS CYCLOPS (relieved by HMS MONTCLARE)	11 'S' Class	9 'S' Class
Blockhouse Flotilla	Shore-based	2 'A' Class 1 'T' Class 1 'S' Class	6 'T' Class 3 'S' Class
Advanced Submarine Training Flotilla Clyde area	HMS WOLFE	6 'A' Class	4 'T' Class
		Full Commission	Imm. Reserve
	Total:–	16 'A' Class 17 'T' Class 12 'S' Class	Nil 'A' Class 10 'T' Class 12 'S' Class
		45	22
Disposition still undecided			13 'S' Class 5 'U' Class 40
		TOTAL:– 85	
Retained for Allies		6 'U' Class	
To be mudberthed or scrapped as Remaining 'A' Class come forward		12 'U' Class TOTAL:– 103	

61. *Minutes of Meeting held by VCNS*

[ADM 1/19301] 28 December 1945

VCNS held a meeting on 28 December 1945 to consider the number of submarines that could be kept in service in the postwar Fleet …

2. At present it was the intention to keep 85 submarines (45 in commission, 40 in Reserve) in the postwar Fleet but this number would have to be reduced owing to the lack of refitting capacity [which] limited the number that could be kept to 58 on a basis of 20 months between refits. FOS/M explained that the figure of 85 was variable … and submarines must always be regarded as different from other craft and that they must

[1] Four boats were transferred to Norway in 1946, but the Chinese transfers did not take place. Others of the class served in the French, Dutch and Danish navies.

be either (a) in full commission, (b) in active reserve (with one-third crew … plus refits) or (c) scrapped …[1]

62. *Mottershead[2] to First Lord of the Admiralty*

[ADM 1/19096] 13 December 1945

I attach a draft report of this afternoon's meeting and will circulate it if you approve.

DofP suggested to me after the meeting that consideration should be given to the cancellation of EAGLE. I gather that the Naval Staff would be quite ready to cancel this ship, but the Air side are anxious to retain her. It appears that very little money has been spent on her so far and for this reason alone he felt that at least cancellation should be considered. I have asked PAS(PS) to let you have the financial position of this ship and suggest that the matter be looked at then.

Possible consideration should also be given to cancelling four of the heavy Cruisers which it was agreed on 15 October to defer.

I believe the Naval Staff are very anxious to keep them in the programme, but in order to show the maximum possible saving now, you may feel that they should be pressed to agree cancellation. This, of course, would mean that they would have to take their chance in future New Construction Programmes. It seems to be difficult to justify retaining in the Programmes ships which were approved under wartime conditions if we do not actually intend to begin work on them yet, even though we firmly believe that they will be required in the future.

Report of a Meeting held on 13 December 1945 to consider further cancellations of ships under construction in past New Construction Programmes

The following were present:–

First Lord, First Sea Lord, Controller, Fifth Sea Lord, Vice Controller, ACNS(A), ACWP, D of P, PAS(PR)

It was approved to cancel:–

(a) Flotilla of GALLANT Class Destroyers (8 vessels)
(b) Flotilla of DARING Class Destroyers (8 vessels hitherto deferred under decision of 15 Oct)
(c) MALTA and NEW ZEALAND (Hitherto deferred by decision of 15 October).

[1] At a subsequent meeting chaired by the Vice Controller on 24 Jan 1946 it was concluded that the refit cycle, plus 12 new construction, could actually sustain a total of 82 submarines. Minutes in ADM 1/19301.

[2] F.W. Mottershead, First Lord's Private Secretary.

The cancellation of an additional four WEAPON Class destroyers was discussed. The Naval Staff were willing that all four should be cancelled. The Controller, however, was anxious to retain two of them (one at Yarrow's and one at Thornycroft's) to avoid dislocation of shipyard labour. It was finally decided that all four of the vessels should be cancelled subject to confirmation that only about 50% of the total cost of the vessels had been spent so far.

There was also discussion about the cancellation of the four Light Fleet Carriers MAJESTIC, LEVIATHEN, POWERFUL and TERRIBLE. It was explained that about ten million pounds had been spent on these four vessels and that the saving from cancellation would be only about two million eight hundred [thousand] pounds. The following arguments were put forward in favour of cancellation of the vessels:–

(i) There would be a saving of £2.8 million.
(ii) The vessels could not take modern heavy strike aircraft.
(iii) High cost of upkeep.
(iv) "Who are we going to fight?".

The following arguments were put forward in support of completing them:–

(i) Even if these four vessels were built, we should still be five short of the requirements for the post war fleet.
(ii) Dominions' requirements.
(iii) These vessels would not be required to carry heavy strike aircraft.
(iv) Ten million pounds had already been spent.
(v) If the vessels were not completed, they would have to be moved from the yards.

ACNS (Air) suggested that if the Government proposed that work on the four carriers should be stopped some value could be obtained from the money already spent if we completed one or two of the vessels, took them into the Royal Navy and sold two COLOSSUS Class Carriers (one to the French and one to the Dutch) for a price at least equal to the cost of completing the two Carriers for ourselves. There was no reason, of course, why we should not obtain a higher price than this from the French and the Dutch.

The First Lord said that if it was confirmed that so high a proportion of the cost of the Carriers had already been spent, he would propose to complete them. He agreed, subject to discussion with the financial authorities, that we should then endeavour to do the deal suggested by ACNS (Air) with the French and the Dutch but at a better price than that suggested …

63. *Mottershead to First Lord of the Admiralty*

[ADM 1/19096] 15 December 1945

At the meeting on 13 December about cancellation of ships under construction in past new construction programmes, two matters were left over for further consideration:–

(a) The cancellation of the second pair of Weapon Class destroyers (CUTLASS and CULVERIN) was subject to confirmation that only about 50% of the total cost of these vessels had been spent so far.

(b) Your decision that the four light fleet carriers should be completed was subject to confirmation that so high a proportion of the cost had already been spent as was suggested at the meeting.

A table showing the estimated amounts already spent on these six vessels and the amounts remaining to be spent is attached. I have shown in pencil the amounts already spent as a percentage of the total cost. You will see that the amount spent on CUTLASS and CULVERIN is somewhat more than that suggested at the meeting. You may feel that the cancellation of these two vessels should stand nonetheless. I understand that in departmental discussions the Treasury have expressed the view that the importance of saving immediate future expenditure should outweigh the disadvantage of wasting past expenditure, even when this waste is considerable.

The amounts which would be saved by cancelling the carriers vary considerably. You will probably wish the decision to complete TERRIBLE and MAJESTIC to stand, but you may wish to consider the cancellation of LEVIATHAN and especially of POWERFUL. Assuming that you decide that at least two of these carriers should be completed, I suggest that PAS(PR) should be asked to start an official paper on the possibility of selling two COLOSSUS Class carriers, one to the French and one to the Dutch, at the best price possible, and certainly at a price not less than the cost of completing the two new carriers.

Figures for the EAGLE are also given. To avoid the necessity for holding a further meeting I suggest that PAS(PR) might also be asked to start an official paper to consider the cancellation of EAGLE. As I mentioned previously, there are said to be conflicting views about this; the Naval Staff are willing to cancel but the Air side are not. I am making enquiries about the four heavy cruisers.

		Amount spent including 'Break Clause' Liabilities	Amount saved by Cancellation
(i) Cancellations decided upon From VE under decisions up To and including decisions at First Lord's Meeting on 15/10		£24,565,500	£86,961,000
(ii) Further cancellations Definitely approved at First Lord's Meeting on 13/12		£4,630,500	£31,769,500
(iii) Further cancellations Contemplated at First Lord's Meeting of 13/12:–			
4 Heavy Cruisers[1]		–	£17,814,800
CUTLASS	*65%*	£440,000	£260,000
CULVERIN	*57%*	£400,000	£300,000
RIFLE		£400,000	£300,000
CARRONADE		£410,000	£290,000
LEVIATHAN	*70%*	£1,900,000	£830,000
MAJESTIC	*71%*	£1,760,000	£730,000
POWERFUL	*61%*	£1,750,000	£1,100,000
TERRIBLE	*79%*	£1,920,000	£520,000
EAGLE	*26%*	£1,950,000	£5,500,000

64. *Private Office note by Mottershead*

[ADM 1/19096] 23 December 1945

Further cancellations of ships building under past New Construction Programmes

With reference to … decisions taken at the meeting in the First Lord's room on 13 December about further cancellations of ships under construction in past New Construction Programmes, the First Lord has now decided, after consultation with the Chancellor of the Exchequer, that all four of the MAJESTIC Class Light Fleet Carriers should be completed, subject only to sale of two or, if possible, three COLOSSUS Class Carriers on the lines of the suggestion of ACNS(A) recorded in the previous note. A proposal to transfer one COLOSSUS Class Carrier to the Dutch is already under consideration … The First Lord wishes the question of selling one or two more COLOSSUS Class Carriers to the French or other buyer to be taken up forthwith. Meanwhile he wishes expenditure on the four MAJESTIC Class Carriers to proceed as slowly as possible in case it should prove impossible to sell the COLOSSUS Class Carriers and hence become necessary to cancel one or more of the MAJESTIC Class.

[1] These were actually large 6″ light cruisers, the *Neptune* class.

The First Lord has also approved the cancellation of the four WEAPON Class Destroyers referred … (ie CUTLASS, CULVERIN, RIFLE, CARRONADE).

After discussion at a Board Meeting on 21 December it has been decided also to cancel EAGLE.

First Lord has now agreed that orders for four of the six heavy cruisers referred to shall not be placed without reference to the Treasury.

65. *Joint Planning Staff Memorandum*

[CAB 84/76] 7 January 1946

JP(45)277(Final) SERVICE COMMITMENTS BETWEEN 1947 AND 1951

As agreed by the Chiefs of Staff we have examined the requirements of our armed forces for the period Spring 1947 to Spring 1951.

We have limited ourselves to this period since we consider that by 1951 atomic weapons will not be generally available … nor [will] the development of other weapons have altered radically the character of war.

2. Our report is quite separate from the proposals[1] for provisional *regular* establishments now being put forward by the Service Ministries and already discussed by the Defence Committee.

3. Our object is to provide the three Service Ministries with an agreed inter-service basis on which the size of forces for the period 1947–1951 can be calculated.

4. … The implications … are:–

(a) During this period there will be large reserves of trained men available …

(b) The prime need of this country is reconstruction …

(c) A major war during the period under review at present appears unlikely …

PART I

World-wide Policing and Occupational Commitments[2]

… The forces arrived at as a result of this examination … we summarise below … as at Spring 1949.

RN

27 Cruisers or larger ships.

60 Escorts or Destroyers …

[1]CP(45)161, reproduced as Doc. No. 46.

[2]The main body of this Part discusses British foreign policy and colonial commitments. The Planners (Captain Guy Grantham RN for the Navy) had to judge what these commitments would be in the absence of direction from the Cabinet or Foreign and Colonial Offices.

PART II

Forces for Expansion and Preparation for War

… We conclude that each Service should maintain a nucleus strength in peace of such an order that they will be able to expand within three years to a force employing the following total manpower figures:-[1]

Army	*RAF*	*Navy*
2,220,000	870,000	645,000

…

TABLE A [extract]
UK UNITS AND FORMATIONS

General Notes:–

1. This table covers all world-wide commitments which require the use of British military forces for policing and occupational duties during the period 1947 to 1951. It does not cover any United Kingdom units or formations which are required as a nucleus for war …
3. Naval units shown are those required on station. There will be an additional requirement to allow for refits and time on passage.

Area	Naval Forces	Remarks
Middle East & Mediterranean	Six cruisers or larger ships Sixteen escorts or destroyers	[some] Ships will be provided from South African or East Indies squadrons
Indian Ocean	Five cruisers Eight escorts	
Far East	Six cruisers Sixteen escorts	
Caribbean & South America	Four cruisers Four escorts	
South Africa	Two cruisers Four escorts	
Home Waters	Four cruisers Twelve escorts	
Occupation – Japan		Ships detached from China Fleet.
Reserves		Drawn from nucleus forces maintained for expansion in war
SUMMARY	Twenty-seven cruisers or larger ships Sixty escorts or destroyers	

[1]These figures, agreed with the Ministry of Labour, were based on what proportion of the employable population would be available for Defence (Annex III, not reproduced).

66. *Chiefs of Staff Memorandum*

[CAB 80/99] 8 January 1946

COS(46)5(O) SIZE OF THE ARMED FORCES AT 30TH JUNE 1946

We have been invited to review our report+ on the size of the Armed Forces at 30 June 1946, with a view to effecting economies in manpower.

2. Such economies could only be derived from one or more of the following sources:–

(a) Reduction in size and scope of our military commitments.

(b) Reduction in the size of the forces estimated as necessary to meet our commitments.

(c) Reduction in the manpower estimated by the Service Ministries to be required to provide the forces referred to in (b) and their administrative backing.

+ COS(45)565(O)

3. The active role of our Armed Forces will be:–

(a) The maintenance of internal security and British prestige in the Colonial Empire, Mandated territories and India.

(b) Occupation of ex-enemy territories.

(c) The protection of British interests in foreign counties and on the high seas.

Our major tasks will be (a) and (b) above and these will fall largely to the Army …

5. We have kept under constant review our previous estimates of the forces required to meet our forecast of military commitments at 30 June 1946. We now submit at Annexes I, II and III our revised estimates. An explanation of the main changes that have been made in our estimates of the forces required and their deployment is given below:–

Navy

6. Our estimates of the number of battleships, destroyers and minesweepers required in the British Pacific Fleet in June 1946 has been reduced. The battleships so released will be transferred to the Home and Mediterranean Stations which will be the main training areas for the Post-War Fleet and which can provide maintenance facilities and amenities ashore at a lesser cost in manpower. The destroyers and minesweepers not required in the Pacific Fleet have now been included in the Reserve Fleet.

7. Although it is considered essential to retain a large force of minesweepers and salvage vessels in commission throughout the summer of 1946 in order to clear sea routes and ports as rapidly as possible, it is intended to make large reductions in these forces in the autumn of 1946 when a large proportion of their task will have been completed …

Recommendation

14. The manpower required for the forces shown in the Appendices is:–

Navy	375,000
Army	1,130,000
Air Force	563,000
TOTAL	2,068,000

We recommend that the Defence Committee give their approval to this estimate as a basis for planning.

ANNEX I

BRITISH NAVAL FORCES REQUIRED ON 30TH JUNE 1946

We set out below the main British Naval units required on 30 June 1946. We have assumed that Australian, Canadian and New Zealand Naval forces will meet commitments in their Home Waters and that some units of the Royal Indian Navy will continue to be available for service outside Indian waters. The figures for the Dominion Forces are not included.

2. A column showing the previous estimate of forces required on 30 June 1946, contained in COS(45)565, has been included for comparison. The previous estimate did not include figures for minesweepers.

Home Fleet	Previous	Revised
Battleships	1	2+
Fleet Carriers	2	–
Light Fleet Carriers	–	2x
Other Carriers (Deck Landing Training with reduced complement)	–	1
Cruisers	4 + 3~	5 + 2Ø
Destroyers	16	16
Escorts	24	14≠
Submarines	30	30
Fleet Minesweepers	–	32
BYMS	–	64

\+ including Vanguard carrying out first of class trials
x preparing for service in the Far East
~ 2 for cadets training and 1 experimental cruiser
Ø 1 for cadets training and 1 experimental cruiser
≠ for Ocean Air/Sea Rescue

Reserve Fleet	Previous	Revised
Battleships	6	6
Fleet Carriers	2	4Ø
Other Carriers	15≠	9≠
Cruisers	16≠	11≠
Destroyers	32	46x

Escorts	100	136[x]
Submarines	40	40
Fleet Minesweepers	–	32
BYMS	–	64

Ø including carriers for trooping and 1 for trials

≠ including cruisers and escort carriers for trooping

X including destroyers and escorts for Naval Air Arm targets, A/A training, Submarine targets, Instructional and Technical School tenders, sea-going training and fishery protection.

Mediterranean Fleet	Previous	Revised
Light Fleet Carriers	2	1
Cruisers	5	5
Destroyers	16	16
Escorts	8	11
Submarines	8	8
Fleet Minesweepers	–	24
BYMS	–	24
East Indies Fleet		
Light Fleet Carriers	2	2
Cruisers	4	4
Destroyers	8	8
Escorts (including Ocean Air/Sea Rescue)	20	20
Fleet Minesweepers	–	24
BYMS	–	19
British Pacific Fleet		
Battleships	3	2
Fleet Carriers	2	2
Light Fleet Carriers	2	2
Cruisers	8	7
Destroyers	24	16
Escorts	16	16
Submarines	8	8
Fleet Minesweepers	–	8
BYMS	–	16
Gunboats (in reserve until required)	5	5
West Atlantic Squadron		
Cruisers	2	2
Escorts	4	4
African Squadron		
Cruisers	2	2
Escorts	4	4

Other Commitments

(a) Assault Craft – It is estimated that a considerable proportion of available LST(3) will be fully occupied in the movement of personnel, vehicles and stores for occupation and rehabilitation purposes in the South East Asia and South Pacific areas …

(b) Coastal Forces – Requirements … will be limited to the equivalent of two flotillas in Home Waters for trials and training and a flotilla in the Mediterranean to meet emergency calls.

(c) Fleet Auxiliaries, Mobile Repair Facilities and Depot Ships – Although a considerable reduction in the number of Fleet Auxiliaries and Depot Ships is being carried out, a proportion will be required to maintain the East Indies and Pacific Fleets, since the reconstruction of shore facilities in Singapore and Hong Kong will not have been completed by June 1946.

The estimates shown under 'Other Commitments' remain substantially the same as those given in COS(45)565 …

67. *Defence Committee Minutes*

[CAB 131/1] 11 January 1946

DO(46) 1st Meeting

1. SIZE OF THE ARMED FORCES AT 30 JUNE 1946 (COS(46)5(O))

THE COMMITTEE had before them a Report by the Chiefs of Staff containing a review of their previous Report* on the size of the armed forces at 30 June 1946.

THE PRIME MINISTER pointed out that the manpower total of the forces which the Chiefs of Staff now estimated to be necessary at 30 June 1946 was a reduction of 156,000 on the total derived from the previous estimate. In paragraph 2 of the Chiefs of Staff Report three sources were quoted from which economies might be obtained. He thought that there was a fourth source, namely, the actual establishments of the various formations said to be necessary. Those establishments required careful scrutiny to make sure that they were not inflated.

* COS(45)565(O)

THE COMMITTEE then examined the detailed estimates given in the Annexes to the Report, as follows:–

ROYAL NAVY (ANNEX I)

Escorts

In response to an enquiry by the Prime Minister why so many escorts wore still required in the various fleets, LORD CUNNINGHAM said that in the Atlantic 19 vessels were still engaged on ocean rescue work at the request of the Americans, who still had a large trans-Atlantic air traffic as far south as Freetown. We provided this service in the Eastern half of the Atlantic. If we did not do so it would mean that the Americans would have to send over several flotillas to be based on our ports. The Admiralty had not felt it possible to refuse the American request. In the Mediterranean and Indian Ocean, we were providing this service for our own air trooping programme. The Admiralty hoped to reduce the number of vessels employed in this service.

Minesweepers

It was pointed out that a large number of minesweeping craft were shown in the revised estimate, whereas none was shown in the estimate made last October.

LORD CUNNINGHAM said that the minesweepers had been omitted from the previous estimate, though their manpower had been allowed for. We were doing a large part of the minesweeping, though the Germans, the French, the Danes, and the Swedes, were also helping. It was hoped that the Russians would soon assist. Efforts were being made to close down British minesweeping in the Mediterranean, and to make the other nations deal with their own waters. But if we had not been doing the work, we would not have been able to get our ships to the various ports. There would be a big reduction in the minesweeping effort in October 1946 and it was hoped that the work would be finished by the end of the year …

The Pacific

THE PRIME MINISTER enquired how long it would be necessary to maintain a comparatively large fleet in the Pacific.

LORD CUNNINGHAM said that the object of keeping the fleet there in its present strength was to show the flag. The Americans had a very large fleet out there and it was not thought right to reduce our fleet too much. We had ships at the present time in Japanese waters (where it would be necessary to maintain a force for occupation purposes) at Tsingtao, at Shanghai, and at Hong Kong. We were also doing some minesweeping for the Chinese. The Pacific Fleet would eventually be reduced to a size somewhat smaller than pre-war.

MR BEVIN felt that the British Pacific Fleet should be kept at good strength until the Control Council in Japan had got into its stride …

68. *Chiefs of Staff Memorandum*

[CAB 80/99] 15 January 1946

COS(46)9(O)(Revise) SIZE OF THE ARMED FORCES AT 31 MARCH 1947

We have been invited to assess the size of the Armed Forces at 31 March 1947, as a basis for estimating service manpower requirements at that date.

2. We find it extremely difficult in the present uncertain state of world affairs in the immediate postwar years to produce an estimate for 1947. The forces which we will require in the various areas must depend very largely on the commitments undertaken by His Majesty's Government and it is not clear at present what all of these will be. We must, therefore, emphasise that our estimates for 1947 are highly speculative and are subject to change in the light if events …

General Considerations

3. The active role of our armed forces at March 1947 is likely to be limited to:–

(a) The maintenance of internal security and British prestige in the Colonial Empire, Mandated territories and India.
(b) Occupation of ex-enemy territories.
(c) The protection of British interests in foreign countries and on the high seas.

4. Our major tasks will be (a) and (b) above and these will fall largely to the Army … The primary responsibility for (c) will rest with the Navy.

Commitments

5. In the following paragraphs we forecast our military commitments at March 1947 and explain the main factors which will govern the deployment of our forces …

United Kingdom

6. The United Kingdom is the main base for training, development and administration of all our forces, including those overseas. The security of this base will, in any future war, become a problem of increasing magnitude and we must, therefore, provide a nucleus organisation for defence and for the protection of our Atlantic communications.

7. It will be our peace time policy to organise our naval forces on the basis of a balanced fleet divided between the Home and Mediterranean stations. This will greatly increase the efficiency or training and widen the scope of trials and the development of tactics and new weapon.

…

Mediterranean Fleet

15. As stated in paragraph 7 above, there will be a fleet stationed in the Mediterranean. Its duties will include the support of our land forces, protection of British interests in foreign countries and 'showing the flag'. Besides forming one of the main training units, this fleet will be well placed as a reinforcement for the Indian Ocean and the Far East …

Indian Ocean

19. Although it is planned to include eventually three cruisers and a small aircraft carrier in the Royal Indian Navy, these units will not be effective by March 1947. It is considered necessary to provide a small force of British cruisers and escorts based on Ceylon for the protection of British interests in the Indian Ocean area and in the Persian Gulf …

Pacific

25. We have allowed for a naval squadron in the Pacific. This will be based on Hong Kong and will use the facilities at Singapore. The squadron's primary tasks will be the protection of British interests in China ports, the discharge of naval commitments in connection with the occupation of Japan and 'showing the flag' in the Far East.

Outlying Areas

27. Warships will be required to protect British interests in the South American republics and in the Caribbean area

Forces Required

28. Our estimate of forces required is given under geographic headings at Appendices I, II and III. We have made no special allowance for the provision of forces for the United Nations Organisation.

Recommendation

29. The manpower required for the forces shown in the Appendices is:–

Navy	225,000
Army	775,000
Air Force	440,000
TOTAL	1,440,300

We recommend that the Defence Committee give their approval to this estimate as a basis for planning.

APPENDIX I

BRITISH NAVAL FORCES REQUIRED ON 31 MARCH 1947

The following are the main British Naval Units required on 31 March 1947. We have assumed that Australian, New Zealand, Canadian and Indian Naval forces will meet commitments in their home waters; the forces given below do not include Dominion forces.

Home Fleet	Reserve Fleet
2 Battleships	6 Battleships
2 Fleet Carriers	2 Fleet Carriers

4 Light Fleet Carriers+
7 Cruisers (including 1 for cadets training and one experimental cruiser)
16 Destroyers
16 Escorts
25 Submarines
16 Fleet Minesweepers

8 Other Carriers
9 Cruisers
58 Destroyers++
140 Escorts++
40 Submarines
32 Fleet Minesweepers
48 Other Minesweepers

\+ Includes 2 with reduced Complements for Deck Landing Training and for experimental purposes.

++ Including Destroyers and Escorts for sea-going training, Naval Air Arm and Submarine targets, Fishery Protection and School tenders.

<u>Mediterranean Fleet</u>
1 Battleship
2 Fleet Carriers
2 Light Fleet Carriers
5 Cruisers
24 Destroyers
10 Escorts (Including 2 for Red Sea)
10 Submarines
16 Fleet Minesweepers
8 BYMS

<u>East Indies Squadron</u>
4 Cruisers
4 Escorts (including 2 for Persian Gulf)

<u>West Atlantic Squadron</u>
4 Cruisers
4 Escorts

<u>British Pacific Squadron</u>
1 Battleship
2 Light Fleet Carriers
5 Cruisers
8 Destroyers
12 Escorts
10 Submarines
8 Fleet Minesweepers
8 BYMS
5 Gunboats (In reserve until required).

<u>Africa Squadron</u>
2 Cruisers
4 Escorts

<u>Specialised Forces</u>

(a) <u>Assault Shipping and Craft</u>

The numbers of assault ships and craft will be related to the training requirements of the Army. These will also be adequate for maintaining naval training. In addition, a nucleus will be required for technical development. This requirement is now under consideration.

(b) <u>Aircraft Requirements of Naval Air Arm</u>

Air crews will be required to man first line aircraft of the Fleet and Light Fleet Carriers in full commission. Additional aircraft will be required to meet the commitments for training, air target towing and communications duties.

(c) Coastal Forces

Requirements for Coastal Forces will be limited to two flotillas in commission, mainly employed on trials and in training and a small reserve …

69. *Defence Committee Memorandum*

[CAB 131/2] 17 January 1946

DO(46)7 PROVISIONAL REQUIREMENTS OF THE POST-WAR ARMED FORCES

Memorandum by the First Lord of the Admiralty and the Secretaries of State for War and Air

1. At a meeting on 30 November 1945, the Service Ministers were requested by the Prime Minister to re-examine the proposals submitted in CP(45)161 and to submit fresh figures based on an estimate of minimum postwar requirements, with a broad estimate of cost.

GENERAL FACTORS

2. The essence of the problem is the considerable number of officers, non-commissioned officers and men, including personnel on Regular engagements which have expired, who are now leaving the Service. The offers to continue in employment in the Services have not so for served to attract officers and men in adequate numbers. This reluctance has undoubtedly been due in part to lack of information on to postwar rates of pay and to similar conditions of service and this part of the problem will, it is hoped, be solved by the publication of the postwar conditions of Service. But it is abundantly clear from enquiries made by officers and men that even more important to them, is the question of ranks and prospects which they can be offered on transfer to the permanent service or on re-engagement. This is a question of establishment and the Services are at present authorised to work only within the limits of the establishment approved in 1939. These figures bear little resemblance to present day requirements. For example, all three Services have branches and trades such as the Air Branch of the Navy and the electrical and radar trades of all three Services which have been created or have developed along new lines since 1939 and any pre-war establishments that may exist for such branches are completely out of date. In consequence it will only be possible to give an indication of the career open to officers and men who desire to remain in the Services when the services have at least a provisional total figure within which they can plan establishments arm

by arm and branch by branch that will give a suitably balanced force. In the absence of such establishments many thousands of highly trained and well-seasoned men will be lost to civil life because it is not possible to offer them acceptable rank:– ie rank which bears some reasonable resemblance to the temporary or acting rank which they have held during the war.

3. Another factor is time. For some time to come there is bound to be a considerable gap between the numbers of men in the Armed Forces serving on Regular engagements – a steadily diminishing body because of the virtual cessation of recruitment for permanent service during the war – and the strengths required. This gap must be filled by National Service personnel; and the larger the gap the more prolonged must be the period which such personnel are required to serve. It is essential to narrow this gap as much and as quickly as possible by securing volunteers in adequate numbers – a policy which will only be successful if reasonable prospects can be offered to officers and men now serving.

INDIVIDUAL FACTORS AFFECTING EACH SERVICE

4 … Royal Navy

The Admiralty in their re-examination of the matter have discovered no ground for modifying their view that, on present computed defence commitments, a force of 170,000 Regular officers and men will be needed in peace apart from a possible extra requirement of 10,000 if permanent National Service is introduced. The principal reasons for the increase over the 1939 figures (133,000) which this represents are the development of the Air Branch, the necessity for nucleus organisations for coastal forces and a Fleet train, the provision of sufficient assault forces for research and development in amphibious warfare and the greatly increased complication in equipment of ships. In the interests, however, of establishing a minimum figure within which planning can proceed, the Admiralty would be content to work on a basis of four fifths of the original Admiralty proposal (ie 180,000 less one fifth = 144,000) for the next year or so; any reduction below this proportion would not enable an appropriately balanced force to meet the Navy's minimum postwar requirements to be achieved …

ESTIMATED COST

5. The estimated annual cost of pay and marriage allowance on the new rates of pay for other ranks and taking a proportionate assumption for officers, for the establishments shown would be in very round figures:–

Navy £32,500,000 (144,000 officers and men)

CONCLUSION

6. We would emphasize that the ultimate size and shape of the three Forces must depend on a full review of the defence commitments of the

country which cannot be completed for some time and a determination of the division of such responsibilities between the three Services. Approval of the provisional requirements outlined above could, however, in our view be given without prejudice to the future. Such approval would give the Services something firm to work on until long-term requirements can be settled. It would reduce the loss to the Services of expensively trained and well-seasoned personnel. It would be a factor tending to shorten the period of National Service. And only if a decision is given now will it be possible to take full advantage of the announcement on pay and conditions of service.

7. The Chancellor of the Exchequer has been consulted on these proposals and raises no objection to them, subject to … consultation between the Service Departments and the Treasury …

70. *Defence Committee Minutes*

[CAB 131/1] 21 January 1946

DO(46) 3rd Meeting

1. SIZE OF THE ARMED FORCES

THE COMMITTEE had before them the following Papers:–

(a) A Report by the Chiefs of Staff giving a revised estimate of the armed forces at 30 June 1946 (COS(46)5(O)) …

(b) A Report by the Chiefs of Staff on the size of the armed forces at 31st March 1947 (COS(46)9(O)(Revise)).

(c) A Memorandum by the Chancellor of the Exchequer covering an Economic Survey for the year 1946 …

LORD ALANBROOKE said that the estimate of the size of the forces required at 31 March 1947 was highly speculative in view of the many unknown factors in the international situation. The manpower figures arising from those estimates showed a reduction of 74 per cent from the figures at the end of the German war.

MR MORRISON[1] drew attention to the fact that the Economic Survey showed that there would be a financial deficiency of £470 million in the year 1946. This deficit would give rise to an inflationary tendency. There was also a deficiency of 1.3 million men based on a figure of 2.6 million men in the forces, and in the Supply Departments working for the forces, at 31 December 1946.

[1]Lord President of the Council.

... MR DALTON[1] said that preliminary examination of the Economic Survey showed that the financial deficit would be very nearly covered if there was a reduction over the year 1946 of £150 million in the expenditure on munitions, and of half a million men in the average strength of the armed forces throughout the year.

THE PRIME MINISTER said that there was no doubt that the nation could not afford either the manpower or the money for forces of the size suggested by the Chiefs of Staff. A cut in the size of the forces was unavoidable. The cut could not be large in June, mainly for reasons of foreign policy which had been explained by the Foreign Secretary at the previous meeting, but it would have to be drastic after that date. He had examined the matter, and he felt that to try and take in detail each of the commitments set out in the Chiefs of Staff Report and to see how they, and the forces required to meet them, could be cut would be an ineffective proceeding. He felt that it would be better for the Government to lay down ceilings for June and December 1946, which could then be examined by the Service Ministries and Chiefs of Staff. In estimating these ceilings, he had taken into account the fact that there was now in existence no foreign Navy worthy of the name other than that of the United States. Similarly, there was no Air Force worth speaking of other than the Russian and the American. It seemed, therefore, that in the immediate future we could afford to make more drastic cuts in these Services than in the Army, where there were a great number of commitments which could not be liquidated. The ceilings he would propose were as follows:–

	30 June 1946	31 December 1946
Royal Navy	330,000	175,000
Army	1,095,000	650,000
Royal Air Force	475,000	275,000
	1,900,000	1,100,000

The following were the principal points made in the subsequent discussion:–

Royal Navy

MR ALEXANDER said that he quite recognised the necessity for keeping the forces at as low a level as possible in the interests of our economic life, but he doubted whether it would be possible to reduce the Navy to the extent suggested by the Prime Minister without entirely wrecking the Age and Service Release Scheme. The reason for this was that it would be found impossible in the time to train sufficient specialists to replace those who would go out of the Navy under the scheme. The

[1] Chancellor of the Exchequer.

release of those specialists was already lagging behind that of the ordinary ratings. Even on the Chiefs' of Staff manpower figures the Navy would have to come down by October to the number of ships required for the following March, because of the difficulty of finding the necessary specialists. To make further heavy reductions would mean immobilising a further large number of ships, and taking the risk of having much of the material in the hands of the Navy fall into disrepair through lack of maintenance personnel. The Navy had considerable commitments, particularly in the Far East. There were more than 190,000 men East of Suez, and a large number of assault craft were still being used in the Far East to fetch and carry. He doubted whether the Navy's commitments could he covered in the revised figures, even If the other difficulties could be overcome. There was little sign yet of any response to the recent conditions of service such as would lead one to hope that a considerable number of specialists would stay on.

THE PRIME MINISTER said that it was not necessary in present circumstances to have a large fleet ready for instant action, as there was no-one to fight. We had to face actualities in our present situation and a certain amount of inefficiency might have to be accepted …

SIR RHODERICK MCGRIGOR[1] said that the Navy had considerable commitments in various parts of the world but they had allowed for the possibility of some re-grouping to be carried out by March 1947. The main difficulty they would be faced with in making further reductions would be the maintenance of the age and service release scheme. The Navy had a special problem owing to the great number of skilled men required in modern ships …

THE COMMITTEE –

(A) Agreed that the Service Departments and the Chiefs of Staff should examine, in the light of the above discussion, the position which would result from reductions of strengths at 30 June and 31 December 1946, to the figures proposed by the Prime Minister …

(B) Took note that when the above examination had been made, the Prime Minister would meet the Chiefs of Staff to consider the situation and to make such adjustments as might prove necessary.

(C) Agreed that in the meanwhile the Manpower Committee and the Service and Supply Departments should take the figures for service strengths proposed by the Prime Minister as a provisional basis for their further planning …

[1] VCNS attending in lieu of the First Sea Lord.

3. PROVISIONAL REQUIREMENTS OF THE POST-WAR ARMED FORCES – DO(46)7 …

THE COMMITTEE:–

Approved the provisional requirements for the postwar armed forces as estimated in the above memorandum.

71. *Director of Plans to VCNS*

[ADM 205/65] 23 January 1946

REDUCTION OF MANPOWER TO 175,000
BY 31 DECEMBER 1946

It is submitted that it should be approved as a point of principle that this 'cut' in manpower does not, in the long-term view, necessitate a reduction in the size of the Fleet to a strength much, if anything, below the planned postwar Fleet.

2. The following facts are relevant:–

(a) We have always considered that we should have to man the Fleet on 170,000 'regulars', plus 10,000 for training conscripts, plus 34,000 conscripts, ie a total of 214,000. The figure of 175,000 represents a 'cut' of 18% on this total.

(b) Most recent planning has been based on the token figure of manning the Fleet on 144,000 'regulars', which figure has been approved by the Defence Committee as a basis for planning. This figure, with conscripts added, produces a total almost the same as that with which we are now confronted.

3. To achieve the 18% 'cut' referred to in para. 2(a) and still man the Post-War Fleet, certain economies will be necessary. This, and the shortages of certain classes of ratings, will probably necessitate accepting reductions in complements and accompanying lessened efficiency.

It may also be necessary, this year, to defer commissioning of some ships for foreign service, because of the shortages of ratings qualified to go abroad.

But it is submitted that this should not be allowed to destroy the aim of manning the Post-War Fleet and meeting our world-wide commitments.

4. It is suggested that the problem with which we are confronted should not be looked at as a manning problem, but rather as a problem in demobilisation. It is a problem of an administrative and logistic nature.

5. Admittedly, to achieve the necessary rate of demobilisation, it may well be necessary to bring home certain ships, particularly from east of Suez. But it is thought that the real solution lies more in the drastic

reductions of shore-based staffs and personnel, beside which the numbers borne in ships are comparatively small.

6. At ANNEX is outlined a possible scheme for withdrawal of forces from abroad and for postponements of building up foreign stations to planned postwar strengths, which would help towards solving the Personnel Departments demobilisation problem.

7. But it is strongly felt that this suggested contribution is but a part of the whole problem. The complete solution should be worked out jointly by the Naval Staff on one side and the Personnel Departments on the other, on a properly planned basis …

ANNEX

INTERIM PROPOSALS FOR THE STRENGTH AND DISPOSITION OF NAVAL FORCES DURING 1946

1. British Pacific Fleet

It is considered that our essential commitments for re-establishing our interests in China and maintaining our share of the Naval occupational forces for Japanese and Korean waters can eventually be met as follows:–

Japan and Korea	2 units (one, at least, being RN)
Shanghai	1 unit
Hong Kong	1 "
Refitting	1 "
Emergency reserve and on passage	2 units
Total	7 "

2. If the Dominion contribution is at least one Cruiser, the RN commitment is for:–

2 CVL and 4 Cruisers	or	1 CVL and 5 Cruisers

which corresponds to the planned postwar strength.

3. For the first six months of this year, however, it is politically desirable to maintain somewhat stronger forces, including some capital ships, in the Pacific.

4. To meet this commitment, therefore, while at the same time contributing to the demobilisation problem, it is suggested that the return of the 2 Battleships and the Fleet Carrier should be phased so that:–

a) between now and June one of the three, taken in turn, is maintained in Japanese waters as already arranged.

b) the last of the 3 ships leaves in June to return to the UK …

5. The strength of the BPF in major units, as previously planned and as now proposed, would be:–

	Present Strength	March 1947	New proposal 31.12.46
Battleships	2	–	–
Fleet Carriers	1	–	–
CVLs	2	2	2
Cruisers	7	5	4

…

7. BPF Destroyers and Escorts

Strengths of the BPF in destroyers and escorts had been planned as follows:–

	Now	March 1947	Post-War
Destroyers	16	8	–
Escorts	16	12	8

It is now proposed that the March 1947 figures be achieved by June 1946 and that the return of further units be then reconsidered.

8. East Indies Fleet

Commitments are considered to be the Netherlands East Indies, rehabilitation etc in Burma, Malaya and Singapore and possible trouble in India in the Spring.

9. Planned strengths for the EIF are as follows:–

	June 1946	March 1947	Post-War
CVLs	2	–	1
Cruisers	4	4	4
Destroyers	8	–	–
Escorts (incl. ASR & Persian Gulf)	20	4	4

10. It is proposed that the March 1947 figures should be reached by 31.12.46. To achieve this, it is proposed that the following should be withdrawn without relief in the immediate future:–

1 CVL (VENGEANCE)
12 Escorts

leaving in the EIF for a period, until the probable situation in India this summer becomes clearer:–

1 CVL (COLOSSUS)
4 Cruisers
8 Destroyers
8 Escorts

to be further reduced by 31.12.46 to:–

4 Cruisers
4 Escorts (includes 2 for Persian Gulf permanently)

11. Air/Sea Rescue

The present requirement for 20 Escorts in the EIF covers the needs of ASR. The commitment is decreasing and may lapse altogether …

12. Mediterranean Fleet

Commitments are considered to be disorders in Palestine, repercussions in the Middle East and possible unrest in the Aegean and Venezia Guilia.

13. The planned strengths of the Mediterranean Fleet are as follows:–

	June 1946	March 1947	Post-War
Battleships	–	1	2
Fleet Carriers	–	2	2
CVL	1	2	2
Cruisers	5	5	5
Destroyers	16	24	24
Escorts	11	10	10

14. It is proposed to maintain the June 1946 figures and not to build up to Post War strength until the manning situation allows.

15. American and West Indies Station

Commitments are considered to be the re-establishment of our position in the interests of prestige and trade.

16. The figures are:–

	June 1946	March 1947	Post-War
Cruisers	2	4	4
Escorts	4	4	4

17. It is proposed to adhere to the June 1946 figures and to reduce the March 1947 requirement to 3 Cruisers and 4 Escorts. The 4th cruiser should therefore join the squadron later in 1947.

18. Africa Station

The commitment is considered to be the re-establishment of our position in South Africa and the East and West Coast of Africa in the interests of prestige and trade.

19. The figures are:–

	June 1946	March 1947	Post-War
Cruisers	2	2	2
Escorts	4	4	4

20. It is proposed to reduce the requirement to the provision of 1 Cruiser and 2 Escorts by March 1947. It is considered that these ships should re-establish the Africa Station as soon as possible in 1946 and that the remaining 1 Cruiser and 2 Escorts should join after March 1947.

21. Home and Reserve Fleets

The commitments are considered to be the desirability of maintaining operational naval units in North Western European Waters and the need to restart training.

22. It is proposed that the Home Fleet should consist of:–

a) Battleships

(i) KGV and HOWE Reduced complements at Portland as at present planned.

(ii) D of Y and ANSON To reduce to Cat. B on return from the Pacific until BBs can be manned for the Mediterranean.

(iii) VANGUARD To commission for trials as at present planned.

b) Aircraft Carriers

(i) 1 Trials Carrier — INDEFATIGABLE followed by ILLUSTRIOUS

1 DLT Carrier — THESEUS

2 For training 1st Line aircraft — INDEFATIGABLE and TRIUMPH

(All the above on reduced complements)

(ii) Reserve Cat.B (or trooping if required)

IMPLACABLE on return from BPF
VENGEANCE " " " "
COLOSSUS " " " "
UNICORN

(iii) Trooping

VICTORIOUS
INDOMITABLE
FORMIDABLE
6 CVEs

c) Cruisers, Destroyers, Escorts etc

To remain as at present planned.

5 Cruisers operational
2 " (1 Cadets training, 1 for trials)
16 Destroyers

23. The increased rate of demobilisation may result in the need to keep ships manned on part complements at home, after their return from abroad, to prevent overcrowding in the depots and/or further congestion of the already strained berthing situation in Home Ports.

24. Assault Forces and Minesweepers

The above proposals do not take account of Assault Forces or Minesweepers which, it is suggested, should be kept the subject of separate investigations.[1]

[1] The lack of any mention of submarines in this paper is striking.

72. *Chiefs of Staff Memorandum*

[CAB 80/99] 10 February 1946

COS(46)39(O)[1] SIZE OF THE ARMED FORCES

Memorandum by the Admiralty

In accordance with instructions* the ceilings of manpower proposed by the Prime Minister for 30 June 1946 and 31 December 1946 have been examined.

* DO(46) 3rd Meeting, Item 1(A).

2. Ceiling of 330,000 for 30 June 1946

The action required to aim at the ceiling for 31 December 1946 will necessitate the immediate acceleration of the present demobilisation plans and will thus facilitate the attainment of the ceiling for 30 June 1946. In this connection, the importance of decisions regarding the disposal of Lend-Lease ships, aircraft and stores, and of our own surplus stores, is stressed.

3. Ceiling for 31 December 1946

The ceiling of 175,000 officers, men and women plus the intake (estimated at 24,000) would be made up (in round figures) of:–

98,000 Regular personnel
24,000 Intake
77,000 Hostilities Only personnel entered since 1943

This will necessitate the release during 1946 of approximately 500,000 men and women. Although this can be achieved as far as actual numbers are concerned, the release of certain categories of officers and men presents great difficulties, if there is not to be an unpalatable invocation of the Military Needs clause of the Release Plan. The implications of this severe and drastic release programme are wide and varied.

4. Effect on Fleet Dispositions

A first and obvious implication will be the effect on Fleet dispositions. Details of the proposed redistribution of the main units are shown in the Annex.

5. Summary of Implications

(a) The necessity to reduce to the minimum possible the number of men non-effective in the demobilisation 'pipeline'.

(b) Consequent on (a) the necessity to reduce the numbers of personnel borne east of Suez.

[1] Subsequently re-published as Annex I to DO(46)20 and considered by the Defence Committee on 15 Feb.

(c) The resultant inability to maintain strong forces in the Pacific after 30 June 1946.
(d) A general reduction of the forces in the Pacific and on the East Indies Station to the lowest limit acceptable to meet our commitments.
(e) A postponement in the planned build-up of the postwar training Fleet in the Mediterranean.
(f) A postponement of the planned dispositions to the America and West Indies and Africa Stations, with consequent effect on British prestige, fostering of trade and readiness for emergency.
(g) The reduction of the commitment for manning LST and major landing craft in the East Indies.
(h) Inability to man fully the postwar Naval Assault Training Force.
(i) Postponement of the planned build-up of the Naval Air Arm.
(j) Dislocation of normal technical training.
(k) Necessity for a general reduction of complements of all ships in commission.
(l) Necessity for a further drastic dilution of complements of ships in Home Waters.
(m) Necessity for a continued re-adjustment of complements during demobilisation and dislocation of administration, preventing continuity of training and continuing into 1947.
(n) Consequent on (j), (k), (l) and (m) the acceptance of a much lower standard of fighting efficiency of ships than ever before.
(o) Hardships to officers and men on regular engagements.
(p) Necessity to expedite the release of personnel locked up in shore bases.
(q) Consequent on (p) the necessity for early decisions on disposal of Lend-Lease craft, stores and aircraft and of all surplus stores.

Detailed remarks on the above are as follows:–

6. Demobilisation pipeline

To release some 500,000 men and women during 1946 it will be necessary to ensure a steady flow through the demobilisation 'pipeline' and the numbers of men 'non-effective' by being locked in the pipeline for long periods must be reduced as low as possible. The further away from home they are employed prior to release, the worse is this situation. Also, the high 'Hostilities Only' content makes it impracticable to use, for manning ships and bases abroad, a large number of men who are due for early release. It is therefore essential to reduce the numbers of officers and men employed East of Suez.

7. Strength of Forces in Pacific and E.I.

This will have an important effect on the strength of naval forces in the Pacific and East Indies. At present approximately 140,000 officers and men are borne East of Suez and it will be necessary to reduce this to approximately 34,000 as soon as possible. The general reduction in main units are shown in the Annex. It must be stressed that these reductions will leave little or no margin for operational needs should there be any deterioration in the political situation on these stations ... the reduction of the escort forces in the East Indies will no longer enable the Royal Navy to carry out any Air Sea Rescue duties in that station.

8. Strength of Forces in the Mediterranean

The strength of forces in the Mediterranean, which is being maintained at approximately its present level, is considered barely sufficient to meet the operational needs of the station in view of the disturbed state of the countries in the area. Apart from this, the build-up of the Mediterranean Fleet as a training fleet which is of great importance to the postwar organisation of the RN, must be postponed and the ships and establishments on this station will suffer much dislocation by reason of the constant changes in personnel throughout 1946 and into 1947.

9. Strength of Forces on Other Stations

It had been planned to build up the naval forces in America, West Indies and Africa Stations during 1946 in order to be ready for emergencies, maintain British prestige and foster trade, an important factor in the restoration of the country's internal economy. This must be postponed and it will only be possible to provide very small forces for those stations at present.

10. Major Landing Craft in East Indies

It is clear that if the LST are withdrawn from SEAC, SACSEA will be unable to meet his commitments for the movement of MT unless a corresponding lift of Red Ensign cargo ships is provided. MWT have recently stated that they cannot do this.

SACSEA's commitments are definite and unavoidable and will continue until the political situation in Indonesia allows the repatriation of RAPWI and Japanese to be completed and his military force to be re-deployed to peace-time stations, which is unlikely to be achieved by December 1946. Since such a large number of personnel, including a high proportion of key ratings, particularly engine-room, are involved in the running and maintenance of these vessels, we cannot both meet SACSEA's requirements and reach the Prime Minister's ceiling of manpower.

11. Combined Operations Training

The postponement of the final postwar organisation of manning Assault Forces will result in a consequent delay in the ability to train any personnel in Combined Operations which it was planned to bring into operation.

12. Naval Air Arm

The effect on the Naval Air Arm will be to reduce the numbers of carriers in commission. This reduction will persist for some time and during its later phase must handicap training. Once the cut in man-power has taken place, recovery will be slow and it will be impracticable to expedite it materially, even in an emergency.

13. Training

The accelerated release rate impinging on a high entry rate necessary for the adequate build-up of the regular content will necessitate emphasis being placed on basic naval training and there will be a consequent falling off in technical training, which will have a marked effect on weapon efficiency generally. On the other hand the implementation of the new Pay Code for the Navy imposes an immediate obligation to increase technical training, so that ratings may qualify for advancement. It will not be possible to meet this obligation efficiently for a considerable period.

14. Complements

The actual composition of the smaller numbers in the Royal Navy on 31 December will, as pointed out in para 5(1) make reductions in 'regular' personnel in ships inevitable. All ships and bases abroad will have to be manned on approximately 4/5 peacetime complements, whilst those at home might have to come down as low as 2/5 plus training content. Every endeavour will be made to keep up the efficiency of ships East of Suez by apportioning to them as many 'regulars' as possible, although this must be done with due regard to the hardship on such officers and men who may be faced with considerable 'foreign service' as a result.

As far as ships at home and in the Mediterranean are concerned, their complements will have to be made up with conscripted men who will have received so little training as to make them of little 'effective' value to the ships and establishments to which they are sent. Further, during the operation of the intensive release programme, there will necessarily be on all stations a continual adjustment of complements which will amount to disintegration and efficiency of ships and material will suffer heavily as a result.

15. Shore Based Personnel

It will be essential to expedite the closing down of shore bases, especially those abroad, if the ceiling figure is to be attained. It will be a matter of great difficulty to achieve this unless an early decision on the disposal of Lend-Lease craft, stores and aircraft can be given and also instructions given on the3 disposal of our own surplus stores. The question of Lend-Lease disposal has already been subject of discussion by the

Manpower Committee (MP(46) 3rd Meeting), but it is emphasised that decisions are also urgently required for disposal of our own surplus stores, which are engaging the services of large numbers of naval personnel.

Conclusion

16. The overall implication of this cut in manpower is that it will be necessary to reduce our naval forces in commission to a strength which will allow no margin for emergencies or deterioration in the general situation and from which it will be difficult to build up again. Furthermore, those ships still in commission which, by reason of drastic reduction and dilution of complements and continual changes in personnel, be reduced to a dangerously low level of efficiency and maintenance.

Annex

The following table shows the proposed redisposition of main units of the Fleet, which, to get officers and men home and through the release machine, will require to be implemented as soon as possible.

(a) British Pacific Fleet

	Present Strength	Now proposed for 31.12.46
Battleships	2	Nil
Fleet Carrier	1	Nil
Light Fleet Carrier	2	2
Cruisers	7	4[x]
Destroyers	16	8
Escorts	16	12
Submarines	10	10
Fleet Minesweepers	8	Nil

[x] on the assumption that the Dominions contribute one cruiser at least.

(b) East Indies Fleet

	Present Strength	Now proposed for 31.12.46
Light Fleet Carriers	2	2[x]
Cruisers	4	4
Destroyers	8	–
Escorts	20	4[xx]
Fleet Minesweepers	24	8

[x] to be reconsidered in March 1946 in the light of political situation in India.

[xx] on the assumption that the present Air Sea Rescue commitment now being undertaken by East Indies Escorts will have lapsed.

(c) Mediterranean Fleet

	June 1946 Strength at present planned	Proposed for 31.12.46
Light Fleet Carrier	1	1
Cruisers	5	5
Destroyers	16	24
Escorts (including Red Sea)	11	10
Fleet Minesweepers	24	16
Submarines	10	10

(d) American and West Indies

	June 1946 Strength at present planned	Proposed for 31.12.46
Cruisers	2	1
Escorts	4	4

(e) Africa Station

	June 1946 Strength at present planned	Proposed for 31.12.46
Cruisers	2	1
Escorts	4	2

(f) Home Fleet

	June 1946 Strength at present planned	Proposed for 31.12.46
Battleships	2	3[+]
Fleet Carriers	2	2[++]
Other Carriers	2[++]	2[++]
Cruisers	7	5
Destroyers	16	16
Escorts	30[x]	16[xx]
Submarines	25	25
Fleet Minesweepers	32	16

[+] 2 with reduced complements.

[++] for trials and training. Reduced complements.

[x] included 16 for A/S training and 14 for Air Sea Rescue.

[xx] for A/S training.

(g) Reserve Fleet

(Including Instructional and Training Tenders)	Proposed for 31.12.46
Battleships	6
Cruisers	15
Destroyers	49
Escorts	126
Submarines	40
Fleet Carriers	4
Other Carriers	5

73. *Defence Committee Memorandum*

[CAB 131/2] 13 February 1946

DO(46)20 MEMORANDUM ON THE SIZE OF THE ARMED FORCES – 30 JUNE 1946 AND 31 DECEMBER 1946

Report by the Chiefs of Staff

The Service Departments have examined the position which would result from reducing the strength of each Service to the figures proposed by the Prime Minister at the Defence Committee Meeting on the 21 January 1946. Reports on the effect on each Service of implementing these reductions are set out in the attached memoranda by the Admiralty, the War Office and the Air Ministry.[1]

2. Broadly speaking, the effect of the cuts will be:–
   (a) A reduction in the size of the Armed Forces to a level which will necessitate the abandoning of certain of our hitherto accepted commitments and
   (b) a general reduction in the administrative efficiency of our Armed Forces, particularly the Navy and Air Force, over the next two years which will make it impossible for the Services to deal with any major emergency.

Size of the Armed Forces

3. The broad strategic implications of the reduction in the size of our Armed Forces to which we would invite the attention of the Defence Committee are as follows:-[2]

...

[1] Annex I which deals with the Navy was previously published as COS(46)39(O), reproduced as Doc. No. 72.

[2] Sub-paragraphs (a) to (e) deal with Army commitments in Germany, Austria, Italy and Greece and RAF squadrons stationed overseas.

(f) Our Naval Forces in the Mediterranean and the Far East will be reduced to the minimum acceptable to meet our commitments. In addition:–
  (i) Only token forces will be available for other foreign stations;
  (ii) it will be necessary to provide freight shipping to SEAC to replace the assault lift which the Navy will no longer be able to man.

(g) In all three Services we shall be without reserves to meet any additional commitments that may arise in any part of the world such as India. No adequate provision has been made for meeting any threat to the security of the United Kingdom.

Efficiency of the Armed Forces

4. Administrative measures required to effect the reductions in strength in the armed forces by the end of 1946 will so lower their efficiency that they will not be capable of expanding to meet a major threat until after the personnel situation has stabilised. Until then, in the Navy, all ships in commission will, by reason of drastic reduction and dilution of complements and continual changes in personnel, be reduced to a dangerously low level of efficiency and maintenance …

Conclusion

6. We could only recommend the Defence Committee to confirm the further reductions in manpower ceilings which they proposed if they are satisfied that there is no risk of our having to be prepared to meet a major emergency during the next two to three years. With this proviso we consider that the reduced target strengths could be achieved, but only if the Defence Committee accepted the implications and conditions which are set out in the attached papers, prepared by the Service Departments. If these conditions are not satisfied the Services, particularly the Royal Navy and the Royal Air Force, would be reduced to a state from which they might not be able to recover for a dangerously long time …

74. *Defence Committee Minutes*

[CAB 131/1] 15 February 1946

DO(46) 5th Meeting

1. SIZE OF THE ARMED FORCES – 30 JUNE 1946 AND 31 DECEMBER 1946

THE PRIME MINISTER said that he thought that the assumption that there was no risk of having to meet a major emergency during the next two or three years, would have to be accepted. In considering the size of the armed forces, it was necessary to assess the size of any hostile forces with which we might be faced. There was no possibility of a war with America, and in his view, there were no hostile fleets in being, or in sight within the next few years, to cause us alarm. He also hoped that the strategic assumption that it was vital to us to keep open the Mediterranean and that in fact we could, should be re-examined. He did not see how we could possibly do it under modern conditions.

(i) Royal Navy (Annex I)[1]

MR ALEXANDER said that although at the moment, there appeared to be no comparable fleet likely to prove hostile in the immediate future, the Russians in their recent election speeches had stressed the need to increase the size of their fleet, and their attitude over the allocation of captured German vessels reflected this intention. In view of the lack of reliable Information on the facilities at the disposal of Russia for increasing the size of her fleet, he did not think that it would be entirely safe to assume that it would not emerge as a menace.

As to the Mediterranean, the cost to us of its closure during the war had been so great, in terms of shipping, that if it was at all possible, we ought to keep it open. If we had been stronger in the air to begin with we might have done so. Atomic bombs might not always be in general use.

SIR RHODERICK MCGRIGOR said that the implications to the Navy of the proposed cuts had been outlined in Annex I. These reductions could only be achieved if the assumption was accepted that there was no defence threat in the next two or three years. The Navy would now be so reduced that it would be capable of little more than police work. Those ships still in commission would by reason of drastic reduction and dilution of complements and continual changes in personnel, be reduced to a low level of efficiency …

(iv) Effect on Foreign Policy

MR BEVIN said that the proposed cuts in the armed forces faced him with grave difficulties in obtaining the support which he thought necessary as a backing to the conduct of the Government's foreign policy … realising full well the financial and man-power implications of maintaining the forces at their present levels, he asked that their strengths should not be reduced appreciably over the next three months. This would provide him with the necessary strength in the most delicate period, and providing a satisfactory solution was found to his problems he would support reductions in the second half of the year … as he was in the process of the formulation of a Far Eastern policy, he considered it dangerous to weaken our naval forces further at present, as we should not

[1] Reproduced above as COS(46)39(O) as Doc. No. 72.

then succeed in influencing decisions in this area to the extent we desired. If all went well, reductions could take place later.

SIR RHODERICK MCGRIGOR said that the Admiralty planned to retain their present fleet in the Pacific until May, and then to reduce it to the minimum for showing the flag and supporting the occupation of Japan …

THE COMMITTEE:–

Agreed that the following assumptions should be accepted as governing our present defence policy:–

(i) That we shall not be called upon to fight a major war during the next two or three years.

(ii) That in any future situation the United States will probably be on our side and will certainly not be against us.

(iii) That no fleet capable of being a menace to our security will exist during the next few years …

75. *Joint Planning Staff Memorandum*

[CAB 84/75] 26 January 1946

JP(45)259(Final) POST WAR NAVAL ASSAULT FORCES

As instructed, we have examined the requirements both in size and composition for the post war naval assault forces …

2. We do not consider that assault forces should be maintained in peacetime to meet any particular operational commitment, since we do not foresee that our forces would be required to carry out a landing in the face of a full scale or organised opposition.

It is, however, very necessary that training and development in this most important phase of operations should be carried out in peacetime.

In the event of an operation, in connection with our Imperial policing tasks in peace requiring any amphibious element, we consider that the naval assault forces and landing craft required should be drawn from those maintained for training.

3. Our report therefore aims at establishing the naval assault training force which we consider will be required for peacetime combined operations training and development for all three services …

In the present stringency both of finance and manpower, we appreciate that such a force cannot be created immediately …

The force which we recommend is one for the subsequent period when our forces will have become more stabilised and able to settle down to their long-term peacetime training and organisation.

It is important to obtain a decision on this force in order that ships and craft now available may be earmarked to meet the eventual requirement.

4. … We have estimated in Annex B[1] the minimum assault force which is required if we are to be able to train on a brigade group basis …

5. The landing ships and craft necessary for a force of the order of a brigade group are already in existence … approval should be sought for their retention …

7. The naval manpower required in peace for the scale of ships and craft set out in Annex B is …

Naval		RM		Total
Officers	Men	Officers	Men	
618	7,409	207	1,980	10,214

…

76. *Defence Committee Memorandum*

[CAB 131/2] 6 February 1946

DO(46)12 PRODUCTION OF WEAPONS, EQUIPMENT AND CLOTHING FOR THE NAVY

Memorandum by the First Lord of the Admiralty

At the Defence Committee on 21 January 1946 (DO(46) 3rd Meeting) I was invited to furnish a list of the new production orders in weapons, equipment and clothing that had been placed by the Admiralty between 1 November and 31 December 1945 and a list of those important items which would still be in production at the end of January 1946 …

I attach these lists at Annexes A and B. I understand that the Service Departments are expected to list only main items in the weapon and equipment categories …..

Production Orders for Weapons, Equipment and Clothing

ANNEX A

Orders placed between 1 November 1945 and 31 December 1945 (Main items only)

(i) Weapons

Naval New Construction – Nil
Guns, Ammunition, Torpedoes – Nil
Anti-Submarine material – 80 Transceivers
Aircraft Production – Nil

[1]Not reproduced. The total requirement was for approximately 500 ships and smaller craft in more than 20 different categories, from 10,000-ton landing ships to 10-ton small landing craft.

(ii) Equipment

Radar – 167 Sets
Radio – 1,452 Sets

(iii) Clothing[1]

ANNEX B

Main items ordered before 1st November 1945, that will still be in production at 31 January 1946

WEAPONS

Naval New Construction

Battleship	1	Sloops	4
Fleet Carriers	2	Frigates	1
Light Fleet Carriers	13	Frigates A/A	8
Cruisers	4	M.F.V.	87
LST(3)	1	Motor Vessels	18
Destroyers	37	Motor Minesweepers	2
Submarines	15	Landing Craft	32

Guns

Up to 4″	998	Over 4″	75

Gun Mountings

Up to 4″	354	Over 4″	153
Directors	740		
Shells	120,030		
Rockets	12,000		

Torpedoes, Mines, Depth Charges etc

Torpedoes	72
Torpedo Bodies	885
Torpedo Heads	1,256
Torpedo Pistols	355
Torpedo Gyros	1,689
Torpedo Engines	25
Torpedo Mountings	16
Depth Charge Throwers	102
Hedgehog Projectiles	384
Mines	3,050

Cordite production at the rate of 25 tons per week

[1] List not reproduced. The Cabinet Defence Committee was furnished with a detailed list of shoes, socks, shirts etc.

Aircraft Production +

Type		Approximate quantity outstanding For delivery after 31 January
(a) Seafire fighters	single-engined	185
(b) Seafang fighters	single-engined	150
(c) Sea Fury fighters	single-engined	100
(d) Sea Hornet fighters	twin-engined	60
(e) Firefly strike/night fighters		300
(f) Firebrand torpedo strike/fighters		110
(g) Sea Mosquito		70
(h) Barracuda bomber reconnaissance/bombers		40
(i) Spearfish torpedo/bombers		30
(j) Sturgeon reconnaissance/bombers		30
(k) Sea Otter amphibians		30
(l) Monitor target towers		10
(m) Jet Spiteful fighters		18

+The aircraft programmes run to the 31 March 1947 and most of the above orders extend to that date. Some of these orders are likely to be reduced as a result of the review of Naval aircraft requirements which is now being made in the light of current discussions on manpower.

EQUIPMENT

Radar approx. total number of Equipments	4,266
Radio approx. total number of Equipments	1,985
Dockyard Installations	
Floating Cranes (150 tons)	2
Fixed Cranes (various)	13

77. *Defence Committee Minutes*

[CAB 131/1] 8 February 1946

DO(46) 4th Meeting

…

EQUIPMENT FOR THE NAVY

The Committee … considered Annex B of the memorandum by the First Lord of the Admiralty (DO(46)12).

Guns

THE PRIME MINISTER enquired why so many guns were still being manufactured.

MR. ALEXANDER said that the majority of the guns were 40mm anti-aircraft and of these he had now suspended 518. Some of the guns were required for arming new vessels:– some were for experimental purposes. Very large cuts had already been made in the programme, but one could not afford to close the production machine down altogether.

LORD CUNNINGHAM said that it was desirable to continue at any rate on a small scale, the introduction of new equipment so as to avoid complete stagnation. He did not think it would be wise to equip new ships with old armament.

Mines

It was explained that the mines now on order were certain of the latest types, of which it was essential to build up over a long period, a reasonable peace reserve.

Shells

THE PRIME MINISTER questioned the advisability of making any shells at the present time. There must be very large stocks in existence with which the Japanese war would here been fought and we simply could not afford to build up further. He well knew the argument that stocks must be maintained in different parts of the world but it must be remembered that there was no Navy worthy of the name which could figure as an enemy for some years to come.

THE COMMITTEE:–

> Invited the First Lord of the Admiralty to review again, in the light of the discussion which had taken place, the outstanding orders for guns, mines, shells and other equipment for the Navy with a view to reducing to the absolute minimum all new production.

Aircraft (DO(46)12 and 13)

THE PRIME MINISTER thought that the outstanding production figures for aircraft, both for the Royal Air Force and for the Navy, appeared to be large in the light of present conditions, and seemed to include some types which might be dispensed with more quickly. He drew attention to the fact that the Cabinet had come to the conclusion that manpower employed on supplies and equipment for the forces must be reduced not to 650,000, but to 500,000, and this would mean that further cuts in aircraft production would have to be made.

In reply it was pointed out that –

(1) A large proportion of aircraft in the Fleet Air Arm at the end of the war were of American origin. Most of the remainder were of obsolete type and there was a limit to which one could go on asking squadrons to man and train on out-of-date material. The aircraft now in production for the Fleet Air Arm were British types specially designed for the work and were better than the American aircraft which were being scrapped.

(2) The programme of production for the Fleet Air Arm was tailing off, and would average up to March 1947, 80 per month. This programme

had been reviewed in the last few days and would probably be reduced to an average of 58 per month, unless this meant a reduction of the aircraft industry below the minimum required for war potential …

THE PRIME MINISTER said that he recognised the necessity for maintaining a war potential, but now was the time when the output of all munitions should be at its very lowest. Output might have to be raised later, but at the present time we had to take into account the absence of possible enemies, and the financial stringency …

78. *Defence Committee Memorandum*

[CAB 131/2] 12 February 1946

DO(46)18 NAVY ESTIMATES 1946[1]

Memorandum by the First Lord of the Admiralty[2]

In accordance with the directions in the Prime Minister's Personal Minute No. 193/45 of the 15th December 1945, I submit for the consideration of the Defence Committee my proposals for the Navy Estimate 1946. I trust that the Committee, in considering these Estimates, will not overlook that the Admiralty combines the functions of a Service and a Supply Department.

2. The new financial provision for which I seek approval is £290,770,000; this may be analysed between the six heads proposed by the Prime Minister as follows:–

		£.
(a)	A sum which can be directly related to the number of men and women in the Naval Forces eg pay, allowance, food, travel etc.	77,805,000
(b)	A sum based on production programme, including research and development and clothing for the Forces.	74,764,000
(c)	Works services.	10,750,000
(d)	Terminal charges, such as pay and allowances during leave after demobilisation, gratuities, deferred credits and outstanding liabilities for completed production.	68,822,000
(e)	Non-effective Votes.	11,704,000
(f)	All other items.	46,925,000
		290,770,000

[1] The Navy Estimates were incorporated into the Service Estimates (DO(46)19) which, subject to a 10% cut in all areas, were approved by the Defence Committee on 15 Feb (DO(46) 5th Meeting Item 2).

[2] Only the most salient features of the Memorandum are reproduced.

3. Details of the services included under each head, together with explanatory notes, are set out in the accompanying Appendices …

PRODUCTION SERVICES

No provision is made for any 1946 New Construction Programme. The construction contemplated is, therefore, to a very large extent completion of vessels under War orders which are being completed because they are needed for the Post-War Fleet. They consist mainly of the larger vessels for which normal replacement had been suspended during the War, or of new types of vessels, eg Light Fleet Carriers needed for the Post-War Fleet. This is illustrated by the following analysis, amongst classes of vessels, of anticipated expenditure on new construction in 1946:–

		£
1	BATTLESHIP (VANGUARD)	1,200,000
2	FLEET CARRIERS	3,350,000
10	LIGHT FLEET CARRIERS	7,650,000
3	CRUISERS	2,500,000
30	DESTROYERS	5,900,000
17	SUBMARINES	1,675,000
–	OTHER VESSELS	2,332,000
		24,607,000

WORKS SERVICES

For new works to be started in 1946 … the principal requirements are:–

Essential improvements to living accommodation at Barracks.
Research and Development Establishments.
Essential building and services at Dockyards (partly in replacement of buildings destroyed) other than Malta, Singapore and Hong Kong.
Essential adaptation of airfields taken over from the R.A.F.
Training Establishments (partly in replacement of buildings destroyed).
Storage Depots.
Rehabilitation of Malta, Singapore & Hong Kong.
Dredging.

General repairs and maintenance have necessarily been at a very low level during the war. The provision now proposed does not enable the arrears to be overtaken, work being strictly limited by the labour likely to be available.

79. *Board Memorandum*

[ADM 167/127] 13 February 1946

B.446 NAVY ESTIMATES 1946

In consequence of the decision of the Board taken at their meeting on 21 December, the Chancellor was asked to make a new provision for Naval services for the financial year 1946 of £291,170,000.

2. Since then two major decisions have been given by the Government having a bearing on the Estimates –

(a) the terminal bearing of naval and WRNS personnel has been fixed at 200,000 including new entries (instead of 225,000 naval and 5,000 WRNS) and it has been decided that these figures shall be achieved by 31 December 1946 instead of 31 March 1947;

(b) a reduced figure for industrial manpower engaged on supplies for the Services to 500,000 to be achieved by 31 December next, the greater part of the cut falling in the earlier part of the financial year. The Admiralty share of this total cannot be more than 110,000 including direct and indirect labour, which represents a cut of about 35,000 on the labour force which would be required to meet the Navy Estimates as they stand at present.

3. The Service and Supply Estimates are to be considered by the Defence Committee on 15 February and the First Lord has submitted a memorandum categorising proposed Naval expenditure for 1946 … The Estimates total as now notified to the Defence Committee is £275,770,000.

4. There is evidence that the Chancellor will call for a considerable cut in the aggregate proposed provision for the fighting services and their supply in the light of the black prospect for the national finances in the years immediately ahead.

5. The situation confronting the Chancellor is broadly as follows. The American loan, assuming that Congress vote one at all, will be £937 millions instead of the sum of between £1,250 millions and £1,750 millions originally hoped for. It is calculated that this sum may be considerably exceeded by the aggregate of our political and military commitments abroad during the next two years, as at present estimated.

6. The picture for 1946 is grim. Even with a cut in our import programme, which will leave the country with very little for easement of the present standard of living, we shall have a deficit of £770 millions on the import and export balance sheet. This is £20 millions more than we contemplated when our loan negotiators went to Washington. Of that sum of £770 millions, no less than £300 millions is accounted for by military expenditure overseas. The Chancellor's conclusion is that unless we can cut our overseas military expenditure drastically and rapidly (the only direct remedy of appreciable effect immediately open to us) we shall be faced with the necessity of cutting rations further and restricting the import of machinery.

7. The problem of finance abroad is paralleled by the problem of manpower at home and the need to close the gap of 940,000 in the manpower budget … is manifest.

8. Under these circumstances, the need to make every possible reduction in naval expenditure during the next few years requires no emphasis, nor does the Chancellor's expected insistence on further reductions call for explanation …

80. *Board Minute*

[ADM 167/126] 14 February 1946

Navy Estimates 1946
4065. The Board had before them a memorandum on the Navy Estimates.

The First Lord informed the Board of the reasons which made essential the maximum possible reduction in defence expenditure and particularly in expenditure abroad. He indicated the extent to which the Navy Estimates would need to be reduced and the heads to which he proposed that the reductions (amounting to nearly £21,000,000, ie 10 per cent of the revised Estimates less terminal charges) should be allocated for the purpose of the consideration of the Estimates by the Defence Committee.

The Board approved the memorandum and agreed to adopt the Controller's proposal that there should be a moratorium in the provision of material for the Fleet, with the object of saving immediate expenditure, even though ultimate expenditure might be increased. Research and development would proceed and in new construction and for experimental use at sea new types of equipment would be fitted, but otherwise provision of new types of equipment to the Fleet would be suspended for a period …

81. *Joint Technical Warfare Committee Memorandum*

[CAB 81/74] 21 March 1946

TWC(46)12 NATURE OF FUTURE WARS
NAVAL WARFARE

…

Functions of the Navy
71. The traditional function of the Navy has been to secure control of sea communications and then to exercise it, thus making use of the sea ourselves and denying its use to the enemy. It is proposed to examine this in the light of the new methods of warfare.
Particular Aspects of the Atomic Bomb in Naval Warfare
72. … probably the most important effect of the atomic bomb is not its direct effect on naval forces but on the civil population of the ports handling our imports …

73. … the depth at which the atomic bomb should be detonated under water to produce the maximum damage to shipping is 500′. An alternative means of attack is to detonate it near the surface and to produce a tidal wave though there is little information on the latter …

74. The following gives expectation of damage to warships and merchant ships from a bomb detonated at 500′ under water.[1]

	Warship	Merchant Ship
Severely damaged or sunk	¾ mile	1 mile
Minor damage only	1½ miles	2 miles

75. The minimum weight of the atomic bomb is estimated to be 10,000lbs and at present no decrease below 7,000lbs can be foreseen within ten years. Until this limitation is overcome or until aircraft to carry this weight can be produced to operate form carriers, the atomic bomb is not likely to be available for naval use.

Biological Warfare

76. Biological weapons could be produced to be carried in naval aircraft though they would only be profitable for use against land targets …

Rocket Delivery of Atomic Weapons from Naval Craft

77. The present limitation of range of the V.2 type of rocket is 400 miles … it might be possible to build submarines specially designed to fire 'strategic' rockets from off an enemy's coast.

The problems involved will be considerable not only in design but in control and accuracy of delivery.

The potential threat to an aggressor will be valuable as it virtually breaks down the idea of a buffer state providing a security barrier if there is accessible sea within range of the target.

Methods of Attack

78. An attack on our sea communications might be made in the following ways:–

(a) By attack on our commercial ports and/or fleet bases in this country.
(b) By submarine attack on our trade routes.
(c) By large scale mining of our approaches and channels.
(d) By conventional means by surface forces after atomic attack on our covering forces either in harbour or at sea.
(e) By direct atomic attack on our convoys.

…

[1] Though not stated, this would appear to assume a bomb of the size detonated in 1945 – about 20 kilotons.

Attack on Ports and Bases

81. … when the supply of atomic bombs is limited … it will be far more profitable … to attack our ports … [which] may have become more vulnerable than our ships which is a new factor …

Submarine Attack

85. The coming of the atomic age has in no way diminished the threat of the new submarines to our trade routes. Quite apart from any question of atomic propulsion, the new and true submarine which very rarely surfaces and has submerged speed of the order of 25 knots, introduces a very real menace to our future sea communications …

88. … it is unlikely that any means of detecting a submerged submarine at over five miles will be found within twenty years …

89. We regard the fast submarine threat as being greatest … when there are insufficient atomic weapons to make a blitzkrieg a really attractive proposition to an aggressor …

Large Scale Mining Operations

91. The mine is an unspectacular weapon [until] the port is closed … No sweeps have yet been devised for the types of mine now being made and the prospect for a future war is most sombre in this direction.

Attack on Sea Communications by Surface Forces

93. The chief influence on the character of naval forces … are:–

(a) There has been a gradual shift of the main offensive power of the fleet from the gun of the battleship to the weapon wielded by the carrier borne aircraft. It is clearly now impossible for the fleet to operate without command of the sea-air.

(b) The increasing range of shore-based aircraft utilised offensively by the enemy and needing high performance fighters and adequate interception methods for defence. Very long-range aircraft on the lines of coastal command in the last war will also be required by the Navy.

(c) The potentialities of the directed rocket both for low angle surface use and as a guided AA projectile may profoundly affect the design of ships. The era of homing missiles has arrived and this will … start a new technical war of counter measures.

(d) The importance of radar, infra-red, asdic etc both for the detection of enemy forces and direction of weapons.

Character of the Main Fleet Units

…

95. The function of the battleship has become much more that of escorting the carrier and … in a bombarding role. Whether … a surface action with guns is likely, is debatable … [but] the side which can afford to have a strong escort will be advantaged.

96. Whether such an advantage should be paid for at the price of reduced air power … is beyond the province of this paper … however, the ratio of the striking power of air forces is more than proportional to their numbers …
97. The carrier is the only means of providing high performance fighters at a distance from a shore base …

Size of Units

98. The conventional battleship has probably reached the zenith of its development and is hardly likely to survive in its present form …
99. In future we regard it as important that the fleet should consist of the maximum number of the smallest units to meet requirements …

Shore-based Aircraft

101. Cooperation between shore-based aircraft and naval forces is likely to be required in future to an increasing degree … An air early warning set may possibly be carried …

Changes in Naval Warfare

116. (a) Necessity for dispersion and secure bases

Diversion and security of our bases is necessary and main bases outside range of likely attack are required. We cannot afford to risk an Atomic Pearl Harbor. The corollary to this is that we must be prepared to operate at great distances from our bases.

(b) The Carrier

Future sea power, except as regards A/S escorts, will probably centre round the carrier and even A/S escorting groups will need carrier support. Carriers will need escorting vessels and all units should be of the minimum size to fulfil their function.

(c) Directed and Homing Weapons

The era of directed and homing weapons has arrived with the prospect of another technical war of measure and counter-measure …

(d) Personnel

The necessity for the highest class of personnel to operate the technical weapons and for the normal and increasing difficulties and complexities of command is clear …

82. *Blue List, 31 March 1946*

[NHB] 3 April 1946

(List of Ships Building)
PART I
SHIPS BUILDING FOR THE ROYAL NAVY[1]

Type and Class	Year of Completion	Month of Completion	Name	Where Building	Remarks
Battleship					42,300 tons
					8 – 15″
Vanguard Class	1946	25 April	Vanguard	Clyde	16 – 5.25″
Aircraft Carriers					
Ark Royal Class					
	Late 1947	–	Ark Royal	Birkenhead	31,600 tons
	–	Uncertain	Eagle	Belfast	8 – twin 4.5″
Lt Fleet Carriers					
Colossus Class	1946	9 April	Triumph	Tyne	14,000 tons
Majestic Class	–	Uncertain	Leviathan	Tyne	
	–	Uncertain	Terrible	Plymouth	
	–	Uncertain	Magnificent	Belfast	
	–	Uncertain	Powerful	Belfast	
	–	Uncertain	Majestic	Barrow	14,000 tons
	–	Uncertain	Hercules	Newcastle	
	–	Uncertain	Albion	Tyne	
Hermes Class	–	Uncertain	Bulwark	Belfast	18,310 tons
	–	Uncertain	Centaur	Belfast	4 – twin 4.5″
	–	Uncertain	Hermes	Barrow	
Cruisers					
Tiger Class	–	Uncertain	Defence	Clyde	8,000 tons
(Improved Fiji)	–	Uncertain	Blake	Clyde	9 – 6″
	–	Uncertain	Tiger	Clyde	10 – 4″
(New Design)	–	Suspended	Bellerophon	–	
	–	Uncertain	Centurion	–	
	–	Uncertain	Edgar	–	
	–	Uncertain	Mars	–	
	–	Uncertain	Minotaur	–	
	–	Uncertain	Neptune	–	
Destroyers					
Chequers Class (12th Flotilla)	1946	May	Chivalrous	Dumbarton	1,710 tons, 4 – 4.5″
Cossack Class	1946	29 April	Comus	Southampton	1,710 tons,
(13th Flotilla)	1946	September	Corso	Cowes	4 – 4.5″
Crescent Class	1946	May	Craccher	Cowes	
(14th Flotilla)	1946	July	Creole	Clyde	1,710 tons,
	1946	August	Cretan	Clyde	4 – 4.5″
	1946	December	Crown	Glasgow	

[1]Not reproduced are details of 4 Oil Fuel Lighters (self-propelled), 3 Rescue Tugs, 2 Mooring Vessels, 1 Torpedo Recovery Vessel, 1 Deep Diving Vessel, 4 750-ton Floating Docks, 5 Fleet Water Carriers, 1 Magnetic Survey Vessel, 7 MTBs, 1 MGB, 21 MFVs, 18 LCTs, 3 LCS(R)s.

1943 Design	1946	July	Battleaxe	Cowes	
Weapon Class	1946	Sep/Oct	Scorpion	Glasgow	3–twin 4″
	1946	November	Broadsword	Southampton	
	1946	November	Crossbow	Tyne	
Battle Class	1946	30 April	Gabbard	Clyde	
(1st Flotilla)					2,315 Tons
					2 twin 4.5″
(2nd Flotilla)	1946	May	St. James	Birkenhead	
	1946	Early July	Sluys	Clyde	
	1946	July	Vigo	Tyne	
	1946	July	Saintes	Tyne	
(3rd Flotilla)	1946	June	Corunna	Tyne	
	1946	End June	Aisne	Newcastle	
	1946	4 July	Barrosa	Clyde	
	1946	August	Jutland	Clyde	2 twin 4.5″
	1946	Early Sept.	Matapan	Clyde	1–single 4.5″
	1946	October	Agincourt	Tyne	
	1946	December	Alamein	Tyne	
	–	Uncertain	Dunkirk	Clyde	
1944 Design	1947	April	Dainty	Cowes	
(Fleet 'D's)	1948	January	Dragon	Glasgow	
	1948	May	–	Glasgow	2,610 tons
	–	Uncertain	Daring	Tyne	3 twin 4.5″
	–	Uncertain	–	Clyde	
	–	–	Diamond	Clyde	
	–	–	–	Clyde	
	–	–	Duchess	Southampton	
Submarines					1,090 tons
"T" Class	1946	Early April	Teredo	Barrow	1 4″ gun
	1946	April	Tabard	Greenock	6 Bow tubes
					5 Ext. Tubes
"A" Class	1946	19 March	Alcide	Barrow	
	1946	19 April	Alderney	Barrow	
	1946	May	Aeneas	Birkenhead	
	1946	May	Aurochs	Barrow	1,120 tons
	1946	June	Alliance	Barrow	1 – 4″ gun
	1946	July	Ambush	Barrow	4 Bow tubes
	1946	August	Artemis	Greenock	2 Stern tubes
	1946	August	Anchorite	Barrow	4 Ext. Tubes
	1946	September	Andrew	Barrow	
	1946	December	Artful	Greenock	
	–	Uncertain	Acheron	Chatham	
	–	Uncertain	Alaric	Birkenhead	
Sloops					
Modified	1946	29 April	Nereide	Chatham	
Black Swan	1946	July	Actaeon	Southampton	1,370 tons
	1946	July	Snipe	Dumbarton	6 – 4″
	1946	September	Sparrow	Dumbarton	
Frigates					
Loch Class (British)	1946	April	Loch Veyatie	Troon	Twin 4″
Bay Class	1946	End July	Surprise	Middlesbrough	
(British)	1946	End July	Alert	Blyth	
	–	Uncertain	Morecombe B.	Sunderland	
	–	–	Herne Bay	Middlesbrough	Twin 4″
	–	Suspended	Luce Bay	Sunderland	
	–	Suspended	Mounts Bay	Sunderland	

...

PART IV
YEARLY SUMMARY OF SHIPS COMPLETING FOR THE ROYAL NAVY

Type and Class	1946	1947	1948	1949	Date Uncertain	Suspended
Battleships						
Vanguard Class	1	–	–	–	–	–
Aircraft Carriers						
Ark Royal Class	–	1	–	–	1	–
Colossus Class	1	–	–	–	–	–
Majestic Class	–	–	–	–	6	–
Hermes Class	–	–	–	–	4	–
Cruisers						
Tiger Class	–	–	–	–	3	–
New Design	–	–	–	–	5	1
Destroyers						
Chequers Class	1	–	–	–	–	–
Cossack Class	2	–	–	–	–	–
Crescent Class	4	–	–	–	–	–
Weapon Class	4	–	–	–	–	–
Gallant Class	–	–	–	–	8	–
Battle Class	13	–	–	–	1	–
Fleet "D" Class	–	1	2	–	5	–
Submarines						
"T" Class	1	–	–	–	1	–
"A" Class	2	1	–	–	10	–
Sloops						
Modified Black Swan	4	–	–	–	–	–
Frigates						
Loch Class	1	–	–	–	–	–
Bay Class	2	–	–	–	2	2
Rescue Tugs						
Nimble type	2	–	–	–	–	–
Minion type	1	–	–	–	–	–
Mooring Vessels	2	–	–	–	–	–

83. *Admiral (Submarines) to VCNS*

[ADM 1/19428] 5 April 1946

SM.320/155

In accordance with your instructions at the meeting held on 3rd April, the following is the revised proposed ultimate disposition of submarine depot ships and 73 submarines.

2. This disposition has been arrived at after further consultation with D of P [and others] and enables submarine and anti-submarine commitments abroad and at home (including that of the Home Fleet) to be met.

3.

		Full Commission	Reserve
China Station (Hong Kong)	ADAMANT	9 'A' Class	2 Fast 'S' Class 2/3 complement
Mediterranean Station (Malta)	FORTH	8 'T' Class	2 Fast 'S' Class 2/3 complement
Home Fleet	MAIDSTONE	6 'T' Class 2 'A' Class	Nil

A/S Flotilla (Portland)	MONTCLARE	6 'S' Class 3 'T' Class	Nil
S/M Training Flotilla	(FORT BLOCKHOUSE)	2 'A' Class 1 'T' Class 2 'S' Class 1 Experimental	9 'T' Class 3 'S' Class
Advanced Training Flotilla (Rothesay)	(WOLFE)	3 'A' Class 2 'S' Class	12 'S' Class
		45	28

84. *Chiefs of Staff Memorandum*

[CAB 80/101] 2 May 1946

COS(46)131(O) CALL-UP OF THE FORCES IN THE TRANSITIONAL PERIOD

Note by the Admiralty

The terms of reference given in COS(46) 61st meeting dated 18th April 1946,[1] do not entirely apply to the Royal Navy in that we have no long-term 'Occupational Commitments', comparable with the Army, from which withdrawals can be made. Therefore, in this paper it is assumed that the British Pacific Fleet and East Indies Squadron will be reduced to the proposed peacetime strength by the end of 1946 and that our Port Parties in Java and in the Far East generally will no longer be required by the end of this year.

2. This leaves our Port Party at Kure and our Naval Parties in Germany (which present proposals will reduce to what is considered the bare minimum) as the only Naval 'Occupational Commitments' and it is not possible to liquidate these.

3. Minesweeping is also a heavy liability; the numbers of ships employed will be reduced progressively, and it has already been decided to lay up as many ships as possible during the winter 1946/7, though some will have to be re-commissioned again next Spring. It is hoped that 1947 will be the last year in which such large numbers of ships will have to be employed on this duty. This, however, must depend on the success of sweeping operations.

4. Since, as had been shown, in the absence of appreciable Occupational Forces little or no economy can be achieved from this source, any retrenchment which can be made in manpower can only be achieved at the expense of commitments regarded as essential; which commitments in many cases have not yet been met. The main peace-time commitments

[1] Not reproduced.

of the Navy (apart from those arising directly from the war, which have been stated above) can be put under two headings:–

(a) To provide peace-time 'Police Forces'.

(b) To provide a nucleus for expansion for war.

5. In considering the 'Police Forces', their main duties can be stated under three headings:–

(a) The maintenance of internal security and British prestige in the Colonial Empire and Mandated territories.

(b) The protection of British interests in foreign countries and on the high seas.

(c) 'Showing the flag' which has a great bearing on our export trade.

It is not considered that these headings require much expansion in this paper, but it is important to realise that in order to have ships available in all parts of the world to land men as may be required to assist in quelling riots or to give succour after a disaster, such as an earthquake, needs a much larger number of men than those actually manning the ships, in order that Officers and men shall not have to spend too much of their service abroad.

6. In order to provide a nucleus for expansion for war it is necessary to have in commission a well-balanced Fleet, including types beyond those required purely for police purposes. This fleet is essential for the necessary training, research, experiment and development on which the efficiency of the war-time Navy depends. It is equally of importance that Senior Officers, Commanding Officers, and indeed all Officers and men, should have experience of working in a Squadron or Fleet.

7. It is also necessary to ensure that sufficient seagoing ships are manned to meet the requirement of giving sea training and experience to all men conscripted, in order that they may form a useful reserve. It is the necessity of getting in this sea time that makes it essential, from the Naval point of view, that the minimum time of service for conscripts must he 18 months.

8. The forces necessary to meet our commitments have again been carefully reviewed and a revised assessment of the minimum strengths which it is possible to accept is set out at [the] Annex.

9. At the same time attention has been directed to every possibility of economics in the manning of this Fleet. By these economies it is now estimated that this Fleet can be manned by a total of 132,000 after December 1947, when demobilisation is complete.

10. The Annex shows only the proposed disposition of the main units of the Fleet. In the estimated man-power costing, allowance has been for the logistic support of the various Squadrons, also including shore training and establishments, administrative staffs, the necessary drafting margin

and the personnel required for Combined Operations and to man all other types of ships and craft not listed as 'main units'.

11. It must be stressed that these reductions that are being imposed continually will lengthen the time before the Navy is capable of being expanded for war; the Fleet shown at Annex will not form a basis for this expansion until the end of 1951.

12. Conclusion

It will be possible to accept a reduction in the total man-power of the Navy from 194,000 to 182,000 after December 1947, but any further reduction will result in an inability fully to meet our commitments and will reduce the Fleet to a state in which it will not form a proper basis for expansion in war.

ANNEX

CLASS OF SHIP	HOME	MEDITER-RANEAN	AFRICA	PACIFIC	AMERICA	EAST INDIES	TOTAL IN COMMISSION	RESERVE	TOTAL
Battleships	2*	2	–	–	–	–	4	4	8
Aircraft Carriers	5ᶲ	2	–	2	–	–	9	20	29
Cruisers	7≠	5	–	4	2	3	23	13	36
Destroyers	48(a)	24	–	8	–	–	80	48	128
Escorts	29(b)	8(b)	2	4	4	4(b)	51	149	200
Submarines	29	8	–	8	–	–	45	28	73
Minesweepers	18(c)	10	–	–	–	–	28	86	114

* With reduced complements.

ᶲ Includes 2 Light Carriers for D.L.T. and development.

≠ Includes 2 cruisers for experiments and Cadets' training.

(a) Includes 32 destroyers for Training duties, Submarine and Air Targets etc, with a reduced complement.

(b) Includes ships required for A/S Training and Red Sea and Persian Gulf Escorts.

(c) Includes 10 for special duties (Fishery Protection etc) with reduced complements.

85. *VCNS to First Sea Lord*

[ADM 205/65] 4 May 1946

The size of the Post War Fleet in PD.0204/45[1] is the same as that in PD.0140/45[2] but the cost of replacement is much reduced owing to the acceptance of a longer life for existing ships.

In the original paper the cost was estimated at £34 million per annum. On the new basis it is about half …

Therefore, the First Lord's query as to what post war fleet could be maintained with a smaller annual expenditure on replacement is really already answered …

86. *Extract of Minutes of First Sea Lord's Meeting*

[ADM 167/127] 5 June 1946

NEW 6″ CRUISER DESIGN

The meeting considered the five sketch designs for a new 6″ cruiser …

The 1944 'NEPTUNE' design with increased amenities.

Sketch 'A' design with 5 twin HA/LA turrets.

Sketch 'B' design with 4 twin HA/LA turrets.

Sketch 'C' the 5-turret design as in sketch 'A' but with revised engine room layout and shortened ship.

Sketch 'D' the 5-turret design as in sketch 'A' but with revised engine room layout keeping same length of ship.

2. The First Sea Lord said that it was for consideration whether it was worthwhile designing a cruiser now on traditional lines or whether we should wait until the trend of armament development became clear. Thus, the choice lay between proceeding with design 'D' or doing nothing.

3. DCNS pointed out that the designs 'A' to 'D' were as advanced as we could get at the moment from the point of view of armament as they embodied 6″ twin turrets, medium range HA armament and torpedoes whose design had only just been commenced …

DECISION

5. It was decided to cancel the 'NEPTUNE' design as this was now out of date and the ship was now larger than we needed, and to proceed instead with design 'D'.

[1] A later version of this paper, dated 12 Sept 1946, is reproduced as Doc. No. 89.

[2] Reproduced as Doc. No. 48.

87. *Board Memorandum*

[ADM 167/127] 8 July 1946

B.469 NAVY ESTIMATES 1946–1947

Departmental requirements for 1946–47, as originally drawn up, amounted to approximately £351¼ millions net. The net requirement as approved by the First Lord for submission to the Chancellor and to the Defence Committee was £291,170,000, a reduction of approximately £60 millions. This reduction is a measure of the efforts made by Departments … to reduce expenditure to the lowest possible limit in the interests of the national economy …

2. Immediately prior to the submission of the figures to the Defence Committee, it was decided that the Vote A numbers[1] should be reduced to 195,000 on 31.3.47 and to 5,000 for the WRNS … a total cash saving of £400,000 …

3. The Defence Committee then imposed a cut in the industrial manpower … to be allowed to the Service Departments during the year; the Admiralty share of this cut was … about 22,000 … evaluated at £15 millions …

4. The cash requirements were thus reduced … to £275,770,000. Upon this figure, the Government imposed a further cut of 10% … the resultant net total of the Navy Estimates became £255,075,000, the figure at which they were finally presented …

16. All possible measures have been taken to control expenditure in the current financial year with a view to ensuring that no substantial commitments are accepted which are not absolutely essential. It has been arranged that all approved requirements of £50,000 or over … shall be re-submitted for Board consideration before an order is actually placed.

…

88. *Defence Committee Memorandum*

[CAB 131/3] 26 July 1946

DO(46)97 SIZE OF THE NAVY

Note by the Secretary

At Annex I and II are copies of minutes exchanged between the Prime Minister and the First Lord of the Admiralty about the minimum man-power requirement for the Navy at the end of 1947 and which the

[1]Personnel numbers.

Prime Minister has instructed should be brought before the Defence Committee for consideration.

ANNEX I

Copy of Minute (M 195/46) dated 4 June 1946 from the Prime Minister to the Parliamentary Secretary, Admiralty

In DO(46)66 the Admiralty asked for 182,000 men as their minimum manpower requirement at the end of 1947. It is recognised that the Navy have no long term 'occupational commitments' and this figure seems very high even when full allowance is made for the Fleet Air Arm. Shortly *before* the war, when we had to reckon with the German, Italian and Japanese Navies, we had rather more than 100,000 men. The figure given in the estimates is 112,000 for 1937 and 119,000 for 1938. The United States are now the only major Naval power in the world and the possibility of war with them is excluded, but the manpower requirement is now said to be much higher than before the war.

I should, therefore, be glad if you would let me have a statement showing in more detail than in Annex I of DO(46)66, both for the present and for the years 1937 to 1938, where the units of the Fleet are, what manpower is involved, and on what duties they are engaged.

ANNEX II

Copy of a Minute dated 24 July 1946 from
the First Lord of the Admiralty
to the Prime Minister

In accordance with your Minute Serial Number M.195/46 of 4 June 1946 I have had prepared the attached three tables, which show:–

A. The overall composition of the Royal Navy in 1938 and as estimated at 31 December 1947.
B. The geographical distribution of the Fleet at the same dates.
C. The breakdown of naval manpower at the same dates under the headings used in Table A.

2. The reasons for maintaining Fleet were set out in paragraphs 4 to 7 of Annex I to Paper DO(46)66. In brief, they are:–

(a) To provide peacetime 'police forces' for the maintenance and protection of British interests and prestige throughout the world.
(b) To provide a nucleus for expansion in war.

3. The Fleet proposed is already smaller than had been calculated as adequate to meet these commitments. In view of shortage of manpower and money our Naval strength has, in view of the Admiralty, been reduced as low as could be justified.

4. It should be borne in mind that we are more rather than less vulnerable in certain parts of the world than before the war. When British interests are at any time suddenly threatened, the most mobile force available and

the handiest for use is the Royal Navy. A visit by a cruiser has often acted as a deterrent, and the presence of HM ships has always been welcomed as a steadying influence by HM Representatives in different parts of the world and by Governors of our Colonial possessions. Withdrawal of our peacetime foreign-based squadrons would be interpreted immediately as a sign that the British Government was less ready to protect its nationals and the situation in many potentially explosive parts of the world would deteriorate. This is not wholly a matter of 'prestige' though prestige enters into it; it is a plain fact that without delay and without logistic difficulty the Royal Navy is ready to bring its influence to bear wherever it is wanted. As will be seen from Table A, Annex I, the number of ships in full commission is considerably less than it was before the war, and Annex II shows how the Admiralty plans the disposition of this reduced Fleet. Annex II shows that our dispositions include fewer ships of all combatant classes except aircraft carriers and escorts and that where increases occur, they are confined to such items as wreck dispersal ships and the ancillary craft which enable a fleet to maintain itself at sea with less reliance on dockyards and shore facilities.

5. This Fleet in full commission is already less than that which will enable the Royal Navy to carry out the commitments inherent in our position as a maritime and commercial power, which we of course intend to maintain.

6. In assessing the size of the Fleet required under (b) to maintain a nucleus for expansion in war, the Admiralty has not confined its consideration to the question "What power is there in sight with which we might have to fight?", but has assumed that the Royal Navy may again he required to engage in global war on a comparable scale to the late war though of a different character as reflected in the changes in the Fleet; and that forces of sufficient strength to provide as nearly as possible an adequate basis for expansion for such a war must be retained in peace.

7. Moreover, it is no longer strategically sound to calculate the strength of the Fleet, class by class, by comparison with the strength of the most likely enemy or enemies. Our strength must be equal to our tasks, the first of which will probably be the protection of our ocean routes by all means including convoys against an immediate, heavy and sustained attack by highly efficient mass-produced submarines equipped with all the newest devices and improvements which are common knowledge among the Allies of the last war.

8. This task alone implies that we must keep in commission and in reserve a large number of escort vessels and carriers, and it involves continuous training of the men who man and will man them, and also uninterrupted research and development in anti-submarine methods ashore, afloat and in the air.

9. Apart from this prime factor, if it were possible to foresee exactly the conditions of a future war, we could perhaps make reductions here and there, though more probably we should be driven to further expansion. But as things are, we can only plan for the most likely possibilities, which probably involve:–

(1) Confining under threat the enemy's surface vessels to his own bases.
(2) Protection of shipping against such enemy surface vessels as may escape to the high seas.
(3) Aircraft strikes from what may well be the only airfields available, namely aircraft carriers.
(4) Safe transport of an assault force.

10. It should here be pointed out that the Naval forces of the British Empire before the war were not of a size capable of dealing with the German, Italian and Japanese Navies together; it was clearly recognised that they would be unable single-handed to handle such a combination. They were capable, with the assistance of the considerable French Navy, of providing adequate security against the German-Italian combination, with a possible small margin for precarious defence against Japan on the assumption that Japanese aggression would inevitably involve the USA eventually.

11. In fact, the French having defaulted, our Navy proved adequate, and only just adequate, to deal with Germany and Italy leaving our Far Eastern possessions bare. Had the Naval forces of either Germany or Italy (let alone both) been resolutely and intelligently handled it is doubted if our adequacy could have been maintained. It must be noted that the forces required to defend sea communications are vastly in excess of those required for attack from secure bases and with all the initiative in choosing the scale and opportunity for attack. But, as pointed out above, the Admiralty considers it unsound to base one's calculations solely on the question "Whom are you going to fight?". Its view is that if we are to hold our world position, we must maintain our sea power and the security of our sea communications on which the life of the UK and the British Commonwealth depends; in fact, in order to keep the peace – to make the penalty for challenging us at sea severe, obvious and certain.

12. The world has not yet re-grouped, nor has it emerged from industrial chaos. Production capacity abroad is uncertain. What is certain is that one very great Power at present bound to us by no ties of friendship is showing in no uncertain terms that it means to have a Navy – while other less great Powers intend to retain, reorganize and rebuild what they have.

13. What is also certain is that any lapse below a clearly commanding lead in Naval war potential over such powers is a direct incentive to a

building competition in which the lead once lost may never be regained. Our purpose should therefore be to adhere as economically as possible to those material assets we possess, and which give us militarily the only advantage over foreign armaments we are likely to enjoy.

14. It is necessary if these material assets are to be of use to ensure that we are capable of expanding our Naval manpower to man them effectively in war. This requirement dictates the maintenance in commission of a proportion for training and development as the nucleus of expansion for war.

15. The Fleet thus provided is in many respects weaker than in 1938 –

(a) As a basis for expansion for war.
(b) To fulfil inescapable commitments required in support of our foreign policy, trade and prestige abroad.
(c) To provide a force at the call of UNO which will be consonant with the dignity of the Empire.
(d) As an insurance premium on which it would be folly to default.

16. Before turning to examine in more detail why, in common with all modern forms of armament, more men are required in 1947 to maintain forces inferior in size to those of 1938, it is desired to point out that in Table A, a large increase in the Reserve Fleet over the 1938 figures has been allowed in December 1947. The increase is particularly notable in escort vessels and minesweepers. The reasons for maintaining an adequate reserve of escort vessels have already been stated. If such a reserve had been available at the outbreak of the last war, we should have been saved much of the immense losses of merchant ships from which we suffered up to the end of 1942, when the newly built escort vessels began to come into service. The same considerations apply to minesweepers, the shortage of which in the first years of the war caused serious losses and seriously restricted our offensive and defensive effort.

17. An examination of Table C will, I think, explain the reason for the increase in Naval manpower over the 1938 figure. The Naval Air Arm, which did not exist as a Naval commitment in 1938, now absorbs 24,000 men in shore stations alone, apart from those needed for the ships of the Fleet and their aircraft, and from men serving in training establishments or included in the margin. The organisation required for the naval element in future combined operations will amount to a total of 10,000. These include:–

The Combined Operations School
The Combined Operations Experimental Establishment
Basic naval training in assault craft
Manning and maintenance of assault ships and craft

For the time being it has been agreed to maintain a nucleus of little more than half of the full numbers, pending the stabilisation of our postwar armed forces. There is an increase of nearly 10,000 in numbers on shore, principally in new entry training establishments, instructional schools, and technical establishments. The number of these establishments has doubled during the war, owing to the increasing complexity of the technical side of modern warfare, and this complexity will increase with the great emphasis which is now being laid on scientific research. As an illustration of this process, it may be mentioned that developments in W/T communication and radar are responsible for a net increase of 4,000 officers and men for maintenance of equipment alone. The Royal Marines show an increase of 4,000 which is largely due to the Government's decision that the Commandos, which did not exist in 1938, shall in future be found by the Royal Marines. The numbers of new entries and of men undergoing initial training show an increase of nearly 10,000; this is due to the introduction of short-term conscription, which will mean a much larger turnover of men, all of whom must be trained. The numbers of officers and men on courses and undergoing training also show an increase of 4,000, for the same reasons as cause the increase in numbers in shore establishments. The overall rise in numbers involves a corresponding increase in the size of the drafting margin, allowance for sickness, leave and crossing reliefs, and in the number of men held in depots awaiting release by 5,500, over the comparable 1938 figures. The rapid turnover produced by short-term conscription will, of course, greatly increase this figure.

18. These figures show, I think that the changes in the composition of the Fleet and in the technique of Naval warfare brought about by the war have been so great that no real ship for ship comparison can be drawn between the Navy of 1938 and the Navy of 1947. The introduction of the large aircraft carrier, the heavy increase in anti-aircraft guns, the immense growth in technical equipment, the development of Radar and W/T, the speed of the modern commerce-destroying submarine, the advent of combined operations, and the introduction of short-term conscription, have radically changed the situation, and their cumulative effect has necessarily been largely to increase the number of men required to maintain a given number of Naval ships units and training depots and schools.

TABLE A – COMPARATIVE TABLES
COMPOSITION OF ROYAL NAVY (DECEMBER 1947)

	A1 In Full Commission		A2 Training, Instruction, Experimental		A3 Reserve Fleet	
	1938	1947~	1938	1947	1938	1947
Battleships	11	3	1	2	4	4
Cruisers	31	20	3	2	25	14
Destroyers	69	40	40	38	6	50
Escorts	20	28	10	25	Nil	145
Submarines	27	25	20	20	12	28
Fleet Sweepers	Nil	16	13	8	20	32
Other Sweepers	Nil	4	6	2	Nil	62
Gunboats	18	Nil	Nil	Nil	Nil	5
Surveying Ships	8	7	Nil	Nil	Nil	Nil
Coastal Forces	18	12	6	10	Nil	32
Depot Ships	4	6	2	Nil	1	1
Repair Ships	1	1	Nil	Nil	Nil	4
Maintenance Ships	Nil	1	Nil	Nil	Nil	14
Wreck Dispersal Ships	Nil	20	Nil	Nil	Nil	Nil
Misc. Ancilliary Craft	2	8	28	52	Nil	17
Fleet Aircraft Carriers	Nil	3	Nil	2	Nil	1
Other Aircraft Carriers*	5	5	2	1	1	6
Naval Air Tenders	Nil	54	Nil	Nil	Nil	Nil
	1938			1947		
Naval Air Arm Aircraft	Nil			204 First Line, 750 Second		
				Line, 100 Reserve and		
Naval Air Stations				1530 Storage		
Combined Operations	Nil			30 (Home and Abroad)		
Craft and Depots	Nil			Sufficient for Battalion Lift		
				together with training and		
				development together with		
				craft in Reserve for lifting		
D. Dockyards and Bases				one Brigade		
	13 (Home and Abroad)			14 (Home and Abroad) + 4		
E. Cmds, Staff & Depots				C&M		
F. NE Training Est.	As requisite for above fleet			As requisite for above Fleet		
G. Instructional Schools	4			11 (approx.)		
H. Technical Training	15			16 (approx.)		
Est.				15 (approx.)		
I. W/T Stations				21 (approx.)		
J. RNVR Divisions	16 (Home and abroad)			12		
K. RN Hospitals	11			13 + 1 Hospital Ship		
L. Boom Defence Org.	10 + 1 Hospital Ship			HQs & 20 vessels in comm.		
M. Royal Marines	HQs & 4 vessels in			As requisite for shore depots,		
(other than in A. & C.)	commission			plus Commandos		
	As requisite for shore depots					

NOTES:– * The number of Aircraft Carriers shown here is less than those shown in DO(46)66. The latter paper included all carriers building or likely to be transferred to Dominion or other Navies.

~ Complements have been reduced to an extent which renders ships only partially effective for war.

TABLE B – PLANNED DISPOSITION OF SHIPS IN FULL COMMISSION (DECEMBER 1947)

Ships	PACIFIC		EAST INDIES		SOUTH ATLANTIC		AMERICA & W.I.		MED.		HOME	
	1938	1947	1938	1947	1938	1947	1938	1947	1938	1947	1938	1947
Battleships	–	–	–	–	–	–	–	–	5	1	6	2
Cruisers	7	4	3	3	2	1	5	2	7	5	7	5
Destroyers	9	8	–	–	–	–	–	–	35	16	25	16
Escorts	7	10	6	4	4	2	2	4	1	8	–	–
Submarines	15	9	–	–	–	–	–	–	7	8	5	8
Fleet Sweepers	–	–	–	–	–	–	–	–	–	8	–	8
Other Sweepers	–	–	–	–	–	–	–	–	–	2	–	2
Gunboats	18	–	–	–	–	–	–	–	–	–	–	–
Surveying Ships	1	1	–	1	–	–	–	–	–	1	7	4
Depot Ships	1	1	–	–	–	–	–	–	1	–	–	–
Repair Ships	–	1	–	–	–	–	–	–	1	–	–	–
Maintenance Ships	–	–	–	–	–	–	–	–	–	–	–	1
Misc. Ancil. Ships	–	5	–	1	–	–	–	–	2	2	–	–
Wreck Dispersal Ships	–	–	–	–	–	–	–	–	–	–	–	20
Coastal Forces	12	–	–	–	–	–	–	–	6	–	–	20
Fleet Carriers	–	–	–	–	–	–	–	–	–	–	–	3
Other Carriers	2	2	–	–	–	–	–	–	1	2	2	1

NOTE:– The above disposition is influenced by the necessity for reconstruction in the 'make–up' of officers and men, which has been dislocated by the war and the release scheme.

TABLE C – COMPARATIVE TABLES
MANPOWER REQUIRED UNDER HEADINGS SHOWN IN TABLE A
A. EFFECTIVE MANPOWER

Item	1938	1947 (Estimated)	
A.1 Ships in full commission	61,300	55,500	
A.2 Ships for Training etc	7,200	10,000	
A.3 Reserve Fleet	5,600	9,000	
B. Naval Air Arm Aircraft and Stations	–	24,000	Ashore only. Those afloat included in A.1
C. Combined Operations	–	5,500	
D. Dockyards and Bases E. Commands and Staff F. NE Trg Establishments G. Instructional Schools H. Tech Trg Establishments I. W/T Stations J. RNVR Divisions K. RN Hospitals L. Boom Defence Orgs	12,200	22,000	
M. Royal Marines	2,500	6,500	Depots and Cdos only. Others included in Section A. etc.
TOTAL EFFECTIVES	88,800	132,500	

B. NON-EFFECTIVE MANPOWER

Item	1938	1947 (Estimated)
New Entry & Initial Training	13,150	23,000
Officers on Courses Men training for non-substantive Rates etc,	5,500	9,500
Margin for Drafting Sickness Leave Release of conscripts etc	11,550	17,000
NON-EFFECTIVE TOTAL	30,200	49,500

SUMMARY	1938	1947 (Estimated)
Effective Manpower	88,800	132,500
Non-Effective Manpower	30,200	49,500
	119,000	182,000

89. *Plans Division Memorandum*

[ADM 1/20906] 12 September 1946

PD/OL.0204/45

PROPOSED PROGRAMME OF REPLACEMENT BY NEW CONSTRUCTION AND EXISTING APPROVED PROGRAMMES AND CANCELLATIONS THEREFROM

1. In considering a programme for replacement of over age ships by New Construction over a period of the next ten years, a Post War Fleet as proposed in PD.0140/45 (Revised) has been used as a basis. Ships of Dominion Navies and ships on loan to Dominions have been considered as part of the Post War Fleet.

2. CAPITAL SHIPS (Proposed postwar strength = 10).

By 1956 the state of the existing Battleship Force will be:– 5 effective ships 10 to 16 years old, 2 over 29 years old and 3 some 40 years old.

3. It is therefore apparent that in 10 years' time, our First Line strength will consist of but 5 ships, with 5 more semi-effective ships suitable only for bombardment or convoy protection.

4. The construction of further Capital Ships be suspended for the time being. If it is found that some type of Capital Ship is required and a modern design, in the light of research and development, can be agreed, it will be possible from the point of view of building capacity to commence a programme of new construction any time after 1949.

5. AIRCRAFT CARRIERS (Proposed postwar strength = 10 Fleets and 25 Light Fleets).

Due to recent developments in weapons and aircraft (eg the atomic bomb and jet propulsion) it is not possible to put forward any concrete proposals for modernisation or new construction. However, it will be noted that with the exception of the ARK ROYAL and HERMES classes, all our carriers have been, or will be completed within 5 years of each other; moreover, our total strength, including all ships under construction, falls short by 10 of the total of carriers proposed for the Post War Fleet. It follows that unless a very heavy replacement programme is to be incurred in about ten years' time, it would be advisable to start new construction after the next 3 years.

6. It is therefore proposed to start new construction at the rate of 1 or 2 ships per year, the first 2 to be included in the 1949 programme and the types to be built being determined by the developments that take place in the interim period.

7. CRUISERS (Proposed postwar strength = 40).

The existing and projected Cruiser new construction already approved will supply all replacements necessary for 9 of the 10 eight-inch cruisers, which will be over age by 1955. It is assumed that the 6 cruisers of the new NEPTUNE Class will be completed. 2 ships (including BELLEROPHON) being ordered in December 1947 and 4 ships in October 1948.

8. Further gradual replacement, however, will be required for Cruisers later than the 8″ Class, of which the remaining ships of the first (LEANDER) Class will become over age in 1958.

9. It is proposed therefore to lay down new construction in 1953 for this purpose, the first 3 ships being shown in the 1952 programme.

10. DESTROYERS (Proposed postwar strength = 136).

Sufficient destroyers have been provided for in existing programmes to make up the active destroyer strength in the Post War Fleet as proposed in PD.0140/45. A certain number of the reserve destroyers will, however, though not over age, be very out of date and war torn, until replaced by new construction after 1949.

11. It is therefore proposed that an average of one Flotilla every two years should be laid down as from 1948 to ensure continuity of work in the specialist destroyer building shipyards, and to enable progress in new design and equipment to be maintained. These ships should be laid down at the rate of 4 each year.

12. SUBMARINES (Proposed postwar strength = 96).

The present submarine strength, including vessels nearing completion, is 16 short of the numbers required to meet the needs of the Post War Navy. It has, however, been decided that repair and refitting capacity will not at present enable us to maintain more than 75 submarines, but this number should increase as our dockyards abroad become rehabilitated.

Meanwhile, it has been approved to build 2 experimental submarines in the New Construction Programme, and the building of 2 further submarines for operational use is under consideration.

13. Until these new vessels have been completed and tried out, no new programme of new construction is contemplated. This is not likely to be before 1949 or 1950.

14. ESCORTS (Proposed postwar strength = 274).

We are 30 short of requirements and many of the existing Escorts are out-of-date. It has been approved to build 2 frigate type Escorts of a new design, capable of rapid production. These vessels will be largely experimental and after experience has been gained with them a clearer view of the modern Escort will be obtained.

15. Until experience shows that a new design can be agreed or that additional experimental Frigates are required for further new development it is not proposed to build any further Escorts for the present.

16. FLEET MINESWEEPERS

It is not considered that any further new construction of Fleet Minesweepers, except to replace casualties or for new development will be required in the next 5 years.

17. SURVEYING SHIPS

Although the construction of 2 new design surveying ships has been approved in the 1945 programme, the need for a further gradual build up in this class will increase as the surveying programme progresses and more trained Officers and Men become available. All except 2 of the existing ships will be overage by 1949.

18. It is therefore proposed to build 7 surveying ships at the rate of one each year, the first ship to be shown in the 1948 programme.

19. REPLACEMENT BY NEW CONSTRUCTION

The attached table shows a proposed future programme for replacement by new construction. It does not take into consideration ships already approved in existing programmes, nor replacement of ships which may be transferred to Foreign Powers.

CLASS	Date of Programme in which included								
	1947	1948	1949	1950	1951	1952	1953	1954	1955
CAPITAL SHIPS	Further Programme at present unforeseen								
FLEET CARRIERS			2	1	1	1	1	2	
LT FLEET CARRIERS									
CRUISERS						3	2	2	
DESTROYERS		4	4	4	4	4	4	4	
SUBMARINES ESCORTS FLEET M/S	Dates of starting New Programme at present unforeseen								
SURVEYING SHIPS		1	1	1	1	1	1	1	

20. Ships in already existing and approved programmes are shown at Appendix A …

APPENDIX A [simplified]

New Construction in existing and approved Programmes as yet uncompleted at 12 September 1946

Ships already laid down

Aircraft Carriers Fleet Carriers	1940 Prog	ARK ROYAL	Launch mid/47. Completes early/50
	1942 Prog	EAGLE (ex-AUDACIOUS)	Launch Mar/46. Completes early/49
Light Fleet Carriers	MAJESTIC Class 1942 Prog	HERCULES LEVIATHAN POWERFUL MAJESTIC	All launched. To complete to towing stage only for completion at a later date
		MAGNIFICENT	Completes May/47 then joins RCN
		TERRIBLE	Launched – Completes late/47
	HERMES Class 1943 Prog	ALBION	Launch Nov/46. Completes mid/49
		CENTAUR	Launch May/47. Completes late/50
		HERMES	Launch early/48. Completes late/51
		BULWARK	Launch Oct/Nov/47. Completes mid/51
Cruisers	1941 Prog	TIGER	Launch Oct/45. Completes Jan/48?
	1942 Prog	BLAKE	Launch Dec/45. Completes Dec/47?
	1941 Prog	DEFENCE	Launch Sep/44. Laid up Gareloch May complete early/49
Destroyers		1 CO Class	
		3 CR Class	2 to be sold to Norway
		4 Weapon Class	A/S Escorts
		11 Battle Class	
		3 Daring Class	
Submarines		12 'A' Class	
Escorts		4 BAY Class	
		2 Bay Class	1 as survey vessel. 1 under consideration as survey vessel
Sloops		3 A/A Sloops	

Ships Approved in Previous Programme but not yet Laid Down

6 Cruisers	1941 Prog	BELLEROPHON	2 to be laid down as soon as
		CENTURION	possible. Remainder later.
		MARS	Only BELLEROPHON has been
NEPTUNE Class	1944 Prog	MINOTAUR	been ordered. All six to be fitted
		NEPTUNE	with new design turrets
		EDGAR	
5 Destroyers		5 DARING Class (Improved Battle)	
2 Submarines		1 Experimental Submarine of 1945 Programme	
		1 Additional Experimental Submarine in New Const. Prog.	
2 Frigates		1945 Programme New Development	
2 Surveying Ships		1945 Programme	

APPENDIX B

1. The following additional cancellations have been made in New Construction since 1 November 1945:–

3 Large Fleet Carriers	MALTA, NEW ZEALAND and EAGLE
20 Destroyers	8 GALLANT Class
	8 'D' Class
	4 WEAPON Class (1943 Programme)
3 Submarines	'A' Class (1944 Programme)

2. These cancellations are in addition to those already shown in the Revised 1945 New Construction Programme CP(45)291, which has received Cabinet approval and were made during 1944 and 1945, up to 30.10.45.

No.	Description	Programme Year
2	Battleships (LION and TEMERAIRE)	1938
1	Cruiser (HAWKE)	1942
2	Large Fleet Carriers (GIBRALTAR and AFRICA)	1943
4	Light Fleet Carriers (4 HERMES Class)	1943
27	Destroyers (2 BATTLE Class Flotillas, 1 WEAPON Class Flotilla and 3 individual ships)	1943
4	Submarines ('T' Class)	1942
30	Submarines ('A' Class)	1943
17	Submarines ('A' Class)	1944
7	Frigates (LOCH and BAY Class)	1943
3	Sloops } A/A Sloops	1941
2	Sloops } A/A Sloops	1942
2	Sloops } A/A Sloops	1944
9	Fleet Minesweepers	1943
3	Motor Minesweepers	1943
265	Coastal Craft	Various
10	Boom Defence Vessels	1943
55	Transport Ferries	1943
2	MTB Carrier Ships	1943
965	Landing Craft (LCS(M), LCG(M), LCA, LCT, LCS)	1942, 1943, 1944
2	Salvage Vessels	1943
1	Repair Ship	1942
2	Cable Ships	1943
2	Destroyer Depot Ships	1942
16	300-ton Concrete Floating Docks	1945
2	6,000-ton Floating Docks	1945
1	15,000-ton Floating Dock	1945
4	Accommodation Arks	1945

90. *Defence Committee Memorandum*

[CAB 131/3] 9 October 1946

DO(46)117 THE INTRODUCTION OF A PERMANENT SCHEME FOR COMPULSORY MILITARY SERVICE

Report By The Manpower Working Party

1. On 22 July the Defence Committee invited the Man-Power Committee to put forward as soon as possible proposals with regard to the introduction of compulsory national service on a permanent basis …

5. The peace-time requirements of the Services in manpower are twofold:–

(a) Man-power required to enable us to start a war at adequate strength.

(b) Man-power required to meet normal peace-time commitments …

10.

	Whole-time embodied Trained force	*Reserves and Basis for Expansion*
Royal Navy	162,000	210,000
Army	320,000	830,000
RAF	299,000	155,000

…

12. (b) *Royal Navy*:– It is not expected that there will be any difficulty in manning the fleet and shore establishments in peace-time solely by volunteers (162,000 trained men plus 8,000 under training) but it will not be possible to build up from voluntary sources the necessary reserves (210,000) to meet the estimated needs of the Navy on mobilisation.

APPENDIX I
SERVICE REQUIREMENTS

Royal Navy

(i) *Regulars* – In addition to providing for the forces to meet the peacetime functions of the Royal Navy, the regular component of the postwar Navy must make provision for the development of the Fleet Air Arm, for nucleus organisations for coastal forces and fleet train, for the provision of sufficient assault forces to carry out research and development in amphibious warfare, and for the greatly increased complication in the equipment of ships. Taking these factors into account, the Admiralty estimate that to meet their anticipated defence commitments 172,000 regular officers and men excluding regular trainees will be required, which includes the staff for the training and administration of National Service entrants (10,000) if compulsory military service is retained.

(ii) *Reserves* – To enable the Fleet to be mobilised in the event of an emergency, it would be necessary to maintain a reserve of the order of 210,000 men. The pre-war figure for reserves was in the neighbourhood of 60,000, and to strengthen this the Admiralty are now planning the future Royal Naval Reserve and Royal Naval Volunteer Reserve which, together with pensioners, the Royal Fleet Reserve and women reserves, should provide not more than 150,000 for mobilisation …

APPENDIX II
POSSIBILITY OF OBTAINING REQUIREMENTS
FROM VOLUNTARY SOURCES

Royal Navy

The Admiralty do not expect difficulty in manning on a voluntary basis the Fleet and shore establishment in peace-time to a strength of 180,000 regulars, including regular cadre of 10,000 for training National Service entrants. This figure, however, cannot be achieved before 1954, and to maintain it an annual intake of volunteers (officers and men) of 16,700 would be necessary, which compares with the standard of voluntary recruitment achieved in pre-war days. As shown above in Appendix I, however, the strength of reserves obtained from voluntary sources is insufficient to meet the extended needs of the Royal Navy on mobilisation …

Compulsory service is not essential for the manning of the peace-time Fleet but is necessary to build up the reserve required for the immediate mobilisation of the reserve Fleet and the Naval Air Arm on the outbreak of war. It is also necessary to provide for the manning of new construction and the increased shore establishments which will form during the emergency period, and for the subsequent expansion to maximum war strength …

APPENDIX III
PERIOD OF COMPULSORY MILITARY SERVICE

Royal Navy

In the case of the Royal Navy, one year's service produces the necessary number of reserves as this is governed by intake and not by length of service, but the time available would permit sufficient sea training to introduce only a proportion of National Service entrants to sea conditions, and would be insufficient to train a number of categories. One-year conscripts would make no contribution towards the manning of the peace-time Fleet.

With a period of 1½ years' service, entrants would be available for 8 to 10 months' sea service after completing their basic training. The number undergoing sea training at any given time on this basis could be accommodated in the Mediterranean and Home Fleets according to present plans, which would thus largely become training fleets. It would not, however, be practicable to employ these men on other foreign stations owing to the heavy trooping commitments involved and the expense and time wasted in transit. Only a very limited number (say, 4,000) of National Service entrants serving at sea would replace men serving on regular engagement, and the majority would have to be borne additional to the normal peace complements of the ships concerned. The reasons for this limitation are, firstly, the lack of technical qualifications among conscript entrants; secondly, frequent changes in complement due to continued drafting to and fro of batches of conscript entrants; and, thirdly, the need to maintain the proper balance between home and foreign service for long-term men …

91. *Defence Committee Minutes*

[CAB 131/1] 16 October 1946

DO(46) 27th Meeting

1. INTRODUCTION OF PERMANENT SCHEME FOR COMPULSORY NATIONAL SERVICE (DO(46)117)

VICE ADMIRAL SIR RHODERICK MCGRIGOR explained the distribution of the proposed whole-time embodied force of 162,000 for the Royal Navy. This comprised:–

(i) 65,000 for ships in commission which included the Home and Mediterranean fleets (32,500), ships in foreign stations (17,500) and ships in home waters for special training and experiment (15,000);

(ii) 10,000 for the reserve fleet which provides the basis for expansion for war;

(iii) 49,000 for shore bases in the United Kingdom (including Naval air stations) which provide for the shore training and administration of naval force throughout the world;

(iv) 9,000 for bases overseas (including Naval air stations) which provide for the maintenance and support of naval forces on foreign stations;

(v) 10,000 for Combined Operations which provide the nucleus and training staff required for assault forces and for world-wide amphibious training, experiments and developments;

(vi) 19,000 as a margin for drafting, leave, sickness and other contingencies.

In comparison with pre-war days, the strength of the main fleet and training ships had been reduced, but on the other hand the Royal Navy was faced with additional requirements in the form of the Fleet Air Arm, the provision of Commando Brigade Groups and those for the other commitments of Combined Operations. He stressed the lessons of the last two wars when submarines and air attacks had brought disaster dangerously near. In the future, as before, maintenance of sea communications was of paramount importance without which, apart from economic considerations, our air forces and army would be unable to operate. At the beginning of the next war we should have no breathing space in which to build up our forces, the threat of air attack was an increasing factor and revolutionary advances in the performance of submarines were already in sight. It followed, therefore, that at the outbreak of war the Royal Navy must be in a position to deploy its full forces in protection of our communications which in turn necessitated the maintenance of a nucleus fleet and trained reserves up to full strength. In the event of war, we might seek assistance from the American Fleet but as past experience had proved it would be unwise to assume that such assistance would be forthcoming in time to participate in defence against the first attacks on our communications. As regards a potential enemy it was noteworthy that the Russian Navy at present comprises 3 battleships, 10 cruisers, 58 destroyers and 216 submarines, with a considerable number of other vessels building and there was little doubt of their intention to build up a powerful navy.

THE MINISTER WITHOUR PORTFOLIO[1] in referring to the submarine threat recalled the great efforts made by the Germans towards the end of the war when they were constructing three submarines a day. Such efforts if they had materialised in 1940 would have brought about disaster. To combat this threat the composition of the Navy had greatly altered in that it now comprised a far greater proportion of smaller craft fitted with complicated equipment, which proportionately required 15–20 per cent more men to man than larger ships. The final composition of the Navy, however, had not yet been resolved and requirements in man-power must be regarded as flexible …

After further discussion there was general agreement that compulsory national service should be adopted as a permanent measure in peace time in order that this country might make the minimum necessary provision for security in war and to carry out its other international responsibilities.[2]

[1] A.V. Alexander, the wartime First Lord of the Admiralty.

[2] At the next meeting of the Defence Committee (DO(46) 28th) the Service Chiefs successfully argued for a call-up period of 18 months followed by 5½ years reserve service liability.

92. *Defence Committee Memorandum*

[CAB 131/3] 8 November 1946

DO(46)135 STRENGTH OF THE ARMED FORCES AT 31 DECEMBER 1946 AND 31 MARCH 1948

Report By The Chiefs of Staff

In accordance with the instructions[1] of the Prime Minister we have prepared an estimate of the size of the Armed Forces considered necessary at 31 December 1946 and 31 March 1948 …

Part I – The requirement at 31 December 1946.

Part II – The requirement at 31 March 1948.

In the Annexes we have set out the points peculiar to each Service. At Appendix to each Annex we show, in tabular form, our estimated requirements by area.

Part I – 31 December 1946

2. The proposed deployment of our forces at 31 December 1946 is shown in the Appendices …

3. We have previously set out our estimate[2] of the forces which we considered would be necessary to fulfil our world-wide commitments at 31 March 1947. The trained manpower required to provide these forces was estimated by the Service Ministries to be as follows:–

Navy	225,000
Army	775,300
RAF	390,000

4. After consideration of these estimates the Defence Committee laid down[3] manpower ceilings as targets for 31 December 1946 as follows:–

Navy	175,000	in all cases less trainees
Army	650,000	
RAF	275,000	

5. In a subsequent paper[4] we explained fully what the implications of these reduced manpower ceilings would be.

6. Our forecast of the serious effects of rapid demobilisation on the three Services has more than been fulfilled and … the numbers of volunteers obtained have fallen short of expectation.

Navy

7. … the Navy is already below the peacetime strength considered necessary to enable it to meet its commitments and will fall still lower …

[1] COS(46)230(O), not reproduced.
[2] COS(46)9(O)(Revise), reproduced as Doc. No. 72.
[3] DO(46) 3rd and 5th Meetings, reproduced as Docs. Nos. 70 & 74.
[4] DO(46)20. Naval Annex, reproduced as COS(46)9(O) (Doc. No. 68).

Summary of Position at 31 December 1946

11. Even taking into account … measures to improve the situation referred to above, none of the three Services will be able to fully meet their commitments and none will have any reserve to meet any unforeseen calls that may arise …

Moreover, our forces will still be too small, and the state of efficiency to which they have been reduced too low, to meet a major threat to our security.

Part II – 31 March 1948

12. Our estimates of the forces required at 31 March 1948 are based on the necessity to provide:–

(a) Forces for our initial defence in the event of war and a nucleus around which to mobilise our full resources.

(b) Forces to meet our security and occupational commitments overseas.

The size of the Army at this date is governed by the extent of our overseas commitments, rather than by the need for maintaining a nucleus for expansion for war. The size and composition of the Navy and the Air Force is governed more by the necessity to provide forces for our initial defence and to maintain a nucleus from which to expand in emergency …

Requirements for Initial Defence and Expansion in War

14. The first task of the Armed Forces in war will be the defence of the United Kingdom, the main support areas and the communications between them. In addition to purely defensive forces this will call for the provision of certain offensive forces which will act as a deterrent to war breaking out and will limit the striking power of the enemy should it do so.

At the outset these tasks will have to be undertaken by those forces in existence in peace-time together with those which can be mobilised immediately. Since we cannot rely on a long warning period, we must maintain the minimum forces which we consider necessary to fulfil these vital roles.

In addition, all three services must be capable of expanding to a balanced force … in war …

16. In addition, nucleus defences for certain bases in other parts of the world must be maintained in peace-time in order that in the initial stages of a war we shall be able to defend the vital Commonwealth communications.

Security and Occupational Commitments Overseas

17. The tasks which our forces are called upon to fulfil under this heading may be summarised as follows:–

(a) To maintain law and order in territories for which we are responsible.

(b) To play our part in the occupation of those ex-enemy countries which will still be occupied in 1948.
(c) To maintain British prestige, to provide an adequate backing to our diplomacy and where necessary to ensure that in areas still under dispute we shall not face a *fait accompli.*
(d) To protect British lives and property in the event of disturbances and to further British trade throughout the world.
(e) To provide forces for use under the Security Council if called upon to do so.

18. At Annex I we give in detail the commitments for which it is considered that specific allowance should be made in 1948 ...[1]

Naval forces will be necessary both in Home Waters and in the Mediterranean, Indian and Pacific Oceans. In addition, allowance has been made for small naval forces in outlying areas such as the West Indies and South Africa.

The forces required for the above will need an adequate scale of administration and training backing in the United Kingdom.

Minimum Forces required to meet 1948 commitments

19. At Annexes II, III and IV we give detailed estimates of the minimum forces which each of the Services would require at 31 March 1948, adequately to meet the commitments shown above. In many cases the forces necessary for out overseas commitments would, in fact, also provide for our initial defence in war and serve as a basis for expansion. Full allowance has been made for this.

These forces expressed in terms of trained personnel (including Women's Services) would be:–

Navy	194,000
Army	611,800
RAF	299,000 ...

The Naval Annex shows what forces could, in fact, be made available within the restricted manpower ceilings which have been put forward for planning purposes ie. 162,800 trained men and the extent to which these forces will fail to meet our commitments. It also shows that, taking into consideration the probable intake of volunteers and the expected rate of releases and call-up of conscripts, the optimum figure of trained personnel that can be reached by March 1948 is 164,000 ...

21. ... We would emphasis again that, as far as the Navy and Air Force are concerned, these figures in no sense represent the forces which we

[1] Annex I not reproduced. It relates mainly to commitments on land, though with general references to naval forces being required in most areas.

consider necessary, nor will the forces that they can sustain meet our requirements and commitments …

ANNEX II

STRENGTH OF NAVAL FORCES ON 31 MARCH 1948

Part I – The minimum forces we consider necessary if we are adequately to meet our commitments.

Part II – The forces that it will be possible to provide under the restriction of man-power at present ordered.

PART I – FORCES CONSIDERED NECESSARY

2. The size of the Naval forces considered necessary on 31 March 1948 is governed by the functions which the Royal Navy is required to carry out in peacetime, namely:–

(A) To train for war.

(B) To protect and further British interests abroad.

(C) To provide a nucleus for expansion for war.

Should we be required to provide forces for the United Nations they would have to be found from those provided for the above roles.

3. … we have assumed that the Royal Navy will be supplemented by Dominion Naval Forces.

(A) *Training for War*

4. *Individual Training* – The increased complexity of equipment and the continuation of conscription together impose a training commitment on the Royal Navy far greater than any previously experienced.

This … has the effect of greatly increasing the shore training establishments required, with the appropriate instructional and administrative staffs. This is one of the factors that makes it possible to man only a much smaller number of ships than previously in comparison with manpower borne. This factor has the further obvious effects of:–

(a) Reducing the size of the commissioned Fleet in peace as compared with that required for war.

(b) Consequently increasing the proportionate size of the Reserve Fleet.

(c) Imposing a further increase in the training commitment owing to the necessity to train a large reserve of skilled officers and ratings to complement the Reserve Fleet when brought forward for service.

5. *Tactical Training* – Over and above the training of the individual it is essential that tactical training be maintained and realistic exercises be made possible. It is considered that these needs can only be met by the provision of sufficient ships of all offensive combatant types to enable the formation of at least two separate forces of all arms. This would permit

realistic exercises to take place and allow practical comparison between differing methods and ideas.

These tactical training forces can conveniently absorb the major part of the individual sea training commitment. This will, however, necessitate stationing these forces at Home or in Mediterranean waters to which Stations the conscript element is confined owing to their limited length of service.

6. *Additional Training Requirements* – The essential experimental work carried out by the various technical establishments and the intensive primary and technical training required by the Schools also call for seagoing ships. These purposes cannot be served by the tactical training forces since their programmes would become impossibly overloaded. Additional ships are therefore needed … manned by special complements …

Total Requirement for Training and Experimental

7. … we consider that ships and craft of the following order will be required:–

4 Battleships (2 as harbour drill ships)
4 Fleet Carriers
6 Light Fleet Carriers (2 for Trials and DLT)
9 Cruisers (including 1 Cadets' Training and 1 experimental)
71 Destroyers
34 Escorts
36 Submarines
22 Fleet Minesweepers

Together with a nucleus of coastal forces, auxiliaries and small craft.

In addition, sufficient landing ships and craft for a Brigade lift and Combined Operations training and development.

(B) *Protection and Furtherance of British Interests Abroad*

8. In the postwar years minor disturbances of many kinds threatening British interests may be expected in all parts of the world, and the mobility of the Navy makes it an effective and economical instrument for settling minor troubles and disputes, often without raising political issues which the moves of army or air forces would involve. Our naval dispositions should provide for ships to reach possible areas of disturbance before trouble can spread and get out of hand.

Apart from guarding British lives and property, 'showing the flag' by HM Ships has been regarded as one of the most effective methods of fostering British foreign trade.

9. The above commitments can, on the Home and Mediterranean stations, be met to some extent by ships whose primary function is that of Training. It will still, however, be necessary to maintain some additional

forces on these stations for 'policing' duties. On all other stations separate forces must be provided to meet these commitments.

10. Although the primary function of these forces is 'policing' of their areas, they are, nevertheless, necessary components of the Empire's war fleet and they have a strategic value in the event of war. They may also be called upon to act on behalf of the United Nations.

It is therefore most necessary that, as far as may be, these forces should be composed in such a manner that:–

(a) They form a tactical unit in themselves.
(b) They are able to maintain training and encourage the development of tactical thought and doctrine …

Size of the 'Police' Forces

11. In order to meet the likely police commitments set out in our overall examination and the above tactical and training requirements, we consider that forces of the following order are necessary in addition to the ships required purely for training and experiments:–

1 Battleship
4 Light Fleet Carriers
14 Cruisers
16 Destroyers
34 Escorts
4 Fleet Minesweepers
7 Surveying Ships
9 Submarines
Together with supporting auxiliaries.

The planned disposition of these forces is given at [the] Appendix.

(C) *Nucleus for Expansion for War*

12. The nucleus for war which is maintained in peace-time governs the rate at which we can expand our forces for war. In order to ensure the defence of the Commonwealth we regard it essential that our nucleus could be expanded on mobilisation sufficiently to provide the forces necessary for the immediate defence of our main support areas and their sea communications. The nucleus should also enable us, in the subsequent period, when all our manpower and resources are being fully organised for war, further to expand our forces to the wartime strength necessary to meet our strategic requirements within the limits of available manpower and production capacity.

Requirement for a Reserve Fleet

13. The Training and 'Police' Fleets cannot, of themselves, provide sufficient forces to meet our requirements at the outbreak of war. It will therefore be necessary for sufficient reserve of ships, men and material to be immediately available for mobilisation which, together with the

ships already in commission, will provide forces to meet our primary requirement – the immediate defence of our sea communications.

During the subsequent period of expansion to our full capacity, we consider that we should be prepared either to expand our striking forces, trade defence forces or assault forces, as the strategy of the war may demand. This will require certain additional ships and trained men in reserve.

14. It has been the practice in the past to allow for a considerable proportion of our forces to be made up during the warning period of strained relations and during the early years of a war. It is now considered that it is only at great risk such a period of grace can be assumed …

In view of the time they take to build, it is therefore important to maintain in reserve the number of ships of the following classes, which we might be required to man on full expansion for war:–

Aircraft Carriers
Battleships
Cruisers
Submarines
Highly specialised and complicated Fleet Auxiliaries

Provided that the production capacity necessary to bring the fleet up to full strength is kept healthy and adequate, we should be able to rely on building a certain number of additional destroyers and smaller ships during the warning period and subsequent period of expansion to our full capacity.

Size of Reserve Fleet

15. Taking into consideration the above factors, we estimate that a Reserve Fleet of the following order will be required:–

6 Fleet Carriers
1 Battleship
10 Light Fleet Carriers
10 Cruisers
40 Destroyers
260 Escorts
50 Submarines
22 Fleet Minesweepers, also Depot ships, Coastal Forces etc and Naval Auxiliary Vessels.

In addition, reserves of Naval aircraft, landing ships and craft will be required.

16. This Reserve Fleet, when added to the Training and 'Police' Fleets, will give a Fleet capable of being mobilised of the order of:–

Fleet Carriers	10	Destroyers	127
Battleships	6	Escorts	328

Light Fleet Carriers	20	Submarines	95
Cruisers	33	Fleet Minesweepers	48

These forces are considered the minimum for our immediate needs and to provide the basis for subsequent expansion to full war strength, on the assumption that they are supplemented by Dominion Naval Forces of the order of:–

Light Fleet Carriers	6	Destroyers	90
Cruisers	7	Escorts	53

17. *Battleships* – It will be noted that the requirement for Battleships has been placed at 6. This is a lower figure than in any previous assessment.

This reduction is, however, considered acceptable for the time being in view of –

(a) The increased power of Naval Aviation in maritime warfare and the possession of Fleet Carriers, which join with the Battleship to form the combined striking power of the Battle Fleet.

(b) The present non-existence of a potential enemy Battleship force of anything approaching equal strength.

However, we possess 10 Battleships, although 5 of them are very old.

If war should come within the next ten years these old ships might well prove of great value for escorting important convoys, shore bombardment and other duties – as has happened in the past. Furthermore, they may prove extremely useful for experiment and development in the mounting of rocket weapons and in the evolution of the future form of the capital ship. It would, therefore, be folly to dispose of them prematurely, and it is considered that all should be retained in reserve.

TOTAL REQUIREMENTS

18. … The ships and vessels set out as necessary to be in commission for Training and 'Police' duties exist. We are, and will be, short of requirements in a number of categories for the numbers necessary to complete the Reserve Fleet. Full requirements have nevertheless been set out as the target of our peacetime strength at any time.

Type of Ship	Training		'Police' Forces	Target Reserve Fleet (Existing numbers are shown in brackets)	Assumed Dominion contributions*	Total
	Tactical Training	Experimental And School Training				
Fleet Carriers	4	…	..	6 (4)	…	10
Battleships	2	2 (harbour drill ships)	1	5 (5)	…	10
Lt Fleet Carriers	4	2 (Trials and DLT)	4	10 (4)	5	25

Cruisers	7	2 (1 Trials, 1 Cadets Training)	14	10 (10)	7	40
Destroyers	32	39	16	40 (35)	30	157
Escorts	16	18	34	260 (160)	33	361
Submarines	20	16	9	50 (35)	...	95
Fleet Minesweepers	...	22	4	22 (22)	...	48

* Some of these will probably be in reserve.

In addition, other types of ships will be required for the Training Fleet (paragraph 7 above) and for the Reserve Fleet (paragraph 15 above).

We show at Appendix, Column IV, the planned disposition of these forces.

MANPOWER

19. The trained personnel required to man the target Fleet detailed above is estimated at 194,000. But, as has been shown, the force considered necessary do not all exist and cannot exist within the next few years. It is estimated that a Navy approximating in strength to that proportion, which will exist, of the target Fleet, could be manned on the figure of 188,500 trained personnel which has been approved in principle.

This latter figure is arrived at as follows:–

(a) Regulars and short-term volunteers	170,000
(b) Additional regulars to train conscripts	10,000
(c) Conscripts (27,000 annually for 18 months)	40,000
(d) Men	220,000
(e) Less men replaced by WRNS	7,500
(f) Total Men	212,500
(g) WRNS	10,000
(h) Total Vote "A"	222,500
(j) Regulars under training	8,000
(k) Conscripts under training	26,000
(l) Total Trainees	34,000
(m) Trained regulars ((a) minus (j))	162,000
Additional trained regulars (b)	10,000
Trained conscripts ((c) minus (k))	14,000
WRNS not replacing men	2,500
Total trained personnel	188,500

PART II – PLANNED FORCES ON RESTRICTED MANPOWER

20. We now proceed to examine the forces that it will be possible to provide under the restriction of manpower at present ordered.

21. During the next five years, the gradual build-up and reorganisation of the regular content of the Navy and the impact of Government decisions on conscription will result in a variation in the numbers of men and women borne at any particular time. Under the most recent recommendations made by the Manpower Committee (known as Scheme D), the total of trained personnel available to the Navy, in March 1948, should be 162,800. This figure is arrived at as follows:–

Regulars	123,700
Conscripted before January 1947	33,900
Conscripted after January 1947	20,400
Total manpower	178,000
Less regulars and conscripts under training	25,000
Trained manpower	153,000
WRNS	9,800
Total trained personnel	162,800

This figure, however, depends on the estimate of the numbers of recruits who will come forward. But ... it will only be possible on the manpower given above to man a considerably reduced force to that which we have set out in Part I as necessary to meet our commitments.

Factors affecting the size of the Fleet

22. The factors that make it impracticable to man a postwar Fleet of anything approaching an equivalent number of ships, as was possible in the past, on the same manpower, are as follows:–

(a) The increased Naval Aviation component of the Fleet, which requires a large percentage of shore backing, both for maintenance and training.

(b) The increased complexity of the technical side of modern warfare necessitates increased technical training on shore and therefore more training establishments and staffs.

(c) The introduction of conscription which necessitates increased training with a consequent further increase in shore training Establishments.

(d) The setting up of a Combined Operations organisation, requiring a naval element.

23. Based on the above considerations and on maintaining the presently accepted standards of training and efficiency ... at the end of the year [1947] the total number of trained personnel will fall to 146,500; it will then only be possible to maintain in full commission a fleet of the following order:–

2 Battleships	32 Destroyers
2 Fleet Carriers	23 Escorts
4 Light Fleet Carriers	17 Submarines
13 Cruisers	16 Fleet Minesweepers

Together with a first line of 168 aircraft and a nucleus of supporting ancilliary craft, combined operations, coastal forces and Boom Defence vessels.

24. … With these reduced forces in commission, particularly the small number of aircraft carriers, our ability to expand to an efficient force for war would be gravely jeopardised.

25. It is therefore considered that such a Fleet is inadequate.

Possible measures to increase the strength of Naval Forces in commission

26. It will be the intention of the Admiralty to consider all possible measures to increase the strength of the Naval Forces that can be kept in commission on the available manpower.

27. At present it appears that an increase in the number of ships in commission could only be achieved by:–

(a) Further drastic reduction and dilution of complements in order that more ships can be manned with the officers and men available.

(b) Reduction of shore training in order to increase the percentage of officers and men available to man ships.

(c) The bearing in ships at Home and in the Mediterranean of a greater proportion of conscripts, resulting in continual changes of personnel.

28. The implications of the above would be an inevitable redaction in the efficiency of personnel, ships and fleets and a further delay in the reorganisation of the postwar Navy …

Conclusion

29. The forces shown in Part I therefore stand as the true estimate of the minimum we consider necessary, which must be attained as soon as availability of manpower permits.

Even if the target figure of 194,000 trained personnel were immediately approved, however, it would not in fact be possible to build up the regular content of the Navy by March 1948 so that that figure would be attained.

It is estimated that, allowing for minor adjustments to the figures in paragraph 21, if it is approved to continue to work towards the figure of 188,600 given in Part I, paragraph 19, and thus towards the ultimate target of 194,000 the highest figure that can be reached by March 1948 is 164,000 trained personnel.

APPENDIX TO ANNEX II
DISPOSITION OF FLEET
(Principal Units only – excluding Dominion Contribution)

Theatre (I)	Naval Forces at 31st December 1946 (II)	Naval Forces which can be provided under Scheme D with man-power reduced in 1948 and continuing until December 1950 (III)	Forces considered necessary at 31st March 1948, adequately to meet our Peace-Time commitments (IV)
Experimental and School Training (Special or reduced complements) – United Kingdom and Atlantic	2 Fleet Carriers 3 Battleships (as harbour drill ships) 1 Light Fleet Carrier 2 Cruisers 33 Destroyers (including 2 in Mediterranean and 1 in Pacific) 25 Escorts 20 Submarines 10 Fleet Minesweepers (including 4 for Fishery protection and 1 West Africa training)	2 Fleet Carriers 2 Battleships 1 Light Fleet Carrier 2 Cruisers 33 Destroyers 25 Escorts (including Fishery Prot.) 20 Submarines 109 Fleet Minesweepers	2 Battleships 2 Light Fleet Carriers 2 Cruisers 39 Destroyers 25 Escorts (including Fishery Prot.) 16 Submarines 10 Fleet Minesweepers
Home Fleet – United Kingdom and Atlantic	3 Fleet Carriers (Trooping) 2 Battleships (reduced complements) 1 Light Fleet Carrier 5 Cruisers 20 Destroyers 8 Submarines 16 Fleet Minesweepers	"Station Forces" – 1 Cruiser (H.F. Flagship) 8 Fleet Minesweepers Tactical Training Force "A" – Nil Tactical Training Force "C" – 2 Light Fleet Carriers 1 Cruiser 8 Escorts	"Station Forces" – 1 Cruiser (H.F. Flagship) 12 Submarines 8 Fleet Minesweepers Tactical Training Force "A" – 2 Fleet Carriers 1 Battleship 1 Light Fleet Carrier 3 Cruisers 16 Destroyers Tactical Training Force "C" – 2 Light Fleet Carriers 1 Cruiser 8 Escorts

Theatre (I)	Naval Forces at 31st December 1946 (II)	Naval Forces which can be provided on 31st March 1948, within Scheme D man-power ceilings (III)	Forces considered necessary at 31st March 1948, adequately to meet our Peace-Time commitments (IV)
Mediterranean Fleet – Mediterranean	2 Light Fleet Carriers 5 Cruisers 16 Destroyers 8 Escorts (including 2 for Red Sea) 8 Submarines 8 Fleet Minesweepers	"Station" Forces – 1 Battleship (M.F. Flagship) 8 Destroyers 4 Escorts (including 2 for Red Sea) 8 Submarines 8 Fleet Minesweepers Tactical Training Force "B" – * 2 Fleet Carriers 1 Battleship 3 Cruisers 16 Destroyers	"Station" Forces – 1 Battleship (M.F. Flagship) 8 Destroyers 8 Escorts (including 2 for Red Sea) 8 Submarines 8 Fleet Minesweepers Tactical Training Force "B" – * 2 Fleet Carriers 1 Battleship 1 Light Fleet Carrier 3 Cruisers 16 Destroyers
East Indies Fleet – Indian Ocean	3 Cruisers 4 Escorts (including 2 for Persian Gulf)	2 Cruisers 2 Escorts (for Persian Gulf)	2 Light Fleet Carriers 3 Cruisers 5 Escorts (including 2 for Persian Gulf)
British Pacific Fleet – Far East	2 Light Fleet Carriers† 3 Cruisers 8 Destroyers 10 Escorts 9 Submarines	2 Light Fleet Carriers 3 Cruisers 8 Destroyers 5 Escorts 9 Submarines	2 Light Fleet Carriers 4 Cruisers 8 Destroyers 8 Escorts 9 Submarines
Africa and West Indies Squadron – Outlying Areas	2 Cruisers 4 Escorts	2 Cruisers 2 Escorts	4 Cruisers 4 Escorts
South African Squadron – Outlying Areas	1 Cruiser 2 Escorts	1 Cruiser 2 Escorts	2 Cruisers 2 Escorts

* NOTE – Tactical Training Forces will alternate between Home and Mediterranean
† Also available for East Indies

In addition, supporting auxiliaries and the following specialised units can be provided:–	In addition, supporting auxiliaries and the following specialised units can be provided:–	In addition, supporting auxiliaries and the following specialised units are required:–
(a) First Line Aircraft … 168	(a) First Line Aircraft … 168	(a) First Line Aircraft … 500
(b) Assault Forces:– 4 L.S.T. 22 Major and 53 Minor Landing Craft in commission	(b) Assault Forces:– 3 L.S.T. 22 Major and 53 Minor Landing Craft in commission	(b) Assault Forces – to be capable of a Brigade Lift, and for training and development – 34 Ships 64 Major Landing Craft 278 Minor Landing Craft
(c) R.M. Commando Brigade of Brigade H.Q. and three commandos	(c) R.M. Commando Brigade of Brigade H.Q. and three commandos	(c) R.M. Commando Brigade of Brigade H.Q. and four Commandos
(d) Coastal Forces – 1 Flotilla in commission 1 reduced Flotilla for training etc.	(d) Coastal Forces – 1 Flotilla in commission 1 Flotilla for training	(d) Coastal Forces – 1 Flotilla plus 1½ Flotillas for Training and 40 Craft in reserve

93. *Chiefs of Staff Minutes*

[CAB 79/54] 3 December 1946

COS(46) 176th Meeting

STRENGTH OF THE ARMED FORCES AT 31ST MARCH 1948 – DO(46)135

The Minister Without Portfolio recalled the Defence Committee's request that he should look closely into the Chiefs of Staff estimate on the strength of the armed forces at 31 March 1948 and make proposals; and explained that he thought that the Conference should approach this matter with a full realisation of the great strain that would be placed on the country's manpower and financial resources and the effect on the Government undertakings in respect of release, if the Chiefs of Staff estimate was to be made in full … the Conference should first go through the commitments on which the estimates were based in order to see whether the forces earmarked for them could be reduced, or any of the commitments themselves dispensed with …

Sir John Cunningham explained that the Chiefs of Staff had done their best to play down this list of commitments. Indeed, some of their assumptions … might be regarded as somewhat optimistic …

THE NAVAL ESTIMATES

Pacific and East Indies

The Minister Without Portfolio questioned the need for a Pacific Fleet of the size contemplated, having regard to the fact that a friendly power, and not a potential enemy, now dominated that ocean.

Sir John Cunningham pointed out that although there might be no potential enemy battle fleet, there were plenty of potentially hostile submarines, and a vast area in which there were many very important British interests. He regarded the naval forces in the Pacific and East Indies as complementary in that one could support the other in emergency and on that basis alone could regard the provision made in the Admiralty estimates as adequate and even then, only when they had been built up to full strength over the next 5 or 6 years …

Mediterranean

Provision for the Mediterranean again had been reduced to the very minimum, as was witnessed by the fact that practically all our naval forces were tied up at the moment on duties in connection with the Palestine situation. Here again … he regarded the Mediterranean and the Home Fleets as complementary.

The Minister Without Portfolio referred to recent public interest in the fact that the number of ships at sea was so small and Sir John Cunningham explained that this was entirely due to the fact that the Navy had had to release the great majority of its trained personnel. Replacements had now to be found and trained, which meant that large numbers of men were now on shore instead of being afloat …

Summing up the Admiralty's plans for the Navy, Sir John Cunningham explained that the Navy had taken great risks in reducing their estimates to the absolute minimum. They had reduced complements drastically and cut everything down to the bone. For a year or two he thought the risks involved in this policy could be accepted, but he would like to make it clear that even under the scheme now put forward it would not be until 1952 that the Navy would be really fit to do its job. Further reduction would have a far reaching effect on these plans and gravely postpone the date when the Navy could be ready.

…

The Minister Without Portfolio said that he was much impressed by the strength of the case put forward by the Chiefs of Staff … The fact remained, however, that the Government was faced with a defence budget which it appeared would absorb practically the whole of the income derived from income tax. It appeared that the defence budget would be of the order of some £900,000,000 … It seemed to him that some cut in the Chiefs of Staff estimates would be essential in the interests of the general economy of the nation and the question seemed to be how should that now be applied …

In reply, the Chiefs of Staff [said] … the estimates … were the minimum which they thought essential of we were to support our position as a great power in the world today … the Royal Navy and the Royal Air Force were in a difficulty. Their figures had been based on the future.[1] They had put forward the minimum which they thought essential if the Royal Navy and the Royal Air Force were to be built up within a reasonable time to a state from which they could expand in an emergency. If they were now called upon to accept a reduction below this absolute minimum, they would not be able to rise to the occasion if the Government were faced with a deterioration in the situation. The date when they could rise to such an occasion would be postponed for years …

The Minister Without Portfolio said that he understood the point of view of the Admiralty and the Air Ministry, but … The question seemed to be whether we could carry this great burden of defence and, at the same time, achieve the national recovery which was essential to our position in the world and, indeed, to our defence. He … thought that they ought to think in terms of an overall budget of some £750,000,000 for the financial

[1] The Army Estimates were based on current, largely immediate postwar, commitments.

year 1947/48. He would like the Chiefs of Staff to look into this figure and advise him as to how they thought the country would stand if the budget were reduced in 1947/48 to something like this figure.

94. *Chiefs of Staff Minutes*

[CAB 79/54] 23 December 1946

COS(46) 187th Meeting

1. GENERAL DEFENCE POLICY

The Minister of Defence explained he had originally asked for this discussion with the Chiefs of Staff in connection with the problem of determining what should be the Service estimates for the year 1947/48. He did not wish specifically to raise this issue, but to discuss the general defence background in such a way as to reach agreement, if possible, on certain basic assumptions which would prove the foundation for determining future British defence policy.

He realised that it was too early yet, to have learnt the full strategic, tactical and technical lessons of the last war, in particular the application of the effect of modern scientific developments on future weapons and warfare. Nonetheless he thought it would be helpful to try and obtain agreement on certain basic strategic assumptions. If these received approval on the highest level, it would be possible to start clearing our minds as to our future defence policy and to lay the foundation for decisions as to the future size and shape of our defence forces after the transitional period was over …

Sir John Cunningham said he was entirely opposed to the re-introduction of the ‘ten-year no war rule’, since this arbitrarily imposed assumption had emasculated the Services in peacetime … So far as the United Kingdom was concerned, we should never again, by adopting the ten year no war rule, automatically wreck the armed forces and hence nearly destroy our ability to wage a major war …

95. *Defence Committee Memorandum*

[CAB 131/4] 7 January 1947

DO(47)3

PRODUCTION, RESEARCH AND DEVELOPMENT PROGRAMMES 1947–48

Report By The Production Committee[1]

1. In September 1946, the Prime Minister informed the Service Ministers and the Minister of Supply in a minute dealing with the preparation of Service Estimates for the next financial year of his intention to set up an *ad hoc* Ministerial Production Committee, and asked that the following papers should be prepared and laid before this Committee:–

(a) An agreed inter-Service programme for defence research and development.

(b) A report stating the dimensions of the Production Estimates for 1947–48 in sufficient detail to enable the Production Committee to see the main elements which go to make up the programmes.

…

Parts I and II below summarise the modified proposals which we recommend for the approval of the Defence Committee.

Part I – Research and Development

4. The following table summarises our financial proposals under this head. The figures include expenditure on works services associated with research and development.

	£m
Admiralty	8.5
Ministry of Supply (Defence) (including £9.4m for atomic energy)	22.4
Ministry of Supply (Air)	35.2
Total	66.1

5. Generally speaking, the programmes put forward by Departments are in large measure a legacy of the war, though some reorientation of effort in such new directions as biological warfare and guided projectiles has been found possible in spite of limitations imposed by shortage of scientific manpower and of building labour and materials …

6. The following is a summary of some of the more important items upon which research and development is now proceeding:–

I – *Admiralty*

(a) Anti-submarine detection and new weapons of attack.

(b) The development of a fast submarine to provide targets on which to develop counter-measures.

[1] Chaired by A.V. Alexander.

(c) Problems connected with providing protection against attack by very fast aircraft.
(d) Carrier operating problems in connection with the use of new fast aircraft.
(e) Constructional problems in the light of information which will become available as a result of ship target trials.
(f) Ship propulsion problems including the development of gas turbines for marine propulsion.
(g) Guided missile problems in conjunction with the Ministry of Supply.
(h) Mining problems, particularly in relation to counter-measures.
(i) Radar and Radio problems, including counter-measures.

…

Part II – Production

11. In the absence of a common strategical background and of any firm decisions as to the size of the postwar Navy, Army and Air Forces, we have observed the following principles in reviewing the report submitted by the Joint War Production Staff:–

(i) First, we have confirmed that all three Service Departments are continuing to make all possible use of existing stocks with the object of reducing their demands on new production to a minimum, and that they fully appreciate the fact that in the interests of economy and the revival of trade there must be a delay in the replacement of obsolescent equipment.

(ii) Secondly, we are satisfied that the requirements include only items:–

(a) Which are absolutely essential for immediate current needs;
(b) Which are compatible with foreseeable changes in design of equipment;
(c) Which must be included in order to maintain essential nucleus war potential by the retention of production capacity and the maintenance of manufacturing technique which it would in the long run be uneconomical to disperse.

The main elements of the Service Programmes are set out in the following paragraphs.

ADMIRALTY

12. The main elements of the Admiralty requirements, which total £70.9 million, are shown at Annex I. They are based on little more than bare maintenance of the existing fleet and the continuation of the construction of ships already being built. Some provision is made for the replacement of the obsolete aircraft with which the Naval Air Arm is equipped today. In the interests of economy, until the lessons of the

late war have been applied and the results of the current programme in research and development are known, it is not proposed to institute a programme for the modernisation of the fleet, and for the same reason it is not intended to commence production yet on new types of equipment.

13. The ship repair programme provides for maintenance of the active fleet at minimum level and for beginning the refitting of the large number of ships which because of manpower shortages had to be put into reserve without their normal refit. This is urgently necessary if the reserve fleet is not to suffer serious deterioration.

Naval Aviation

14. We have closely examined the requirements of naval aviation and at our instance the number of combat aircraft for which the Admiralty proposes to indent has been considerably reduced from the original figure …

20. … none of the Services proposes to initiate in the next financial year a policy of modernisation on any but the most modest scale … The stagnation imposed by the policy adopted in preparing this year's production estimates should therefore not be allowed to continue any longer than is absolutely necessary …

ANNEX I

ADMIRALTY

The main headings which go to make up the Admiralty total of £70,877,000 and the policy underlying these headings are as under:–

(a) *Warship Construction and Equipment …*	13,732.00
(b) *New Construction other than Warships …*	1,888.000
(c) *Ship Repairing …*	15,679,000
(d) *Technical Equipment …*	4,421,000
(e) *Naval Armament Stores …*	6,384,000
(f) *Machinery (other than for new construction) …*	6,100,000
(g) *Naval Aviation Requirements*	
(i) Aircraft (425 combat and 26 non-combat, plus backlog of 70 aircraft from 1946–47, and spare engines)	7,100.000
(ii) Aircraft spares, equipment and stores	3,000,000
(iii) Modifications and repairs etc	1,100,000
(iv) Production labour in Naval Aircraft Establishments	800,000
(h) *Non-Warlike Stores*	
(i) *Maintenance Stores …*	5,983,000
(ii) *Motor Transport …*	1,361,000

(iii) *Clothing, Mess Gear and Medical Stores* … 3,329,000

Net Admiralty requirement 70,877,000

…

APPENDIX A TO ANNEX I

Revised Aircraft Production Programme for the Royal Navy in 1947–48 by types:–

		Reduction
(i)	*Combat Aircraft* –	
80	Seafire 47 single-seat fighters instead of 100	20
135	Sea Fury single-seat fighters	…
120	Firefly IV strike/fighters	…
12	Sea Mosquito strike instead of 24	12
33	Sea Hornet strike/fighters-night fighters instead of 45	12
30	Sea Vampire jet fighters	…
15	Westland 17/46/P(N.11/44) strike/fighters	4
425	Combat aircraft instead of 473	48
(ii)	*Non-combat aircraft* –	
23	Sturgeon target towers for anti-aircraft exercises	7
3	Mosquito T.III dual trainers	…
No	Dove for communication duties instead of 2	2
No	Auster light trainers instead of 15	15
26	Non-combat aircraft instead of 50	24
(iii)	*Backlogs from the 1946–47 Production Programmes* –	
24	Firefly IV strike/fighters	…
23	Firebrand V single-seat strike instead of 59	24
11	Sea Hornet strike/fighters-night fighters	…
No	Westland 17/46/P(N.11/44) strike/fighters instead of 1	1
No	Spearfish bombers instead of 24	24
70	Aircraft instead of 119	49
	Total 521 aircraft instead of 642 aircraft, a reduction of	121

96. *Lang to Wilson Smith*[1]

[ADM 1/20417] 18 December 1946

Cuts in Naval Estimates

The following is the present situation:–

(a) Seagoing Fleet is, in several directions, below the minimum to meet peacetime commitments. Very little pruning is possible.

[1] J.D. Lang, Permanent Secretary to the Admiralty; Sir Henry Wilson Smith, Permanent Secretary at the Ministry of Defence.

(b) Reserve Fleet is below requirements in aircraft carriers, destroyers and escort vessels. It has not yet been possible to refit the majority of ships in reserve. The necessity for keeping so many destroyers and escort vessels is on account of the advent of the fast submarine which entails defence of convoys and fleets in depth and so more escorts. Air attack also entails more escorts owing to the need for air pickets.
(c) New Construction. Very little proceeding. A number of ships under construction have been suspended temporarily.
(d) Combined Operations. Assault lift for one Brigade Group is being kept principally in reserve.
(e) Naval Air. Owing to disappearance of hostilities personnel and of American type aircraft, this is being built up almost ab initio both in personnel and aircraft …
(f) Royal Marines. In process of reorganisation with a view to economy. Royal Marine Commandos are relieving Army personnel on garrison duties abroad.
(g) Training. A very large training commitment both of long and short service personnel and of conscripts exists owing to disappearance of hostilities officers and ratings. This entails an increased number of shore establishments and training afloat, including special training ships and squadrons.
(h) Fuel. A start is being made to build up fuel reserves which have fallen very low.

…

General Effect of Cuts

The following remarks are made regarding the general effect of the [proposed] cuts in relation to the build-up of the Post-War Fleet:–

(a) 10 Million Pound Cut
The long-term effect is not likely to be serious.

(b) 25 Million Pound Cut …
   (i) Gravely to lower the standard of training in the Fleet.
   (ii) To cripple the capacity of the Navy (particularly Naval Aviation) to expand.
   (iii) To reduce the capacity of the Dockyards to maintain the active Fleet.
   (iv) To abolish maintenance of the Reserve Fleet.
   (v) To reduce Combined Operations to an experimental basis.

The capacity of the Navy to meet a future emergency would thereby be seriously jeopardised immediately and the position would become progressively worse.

(c) 40 Million Pound Cut
The serious situation, which would have to be faced if the cuts proposed under this heading were imposed, is self-evident. The whole Naval structure would be radically undermined and it is considered that the cuts go far beyond the maximum by which the Naval estimates can be pruned if the Navy is to retain its capacity to maintain its present functions.

97. *Defence Committee Minutes*

[CAB 131/5] 14 January 1947

DO(47) 2nd Meeting Defence Estimates 1947–48

The Minister of Defence said that in the short time available he had endeavoured, with the assistance of the Service Ministers, the Minister of Supply and his military advisers, to integrate the three Service estimates for 1947–48, and to submit the overall requirements in a composite and balanced form in so far as this was possible. In the absence of a long-term defence policy the 1947–48 estimates were necessarily prepared on an *ad hoc* basis. He had, however, already initiated discussions with the Chiefs of Staff in regard to the preparation for the Defence Committee of long-term defence proposals which would take account of the changes in modern weapons and the advent of the United Nations Organisation.

When scrutinising the estimates submitted by the Service Departments, he had been influenced by two main factors; firstly, the necessity to meet current operational commitments and to provide the requisite backing of armed force for our foreign policy; secondly, the obligations assumed by the Government in regard to the release of manpower from the Services which entailed a rapid run-down in trained men after 1 January 1947, with a consequential training problem. Whereas the provision for the Services during the current financial year had been £1,667 million, the original figures submitted by Departments for 1947–48 had totalled £2,467 million, a reduction of £800 million. In spite of this substantial reduction in expenditure he had felt that further economies were possible and with the co-operation of the Service Departments he had succeeded in reducing these original figures by a further £100 million, bringing the total now submitted for 1947–48 to £968 million …

In the field of production, he was satisfied that all three Service Departments were continuing to make all possible use of existing stocks with the object of reducing their demands on new production to a minimum …

While he fully appreciated the vital need to economise and to balance the national budget, in his view any further major cuts in the estimates of the three Services would have such adverse effects that he would not be able to report to Parliament that the Services were either efficient or adequate to meet our obligations.

The Prime Minister said that, while balanced and efficient nucleus forces must be preserved for expansion in the event of war and adequate military backing for our foreign policy must be maintained, the money and manpower allotted to the Services must be within the national resources.

The Chancellor of the Exchequer ... questioned the proposed manpower ceiling of 189,000 for the Royal Navy and suggested that the manpower requirements of the Army and the RAF might also be reduced. He would favour making reductions in the Defence Estimates for 1947–48 on the understanding that higher Defence Estimates would be accepted in later years when the economic position might be less strained ...

The Committee considered the detailed man-power requirements of the Services.[1]

Royal Navy

The First Lord of the Admiralty, in explaining the man-power requirement of 189,000 for the Royal Navy, said that Naval Aviation now absorbed some 63,000 men as opposed to a comparable pre-war figure of some 8,000–9,000, which took account of the services then rendered by the RAF. There was a heavy manpower commitment of about 12,000 for the maintenance of some 300 ships in reserve, ranging from battleships to minesweepers; this maintenance was essential to prevent uneconomical deterioration. As regards ships now in commission, it was not possible to compare these with those in 1938, for technical equipment was now infinitely more complicated, requiring increased complements in ships and an increased training organisation.

The First Lord gave figures illustrating the increased man-power requirements in 1946 compared with 1938. For instance, the total of non-effectives, including those on courses, leave and sickness, was 58,000 as against 38,000; while the training requirement was 22,000 as against 12,200. Combined operations and Royal Marine Commandos called for an increase of some 9,500. Though the complement of ships in commission was 5,000 less in 1946 than in 1938, this was balanced by an increase of 4,500 in the reserve fleet. He also outlined the composition and disposition of the fleet in 1948 as shown in DO(46)135 Annex II (Appendix),

[1] The Defence Committee agreed to further review the financial and manpower requirements before submitting the Defence Estimates to the Cabinet.

emphasising that the complement of all ships in commission was one-fifth below their full requirement and that the naval forces abroad were the absolute minimum considered necessary to meet current commitments overseas.

He pointed out that at the outbreak of the late war the German Fleet possessed 65 submarines, whereas the Russian strength in submarines to-day was 230. In addition, the Russian fleet included 17 cruisers and 69 destroyers, a large proportion of which were new ships. The Royal Navy's superiority in ships in commission over the Russian Fleet was, therefore, small.

He stressed that any reduction in manpower would prejudice the efficiency of the fleet in 1951 and 1952; after the 1931 cuts it had been found impossible to increase the regular long-service component (for the build-up in 1934 and 1935) at a rate in excess of 1,500 a year and while some increase in this rate might now be achieved its probable magnitude could not be assessed. This factor, coupled with the fact that, as during the war the long-service intake had been curtailed, the target of 189,000 now contained a high proportion of trainees and only a relatively small number of long-service men, indicated that the manpower ceiling could not be reduced without affecting the rate of build-up of the long-service component …

98. *Plans Division Memorandum*

[ADM 1/20906] 26 February 1947

PD.012/47 1947 NEW CONSTRUCTION PROGRAMME
INTRODUCTION

By reason of the demand that expenditure in 1946 and 1947 should be reduced to a minimum, no Naval New Construction Programme was presented for 1946.

2. In order to meet what were considered essential current requirements for training and operational purposes, a 1947 New Construction Programme was submitted in PD.061/46 dated 16 December 1946 to DCNS. It contained items which had received Board approval or which were still under consideration by the Board, and also some items approved in previous programmes which had been amended from the original order.

3. In January 1947 and before PD.061/46 could be taken for consideration by the Board, the programme as submitted became obsolete for the following reasons:–

(a) The decision in D.21430/46 that items of new construction outstanding from previous programmes, on which it is not now proposed to start work in 1947/48, should be considered as definitely cancelled, and that fresh authority be sought through the annual Programme Statement to the Cabinet, should it become desirable at some future date to start work on such items.

(b) The cuts in the 1947/48 Naval Estimates, which it is understood are likely to limit the sum available for new construction to £270,000 during the financial year 1947/1948.

4. Proposals for the composition of the Post War Fleet, originally submitted PD.0140/45, and a proposed Programme of Replacement by New Construction, originally submitted in PD/0L.0204/45, have, therefore, had to be suspended. It is, however, abundantly clear that a considerable replacement by new construction is required as soon as it can be supported financially, and this is particularly so in the case of escort vessels. The very modest composition of the programme for presentation now proposed in this paper and which was proposed in PD.061/46, is therefore no true measure of Naval requirements, and is dictated solely by the requirements for the most stringent economy.

5. Meanwhile, some of the fruits of Research and Development should be more readily available for embodiment in future new construction, upon which it is hoped to be able to embark immediately the national economy permits.

6. OUTLINE OF REQUIREMENTS OF NEW CONSTRUCTION TO BE CONSIDERED FOR INCLUSION IN 1947/48 PROGRAMME

6 MINOTAUR Class Cruisers
2 New type Escort Vessels
1 Fleet Aircraft Direction Escort
2 New Design Submarines
2 Surveying Ships
1 Landing Craft Headquarters (by purchase from USA)
1 Landing Ship Dock
1 Prototype Landing Craft Personnel (Large)
2 Development Build-up Amphibians
1 Assault Amphibian
2 A/S Coastal Force Craft (from Fairmile M/Ls in reserve)
2 Convertible MTB/MGBs
6 High Speed Towed Targets
1 Prototype Small Expendable Distant Controlled Target
1 Hydrofoil Craft
Other Small Craft

Note:– 2 Fast Fleet Oilers are not included, as it was directed in TSD.2018/46 that they should be postponed for further consideration in the 1948/49 Programme.

7. For the above items, approval has been given or is sought as follows:–

(a) Board and Treasury Approval has already been given as follows:–

1941 Supplementary Programme	1 Cruiser of MINOTAUR Class
1944 Programme	5 Cruisers of MINOTAUR Class
1945 Programme	2 Fast Fleet Oilers
	1 New Design Submarine
	2 New type Escort Vessels
	2 'A' Class Surveying Vessels

(b) Board Approval only has been given for:–

The Fleet Aircraft Direction Escort
The 2nd New Design Submarine
The 2 Surveying Ships (PEGWELL BAY and THURSO BAY)
The 2 Development Build-up Amphibians
The 2 A/S Coastal Force Craft
The 2 Convertible MTB/MGBs
The Prototype Landing Craft Personnel (Large)
Design work on the Prototype Small Expendable Distant Controlled Target

(c) COS Approval has been given for:–

The Landing Craft Headquarters
The Landing Ship Dock

…

25. In considering the limited amount of money likely to be available for the foregoing projects, it is recommended that they should be placed in the following order of priority:–

(a) 2 New Design Submarines. These are to be fast submarines with a new type of propulsion. It will be from trials and exercises with them that we shall be guided in the selection of the most effective tactics, weapons, and training to be adopted to counter an enemy threat.

(b) 2 New Type Escort Vessels. Escort Vessels will be of predominant importance for the defence of our sea communications in any future emergency, to meet the threat of attack by enemy aircraft and submarines. We are already short of the estimated number required, and many of such as we possess are ill-armed and too slow for the war of the future to deal with the fast submarine and modern air weapons. It is from these prototype new Escort Vessels that we hope to obtain the necessary information on which to base mass production by prefabricated methods to expand in the future.

(c) 1 Fleet Aircraft Direction Escort. The necessity to progress with this type of ship was clearly shown in the war in the Pacific.

(d) 2 of the 4 Surveying Vessels. There is an acute shortage of Surveying Vessels to carry out the vast amount of outstanding and essential surveys.

99. *Report by the Principal Personnel Officers' Committee*

[DEFE 5/1] 19 March 1947

PPO/P(47)24(Final) MANPOWER –
STRENGTH OF THE ARMED FORCES AT 31 MARCH 1948

It will be recalled that, in his memorandum[1] on the Defence Estimates 1947–48 the Minister of Defence estimated the following numbers of men and women to be serving in the Forces on 31 March 1948:–

Navy	189,000
Army	590,000
RAF	315,000
Total	1,094,000

2. These figures were based on the estimates of the Chiefs of Staff[2] of the size of the Forces considered necessary … The figure for the Navy was subsequently reduced by 7,000 and the total figure of 1,087,000 was incorporated in … the Statement Relating to Defence (Cmd.7042).

3. We feel it to be our duty to inform the Minister of Defence, the Service Ministers and the Chiefs of Staff of the present position. There is, in our opinion, a grave risk of an unacceptable shortage in the more highly trained and responsible elements in all three Services …

4. The present rate of voluntary recruitment direct from civil life must be regarded as creditable in all three Services …

5. Recruitment (under the 'Bounty' scheme) of trained personnel and re-engagements have not been satisfactory in any Service and it is on this account that the greatest anxiety is felt.

[1] DO(47)4, not reproduced.

[2] DO(46)135, reproduced above as Doc. No. 92.

ROYAL NAVY

Male ratings

6. The situation on 31 December 1946 was …:–

Regular engagements	84,000	
Bounty engagements	4,000	
National Service	83,500	
Male rating strength of Navy	171,500	(excluding 3,000 locally-entered personnel abroad)

…

7. During 1946 the Navy obtained volunteers … as follows:–

Regular re-entries	1,255
Bounty engagements	3,964
Regular recruits from civil life	16,440
WRNS	2,460
	24,119

…

9. There are indications that the Navy will meet its immediate target of 19,500 volunteer male rating recruits from civil life in 1947. It is necessary to increase this to about 22,500 a year to build up the regular strength of the Navy to 144,000 officers and men in 1951.

10. The response to the Bounty scheme has not been so good … If this continues it will be reflected in a low strength of the Navy in 1949–1951.

11. The burden of training men for short term … National Service is a heavy drain on both manpower and accommodation whilst the regular strength is being built up …

13. The Navy is fortunate in having an adequate number of Chief Petty Officers and Petty Officers … but there is a very marked shortage of leading ratings and experienced able rates …

15. The very large number of men released since VE Day has left the Navy, like other services, unbalanced … the resultant effect is that ships and establishments are kept going at a lower standard of operational efficiency …

PART III

THE NINE-YEAR PLAN, MARCH 1947 – NOVEMBER 1948

Until early 1947 attempts to plan the postwar Fleet lacked much by way of overall strategic guidance, and were constantly buffeted by ever-increasing demands for immediate savings in both money and manpower. Henceforth, the Chiefs of Staff were able to plan ahead with a little more consistency and the Admiralty's plans for the Navy reflected this. The process began in March 1947 with a large study by the Joint Planners *Review of Defence Problems* [100]. Perhaps the key conclusion, or at least assumption, was that a deliberately started war was unlikely before 1956. This was soon to be translated into a planning target of 1957 as the date when the Forces needed to be ready for such an event. The forces required for this reflected the experience of the recent war with an emphasis on carriers and escorts. It still assumed a period of warning during which a large reserve fleet could be brought into service.

This work was then carried forward to propose a *Future Defence Policy* published by the Chiefs of Staff in May [102], the first postwar attempt to establish an overarching policy for the composition and employment of the Armed Forces. The Soviet Union was now recognised as a 'potential enemy' who might have atomic weapons by 1956–57 (The Russians were to explode their first device in 1949) and Britain 'must have the active and very early support of the United States'. Defence priorities were the UK base, the Middle East and control of sea communications. The paper re-iterated that the main threats to the latter were submarines, air attack and minelaying. The new Defence Policy was approved by the Prime Minister on 11 June [103]; 'The United Kingdom [now] had an approved anti-Soviet defence strategy.'[1] In parallel, the Planners made more detailed recommendations about the naval forces that would be required on the outbreak of war [101].

Meanwhile, the Board considered the future of naval aviation [104]. The aspirations set out in 1945 [23] remained largely in place but given an RN manpower limitation of 170,000 the plan would have to be moderated to 10 carriers in commission with 450 front-line aircraft. Under already approved programmes, by 1956 the RN would have 24 carriers but on the outbreak of war would require 30. A large programme of modernisation was required even to achieve the lower figure as most existing carriers could not operate modern aircraft. These numbers were of course wholly unrealistic and even after the country started to re-arm in the early 1950s nothing like these totals was ever achieved.

In July the Defence Committee approved a revised Construction Programme for 1947–48 [105, 106]. In view of extant shipbuilding from

[1]Lewis, *Changing Direction*, p. 334.

earlier programmes (12 carriers, three cruisers, 16 destroyers plus smaller vessels) the new programme was confined to a single submarine, two survey ships and a number of amphibious vessels. The six big cruisers, previously cancelled from the 1941 and 1944 programmes, were not re-instated as DofP had suggested in February [98].

The explicit identification of the Soviet Union as a threat prompted the Joint Planning Staff to review the state of preparedness of the Forces [107]. Their conclusions were gloomy, but mitigated by the view that the Russians were not in much better shape [109]. They did, however, have an estimated 230 submarines; Germany had started the recent war with just 65.

By now an intensifying financial crisis was putting further pressure on the Forces to reduce commitments and capabilities [108], led by the Prime Minister himself,[1] which was to lead in succeeding months to repeated reviews of the future shape and size of the Forces. These reviews saw an increasing tension between the needs of the recently adopted defence policy and a growing awareness of the Soviet threat on the one hand, and the pressing needs for economy on the other. Risks would have to be taken.[2] 'Given [the] economic and political background, it is a little disappointing that the Admiralty's policy makers could not be more realistic in their future fleet planning.'[3]

The 1957 planning target led to occasional references to the 'nine-year plan' though in reality this remained more a timescale than a single plan. A detailed Admiralty report for the Chiefs of Staff [110, 111] on naval peacetime requirements over the same time period, again optimistically, identified the need for six battleships, 31 carriers, 35 cruisers, 80 submarines and over 400 destroyers and escorts plus modest contributions from the Dominions; 211,500 men and women would be required in peacetime. Tellingly, 'there was no hope of the Government authorising expenditure on the scale envisaged'. No explanation was offered for the size of forces required, 'a good illustration of the unrealistic … terms in which the Naval Staff were still thinking',[4] or how they might be employed against the likely enemy, the Soviet Navy.

In the meantime, the short-term future was considered by DofP [112]. The projected regular and conscript numbers would mean a shortfall of over 15,000 personnel by March 1949. This required a revised forecast

[1]DO(47)63, 2 Aug 1947 in CAB 131/4, not reproduced.

[2]DO(47) 22nd meeting, 29 Sept 1947 in CAB 151/5, not reproduced.

[3]Grove, *Vanguard to Trident*, p. 31.

[4]Grove, *Vanguard to Trident*, p. 34.

of the Fleet's dispositions over the same period and the disposal of some older battleships and cruisers.

In August the Board had to re-examine its recent long-term plan in the light of a probable annual budget of £180 million out of a defence total of £600 million [113–15]. The Navy's budget could even be as low as £160 million [116]. Any build-up of forces would be postponed for five years and resources concentrated on maintenance and modernisation of existing ships (especially carriers). The only new construction would be prototypes. Ships in commission, with either full or reduced complements, would total three battleships, nine carriers, 16 cruisers, a little over 100 destroyers and escorts, 40 submarines plus smaller and auxiliary units. By the end of 1951 the Navy would consist of 157,000 personnel. The scale of cuts being asked for would 'seriously impair the ability of the Navy … when the risk of war increases' [117].

In September A.V. Alexander, by now Minister of Defence, presented a consolidated tri-service plan to the Defence Committee [118]. Financial pressures and the need to release more manpower for the civilian economy were, as ever, the driving forces though it was now hoped to arrive at longer-term conclusions and in particular for the financial year 1948–49 (which wasn't so long-term). Despite a target for overall defence spending of £600 million, the Minister could only bring spending down to £711 million, and that was by accepting strategic risk (which he did not quantify). For the Navy, it meant a budget of £155 million and further manpower reductions to a total of 147,000 by 31 March 1949. A large part of the Reserve Fleet, which cost money and manpower to maintain, would be scrapped including five battleships and 11 cruisers. Overseas squadrons would be smaller and much of (a greatly reduced) Home Fleet would be immobilised in 1947–48. The Navy's National Service intake would be a token 2,000 out of a combined services total of 150,000. In subsequent Defence Committee discussions [119, 120] the scale of disruption to the Navy the proposed reductions would inflict was made clear; "I do not see how the Navy can possibly do more". At the end of the month the Prime Minister accepted the risks entailed and the proposals were approved [121]. This probably represented the low-point for the postwar Navy.

With a £600 million defence budget still the Government's intention, the Joint Planning Staff was directed to examine the long-term size and shape of the armed forces [122]. The JPS was blunt. The force structure they developed was 'the barest minimum … neither strong in all arms nor fully equipped with modern weapons … There is no question of our recommending them.' But it would still cost, not £600 million but £740 million, of which £208 million would be spent on the Navy (the smallest amount of the three Services). If further cuts were required, DofP suggested that the Navy and Air Force should have priority – an early example of inter-service wrangling over resources.

The Admiralty's assessment of its required forces assumed a heavy reliance on the United States, but this fleet still could not be accommodated within a £600m defence budget. Once again, though listing the forces required in peacetime and on the outbreak of war, the Admiralty's submission said little about how these requirements had been derived, other than that they would provide a single 'Battle Force' and the ability to escort four convoys at a time. The Americans would have to provide half the convoy escorts and there would be no amphibious force.

While the implications of this dire position were being considered [123], the Board turned its attention to carrier modernisation [124]. A detailed study had shown that only the six largest ships under construction, and none of those already in service, would be able to operate all modern aircraft types by 1952. There were three elements to the problem; the completion of the *Ark Royal* and *Hermes* classes, modernisation of the six existing fleet carriers, and completion/modernisation of the *Colossus*- and *Majestic*-class light fleet carriers, some of which were destined for Australia and Canada.

The Admiralty also made proposals to the Defence Committee on the disposal of ships in reserve [125, 126]. The principal outcome was to demonstrate that with five modern battleships (and Russia possessing none) there was no case for also retaining five older ships, which were therefore to be scrapped.

At the beginning of 1948 the Defence Committee considered the outcome of the attempts to shape the armed forces within the £600m budget [127]. It was explicit that a risk of war must be accepted, and that the risk would increase from about 1952 onwards until 1957. Thereafter the Forces must be strong enough to deter war. The threats were the 'Cold War' (perhaps the first time the phrase appeared), the risk of a 'conventional war' in the near future and a risk of atomic war after 1957. These required a deterrent striking force, the defence of the UK, safeguarding sea communications and the defence of overseas bases. The immediate need for economy was accepted, but increases in defence spending would be required within two to three years. In the short term, existing commitments would see the largest expenditure on the Army but neither the Chief of the Air Staff nor the First Sea Lord accepted that this position should endure. On 15 January the Defence Committee confirmed that a figure of £600 million per annum after 1948–49 would be allocated to Defence.[1]

[1]DO(48) 3rd Meeting, CAB 131/5, not reproduced.

The resultant force structure for the Navy would leave it with a peacetime fleet in commission of three battleships, 10 carriers, 17 cruisers, over 100 destroyers and escorts, 40 submarines and 300 frontline aircraft. Even allowing for the growing obsolescence of this force, from today's perspective it is still an impressive fleet, the world's second-largest (apart from submarines) and maintained at a time of national economic emergency.

In January it was also confirmed that the date of 1957 should be adopted for all planning purposes, including rearmament [128], almost a new 'Ten-Year Rule' and formalising the 'nine-year plan'.

Reverting to shorter-term matters, in March 1948 DofP produced a useful audit of ships in commission and those forecast for the end of 1950 [129]. By then there would be no battleships in commission as manning anti-submarine escorts and minesweepers was a higher priority. The fleet in commission would include nine carriers, 15 cruisers, 73 frigates and destroyers, 42 submarines and 12 ocean minesweepers, requiring 30,400 men for ships in full commission out of a total of 147,000. The reality at the time, however, was somewhat different. In the Home Fleet only a single cruiser and five destroyers were fully operational.[1]

In line with the 1957 planning date, the Planners in conjunction with the Joint Intelligence Committee produced a forecast for that year [130]. Notwithstanding the decisions already made concerning battleships it assumed that, including Commonwealth forces, on the outbreak of war there would be three battleships available plus 13 carriers, 21 cruisers and 140 destroyers and frigates.

A review of the naval aircraft programme [131] reiterated the already known inability of most existing carriers to operate modern aircraft. Even the recently modernised *Illustrious* would only be able to take the turboprop Gannet. Aircraft under development or consideration included what later became the mainstay of the Fleet Air Aim in the 1960s, the Buccaneer, Sea Vixen, Scimitar and Gannet.

In June the JIC returned to forecasting the situation in the key date of 1957 [132]. Still predicting the presence of battleships in the Fleet their report estimated that, with *four months*' notice of the outbreak of war (for mobilisation to be ordered), at the start of hostilities the Fleet would include a wholly unrealistic (and largely unmodernised) total of over 350 destroyers and frigates in addition to 17 carriers.

More usefully, the JIC estimated that the Soviet fleet in 1957 would include 33 cruisers, 113 destroyers and approximately 500 submarines,

[1] 'State of the Home Fleet 1 March 1948' in ADM 205/69, not reproduced.

split between Northern Europe (including the Baltic), the Black Sea and the Far East. The report cast doubt on the efficiency of much of this force. Somewhat bizarrely, the JIC had a much firmer grasp on the scale of future Russian capabilities than it did Britain's own.

In preparation for a new paper on the size and shape of the armed forces, in July DofP updated the roles of the Navy [133]. Existing tasks were re-stated; the control of sea communications, denying the use of the sea to the enemy, to move and sustain the Air Force and Army, to provide sea-based air support and to assist the RAF with the strategic air offensive (a highly contentious ambition). To these was added a caveat that the Navy would have insufficient strength to perform all these roles, but would need to be able to control the North Atlantic and the Mediterranean and deny them to the enemy whilst maintaining a sufficient nucleus to build up forces for the other tasks.

In the same month detail was added to the use of 1957 as the date for force planning purposes [134]. Admiralty departments were instructed to prioritise technical developments which could produce new weapons by that date. Only then could attention be turned to longer-term projects. An annex detailing the Fleet for 1957 once again featured battleships plus a significant number of carriers and cruisers, and over 300 destroyers and frigates. 1957 was starting to look like an assumption-based planning guide rather than an objective prediction, and future force levels looked equally unrealistic.

A major review of the 'Defence Position', essentially a stocktake, was undertaken in the summer of 1948 [136, 137], as a response to a growing awareness of the poor state of Britain's defences and the worsening of the international situation (the Berlin Blockade had started on the 24 June). The deficiencies identified (in addition to inadequate numbers) were staff, manpower, equipment, ammunition and fuel – which didn't leave much by way of strengths. The Navy had 145,000 personnel (much less than either of the other two services). It would not be able to carry out all its tasks in the event of war, but its strength compared to the Russians was better than the Army or Air Force comparisons. The forces were 'not in a fit state … to commence a major war' as a direct consequence of current policy to prepare for 1957.

On 30 July the Defence Committee decided, in response to increased tensions with the Soviets, to improve preparedness with all steps that could be taken without publicity and without serious economic impact. Defence priorities in the event of war were set out: first, the defence of the UK and sea approaches; second, control of sea communications; third, the Middle East. Provision of bases for the US Air Force and for fighting on the Continent were less important, and no mention whatever was made of the Far East. Immediate tasks for the Navy in improving its preparedness were refits of escorts and smaller craft, updating equipment in ships and preparation of naval aircraft and armament stores [138]. The financial caveat meant that the measures taken were modest, but did suggest that the 1957 planning date might be too late.

A further stocktake in September concluded 'that the present state of the forces gives the gravest cause for alarm' [139, 140]. A table attached to the report identified serious deficiencies in carriers, escorts and minesweepers. The Services were instructed to review their peacetime manpower requirements, which the Second Sea Lord reported was 160,600 for the Navy [141], over 15,000 more than currently authorised [139].

In October yet another review of the future size and shape of the Forces looked ahead to 1949, 1952 and 1957 [142]. By the latter date it was planned to have in commission four battleships (which had now re-appeared), eight carriers, 19 cruisers, 118 destroyers and frigates, 51 minesweepers and 45 submarines; an impressive force though the number of carriers looks very low in relation both to previously stated requirements and the numbers of large gun-armed ships (battleships and cruisers).

Another area of concern was guided weapons, on which progress was slow [143]. The Admiralty expressed dissatisfaction with their management by the air side of the Ministry of Supply, though little action seems to have been taken. Sea Slug was wanted in service by 1956 but actually took another six years after that to bring into operational service.

100. *Joint Planning Staff Memorandum*

[CAB 84/84] 31 March 1947

JP(46)164 (Final) REVIEW OF DEFENCE PROBLEMS[1]

SECTION IX

THE SHAPE AND SIZE OF THE FORCES

…

508. The principal factors, apart from manpower, affecting the shape and size of the forces over the next ten to fifteen years and possibly longer are:–

The risk of war and the probable warning.
The nature of future war and its probable duration.
Disarmament.
Expansion requirements in war.
Our relations with the United States.
Extent of responsibilities accepted by the Dominions.
Conscription.
Availability of equipment
Research and development.
National economic position …

509. … we have concluded that:–

(a) The risk of accidental war is more apparent than real and should diminish with the settlement of immediate post-war problems.
(b) Planned war is unlikely before 1956.
(c) From about 1956–1960 there is likely to be a critical period in international relations …

510. The implications of these conclusions are:–

(a) We should at present aim at raising the level of our armed forces to the strength necessary to meet our minimum defence requirements by 1956.
(b) We must decide on the general pattern of re-equipment on the basis of scientific development over the next few years and be prepared to go into production to achieve the greatest measure of re-equipment by 1956. For economic reasons, however, rearmament may have to be subordinated to our economic recovery for at least the next five years.
(c) … we should at present plan on a period of about twelve months in which to complete our preparations.

…

[1] Signed by DofP, Captain C. Lambe, for the Navy.

517. The Navy in future war, apart from a greatly reduced surface threat, is likely to be faced with responsibilities for the defence of shipping similar to, but heavier than, those in the past and may well be deprived of some of its base facilities in the United Kingdom soon after the outset of war. It is improbable, however, that the enemy threat to sea communications will develop as quickly as that directed by aerial bombardment against the United Kingdom itself …

… warships cannot be produced in large numbers in a short time and the Navy must, therefore, take greater account of the possibility of a long war than the other Services.

…

531. … the requirements of the three Services … may be summarised as follows:–

Royal Navy		
Battleships	Nil*	* 5 Battleships in Reserve.
Carriers	30	
Cruisers	25	
Destroyers	96	
Escorts	250	
Submarines	80	
Minesweepers	198	
Amphibious Forces	–	
Fleet Train	–	

532. We estimate that the manpower needed to provide these forces will amount to 2,305,500 made up as follows:–

Royal Navy	*Army*	*Royal Air Force*
328,500	1,377,000	600,000

…

Forces Required at Outbreak of War

Naval Forces

Battleships

534. Large-scale engagements by heavy surface forces are only likely in the next war if Russia builds her own or uses captured battleships. In consequence we have recommended that the five existing modern battleships should be kept in reserve … and all other battleships should be scrapped now.

Carriers

535. We envisage that the main roles of naval aircraft will be anti-submarine and air defence. Air striking forces against either enemy ships or shore targets are only likely to be needed at a much lower priority. It is therefore more on numbers of small carriers rather than a few large carriers that we should concentrate.

536. Whatever type or size of carrier force we possess in future, however, there will be a need for a far greater degree of cooperation between carrier-borne and shore-based maritime air forces than even in the last war. A continuing study of the joint air/naval problem of controlling sea communications must, therefore, be carried on in peace …

Escorts

537. We do not yet know what design of escort vessel is required against the fast submarine. It is, however, clear that our existing ships will, almost without exception, be of insufficient speed to hunt a submarine to a kill. As soon as research renders it possible, therefore, it is of prime importance that an annual building programme for escort vessels be started without delay.

Submarines

538. One quarter of the planned submarine strength of 80 is required for anti-submarine training and such submarines must be of modern type. The remainder are required for attack on enemy seaborne movement, reconnaissance and intelligence. Allowing one submarine out of five on patrol at any one time, the resulting effective strength is undoubtably small. It is axiomatic that if we are to be strong in anti-submarine defence, we must be ahead in offensive submarine development. There may also be big developments in the use of submarines against submarines.

Amphibious Forces

539. We foresee no need in the early stages of a war for assault forces as employed in World War II. There will, however, be early and urgent call for amphibious forces capable of moving formations rapidly from beach to beach and for beach maintenance. These must exist in peacetime.

…

The Size of the Forces in Peace

551. … we have examined our minimum defence requirements with a view to reducing the size of the permanent forces in peace and, in the case of the Navy and Army, we have found it possible to recommend permanent peacetime establishments considerable smaller than those considered at the outbreak of war …

553. Disregarding the temporary commitments created by post-war conditions, we have examined … the forces we consider we must maintain on a permanent basis in peace, on the assumption that we must be able to expand these up to our minimum requirements at the outbreak of war, given twelve months' warning … the minimum active forces we consider necessary are summarised below:–

Royal Navy		
Battleships	2*	* For experiment and Training
Carriers	12	
Cruisers	18	
Destroyers	73	
Escorts	40	
Submarines	30	
Minesweepers	16	
Amphibious Forces	–	
Fleet Train	–	

554. The total manpower required by the Services in peace is estimated as being about 1,016,250 men, made up as follows:–

RN	185,250	(including 21,000 National Servicemen)
Army	431,000	(including 166,000 National Servicemen)
RAF	400,000	(including 45,000 National Servicemen)

…

The Cost in Manpower and Money

566. The provision and maintenance of the forces we recommend will require … will entail an estimated annual expenditure, excluding Research and Development, or the order of £835 million, made up as follows:–

	£ million
Royal Navy	190
Army	345
Royal Air Force	300

567. Although under the most favourable circumstances it is improbable that we could create the forces recommended in less than five to seven years and probably equally true that the full cost of modernising their equipment would not arise any earlier, we realise that the target expenditure exceeds that provisionally forecast by the Minister of Defence for a normal peacetime year by nearly 40 per cent.

…

ANNEX N

THE SHAPE AND SIZE OF THE ROYAL NAVY

The factors affecting the shape and size of the Royal Navy

1. … the Naval Forces required in the various theatres of was have been assessed against the background of our proposed British strategy for a war against Russia in 1956 in which the United States is allied to us but not necessarily from the very start.

This background now requires amplification in order to justify the assessment made and to expound the many assumptions upon which our calculations are based.

The threat to sea communications

2. Unless Russia launches a big building programme of capital ships and carriers, the chief threat to our sea communications will be initially confined to:–

Fast submarines.
Shore-based air attack.
Minelaying in coastal waters.

The surface raider, even if used in small numbers, will find it increasingly difficult to remain undetected as the range of shore-based aircraft and the efficiency of radar increase. We must be prepared to destroy such ships.

It is therefore primarily against the above methods of attack that the future Navy will be required to shield the sea communications of the Commonwealth at the outbreak of war.

At a later stage in the war, there is the possibility of Russian naval strength being increased by the cooperation of part at least of the French Navy and by units of other Western European Powers. We do not, however, consider that this accretion of enemy strength will materialise within the first three months.

Expansion of the Navy during the period of warning

3. Unlike the other Services, the Navy possesses the valuable ability to maintain its weapons in reserve in peace. Excepting naval aircraft, there is no reason why a proportion of the wartime fleet should not be kept in reserve but ready for action within the warning period which we foresee. This period is unlikely to exceed one year.

4. Given an adequate number of peacetime trained reservists, a proper reserve of stores and a steady and continuous programme of modernising and refitting of our reserve ships and weapons, there is no reason why more than a proportion of the naval forces required in war should be kept in full commission in peace. This proportion must, however, be adequate to meet the peacetime calls upon the Navy and to support on service and in the reserves the number of highly trained and experienced personnel required on mobilisation.

5. This proportion is, however, much higher in the case of aircraft carriers than in other types of ship since the expansion of this part of naval force is governed by the rate at which the aircraft industry can be expanded as well as by the limitations imposed on the size of the reserve of aircrews and maintenance staffs and by the need to keep them in constant practice.

6. Parallel with this is the need for an increased anti-submarines and A/A School capacity to compete with the heavy programme of refresher training which will be required for reservists at the outbreak of a war and

for the big expansion of this type of training which will undoubtably be hurriedly needed if the war becomes drawn-out. A proportion of the school capacity might well be overseas but it must be in existence and properly equipped before the emergency arises.

Naval Reserves

7. It should thus be our aim to build up reserves of trained naval manpower upon the following principles:–

(a) The qualification and experience of men in the various regular reserves must be such that when, upon expansion, the national service reserve men are added to their number and the whole added to the peacetime strength of the Navy, the consequent dilution of skill is not unacceptable.

(b) Numbers available in reserve must be sufficient to meet the maximum possible rate of intake during the warning period and first few months of war.

(c) The period of warning will not exceed one year and may be as little as six months.

(d) The full strength of the Reserve Fleet (less about one-eighth refitting) will be available for manning and operations at not more than one year's notice and a large proportion at six months or less.

(e) If war breaks out at shorter notice than that envisaged, priority of commissioning of types of ships will be dictated by the rate of development of the various enemy threats (eg it may be necessary to accelerate the commissioning of reserve escort vessels at the expense of reserve minesweepers).

(f) Reserves must also be suitable to cover the various and extra calls upon naval manpower which will arise from the outbreak of war, eg ratings for merchant ships, port and base staffs, harbour defences, extra communications etc, for at least the first four months of war.

Further expansion after the start of the war

8. No allowance has been made for a rate of intake after the outbreak of war in excess of that of the preceding months for the following reasons:–

(a) If we are to hold the ring for the first few months without allies, we cannot afford to withdraw personnel from active operations to expand naval training.

(b) If the war is to be fought to a successful conclusion, the active support of the United States as a belligerent is imperative within three months. This in itself will provide a considerable expansion of the naval strength available to the Allies.

9. Once America declares war, the effective strength of the Royal Navy would have to be cut in order to start the expansion programme which, though late in time, would be necessitated by the prospect of a long war.

Concept of Naval Operational Bases

10. In World War II, the inadequacy of the Scapa Flow defences forced upon us at least a temporary dispersion of our home naval forces amongst lesser anchorages. New forms of potential attack on fleet anchorages in another war will force similar measures upon us, at least at the outset, in the British Isles and eastern Mediterranean. It must therefore be our aim:

(a) To avoid as far as possible basing naval forces in the neighbourhood of important economic targets.
(b) To base as great a proportion as possible of our Atlantic forces on the North American continent.
(c) To be prepared to use remote anchorages such as Loch Ewe, Bantry Bay, Tobruk and Benghazi to the greatest extent possible.
(d) To provide means whereby operational bases can be easily moved from one anchorage to another (eg Fleet Support Ships).

The Navy by Types of Ship

11. With this background it is possible to draw certain conclusions as to the shape and size of the Commonwealth naval forces required to be operational at the start of a war in 1956.

Battleships

12. In war, we shall only require battleships in the unlikely event of Russia having built this type of ship or if Russia employs captured French battleships. In peace, however, such ships are of great value in place of shore training establishments.

The four King George V class and Vanguard should be kept in reserve against this contingency or for eventual conversion to heavy GAP ships. All other battleships should be scrapped now unless required for accommodation.

At a cost of 1,250 men, we regard this reserve as a reasonable insurance against unforeseen developments.

Carriers

13. Naval aircraft will be required for the following main roles:

(a) Anti-submarine.
(b) Air defence of naval forces and convoys.
(c) Reconnaissance and airborne early warning.
(d) Striking enemy warships or coastal shipping.
(e) Army support.

The last three roles will require insignificant numbers of aircraft compared to the first two.

14. In all the above roles, naval aircraft will be cooperating with shore-based RAF aircraft. The numbers and types of carriers will therefore depend upon:–

(a) The frequency of convoys in areas open to submarine attack.
(b) The frequency of convoys in areas open to enemy air attack.
(c) The scope of maritime cooperation to be provided by the RAF.
(d) The size and organisation of our heavier naval surface forces.
(e) The scale of attack required on enemy seaborne movement.
(f) The probable requirements for reinforcement and replenishment of aircraft.

15. Conditions in the United Kingdom will probably necessitate the basing of our Atlantic trade defence carriers on Canada. The point at which a homeward-bound convoy is transferred to RAF air escorts based in the UK will require nice judgement, bearing in mind the risk run by the carrier herself on the one hand and the effort needed to maintain adequate air escort from shore bases on the other …

16. … the total number of carriers required at the outbreak of war is tentatively estimated at 34 of which the majority will be of the Trade Defence type …

(a) Home and Mediterranean Battle Forces	8
(b) Anti-Air and Anti-submarine support of convoys	12
(c) Trials and Training	3
(d) Far East Defence and Trade Protection	2
(e) Reserves for above	6
(f) Ferry Carriers	3
Total	34

Cruisers

17. The functions of a cruiser in 1956 will be:–

(a) Heavy or Medium A/A defence.
(b) medium anti-surface-ship escort.

Cruisers may also be of use as bombarding ships … but this role is of minor importance … The GAP is unlikely to be in production in quantity by 1956 but it may be fitted in the first hulls … we estimate the requirement is:–

(a) Home and Mediterranean Battle Forces	12
(b) Close escort of vital convoys	4
(c) Four hunting groups	8
(d) Reserves	6
Total	30

It will be of great importance that as many cruisers as possible are converted to A/A as their primary role before the outbreak of war.

Destroyers

18. Until our last war anti-submarines escorts are replaced by new construction of greater speed, the destroyer is the only class of ship capable of hunting a modern fast submarine successfully ... The function of the destroyer will not greatly change in other respects.

(a) Home and Mediterranean Battle Forces		48
(b) Hunting groups		24
(c) Reserves		34
	Total	106

High-speed surface ships will be at a premium in the anti-U-boat battle and no present day destroyers which are capable of being made operational in 1956 should be scrapped.

Escorts

19. Many of our existing escorts are likely to be incapable of modification to the needs of attack and defence against the future fast submarine. The need to replace such ships by new construction is therefore urgent ... Although the Navy is always likely to have uses for small ships in numbers, we must be certain that our ability to construct new escorts ... is not unduly impaired by the cost in manpower and money of retaining in reserve obsolete ships for which no *immediate* use can be foreseen at the start of another war ...

A recent theoretical appreciation of the numbers of escort vessels required ... arrived at a figure of 636 ... clearly beyond our capabilities and, for 1956, we estimate ...:–

(a) Convoy Escort (10 groups)		120
(b) Independent hunting		60
(c) Coastal convoys		50
(d) Support of Fleet operations		50
	Total	280

Pickets

20. Pickets ... will be required:–

(a) To give early warning ...

(b) To control fighter operations ...

2 Battle forces, 6 each		12
Reserve		3
	Total	15

Submarines

21. If we are to be strong in anti-submarine defence, we must be ahead in offensive submarine development. Submarines are also required for training in A/S warfare, reconnaissance, intelligence and attack on important enemy seaborne movement and may, in future, be used more and more as anti-submarine vessels. To maintain one submarine

continuously on patrol at any distance … requires five submarines … we estimate the following numbers are needed:–

UK theatre		40
Mediterranean		20
Training		20
	Total	80

Minesweepers

22. … The minesweeping technique of 1956 cannot yet be adequately forecast … the estimate below cannot be more than a guess at present:–

(a) Fleet minesweepers		48
(b) Danlayers		12
(c) Coastal minesweepers		138
	Total	198

Amphibious Forces

23. We foresee no requirement for assault operations against defended positions in the early years of another war … our effort … should be confined to experimental development. There is, however, a very great need to be able immediately to move Army and Air forces rapidly … upon such moves, the success of our strategy in the Middle East may well depend … amphibious forces, organised for rapid beach movement and supply rather than for assault, should exist in peacetime. We have assessed the minimum requirement … as a lift for one Brigade Group.

Logistic Support

24. … The Fleet Train requirement … is estimated … at about three-quarters of the support for the fleet planned for the Pacific in 1946.

Miscellaneous

25. … a requirement for Boom Defence, Surveying Ships, Coastal Craft, Net Layers etc.

Dominion Contribution

26. Present indications are that, in peace, the Dominions will maintain the following naval forces either in commission or in ready reserve …:–

	Carriers	*Cruisers*	*Destroyers*	*Escorts*
Canada	1	2	10	12
Australia	2	2	10	12
New Zealand	1	1	5	6
Totals	4	5	25	30

…

Manpower Required for the Royal Navy at Outbreak of War

28. It is estimated that, to man the fleet … above, including trainees, wartime shore commitments etc, a gross manpower figure of some 328,000 men and women is needed.

Capacity to Expand

29. There are two main limitations on the Navy's capacity for expansion:–

    (a) Dilution of skill and experience must not exceed a certain proportion if ships are to remain efficient for operations.
    (b) The rate at which men called up can be redeployed to their wartime billets.

30. The skilled reserves available to the Navy in an emergency consist broadly of pensioned officers, pensioned men (22 years' service), Royal Fleet Reserve men (12 or 7 years' service) and the various ancilliary reserves such as the RNR, RNVR and RN Patrol Service … the greater part Leading Rate or above. [For] … unskilled we have numbers of National Servicemen, few of whom [are] … up to Able Seaman standard …

31. We are advised that … the peacetime strength of the Navy should be half of 328,500, ie 164,250.

32. There is also the physical limitation to the rate at which men can be called up and redeployed to their wartime billets … at 10,000 per month in sixteen months we should be able to increase from a peacetime strength of 164,250 to the required figure of 328,500 and, on this count also, it would appear that a regular strength in peace of not less than 164,250 is required.

…

35. The expansion in emergency of naval aviation is, however, limited chiefly by the time taken to train pilots and skilled maintenance ratings (two years), the rate at which the aircraft industry can expand and the rate at which merchant ships can be converted into trade defence carriers.

36. … in order to expand a peacetime force of … twelve carriers to twenty, within five months of mobilisation, the following measures would be necessary:–

    (a) A peacetime strength of 500 aircrews and first-line aircraft.
    (b) A first-line reserve of 300 aircrews and aircraft.
    (c) A stored reserve of 500 operational aircraft.
    (d) A monthly peacetime production of eighty-five aircraft.
    (e) A warning period of one year to eighteen months.

…

Strength of Reserves required for War

37. From the foregoing … the total reserve strength of the Navy also needs to be of the order of 164,250 men and women. By mid-1957, on present plans, the following reserves of trained men and women (excluding National Servicemen) should be available …:–

Regular Reserves		57,000
Ancilliary Reserves		25,000
WRNS Reserve		8,000
	Total	90,000

38. There remains, therefore, a gap of some 74,250 which can only be filled by National Servicemen. At the present rate of intake (13%) … a reserve of 103,000 would be available in 1957. This figure is too high … the following numbers might be acceptable:–

National Servicemen required in uniform at any one time (… 18 months' service, ie 14,000 per year or 7%)	21,000
Reserve of National Servicemen available in 1957	55,000
Total	76,000

39. By this means the total strength of all Reserves available to the Navy would be about 166,000 in 1957 – an acceptable figure.

Peacetime Naval Forces

40. The Navy's functions in peace, apart from forming part of the armed strength of the Commonwealth (… a potent factor in averting war) are as follows:–

(a) To provide a trained force as a basis for expansion in war.
(b) To experiment and develop new weapons and techniques.
(c) To provide a mobile police force …
(d) To train the reserves required for expansion in war.

41. … the peacetime Navy would be made up as follows:–

Regulars and short-term volunteers	157,050
Regulars for training National Servicemen	5,200
National Servicemen	21,000
	183,250
Less men replaced by WRNS	6,000
Total men	177,250
Total WRNS	8,000
Grand total, men and women	185,250

42. A manpower force of this size should enable the Navy to retain in peacetime … in full or partial commission:–

Battleships	2	for experiment and training
Carriers	12	
Cruisers	18	
Destroyers (including pickets)	73	
Escorts	40	
Submarines	30	
Minesweepers	16	

43. These figures accord closely with the numbers calculated purely on peacetime requirements and may therefore be considered acceptable, except for the aviation component, which may well require to be increased at the expense of other type of ship in order to provide the expansion required in war.

Conclusions on naval manpower:–

44. We conclude that:–

(a) The target for expansion in emergency should be 328,500 by D+4 months.

(b) The peacetime strength should be 185,250, including 21,000 National Service.

(c) The annual National Service intake should be reduced from the present 13% to 7%.

The cost

45. Any estimate of the annual vote required to support a Navy of 185,250 in about ten years' time must necessarily be highly speculative … on the best information available, we estimate an annual cost of the order of £190 million (excluding research and development) …

Conclusion on the cost

47. … a cost of about £1,000 per head per annum is not unreasonable if the service is to be properly prepared for an emergency arising in 1956 or later.

…

101. *Joint Planning Staff Memorandum*

[DEFE 4/4] 19 May 1947

JP(47)67 (Final). THE FUTURE SHAPE AND SIZE OF THE ARMED FORCES

As instructed, we attach at Annexes I, II and III respectively assessments by the Service Ministries of the naval, army and air forces required on the outbreak of was in order to implement the strategy outlined in our report on Future Defence Policy.[1]

2. When agreed, these assessments will provide Service Ministries with a target to be reached by the outbreak of war, from which it will be possible for them to calculate:–

(a) The stages by which we should work up to this target.

(b) The cost in manpower and money …

In order to do this, it will be necessary to lay down a time limit by which the target forces should have been reached. We suggest that in the first instance this limit should be fixed at the period 1956–1960 …

[1]JP(47)55 (Final), 7 May 1947 in DEFE 4/4. This formed the basis of DO(47)44, reproduced as Doc. No. 102.

ANNEX I

Naval Forces Required on the Outbreak of War

In this annex the Naval Forces required on the outbreak of war to fulfil the tasks which will fall upon the Royal Navy, are assessed.

COVER FORCES

Control of sea communications can only be exercised under the cover of forces able to outmatch and forces with which the enemy may challenge that control. On the assumption that the 'early and active support of the USA' will enable us to regard the Pacific as an area of American responsibility, this necessitates two Battle Forces capable of meeting any enemy challenge in Home and Foreign waters respectively.

FLEET CARRIERS

Battle Forces must be capable of finding, fixing, closing and destroying any enemy forces under all conditions. This demands a balanced force, including Fleet Carriers. To provide reconnaissance, strike and fighter aircraft and to admit of flexibility or prolonged operations, 4 carriers in each Force will be required, with a margin to cover refits and damage repairs … Total 10.

CAPITAL SHIPS

If the Battle Forces are to be capable of meeting any enemy challenge and of closing and destroying the enemy's forces wherever and in whatever conditions they may be found, they must include Capital Ships. It is impossible exactly to forecast what the future form of the Capital Ship will be, or what strength in Capital Ships may be necessitated by foreign warships construction and development … provided an enemy does not possess more than 4 Capital Ships … our minimum requirements will be for 2 Capital Ships in each Battle Force, with [a] margin to cover refits and damage repairs … Total 6

LIGHT FLEET CARRIERS

Just as Fleet Carriers have become an essential part of a balanced Battle Force, so Light Fleet Carriers must work with Cruisers in the provision of forces for the direct control of sea communications …–

12 for direct control of sea communications
4 as Replenishment Carriers for the Battle Forces
4 to maintain essential training
5 spares … Total 25

DESTROYERS

Destroyers will be required for the multifarious duties of fast A/S escort, supplementing AA defence, forming surface striking forces and supporting the Army's land battle …:–

To work with the Battle Forces	48 + 12 spares
" " " Cruisers and Light Fleet Carriers	48 + 12 spares
	Total 120

AD PICKETS

Modern developments require that the air defence of a fleet must be extended by the use of air defence pickets, stationed at a distance from the Fleet … at least 6 with each Battle Force, for a total of 12 with 3 spares.

ESCORTS

To meet the threats of submarine and air attack, Escorts in large numbers will be required. On the assumptions that the Pacific is an area of American responsibility and that the threats to our sea communications in the Indian Ocean can be ignored at the outset, the requirement is:–

Atlantic convoys	10 groups	
Mediterranean convoys	6 "	
Independent hunting	5 "	
British coastal convoys	50 ships	
Fleet Train	30 "	Total 332 Escorts

MINESWEEPERS

The mine will constitute one of the chief threats to our sea communications. Minesweepers will be required in large numbers …:–

Fleet minesweepers	48
Danlayers	12
Coastal minesweepers	140
Total	200

SUBMARINES

Submarines will be required for offensive operations against enemy seaborne movement, for reconnaissance and for clandestine operations. In addition, the efficiency of our anti-submarine forces will largely depend on continued training with our own submarines …:–

Northern waters	40
Mediterranean	20
Training	20
Total	80

COASTAL FORCES

MTB/MGB	50
ML	100

MINELAYERS

7 small minelayers

DEPOT SHIPS

2 Destroyer Depot Ships

5 Submarine Depot Ships

FLEET TRAIN

It will be essential to provide for the logistic support of the Fleet on a mobile basis and not to rely on fully equipped peacetime dockyards and bases …

COMBINED OPERATIONS AND CRAFT

a brigade lift, but not on a full assault scale …

102. *Defence Committee Memorandum*

[DEFE 5/4] 22 May 1947

DO(47)44 FUTURE DEFENCE POLICY

Report by the Chiefs of Staff

OBJECT

The object of this paper is to set out the fundamental principles which should govern our Future Defence Policy and to arrive at a clear statement of the basic requirements of our Strategy, on which the shape and size of our armed forces can subsequently be planned.

We have accordingly arranged the paper in two parts:–

PART I – Commonwealth Defence Policy. This Part concludes with a definition of the fundamentals of our Defence Policy.

PART II – The Strategy of Commonwealth Defence. This Part begins with a statement of the basic requirements of our Strategy and concludes with a statement in general terms of the basic tasks of our armed forces and the principles which should govern their shape and size in order to fulfil this Strategy.

…

PART I – COMMONWEALTH DEFENCE POLICY

International Relations

2. The fulfilment of the main object of the United Nations, the maintenance of world peace, depends on the ability and readiness of the Great Powers to keep the peace.

The supreme object of British policy is to prevent war, provided that this can be done without prejudicing our vital interests.

3. The United Kingdom, as the senior member of the British Commonwealth and a Great Power, must be prepared at all times to fulfil her responsibilities not only to the United Nations but also to herself as a Great Power. To fulfil her obligations, she must achieve a strong and sound economy which will give her the ability to expand industry and the armed forces immediately on a war basis.

4. Because of the Veto, the United Nations Organisation provides no security against war between the Great Powers. In this situation, we

believe that the only effective deterrent to a potential aggressor is tangible evidence of our intention and ability to withstand attack and to hit back immediately. No measure of disarmament should be accepted without adequate guarantees of security. Our aim must be to refashion our forces and our war potential to meet the needs of the future. We must remain strong enough to demonstrate our ability to withstand and our intention to counter aggression at any time.

5. Whether, therefore, we are acting in pursuit of national policy or in support of the United Nations, it is necessary to maintain British forces in peacetime to deter aggression which might lead to a major war and to defend our own interests. In support of these forces there must be reserves of essential resources.

Importance of Commonwealth Unity

6. The security of the United Kingdom is the keystone of Commonwealth defence …

Possible Threats to World Peace

7. Although we do not regard a future war as inevitable, we cannot yet be sure that all the Great Powers are determined to keep the peace. Until the general political atmosphere improves, we cannot, therefore, rule out the possibility of war with Russia, either by actual aggression on her part or by a miscalculation of the extent to which she can pursue a policy of ideological and territorial expansion short of war with the Democratic Powers.

8. The issue which cannot be avoided is that our Defence Policy must at present be based on the possibility of war with Russia …

9. We are convinced that we can reduce the risk of war if from now onwards we and our potential allies show strength and a preparedness to use this strength if necessary. Subject to this, we believe that the likelihood of war in the next five years is small; that the risk will increase gradually in the following five years, and will increase more steeply thereafter as the rehabilitation of Russia gathers momentum.

Characteristics of Russia as a Potential Enemy

10. The power of Russia as a potential enemy rests on the following factors:–

(a) Her very great superiority in manpower.
(b) She has vast territory and great resources …
(c) Her present political organisation and the degree of control exercised over the people … In addition, the high standard of security achieved renders our collection of intelligence difficult and makes it the more likely that Russia will have the advantage of surprise at the outset.
(d) She makes full use of Communist Parties in other countries …

On the other hand, Russia suffers from the following elements of weakness:–

(e) Large parts of Russia have been completely devastated.

(f) The population is ignorant and ill-educated and … though her industrial potential and technical ability are growing, she has still a long way to go.

(g) Her transportation system is vulnerable and comparatively undeveloped.

(h) Her oil production is barely sufficient for her needs and her main sources are badly placed strategically.

11. Against Russia as a potential enemy we must redress the balance in favour of the Commonwealth by:–

(a) Increasing and exploiting our present scientific lead. This applies particularly to the development of mass destruction weapons.

(b) Seeking to unite with us all powers which are determined to resist aggression.

European Allies

12. In the past we have relied on building up an alliance of European countries to unite with us from the very beginning in resisting aggression. There is now, however, no combination of European Powers capable of standing up to Russia …

Support from the United States

13. We must have the active and very early support of the United States … because of her manpower, industrial resources and her lead in the development of weapons of mass destruction …

Threat of Russian Expansion

14. The Russian policy of territorial and ideological expansion by the absorption of Satellite States and by the spread of Communism in peace constantly threatens various countries whose continued integrity and independence profoundly affect Commonwealth security. Our interests are challenged, not only throughout Europe but also in the Middle East and throughout the world.

15. The area in which Russian expansion would be easiest and at the same time would hurt us most would be the Middle East. We may be sure that if we abandon our position there in peace Russia will fill the vacuum.

16. … The first impact of Russian expansion into the Middle East would therefore be upon our oil supplies and upon Commonwealth sea and air communications. The importance to us of present and potential oil supplies in the area is as great, if not greater, than ever, particularly in peace. The importance of the Middle East as a centre of Commonwealth communications remains, and will remain, beyond question …

20. … if Russia secured control of this area not only would we lose very important resources and facilities but she would acquire a position of such dominating strategic and economic power that it would be fatal to our security …

Implications of New Weapons

22. The main implications of the new weapons likely to be available by the critical period about 1956 may be summarised as follows:–

(a) … the use of mass destruction weapons against economic key targets and the civil population

(b) Owing to the vastly greater destructive power of atomic and biological weapons, acceptable standards of defence have gone up immeasurably. Within the next ten years there is little possibility that these higher standards of defence can be reached.

(c) There are greater possibilities than before of surprise attack, since the preparations required to deliver decisive attacks with the new weapons …

(d) The potential threat to our sea communications will be greater than at any time in the last war.

Russian Technical Development

23. … We must expect that from 1956–57 Russia will probably be in a position to use some atomic bombs and biological warfare; that she may have developed … rockets, pilotless aircraft, a strategic bomber force and a submarine force; and that she will continue to maintain very large land forces …

FUNDAMENTALS OF OUR DEFENCE POLICY

33. (a) The supreme object of British policy is to prevent war, provided that this can be done without prejudicing our vital interests …

(b) The most likely and most formidable threat to our interests comes from Russia, especially from 1956 onwards …

(c) The most effective step towards preventing war is tangible evidence that we possess adequate forces and resources, that we are fully prepared and that we have the intention and ability to take immediate offensive action.

(d) Essential measures required in peace to give us a chance of survival and victory in the event of war … Being ourselves prepared, equipped and able to use weapons of mass destruction …

PART II – THE STRATEGY OF COMMONWEALTH DEFENCE

34. … in a future war, time will be an all-important factor. The days when we could afford to remain on the defensive, while gathering our great strength for the knock-out blow, ended with the advent of the first atom bomb. A far higher degree of preparedness in peace is now imperative …

35. Our first consideration must be the defence of the United Kingdom, which is both the focus of Commonwealth strength and also its most vulnerable point … The control of sea communications is essential …
BASIC REQUIREMENTS OF OUR STRATEGY

36. (a) The defence of the United Kingdom and its development as an offensive base.
(b) The control of essential sea communications.
(c) A firm hold in the Middle East and its development as an offensive base.

…

39. … the security of the sea communications of the United Kingdom is an essential part of the defence of the United Kingdom both against invasion and to sustain the whole war effort of the country. This security must be extended worldwide to cover communications with the Dominions, with the United States and with sources of raw materials and essential supplies throughout the world.

The threat in Home waters and the North Atlantic would be immensely magnified by an enemy advance to the Channel ports and the Atlantic seaboard …

40. We must also exercise control of sea communications to gain flexibility and mobility of deployment of all the Armed Forces wherever they may be required and to deny those advantages to the enemy. By control of the sea communications through the Mediterranean we could most quickly deploy our forces for the defence of the Middle East and obtain rapid assistance in that theatre from the United States and the Dominions, while at the same time by denying the use of that sea to the enemy, we confine him to difficult land communications and prevent him from obtaining a foothold in North Africa from which he might advance to outflank our defence of Egypt or to establish bases from which to threaten our Atlantic communications.

41. To enable us to exercise control of sea communications through the Mediterranean, we must retain our existing strategic possessions there and obtain additional base facilities on the North African coast …

42. To attain security and control of sea communications, naval and air forces, adequate and suitably organised to meet any threat or challenge, and bases for their effective operation will be required. At present it appears that the chief threats to our sea communications will be from fast submarine attack, air attack and minelaying. But the threat of surface attacks on our shipping must still be guarded against and the capacity of the potential enemy to challenge our control of sea communications must be constantly watched and provided against …

103. *Chiefs of Staff Minutes*

[DEFE 4/4] 11 June 1947

COS(47) 74th Meeting[1]

1. FUTURE DEFENCE POLICY

The Conference had before them a report by the Chiefs of Staff (DO(47)44), the object of which was to set out the fundamental principles which should govern our future defence policy and to arrive at a clear statement of the basic requirements of our strategy, on which the shape and size of our armed forces could subsequently be planned …

The Minister of Defence said that although the Chiefs of Staff considered the likelihood of war during the next five years to be small, an agreed defence policy was required now … so that we could build up correctly composed nucleus forces on which to expand when the threat of war increased. The difficulty was to reconcile our defence requirements with our limited resources in finance and manpower …

The Chiefs of Staff … emphasised that the best deterrent against a future was would be our known preparedness to defend ourselves and to hit back …

THE CONFERENCE:

Approved the recommendations in … DO(47)44…

104. *Board Memorandum*

[ADM 167/129] 22 May 1947

B.513 THE FUTURE OF NAVAL AVIATION[2]

A stage has now been reached in planning for the future of Naval Aviation when it is most desirable to announce, even if only in the broadest terms, an accepted policy. This is particularly necessary for forecasting manpower and training requirements, compiling aircraft production programmes and in building up an effective Naval Air Reserve ready for active service at short notice.

2. The Aim

It has been assessed (PD.0140/45. Revised November 1946) that, in order to secure a balanced Fleet, the Naval Aviation component of the Target Post War Fleet (excluding Dominion contribution) should be:–

[1] Chaired by the Prime Minister.

[2] Drafted by Director of Plans, Capt J. Stevens and originally dated 6 March 1947, reference PD/OL.020/46.

4	Fleet Carriers	In Commission
8	Light Fleet Carriers	
500	Front Line Squadron Aircraft	
2	Light Fleet Carriers for Training and Experiment	
6	Fleet Carriers	In Reserve
10	Light Fleet Carriers	

3. The expected deficit in ships actually available will reduce the above figures, so that the Actual War Fleet (circa 1956) – (excluding probable transfers to Dominion and foreign Navies) – which it is possible to take as the aim, becomes:–

4	Fleet Carriers	In Reserve
2	Light Fleet Carriers	

In the event of war, the necessary expansion of our forces would demand the conversion of additional ships to carriers to make good the deficit.

4. The total Vote 'A' required for the Actual Post War Fleet referred to above would be 222,500 (ie 170,000 regulars plus 10,000 regulars to train conscripts plus 2,500 WRNS not replacing men, plus 40,000 conscripts).

5. It is apparent that limitations imposed by finance may render the attainment of the aim for the Post War Fleet impossible. This poses the question of how reductions in the strength of the Fleet up to which we would wish to build, both in ships and manpower, should be apportioned.

Whilst the need to preserve a correctly balanced Fleet both in peacetime and during expansion in an emergency must be kept in mind, the achievement of such a balance is complicated by the fact that there is a minimum strength in Naval Aviation below which we must not fall in peacetime if this arm of the Service is to expand, when required, pari passu[1] with the remainder of the Fleet. The reasons for this are:–

(a) It takes some two years to train a Pilot to operational standard.

(b) It takes very little less time to train Maintenance and certain other ancilliary ratings in the all-important Leading Rate categories.

(c) It is likely that at least two years must elapse from the start of any expansion scheme before the aircraft industry can show any appreciable increase over its present planned peacetime output of Naval types.

(d) Besides a considerable increase in the Naval Aviation element of the Fleet in mobilisation there will be a simultaneous increase, for

[1] equal footing.

which provision must be made, in the shore training necessitated by the starting up of a War expansion programme.

It follows, therefore, that in order to ensure a balanced Fleet in war, it is necessary to accept some degree of un-balance in peace in favour of Naval Aviation.

6. Manpower allocated to Naval Aviation

It also follows from the above contentions that man-power allocated to Naval Aviation cannot be a fixed percentage of the total Naval manpower.

Up to the present it has been arbitrarily assumed that the proportion of personnel allocated in peace time to Naval Aviation, including crews of carriers and complements of Air Stations, should be 1/3 of the total Naval manpower. This is a fallacy; manpower for Naval Aviation should be allocated according to requirements and not on a fixed percentage basis. It is apparent that the Navy cannot reach its full planned peace time strength until 1956, even if Governmental approval to the manpower figures considered necessary were forthcoming, which is far from certain. But, taking the planned figures as a basis, it is calculated that when they are achieved, the Naval air component would amount to some 80,000 officers and men (just under 40 per cent), including crews of carriers and complements of air stations, or some 38,000 officers and men (ie 17 per cent) if Naval air personnel only are considered …

7. Minimum strength of Naval Aviation in Peace and War

The strength of Naval Aviation in commission in peace in the Target Post War Fleet:–

4 Fleet Carriers
10 Light Fleet Carriers (2 reduced complements for training and experiment)
500 Front Line Squadron Aircraft

approximate to the theoretical minimum strength necessary to ensure ability to expand on mobilisation to the strength of:–

10 Fleet Carriers
25 Light Fleet Carriers (including 5 from Dominions)
1500 Front Line Squadron Aircraft

which it has been calculated would be necessary in war.

8. A re-examination, not yet completed, of the strength of the Fleet which we may be forced to accept by limitations of finance and man-power, suggests that, if we are reduced to a total Vote 'A' of 170,000 or even less, it will still be necessary to keep in commission at least:–

2 Fleet Carriers } (2 reduced complement for
8 Light Fleet Carriers } Training and Experiment)
450 Front Line Squadron Aircraft

in order that the capacity to expand may not be destroyed.

These figures are given as an indication of the lines on which it is conceived the principles enunciated in paras 5 and 6 above, would have to be applied in the event of a forced reduction of our total peace-time strength.

9. Ability to Expand

Besides the existence of trained personnel in the formed squadrons of the peace-time Fleet in commission, available to assist in complementing the reserve squadrons, the ability to expand also depends on an adequate reserve organisation and, during the years of peace, an aircraft replacement programme sufficient to maintain war potential in the aircraft industry.

10. Naval Air Reserves

It is estimated that the minimum strength of the Air Reserve required is 300 aircrews trained to operational standard and supported by the equivalent number of maintenance and ancilliary personnel. This number must be increased by 700 as soon as the warning period is reached.

11. Aircraft Production

It is estimated that a production rate of 85 operational aircraft per month will maintain a Front Line of 500, a Reserve of 300 and a stored War Reserve of Aircraft sufficient to cover the initial stages of a war.

This peace-time production rate is considered just sufficient to ensure that the aircraft industry is capable of expansion at the required rate in an emergency.

12. Carrier Building and Modernisation

We shall, by 1956, with the present approved programme, have 8 Fleet and 16 Light Fleet Carriers. If the air expansion envisaged is achieved, we shall need 30 carriers shortly after the declaration of war; thus, if a war came in 1956, we should be 6 short of the number of carriers needed. This takes no account of the requirement for ferry and replenishment carriers.

To make up this deficiency it has been proposed that a number of suitable ships should be converted to carriers, the exact number needed depending on the state of the building programme. It is estimated that these ships could be converted within 18 months provided flight deck machinery, which takes longer to make, is kept available in store (Lift mechanisms, arrester gear and catapults).

Of the 8 Fleets and 16 Light Fleets which we shall have in 1956, all but 2 ARK ROYALs and 4 HERMES will need modernisation to operate the new aircraft which will by then be in service. Without this modification:–

(a) 3 of the Fleets and 12 of the Light Fleets will be unable to operate any aircraft.

(b) 3 other Fleets may be able to operate suitable future A/S aircraft but they will not be able to operate modern fighters.

This question of modernisation is now being examined by a committee under the chairmanship of ACNS. Their proposals will be submitted to the Board shortly.

13. Conclusions

That the Board should approve:–

(a) The principle that a degree of unbalance in favour of Naval Aviation in the Fleet must be accepted if, for financial or other reasons, a reduction of Naval strength has to be made during the period when the Navy is being built up to its ultimate balanced peace-time strength; the acceptance of this temporarily unbalanced state being necessary because Naval Aviation takes longer to expand both as regards its personnel and material than does the rest of the Naval Service.

(b) The principle that manpower for Naval Aviation is allocated according to requirements and not on any fixed percentage basis, to ensure the ultimate requirements of a balanced Fleet.

14. That the Board should approve that planning for Naval Aviation should be carried out with the following aims:–

(a) To build up by 1956 a front line of 500 aircraft exclusive of any Dominion contribution.

(b) To build up by 1956 reserve squadrons comprising 300 aircraft together with supporting air crews, maintenance and ancilliary personnel.

(c) To build up by 1956 a full complement of operational, training, ancilliary and War Reserve aircraft thereafter maintained by a monthly production of 85 operational types.

(d) To complete the carriers now building and to effect modernisation of existing carriers as may be decided in the light of the recommendations of the Committees now investigating the problem.

(e) To acquire by 1956 a reserve stock of Flight Deck machinery ready for use in ships to be converted to carriers, including operational, replenishment and ferry carriers.

15. That the Board should direct that the entry and training of personnel for Naval Aviation and the provision of aircraft, within such limits as may be imposed by Government decisions, should be carried out so as continuously to build up to the planned strength of Naval Aviation in the actual Postwar Fleet.

105. *Defence Committee Memorandum*

[CAB 131/4] 12 July 1947

DO(47)52 NAVAL NEW CONSTRUCTION PROGRAMME FOR 1947–48

Memorandum by the First Lord of the Admiralty

My predecessor, in presenting a small (revised) Programme of Naval Shipbuilding for 1945 (CP(45)291) referred to the need for a breathing space for the assimilation of the lessons of the war, and for progress on outstanding vessels to proceed as slowly as might be necessary, in order that priority could be given to Merchant Ship Construction in the building yards.

2. In pursuance of this policy and bearing in mind the need for strict economy, no programme of New Construction for 1946–47 was presented, and for 1947–48 I am putting forward proposals limited, with the exception of two Surveying Ships and some Landing Craft, to experimental vessels, in order that essential experience in operation may be gained of new scientific and technical developments of far reaching effect or that vessels may be developed to serve as prototypes for mass production in the event of large numbers being required in an emergency.

3. Before giving details of my proposals, I think it may be useful to refer to New Construction remaining to be completed from previously approved Programmes, as this information has not been disclosed in the Navy Estimates for the year:–

Fleet Carriers	2
Light Fleet Carriers	10
Cruisers	3
Destroyers	16
Submarines	7
Frigates	2
Escort Vessels	2
Non-Magnetic Surveying Ship	1
Surveying Ships	4
Diving Vessel	1
Motor Torpedo Boat	1
Motor Gun Boat	1
Controlled Target Boats	5

Details of these vessels, with the possible completion dates as far as can be foreseen, are given by Programmes in Table I. The preference accorded to merchant shipbuilding referred to above renders the completion dates highly speculative, and it is by no means improbable that further retardation may occur, with some additional, though at present incalculable, financial effect on the estimate given in Table III. The eight destroyers of the 1944 Programme, known as the 'Daring' Class, may also be subject to delay as they are to embody new types of machinery for which stringent tests on shore are necessary prior to installation. Four of these vessels will operate on Alternating Current Electric Supply instead of the Direct Current Supply customary in HM Ships, an experiment from which, if successful as is confidently expected, most important advantages will accrue.

4. The demands upon the limited funds available for Naval Services have, to my regret, prevented a resumption of work upon the non-magnetic ship *Research*, on which considerable progress had been made when construction at Dartmouth had to be abandoned at the outbreak of war. In view of the important role this vessel was designed to fill in the international field, I intend to keep the matter under close review.

5. To meet essential needs, I have found it necessary to modify in a slight degree the character of a small number of vessels approved in prior Programmes. Two Frigates of the 1943 Programme are being completed as Surveying Ships, of which there is at present an acute shortage. One of the two Escort Vessels mentioned in paragraph 3 was described and approved in the 1945 Programme as for Anti-Submarine duties, but will now be designed for Aircraft Direction duties; both vessels will be laid down in 1947–48. The construction of the Experimental Type Submarine approved in the 1946 Programme has been deferred until the current year in order that it may incorporate, in common with a second Experimental Submarine which I am proposing in the 1947–48 Programme, an entirely new method of propulsion. I will refer more fully to this when dealing with the 1947–48 Programme.

6. All other outstanding vessels of Programmes up to 1945 have now been cancelled and a list of cancellations further to that given in CP(45)291 is contained in Table IV. I must, however, make a qualification in regard to the 6 Cruisers, one of the 1941 Programme and the remainder of the 1944 Programme. They were to be constructed to a new design which is not yet ready. I think it proper therefore that they should be formally cancelled from these old wartime programmes. The need for these vessels, however, has not lapsed, and it is my intention to propose their inclusion, to such number as may then seem desirable, in a future Programme, as soon as the design is finalised and construction can be commenced.

OUTLINE OF 1947–48 PROGRAMME

7. Turning to the current year, the Programme for which I ask approval is as follows:–

1 Submarine of new design
2 Surveying Ships

2 Build-up Amphibians
1 Assault Amphibian
2 Convertible Motor Torpedo Boats/Motor Gun Boats
1 Landing Craft, Personnel
1 Expendable Director Controlled Target Boat
1 Landing Craft Headquarters
1 Landing Ship Dock
A number of miscellaneous small craft and motor boats

SUBMARINES

8. In the concluding stages of the late war, the Germans had succeeded in developing a Submarine of revolutionary design, capable of very high submerged speeds, by the use of hydrogen peroxide (HTP) as a propellant. I consider it essential that we should have experience in the construction and use of such submarines in order to train the Fleet to operate fast submarines and, what is equally important, to develop counter measures.

9. I propose, therefore, to use the Experimental Submarine of the 1945 Programme in connection with this development, equipping it with HTP machinery, and in view of the great importance of this project and the grave disadvantages and risks in having available for this purpose only one Experimental Submarine, an accident to which would postpone experiment and development for several years, to provide an additional Experimental Submarine in the 1947–48 Programme. Until experience has been gained in the development of the two Experimental vessels. I propose not to proceed with the construction of the three remaining Submarines of the 1944 Programme, which have accordingly been cancelled, or to lay down further operational vessels.

10. It will, however, be some time before these new submarines can be completed. In order to provide essential training in fast submarine operation and detection at the earliest opportunity, we are, with the sanction of the Treasury, proceeding with the conversion of an 'S' Class Submarine to enable a high submerged speed to be achieved by increasing the battery strength.

SURVEYING SHIPS

11. To meet the extensive programme of surveying to which my predecessor drew attention when seeking approval of the 1945 (Revised) Programme, embodying the accurate charting of the many wrecks round our coasts, the complete re-survey of all Estuarial waters, and a large amount of work in foreign parts, our existing resources are totally inadequate. I am, as explained in paragraph 6, adapting two Frigates of the 1943 Programme for the purpose, and construction of the two new vessels of the 1945 Programme can commence in the latter part of the current year on completion of the design. These last two will take several

years to complete, and in order further to augment with expedition our resources for this essential work, I seek approval to complete two other Frigates as Surveying Ships, utilising for the purpose two ships already formally cancelled from the 1943 Programme, the partially-completed hulls and machinery being still available.

BUILD-UP AMPHIBIANS[1]

12. To meet a long-term requirement of the Chief of Combined Operations Staff for an amphibian to replace the Landing Craft (Mechanised), a design of a 'build-up' Amphibian is now approaching completion. The function of the craft is to disembark stores and equipment (including vehicles) on to dry land over all types of beaches (excluding rocky foreshores). For the purpose of developing this type of craft, I propose to proceed with the construction of two, with different types of suspension, to undergo trials which would be carried out under Navy and Army direction.

ASSAULT AMPHIBIANS

13. Requirements have been raised by the Chief of Combined Operations Staff for a craft for disembarkation of troops in an amphibious assault against a defended coast, with such of their immediate requirements of weapons as can be carried without prejudice to the design as an Assault Personnel Carrier. These craft are to be capable of negotiating barriers which prevent a normal landing craft disembarking troops on dry land or in shallow waters. Some preliminary design and development work and model trials have been carried out, and I now propose to proceed with the construction of one Assault Amphibian in order that essential practical experience can be gained.

CONVERTIBLE MTB/MGB

14. To meet future requirements for a craft to fulfil the functions of a Motor Torpedo Boat or Motor Gun Boat, it is important to develop a prototype design to solve the many problems of construction and hull form, for improvement of sea keeping qualities, and production of higher speeds I propose to proceed with the construction of two large craft, the primary object of building two being to compare the respective merits of hard chine and round bilge for hulls of craft over 100 ft. in length, with speeds of over 40 knots.

LANDING CRAFT PERSONNEL

15. Hitherto Landing Craft, Personnel, have been of American origin. Those in use have seen upwards of five years' service and are rapidly wearing out. To meet the requirements of the Chief of Combined Operations Staff for a general-purpose beaching craft to carry out such

[1]A tracked amphibious vehicle.

ancillary duties as collection and delivery of despatches, I seek approval to construct one vessel which will serve as the British prototype for future construction of this class of work.

EXPENDABLE D/C BOAT

16. There is a requirement for unarmoured Director Controlled Target Boats for gunnery training. The boats are to be capable of being carried in a Cruiser or larger ship so as to be available for practices in any area. Trials have been carried out with a 25 ft. converted Motor Boat, but it is evident that requirements as regards speed and sea keeping qualities cannot be met thereby. The design of a suitable boat is now proceeding, and I seek approval to build one prototype vessel.

LANDING CRAFT HEADQUARTERS

17. Landing Headquarters are needed in the Post War Assault Force. Those which were operated, and found indispensable, during the late war were all obtained from the United States under the terms of the Lend-Lease Agreement. The craft are of highly specialised nature and have no counterpart in British construction. One such craft is at present in constant use for instructional purposes. The return of this vessel to the United States would, therefore, cause a cessation of this aspect of instructional training in Combined Operations in the interim period until a replace vessel of British design and construction could be produced, which would take at least three years. I therefore propose to enter into negotiations for the purchase of this vessel, the retention of which has been endorsed by the Chiefs of Staff. The Treasury has sanctioned the dollar expenditure involved ($95,000).

LANDING SHIP DOCK

18. A Landing Ship Dock is required for docking and repair of Landing Craft at or near the seat of operations, and its use will be necessary in connection with peace-time exercises. One such ship is now in use, of American origin, and I have considered whether it would be advisable to attain our end by purchasing her. The dollar expenditure would, however, be very considerable, and the sterling equivalent would not be far short of what is necessary to build a new ship in this country with all the advantages of modern equipment. Completion under present priority for naval work will probably not be effected until 1952, but this is acceptable to the Chiefs of Staff.

SMALL CRAFT AND MOTOR BOATS

19. I ask approval in the normal way for the miscellaneous small craft required to serve the Fleet and for other various duties.

COST OF PROGRAMME

20. The sum of £240,000 has been included in Navy Estimates for the current year for the commencement of the New Programme in

anticipation of its approval. The total cost of this Programme is estimated at £1,955,000.[1]

GENERAL

21. The foregoing represents all the New Construction that I consider essential for the current year, but there are two further requirements of an experimental nature which I must mention.

22. One is a Fleet Aircraft Direction Escort which experience, particularly in the Pacific, in the late war showed to be essential for the early detection of hostile aircraft attack and the co-ordination of counter-measures. It is necessary for the Fleet to have practical experience in the use of such ships and, pending the production of the final form of radar to be employed, I am satisfied that the object can be achieved by the adaptation of existing Fast Minelayers, and, in the first instance, I intend to proceed with the conversion of one.

23. The other requirement is for the development of A/S Coastal Forces Craft to operate in the coastal traffic lanes and approaches to harbours. This purpose can be satisfied by the conversion of two existing Fairmile Motor Launches.

[1] Tables II & III, which summarise expenditure on new construction in each financial year 1946–47 to 1951–52, are not reproduced.

TABLE I – STATEMENT OF SHIPS REMAINING TO BE COMPLETED FROM APPROVED PROGRAMMES
(excluding Harbour Service Craft and Motor Boats)

Programme Year	Class of Ship	Name	Date of			Remarks
			Laying Down	Launch	Completion as at present foreseen	
1935	Magnetic Survey Vessel	*Research*	9.9.1937	4.4.1939	Uncertain	Work suspended
1940	Fleet Carrier	*Ark Royal*	3.5.1943	Mid-1948	End of 1950	
1941	Cruisers (*Tiger* Class)	*Tiger*	1.10.1941	25.10.1945	Early 1949	
		Defence	24.6.1942	2.9.1944	Uncertain	Work suspended
1942	Fleet Carrier (*Ark Royal* Class)	*Eagle*	24.10.1942	19.3.1946	June 1949	
	Light Fleet Carriers (*Majestic* Class)	*Hercules*	14.10.1943	22.9.1945	Uncertain	Work suspended
		Leviathan	18.10.1943	7.6.1945	Uncertain	Work suspended
		Majestic	15.4.1943	28.2.1945	Uncertain	Work suspended
		Magnificent	29.7.1943	16.11.1944	End 1947	(To be transferred on loan to R.C.N.
1943		*Powerful*	27.11.1943	27.2.1945	Uncertain	On completion)
		Terrible	19.4.1943	30.9.1944	Uncertain	Work suspended
	Cruiser (*Tiger* Class)	*Blake*	17.8.1942	20.12.1945	March 1949	Building in HM Dockyard
	Light Fleet Carriers (*Hermes* Class)	*Albion*	23.3.1944	6.5.1947	March 1950	Devonport
		Centaur	30.5.1944	22.4.1947	December 1949	Work suspended
		Hermes	21.6.1944	Late 1948	End 1950	
		Bulwark	10.5.1945	Early 1948	Mid-1950	

	Destroyers (Fleet Weapons) (*Battleaxe* Class)	Four	Between April and December 1944	Between June 1945 and August 1946	Between July and December 1947	
	Destroyers (Fleet Battles) (*Agincourt* Class)	Four	Between December 1943 and April 1944	Early 1945	Between June 1947 and January 1948	
1944	Submarines ('A' Class)	Six	Between Feb 1944 and August 1945	Between Sep 1945 and March 1947	Between June and November 1947	One building in HM Dockyard
	Frigates (*Bay* Class)	Two	April and Oct 1944	November 1944 and June 1945	Uncertain	
1945	Surveying Vessels	Two	April and Aug1944	April and May 1945	Uncertain	Originally commenced as *Bay* Class Frigates. Completing in HM Dockyard
	Diving Vessel	*Reclaim*	9.4.1946	September 1947	Uncertain	
	Floating Dock	AFD 35	…	…	Uncertain	
	Destroyers (*Daring* Class)	Eight	Between Sept 1945 and October 1947	Uncertain	Between October 1949 and Sept 1950	
	M.T.B.	One	10.9.1947	June 1947	Uncertain	
	M.G.B	One	11.9.1945	May 1947	Uncertain	
	C.T. Boats	Five	April–August 1945	Uncertain	Uncertain	
	Experimental Submarine	One	…	…	…	
	Surveying Vessels	Two	…	…	…	
	Escort Vessels	Two	…	…	…	To be laid down in 1947. One as A/D, one as A/A

TABLE IV – LIST OF CANCELLATIONS
FROM 1 NOVEMBER 1945 TO DATE

No.	*Description*	*Programme Year*
3	Large Fleet Carriers	1 – 1942
		2 – 1943
*6	6-inch Cruisers	1 – 1941
		5 – 1944
20	Destroyers	4 – 1943
		16 – 1944
3	LCS(R)	1943
16	90-ft Motor Fishing Vessels	1943
19	61½-ft Motor Fishing Vessels	7 – 1943
		12 – 1944
19	75-ft Motor Fishing Vessels	2 – 1943
		17 – 1944
4	45-ft Motor Fishing Vessels	1 – 1943
		3 – 1944
5	LCT(8)	1944
5	105-ft Motor Minesweepers	3 – 1940
		2 – 1941
1	MTB	1942
2	Aircraft Transports (Small)	1943
*2	Tugs	1 – 1943
		1 – 1944
*3	Submarines (Improved 'A')	1944

Vessels marked thus * had not been ordered

106. *Defence Committee Minutes*

[CAB 131/5] 16 July 1947

DO(47) 16th Meeting

Naval New Construction Programme:– 1947–48

The First Lord of the Admiralty explained that, with the exception of two surveying ships and some landing craft, his proposals for new construction were limited to experimental vessels designed to ensure that essential experience would be gained on new scientific and technical developments, or to produce vessels which would serve as prototypes for mass production in the event or an emergency. The total cost of the programme would be £1,966,000 over a period of five years, towards which an expenditure of £240,000 had been included in the Navy estimates for 1947–48. The amount of money to be devoted year by year to this and the earlier programmes would come forward for approval in each year's estimates. He pointed out that steps had been taken to cancel or suspend work on a wide variety of Ships, the construction of which had been previously approved, and that no new construction programme had been put forward for 1946–47. On further points of detail, the First Lord of the Admiralty explained:–

(a) That, with the approval of the Treasury, it was proposed to purchase from the Americans a landing craft headquarters at a cost of $95,000. This vessel was essential for combined operations training, the needs of which covered about half the total new construction programme.

(b) That it had been decided to build a landing ship dock to replace one of United States origin which had now been returned to the United States. The purchase of the United States landing ship dock would have involved heavy dollar expenditure.

(c) That, though his proposals envisaged a considerable rise in expenditure on new construction in the financial year 1948–49 through the resumption of work on cruisers and light fleet carriers on which work had been suspended, it was hoped that a number of vessels on which construction would be resumed would be bought by the Dominions. In any event, the amount of money to be spent on new construction in 1948–49 would come up for discussion when next year's estimates were considered by the Defence Committee.

The Chief of Combined Operations emphasised the importance of the combined operations requirements included in the programme. He hoped that it would be possible to include in the next programme one or more supporting craft. At present no craft of this kind were available for combined operations purposes.

The Parliamentary Secretary, Ministry of Transport, said that the proposed new programme would not interfere with the merchant shipbuilding programme.

The Prime Minister said that the new programme seemed to be a modest one and might be accepted, on the understanding that the expenditure to be incurred year by year on this programme and on earlier programmes would come up for consideration in each year's estimates. On the question of procedure, however, the traditional practice by which the First Lord put his proposals for new construction direct to the Cabinet was no longer appropriate. He thought that in future the procedure adopted should conform with the new defence organisation which had been set up. For this purpose, each new construction programme should go to the

Joint War Production Staff and to the Ministerial Production Committee, before being submitted to the Defence Committee.

The Committee:–

(1) Approved the proposals in DO(47)52 on the understanding that the expenditure to be incurred on them and on earlier construction programmes would come before the Committee for consideration in each year's estimates.

(2) Agreed that the procedure for submitting future Naval new construction programmes should follow the lines outlined by the Prime Minister.

107. *Joint Planning Staff Memorandum*

[DEFE 6/3] 8 July 1947

JP(47)97(Final) POSITION OF ARMED FORCES – SUMMER 1947

We have reviewed the present position of the Armed Forces:–

ANNEX I	–	Naval Forces
ANNEX II	–	Land Forces
ANNEX III	–	Air Forces[1]

…

2. The detailed considerations in the Annexes show that in general terms this country is in no position at the present moment to undertake a major war against a first-class power organised and ready for war. All three Services are in process of running down and are consequently a good deal disorganised. The trained manpower which was the source of their strength at the end of the war is rapidly being released and the Services are now inevitably dependent to a great extent upon the raw and untrained intake. Arrears of re-equipment and reconstruction are mounting up.

3. Except for their preponderance of manpower, the Russian situation is not very much better. Russia could not in existing circumstances embark upon a major war of any duration, nor could she at the moment mount even a brief threat of serious proportions with independent air forces or at sea.

4. We feel it is safe to conclude, therefore, that the existing situation can be accepted. If a political crisis should precipitate a war for which neither side was attempting to prepare, we believe that with improvisation and with assistance from the United States of America we should be able to hold our own.

[1] Annexes II & III not reproduced.

5. On the other hand, the situation of our own Armed Forces is likely to grow worse over the next few years, since the men trained in the last war will be less readily available and less skilled with the passage of time; moreover, existing equipment will grow less serviceable as time goes on. The position can only begin to improve in perhaps three or four years when there is a larger supply of trained technical personnel available in the Services, and provided that the financial expenditure authorised for Defence permits the production of new equipment and material. Although in three- or four-years' time the Army will be considerably smaller in numbers than it is today, its means of expansion will have greatly improved.

Against this, however, the Russians are likely to devote far more money and manpower, in proportion, to the defence services than we can and their position will, therefore, improve faster …

ANNEX I

NAVAL FORCES

Naval forces available in Emergency at 31 July 1947

The attached Table gives a reasoned assessment of the Naval Forces which could be produced in Emergency as at 31 July 1947, and the build-up which could be reasonably expected by 31 August, 30 September and 30 November.

Assumptions

2. The assumptions relating to this present assessment are as follows:–

(a) Except for the basic training of new entries which would continue, all Technical Training would be stopped for the first two months of the emergency and the personnel thus released would be utilised for manning purposes. (Should the emergency be protracted beyond this date re-commencement of Technical Training would be imperative and allowance is made for this fact).

(b) All ships employed for training and experimental purposes would be brought forward for service.

(c) Pensioners, Reservists and ex-National Servicemen would require to be recalled at the following rates which can be handled by the manning depots:–

During first month	–	36,000
second month	–	26,000
third and fourth months	–	a total of 38,000

(d) Royal Dockyards would be required to bring forward the necessary ships but their full output would be used on this work alone.

State of Readiness

3. The ships shown in Column 2 of Appendix A are all manned with reduced complements in varying degrees and will remain so for various periods amounting in some cases (particularly in the case of ships abroad) to some weeks. Their operating capacities will therefore be limited to a corresponding degree.

Manning Requirements

4. The manning requirement will call for some measure of trooping capacity to foreign stations.

5. Manning allowances include provision for:–

(i) Starting up a DEMS organisation.

(ii) Manning and providing for the defences of a nucleus of shore bases.

(iii) Completion of a Brigade Lift of Combined Operations craft by the end of the fourth month. (Note – Transport facilities only will be available and the Brigade would not be equipped for an assault).

Locations of Naval forces at 31 July 1947

6. Attached at Appendix B is a 'station' breakdown of the disposition of the major forces shown in Column 2 of Appendix A (ie the ships available on 31 July). This statement is not carried further owing to the uncertainty of the dispositions which will be found necessary after the state of Emergency is proclaimed.

Commonwealth Contribution

7. No allowance has been made herein for any Commonwealth contribution from whom, however, the following maximum major forces might be made available during the total period under review:–

	Australia	Canada	New Zealand
Light Fleet Carriers	–	1	–
Cruisers	3	1	1
Destroyers	5	3	–
Escorts	4	2	2

Administration

8. The following points affecting administration must be taken into account:–

(a) Ammunition, stores and fuel are available for the forces envisaged, but operations on a war scale could not be supported on existing stocks for more than a few months. In the case of aviation fuel, it would be a matter of weeks. Continuance of operations would therefore depend on the uninterrupted flow of supplies from overseas.

(b) All our defended ports are in peacetime state and at no notice for war. It would take months to lay the defences at even a few ports.

APPENDIX A

Type of Ship	31 Jul	31 Aug	30 Sep	30 Nov
Battleship	1	2	3	4
Fleet Carrier	–	2	2	3
Light Fleet Carrier	4	5	6	6
Cruiser	21	21	22	24
Destroyer	32	67	71	79
Escort	44	54	60	72
Submarine	27	36	46	55
Fast Minelayer	1	1	1	2
Fleet Minesweeper	24	37	44	44
Coastal Minesweeper	24	32	35	45
Netlayer	1	1	1	2
Coastal Craft	12	12	22	32
Surveying Ship	5	5	5	5
Surveying Launch	6	6	6	6
Destroyer Depot Ship	1	1	1	2
Submarine Depot Ship	4	4	4	5
Fast Tanker	–	1	1	1
Fleet Tug	5	5	5	7
Salvage Vessel	2	2	2	4
Hospital Ship	1	1	1	1
Fighter Direction Ship	–	1	1	1
Boom defence Vessel	20	25	35	50
Front Line Aircraft	96	216	240	288
Combined Operations	To bring up to Brigade Lift in 4 months			

NOTE:– No allowance has been made for any Dominion contribution.

APPENDIX B

Breakdown of Major Forces by Stations

Class of Ship	Home Fleet	Mediter-ranean	America & W Indies	East Indies	Pacific	South Atlantic	Training, Experi-mental	TOTAL
Battleships	1	–	–	–	–	–	–	1
Fleet Carriers	–	–	–	–	–	–	–	–
Light Fleets	–	2	–	–	2	–	–	4
Cruisers	5	5	2	3	3	1	2	21
Destroyers	11	13	–	–	8	–	–	32
Escorts	–	15	4	4	5	1	15	44
Submarines	–	–	–	–	5	–	22	27

108. *Chiefs of Staff Minutes*

[DEFE 4/5] 31 July 1947

COS(47) 98th Meeting ARMED FORCES –
REDUCTION OF OVERSEAS COMMITMENTS
AND OVERALL SIZE

The Minster of Defence referred to a minute he had received from the Prime Minister … [concerning] the reduction of the forces stationed overseas theatres by about 150,000 by 31 December 1947, and on the question of securing a quicker run-down of the total size of the armed forces by the end of March 1948 …

Sir John Cunningham said that the numbers of Royal Naval personnel which could be withdrawn from overseas theatres … were likely to be extremely small, since there was only a total of some 46 in Venezia Guilia, 37 in Italy … 65 in Greece, 300 in Palestine and 129 in Egypt.

As regards personnel afloat … the greater part of this expenditure was incurred in British controlled territories such as Malta. The greater part of the Royal Naval personnel due to be released by the end of 1947 had already arrived or were enroute to the UK …

Sir John Cunningham said that all Royal Naval ships already carried a complement 20% below normal and if the Royal Navy was called upon to withdraw additional personnel from overseas before December 1947, the only fleet which it would be possible even to consider reducing was the British Pacific Fleet which was already short of a cruiser and 4 escort vessels. The carriers which formed the main part of the British Pacific Fleet provided in fact the only mobile air force north of Malaya. He pointed out that they were most useful in the event of it being necessary to carry out emergency moves and to meet such a contingency, their continued presence in Far Eastern waters was therefore most advisable …

The Minister of Defence … as regards a quicker run-down of the total size of the armed forces … below 1,000,700 by the end of March 1948 … appreciated that all possible economies had been taken into account in reaching that figure. He agreed, therefore, to recommend to the Defence Committee that no further reduction was possible …

109. *Joint Intelligence Sub-Committee Memorandum*

[CAB 158/1] 6 August 1947

JIC(47)7/2 Final SOVIET INTERESTS, INTENTIONS AND CAPABILTIES

. . .

Navy

83. *General* – The Russian Navy is divided according to the four main strategic areas, which differ to a great extent in geographical and climatic conditions. These areas are:–

(a) Northern Waters, including the White Sea
(b) The Baltic
(c) The Black Sea
(d) The Far East

84. Of these areas, the Black Sea is the only one which is not connected to the other three by water under the control of the USSR. It is possible, however, that in the future the Black Sea may be linked by canal systems with the Baltic and the White Sea for the passage of destroyers, submarines and light craft.

85. The Baltic is already connected with the White Sea by the Stalin Canal, which is navigable by destroyers and smaller vessels when specially lightened, for about six months in the year.

86. In Northern Waters, the ports of Murmansk, Polyarnoe and the Petsamo district are ice-free all the year round. These three ports and the White Sea are connected with the Far East by the Northern Sea Route, which is navigable in normal years, in either direction, for a period of two or three months beginning in mid-July.

87. Up to the end of the war Russia possessed no ice-free ports in the Baltic or the Far East. In the Far North, Murmansk and Polyarnoe were available to her all the year round and the Black Sea ports were kept in use all the year round with the aid of icebreakers. This factor imposed considerable restrictions on the Soviet Navy in respect of training programmes and shipbuilding and was largely responsible for the lack of 'sea sense' in Soviet Naval personnel.

88. Since the war, the Soviet Union has gained more ice-free ports than have ever before been controlled by the Russian Empire. She now has Petsamo in the Far North, Tallinn, Libau, Memel, Kaliningrad (Konigsberg) and Baltusk (Pillau) in the Baltic and agreements with China giving her access to Port Arthur and Dairen in the Far East. It should be noted that of all these ports, Port Arthur and Dairen are the only ones whose land communications with the USSR are not at present wholly under Soviet control.

89. *Naval Forces Available* – The Russians possess no modern battleships and the employment of their four old heavy ships (including the *Royal Sovereign** and the ex-Italian *Cesare*) is likely to be in the role of floating batteries for use as a mobile supplement to military bombardment in the course of predominantly land operations.

* The *Royal Sovereign* and *Milwaukee* are due to be returned to Great Britain and the United States respectively when the Russians receive their share of the ex-Italian Fleet.

90. Russia possesses six Russian-built Cruisers of modern type, of which two each are at present in the Baltic, Black Sea and Pacific Ports. With 7.1-inch guns and a high speed, these ships are the most formidable units possessed by the Russian Navy. Five uncompleted ships of this type were launched during the war years but it is probable that work is only proceeding on one of them. There are believed to be three more, probably of the same class, on the stocks. In addition, the Russians have the ex-German *Nurnberg* and the ex-American *Milwaukee* and they have been allocated the *Duca D'Aosta* as part of their share of the Italian Fleet. The endurance of Russian-built Cruisers is less than that of the corresponding British types.

91. The Russians have not as yet developed a fast type of Merchant ship which would be suitable for conversion to an armed merchant cruiser, but the possibility of such construction cannot be excluded.

92. The Russians have at least five modern Flotilla Leaders of Soviet design and about thirty modern Russian-built Destroyers, armed with 5.1-inch guns. They have five ex-German and three ex-Italian Destroyers all of modern type. The endurance of Russian-built Destroyers is considerably less than that of corresponding British types.

93. The strongest single arm of the Russian Navy is undoubtably submarines, of which it possesses approximately 230 at the present time a few of which are reaching the age of ten years. Although this number includes many submarines of obsolescent or coastal types, the Russians possess sound Russian-built types of large range ocean-going submarines, medium submarines and coastal types.

94. As their share of the German Fleet, the Russian have been allocated 10 ex-German U-boats of the most modern type. In addition to these, it is believed that at least ten more U-boats of various types were acquired by the Russians in sea-going condition and up to forty more U-boats have been salvaged or removed in an unfinished state to Russian Baltic yards. These are believed to include a number of the latest German electric boats with a high underwater speed ...

110. *Board Memorandum*

[ADM 167/129] 26 July 1947

B.520 FUTURE DEFENCE POLICY
NAVAL PEACETIME REQUIREMENTS[1]

SCOPE OF MEMORANDUM

The Chiefs of Staff have invited the Admiralty (COS(47) 70th Meeting, Item 5) to estimate:–

(i) the cost in manpower and finance of the peacetime Navy which it would be necessary to maintain to meet peacetime requirements and be capable of expansion on mobilisation to man and support the forces given in JP(47)67 as amended by JP(47)71,[2] particulars of which are given in paragraph 5 below.

(ii) the cost in manpower and finance of the Naval forces required in 1948/49.

2. For the purposes of preparing the estimates under paragraph 1, it has been assumed that:–

(a) the target peacetime fleet must be built up by 1956/57.

(b) there would be a year's warning from 1955 onwards of any greatly increased likelihood of an outbreak of war.

3. The memorandum is divided as follows:–

Part I – Target peacetime forces.
Part II – Reduction of expenditure to meet financial limitations.
Part III – Forces for 1948/49.

PART 1 – TARGET PEACETIME FORCES

FUNCTIONS OF PEACETIME NAVY

4. The functions of the peacetime Navy are to:–

(a) provide the nucleus on which to expand on the outbreak of war,

(b) provide the means of training for war,

(c) provide the 'police' forces for the protection and furtherance of British interests at home and abroad.

(a) governs the total size of the Fleet, active and reserve.

(b) and (c) governs the number of ships it is necessary to keep in active commission, with full or reduced complements.

UN Forces, if required, would be found from within those provided for other roles.

[1] Forwarded to the Ministry of Defence as COS(47)166(O), 13 Aug 1947 (DEFE 5/5).

[2] Not reproduced.

NUCLEUS FOR EXPANSION FOR WAR

5. Forces

It has been accepted by the Chiefs of Staff that the forces shown in the following table should serve as an indication and guide, prepared with the knowledge at present available, of the size and shape of the naval forces needed at the outbreak of war.

Type of Ship (i)	Assessed total requirement (ii)	Assumed Dominion contribution (iii)	RN Forces required (iv)
Capital ships	6+2 in reserve	Nil	6+2 in reserve
Fleet Carriers	10	Nil	10
Light Fleet Carriers	25	4	21
Cruisers	35	5	30
Destroyers	120	20	100
AD Pickets	15	Nil	15
Escorts	332	32	300
Minesweepers	200	Nil	200
Submarines	80	Nil	80
MTB/MGB	50	Nil	50
ML(A/S) and (HD)	100	Nil	100
Minelayers	7	Nil	7
Destroyer Depot Ships	2	Nil	2
S/M Depot Ships	5	Nil	5
Fleet Train	To support	–	To support
For Combined Operations, provision should be made for a Brigade Group lift with its full complement of supporting arms and craft, and additional provision to allow training and experimental establishments to continue separately on the outbreak of war. No Dominion contribution is assumed.			

The number of aircraft, airfields and air establishments required immediately on mobilisation to complement and support the Aircraft Carriers given in the above fleet are:–

900 Front line aircraft, including assumed Dominion contribution of 100 aircraft.

2000 Reserve aircraft }
1100 Training aircraft } Not including Dominion holdings

36 airfields and establishments (including satellites) and including 2 or 3 in the Dominions.

6. Manpower

The total uniformed manpower required to man and support the above fleet on mobilisation, exclusive of Dominion contributions, is estimated to be 382,000.

7. Requirement for expansion

In order to expand to the above fleet on mobilisation, the target peacetime Naval forces must be of sufficient size:–

(i) to provide the ships and supporting services required on mobilisation, exclusive of what can be provided during the warning period;
(ii) to allow of sufficient personnel being borne as will, with the addition of the Reserves, man the fleet on mobilisation.

These two aspects of expansion are next examined.

8. Ships

It is not considered sound to assume that it will be possible to supplement the Fleet in existence in peace by New Construction within the warning period of one year, except for a number of small Minesweepers and Coastal Forces craft. Such New Construction of larger units as can be commenced would not be available in less than 18 months. No deduction in the main units of the Fleet required on the outbreak of war, to arrive at the strength required in peace can, therefore, be made on this count. Ability to construct or convert a number of small Minesweepers and Coastal Forces craft is assumed to be possible within the warning period, together with the conversion from trade of a number of ships required for the Fleet Train and of tugs and naval servicing craft.

9. It follows, therefore, that all the fleet units shown in column (iv) of the table given in paragraph 5 above, with the exception of a number of small minesweepers, Coastal craft and Fleet Train units, must exist in the peacetime Naval forces, either in active commission or in reserve.

10. Manpower required in peace

Besides providing the actual numbers of men needed to man the Fleet, active and reserve, required in peace, the peacetime manpower strength must:–

(a) provide a large enough nucleus of trained and experienced personnel around which the full mobilised strength can be formed;
(b) year by year pass sufficient men to the reserve to ensure that the total reserves required to fill the gap between peace and war strengths is always available.

11. The basic factor governing expansion of personnel is that the nucleus referred to in paragraph 10(a) must be at least half the number required for the mobilised Fleet, ie the regular content in peace must be at least half the total manpower strength required on mobilisation … The number of regulars in peace, including 10,000 women, must, therefore, [be] not less than 191,000, ie half the total numbers required for the mobilised fleet (para 6) …

14. In order to be capable of expansion to 382,000, the target peacetime Navy must, therefore, consist of:–

Regulars, men	181,000
NS men	20,500
WRNS	10,000
	211,500

15. Individual training

The increased complexity of equipment and the continuation of conscription together impose a training commitment on the Royal Navy far greater than any previously experienced.

The training commitment demands more shore training establishments with the appropriate instructional and administrative staffs. This in turn has the further effects of:–

(a) reducing the number of ships that can be kept in commission in peace with a given number of men;
(b) consequently increasing the proportionate size of the reserve fleet;
(c) imposing a further increase in the training commitment owing to the necessity for training a large reserve of skilled officers and ratings to complement the reserve fleet when brought forward for service.

16. Tactical training

Over and above the training of the individual, it is essential that tactical training be maintained and realistic exercises be made possible. It is considered that these needs can only be met by the provision of sufficient ships of all offensive combatant types in commission to enable the formation of at least two separate forces of all arms …

These tactical training forces can conveniently absorb the major part of the individual sea training commitment. This will, however, necessitate confining these forces to Home, North Atlantic and Mediterranean waters, to provide for the continuous changes in personnel which would be necessary.

17. Additional training requirements

The essential experimental work carried out by the various technical establishments and the intensive primary and technical training required by the schools also call for seagoing ships … Additional ships are, therefore, needed for these requirements which would be manned by special complements suitable to their functions …

111. *Board Minute*

[ADM 167/128] 31 July 1947

Future Defence Policy:– Naval Peacetime Requirements

4171. The Board discussed a memorandum on future Defence Policy, together with a forecast of expenditure 1948/49 to 1956/57 and stabilised requirements thereafter.

After several Members of the Board had raised questions concerning the basis on which the requirements had been assessed, the Board agreed that the memorandum was appropriate as a reply to the enquiry which the Minister of Defence had put to the Chiefs of Staff. There was, however, considerable doubt whether the programme was realistic from the point of view of the shortage of capacity in shipbuilding yards, dockyards and in the works field (especially the two latter). There was full realisation that there was no hope of the Government authorising expenditure on the scale envisaged in the memorandum.

It was agreed that the memorandum should be forwarded to the Ministry of Defence with a covering note indicating that the Admiralty recognised that the proposals contained in it represented an ideal that was impossible of attainment within the period chosen for planning purposes, and that the programme would need to be considered in conjunction with similar memoranda from the War Office and Air Ministry in order to determine what adjustments should be made in the programmes as a whole to bring then within the bounds of possibilities.

112. *Memorandum by Director of Plans*

[ADM 1/20667] 1 August 1947

COMPOSITION AND DISPOSITION OF THE FLEET, 1948/49

Manpower available

The run-down of the personnel of the Navy between 31 December 1947 and 31 March 1949 involves a total reduction of 15,450, from 181,700 to 166,250, made up as follows:–

	Males	WRNS	Total
Numbers required by the Forecast of the Fleet for 31 December 1947…	173,318	8,383	181,701
Forecast strength on 31 March 1949	157,000	9,250	166,250
Difference in strength	–16,318	867	–15,451

2. This run-down of 15,450 is obligatory and is determined by the estimated intake of regulars in conjunction with the National Service release programme. It assumes that:–

(i) the regular intake will be up to expectations.

(ii) no cut is imposed in the 1948/49 estimates either in manpower or money which will necessitate accepting a lower terminal figure than 166,250.

3. From a practical point of view, it is necessary to plan for the attainment of the reduction to be reached somewhat in advance of the date by which it is due:– The aim is therefore to prepare a Forecast of the Fleet for 31 December 1948, which conforms to the figure of 166,250; the timing of the reductions has to be spread evenly through 1948.

Reductions in shore commitments

4. Part of the required saving will be achieved by the closing down of commitments which, although not included in the Forecast of the Fleet for 31 December 1947, will still be in the process of running down on that date and for which allowance has consequently been made … Further savings will be made by minor reductions in the complements of Shore Establishments and Shore Commands, mostly effected by a percentage cut.

5. It is further proposed that, subject to investigation, the following reductions ashore should be made:–

(i) Closing of RN Hospital Sherborne.

(ii) Closing of Falkland Islands W/T Station.

(iii) Re-organisation of FOSNI, LOCHINVAR and COCHRANE with the object of achieving a saving equivalent to the total elimination of LOCHINVAR.

(iv) Amalgamation of BOSCAWEN and OSPREY.

(v) Abolition of VERNON II.

(vi) Abolition of IMPREGNABLE.

(vii) Reduction in Royal Marine Commitments.

6. The reductions visualised in paragraphs 4 and 5 will, it is estimated, together with the concomitant reduction on 'Margin', produce a saving in personnel requirements of 6,800, leaving a further reduction of 8,650 officers and men to be made.

Reduction in Naval Aviation

7. Naval Aviation has perforce to contract in overall numbers during the period between 31 December 1947 and 31 December 1948 before it can again expand and will suffer a physical reduction of 2,250. Nevertheless, because the ratings, by categories, will be better balanced, it is not expected that any appreciable reduction in Naval Aviation complement strengths will be necessary. This 'windfall' of 2,250 reduces the further saving to be made to 6,400.

Possibility of further reductions in shore commitments

8. The shore sections of the Forecast of the Fleet 1947, have been carefully examined and it is considered that further pruning in addition to the above is not possible at present without seriously affecting the functions of the services concerned. Efforts will continue, however … to effect reductions wherever it is practicable for them to be made.

Reductions in the Fleet

9. It therefore remains to examine how far the saving of 6,400 yet to be made can be achieved by reductions in the remaining sections of the Navy:–

Ships in full commission.
Ships in commission with special complements for Experiment and Development, School Training etc
Reserve Fleet
Combined Operations

10. After an exhaustive examination of all the possibilities, the following reductions and adjustments are proposed:–

(i) Ships in full commission

Home Fleet	add	1 Fleet Carrier
		1 Fleet Replenishment Ship (NORTHMARK)
	reduce	1 Cruiser
		4 Destroyers (already in hand)
		4 Fleet Minesweepers
		9 Submarines (5 transferred to Training)

The retention of VANGUARD in commission for her extended trials, in addition to DUKE OF YORK, is considered necessary.

Mediterranean Fleet	reduce	1 Cruiser
		3 Fleet Minesweepers*
		4 Frigates on loan from BPF*

* This may be impossible if there is no decrease in illegal immigration.

	add	4 Submarines (a completion to planned strength)
		The possibility of having one depot ship for destroyers and submarines, instead of one for each type of vessel, is being investigated.
East Indies	reduce	1 Cruiser (BPF to lend cruiser or fast minelayer as necessary)

British Pacific Fleet	replace	a second Cruiser by second Fast Minelayer
	reduce	2 Frigates, in addition to the permanent reduction of the 4 on loan to the Mediterranean.
America and WI	reduce	2 Frigates

(ii) Ships with special complements

Battleships	Reduce	1 training seamen at Portland and transfer trainees ashore.
	Replace	1 training seamen at Portland by Fleet Carrier (already in hand).
	Reduce	RENOWN …
Aircraft Carriers	Replace	1 Fleet Carrier by 1 Light Fleet Carrier
Cruisers	Postpone employment of CUMBERLAND as trials cruiser.	
Destroyers and Frigates	Keep Boys' Training Flotilla of 4 ships instead of … using Home Fleet destroyers, which have been reduced by 4. Reduce 1 Air Target vessel in Med. The net addition is therefore 3.	
Fleet Minesweepers	Reduce 1 employed in Minesweeping Supervision in Germany.	
Submarines	Add 5 (instead of Home Fleet).	
Ferry Carriers	Add 1 (CAMPANIA).	

(iii) Reserve Fleet

Reduce following ships to Category C (Disposal Reserve):–

NELSON, RODNEY (already proposed)

Two ships out of RENOWN, QUEEN ELIZABETH and VALIANT, leaving six battleships in commission or in A or B reserve. (This is not in line with the CoS recent assessment of forces required on mobilisation, which included 6 Battleships … plus 2 in reserve).

BERWICK, ORION, AJAX, SUFFOLK … subject to retention if other cruisers are sold to Norway or loaned to India.

The above proposals save 745 on the battleships and 590 on the cruisers.

(iv) Combined Operations

Reduce present allocation of manpower of 4,200 (including margin) by at least 200; this is considered feasible and detailed proposals will be worked out.

Postpone the setting-up of a CTE in the Middle East until the position eases and so avoid an increase of 400. The Admiralty have said that they would try to provide the manpower in 1949, but it appears doubtful whether, in point of fact, the Army will be able to allocate trainees from the Middle East Commands.

11. Allowing for unforeseen additional commitments of 300 on ships and 200 on the Reserve Fleet, the saving effected by the proposals in paragraph 10 amount to 4,200 on ships and Reserve Fleet and 200 on Combined Operations.

<u>Total manpower savings</u>

12. If the above proposals are approved, the position will be:–

Savings on shore commitments	6,800
Contraction in Naval Aviation	2,250
Savings on ships and Reserve Fleet	4,200
Savings on Combined Operations	200
	13,450

There is thus still a gap of 2,000 between the figure so far saved and figure desired to be saved (15,450). If the unforeseen commitments, for which an allowance of 500 has been made, do not arise, the gap would be 1,500.

<u>Possible methods of covering the remaining gap in manpower</u>

13. Although the overall figure for the Navy will continue to drop from 166,250 at 31 March 1949 to 162,850 at 31 December 1949, a build-up of regulars will be achieved in 1949, which will compensate for the lower total figure. In fact, the most difficult period is expected to be during the six months from October 1948 to April 1949. This being so, the question of the gap can be considered in two ways:–

(a) Realise that there is a gap of 1,500–2,000 in the plan, but accept the risk of its existence and deal with it as occasion demands either by immobilising some ships temporarily, or for the time being cutting non-substantive training at the technical schools.

(b) Make further definite cuts in commitments, eg ships in commission, ships in Reserve Fleet.

14. It is proposed that the risk should be taken and that the procedure in paragraph 13(a) be adopted …

<u>Conclusions</u>

16. Approval is therefore sought for:–

(a) the acceptance of the fleets shown in Appendix I, column II as the target for 31 December 1948.

(b) the early investigation of the proposals for reductions ashore as specified in paragraph 5, with Board instructions to those concerned that every effort must be made to achieve the reductions or, where applicable, equivalents of a like kind eg another hospital in lieu of Sherborne, with the same saving.

(c) D of P to collate and put forward to the Board, on a separate paper, proposals for reducing 4 battleships and 4 cruisers to the Disposal Reserve (paragraph 10(iii)).

(d) the acceptance in principle of the proposals for reducing present commitments of Combined Operations by at least 200, and postponing the setting up of the CTE in the Middle East until the position eases.

(e) the acceptance of the existence of the gap of 1,500–2,000 in the manpower budget (paragraph 13(a)).

17. If the proposals in paragraph 16 receive approval, it will then be necessary to proceed with the preparation of phased plans for spreading the reductions evenly throughout 1948.

113. *Chiefs of Staff Minutes*

[DEFE 4/6] 20 August 1947

COS(47) 106th Meeting
FUTURE DEFENCE POLICY – STRENGTH OF THE ARMED FORCES

. . .

Sir John Cunningham said that the Admiralty had also decided to adopt a somewhat similar policy [as the RAF] as a basis for assessment for the size and composition and expenditure on the Royal Navy. It was proposed to concentrate on providing the minimum forces to meet immediate tasks which were:–

(a) To provide forces to meet our essential foreign station commitments.

(b) To provide for proper training. This in itself demanded ships of all types in commission and modern aircraft.

(c) To be prepared to provide a contribution to UNO security forces. This contribution could probably be provided out of the ships required in commission for training purposes.

It was also proposed to postpone for the next five years any attempt to build up the Naval Forces which would be required in war and to concentrate on:–

(a) The construction of experimental and prototype vessels. No other new construction would be attempted.

(b) The modernisation of such vessels, notably aircraft carriers which would otherwise be ineffective or unable to operate modern aircraft.

(c) The maintenance, by refit, of existing forces.

He emphasised that the above outlined policy could only be followed if the Royal Navy accepted only a token part of their share of National Service personnel …

Sir John Cunningham … was not convinced that during the next five years the possibility of war could be completely disregarded. To state that there would be no war in the next five years as a governing factor in determining the shape and size of our forces was to render us defenceless over that period …

114. *Board Memorandum*

[ADM 167/129] 28 August 1947

B.526 FUTURE DEFENCE POLICY –
REVISED NAVAL PROGRAMME TO MEET SUGGESTED LIMITATION OF DEFENCE EXPENDITURE

At their meeting on 31 July the Board reached certain conclusions on future defence policy as outlined in the documents circulated with Board Memorandum B.520 of the 26 July. This policy was related to the maintenance of peacetime requirements and the desirability of being able to expand on mobilisation to man a certain force which was planned to be built up by 1956–7. Since July the Minister of Defence has called for a complete re-examination of the basis which led to the previous assessment of forces based on:–

(a) an assumption that the risk of a major war is ruled out during the next five years and that the risk would increase only gradually during the following five years because we could not contemplate undertaking a major war until our economic and industrial strength has been recovered. We should, if such a war did occur, have to fight with what weapons we have:– during the next five years it should be assumed that the risk of a major war will vary directly with our visible offensive strength;
(b) an assumption that an annual expenditure of £600,000,000 will be the maximum allowed to the Armed Forces, including expenditure on production and defence research and development for an indefinite period starting with 1948–49;
(c) acceptance of the situation that the financial limit imposed may prevent the country having the defence forces hitherto considered necessary on the outbreak of war:– the serious risk involved in this is to be assumed as accepted by the Government. In determining the build-up of the forces during the next five years we

should concentrate on those which give us the best chance of survival and should avoid dissipating our resources.

2. The Minister of Defence has stated the following principles which should govern the composition of our forces:–

(a) Priority must be given to forces which in peace give the best visible show of strength and therefore have the greatest deterrent value;
(b) Long term research and development should have high priority in defence expenditure;
(c) We must provide the minimum forces necessary for our essential overseas garrisons and stations;
(d) No additional provision should be made for forces which might be required by the United Nations.[1]

3. The memorandum in Annex A (Future Defence Policy – Revised Naval Estimates for Period 1948/49 to 1952/53) which has been prepared by Plans Division in conjunction with DPS, the general lines having been endorsed by VCNS, is intended as a draft of the memorandum to be placed before the Minister of Defence as the Admiralty's assessment of the measures required to bring the Navy Estimates down to a figure which would represent a reasonable share for the Admiralty out of the £600,000,000 a year. I have been engaged in an endeavour to state what sum of money would be required to provide for the policy outlined in Annex A. It is out of the question with the very limited notice which has been given to produce estimates of cost on the same detailed basis as was done for the Board on 31 July, covering a forecast of expenditure for 1948/49 until 1956/57 and for a stable year thereafter … on the hypothesis that the Admiralty share might be, say, £180,000,000.

4. This line of approach was discussed at a meeting attended by the Controller, Fourth Sea Lord and Fifth Sea Lord a few days ago and since then the Controller has held a meeting of the Heads of his Departments and of Fourth Sea Lord's Departments with a view to indicating to what extent the programmes at which they would aim in the light of the policy outlined in Annex A could be met.

5. The result is to show that a sum of £180,000,000 for 1948/49 would probably not suffice to maintain the Fleet as outlined in that document. Probably £190,000,000 would suffice for that purpose if the utmost economy and care is employed in spending it …

6. It is a reasonable assumption (though subject to the qualification that the above figures are not accurate assessments) that the sum of

[1]COS(47)106th Meeting, 20 Aug 1947 in DEFE 4/6, not reproduced.

£180,000,000 would suffice for succeeding years as long as the policy outlined by the Minister of Defence continues and its practical form in the Navy is that described in Annex A:– the problem of making both ends meet within £180,000,000 would be rather easier in the three or four years following 1948/49 because the full effect of the reduction in the level of Naval personnel would be felt and the amount required for new construction and aircraft would fall off sharply.

7. It should be emphasised in connection with any substantial cut below £180,000,000 which might prove to be necessary if the Government were to refuse absolutely to face any excess beyond £600,000,000 for the Defence Votes for 1948/49 (and assuming the Admiralty could not succeed in gaining support for the Admiralty's share of £600,000,000 to be £180,000,000) that it would not be possible to confine any reduction solely to the heavy spending Votes (8 and 9). The cut that might have to be made in such Votes would almost certainly involve a substantial reduction in the aircraft programme (£17,000,000 for 1948/49), cancellation of new construction now building (albeit a wasteful form of economy), some reduction in dockyard strengths (involving discharges in the Home yards), but a cut of magnitude would also undoubtedly involve a reduction in the size of the Fleet to be maintained (which would have to take the form of reducing still further the Fleet in commission, or of scrapping more Reserve Fleet ships, or a combination of both) and also in Fleet personnel (involving some restriction in the recruitment of regular forces).

8. It is proposed, assuming that the Board approve Annex A as the basis of a reply to the Minister of Defence, to add at the end of it the paragraphs shown in Annex B.

ANNEX A
FUTURE DEFENCE POLICY – REVISED NAVAL ESTIMATES FOR PERIOD 1948/49 TO 1952/53

Memorandum By Admiralty[1]

RE-EXAMINATION

A re-examination of the Naval forces required in the next five years has been made in accordance with the assumptions and principles given in the memorandum by the Minister of Defence dated 23 August 1947. The limit of £600 million annually for the Armed Forces has been the most powerful factor in framing the new estimate of requirements.

[1] Submitted to the MoD as COS(47)178(O) 29 Aug 1947. DEFE 5/5.

NAVAL APPROACH TO THE PROBLEM

2. (a) To concentrate on providing the minimum forces to meet our immediate tasks:–
    (i) To provide the forces to meet our essential foreign station commitments.
    (ii) To provide for proper training. This in itself demands ships of all types and modern aircraft.
    (iii) To be prepared to provide a contribution to UN Security Forces, but no additional provision to be made for this.
   (b) To postpone for the next five years any attempt to build up the forces which would be required in war and therefore to concentrate, on the material side, on:–
    (i) Maintenance by refit of the existing forces;
    (ii) Modernisation of such vessels, notably aircraft carriers, which will otherwise be ineffective or unable to operate modern aircraft;
    (iii) To limit the laying down of New Construction to experimental and prototype vessels.

NAVAL FORCES

3. The minimum forces required for foreign stations (paragraph 2(a)(i)) are substantially the same as those resulting after the recalls recently made for the purpose of reducing expenditure abroad. The forces needed in Home Waters to provide for the commitment in paragraph 2(a)(ii)) above consist of a Home Fleet and a number of ships with special complements for experiment and school training. Details of the ships required to cover these commitments are given in Appendix A.

NAVAL AVIATION

4. (a) Front Line. 190 Front Line aircraft are required to complement the Carrier Fleet (see Appendix A) with normal allowance for re-equipping and re-commissioning.
   (b) Training and Miscellaneous. This is being kept to the bare minimum necessary to maintain a Front Line of 190, no allowance being made to build up any reserve of aircrews, apart from maintaining existing RNVR squadrons. Flying training over the next few years is of necessity at high level because of the need to replace temporary extended service pilots by regulars.
   (c) Aircraft. It is being planned to maintain the Front Line and training strength with the minimum of production of new aircraft over the next five years, whilst at the same time making fullest use of the remaining strength of wartime aircraft, which it is estimated will be entirely exhausted by the end of the five years. It is not planned to carry out any re-equipment for the sake of

re-equipment, but the aim is to replace worn out aircraft with new and modern types rather than with obsolescent ones.

(d) Airfields. Reductions of previous numbers planned are dependent on reduction of aircraft in storage and a reduced training commitment in maintenance ratings, and the paying-off of one airfield abroad.

MANPOWER

5. It is desired to maintain the policy of building up the regular male content of the Navy to the figure of 144,000, provisionally approved by the Defence Committee (DO(46) 3rd Meeting Item 3) … the figure of 144,000 regulars will not be reached for five years.

6. The Admiralty is anxious to reduce the National Service intake for the Navy to a token figure of 2,000. The usefulness of National Service men to the Navy is limited by the degree of dilution acceptable on mobilisation and, with overall figures for the Navy of the size now contemplated for the next five years, it has become apparent that the effort necessary to train NS men during this period is not commensurate with other claims on naval manpower. These facts, coupled with assumption (ii) in the Minister of Defence's memorandum regarding the risk of a major war, makes it uneconomic for the Navy to include more than a token number of NS men in their total manpower.

7. On the basis given in paragraphs 5 and 6 above, Appendix B gives an estimate of the manpower bearings over the next five years. If a greater number of NS men had to be included, the totals would be greater and further provision would have to be made for their training.

NEW CONSTRUCTION, MODERNISATION AND CONVERSION

8. New construction and conversions in a state of partial completion (except Dominion requirements and prototypes) will be slowed down as and where this would effect economy.

9. Further new construction and conversion during the next five years will be limited to prototypes of vessels not larger than frigates.

10. Modernisation will be limited in the next five years to two Fleet Carriers and two Light Fleet Carriers. This is necessary so that they may be made capable of operating modern aircraft.

STOCKPILING

11. It will have to be accepted that a back log will accumulate and the provision made in the next five years will not be more than half that allotted in the first five years of the original plan.

RESERVE FLEET

12. The Reserve Fleet is costly both in manpower and money for maintenance and a number of ships will be placed on the disposal list. This process must, however, be limited to disposing of ships which, from age

or deterioration, are no longer worth the expense of upkeep, in view of the decision to disregard the risk of a major war during the next five years.

APPENDIX A
ESTIMATE OF MINIMUM FLEET BETWEEN 1948/49 AND 1952/53

Theatre	Composition and numbers	Remarks
Home Fleet	2 Battleships 1 Fleet Carrier 1 Light Fleet Carrier 4 Cruisers 16 Destroyers 4 Fleet Minesweepers (1) 1 Fleet Replenishment Ship	(1) for duty in Med. when req'd
Mediterranean	2 Light Fleet Carriers 4 Cruisers 12 Destroyers 4 Frigates (Hunts) (a) 8 Frigates (Other) (b) 6 Submarines 2 Submarines (2/3 Comp.) (c) 4 Fleet Minesweepers 1 Submarine Depot Ship	(a) in lieu of destroyers (b) 2 for Red Sea (c) fast S/M targets for A/S trg
East Indies	2 Cruisers 4 Frigates (d)	(d) 2 for Persian Gulf
British Pacific Fleet	2 Light Fleet Carriers (m) 2 Cruisers } (e) 2 Fast Minelayers } 8 Destroyers 4 Frigates 6 Submarines 2 Submarines (2/3 Comp.) (f) 1 Submarine Depot Ship	(m) available for East Indies (e) or 3 Cruisers (f) fast S/M targets for A/S trg
America and West Indies	2 Cruisers 2 Frigates	
South Atlantic	1 Cruiser 2 Frigates	
Total of ships in full commission	2 Battleships 1 Fleet Carrier 5 Light Fleet Carriers 15 Cruisers 2 Fast Minelayers (g) 36 Destroyers 4 Frigates (Hunts) (h) 20 Frigates (Other) 12 Submarines 4 Submarines (2/3 Comp.) (i) 8 Fleet Minesweepers 2 Submarine Depot Ships 1 Fleet Replenishment Ship	(g) in lieu of cruisers (h) in lieu of destroyers (i) fast S/M targets for A/S trg

Ships with special complements. Experimental, School Training etc	1 Battleship 2 Fleet Carriers 1 Light Fleet Carrier 1 Cruiser 21 Destroyers } 8 Frigates (Hunts) } 46 17 Frigates (Other) (j) } 24 Submarines 12 Fleet Minesweepers (k) 1 Ferry Carrier 1 Fighter Direction and R/P Training Ship	Plus CUMBERLAND as Trials Cruiser when manpower permits (j) 1 Fishery Protection (k) 7 Fishery Protection
Total of ships in commission with full and special experimental and training complements. ie all ships excluding reserve	3 Battleships 3 Fleet Carriers 6 Light Fleet Carriers 16 Cruisers 2 Fast Minelayers 57 Destroyers 12 Frigates (Hunts) 37 Frigates (Other) 40 Submarines 20 Fleet Minesweepers 2 Submarine Depot Ships 1 Fleet Replenishment Ship 1 Ferry Carrier 1 Fighter Direction and R/P Training Ship	Plus CUMBERLAND later

APPENDIX B
BUILD-UP OF MANPOWER TO END OF 1952

Date	31 Dec 1947	31 Mar 1948	31 Dec 1948	31 Mar 1949	31 Dec 1949	31 Mar 1950	31 Dec 1950	31 Mar 1951	31 Dec 1951	31 Mar 1952	31 Dec 1952
Regulars	114,750	116,800	122,950	124,550	129,400	130,100	132,200	133,400	137,050	138,800	144,000
Locally Entered Personnel	2,700	2,650	2,500	2,500	2,500	2,500	2,500	2,500	2,500	2,500	2,500
National Servicemen	56,500	40,450	17,100	10,500	2,000	2,000	2,000	2,000	2,000	2,000	2,000
Total Males	173,500	159,900	142,550	137,550	133,900	134,600	136,700	137,900	141,550	143,300	148,500
WRNS	8,000	7,900	8,100	8,100	8,200	8,200	8,300	8,300	8,400	8,400	8,500
TOTAL NUMBERS	181,950	167,800	150,650	145,650	142,100	142,800	145,000	146,200	149,950	151,700	157,000

NOTE:– The figure of 167,800 for 31st March 1948 is 10,500 less than the figure of 178,300 originally planned for that date.

115. *Board Minute*

[ADM 167/128] 29 August 1947

Future Defence Policy:– Revised Naval Programme to meet suggested limitation of Defence Expenditure

4175. Since the last meeting of the Board (Board Minute 4171) the Minister of Defence had called for a complete re-examination of the basis of the previous assessment of Service requirements.

The Board considered the draft of a memorandum which had been prepared estimating the requirements for the Navy for the years 1948/49 to 1952/53 in accordance with the assumption and principles set out in the memorandum by the Minister of Defence, and indicating the minimum financial provision which would be needed in 1948/49 to meet those requirements.

The Board agreed that the figure to be given for the minimum financial provision estimated to be required for 1948/49 should be £185,000,000 and that the list of deficiencies set out in sub-paragraphs (a) to (k) of paragraph 13 of the draft memorandum as arising with a provision of £180,000,000, should then be omitted, except that it should be made clear that with a provision of £185,000,000 it will not be possible to make progress with the heavy backlog of refitting work of ships now in reserve and that there is some doubt of the dockyard labour being available to undertake the projected modernisation of aircraft carriers. It was decided that no reference should be made in the memorandum (as in paragraph 14 of the draft) to the effects of a reduction in the financial provision below the figure to be given as the minimum provision required. For the First Sea Lord's information, a statement would be prepared setting out the consequences of a reduction in the provision by £10,000,000 and by £20,000,000.

It was agreed that paragraph 5 of the draft memorandum should be revised so as to avoid relating the build-up of the regular male content of the Navy (to 144,000 at the end of 1952) to the bid on account of the same figure which had been provisionally authorised in 1946 for the naval bearing. It was pointed out that if no more than 2,000 National Service men were taken annually for wholetime service in the Navy over the next five years, it was likely that special provision would be required to ensure that a larger proportion of National Service men of the years 1949 to 1952 would be available to the Navy on mobilisation.

The Board discussed the reference in paragraph 12 of the draft memorandum to the placing of ships of the Reserve Fleet on the disposal list. The First Lord stated that no decision on the disposal of ships of the Reserve Fleet could be reached until he had fully considered the issue, and asked that a separate paper on this question should be prepared for his consideration.

The memorandum as revised in the discussion at the Board was approved for transmission to the Minister of Defence …

116. *Chiefs of Staff Minutes*

[DEFE 4/6] 30 August 1947

COS(47)112th Meeting

FUTURE DEFENCE POLICY – STRENGTH OF THE ARMED FORCES

…

Admiralty Memorandum[1]

Sir John Cunningham said that achievement of the financial and manpower figures quoted in the memorandum by the Admiralty involved drastic reductions in the Royal Navy. The forces estimated represented the absolute minimum required to fulfil the tasks specified for the Royal Navy by the Minister of Defence. He did not believe it was possible to assess the size and composition of naval forces which might be required after a period of five years. Such an assessment would have to be made nearer the time in the light of the position at home and abroad. He pointed out that the total financial expenditure of £185 millions estimated as being required during the year 1948/1949 included £3½ millions for war terminal charges and £7¾ millions for research and development. Thus, the true amount which it was estimated would be required to be expended on the Royal Navy during that year was just under £174 million.

He emphasised that the limit of £600 millions annually for the armed forces had been the most powerful factor in framing the Naval estimates. This was an assumption which had been given to the Services and he thought it was important to draw a distinction between it and the assumption that it was not contemplated undertaking a major war until our economic and industrial strength had recovered. This latter assumption implied that we must face the risk of losing any major war, if involved in one, before our economic and industrial strength was recovered and also for an indefinite period thereafter until our armed forces were recreated …

…

The Minister of Defence … wished to make it clear that he would have to present to the Cabinet the implications of reducing the expenditure of the forces to £600 millions for 1948/49. Since there had been

[1] B526 Annex / COS(47)178(O), Doc. No. 114.

no agreement in the COS Committee – a fact he deplored since it was a reflection on the Joint Staff system – he would have to ask for assessments on arbitrarily imposed cuts on the present estimates … estimates of the armed forces might be as follows:–

Royal Navy	£160 millions
Army	£270 millions
Royal Air Force	£170 millions

…

In subsequent discussion … it was agreed that Service Ministries should prepare a statement showing the methods and implications of reducing their estimates for 1948/1949 to the figures outlined above by the Minister of Defence …

117. *Chiefs of Staff Memorandum*

[DEFE 5/5] 1 September 1947

COS(47)184(O)

FUTURE DEFENCE POLICY – STRENGTH OF THE ARMED FORCES

Memorandum by the First Sea Lord

In arriving at an estimated expenditure for 1948–49 of £185 millions (… a net figure of £173¾ millions) cuts in projected expenditure have been envisaged which seriously impair the ability of the Navy subsequently to expand commensurately with its responsibilities if and when the risk of war increases … both by reason of accepting a lower standard of maintenance of material and of training of personnel …

It should be emphasised that to achieve the reduction in naval manpower and in expenditure, outlined in Admiralty memorandum of 29 August,[1] considerable reductions will have to be made in the number of ships at present maintained in reserve. The scheme now under examination in the Admiralty envisages the immediate scrapping of a number of cruisers and possibly even some battleships (apart from smaller craft).

[1] B.526 / COS(47)178(O), Doc. No. 114.

118. *Defence Committee Memorandum*

[CAB 131/4] 15 September 1947

DO(47)68 DEFENCE REQUIREMENTS

Memorandum by the Minister of Defence

I – Introductory

During recent months I have been engaged, in consultation with the Chiefs of Staff, upon an examination of our future defence policy and of the size and composition of our peacetime Armed Forces.

2. Simultaneously I have been considering the possibilities of making short term reductions in the size of the forces in order to reduce their requirements of foreign currency and to release as many men as possible for work in productive industry. Early in August I recommended to the Defence Committee that in order to assist us in our financial and economic difficulties the strength of the forces at 31 March 1948, which under previous plans would have been 1,087,000, should be reduced by a further 80,000 to 1,007,000 and that as many as 210,000 men should be withdrawn from overseas stations by the same date.

3. This proposal was approved by the Cabinet on 5 August (CM(47) 68th Conclusions, Minute 2). I continued to seek further rapid reductions in numbers, but I was soon forced to the conclusion that we had gone as far as we ought to go in the way of making piecemeal and arbitrary reductions in the absence of any clear idea of longer-term policy or of the size and composition of the forces which would be required to carry it out in 1948–49 and subsequent years.

4. I have therefore during the past few weeks spent much time in consultation with the Service Ministers and the Chiefs of Staff on longer-term issues, particularly as they affect the requirements of manpower and money for the financial year 1948–49. I have now reached the stage where I feel that I must acquaint my colleagues with the general picture, in order that they may judge the current situation against its correct background.

5. On 18 February I issued a directive to the Chiefs of Staff asking them to consider the fundamental principles of our post-war defence policy and to give me their views on the form and nature of our forces over a long-term period. To impart reality to their deliberations I gave it as my view that expenditure on the forces in peacetime would be severely limited and that it could not be expected that the defence share of the national budget, after clearing up the aftermath of war, would be likely to exceed £600 million a year.

6. On 30 May I issued a further directive to the Chiefs of Staff amplifying my earlier views, re-emphasising the financial limitations

within which their planning would have to take place and laying down a precise timetable for the submission of reports on –

(a) the size and composition of our forces in a normal peacetime year;
(b) the size and composition of our forces in the financial year 1948–49;

Both costed in money and manpower.

7. This information was provided in individual reports from the Service Departments early in August, and it was at once clear to me that the money and manpower which would be required if these proposals were adopted would be far beyond the capacity of the country in this time of economic stress. I do not propose to go into detail at this stage, but it will be sufficient if I say that the Defence Estimates for 1948–49 would have amounted to more than £900 million.

8. It was obvious, therefore, that some drastic change of the policy which hitherto the Chiefs of Staff have followed would be necessary. After consultation with them I issued a further directive on 23 August calling for an urgent re-examination on the following basis:–

General Assumptions

(i) It is not possible to contemplate undertaking a major war until our economic and industrial strength has recovered. It must therefore be accepted that an annual expenditure of £600 million will be the maximum allowed to the Armed Forces, including expenditure on production and defence research, for an indefinite period;
(ii) It must be accepted that the risk of a major war is ruled out during the next five years and that the risk will increase only gradually during the following five years. This risk will vary directly with our visible offensive strength. If attacked we must fight with what we have;
(iii) It must be accepted that the financial limit imposed may prevent us having the defence forces hitherto considered necessary on the outbreak of war. It will therefore be necessary to build up only the forces which give us the best chance of survival and to avoid dissipating our resources. This will mean taking serious risks.

Principles which govern the Composition of our Forces

(iv) Priority must be given to forces which in peace give the best visible show of strength and therefore have the greatest deterrent value;
(v) Long-term research and development should have high priority in defence expenditure;
(vi) We must provide the minimum forces necessary for our essential overseas garrisons and stations;
(vii) No additional provision should be made for forces which might be required by the United Nations.

9. It will be observed that under the terms of this directive our policy for the next five years would bear no relation to any state of preparedness for war, but would be concentrated on maintaining the forces in being at the minimum level, while at the same time endeavouring to provide for essentials and to maintain the best possible show of deterrent strength.

10. Such a policy as that outlined in the previous paragraph necessitates settling an order of priority between the various competing requirements for the limited resources of manpower and money which we shall be able to afford for defence purposes during the next few critical years. So far, I have received no collective appreciation by the Chiefs of Staff on what these priorities should be. I have, however, given a good deal of thought to the problem and, in my opinion, the broad basis of priority, as between the respective Services, is as follows:–

(a) Defence research and development for all three Services. This is all-important.

(b) Maintenance of the Royal Air Force at a level sufficient to preserve its essential structure and to maintain the best possible show of deterrent strength.

(c) Maintenance of the Navy at the minimum level required to safeguard our sea communications, to carry out such commitments overseas as are laid upon it and to preserve a nucleus on which we could expand if it should become necessary to do so. This policy will necessitate a scaling down of Naval plans, more especially as regards large capital ships; it implies concentration on the Naval Air Arm and retention of cruisers and below in adequate numbers.

(d) Employment of the Army as a training organisation for the National Service intake upon which its long-term defence policy must rest and to provide the minimum strength needed to meet its overseas commitments. These commitments will undoubtably have to be substantially reduced.

11. More work is still required on our long-term policy and on its application in the years after 1948–49. I can. however, see no escape from an approach to the problems of 1948–49 against the general background which I have sketched above – and it is only after an examination on that basis of defence requirements during the next financial year that one can form a correct judgment on the immediate situation.

II – 1948–49 Defence Requirements

12. I have already mentioned that the figures for 1948–49 which were originally prepared by the Service Departments, plus the requirements of the Ministry of Supply for defence research and development, inspection, and war terminals, amounted to more than £900 million.

13. After intensive examination on the basis of mv latest directive, this figure was reduced to approximately £825 million, divided between the three Services and the Ministry of Supply as follows:–

	£ million	
Navy	185*	* Including £7.75 million for research and development
Army	386	
Air Force	206	
Ministry of Supply	70	
Total	827	

14. At this point, I must make it clear that 1948–49 can in no sense be regarded as a normal peacetime year, so far as expenditure on the Services is concerned. Even if £600 million is feasible as a target from 1949 onwards, it cannot be reached next year. Examination of the table above will show that expenditure on war terminal charges … will still amount to about £70 million.[1] This is an inescapable liability. In addition, many of the commitments imposed upon us as a result of the war and the disturbed situation which it created will still remain …

15. I am, nevertheless, certain that a total of £825 million for the defence budget in the financial year 1948–49 is far higher than anything that the Government or Parliament would be prepared to contemplate. After the most searching enquiry, I have ascertained that considerable further economies can still be made provided His Majesty's Government accept the strategical risks and political consequences involved, though I must emphasise that many of them will be contrary to the present views of the Service Ministers and the Chiefs of Staff. This is, of course, not the time to settle the money provision for defence in the next financial year, and at this stage I will go no further than to suggest in the most tentative way that it should, subject to further close examination, be possible to arrive at a total for the 1948–49 defence estimates of something in the neighbourhood of £710 million, including terminals, divided between the three Service Departments and the Ministry of Supply very roughly as follows:–

	£ million	
Navy	155*	* Including research and development
Army	316	
Air Force	180	
Ministry of Supply	60	
Total	711	

[1] Only about £3.5m of 'terminals' were attributed to the Navy.

16. To arrive at such figures as these, large reductions in the strength of the forces both during the remainder of the current financial year and over the whole of 1948–49 will be necessary. I shall deal later in this memorandum with the possibility of making further reductions between now and 31 March 1948. My tentative proposals for man-power strengths during 1948–49 would involve a run-down to the following figures at 31 *March* 1949 (a reduction of nearly 300,000 on the present approved figure of 1,007,000 for 31 March 1948 and of nearly 500,000 on the figure as it will be on 30 September 1947):–

Navy	147,000
Army	339,000
Air Force	227,000
Total	713,000

17. The effect on the Services of such considerable reductions in manpower and money as those which I have in mind will inevitably be very serious … The target figures I have just given for the strength of the Forces at 31 March 1949 will not admit of more than the following intake of national servicemen in the coming financial year:–

Navy	2,000	(practically a token figure)
Army	100,000	
Air Force	48,000	

…

19. An indication of the consequences which flow primarily from the reductions in manpower foreshadowed for 1948–49, for each Service, is as follows:–

NAVY

(a) A large scrapping programme of ships at present in reserve will have to be carried out. This is likely to be of the following order:–
 5 battleships
 11 cruisers
 55–60 destroyers and frigates
 1 aircraft component repair ship
 Some submarines
 Considerable numbers of combined operations craft, fleet train and small craft.

(b) A drastic, but it is hoped in some cases temporary, reduction of strength on foreign stations including the following measures:–
 Reduction of the American and West Indies Squadron to:– 1 cruiser and 1 frigate.
 Reduction of the British Pacific Fleet to:– 2 cruisers and 4 frigates.

Reduction of the Naval Dockyard at Hong Kong to care and maintenance.

(c) The abandonment of the Admiralty's wreck dispersal organisation, with probable serious effects on commercial shipping.

(d) Reduction of the Royal Marines by the equivalent of two Commandos.

(e) Reduction of the Combined Operations organisation.

(f) Reduction of the Home Fleet to a strength of:–

1 battleship
1 fleet carrier
3 cruisers and
8 destroyers (plus a training squadron)

And virtual immobilisation even of this reduced strength for a period of about eight months between October 1947 and May 1948 in order that men due for release in these ships may be removed without relief …

20. The strategic consequences of measures of this kind are extremely grave, and must bring with them undesirable political consequences, particularly in the virtual abandonment of our position in the Pacific and the serious weakening of our strength in the Middle East and in Germany. None the less, the Defence Committee must appreciate that if in our present economic situation there must be reductions in the forces of the kind outlined above, then there is no escape from the unpleasant decisions required.

21. To bridge the gap between the £825 million mentioned in paragraph 13 above and the tentative figure of £710 million mentioned in paragraph 15, considerable further reductions will be necessary … The following paragraphs will, I hope, serve to give some broad indication.

NAVY

(a) Virtually all work on new construction will be suspended, with the exception of one aircraft carrier and certain prototype vessels which are urgently needed for research and development.

(b) All alterations and additions in ships and fleet establishments intended to improve amenities will have to be postponed.

(c) The dockyard labour force in the United Kingdom will have to be very considerably reduced. *This will almost certainly involve putting one of the southern dockyards, probably Chatham, on a care and maintenance basis.*

(d) The re-equipment of the Royal Dockyards with modern machinery and plant will be still further delayed.

(e) General reductions in the store, armament and inspection organisations will be necessary.

(f) A further cut in the Admiralty's oil fuel programme, including stopping building new fleet oilers, will have to be made.
(g) *The naval aircraft programme will be severely cut and all modernisation of aircraft carriers will be deferred. Five air stations will be closed.*
(h) No new major works projects will be started in 1948–49 and the provision for new minor works projects will be limited to about £100,000.
(i) Certain items in the present approved works programmes will be cancelled and the housing programme for naval personnel at home and abroad and the modernisation of naval barracks will be further slowed down …

22. The drastic effect of cuts of this kind on the Services will be readily appreciated. Some of them, notably the reductions in the production and works programmes, cannot be regarded as more than temporary suspension of expenditure which will be necessary in the near future if the reduced forces with which we shall be left are to be efficient and contented. The effect on the country's industrial war potential of reductions in the Service production programme of the order which I have in mind has yet to be assessed, and it may well be that it will be impossible to go as far as I have suggested. This point is being investigated by my Department in consultation with the Ministry of Supply and the Admiralty. The reduction in the works programmes means that all improvements in conditions of life in the Services will be virtually abandoned for the time being. Even though, in my view, this can be defended as part of an essential reduction in the national investment programme, it will inevitably have its effect upon Service morale and upon recruiting, and it must be remembered that the continued recruitment of regulars in all three Services is essential to the future manpower needs of the Forces. *The political and industrial effect of so drastic a step as the closing of one of the southern dockyards will need the most careful examination …*

23. All these matters will require further consideration by the Defence Committee and the Cabinet when the time comes to settle the total of the Defence Estimates for 1948–49. At the moment I do not seek authority for any of them, and my sole purpose in referring to them in this paper is to warn my colleagues of the extreme measures to which it appears likely that we shall be forced if the defence budget is to be reduced to a figure which can be regarded as reasonable in the present critical situation of this country.

24. What I do ask the Defence Committee to consider here and now in relation to 1948–49 is whether, given our current and prospective economic difficulties, we must be prepared to accept the very serious

consequences of the substantial run-down in numbers by 31 March 1949 as described in paragraph 19 above … If the Committee are prepared to face the risks outlined above, I ask them to approve, as a basis of planning, the figures contained in para. 16.

III – Current Strength of the Armed Forces

25. Against the background sketched in Parts I and II of this Memorandum, I turn to the question of the strength of the Armed Forces between now and 31 March 1948. The present approved estimate for that date is 1,007,000 which must be compared with my provisional forecast of strengths of approximately 713,000 at 31 March 1949 (see paragraph 16 above). The immediate question for decision is whether it is feasible to contemplate a lower figure than 1,007,000 by 31 March next.

26. To increase the pace of the run-down in the Armed Forces will reduce their efficiency and their ability to undertake their current commitments. As my colleagues are aware I have emphasised on more than one occasion the serious position in which the Services find themselves from the loss of trained men; to increase that loss will present them with further formidable difficulties. None the less if it is the view of the Defence Committee that, in the light of the current financial and economic situation, still further contributions must be made by the Services in the release of manpower, I consider, after consultation with my Service colleagues, that, subject to the fulfilment of certain conditions, a further reduction can be made …

27. If, and only if, it is possible to fulfil these conditions[1] I consider that the strengths of the Forces at 31 March 1948 could be reduced by a further 70,000 to 937,000. The detailed breakdown of the latter figure as compared with that announced by the Prime Minister in the House of Commons at the beginning of August would be:–

	Present	*Proposed*
Navy	178,000	147,000
Army	550,000	527,000
Air Force	279,000	263,000
	1,007,000	937,000

28. I do not see how larger reductions between now and the end of this financial year can be regarded as feasible …

29. I ask the Defence Committee:–

(i) *to take note of* the position at present reached on the long-term requirements of Defence within strictly limited resources of money and man-power;

[1] These conditions have not been reproduced. They relate to withdrawal of forces from Austria, Italy, Greece and Japan, the deferment of call-up of National Service conscripts and the effect on shipping of increased repatriation of personnel serving abroad.

(ii) *to take note of* the provisional forecast of the financial requirements of the Defence Estimates for 1948–49;

(iii) *to decide whether* the serious risks and the political consequences involved in the large-scale reductions in the strengths of our Forces forecast for 1948–49 must be accepted;

(iv) *to approve* the proposal that the National Service intake in 1948–49 shall be reduced to approximately 150,000 (Army 100,000, Air Force 48,000, Navy 2,000) …

(v) subject to the decisions on (iii) and (iv) *to approve* the following estimate for the strength of the Forces at 31 March 1949:–

Navy	147,000
Army	339,000
Air Force	227,000
	713,000

(vi) *to agree*, subject to the conditions in paragraph 26, that there should be a further reduction of 70,000 in the strength of the Forces to 937,000 at 31 March 1948 and that this is the limit of reduction for the current financial year involving, as it would, a drop of 150,000 from the original approved planning figure of 1,087,000;

(vii) *to take note that*, if the above decisions are taken, the planned run-down of the Forces, as now revised, would be:–

	30.9.47	*31.3.48*	*30.6.48*	*31.3.49*
Navy	182,000	147,000	147,000	147,000
Army	714,000	527,000	448,000	339,000
Air Force	307,000	263,000	250,000	227,000
	1,203,000	937,000	845,000	713,000

119. *Defence Committee Minutes*

[CAB 131/5] 18 September 1947

DO(47) 20th Meeting

1. Defence Requirements

The Committee had before them a memorandum by the Minister of Defence (DO(47)68) describing the stage reached in his study of the long-term requirements of defence, setting out his estimate of the reductions in the strength of the Armed Forces that might be made by 31 March 1948 and 31 March 1949 and giving an assessment of the risks and consequences involved in these reductions …

The Prime Minister said that, in his view, there had not been sufficient appreciation of the need to bring the strength of the Armed Forces within the limits of what the country could afford in terms of money and manpower, and that he was disappointed in the extent to which the Chiefs of Staff had found it possible to submit proposals on a joint basis. He also found it difficult to understand why the reductions proposed in DO(47)68, which still provided for an expenditure of over £700 million in 1948–49, should have the effect of virtually immobilising the Armed Forces. Thirdly, he thought that the Committee should be told what were the assumptions with regard to the tasks to be discharged by the Armed Forces on which the proposals in DO(47)68 were based. In the present transitional period, the strength of the Forces should be based on some such assessment and not be merely the result of a reduction from a previously approved figure …

The Foreign Secretary said that he found it difficult to take an optimistic view of the international situation at the present time … He recognised our economic difficulties, but if the United Kingdom were to have any influence in international affairs, he must have an adequate backing of armed force.

The First Lord of the Admiralty stressed the fact that in 1948–49 the Navy would still be struggling to achieve an equilibrium after the loss of skilled men through demobilisation. A substantial number of regular recruits was being obtained, and he hoped that, in order to avoid further disorganisation, the intake of National Service men into the Navy might, for the time being, be limited to a token number. New construction had been virtually eliminated and if the proposals for 1948–49 outlined in DO(47)68 were accepted many ships would have to be scrapped. This would mean the loss of much material, the preservation of which would have been a valuable insurance against future emergencies. He emphasised the importance of the role of the Navy in preserving law and order *(eg* in the West Indies) and in maintaining the prestige of the United Kingdom in foreign countries …

The Chancellor of the Exchequer said that he recognised the risk involved in assuming that there would be no major war for five years, but that, in his view, the greater danger was the possibility of early economic disaster …

120. *Defence Committee Memorandum*

[CAB 131/4] 25 September 1947

DO(47)74 DEFENCE REQUIREMENTS

Memorandum by the Minister of Defence

The Defence Committee, at its meeting on 18 September (DO(47) 20th Meeting, Minute 1) invited me "to consider and report on the possibility of further accelerating the run-down of the Services to the figure of 713,000."

2. … I have conducted, in consultation with the Service Ministers and the Chiefs of Staff, a most searching and detailed examination into the possibilities of improving the planned run-down of the Forces as set out in the table contained in paragraph 29 (vii) of my memorandum DO(47)68. While my investigation has necessarily covered all three Services, study of that table will show that the possibility of any substantial acceleration in the run-down primarily arises in connection with the Army, not so much because of its total size as because of the extent to which its current numbers exceed the numbers forecast for 31 March 1949. In the paragraphs which follow, I therefore pay particular attention to the case of the Army, but I am bound to say at once that neither there, nor in the case of the Navy or the Air Force, am I able to recommend any acceleration of the run-down previously submitted to the Defence Committee.

3. … I must emphasise once more the magnitude of the effort contemplated in my original proposals … the estimated reduction of the Forces from 1,227,000 at 30 September 1947 to 713,000 at 31 March 1949 would involve the release of no less than 800,000 men and women; that is to say, the release of eight out of every twelve who will be in the Forces at the end of the month.

4. These original proposals involv[ed] … acceptance of serious strategic risks and political consequences in the interests of a major contribution to our current financial and manpower needs. Nonetheless, I have endeavoured … to find some means of accelerating still further the pace of run-down. I have examined that question both in relation to the current financial year and in relation to the financial year 1948–49, and my conclusions as regards each Service can be summarised as follows.

NAVY

5. The figure of 1,087,000 originally approved for the strength of the Forces at 31 March 1948 included 182,000 for the Navy. The proposals contained in DO(47)68 contemplated that the Navy would run-down to a figure of 147,000 at 31 March 1949 and, what is more, would reach that figure of 147,000 by 31 March 1948. For the Navy to come down to 147,000 even by 31 March 1949 will involve the most serious consequences set out in paragraph 19 of DO(47)68; to come down to that

figure by 31 March 1948 will involve the immediate implementation of major measures of reorganisation and re-deployment. The present plan envisages, therefore, that the figure for 31 March 1949 will be reached in six months from now. It is only with great sacrifice that this can be brought about. I do not see how the Navy can possibly do more …

…

CONCLUSION

13. I therefore ask the Defence Committee to approve the various proposals recapitulated in the following paragraph of this memorandum and, in particular, if they accept the risks and implications involved, to agree to the planned run-down in manpower to 713,000 by 31 March 1949…

14. I ask the Defence Committee:–

(i) to decide whether the serious risks and the political consequences involved in the large-scale reductions in the strengths of our Forces forecast for 1948–49 must be accepted …

(ii) to approve the proposal that the National Service intake in 1948–49 shall be reduced to approximately 150,000 (Army 100,000, Air Force 48,000, Navy 2,000);

(iii) subject to the decisions on (i) and (ii), to approve the following estimate for the strength of the Forces at 31 March 1948:–

Navy	147,000
Army	339,000
Air Force	227,000
	713,000

(iv) to agree that the further reduction of 70,000 in the strength of the Forces to 937,000 at 31 March 1948, as approved by the Committee on 19th September (DO(47) 20th Meeting, Minute 1) is the limit of reduction for the current financial year involving, as it would, a drop of 150,000 from the original approved planning figure of 1,087,000;

(v) to take note that, if the above decisions are taken, the estimated run-down of the Forces, as now revised, would be:–

	30.9.47	*31.3.48*	*30.6.48*	*31.3.49*
Navy	182,000	147,000	147,000	147,000
Army	738,000	527,000	442,000	339,000
Air Force	307,000	263,000	250,000	227,000
	1,227,000	937,000	839,000	713,000

121. *Defence Committee Minutes*

[CAB 131/5] 29 September 1947

DO(47) 22nd Meeting
Defence Requirements
… *The Prime Minister* said that, in his view, the Committee had no option but to recommend to the Cabinet that the strategic risks and the political consequences outlined by the Minister of Defence should be accepted, and that the proposed run-down in the strength of the Forces should be approved … Meanwhile the Minister of Defence should devote the utmost efforts to ensuring that the country was provided with the most efficient means of defence within the manpower ceilings now recommended … The Committee … agreed to recommend [this to] the Cabinet …

122. *Joint Planning Staff Memorandum*

[DEFE 6/3] 11 November 1947

JP(47)129(Final) SHAPE AND SIZE OF THE ARMED FORCES

As instructed[1] we have made an examination with the object of arriving at

> "an assessment of what should be the long-term shape and size of our armed forces in peacetime on the basis of an annual defence expenditure, including research and development for the armed forces, not exceeding £600m."

2. We cannot refrain from pointing out that the wording of this instruction implies, without precisely stating it, that armed forces which mean anything at all can, in fact, be provided by an annual expenditure arbitrarily fixed at £600m. We feel that this method of approach is unrealistic and dangerous. If defence and security are to be obtained, they must be paid for. It is no good buying something else which costs rather less. If a man requires a suit of clothes, he must pay what it costs. If he cannot afford a complete suit of clothes, it will be no good his buying part of a suit only and then pretending that he is fully dressed when, in fact, he has no trousers.

3. In our approach to the problem we first tried to find the absolute minimum requirement of the three Services in peacetime, ie the least amount of cloth and the cheapest kind which will give us a suit at all. What has made this even more difficult is the requirement in our terms of

[1] COS(47) 120th Meeting, Item 4.

reference that the suit must not only do for every day but must be capable of being repaired and renewed within a year for the special occasion of war.

ESTIMATE OF MINIMUM FORCES REQUIRED – ANNEX I

4. In Annex I we have followed as closely as possible the guidance given us in our terms of reference. We started from the statement of our Future Defence Policy[1] and the Minister's Directive.[2] We used the estimates already made by all the Service Ministries to implement this policy and we cut them and pruned them and reshaped them as far as we could. The forces which we arrived at are shown in the Appendices to Annex I, which contains an explanation of the varying basis on which each was estimated and the implications of accepting them …

Conclusions of Annex I

11. The results of this part of our examination are shown in full in Annex I. They are disappointing. The forces which are shown as the barest minimum are neither strong in all arms nor fully equipped with modern weapons. They rely, moreover … on a considerable degree of American aid against a major power. There is no question of our recommending them.

And yet the average annual cost including research and development is £740m:–

	£m
Research and Development	42
Navy	208
Army	250
RAF	240
Total	740

12. It is, therefore, already clear that even with these exiguous forces we are still a long way over the financial limit imposed on us. We therefore proceeded with a further effort to reduce cost without a further sacrifice of security …

POSSIBLE METHODS OF MAKING FURTHER CUTS – ANNEX II

16. Since we realised that we had not yet achieved the target we went on to consider whether any radically different method of approach might lead to a solution.

17. In this part of our examination we kept before us the emphatic priority given to us in our terms of reference for forces which could be expected to deter aggression.

[1]DO(47)44, reproduced as Doc. No. 102.
[2]COS(47)173(O).

We had no difficulty in agreeing a broad definition of deterrent power. We defined it as the power which might be expected by the aggressor to exact a greater price for victory than he was willing to pay.

In translating this power into actual visible strength and relating it to the aggressor we had in mind, our opinions diverged …

20. This divergence of view is reflected in the three examinations attached to Annex II[1] …

26. In his paper, Director of Plans, Admiralty, argues from the proposition that although it is agreed by all of us that adequate defence requires three effective Services, financial stringency may make it necessary to lay down priorities between them. He argues that in both peace and war the RAF and the Navy should have priority – if there must be a priority – over the Army.

27. His contention is as follows. In peace the Air Force must provide the deterrent and the Navy, by reason of its flexibility and mobility can most economically provide for police duties. In war, the security of the UK must have absolute priority and this requires as a first charge the provision of adequate air forces and, for the control of sea communications on which the life of [the] UK depends, an adequate Navy.

28. On this basis, he calculates that with a Navy and RAF on the lines of the estimate in Annex I and an Army whose expenditure was limited to £150 million, defence services could be provided for an average annual cost of £640 million.

29. … We are all agreed that it would be a counsel of despair to cripple the Army in this way. The lessons of the recent war have emphasised the interdependence of the three Services on one another. Each Service plays a vital part. In spite of arguments that the development of the atom bomb may have altered priorities between the three Services there is no evidence that it has in any way altered these basic principles …

CONCLUSIONS

30. Our conclusions are:–

(a) In present conditions of high costs, it is not possible to provide adequate defence services within a financial ceiling of an average annual expenditure of £600m.

(b) Even the forces shown in Annex I, the cost of which is £740m, including research and development, are not complete in all arms nor fully equipped with modern weapons. They rely, moreover, on a considerable degree of American aid. There is no question of our recommending them.

[1]Not reproduced. The Admiralty's paper is summarised in paragraphs 26–28.

(c) If HMG insists on imposing an arbitrary limit of £600m then, in our view, there should be no question of the Chiefs of Staff making recommendations to this end. It should be made clear to HMG that if they are insistent upon this financial limit, they would have to accept responsibility for ordering reductions which are incompatible with security, and for the decision on the means by which the financial limit was to be reached. In our view this decision will bring them, depending upon their interpretation of deterrent power, to a choice between two broad courses which we have discussed in Annex II.

ANNEX I
FORCES USED AS A BASIS FOR THIS PAPER AND SUGGESTIONS FOR POSSIBLE FURTHER REDUCTIONS

…

Royal Navy

3. Originally, the Admiralty prepared a detailed appreciation on the size of the fleet required to assure Commonwealth security in the event of a possible future war. Even after making an allowance for a contribution from Commonwealth resources, it was realised that owing to financial and manpower stringency it would be necessary to accept the fact that it would only be possible to mobilise a reduced fleet for a defensive war pending the build up to full effectiveness.

4. When further reductions became necessary certain basic assumptions had to be made:–

(a) The Pacific could be regarded as an area of American responsibility.

(b) The US Navy would reinforce our own in other theatres.

The forces which evolved from these assumptions are … the bare minimum necessary and … fall far short of the assessment of our true needs. Even these forces, however, are unattainable within the £600m limit …

5. To accept still smaller forces, not only must grave risks be accepted, but greatly increased American air must be assumed from the outset.

6. Our estimate of naval forces, shown at Appendix A, is based on the acceptance of the following risks:–

(a) The provision of but a single Battle Force, on the assumption that the US Navy would provide the second Force which we would lack.

(b) With this single Battle Force, we would have no margin of superiority over, and possible even an inferiority in numbers to the strength which the enemy might acquire in Home Waters.

(c) It would only be possible to provide Light Fleet Carriers for 4 convoys simultaneously or 4 Hunting Groups, but not both.

(d) We would have to rely on the Americans for half the escorts required for Atlantic convoys.

(e) No organised lift of combined operations ships and craft would be available.

In addition, there has been a purely arbitrary cut in our submarine force.

7. To accept these risks and limit the Navy to the forces shown in Appendix A would mean that, for the first time, we should be dependent on immediate and heavy reinforcement by another power. By themselves such forces would not be adequate "to secure to our own use sea communications, not only in the approaches to the United Kingdom, but worldwide with the Dominions, the United States and sources of supply, and also through the Mediterranean to the Middle East; and the same time denying them to the enemy." [DO(47)44] …

APPENDIX A
ROYAL NAVY

TYPE OF SHIP	FORCES REQUIRED AT THE OUTBREAK OF WAR			FORCES IN COMMISSION IN PEACE		
	Assumed requirement at the outbreak of war	Assumed Commonwealth contribution	RN Force requirement	In full Commission	Training, experiment schools etc	TOTAL
Battleships	3	–	3	2	1	3
Fleet Carriers	5	–	5	1	2	3
Lt Fleet Carriers	16	4	12	5	2	7
Cruisers	28	5	23	15	2	17
A/D Pickets	8	–	8	–	–	–
Destroyers	80	20	60	36	21	57
Escorts	262	32	230	24	25	49
Minesweepers	200	–	200	8	12	20
Submarines	65	–	65	12	28	40
MTB/MGB	50	–	50	–	12	12
ML (A/S and ND)	100	–	100	–	–	2
Minelayers	7	–	7	2	–	1
Dest, Depot Ships	2	–	2	1	2	4
Sub. Depot Ships	5	–	5	2	–	1
Fleet Replenish.		–		1	1	1
Fighter Dir. Ships				–	–	–
Fleet Train				–		
CO Ships & Craft	For training and experiment plus emergency use of existing ships and craft retained in reserve				5 LST 6 LCT	
Front line aircraft	825	120	705	300	–	300
Approx. manpower req'd	285,000			150,000		

The average annual cost of this force is estimated at £208m …

ANNEX II

POSSIBLE METHODS OF MAKING FURTHER CUTS

NAVY

Tasks of the Royal Navy in Peace

1. As a result of its great mobility, the Navy has special value in peace for maintaining our interests and prestige and lending support to our foreign policy throughout the world. The visits of Royal Naval units to ports in the Mediterranean, Persian Gulf and China coast during the periods of tension have often eased a dangerous situation.

Tasks in War

2. Security of the United Kingdom. The first duty of the Royal Navy is in conjunction with the RAF to secure this country from invasion by sea. The design of the Army is based on the assumption that this task will be successfully undertaken.

3. Security of the Middle East. Similarly, naval forces must be positioned at the outbreak of war to secure our vital bases in the Mediterranean.

4. Security of the Sea Communications. It is suggested that control of the sea communications between this country and America, and between this country and the Middle East, should rightly be the joint concern of the US and ourselves. In the opening stages of war, it would, therefore, be reasonable to expect the US to assume the main responsibility for controlling the Atlantic communications and to provide a major share of the forces required for the protection of the sea routes to the ME.

There is little threat to our sea communications in the Indian Ocean, and the Pacific is already accepted as a sphere in which the US and Australia will assume responsibility.

123. *Chiefs of Staff Minutes*

[DEFE 4/9] 27 November 1947

COS(47) 148th Meeting SIZE AND SHAPE OF THE ARMED FORCES

The Minister of Defence said he has asked to see the Chiefs of Staff to impress upon them the urgency of completing their recommendations to him on the future size and shape or the armed forces … He has already put before the Defence Committee tentative estimates for the three Services for 1948/49 based on reaching a manpower strength of 713,000 at 31 March 1949. He had indicated that this might involve expenditure of £711 million …

Lord Tedder[1] said the Chiefs of Staff had provided His Majesty's Government with their recommendations on future defence policy which had been approved by the Prime Minister … The 1948/49 estimates were inevitably based on a transition period, since the structure of all three Services was governed principally by the reduction of the forces … The Chiefs of Staff were faced with an enormous problem in deciding the structure and development of the armed forces over the next ten to fifteen years … In conformity with the time factor, namely that the risk of war over the next five years was slight, the size and cost of the armed forces in this period was to be as small as possible.

The Navy and the Air Force had prepared their long-term plans under this conception …

Sir John Cunningham said he agreed with the basic approach to the problem outlined by Lord Tedder. The Naval plan was based on the priorities given by the Minister of Defence and their expenditure was – in conformity with the time and economic factors – the minimum necessary to keep a nucleus fleet in being over the next few years and thereafter on which to build to provide the Naval forces required for their functions at the outbreak of war …

124. *Board Memorandum*

[ADM 167/129] 17 November 1947

B.533 CARRIER MODERNISATION POLICY

The report … of a committee under the chairmanship of Rear Admiral G N Oliver, ACNS, set up at the end of 1946 to investigate the "modernisation of existing Fleet Carriers" discloses that, by 1952, only 7 of the then existing Carriers will be able to operate any front-line aircraft. Six (2 ARK ROYAL and 4 HERMES class), all of which are now under construction, will be able to operate all front-line aircraft; one, ILLUSTRIOUS, will be able to operate the projected A/S aircraft (GR.17) but no other types. The Committee therefore recommended the following policy:–

(i) Modernisation of the 6 existing Fleet Carriers, 2 at a time, so that they can operate all front-line aircraft existing in 1952. (Capacity would be of the order of 48 aircraft, ie rather more than a HERMES but not much above half an ARK ROYAL). Two assumptions are made here:–

(a) 8 Fleet Carriers are required. (our present estimated requirement is 10).

[1] Chairman of the COS Committee.

(b) we can expect aircraft speeds in future to stabilize at around 600mph for long enough to justify this work.

(ii) Modernisation of the 14 existing Light Fleet Carriers to the limit possible with their structure … this would enable the[m] to operate the … GR.17 and a "fighter of limited capacity". Indications now are, however, that modernisation should enable these ships to operate the A/S aircraft … the Strike aircraft (Wyvern II) and probably also the new Jet-propelled Day Fighter, the N.7/46.

…

3. The Light Fleet Carriers in question consist of 8 COLOSSUSs and 6 MAJESTICs.

(a) Of the 8 COLOSSUS, one is on loan to France and another is about to be sold to Holland … only 6… need be considered by the Board.

(b) Of the 6 MAJESTIC, one is on loan to Canada and 2 are to be sold to Australia … the full cost of modernisation would fall on Navy Votes only in the case of the remaining three (now under construction).

4. There is a substantial difference between the COLOSSUSs and the MAJESTICs in that the former have been completed and are in service, while the latter are not completed and have already been partly modernised in design.

5. Financial Implications

The total cost envisaged is about £27 million:–

(a) modernisation of 6 Fleet Carriers at £3 million each (which allows £½ million for new armament) … £18.0 million

(b) conversion of 6 COLOSSUS Light Fleets plus completion to modernisation standard of 6 MAJESTICs at something up to £¾ million each (12 ships)

£. 9.0 million

£27.0 million

(The total may possibly be reduced to £24¾ if Canada and Australia pay for their respective MAJESTICs) …

7. Board decision is required on the proposal … that drawings and specifications should now be prepared for the modernisation of two of the existing Fleet Carriers (VICTORIOUS and FORMIDABLE) and for the conversion of the COLOSSUS Class Light Fleet Carriers to modernised MAJESTIC standard.

8. The Board are also asked to consider whether Treasury and, if considered necessary, Defence Committee approval should be sought for:–

(a) completion of the ARK ROYAL and HERMES classes;

(b) modernisation of the existing Fleet Carriers;

(c) completion of the MAJESTIC class Lt Fleet Carriers to modernised standard;
(d) conversion of the COLOSSUS class to similar standard ...

125. *Defence Committee Memorandum*

[CAB 131/4] 15 December 1947

DO(47)96 DISPOSAL OF CERTAIN OF HM SHIPS

Memorandum by the First Lord of the Admiralty

The Minister of Defence, in paragraph 19 of his Memorandum DO(47)68, dated 15 September 1947, postulated that one of the consequences of the reductions in service manpower foreshadowed for 1948–49 would be the necessity to carry out a large scrapping programme of ships at present in reserve. He stated, on my advice, that such a programme would be likely to be of the following order:–

5 Battleships
11 Cruisers
55–60 Destroyers and Frigates
1 Aircraft Component Ship
Some Submarines

Considerable number of Combined Operations craft, Fleet Train and small craft.

2. On further consideration the Admiralty has come to the conclusion that the scrapping of the above numbers of ships of the categories of Cruiser and below would reduce the fleet strength in an emergency to such a degree that the strategic consequences could not be accepted. I have, therefore, decided that the numbers of such ships to be scrapped should be considerably reduced, particularly in the Destroyer and Frigate categories, and that compensating economies in manpower and expenditure should be effected by alternative means, including the reduction of more ships in the Reserve Fleet to a lower category of reserve. The programme of disposal, etc thus approved is as follows:–

To be scrapped:– 7 Cruisers
10 Destroyers
7 Frigates
9 Minesweepers
Up to 8 Submarines
1 Aircraft Component Ship

To be reduced to a lower category of reserve:– 30 Frigates

Action proceeds on these lines.

3. This programme does not include the scrapping of the five Battleships on which I am not prepared to take a decision without further consultation with my colleagues on the Defence Committee and without their being more fully apprised of the strategic, political, financial and man-power implications of this course than was possible when DO(47)68 was under consideration.

4. Appendices I and II[1] show the Capital Ship strength available to the Royal Navy and to foreign powers respectively. Summarised, the capital ships in existence or laid down, are distributed as follows:–

	Effective Modern Units	*Others*	*Total*
United States	14	6	20
Britain	5	5	10
France	2	1	3
Russia	...	5	5
Italy	...	2	2
Turkey	...	1	1
Argentina	...	2	2
Brazil	...	2	2
Chile	...	1	1

5. It can be seen that in certain circumstances we might have to guard against a possible combination of two effective modern battleships, three effective but not modern, and four very much less effective units, *ie* the total European Battleship strength. The first are French ships which have been modernised in the United States, the second category are Italian or ex-Italian, and the last four are not considered to present any major threat on account of their age and poor equipment. To meet such a contingency, we have available at present to the Royal Navy five effective modem ships and five others. Allied to the United States, we should have a total of 19 effective modern Battleships and 11 others. If our five less effective units were scrapped, we should be left in the Royal Navy alone with five effective modern ships, which by themselves are considered more than a match for the five best units which could in the worst possible case be operated against us.

6. It is clear that from considerations of our own defence and the balance of sea power, even without any aid from the United States, the retention of more than our five most modern Battleships is hard to justify under the present circumstances of urgent need for economy in money and manpower, even when we consider the possibility of all the foreign capital

[1] Appendices not reproduced.

ships in Europe coming to be at the disposal of an enemy. The capacity of any potential enemy to challenge our control of sea communications, by embarking on a programme of new construction must, of course, be constantly watched and provided against.

7. It might be deemed advisable to retain the additional five Battleships for use as bargaining counters at any future Disarmament Conference. Although I would not attach great significance to the point, the fact that we had carried out a scrapping programme of such considerable proportions since the end of the war should weigh in our favour at any Disarmament Conference that may take place in the future.

8. If it were considered desirable to retain the five old Battleships, *Nelson*, *Rodney*, *Renown*, *Queen Elizabeth* and *Valiant*, several most important considerations would have to be faced.

9. An analysis of the cost and time involved in various alternative methods of dealing with the older Battleships gives the following results:–

(i) *Cost of Refitting* to render seaworthy and fit for limited operational service *eg* accepting present limitations as regards speed:–

Nelson, 20 years old, is in poor condition and would, it is estimated, cost not less than £2 million to refit. The work would probably take two years to complete.

Rodney, 20 years old, is in an extremely poor condition and has of necessity been berthed in a graving [dry] dock as she would otherwise have sunk at her moorings through continual leaks. It has been assessed that it would cost not less than £2 million to make the ship operational and that a considerable labour force would be required to have the ship in hand for more than two years.

Renown, 31 years old, would cost approximately £1 million and take about 18 months to refit.

Valiant, 31 years old, would need a refit costing £750,000.

Queen Elizabeth, 32 years old, would cost approximately £1 million and take about 18 months to refit.

NOTE: Of the five vessels, the last three as named above, were modernised to some extent during the recent war:– no similar work has, however, been done on *Nelson* and *Rodney*.

(ii) *Cost of Modernising* – Neither of the ships *Nelson* or *Rodney* is really suitable for modernisation nor *Renown*, *Valiant* or *Queen Elizabeth* for further modernisation, as with the exception of *Renown* their speeds on completion would still be inadequate for operation with a Carrier Task Force. It has been assessed that it would cost approximately £4–5 million to modernise each ship if the lack of speed were to be accepted. The work, which would have to be undertaken in Royal Dockyards, would take at least four years for each ship thereby absorbing a very large part of the Dockyard resources for 8 to 10 years, at the expense of the maintenance of the rest of the Fleet.

(iii) *Cost of Maintenance in Extended Reserve* – The cost of maintaining the five old Battleships in the lowest form of Reserve in which any form of maintenance is carried out might not be higher than £25,000 per annum, but unless they were refitted first (at a total cost of approximately £7 million) they would rapidly deteriorate and the essential refitting costs would materially and progressively increase the longer the refits were postponed. The crews required to maintain the five ships in the above category of Reserve would be 15 officers and 380 ratings at a cost of £100,000 per annum. It must be realised that the disposal of these ships and the release of their crews to other duties has been definitely counted upon as one of the means of reducing the man-power strength of the Navy to 147,000 by 31 March 1948.

(iv) *New Construction* – There is no intention at present of embarking on a programme of Capital Ship replacement and there cannot to my mind be any question of doing so at least until the results of research and development have progressed sufficiently to throw more light on the form and armament of the Capital Ship of the future. The cost that would be involved in the construction of a new Capital Ship is to be gauged by the £13–14 million spent on HMS *Vanguard; the figure would in all probability be materially higher in any future instance.*

10. In the circumstances outlined the Naval Staff are satisfied that there will be no use in their present condition for the five Battleships under consideration for the next ten years. Their value, even if modernised as far as practicable at the considerable cost indicated, would be doubtful and we shall in any event require the money for the modernisation of our Aircraft Carriers which must be given first priority. I agree and conclude that a decision should now be taken on the scrapping of at any rate *Nelson, Rodney*, *Queen Elizabeth* and *Valiant* and that the scrapping of *Renown* should also be considered …

126. *Defence Committee Minutes*

[CAB 131/5] 19 December 1947

DO(47) 27th Meeting

1. Disposal of Certain Warships

The Prime Minister said that when the Defence Committee had considered the question of reductions in the strength of the Armed

Forces on 18 September (DO(47) 20th Meeting, Minute 1) they had been informed by the Minister of Defence, on the basis of information given to him by the Admiralty, that a consequence of the proposed reduction in the strength of the Navy would be that a scrapping programme of the order of that set out in paragraph 1 of DO(47)96 would have to be carried out. It now appeared, however, that the necessary economies could be secured by means of the very much smaller programme set out in paragraph 2 of DO(47)96. He found this discrepancy disturbing, since it suggested that when the question of manpower reductions was being considered by the Defence Committee in September the Admiralty had seriously over-stated the consequences of the proposed cut in the strength of the Navy. He recognised that the scrapping programme put forward in DO(47)68 had not been a firm one, but the Admiralty should see to it in future that their estimates did not err so much in the direction of over-statement.

The First Lord of the Admiralty and *The First Sea Lord* explained that the scrapping programme given in DO(47)68 had been drawn up at very short notice and had necessarily been a tentative one. This fact had been brought out in paragraph 19(a) of DO(47)68 where it was stated that the programme was "likely to be of the following order." Moreover, the revised proposals did not mean that any more ships would be kept in commission, and it would be observed that, though it was now proposed to scrap only 17 destroyers and frigates, as compared with the original estimate of 55 to 60, 30 frigates were to be reduced to a low class of reserve in which their retention would make only a negligible demand on manpower …

There was general agreement that, in the light of the considerations set out in DO(47)96, all five battleships should be scrapped …

127. *Defence Committee Memorandum*

[CAB 131/6] 5 January 1948[1]

DO(48)3 SIZE AND SHAPE OF THE ARMED FORCES

Report by the Chiefs of Staff to the Minister of Defence

You have asked for a collective report from us on the Size and Shape of our Peacetime Forces so that you may be able to obtain approval for a policy which will form the basis of your 1948 White Paper and which will, *inter alia*, enable you to settle in principle the main issues on the shape and size of our peacetime forces; to determine the defence risks that must

[1] Originally presented to the Minister of Defence on 11 Dec 1947 as COS(47)263(O) in DEFE 5/6.

be faced through having to impose a financial ceiling of £600 million or thereabouts on the cost of the Armed Forces; and to find a solution for the distribution of the National Service intake between the three Services.

2. In all our discussions we have used as a basis the future defence policy already approved by His Majesty's Government (DO(47)44) and the instructions you gave and the priorities laid down for planning of the future Armed Forces in COS(47)173(O).

The Principal Agreed Factors affecting a Long-Term Plan for the Armed Forces

Time Factor

3. To be dogmatic regarding the risk of war is unjustifiable and dangerous. The belief is held by some that, through fear of the atomic bomb, a potential enemy will recoil from war until she herself has modern weapons. On the other hand, it can be argued that she might come to the conclusion that in the scientific race she was being increasingly outstripped and that it was to her advantage to strike before the odds against her became too great. We are, however, agreed that, because of the economic factor referred to below, the risk of war until about 1952 must be accepted when planning our Defence Forces. This risk will gradually increase throughout the period until about 1957, and on and after this date the risk will increase so steeply as to mean that our forces must be strong enough to deter war, and give us a reasonable chance of defending ourselves. We would also add that the stronger we can be in the interim period, the more are we likely to diminish the ultimate risk.

Nature of Threat

4. On present intelligence and scientific advice, we agree that there is little or no possibility of atomic attacks on this country before 1952. Between 1952 and 1957, a possibility of attacks by weapons of mass destruction exists, but for a variety of reasons, we think the chances are slight. After 1957, this form of attack is a distinct possibility. Furthermore, for the next 5–10 years the threat of use of these weapons is the only effective backing to our foreign policy or deterrent to a would-be war-monger. Nevertheless, from 1957 onwards we must be fully prepared for the possibility of atomic warfare on a scale which might well prove fatal to us.

The nature of the threats we have to consider are, therefore:–

(a) The "cold war" now in progress.

(b) A conventional war in the comparatively near future.

(c) A war with mass-destruction weapons after 1957.

Considering these threats:– *(a)* must be fought largely on the political front. Against *(b)* we cannot afford to prepare and, as has already been said, the risk must be accepted. But it follows that it becomes all the more necessary to prevent war and therefore to commence building up a deterrent force. To provide against *(c)* there must be no diversion of our limited resources from the development of modernised forces organised and equipped to provide:–

(i) Offensive striking forces, suitably based and ready at once to implement the threat to deliver mass-destruction weapons on selected objectives.
(ii) Active and passive defence forces, for the security of the United Kingdom, mainly against air attack.
(iii) Combined sea and air forces, mainly anti-submarine and anti-air to safeguard sea communications.
(iv) Forces for the defence of Overseas Bases.

Economic

5. We accept that in our present circumstances we cannot obtain economic recovery and at the same time build up or even maintain large forces. We agree that it is vital to put our economic house in order at once and to build up a strong financial and industrial peace economy. Nevertheless, we must emphasize that any limit or allocation between the Services which is now imposed cannot be permanent. If we are to meet the risk of war, it is essential that more money should be spent on defence after the next 2 or 3 years. Some change in the proportionate allocation between the Services will also be necessary if we are to meet our first commitment, which is to deter war, or if that fails to be ready to meet it.

National Service

6. We accept the value of the recognition of the principle of universal National Service. We recommend that it be retained, because of its long-term advantages, namely, that it will build up in the nation a good reserve of disciplined and physically fit men to meet the many needs which are bound to arise in a future war. Moreover, National Service is in itself a deterrent influence and its abolition would be a discouragement to our friends and an invitation to our enemies. As we show later, we think its form and application need further study.

Problems to be Resolved affecting Planning of our Future Armed Forces

7. Our object has been to find a common basis for the planning of the three Services which would form a balanced and efficient defence force, the cost of which would have been within the money limitations and which would at the same time have absorbed the expected numbers of conscripts from National Service.

8. There are the following obstacles to the production of a solution compatible with these factors:–

(a) *The Role of the Army in War …*

(b) *Occupational Commitments ...*

(c) *The National Service Act* ... The ultimate form of distribution and training and the percentage of conscripts absorbed in each Service will depend on the determination of the role of the Army at the outbreak of war and the ability of the Navy and RAF to utilise the entry in an economical and profitable manner.

9. The approach by the Navy and the RAF has been to base their plans precisely on the priorities laid down, which call for a deterrent force and a minimum nucleus to meet war requirements and on which expansion can best be based if time and resources allow. The approach by the Army so far has been confined to the provision of the forces necessary to meet peacetime commitments, to train the National Service intake and to make a very modest provision for such production of new equipment as is necessary to keep alive production techniques, thus making possible the modernisation of Army equipment on an adequate scale should the need arise. Whilst, therefore, the forces we indicate to you in the case of the Navy and the RAF are based on a long-term 12-year plan, the approach by the Army has been limited to a plan for the next 5 years on a purely peace basis.

The Size and Shape of the Armed Forces in the Near Future

10. We suggest that you should accept as a temporary measure, which must by its nature be continuously reviewed, an estimate of forces as set out in the three Annexes to this paper. You will see that the Navy and RAF have produced a long-term plan and that the Army has adopted a level peacetime expenditure. For the reasons given above, we think that this is the only method of estimating in present circumstances ...

11. Considering that many problems are not yet solved and that there are many variable factors, we suggest that it is misleading to look at the average annual expenditure on the forces shown in the Annexes over a period of twelve years. While these problems are being examined, it is safe, without jeopardising the future shape and size of the forces, and particularly the Navy and the RAF, to look to the immediate future only. On this basis the annual expenditure on defence would be of the following order:–

	£ Millions
Research and Development	42
Navy	180
Army	250
Royal Air Force	190
Total	662

12. The CAS and First Sea Lord must emphasise that the Navy and RAF can only accept this small allocation of money for the immediate future on the absolute and specific understanding that it is the beginning of a

twelve-year programme which must continue as planned if these two Services are to provide any form of deterrent or security as the danger of war increases. The CAS and First Sea Lord must further point out that this programme could only start in 1949. Next year's estimates must be considered as a separate problem.

After the next few years we must begin building up the deterrent force, its maintenance and airfield facilities in localities well-placed strategically. Similarly, the modernisation of the Navy, which will take many years to complete, must be commenced …

The CAS and First Sea Lord are concerned to point out that this immediate solution, which leaves the Army as the largest and most expensive Service, is, in their view, inconsistent with the priorities which they believe should be applied if Defence expenditure has to be kept within a financial limit; that it is only justified as a short-term measure by the present Army commitments and consequent impossibility of an early and drastic reduction of Army strength; and that, if a financial limit still has to be imposed beyond the next few years, when a rise in Air Force and Navy expenditure becomes essential, then decisions will have to be taken which will enable a corresponding reduction in Army expenditure to be effected.

13. We are not entirely satisfied with the forces recommended …

14. We, therefore, want to leave you under no misapprehension. We have not solved the long-term problem, nor shall we solve it without continuous study and the preservation of a flexible outlook, not only on the development of weapons, but on the changing economic situation, both in this country and in the countries of Western Europe.

Comments on the Size and Shape of the Armed Forces

15. In the foregoing paragraphs we have discussed the size and shape of the Armed Forces in the immediate future; have brought out two major issues, namely, the role of the Army on the outbreak of war and the method of distributing and training the National Service intake; and have indicated others needing examination. Because of the need to resolve these two major issues and because of the factors given in paragraph 8*(b)*, the forces shown in the Annexes are not planned on the same basis. They, nevertheless, represent the conception which we recommend should be accepted for the time being. The forces described are not balanced forces working to the same concept and they are imperfect in that they are not within the financial limitations imposed. However, with further examination it may prove possible to modify this imperfection in such directions as the reduction of Administrative Overheads and adjustments to the Works and Production Programmes.

Recommendations

(1) The conception for the planning or the Armed Forces in the immediate future, outlined in paragraphs 10–12, be accepted for the Defence White Paper …

(4) The Size and Shape of the Armed Forces described in Annexes 1–3 be accepted for immediate planning purposes …

ANNEX I
ROYAL NAVY

Type of Ship	Forces Required at the Outbreak of War			Forces in Commission In Peace		
	Assumed requirement at the outbreak of war	Assumed Commonwealth contribution	RN Force required	In full commission	Training, experiment, schools etc	Total
Battleships	3	…	3	2	1	3
Fleet Carriers	5	…	5	1	2	3
Lt Fleet Carriers	16	4	12	5	2	7
Cruisers	28	5	23	15	2	17
A/D Pickets	8	…	8	…	…	…
Destroyers	80	20	60	36	21	57
Escorts	262	32	230	24	25	49
Minesweepers	200	…	200	8	12	20
Submarines	65	…	65	12	28	40
MTB/MGB	50	…	50	…	12	12
ML (A/S & ND)	100	…	100	…	…	
Minelayers	7	…	7	…	…	…
Dest. Depot Ships	2	…	2	1	…	1
Sub. Depot Ships	5	…	5	2	2	4
…						
Front Line Aircraft	825	120	705	300	…	300
Approximate man-power required	285,000			150,000		

128. *Director of Plans to Head of Military Branch*

[ADM 116/5966] 22 January 1948

DATE WHEN RISK OF WAR BECOMES GRAVE

In DO(48)2 – SHAPE AND SIZE OF THE ARMED FORCES – it is stated that "the risk of war within the next five years is small and that risk must be accepted. Thereafter, the risk will tend to grow until in about 1957 the threat of war may become grave." This statement was accepted by the Defence Committee in their meeting on the 8 January (DO(48) 2nd Meeting). The Joint Planning Committee at its meeting on the 21 January after consulting the JIC considered that this date of 1957 should now be accepted as a planning date for all purposes (operational, administrative, rearmament and research). It was therefore agreed that this decision of the Defence Committee should be circulated fully within the Ministries concerned. It is requested that M. will prepare a Secret Acquaint, or some such other document as is thought appropriate, to carry out this purpose. All that need be said, I think, is that –

> "The Defence Committee of the Cabinet has decided that the threat of war may become grave in about 1957. For all planning purposes therefore the date 1957 is to be taken as the date to which the Navy is to be prepared to meet this threat."

129. *Director of Plans to VCNS*

[ADM 1/21473] 1 March 1948

PD.R51/86 SHIPS IN COMMISSION

As directed, I have prepared a statement of ships in full commission, the manpower required to man them and the additional ships we hope to commission during the next two years. Figures giving an ideal Peace Time Fleet are also shown …

The following tables show the state of the Fleets in full commission under various conditions and at certain times. The manpower figures given show the numbers required to man the ships given in the tables and the total numbers in the Navy at this time. How the remainder of the manpower is employed has not been shown as it is estimated it will remain approximately constant up to the end of 1950 and has gone up proportionately in the Ideal Peacetime Fleet.

	Fleets at Present in Full Commission	Forecast Fleet in Full Commission For 31.12.49	Estimated Fleet in Full Commission 31.12.50	Ideal Peacetime Fleet in Full Commission
Home Fleet				
Battleships	2 (DUKE OF YORK, VANGUARD)	–	–	2 (1 for training)
Fleet Carriers	1	1	1	–
Light Fleets	2	2	2	2
Cruisers	4	4	4	5
Destroyers	16	16	16	16
Frigates	–	–	8	8
Submarines	26	26	26	31
Ocean Minesweepers	–	6	6	8
Fast Minelayers	–	–	–	1
Mediterranean Fleet				
Battleships	–	–	–	1
Light Fleets	2	2	2	2
Cruisers	4	4	4	4

Destroyers	12	12	16	17
Frigates	9	9	9	9
Submarines	8	8	8	8
Ocean Minesweepers	–	6	6	8
Destroyer Depot Ship	–	1	1	1
Fast Minelayer	–	–	–	1
Far East				
Cruisers	3	2	2	3
Destroyers	5	6	6	5
Frigates	5	7	7	5
Submarines	–	8	8	8
Submarine Depot Ship –	–	–	1	
East Indies				
Cruisers	2	2	2	2
Frigates	4	5	5	5
America and West Indies				
Cruisers	2	2	2	2
Frigates	4	4	4	4
South Atlantic				
Cruisers	1	1	1	1
Frigates	2	2	2	2
Carrier Task Group				
Fleet Carrier	–	–	–	1
Aircraft Repair Ship	–	–	–	1
Destroyers	–	–	–	8
Approximate Manpower Required for Active Fleets In Full Commission	30,000	29,000	30,400	47,000
Total UK Naval Manpower Required	145,000	145,000	147,000#	160,600

Estimation only of manpower which will be available.

Note 1:– The following major changes are planned to take place before the end of 1949:–

(a) VANGUARD reduce and join the Training Squadron.
(b) DUKE OF YORK reduce to reserve or immobilise.
(c) SUSSEX to reduce to reserve.
(d) Six Ocean Minesweepers commission for service at home.
(e) One Destroyer and two frigates commission for service in the Far East.
(f) One Frigate to commission for service in the East Indies.

Note 2:– It is hoped that it will be possible to commission one Destroyer Depot Ship in addition to the above for service in the Mediterranean at the end of 1949 or early in 1950. This ship is urgently required.

Note 3:– The following further changes are planned to take place before the end of 1950:–

(a) Eight Frigates to commission for service at Home.
(b) Four Fleet Minesweepers to commission for service in the Mediterranean.

2. Neither VANGUARD nor DUKE OF YORK have been included in the forecast for 31.12.49 as it had been planned for VANGUARD to join the training squadron and for DUKE OF YORK to be immobilised or placed in reserve. This would have resulted in a saving of some 1,300 men, which would have allowed us to man six additional ocean minesweepers at Home and help towards the build-up of reserve fleet complements, thereby improving the maintenance of reserve fleet ships whose condition is at present deteriorating seriously.
3. The other commitments in notes 1(e) and (f) and 2 are urgent requirements which have been found to be necessary and which have been allowed for.
4. DUKE OF YORK has already remained in commission longer than anticipated and the reserve fleet manning problem has become acute as a result.
5. The major threats we shall have to meet in war will be minelaying and submarine attack and it is essential that we should be better prepared to meet them by having more suitable ships in commission in peace to counter them.
6. Employment of Battleships in War

It is planned for two battleships to be brought forwards and commissioned by D + 3 months …

130. *Joint Planning Staff Memorandum*

[DEFE 4/12] 8 April 1948

JP(48)11 (Final) BASIC ASSUMPTIONS FOR PLANNING

As instructed, we have prepared an appreciation covering the basic assumptions that should be made on the world wide strategic situation at the outbreak of war in 1957.

…

OVERALL UK DEFENCE POLICY

Our overall strategy is based on three main fundamentals:–

(a) The defence of the UK,
(b) The control of our essential sea communications.
(c) A firm hold on the Middle East.

…

APPENDIX

On the assumptions we have made concerning the manner in which war will break out and the warning period we shall have, we list the major operational Commonwealth forces which Service Ministries estimate to be available at the outbreak of hostilities …

2. NAVY

Country	Fleet Carriers	Battle-ships	Lt Fleet Carriers	Cruisers	Destroyers	Frigates	Fleet Mine-sweepers	Sub-marines	Front line aircraft
UK	5	5	12	23	62	229	60	65	300
Canada	–	–	2	2	11	6	9	–	60
Australia	–	–	2	4	16	21	32	–	60
N. Zealand	–	–	–	2	–	7	–	–	–
S. Africa	–	–	–	–	–	3	2	–	–
Pakistan	–	–	–	–	2	4	4	–	–
Malaya	–	–	–	–	–	2	–	–	–
TOTAL	5	5	16	31	91	272	107	65	420

Note: Auxiliary and light craft have not been included.

3. With the exception of two battleships and three fleet or light fleet carriers, the UK ships can be manned and in an operational condition on the outbreak of war, provided that:–

(a) Mobilisation is commenced four months before the outbreak of war.

(b) They are maintained … in an operational condition (not more than 3 months' notice).

(c) A manpower of 285,000 regulars and reserves is available.

4. We are not able to estimate how far these conditions will be met. We have assumed, however, that mobilisation will not be commenced until a few days before the outbreak of war, at which time our major warships in commission will be:–

Country	Fleet Carriers	Battle-ships	Lt Fleet Carriers	Cruisers	Destroyers	Frigates	Mine-sweepers	Sub-Marines	Front line aircraft
UK	3	3	7	17	57	49	20	40	300
Canada			1	1	6	2	2		60
Australia			2	2	8	11	16		60
N. Zealand				1	2	6	1		
S. Africa						2	2		
Pakistan						2			
Malaya						2			
TOTAL	3	3	10	21	73	74	41	40	420

… we anticipate that between a third and a half of the reserve fleet can be commissioned within one month after the outbreak of war and that the whole of our seagoing fleet will be commissioned within the first three months.

5. We assume a similar mobilisation will be undertaken by the other countries of the Commonwealth.

MERCHANT SHIPPING

6. Taking account of the present trends in merchant shipping, we assume that the United Kingdom and Dominion shipping of 100 gt and over available in 1957 will be:–

Type of Ship	Gross Tons
Tankers	5,000,000
Passenger Liners (ocean)	1,000,000
Passenger Liners (coastal)	150,000
Passenger (cargo ships) (ocean)	3,500,000
Passenger (cargo ships) (coastal)	350,000
Other Cargo Ships (ocean)	12,000,000
Other cargo Ships (coastal)	2,000,000
Total Non-Tankers	19,000,000

We assume that between a quarter and a third of this tonnage will be available for military purposes at the outbreak of war …

131. *Board Memorandum*

[ADM 167/131] 18 June 1948

B.556 NAVAL AIRCRAFT IN SERVICE, UNDER DEVELOPMENT AND PROJECTED (FRONT LINE ONLY)

Section I – Policy

Consideration of the functions of Naval Aviation in a future war indicate that the following roles must be provided for:–

(i) Day fighter (interceptor)
(ii) Day Fighter (long range escort or support)
(iii) Land Assault (reconnaissance, spotting, ground attack, supply)
(iv) Strategical reconnaissance (photographic)
(v) Night Fighter (two seater)
(vi) Strike (single or two seater)
(vii) Strike Navigating
(viii) Anti-submarine
(ix) Reconnaissance (sea)
(x) Rescue and Search

2. Certain of these roles can, of course, be performed by one basic design of aircraft …

3. The period since the end of the war has necessarily been marked by a drastic reduction in the number of new aircraft … under development and by a shift of stress from short term requirements, to meet urgent operational needs, to long term requirements for which more orderly plans of development are possible.

4. The far reaching effects of … modern gas turbine aircraft on tactics, carrier handling etc. … are becoming clearer. Some of the main problems are …:

(a) Weight. The two seater aircraft of the future … is likely to weigh between 25,000 and 30,000 lbs …

(b) Endurance … the jet engine gives it best performance at about 35,000 feet. Consumption of fuel increases rapidly as operating height is reduced, and at sea level it is approximately four time as great …

5. Unless existing carriers are modernised … they will be unable to operate any of the types of aircraft under development and projected and by 1952 or thereabouts the following situation will have developed:–

(a) Only the 2 Ark Royals and the 4 Hermes, now under construction, will be able to operate all types.

(b) One – ILLUSTRIOUS – will be able to operate satisfactorily the projected A/S aircraft (GR 17/45) but no others.

(c) The remaining 19, 5 Fleets and 14 Light Fleets will not be able to operate satisfactorily any of the current types …

Section II – Aircraft

(i) Types in, or shortly becoming available for, frontline service.

(a) Seafire – single seat fighter … The Seafire 47 … is not expected to remain in the frontline after the end of 1949 …

(b) Sea Fury – single seat fighter … Three frontline squadrons have so far been formed, one of which is allocated to the RCN …

(c) Sea Hornet – twin engined fighter, an interim measure. Three Marks are on order; the Mark 20, a strike/fighter single seat version … The Mark 21, a two-seater night fighter … The Mark 22, a single seat strategical reconnaissance version … No squadrons of Sea Hornet Marks 21 and 22 have yet formed.

(d) Firefly – two seat strike/fighter and night fighter … All Mark 1 Firefly will have been replaced in the frontline by the Mark 4–5 by … early 1949.

(e) Firebrand – single seat torpedo strike aircraft – being held available until its modern counterpart – the Wyvern 2 – comes into production.

(f) Barracuda – bomber/reconnaissance aircraft … obsolete, one squadron is retained for the anti-submarine role.

(g) Sea Otter – an amphibian … used primarily for search and rescue … It cannot be catapulted.

(ii) Types under development.

(a) Hawker N7/46 (name to be allocated).[1] A single seat turbo jet interceptor fighter … It is not anticipated that this aircraft will start to come into service before 1952 in replacement of the Sea Fury.

(b) Attacker – a single seat fighter … An order to 60 Attackers will be placed … to enable early Squadron experience in the operation of jet fighters …

(c) GR17/45 (name to be allocated).[2] Designed specifically for anti-submarine work … not expected to come into service before 1952/53.

(d) Westland Wyvern – a single seat strike fighter …

(e) Supermarine S14/44 (Seagull). A monoplane amphibian flying boat designed for Search and Rescue … No order … until replacements for Sea Otter begin to be required …

(iii) New projects in hand or contemplated.

(a) Supermarine twin jet interceptor fighter to specification N9/47[3] … [also] Strike Support role.

(b) N40/47 – a projected two seat night fighter.[4]

(c) Two seat strike aircraft … eventual replacement for the Wyvern 2.[5]

(d) Helicopters … specifications are now being prepared for two types …:–

Light Helicopter.

(i) Communications aircraft between ships at sea.
(ii) Communications aircraft in land assault operations.
(iii) Supply link between aircraft repair ships and supporting air strip.
(iv) Radar calibration.
(v) Photographic marking of special trials …
(vi) Sea and Rescue at sea and ashore.
(vii) Photographic survey work.

Heavy Helicopter.

(i) Submarine detection.
(ii) Mine spotting.
(iii) Photographic survey.

[1] Sea Hawk.
[2] Gannet.
[3] Scimitar.
[4] Sea Vixen.
[5] Eventually, the Buccaneer.

APPENDIX I

NEW AND PROJECTED TYPES OF AIRCRAFT THAT CAN BE OPERATED BY THE FLEET AND LIGHT FLEET CARRIERS IN THEIR PRESENT CONDITION

Type of aircraft and role	Seafire 15 & 17 Day Fighter	Seafire 47 Day Fighter	Firefly 1 & 4/5 Strike Night Fighter	Sea Fury Day Fighter	Sea Hornet All Purpose	Barracuda 3 A/S	Firebrand Strike	Wyvern 2 Strike	Attacker E.10/44 Fighter	Hawker N7/46 Fighter	Fairy or Blackburn GR17/45 A/S	Supermarine N9/47 Interceptor	Night Fighter Project N40/46
Estimated date out of frontline service	1948/49	End 1949	1 1948 4/5 about 1954	About 1954	About 1954	1950	1950 or earlier	–	–	–	–	–	–
Estimated date into service	–	–	–	–	–	–	–	1951	1950	1952	1952/53	1953	1953/54
Class of Ship													
ILLUSTRIOUS	Yes	Yes	Yes	Yes	DPO	Yes	Yes	Yes[x]	No	No	Yes	No	No
FORMIDABLE VICTORIOUS	Yes	Yes	Yes	Yes	DPO	Yes	Yes	DPO[x]	No	No	DPO (lifts)	No	No
INDOMITABLE	Yes	UH spread or partly folded LH Yes	Yes	UH spread or partly folded LH Yes	DPO	Yes	Yes	DPO[x]	No	No	DPO		
IMPLACABLE INDEFATIGABLE	Yes	UH spread or partly folded LH No	Yes	UH spread or partly folded LH No	UH	Yes	Yes	DPO[x]	No	No	Yes (Fairey) DPO (Blackburn)	No	No

COLOSSUS MAJESTIC	Yes	Yes	Yes	Yes, but arresters need modification	Yes+	Yes	Yes	No	No	No	Yes+	No	No
HERMES	Yes	Yes	Yes	Yes	Yes	Yes	Yes	Yes	Yes^	Yes	Yes	Yes	
ARK ROYAL EAGLE	Yes	Yes	Yes	Yes	Yes	Yes	Yes	Yes	Yes^	Yes	Yes	Yes	

DPO Deck Park Only UH Upper Hangar LH Lower Hangar

x Speed into wires may be critical. + Very limited operation possible. Aircraft would have to be fuelled and armed on deck and only land on without load and with little fuel.

^ Limited endurance of the Attacker may render it necessary to operate in the overload condition.

132. *Joint Intelligence Committee Memorandum*

[CAB 158/1] 12 June 1948

JIC(48)42(O)(Final) FORECAST OF THE WORLD SITUATION IN 1957

ASSUMPTIONS

In forecasting the world situation in 1957 the following three basic assumptions have been made:–

(a) The British Commonwealth and United States remain democratic in their system of government and closely associated with one another.
(b) The Soviet Union continues under the present type of regime and associated foreign policy.
(c) The economic recovery programme has been implemented in Europe.

...

MILITARY CAPABILITIES

The effectiveness in 1957 of the three Services of both sides in the expected conflict is estimated as follows (excluding the United States):–

Navies

British Commonwealth

Given certain favourable condition, the total naval forces of the British Commonwealth will consist at the outbreak of war of the following units:–

3 battleships	272 frigates
4 fleet carriers	107 minesweepers
14 light fleet carriers	65 submarines
31 cruisers	420 frontline aircraft
91 destroyers	

Certain additional units could be rapidly commissioned after the outbreak of war.

Soviet Union

The Soviet Union is expected to make a considerable effort in the development of her navies in the North-West, the Black Sea and the Far East. The greatest menace is expected to be the submarine fleet which will probably number 500, a large proportion of which will have high underwater speed.

It is known that the Russian are taking a great interest in the building of midget submarines and in fast coastal craft of all types, and it is estimated that they will have large numbers of these by 1957.

Advantage is being taken of German technique and experience in the development of surface ship designs, and the Russian surface fleet is expected to have much better ocean-going qualities than hitherto and to consist of:– 33 cruisers, 25 large destroyers and 88 destroyers.

Owing to a shortage of technicians and of sea-going experience, it is expected that the potential strength of such large numbers of surface ships and submarines will be to some extent offset by crude tactical handling.

The total naval personnel strength is estimated to be 865,000 including marines and coastal defence and naval air personnel …

Military Capabilities of the British Commonwealth … and the Soviet Union in 1957

NAVIES

British Commonwealth

25. The major warships likely to be in commission in 1957 will be as follows:–

Country	Battleships	Fleet Carriers	Light Fleet Carriers	Cruisers	Destroyers	Fleet Frigates	Minesweepers	Submarines	Frontline Aircraft
UK	3	3	7	17	57	49	20	40	300
Canada	–	–	1	1	6	2	2	–	60
Australia	–	–	2	2	8	11	16	–	60
N. Zealand	–	–	–	1	–	6	–	–	–
S. Africa	–	–	–	–	–	2	1	–	–
Malaya	–	–	–	–	–	2	–	–	–
Total	3	3	10	21	71	72	39	40	420

26. The number of warships in commission on the outbreak of war could, however, be increased to that shown below if:–

(a) Mobilisation is commenced four months before the outbreak of war.

(b) Ships in reserve are maintained from a material point of view in an operational condition (ie at not more than 3 months' notice)

(c) A manpower of 285,000 regulars and reserves is available.

Country	Battleships	Fleet Carriers	Light Fleet Carriers	Cruisers	Destroyers	Frigates	Fleet Minesweepers	Submarines	Frontline Aircraft
UK	3	3	10	23	62	230	66	65	300
Canada	–	–	2	2	11	6	9	–	60
Australia	–	–	2	4	16	21	32	–	60
N. Zealand	–	–	–	2	–	6	–	–	–
S. Africa	–	–	–	–	–	3	2	–	–
Malaya	–	–	–	–	–	2	–	–	–
Total	3	3	14	31	89	268	109	65	420

Estimate of Soviet Naval Forces in 1957

27. At the present time the Soviet Navy possesses four old battleships, seven modern cruisers of 10,000 tons, high speed and armed with 7.1-inch guns, three cruisers (ex-German, American and Italian) of varying characteristics, at least five modern flotilla leaders and upwards of 35 modern Russian-built destroyers with 5.1-inch guns. The Soviet Navy has five ex-German destroyers and will shortly take delivery of three ex-Italian destroyers which have been allocated to it.

28. The Russian submarine fleet (including the ten ex-German submarines allocated by Treaty) consists of 75 large and about 200 medium and small submarines of varying age, construction having continued steadily over the last ten years. None of the Russian ocean-going submarines has, so far as in known, been fitted with snort equipment which seriously reduces their potential by modern standards. The ex-German submarines were, however, fitted with schnorkel and it can be expected that the Russians will convert their present fleet and incorporate it in all ships now building and in future construction.

29. It is the declared intention of Stalin and the Soviet Government to build a powerful ocean-going navy and fleet of merchant ships, and it is believed that high priority is being given at any rate to the naval side of the project.

30. Although Soviet shipyards, particularly those in the Black Sea, suffered damage during the war, the main yards at Leningrad, Molotovsk and in the Far East are probably all capable of constructing modern warships, and work is known to be in progress. It is, however, considered unlikely that the Soviet Union will embark on a programme of construction of battleships and aircraft carriers and it is thought that the building programme is limited to cruisers, destroyers and submarines, and also small battle units and coastal craft, in the development of which they are showing considerable interest. Designs have recently been prepared with German assistance for large destroyers of about 4,000 tons, similar to those projected by the Germans for use in the North Sea and Atlantic. Development of Walther type high speed submarines is being energetically pursued, but even if this is successful the completion of a large number is not expected before 1957. Nevertheless, it is expected that a type of submarine with comparatively high underwater speed (eg Type XXI or an improvement on it) will have been built in large numbers by that date. Moreover, designs for submarine depot ships based on German experience are known to have been prepared for the Soviet Navy.

31. The following figures, though highly speculative, are considered to be a reasonable estimate of the Soviet Navy in 1957. No attempt has,

however, been made to estimate the numbers by areas of small battle units and coastal craft, but these can be assumed to be large.

(a) *Northern and Western Europe including the Baltic.*
1 cruiser, 2 flotilla leaders, 10 destroyers from those now in commission and, in addition, 10 cruisers, 25 large destroyers (of about 4,000 tons), 10 destroyers, 7 submarine depot ships, 200 ocean going submarines and 100 coastal submarines. A large proportion of the submarines will have high underwater speed.

(b) *Black Sea.*
2 cruisers and 4 destroyers from those now in commission and, in addition, 8 cruisers, 20 destroyers, 4 submarine depot ships and 50 intermediate type submarines of high underwater speed.

(c) *Far East*
3 cruisers, 2 leaders and 10 destroyers from those now in commission and, in addition, 9 cruisers, 30 destroyers, 6 submarine depot ships and 150 ocean-going submarines, many of which will have high underwater speed …

34. The estimated naval strength in 1957 is 33 cruisers, 25 large destroyers, 88 destroyers, including flotilla leaders, 500 submarines and large numbers of small battle units and coastal craft. To man this fleet will require 105,000 officers and men. Attendant auxiliaries are estimated to require 45,000 officers and men. This makes a total of 150,000 seagoing personnel. On the ratio of three to one shore personnel in the Navy are estimated at 450,000. This makes a grand total of 600,000, excluding a force of Marines and Coastal Defence Service estimated at 220,000, and personnel of Naval Air Force estimated at 45,000 (see paragraph 63) … Since the end of the war the Soviet Union has regained control of more territory … but it will be many years, and certainly not by 1957, before the effect of the increase of her maritime population will be reflected in any significant increase of the efficiency of her Navy.

35. … The most efficient arm of the Navy will be the submarines but, unless the quality of Commanding Officers is considerably improved in comparison with that obtaining in the Second World War, the potential menace will be considerably less than the number of submarines available would appear to indicate. Some steps appear to be in hand to improve attacking efficiency but there is a long way to go to approach a reasonable performance by our standards. The small submarines, in which personal bravery is the predominant factor for success, will be a danger. Surface units will be inexperienced in modern warfare at sea. A policy of ocean raiding would not be suited to the Soviet temperament but individuals might be successful in this sphere. Although reliance on Western ideas is denied in the Soviet press, energetic steps have been taken behind the

scenes to collect all available German knowledge and some improvement in staff work, technical efficiency and sea sense compared with the last war can be expected. We therefore consider that although any Soviet ship would compare unfavourably in fighting efficiency with her counterpart in the British or United States Navies, the Soviet Navy *as a whole* could operate such numbers of fast modern surface ships and submarines at such widely scattered points as to present a serious menace to our sea communications …

133. *Director of Plans to VCNS*

[ADM 205/69] 20 July 1948

THE ROLES OF THE NAVY IN WAR.

The Chiefs of Staff (COS(48) 82nd Meeting, item 7) have asked the Service Ministries to redefine the roles of their Services as a preliminary to the statement of their requirements for inclusion in a new edition of "Shape and Size of the Armed Forces" paper.

2. In DO(47)44 para 47(a) the task of the Navy was defined as follows:–

"The task of the Navy, assisted by the RAF, will be to secure our own use sea communications, not only in the approaches to the United Kingdom but world-wide with the Dominions, United States and sources of supply, and also through the Mediterranean to the Middle East; at the same time denying then to the enemy".

This definition while correct is not, in the opinion of D of P very clearly worded and is somewhat hard to argue from. D of P therefore suggests that the roles of the Navy in war should be defined as follows:–

"The roles of the Navy, which can only be achieved by operating in the closest cooperation with the RAF, are:–

- (a) To control sea communications thereby ensuring that:–
  - (i) United Kingdom can remain a main support area and become a defence base. This necessitates complete control of the Atlantic sea communications and control, in conjunction with the Commonwealth and Allied forces, and world-wide sea communications.
  - (ii) The Middle East base and its supply lines are safe-guarded. This, in particular, necessitates control of the Mediterranean sea routes.
- (b) To deny to the enemy the use of the sea so that:–
  - (i) The United Kingdom and the Commonwealth are defended against seaborne invasion.

(ii) The enemy are unable to use the sea for the deployment or maintenance of their Air forces and Armies.

(c) To move and maintain the Air force and Army overseas in accordance with our strategy and, if required, to withdraw them. This role includes the requirements for seaborne assault and seaborne flank support when necessary.

(d) To provide seaborne tactical air support when shore-based air cover is not available.

(e) To assist the R.A.F. with a strategic air offensive if so required."

3. It is also proposed to add the following note:–

"On the outbreak of war the Navy cannot have sufficient mobilised strength to carry out all these roles in their entirety, but it must have sufficient strength to be able to deny to the enemy the use of the main ocean, the Narrow Seas and the Mediterranean:– it must have sufficient strength to be able to control the North Atlantic and the Mediterranean, and it must have a nucleus strength from which to build up forces to undertake the other roles, otherwise it will be impossible to go over from the defensive to the offensive."

4. Your direction on this matter is requested.[1]

134. *Special Military Branch Acquaint 3358*

[ADM 116/5966] 23 July 1948

TARGET DATE FOR RE-EQUIPMENT OF THE FLEET

Assumptions as to risk of Future War

2. HM Government have assumed for all planning purposes that the likelihood of war during the years until 1952 will be small. The risk will then increase gradually in the following 5 years and increase more sharply and steeply thereafter.

3. No warning period can be promised, in relation to any date either before or after 1957.

Assumptions of Nature of Future War

4. HM Government have accepted the assumption that no probable enemy will be able to use weapons of mass destruction (atomic and biological weapons) before 1954 and, possibly before 1957. Thus, between now and 1954–1957 the actual threat to be encountered will probably be confined to conventional weapons … of an advanced type and to include fast and deep diving submarines, unsweepable mines, considerably faster

[1] Minute copied to the First Sea Lord, who approved it on 21 July.

aircraft, airborne guided bombs, homing torpedoes, rockets and some form of guided missiles.

Implications of the Assumptions

5. It is emphasised that the dates quoted above will not be adjusted annually. Thus, these assumptions are entirely different in character from the rule applying between the First and Second World Wars, by which it used to be reaffirmed annually that war was unlikely within the next 10 years.

6. The target date for re-equipment of the fleet as an effective fighting force is, therefore, 1957 …

Instructions for Admiralty Departments

7. (a) First priority should be given to those essential projects which offer the technically most advanced solution that can be matured in time to enable the Fleet to be rearmed by 1957 …

(b) When new or existing projects cannot be matured in time to enable the Fleet to be rearmed by 1957, rearming with the latest available equipment will by then require to have been carried out.

(c) By far the greatest risks will arise in a war fought by an enemy with mass destruction weapons. Responsibility for development of these weapons, however, and their countermeasures, rests mainly with the Ministry of Supply. The Admiralty is free, therefore, to give priority to the development of advanced naval weapons and their counter-measures. The highest priority should be given to advanced weapons which will still be required in a war fought with mass destruction weapons or other weapons likely to emerge after 1957.

(d) It is necessary to adhere to a phased programme allowing for research and development, production and installation.

It is estimated that to complete major projects, now under research and development, to the production stage, will take 1–2 years. It is also estimated that to install such completed equipment in the Fleet will require up to 5 years.

Therefore, only 2–3 years are left for research and development on major weapons requiring to be installed by 1957. It is in consequence essential to concentrate during the next 2–3 years all research and development effort on these immediate tasks, to the exclusion of longer-term projects.

When the time required for production and installation is less than that estimated above, a greater period can be allowed for research and development in the phased programme.

Only those research and development resources, if any, that are not essential for the immediate tasks in the phased programme may be employed on longer term projects during the next 2–3 years. After the research and development phases of this programme are completed, it may be possible to switch the effort of research and development towards longer term projects. Fresh directions will then be issued.

(e) Under present conditions changes of effort from one field to another cannot, for purely material reasons, be effected quickly. The above considerations will unquestionably necessitate a ruthless pruning of programmes. This process should be carried out at once; there is no time to be lost.

8. … it is highly improbable that the Government will be prepared to authorise additional expenditure during 1948/49.

As regards modifications in staff numbers, it is also unlikely that it will be possible to make additions (except to such extent as countervailing reductions elsewhere may assist) during 1948/49.

Guidance cannot at present be given as regards the extent of the money and manpower that will be available in later years …

ANNEX

CATEGORY			NUMBER	
Battleships			5	
Fleet Aircraft Carriers			8	includes 3 unmodernised
Lt. Fleet Aircraft Carriers			12	" " "
Cruisers			23	
Monitors			2	
Fast Minelayers			2	
Destroyers			62	
Frigates	Ex	Destroyer	59	
"		Hunt	49	
"	A/A	Black Swan	23	
"		Bay	21	
"	A/S	Loch	19	
"	A/S	Castle	24	
"		River	23	
"		Flower	–	
"		New A/A	3 ?	
"		New A/S	4 ?	
"		New A/D	4 ?	
		(Total)	231	
Submarines			65	
Midget Submarines			8	
Fleet Aircraft Direction Escort			3	
Ocean Minesweepers			66	
Danlayers			12	
Coastal Minesweepers MMS			76	

Gunboats		–
Trawlers A/S M/S		3
Coastal Force Craft	HDMLs	?
	M/SMLs	50
	MTBs	50
	A/S	28
Surveying Vessels		11
S/M Depot Ships		5
Destroyer Depot Ships		2
Aircraft Transports		1
Aircraft Repair Ships		3
Repair Ships		5
Escort Maintenance Ships		4
Armament Maintenance Ships		1
Coastal Force Maintenance Ships		1
NSC Maintenance Ships		2
LT Maintenance Ships		2
LC Maintenance Ships		2
Maintenance Craft		12
Netlayers and Target Towing		2
S/M Target Vessel		1
CF Tender		–
Radar Training Ship		1
Fleet Replenishment Ship		3
Fleet Issue Ship		1
Boom Defence Vessels		17
Wreck Disposal Vessels		12
Wreck Disposal Store Carriers		2
Fleet Tugs		7
Salvage Vessels		3

135. *Defence Committee Memorandum*

[CAB 131/6] 20 July 1948

DO(48)45

MANPOWER REQUIREMENTS OF THE SERVICES IN EMERGENCY

Memorandum By The Minister Of Defence

A Working Party, comprising representatives of the three Service Departments, the Ministry of Defence, the Ministry of Labour and the Home Office, was set up recently by the Minister of Labour and

National Service and myself to review the manpower requirements of the Services for an early emergency, and to discuss methods of meeting those requirements.

APPENDIX A

THE SERVICES' REQUIREMENT IN MANPOWER

Royal Navy

Apart from a small number of naval pensioners and reservists and released personnel required before 'D-Day' for mobilisation staffs and other key posts, the Navy would aim to recall about 55,000 (all ranks, men and women) in the organised Naval Reserves on or immediately after 'D-Day' ('D-Day' being assumed as the date of any general recall to the colours when the emergency has become clear and open). A certain proportion of the personnel recalled could be women. In addition, the Navy would require about 50,000 released personnel on or as soon after 'D-Day' as possible, and those in certain categories, particularly electrical, aircraft maintenance, radar ratings, coders and cypherers, immediately …

136. *Defence Committee Memorandum*

[CAB 131/6] 26 July 1948

DO(48)46 THE DEFENCE POSITION

Memorandum By The Minister Of Defence

The Ministry of Defence, the three Service Ministries and the Ministry of Supply have reviewed the present state of Defence preparations.

2. This report covers:–
   (i) Present Policy.
   (ii) The Order of Battle of our Armed Forces at the present time.
   (iii) The main deficiencies and gaps.
   (iv) The remedies to enable us to fight with what we have got.

Present Policy

3. Government approved policy which provides the foundation for the present condition of the Armed Forces may be summarised as follows:–
   (a) *The Time Factor* – If by a miscalculation or by design war is forced upon us within the next few years, we must fight with the forces and weapons we possess. The long-term planning date for the readiness of peacetime forces capable of immediate expansion is 1957.
   (b) *Priorities* – First national priority for our efforts and resources is a strong industrial and financial economy as the prerequisite for defence. The financial limit imposed may prevent our having the forces hitherto thought necessary on the outbreak of war. At present

it is the policy to build up forces which give us the best chance of survival. This means taking serious risks. Priority is given to Defence Research, the forces which give the best visible show of strength and therefore have the greatest deterrent value, fulfilling our wartime and peacetime commitments, and training the National Service intake.

(c) *Finance* – Expenditure on the Armed Forces since the war has been progressively reduced and, on present plans, the budget is unlikely to exceed £600 million a year.

(d) *Manpower* – The policy is to reduce the permanent strength of the forces to the minimum compatible with fulfilling present commitments, while preserving the efficiency and technique of the various arms. The National Service Act is designed to build up the strength of the forces by the middle 50s; meanwhile to rely on 4 million trained men and women released from wartime forces.

(e) *Production* – The Services have been living mainly on stocks. Production has been on a small scale and designed mainly to meet urgent current needs and to retain the technique and potential capacity for war production. Disposals have been accelerated to make goods available for civil use and to release accommodation. Most surpluses have now been cleared.

Order of Battle and Operational Readiness

4. The detailed Orders of Battle for each Service are at Annexes I, II and III. The Comments on each of the Services are as follows:–

Royal Navy – See Annex I

5. Without the remedies recommended below, the Navy will not be in a position to carry out its role efficiently on the outbreak of war. Losses of merchant ships at sea and possibly in harbours must then be expected with consequent dislocation to our home supplies and the redeployment of our Air Force and Army. A major factor affecting the operational efficiency of the Navy is the lack of fuel stocks. The comparative fighting strength of the Navy to the Russians is much more favourable than in the case of the other two Services, but anti-aircraft defence and naval aircraft should be regarded as priority for strengthening.

6. Present Strength – 145,000 …[1]

…

The Main Deficiencies

13. These, apart from the fundamental smallness of our forces, may be summarised as follows:–

[1]The strengths of the Army and RAF were 460,000 and 245,000, respectively (paragraphs 9 & 12, not reproduced).

(a) Staff to work on mobilisation and re-equipment details.
(b) Manpower.
(c) Equipment and ammunition.
(d) Fuel.

14. All the Service Ministries would require an increase of Staff to prepare fully for mobilisation and re-equipment …

Manpower

15. The main deficiency in all three Services is lack of experienced men. A high proportion of all Services, both regular and National Service, are young men in training. The chief consequences are a minimum maintenance of reserves, lack of repairs and refits, shortages in skilled trades particularly engineering, electrical and radar. It would be necessary to increase the total strengths of the forces by about 350,000 on or about 'M' Day.

Equipment and Ammunition

16. The position is mixed. In some items we are reasonably placed; in others very short …

Fuel

17. Admiralty reserves are 497,000 tons in United Kingdom compared with a normal reserve of 2 million tons; enough to fill up the reserve fleet and, thereafter, to refuel the total fleet once …

Remedies

18. Broadly speaking, "to fight with what we have got" requires action which could be taken in four progressive stages, namely:–

(a) Recruit civilian manpower to the Ministries and to reserve and maintenance depots.
(b) Stop present releases and begin fuel restocking.
(c) Restart armament production.
(d) Mobilisation.

19. The sooner (a), (b) and (c) are begun the better the position if war comes. When armament production is restarted little results will be obtained within six months and it will be twelve to eighteen months in some cases before substantial new production materialises. Measures designed to strengthen the manpower of the Forces could be cancelled if the situation warranted without having upset too greatly the long-term plans of the Services …

Conclusions

25. Our forces are not in a fit state at present to commence a major war:– this is the inevitable result of the approved Defence policy set out in paragraph 3 above. Broadly speaking they are probably in as good a general condition in relation to their numbers as any other forces in the world. Against the Russians their gravest disadvantage would be on the

ground against superior numerical odds of manpower, equipment and ammunition. Little or no help could be expected from France and Benelux through lack of equipment. The main advantage is Allied possession of the Atom Bomb. If we had no time for preparation, present forces on the Continent could be swamped if the Russians chose to do so. The Air threat to the United Kingdom would be most grave if the Russians overran the Continent. The Navy could, particularly with American assistance, hold its own provided fuel stocks were available. American and Dominion help would almost certainly be forthcoming in reasonable time. Immediate assistance would be American Forces of all three services at present in Europe, shipping and fuel.

26. We are living on stocks with inadequate reserves. Recruiting of civilian manpower, stoppage of releases, calling up of reservists, and restocking fuel and equipment reserves are first priorities. It would be an appreciable time after orders were placed before equipment supplies came forward in substantial quantity. American Lend/Lease assistance, particularly fuel, must begin before the outbreak of war. The sooner it begins the better the position of United Kingdom Forces in the event of war.

ANNEX I
NAVAL FORCES, JULY 1948

	In Commission		To be Commissioned by	
	Current Peacetime Complement	Reduced Complement	D+3 months*	D+ 6 months*
Fleet Carriers	1	1	2	2
Battleships	1	2	3	3
Light Fleet Carriers	4	...	6	6
Cruisers	14	2	19	23
Destroyers	33	...	62	62
Frigates+	42	21	119	131
Submarines	33	...	63	63
Fast Minelayers	...	...	3	3
Fleet Minesweepers	17	...	40	44
Coastal Minesweepers	11	1	42	83
Coastal Forces (MTBs)	10	2	24	36
Surveying Ships	7	...	3	3
Submarine Depot Ships	3	...	4	4
Destroyer Depot Ships	...	...	2	2
Escort Maintenance Ships	...	...	...	4++
Accommodation Ships	...	...	...	1
Repair Ships	...	1	1	1
Fleet Replenishment Ship	...	1	1	1
Boom Defence Vessels	17	...	48	77
Harbour Craft Maintenance Ship	...	...	...	...
Aircraft Transport	...	...	1	1
LST	5	...	28	40
LCT	1	...	30	30
Store Carriers	3	...	5	5
Netlayers	...	...	1	2
Fleet Tugs	7	...	7	7
Salvage Vessels	2	...	3	12
ND Training Ship	...	1	...	...

* The figures for D+3 and D+6 months are planning figures and are subject to revision in the light of current examinations of dockyard and manning capabilities.

[+] Destroyers earmarked for conversion to Frigates are shown as such.

[++] One Escort Maintenance Ship is at present on loan to the Dutch.

Minor landing craft and fleet auxiliaries and ships which it is not possible to commission within 6 months are not included in this list.

DISPOSITION OF NAVAL FORCES 1 JULY 1948

	Home	Mediterranean	Pacific	East Indies	South Atlantic	America & WI	Home Trg & Experimental
Fleet Carriers	1	...	...	...	...	...	1
Battleships	1	...	...	...	...	...	2
Light Fleet Carriers	2	2	...	...	...	...	...
Cruisers	4	4	2	2	1	1	2
Destroyers	16	12	5	...	...	...	...
Frigates[+]	18	10	5	5	2	2	21
Submarines	12	8	1	...	...	...	12
Fast Minelayers	...	...	...	...	...	...	...
Fleet Minesweepers	...	8	...	...	...	...	9
Coastal Minesweepers	8	3	...	...	...	...	1
Coastal Forces (MTBs)	10	...	...	...	...	...	2
Surveying Ships	4	1	1	1	...	...	...
Submarine Depot Ships	2	1	...	...	...	...	...
Destroyer Depot Ships	...	...	...	...	...	...	...
Escort Maintenance Ships	...	...	...	...	...	...	...
Accommodation Ships	...	...	...	...	...	...	...
Repair Ships	...	...	...	...	...	...	1
Fleet Replenishment Ship	...	...	...	...	...	...	1
Boom Defence Vessels	7	2	3	3	1	1	...
Harbour Craft Maintenance Ship	...	...	...	...	...	...	1
Aircraft Transport	...	...	...	...	...	...	...
LST	1	4	...	...	...	...	...
LCT	1	...	...	...	...	...	...
Store Carriers	2	...	...	...	1	...	...
Netlayers	...	...	...	...	...	...	...
Fleet Tugs	3	2	1	1	...	...	...
Salvage Vessels	1	...	1	...	...	...	...
ND Training Ship	...	...	...	...	...	...	1

137. *Defence Committee Minutes*

[CAB 131/5] 27 July 1948

DO(48) 13th Meeting

...

Defence Preparations

The Committee had before them ... (DO(48)46) reviewing the present state of preparedness of the Armed Forces ...

Royal Navy

The Minister of Defence said that the general state of readiness of the Royal Navy was described in paragraph 5, which showed it would be unable to carry out its role efficiently on the outbreak of war unless the measures recommended in paragraph 21 were taken. The most serious deficiency was the shortage of fuel stocks, but subject to this, the Royal Navy was in a better position than the other two Services, and in view of the assistance that might be expected of the United States Navy, was much better placed to fight a war than it had been in 1940.

The First Sea Lord said that it was very difficult to obtain intelligence of Soviet naval activity. It was known, however, that the Soviet contemplated having a fleet of some 347 submarines by 1950 of which about 100 would be old types. Soviet bases in the north (Petsamo, Murmansk and Archangel) were not very well developed, but account had to be taken of the Russian canal system which would enable submarines to be moved from their main submarine base in the Caspian to the Arctic. A particular cause for anxiety lay in the fact that the Russians were skilled in minelaying, while we were very short of minesweepers and high-speed anti-submarine vessels. It was important that steps should be taken to accelerate the refit of these smaller ships, most of which were in reserve …

138. *Defence Committee Memorandum*

[CAB 131/6] 11 August 1948

DO(48)53 PREPARATIONS FOR DEFENCE

Report by the Chiefs Of Staff and the Joint War Production Staff

On 30 July the Defence Committee agreed that any steps to place the Armed Forces in the best possible position to fight in the event of war in the near future, which could be taken without publicity and without serious impact on the economy of the country, should be taken forthwith; and invited us to submit a co-ordinated appreciation setting out the tasks of the Armed Forces, a list of the preparatory measures necessary to perform these tasks and what effect these steps would have on the national economy and how far it could be carried out without publicity.…

ANNEX I

TASKS OF THE ARMED FORCES

1. The immediate military responsibilities of the United Kingdom forces in a war against Russia in 1948–49 are set out below, but the ability of the Armed Forces to fight effectively will depend largely on how far in advance of the outbreak of war decisions in Annex II[1] are taken by Ministers.

[1]Not reproduced.

(a) *Defence of the United Kingdom –*

Task	*Service responsible*
(i) Air Defence (ii) Defence of the sea approaches and ports	All three Services

(b) *Control of essential sea communications –*

(i) Provision of the naval forces for the control of The North Atlantic and Mediterranean sea Communications	RN
(ii) Employment of the air forces for the defence of these sea communications	RN and RAF
(iii) Institution of convoys in the Atlantic Ocean and Mediterranean Sea	RN

(c) *Middle East –*

(i) Defence and development of Middle East base (ii) Re-deployment and reinforcing of existing forces	All three Services

(d) *Bases for United States Strategic Air Forces in United Kingdom and Middle East –*

(i) Preparation and stocking of the airfields in East Anglia, Canal Zone, Aden and Sudan	RAF

(e) *Fighting on the Continent –*

(i) Re-deployment on the Rhine of existing forces in Europe	Army and RAF
(ii) Provision of essential administrative backing to our forces on the Rhine	Army

2. Broadly, the priority of the tasks of the Armed Forces is in the order given above. Many of the measures to fulfil these tasks, however, can and should be carried concurrently …

ANNEX III

MEASURES TO BE TAKEN TO PREPARE THE FORCES

We have found it impracticable to draw up a list of exact priorities for the various measures which can be put in hand as many of them can and should be put in hand concurrently. We have, however, allotted priorities by groups.

2. In deciding the priorities there are three overriding considerations which affect all three Services:–

(a) The need to build up our fuel stocks.
(b) The need to ensure our ability to mobilise rapidly.
(c) The need to progress our plans for war …

ANNEX IV
CONSEQUENCES OF MEASURES REFERRED TO IN ANNEX III

...

5. *Keeping Essential Ports Open to Shipping*
   (i) *Refits of Small Craft*
   Steps have already been taken to accelerate the refits of small craft and no difficulty is expected about overtime or publicity; any extra staff needed will be recruited gradually. About 5,000 tons of steel will be required for refits both in dockyards and by contract.
   (ii) *Seaward Defences of Ports and Bases*
   Additional men are being entered in Boom Defence Depots, for the overhaul of material and for the laying of trots in certain port approaches if this can be done unobtrusively ...
6. *Security of Sea Communications*
   (i) *Refits of Escort Vessels*
   In addition to accelerating refits of escort vessels in the Royal Dockyards, it is proposed to place a small number of contracts with private yards if this will not cause any significant diversion of civilian resources.
   (ii) *Replacement of Wartime Equipment in Ships*
   The essential preliminary to the replacement in ships of wartime equipment is the inspection of the equipment; this is going on.
   (iii) and (iv) *Work on Naval Aircraft and Armament Stores*
   A modest start is being made on the preparation of aircraft for the front line and on the assembly or armament stores, without publicity, to the extent to which labour can be made available where it is wanted ...

139. *Chiefs of Staff Memorandum*

[DEFE 5/12] 21 September 1948

COS(48)212(O) THE STATE OF THE ARMED FORCES

Attached to this memorandum are statements on the present condition of the Royal Navy, Army and Royal Air Force ...

The Royal Navy is ill prepared for the role expected of it in the event of war. It is insufficiently trained and its fighting efficiency very superficial at present. The Reserve Fleet is in a poor state of maintenance; there is an adequacy of reserves of fuel and supplies and a lack of modern equipment. It will moreover be impotent to meet the long term threat unless the manpower requirements are met and unless the phased programme of production requirements is started now and fully implemented ...

We conclude – that the present state of the forces gives the gravest cause for alarm ...

ANNEX I
STATE OF THE NAVY SEPTEMBER 1948
Statement by First Sea Lord

The problem confronting the preparedness of the Navy for war is twofold; firstly, to be prepared to meet an emergency at any time in the immediate future whilst at the same time performing normal peacetime functions; secondly to build up and modernise the Fleet so that by about 1957 it is ready to meet the Russian threat ...

PART I
THE NAVAL MANPOWER SITUATION

To enable the Navy to carry out its peacetime tasks and be prepared for expansion in war, a UK manpower ceiling of 160,600 is required of whom at least 135,000 should be regular male personnel ... however, at present the Navy is below the ceiling of 145,000 approved for the current financial year.

PART II
NAVAL PREPAREDNESS TO MEET A SHORT TERM EMERGENCY

1. The Seagoing Fleets

The efficiency of the seagoing fleets has been reduced by four factors:–

(a) the personnel difficulties of the transition period.
(b) the effects of immobilisation.
(c) the postwar moratorium of the re-equipment of ships.
(d) the reduced complements of seagoing ships ...

2. The Reserve Fleet

It has been impossible to maintain ships in the Reserve Fleet at the proper standard due to lack of money, or naval manpower, of dockyard facilities ... The majority of ships have not been refitted since the end of the war ... many ships were placed in Reserve without refit on completion of arduous war service ...

3. Naval Aircraft

The principal immediate weaknesses are:–

(a) No jet aircraft are yet in service in the front line. Rearming is expected to start in 1951 ...
(b) The shortage of A/S aircraft and material ...
(c) ... reserve aircraft have not been brought up to date ...

(d) The large number of different types still in service …
(e) The difficulty of obtaining spares …

…[1]

PART III

NAVAL PREPAREDNESS TO MEET THE LONG TERM THREAT

The table at Annex to this paper shows … a serious discrepancy between the planned fleet and that fleet which … would be required on the outbreak of war. The principal deficiencies … are in aircraft carriers, escorts and minesweepers …

ANNEX

UNIT	Full Commission	Special Complement (training & trials)	Reserve Fleet		Peacetime Fleet Req'd in Commission	Planned Fleet for 1957	Fleet Req'd on outbreak of war
			14–30 days.	Need Refit			
Battleships	2	2	–	1	2	5	5
Fleet Carriers	–	3	–	3	1	8	10
Light Fleet Carriers	4	2	–	–	4	12	21
Cruisers	17	1	5	6	17	23	30
Destroyers	31	6	17	12	46	62	100
Frigates	25	30	44	126	33	230	300
Submarines	27	–	11	27	45	65	80
Midget Submarines	–	–	–	–	–	8	–
Fleet AD Escorts	–	–	–	–	–	5	15
Minesweepers (Ocean)	7	6	21	32	16	66	208
Minesweepers (Coastal)	10	13	13	36	8	171	674
Minelayers	–	–	2	1	2	3	7
Front Line Aircraft	169	–	–	–	–	300	800

140. *Chiefs of Staff Minutes*

[DEFE 4/16] 24 September 1948

COS(48) 136th Meeting

STATE OF THE ARMED FORCES

The Staff Conference had before them a memorandum by the Chiefs of Staff on the State of the Armed Forces[2] …

Lord Fraser said that from all accounts the Russian submarine fleet was a really formidable threat. They had a total of about 290, of

[1]Further sections deal with oil stocks, clothing, stores, ammunition, port defences, communications and arming of merchant ships.

[2]COS(48)212(O), Doc. No. 139.

which some 100 could be employed against our sea communications. The Germans started the war in 1939 with 50 U-boats. As regards surface ships the Russian had 2 battleships, 9 cruisers and 43 destroyers. During a visit to Russian ports he (Lord Fraser) had personally seen the battleship 'October Revolution' and some destroyers, which gave every indication of efficiency. As regards our own Fleet a large number of ships had not been refitted since completing their war service. In reply to a question, he said that we needed our cruisers in peacetime for a variety of commitments. The timely arrival of a cruiser had a very salutary effect when trouble broke out in remote parts of the world.

The Minister of Defence referred to the strength of the Fleet as shown in the Annex to the Chiefs of Staff paper. It seemed that with the ships at present in commission, together with those that could be fully commissioned in a short space of time, the Navy could dispose 4 battleships, 9 carriers, 23 cruisers, 54 destroyers and a considerable number of smaller anti-submarine and minesweeping vessels. Surely this fleet would be more than a match for the Russian Navy.

The Prime Minister thought that we were paying an enormous compliment to the Russian navy by maintaining such a large fleet. This view was emphasised by the fact that the Russian fleet could not possibly concentrate. Some ships were in the Far East, others in the Black Sea and the remainder in the Baltic and White Seas. The Russians had shown no form during the last war. It had often been claimed that it took many years to build a fleet. Was it really thought that the Russians would take the offensive at sea if war broke out in 1949 or 1950?

Lord Fraser said that the Russians could take the offensive with their submarines. If we had no battleships there would be nothing to stop the Russians using their battleships. Naval warfare was not only a matter of fleet actions. The indications were that the Russians were developing their fleet. If these indications proved false, then we could think again about the size of our own navy …

The Minister of Defence said that if the Army requirement of 433,000 men was accepted, together with 250,000 for the RAF and 160,000 for the Navy, this would mean a personnel total for the forces of 843,000. Each man, taking everything into account, cost about £1,000 a year. This would mean a defence budget of £843 millions before we even started to re-equip the forces … [He] said that he has all along been handicapped by the failure on the part of the Chiefs of Staff to present to him a long term plan for the size and shape of the forces within an approximate financial limitation of £600 million a year. He recognised that this would mean the acceptance of risks but the responsibility for the acceptance of risks devolved on the Government …

141. *Principal Personnel Officers' Memorandum*

[DEFE 4/16] 28 September 1948

PPO/P(48)27

MANPOWER REQUIREMENTS OF THE ARMED FORCES IN 1949

Report to the Chiefs of Staff Committee

1. The plan for the run-down of the Forces during the last quarter or 1948 and during 1949, if implemented, would have left the Forces … at too low an overall strength to fulfil their commitments …

ANNEX I

MANPOWER REQUIREMENTS OF THE NAVY

Memorandum by the Second Sea Lord

The Chiefs of Staff at COS(4) 124th Meeting invited the Principal Personnel Officers' Committee to prepare a joint service statement of the manpower requirements of the Armed Forces for 1949.

2. I attach … a statement of the manpower requirements of the Navy in peace, It will not be possible for the Navy to achieve this figure during 1949 …

(a) The real deficiency is not so much in numbers as in experienced men of the Able and Leading rates and in certain specialist branches.

(b) An annual intake [of National Servicemen] greater than 10,000 involves opening additional Training Establishments which in turn means the withdrawal of trained regulars from the seagoing fleet.

…

4. (b) The Fleet, Naval Establishments and bases required to be manned on mobilisation and the first three months of war require approximately 285,000 UK personnel. For expansion to this size, it is also essential that the number of regular male personnel in peace should not be less than 135,000. The requirement of Reserves needs an annual entry of 10,000 National Servicemen.

ANNEX [*simplified*]

Ships and Establishments Essential in Peace

I – ACTIVE FLEETS AND OVERSEAS COMMITMENTS	Manpower required
Home Fleet	14,870
Mediterranean Fleet	17,360
Far Eastern Fleet	7,170
East Indies Squadron	3,420
South Atlantic	1,390
America and WI	2,530
Carrier Task Group	4,250
Combined Operations	1,600
RM Commandos	2,150
Occupational Forces	200
TOTAL:	54,940
II – HOME STATIONS	
Naval Aviation Ashore	13,000
Ships based on UK	3,020
Commands and Staffs	500
Reserve Fleet	12,430
Dockyards, Base ships and depots	8,370
Training ships (New Entry & Cadets)	2,400
New Entry Training Establishments	7,000
Ships for Technical Training	8,490
Advanced and Technical Training Establishments	6,100
Trials Ships	2,040
Trials Establishments	720
Miscellaneous	3,290
TOTAL:	67,360
III – NON EFFECTIVES	
New Entry and Initial Training	17,000
Advanced and Technical Training	5,100
Training afloat	1,200
Margin for drafting, sickness and passage	14,700
Demobilisation staff and pipelines	1,000
On loan to other navies	1,500
TOTAL:	40,500
Total I to III	162,800
Add nurses & VADs	600
Deduct locally entered personnel	3,000
Grand Total UK Manpower	160,600

142. *Chiefs of Staff Memorandum*

[DEFE 5/12] 2 October 1948

COS(48)227(O) SIZE AND SHAPE OF THE ARMED FORCES

ANNEX I

THE ROLE OF THE NAVY IN WAR

The tasks of the Navy, which can only be achieved by operating in the closest cooperation with the RAF, are:–

(a) To control sea communications in order to ensure:–
   (i) that the United Kingdom can remain a Main Support Area and become an offensive base. This necessitates complete control of Atlantic sea communications and, in conjunction with Commonwealth and Allied forces, of world-wide sea communications.
   (ii) that the Middle East Base and its supply lines are safeguarded. This in particular necessitates control of Mediterranean sea routes.
   (iii) the movement and maintenance of the Army and Air Force overseas in accordance with our strategy and if required their withdrawal. This role includes the requirement for seaborne assault and flank support when necessary.
(b) To deny the enemy the use of the sea so that:–
   (i) the United Kingdom and the Commonwealth are defended against seaborne invasion.
   (ii) the enemy are unable to use the sea for the deployment or maintenance of their armies and air forces.
(c) To provide seaborne tactical air support when shore-based air support is not available or adequate.
(d) To assist the RAF with a strategic air offensive if so required.

Note:– On the outbreak of war the Navy may not have sufficient mobilised strength fully to carry out all these tasks simultaneously. It must have sufficient strength to be able to deny to the enemy the use of the main oceans, the narrow seas and the Mediterranean. It must also have a nucleus strength from which both to build up forces capable of undertaking its full tasks and also to seize the initiative and thus impose on the enemy a feeling of insecurity.

PLANNED SHAPE AND SIZE OF THE FLEET

Type of Ship	1957			1952			1949		
	In Commission	Reserve	Total	In Commission	Reserve	Total	In Commission	Reserve	Total
Battleships	4	1	5	4	1	5	3	2	5
Fleet Carriers Modernised	3	2	5	3	–	3	–	–	–
" " Unmodernised	–	3	3	–	5	5	3	3	6
Light Fleet Carriers Mod.	5	4	9	5	–	5	–	–	–
" " " Unmod.	–	3	3	–	5	5	5	1	6
Cruisers	19	4	23	19	10	29	19	10	29
Fleet AD Escorts	–	5	5	–	1	1	–	–	–
Destroyers	46	16	62	52	51	103	56	59	115
Frigates (incl ex-destroyers)	72	158	230	52	140	192	45	125	170
Minesweepers (Ocean)	25	41	66	25	41	66	29	37	66
Minesweepers (Coastal)	26	145	171	18	56	74	18	54	72
Submarines	45	20	65	34	31	65	34	31	65
MTB/MGB	12	38	50	12	26	38	12	24	36
ML (A/S & HD)	4	96	100	4	–	4	3	1	4
Fast Minelayers	2	1	3	2	1	3	2	1	3
Coastal Minelayers	–	1	1	–	1	1	–	1	1
Midget Submarines	3	5	8	–	4	4	–	4	4
Aircraft Repair Ships	1	–	1	–	1	1	–	1	1
Destroyer Dept Ships	1	1	2	1	1	2	1	1	2
Submarine Depot Ships	4	1	5	3	2	5	3	2	5
Fleet Replenishment Ships	1	–	1	1	–	1	1	–	1
Fighter Direction Ships	1	–	1	1	–	1	1	–	1
Fleet Train									
CO Ships & Craft	5 LST 6 LCT	Balance of Brigade Lift	Sufficient for Brigade Lift	5 LST 6 LCT Small craft	Balance of Brigade Lift	Sufficient for Brigade Lift	3 LST 1 LCT Small craft	Balance of Brigade Lift	Sufficient for Brigade Lift
Front Line Aircraft	300	405	705	190	NA	190	150	NA	150
Peacetime Manpower		160,600			150,000			148,000	

143. *Chiefs of Staff Memorandum*

[DEFE 5/8] 2 November 1948

COS(48)148 GUIDED WEAPONS

Memorandum by the First Sea Lord

The Defence Research Policy Committee's Annual Review dated 19 October 1948[1] draws attention to the lack of progress in the guided weapon field … it recommends … allocating the same priorities in staff, equipment and materials as is accorded atomic energy.

2. … the development of these weapons is of the highest importance in order that we may assess their value in meeting future air attack.

3. Our present defence, which lies in the gun and fighter aircraft, becomes more difficult as the speed of the attacker becomes faster and faster. The guided missile is a weapon which may prove of immense value in this respect.

4. In the near future we aim to use the guided missile probably in limited numbers in conjunction with the fighter and the gun, and we had arranged to include some of these weapons in the Fleet planned for 1957.

5. … the size and nature of these guided weapons and their launching devices will almost certainly have a radical effect on ship design and construction …

6. Although progress has been made on SEA SLUG[2] it seems … that [it] can only be in operational service by 1956 if we take the most determined and decisive measures to speed up the research and development work. The same is believed to be true of the other three guided projects, RED HEATHEN, BLUE BOAR and RED HAWK.[3]

7. The Admiralty feel[s] … the present organization appears to be somewhat inappropriate in that responsibility for developing … Naval and Army weapons … has been placed on the air side of the Ministry of Supply.

8. In the Admiralty view the development of SEA SLUG and RED HEATHEN … should be placed in a separate category under its own Controller, as has already been done in the case of atomic energy …

[1] DRP(48)139, not reproduced.

[2] A medium-range surface-to-air missile, Sea Slug entered operational service in 1962.

[3] A land-based SAM, a guided anti-ship bomb and an air-to-air missile, respectively.

PART IV

THE REVISED RESTRICTED FLEET, DECEMBER 1948 – JUNE 1950

At the end of 1948, in the midst of the Berlin crisis, the Defence Committee again considered requirements for 1949–50 [144, 145]. Within a deteriorating international situation, the Forces faced increasing obsolescence and could no longer live off diminishing wartime stocks of equipment and stores. The Minster of Defence (A.V. Alexander) stated that within the £700 million defence budget the Chancellor now wished to allocate, £177 million would go the Navy with a manpower strength of 145,000. The Admiralty stressed that under these circumstances, the Navy's readiness would decline to the point it had been prior to the Berlin crisis. Even with a budget of about £190m they would have to abandon the first part of the plan to prepare for war by 1957. Refitting of ships would be badly hit and the number of front aircraft would not rise above its current low total of 170. A decision on the size of the defence budget was deferred for later consideration.

In the new year the Admiralty Board had to accept that the Navy was most unlikely to get any more than £190 million for 1949/50 [147–149]. It eventually had to settle for a little less. The principal outcomes of this were the deferral of the 'nine-year plan' by a year and the cancellation of three cruiser refits. At one of its meetings the Board also noted that the WRNS had become a permanent part of the RN with effect from 1 February 1949 [149].

Following settlement of the Service Estimates for 1949/50, a detailed report on production (equipment) programmes for the same year noted the effect of financial limitations for the Navy [150]. Though one fleet carrier modernisation was to start, in general carrier modernisation was being delayed as were improvements to gunnery equipment. The report highlighted the need for long-term plans rather than wasteful and inefficient annual allocations (a perennial Defence concern). The legacy construction programme was still an impressive one, however, including seven carriers, three cruisers and seven destroyers, while a further three small carriers were suspended. Over 300 aircraft were in production, mainly the Sea Fury and Firefly.

DofP returned to the subject of cruisers, both old and new [151, 152]. Decisions were required as to which ships should be retained and which disposed of. The prewar *Southampton*s were favoured due to their peacetime construction and greater scope for modernisation. New cruisers were planned for 1954; he recommended the new 6″ and 3″ guns but probably not Seaslug. Manning considerations also drew renewed attention to the battleships, all of which were either in the Training Squadron or in Reserve [153].

In addition the Board paid attention to other detailed matters, such as landing ships [146], the Reserve Fleet [154] and several ship conversions [155].

In April 1949 ACNS produced a major study on the 'Ships of the Future Navy' [156]. He identified Russia as the only conceivable enemy, and assumed America as an ally. That perennial aspiration a 'balanced fleet' was required but financial stringency demanded some prioritisation. The paper laid out a detailed list of threats and tasks before considering what types of ship would be required to meet them. ACNS concluded that the Navy needed carriers, a new 'cruiser/destroyer', escorts, submarines, minesweepers and coastal craft. Guided weapons ships would eventually be required, but were still some way off. Battleships were required only to counter other battleships, and the Russians had none. The existing five ships should go into reserve.

The paper went on to consider cruiser and destroyer numbers, comparing the 'nine-year plan' with a new 'Restricted Fleet', and then substituting 50 of the proposed cruiser-destroyers for both existing types. Nothing was to come of the latter idea,

In parallel with ACNS's musings, the 'Harwood Report' [157, 162] had been commissioned to consider the size and shape of the Armed Forces between 1950 and 1953, assuming an annual defence budget of just £700m as mooted by the Chancellor. The Chiefs of Staffs wanted to demonstrate that such a limited budget was insufficient and Harwood did just that. Naval manpower would have to be cut to 90,000 by 1953. Forces would be withdrawn from most overseas stations and bases abandoned or reduced to care and maintenance. At home, Sheerness, Portland and possibly Chatham would be closed and both the Royal Marines and WRNS abolished.

Perhaps the most far-sighted proposal was a 'peripatetic' task group to visit overseas areas rather than smaller forces permanently on station – which is exactly what the RN adopted in the 1970s and beyond. The Harwood Report was also realistic in noting a wartime legacy of obsolescent ships in reserve and a large number of shore establishments, many of which needed to go in order to modernise the Fleet irrespective of any financial cut imposed. The active fleet in 1950–53 would comprise five carriers, seven cruisers, 40 destroyers, 32 frigates, 28 submarines and 40 minesweepers which, however galling it would be to the Naval Staff, was much more realistic than some of the force levels previously mooted.

The Chiefs of Staff immediately instituted their own studies to review Harwood [158]. When the Board considered the Report in April [159], their initial conclusions were that the peacetime forces recommended were inadequate but that those proposed for war were broadly sufficient. In both cases, however, the Fleet was 'unbalanced'. Nor could they agree to the loss of the Marines or the WRNS. Though anxious not to reject the Harwood Report out of hand, the Navy's leadership expressed firm reservations. In reporting to the other Chiefs the First Sea Lord made plain that, were Harwood to be adopted, most overseas commitments would have to be abandoned with significant political and diplomatic repercussions [160]. The proposed administrative savings to be achieved were regarded as optimistic – again, a recurrent feature of reviews of defence. The First Sea Lord (Lord Fraser of North Cape) went on to recommend that the Chiefs submit their own proposals based on what was required to execute the Government's own policies [161].

When the Chiefs reported to the Defence Committee in June [163] they made clear that Harwood had confirmed their previous belief that £700 million was 'seriously inadequate' – which must be what they intended all along. The Admiralty's earlier conclusions [160, 164] were reiterated. The Minister of Defence stated the crux of the matter; 'on any reasonable assumption about the size of the future defence budget, the rising curve of re-equipment expenditure can only be financed by a decline in the size of the forces'.[1] This dilemma has bedevilled defence planning right up to the present day. He later went on to identify another perennial issue; 'teeth v. tail' and the search for 'administrative economies'.[2]

In parallel to deliberations on the Harwood Report, the Board considered what the 1949/50 Construction Programme would look like [165]. A revised version that better reflected decisions arising from Harwood was finally submitted to the Defence Committee in December [183]. In response to Harwood itself, DofP proposed a 'Restricted Fleet' [166] that, with later amendments, became the 'Revised Restricted Fleet'.[3] One immediate consequence was to be the closure of Sheerness Dockyard.

Detailed development of the Revised Restricted Fleet began with a detailed comparison with the previous year's plan [167]. Most categories of ship were reduced in numbers though, with the exception of existing Light Fleet Carriers (which could not operate modern aircraft), not by much. Over five years, it represented a cumulative 17 per cent financial saving over the previous plan though still a larger annual budget than that proposed by Harwood. Instead of 145,000 the peacetime Navy would now number 121,500 – still huge by today's standards. The Board, unsurprisingly, considered DofP's proposal far preferable to Harwood [168] though perhaps Harwood did serve to make further reductions on the previous year's plan more palatable. The ships to be maintained in full commission included five carriers, 13 cruisers, 70 destroyers and frigates, and 20 submarines plus several more vessels with 'special complements'

[1]DO(49)51, 25 June 1949 p. 2 in CAB 131/7, not reproduced.
[2]DO(49)66, 18 Oct 1949 p. 2 in CAB 131/7, not reproduced.
[3]Grove, *Vanguard to Trident*, p. 51.

employed on trials and training duties. The Board agreed that this plan would form the basis of the Navy's submission on the future size and shape of the Forces as a response to Harwood [169, 170].

Money was not the only challenge facing the Board. Retention of manpower was poor, with the prospect by mid-1951 of "not manning difficulties but a first-class breakdown" [171, 172].

While the Navy was considering the Revised Restricted Fleet the Joint Planners were, perhaps for the first time, thinking about future force requirements in an alliance context [173] (The Washington Treaty establishing NATO had been signed on 4 April 1949). The global requirement was stated as 68 carriers with nearly 3,000 aircraft, over 70 cruisers, nearly 1,200 destroyers and frigates and almost 200 submarines. Other than the need to maintain powerful task groups in the four main areas – Atlantic, Mediterranean, Middle East and Pacific – there was little indication of how these ambitious force levels were calculated, and no reference to the scale of a Soviet threat at sea.

In September attention turned to the Estimates for the next three years [174, 175]. The salient points agreed were that the Navy's peacetime strength would reduce to 124,000 personnel, that the Service would phase out the use of conscripts and the naval budget would stabilise at £201 million by 1950–51, though there were concerns about the effect of the devaluation of Sterling against the US Dollar.

The same timescale was used, post-Harwood, to plan the size and shape of the forces within a total budget of £810 million per annum [176], £700 million having been shown to be quite inadequate. The Revised Restricted Fleet was the Navy's part of this.[1] On the forecast Estimate of £201 million per year, in 1950 the Navy would maintain in commission a single battleship, seven carriers, 15 cruisers, almost 100 destroyers and frigates and 33 submarines. The Reserve Fleet would be of a broadly similar size, but with many more frigates. By 1957 large increases were forecast in coastal minesweepers and naval aircraft but otherwise there was to be little significant change; until 1953 new construction programmes would focus mainly on minesweepers.

When the proposals were submitted to the Defence Committee in October 1949, the memorandum [177] contained a useful summary (paragraphs 5–7) of deliberations to date. Following extensive discussions [178–81] the Prime Minister and the Chancellor of the Exchequer agreed to a defence budget for 1950–51 of £780 million, in part as a consequence of the recent devaluation of Sterling.[2]

[1] 'Future Composition of the Navy', p. 23.

[2] Bill Jackson & Edwin Bramall, *The Chiefs: The Story of the United Kingdom Chiefs of Staff* (London, 1992), p. 279.

A short, undated, memorandum by DofP from around this time estimated the likely loss rates of ships during a future war set against the predicted force shortfalls at the outbreak of war [182]. The biggest deficiencies were in frigates and minesweepers, reflecting the view that the principal Soviet threats at sea came from submarines, air attack and mining.

In December the 1949–50 new construction programme was finally presented to the Defence Committee [183, 184]. Like its predecessors in 1945 and 1947 it was a modest one and reflected the recent financial settlement for the Navy. There were still plenty of ships under construction, including carriers, but these were delayed items from wartime programmes. Work on some was proceeding, while others were 'suspended'.

Soon after, the Committee was presented with a paper outlining defence efforts being made by the other Commonwealth countries [185]. Though the Admiralty often expressed ambitions for greater Dominion contributions as part of the 'Empire' or 'Commonwealth' Fleet, the Defence Committee memorandum showed that all were, in fact, providing much larger forces than before the War.

A report by the Joint War Production Staff just before Christmas showed increases in spending across all Service departments with the Admiralty receiving the biggest proportionate increase [186]. The largest element was continuing construction of delayed wartime orders and an increasing number of repairs, modernisations and conversions. The re-capitalisation of the Navy was now underway, though at a smaller scale and slower pace than the Admiralty had argued for. In common with the other Services, the Navy had largely used wartime stocks of equipment and supplies, so greater expenditure was required on these as well. It became apparent in the New Year that these equipment programmes could not be met from the £780 million Defence Vote, but the Government was not prepared to authorise Supplementary Estimates to cover the shortfall [187]. With the Admiralty's overall budget now set at £193 million, some small reductions in capital expenditure were required. The principal effect of this was to further delay improvements to readiness.

In February the Board authorised a prototype 'limited' destroyer-frigate conversion, what became the Type 16 [188]. The following month, ACNS conducted a review of the overall conversion and modernisation programme for frigates, together with the future number of minesweepers [189]. It showed some significant shortfalls against the identified, but ambitious, requirements.

The Board's attention also turned to the cruiser programme [190, 191]. The 1957 requirement was for 18 in total and with 24 available plus three still in build, nine ships would go for disposal. All, including the still incomplete *Tigers*, were of prewar or wartime design and construction. The report highlighted in particular the need for modern AA defences, but by the time new 3″ guns and modern fire control would be available, most ships would be too old to make extensive modernisation economical. As to new construction, it was planned to start a large cruiser in 1957 together with the small 'cruiser-destroyer' starting in 1953.[1]

The future scale of modernisations and conversion was therefore becoming clearer. So in April and May the Board considered which ships were surplus to the requirements of the Revised Restricted Fleet [192, 193], the size of which was governed by what was 'economically possible'. The principal casualties were slow wartime frigates, few of which had been modernised or even properly preserved since the War. The Board also approved the design of the 'Second Rate' frigate, which became the Type 14 [194].

A definitive statement of defence policy had not been made since 1947. Since then, the financial crisis of that year had, at least in part, abated, the Berlin crisis had intensified the Cold War and the NATO alliance had been formed. The Chiefs of Staff therefore formulated a fresh statement on Defence Policy and Global Strategy for the Cabinet [196]. It was accompanied by a brief on the current and planned (1957) naval force levels [195], unchanged from the Revised Restricted Fleet of the previous September [176]. The strategy paper identified British aims in both 'cold' and 'hot' wars and stated western Europe, the Mediterranean, the Far East and sea communications as the principal theatres, notably excluding the Middle East though the Russian threat to the area was mentioned. As to defence priorities, it was 'First Things First' – the home base, sea communications, the front in Europe, a strategic offensive (bomber) force, holding Cold War positions throughout the world and, specifically, the 'Egyptian base'. This paper was the definitive statement of the UK's defence policy just prior to part of the Cold War becoming hot, in the Far East.

The Pink List of 6 June 1950 provides a closing snapshot of the Fleet [197], somewhat recovered from the nadir of 1947. The active Home Fleet included three carriers and three cruisers, plus 14 destroyers. The Mediterranean Fleet comprised a single small carrier, four cruisers, 16 destroyers and frigates and seven submarines. The South Atlantic and America and West Indies Stations between them had a pair of cruisers and four frigates. In the East Indies and the Far East there was another small carrier (soon to see action off Korea), five cruisers, seven destroyers and

[1] Neither type was ever built.

13 frigates. Many more ships were allocated to the Portsmouth, Plymouth, Rosyth, Nore and Submarine Commands as well as the Reserve Fleet. Under construction were 10 carriers, three cruisers and eight destroyers

On 25 June 1950 North Korea invaded the South, sparking the Korean War. British involvement in this conflict and the wider implications of the war soon overturned existing planning assumptions for the Fleet.[1]

[1] Volume II.

144. *Defence Committee Memorandum*

[CAB 131/6] 6 December 1948

DO(48)83 DEFENCE REQUIREMENTS 1949–50

Memorandum by the Minister Of Defence

1 – *Explanatory*

For some months past I have been examining with my Service colleagues and the Chiefs of Staff the Defence requirements for 1949–50 in terms of men and money.

2. A year ago, I sought and obtained acceptance of a defence Budget of £692.6 million for 1948–49. The manpower strengths set out in the 1948 Defence White Paper were as follows:–

	1 April 1948	*31 March 1949*
Navy	145,000	145,000
Army	534,000	345,000
Air Force	261,000	226,000
Total	940,000	716,000

3. When I put forward to the Cabinet in January 1948 (CP(48)2)[1] my proposals for 1948–49, I emphasised that it had been necessary to take very considerable risks and that I was bound to warn my colleagues that, should these mature against us, or should we be faced with additional commitments which had not been taken into account in preparing the estimates, I should be compelled to seek authority for reasonable Supplementary estimates. At the same time the Cabinet had before it the report of the Joint War Production Staff which pointed out that there could not be indefinite delay in the modernisation of our armed forces; and that, since the programmes then submitted assumed the extensive use of obsolescent equipment, future programmes must contain increased provision for the production of equipment.

4. In the event, the position has deteriorated …[2] The position was specially reviewed last summer and at its meeting on 28 August (CM(48)57)[3] the Cabinet approved a number of emergency measures designed (a) to remedy some of the most serious deficiencies in equipment and (b) temporarily to stabilise the strength of the Forces.[4] These decisions further upset the plans made a year ago for 1948–49…

[1]Not reproduced.

[2]Due to ongoing commitments in Austria, Trieste, Greece and Malaya, the Berlin crisis and deteriorating relations with the Soviet Union.

[3]Not reproduced.

[4]None of these measures applied to the Navy, and its manpower total remained unchanged.

II – *1949–50 Defence requirements*

7. In 1949–50 the Services will unfortunately still be charged with responsibilities of which we had hoped that they would be relieved ... they can no longer continue to depend to the same extent as hitherto on wartime stocks for their current needs of equipment and stores, which in 1949–50 must be met from fresh production. This will involve a considerable increase in inescapable expenditure ... the requirements of the Services in both men and money will be greater in 1949–50 than I would have wished.

8. I obtained reports from the Service Departments of their requirements for 1949–50 in the light of present circumstances. These reports assumed average man-power strengths for next year as follows:–

	Average
Navy	145,000
Army	434,000
Air Force	237,000
Total	817,000

The total Defence Budget was estimated to be about £833 million. The Chancellor had indeed indicated to me that the economy of the country could not sustain a Defence Budget of more than £700 million, plus the provision of about £12 million for the pay increase announced on 12 November.

9. I therefore requested the Service Departments to revise their plans and to state the effect of accepting a total Defence Budget of £700 million. I indicated that, after making provision for pay increases and for Ministry of Supply and Ministry of Defence expenditure, there would remain some £627 million, which I suggested should provisionally be allocated:–

	£ million
Admiralty	177
War Office	270
Air Ministry	180

Navy

10. The Admiralty pointed out that they had already reduced their strength to 145,000 before the beginning of this year and that there never had been any intention that it should fall below this figure. No saving could therefore be expected from cuts in manpower. The approved Navy programme had envisaged an expenditure of £160 million for the current year. A special shadow cut of £7 million was applied on the understanding that a supplementary estimate up to that amount would be allowed if the programme progressed at such a rate as to show that the money would be required, as indeed it will be. In 1949–50 they would have to spend £5 million on emergency measures already in hand and a further £19 million on account

of higher prices, higher civilian wages, increased non-effective charges, maintenance, production in respect of items in regard to which wartime surpluses no longer existed, increased expenditure on works:– this figure also allowed for a fall in receipts. In addition, they would have to provide for the sanctioned stockpiling of oil fuel (an approved programme for which had, it will be remembered, suffered a serious setback by the help which the Admiralty was called upon to make to civilian needs a year ago) and for essential refits on Reserve Fleet ships. If, therefore, the Admiralty were held to £177 million they would be forced:–

(i) To abandon all further measures, both long- and short-term, designed to improve the Navy's state of readiness, and to cancel some similar measures already in hand;
(ii) to abandon all improvements to machinery and equipment ashore and afloat;
(iii) to abandon measures designed to remedy the most serious deficiencies in present stocks of naval ammunition;
(iv) to reduce the already inadequate provision for works …;
(v) as a last resort, to reduce the manpower strength.

The cumulative effect would be that the state of material readiness of the Navy would go back practically to the level at which it stood before the emergency of last summer, and if (v) proved to be necessary some immobilisation of ships now in commission would be inevitable …

General

13. … I am fully convinced that a Defence Budget of £700 million … is quite inadequate to support effective Armed Forces.

REVISED PROPOSALS

16. If we are to remedy some of the most striking deficiencies in our Defences it is clear that no smaller total provision than £770 million will suffice. To go below that figure would have serious consequences on our ability, should need arise, to fight with what we have got. The task which each Service has to perform, both in the immediate future and in a major war, has been most carefully reviewed. It is not possible to place the major share of any economies on one Service either in present circumstances or in view of the role of each in the support of the three main continuing pillars of our overall strategy, viz., defence of the United Kingdom, maintenance of sea communications, and Middle East defence … To secure a substantial reduction below £770 million would involve a slowing down, if not cancellation, of many of the measures in the emergency programme which only as recently as last September we informed the House of Commons that we had accepted as essential for the well-being of our Forces. Some retardation may be possible, but complete cancellation is, in my view, out of the question. Moreover, there

is no more certain way of wasting money than to start a programme and then drastically curtail it just as it is getting into its stride …

17. I have, however, considered the effect on our Defences of a Defence Budget of £750 million … as follows:–

Admiralty – about £190 million (including Research and Development) …

18. With a [Defence] Budget of £770 million the Admiralty would have to eliminate all provision for the first instalment of the plan to prepare the Navy for a major threat of war by 1957, and the other two services would also be unable to make provision for long-term re-equipment. A reduction to about £750 million would affect the three Services in the following ways:–

Navy

19. The Admiralty would have to abandon or curtail the following vital measures:–

(1) Provision of anti-submarine and anti-aircraft weapons and ammunition, radio and radar equipment, replacement of obsolescent and unserviceable items; and the replacement of over-age submarine batteries.

(2) The replacement of obsolete aircraft and aircraft stores.

(3) The provision of boom defence equipment and degaussing material for merchant ships.

(4) Stockpiling of oil fuel.

(5) Refitting of Reserve Fleet ships at present rate (which would involve further serious deterioration in their condition)

Recommendations

23. I invite my colleagues:–

(i) to agree that it is not possible to reduce the Defence Budget to £712 million, as this provision would compel us to abandon many present commitments; to reduce the Forces to an extent which would make them ineffective and permit of a more token intake of national servicemen in 1949; and to deny them the equipment which is essential if they are to be effective;

(ii) to approve, for submission to the Cabinet, a Defence Budget for 1949–50 of £770 million, of which the precise distribution will be further considered by myself, my colleagues in the three Service Departments and the Minister of Supply.

145. *Defence Committee Minutes*

[CAB 131/5] 8 December 1948

DO(48) 23rd Meeting Defence Requirements 1949–50

The Committee had before them a memorandum by the Minister of Defence (DO(48)83) setting out, in terms of men and money, his estimate of the defence requirement for 1949–50…

The Chief of the Air Staff[1] said that the Chiefs of Staff fully appreciated the difficulties in the economic situation and had done their best to reduce the bill for defence to the minimum. In their opinion a Defence Budget of £770 million would just, but only just, enable the three Services to perform their essential tasks which fell broadly into four groups.

In the first place they had to play their part in fighting the cold war …

Secondly, the Armed Forces had to be ready to fight with what they had got …

The third task of the Armed Forces, to which the Minister of Defence had already referred, was to inspire confidence in our ability to meet our Treaty obligations and provide our Allies with some help in building up their defences …

Finally, the Armed Forces had to be ready, in 8–10 years' time, to meet the possibility of premeditated war and this meant that they must gradually begin to build up their structure and armaments.

The Chiefs of Staff were looking at the problem not as one which was the province of three separate Services but as a national problem to which a single solution had to be found … In the future the Chiefs of Staff hoped to be able to achieve a better balance between the Forces and a special team was already at work in an endeavour to discover a fresh approach to the very difficult problem.[2] But this investigation could not possibly have any bearing on the size and shape of the Armed Forces in 1949–50 and the financial provision that should be made for them in that year. While recognising that the bill was a formidable one the Chiefs of Staff were firmly of the opinion that any drastic cut in the figure of £770 million would have disastrous effects both on all three Services and on national defence as a whole …

The First Sea Lord said that a reduction or the overall Budget to the figure of £712 million would mean that the Royal Navy would get £20 million less than in 1948–49. This would have a very serious effect on the whole structure and in particular would mean that a part of the

[1] Marshal of the Royal Air Force Lord Tedder, Chairman of the Chiefs of Staff Committee.
[2] The Harwood Committee which reported the following year; reproduced as Doc. No. 157.

Home Fleet would have to be immobilised, refitting of the Reserve Fleet would practically have to be stopped and the refitting of sea-going Fleets slowed down. The Navy would be unable to take any further National Service entrants, regular recruitment would have to be slowed down and Naval aviation would have to be stabilised at its present deplorably low figure of 170 front-line aircraft …

The First Lord of the Admiralty recalled that the question of the peacetime strength of the Navy had been very gravely considered some two years ago, and it had been decided to reduce the total strength to 145,000, on the understanding that the Admiralty could base their plans on the assumption that this figure would be maintained for some years. This figure could not be regarded as extravagant having regard to the fact that the Fleet Air Arm accounted for between one-third and one-quarter of the total Naval manpower. The minimum provision of £190 million in 1949–50 for which the Admiralty had asked would provide only £7 million for new services. He had examined the Estimates carefully and he was satisfied that no reduction could be made in this figure. In considering this matter, the Committee should bear in mind the extent of the Naval commitments overseas; and the fact that in a number of foreign stations it was essential for the Navy to maintain very considerable ship repair facilities …

The Prime Minister asked why the difference of some £60 million between the figures of £770 million and £712 million made, as it seemed, all the difference between an effective and an ineffective defence … The Committee, however, could not settle a final budgetary figure which would be recommended to Cabinet as this was dependent on other circumstances which he would discuss further with the Foreign Secretary, Chancellor of the Exchequer and the Minister of Defence.

146. *Joint Planning Staff Memorandum*

[DEFE 6/7] 8 December 1948

JP(48)123(Final) REQUIREMENTS FOR LANDING CRAFT, TANK IN THE EVENT OF WAR

As instructed, we have prepared in consultation with Combined Operations Headquarters a report showing British requirements for LCT in war …

2. Thirty modern ocean-going LCT now exist. The earlier war-built types which have limited sea-going qualities are being disposed of. Two of the modern craft are in the Mediterranean …

4. It has been agreed by the Chiefs of Staff that we should have available immediately on the outbreak of war sufficient landing ships and craft for a Brigade Group lift.
5. The right proportion of ocean-going LCT for a force of this size is twenty-four. Twenty-eight LCT(8) now in Home Waters therefore allow a prudent margin for contingencies …

147. *Board Memorandum*

[ADM 167/133] 1 January 1949

B.577 Navy Estimates 1949/50

The First Lord wishes to report to his colleagues the developments of the last few weeks concerning Navy Estimates for the next financial year.
2. The final Sketch Estimates … amounted to … a net estimated expenditure of £220,468,900 (including approximately £12,000,000 for research and development). These were the figures on which negotiation with the Ministry of Defence and the other Service Departments was commenced. Corresponding Sketch Estimates from the other Departments would have required a total of £833,000,000 for defence expenditure in 1949/50, as contrasted with a total expenditure of £692,000,000 provided in the Estimates for 1948/49. Even allowing for the cost of certain measures to make good deficiencies in preparedness for emergency, the total defence expenditure forecast in these Sketch Estimates was of a size that it was clear the Chancellor of the Exchequer would resist strongly.
3. In the course of discussions between the Service Departments and the Ministry of Defence, the Admiralty accepted as inevitable the postponement of the first year of the 9-year plan on which the Sketch Navy Estimates had been based. This, and the spreading over a longer period of the majority of the deficiency measures, enabled the Admiralty to bring the total proposed Navy Estimates for 1949/50 to £196,000,000 (including £11,000,000 for Research and Development). These measures involved reducing the total provision for emergency items to just over £11,000,000 as compared with a figure of £18,000,000 if full provision were to be made according to the minimum programme which the Admiralty considered desirable.
4. There has been a bitter fight between the Minister of Defence and the Chancellor of the Exchequer on the total of Service Estimates and, in particular, on the amount to be allotted to the Navy. The Chancellor started on the basis of a total of no more than £712,000,000, which would have given the Admiralty something in the neighbourhood of £180,000,000 total. He has been persuaded to increase that figure to £750,000,000,

but is resisting strenuously anything more than that. The final proposals of the Minister of Defence have taken the form of a defence expenditure of £763,000,000, of which the proposed Admiralty share would be £190,000,000. It may be possible in the final arguments to obtain £1,000,000 or £2,000,000 more for the Admiralty than £190,000,000, but this is most unlikely:– there is more than a risk that, in the final bargaining, if the Cabinet as a whole are disposed to back the Chancellor in his figure of £750,000,000, we shall have to suffer a further cut of £1,000,000 or £2,000,000 below £190,000,000.

5. The Finance Committee met just before Christmas to consider how the various Vote totals could be adjusted to bring naval expenditure down to £190,000,000 in 1949/50. On the production Votes (8 and 9), the Controller had already prepared proposals based on a total estimate of £193,000,000. These proposals involved reducing the expenditure on the emergency items to £8,000,000 only. The Finance Committee took the line that no further reductions should be made in these Votes, but by severe pruning of services in the other Votes, succeeded in scaling down the total to £190,000,000 ….

6. It is to be emphasised that the consequence of these measures will be:–

(a) that the rate of remedying deficiencies in preparedness for emergency will be markedly slowed down;

(b) that almost no provision will be possible for certain deficiencies, such as uniform clothing where in any event the prospect of securing an allocation of the necessary materials would be slight;

(c) that the 9-year programme for bringing the Fleet to a state of readiness to undertake a major war will be completely postponed for a year:–

(d) a cut of approximately one-twelfth of the Admiralty's R and D effort, plus a potential shadow cut equivalent to a further one-fifteenth;

(e) very severe restriction, amounting almost to practical elimination, of any new works which have not been started in 1948/49;

(f) a practical cessation of development of, indeed, a possible reduction in, the policy of utilising civilians to replace naval personnel in Fleet Establishments;

(g) a resumption of the process of pruning Admiralty and ex-Headquarters staffs;

(h) acceptance of the situation that any further measures designed to remedy deficiencies in preparedness for an emergency can only be undertaken at the cost of finding the money from some other source which, in general, will require the postponement or cancellation of some other service.

148. *Board Memorandum*

[ADM 167/133] 27 January 1949

B.579 Navy Estimates 1949/50

In the examination of the sketch Navy Estimates by the Ministry of Defence and the Treasury – which followed the tabling of sketch estimates based on a total provision of £190m (Board Memorandum 577) the Treasury concentrated attention on the big spending Votes pressing for larger shadow cuts, assumption of increased Appropriations in Aid, some slowing down in the attenuated programmes covered by the sketch estimates and a larger saving in staffs generally. They apparently advised the Chancellor over the whole field of service estimates, though it is not known to what extent they assumed potential savings in the Navy field that it should be possible to save £13m out of the £763m total and thus bring the figure to £750m. The Minister of Defence and the Service Ministers decided that if they could secure a total of £760m from the Chancellor without risking an appeal to the Cabinet which might support the Chancellor's view about the adequacy of £750m, it would be worth the sacrifice of the odd £3m. The Chancellor eventually accepted this arrangement and the Admiralty's contribution to the saving of £3m has been agreed at £.75m …

3. Certain adjustments in the programmes … have now been made …:–
   (1) The order of priority of work in the Dockyards has been revised to admit inter alia of a start being made on the modernisation of FORMIDABLE; priority has been given to work on certain other ships; the refits of ROYALIST, NORFOLK and SUSSEX have been deleted from the programme.
   (2) Increased provision has been made for LL Sweep batteries (£67,000) and mine location equipment (£35,000), with compensating adjustments in the provision for other items of equipment under Votes 8 and 9.
   (3) The production of torpedoes and the purchase of degaussing equipment and guns for DEMS will proceed at minimum pace.
   (4) The need for heavy armour plate trials and the possibility of a reduction of the Ship Target Trials programme will be examined.

149. *Board Minutes*

[ADM 167/132] 1 February 1949

Women's Royal Naval Service

4270. The Board took note that on 1 February 1949 the Women's Royal Naval Service became part of the permanent organisation of the Royal Navy …

Navy Estimates 1949/50

4271. … the Board took note of a further memorandum on the Navy estimates 1949/50, indicating that a total of £189,250,000 had now been approved and explaining the further cuts which had been made in order to reach this figure.

The Board were informed that during the negotiations the Chancellor of the Exchequer had made it clear that he would not be prepared to contemplate Supplementary Estimates for the Services in 1949/50. It was expected, however, that should additional funds become available during the financial year by reason of an increase in Appropriations-in-Aid above the figure on which the Estimates were now based, the additional money thus found could be used to meet additional commitments, in which event priority would be given to the items which had been deleted in order to reach the final figure of £189,250,000 …

150. *Defence Production Committee Memorandum*

[CAB 131/7] 18 February 1949

DPC(49)1 SERVICE PRODUCTION PROGRAMMES 1949–50

Report by the Joint War Production Staff

1. *Comparison of 1949–50 and 1948–49 Programmes*

The production programmes of the three Services for 1949–50, expressed in terms of money, compare as follows with the amended programmes planned for 1948–49:–

	1948–49	*1949–50*
	£000	£000
Admiralty	46,229	65,542
War Office	50,750	69,472
Air Ministry	68,250	79,003
Ministry of Supply	2,200	1,920
Total	167,429	216,937

… The Admiralty is … its own Supply Department and its total also includes disbursement on ships and other items which take a long time to build and which may have been delivered before the financial year begins, or will not be delivered until after is has ended. For this reason, the totals for each Service are not strictly comparable …

8. *Main features of each programme*

Admiralty

The programme provides for the maintenance of the Active Fleet expected to be in commission and for some progress to be made during the year with reconditioning some ships of the Reserve Fleet. The programme also provides, as in 1948–49, for expenditure on the residue of new construction programmes approved in previous years. There is also a token provision for a small 1949 Construction Programme, including a few auxiliary vessels. The programme of conversion, repair and refit of ships planned in connection with the 'nine-year plan' has had to be postponed, and the Admiralty cannot start on their modernisation plan except for the taking in hand of one Fleet Aircraft Carrier towards the end of the financial year. The capacity of the dockyards will be fully occupied by repairs to His Majesty's ships and a small programme of conversions of submarines, destroyers and other vessels. The relatively small residue of repair work will continue to be carried out in private yards. The naval aircraft programme, apart from the provision made to meet a possible early emergency, is related to the maintenance of a front-line strength at present estimated at 182 aircraft …

9. *Deferment of modernisation of the Forces*

Shortage of money has made it impossible to plan scientifically the modernisation of the Forces. Fair progress has been made with some types of aircraft, and with certain radio and radar equipment where the replacement of the old types had become unavoidable. The main object of the recent emergency measures was to enable the Services to make good the most vital immediate deficiencies, not to undertake the modernisation of their equipment except in so far as this was a necessary consequence … In the case of the Navy the Admiralty's inability to begin the programme of modernising aircraft carriers will postpone the time when they will be able to operate modern types of aircraft now coming into production. Moreover, the long-term task of modernising the gunnery equipment of the Fleet cannot be effectively started …

14. *War Potential*

Very little can be done with present funds to place orders to maintain techniques in being in firms which will be very valuable in war time. The refit of submarines by contract is one of the few examples of what is being done. The emergency measures approved in the summer were of considerable value in this connection, but the curtailment of orders as a result of the decision to cut the emergency programme has caused a setback …

In the case of the Royal Navy, an early emergency would concentrate effort on the reconditioning of existing ships, weapons and equipment. The Admiralty's main production potential consists of the Royal Dockyards and private shipyards and the latter, owing to the flourishing state of the shipbuilding industry, are being maintained at a satisfactory levels …

17. *Need for long-term production plans*

In previous reports we have stressed the necessity both from the strategic and the financial point of view of long-term planning. We can hardly overemphasise the fact that if we are to achieve the orderly modernisation of our Forces and to be sure of getting the manufacturing capacity we need for Services' production, orders must be placed a long time ahead. The present system of uncertain annual allocations prevents the best use being made of the limited industrial capacity available for Service production; it dissipates industrial and Service manpower; and its results discourage the Armed Forces. In short, it is wasteful of manpower, manufacturing capacity and money.

We are unable to proceed with a long-term production programme without a fairly clear indication in advance of what the future shape, size and function of each of the armed Services is to be and how much money is to be available for production …

APPENDIX[1]

ITEM 1

CONSTRUCTION OF NAVAL VESSELS

The amount of new construction to be progressed during the year is small and apart from a token provision for a small 1949 New Construction Programme, is the residue of approved programmes of earlier years. It represents, broadly speaking, the minimum rate of construction which must be maintained on those ships already laid down on which work is continuing …

The programme includes expenditure on the following major warships:– it does not include £198,000 for *Terrible* and *Majestic* for the Royal Australian Navy.

Aircraft Carriers	Cruisers
Ark Royal	*Tiger*
Eagle	*Defence*
	Blake
Light Fleet Carriers	Destroyers
Hercules	*Alamein*

[1] In the interests of space, the detailed costings under Items 1–7 are not reproduced.

Leviathan	*Diamond*
Magnificent	*Defender*
Powerful	*Decoy*
Albion	*Diana*
Bulwark	*Duchess*
Centaur	*Broadsword*
Hermes	

ITEM 2

MACHINERY FOR SHIPS AND SHORE ESTABLISHMENTS

This item includes the cost in 1949–50 or replacement machinery for ships in service and some items of machinery for the programme of modernising aircraft carriers, for the conversion of an initial number of destroyers to A/S frigates and of some T Class submarines to fast battery types …

ITEM 3

REPAIR AND REFIT OF NAVAL VESSELS AND MARINE CRAFT

The Admiralty total represents the conversion, repair and refit programme to be carried out in United Kingdom yards.

The Royal Dockyard programme includes two submarines to be converted to fast battery type and two destroyers to frigates. Large repairs will be carried out on 15 vessels (1 fleet carrier, 3 cruisers, 3 destroyers, 4 frigates, 3 submarines and 1 repair ship).

The work to be placed out on contract in private yards will comprise repairs and refits to 58 vessels, including 3 depot ships, 14 frigates, 8 destroyers and 8 submarines … The programme at home will be supplemented by work in Naval dockyards abroad …

ITEM 4

AIRCRAFT

Naval Aircraft Programme

The intention is to maintain a front-line strength for the Royal Navy of 182 aircraft as against 157 for 1948–49. Training and Miscellaneous Units and RNVR squadrons will hold from 270–300 aircraft of current and obsolescent operational types.

The programme comprises the following:–

254 aircraft to meet normal requirements.

20 aircraft in arrears from the previous year's programme.

66 Fireflys as an emergency reserve.

64 aircraft for delivery … to the Royal Canadian and Royal Australian Navies.

Details of the programme by types of aircraft are given in Annex A …

The programme is based on the maximum use of existing stocks of aircraft including types no longer in production; continued reliance on piston-engined aircraft because of the setback in production of more modern types … and the requirements for working reserves and to cover annual wastage …

An order is about to be placed for 150 jet Naval fighters to specification N7/46,[1] deliveries of which are expected to begin in the first half of 1951 …

ANNEX A

Naval Aircraft Production Programme for the Royal Navy and the Dominions for 1949–50

	Backlog from	1949–50		
Combat types for front line and training –	*1948–49*	*RN*	*Dominions*	*Total*
Sea Fury Mk II single-seat fighters	…	103	32	135
Firefly Mk 5 fighter/anti-submarine	…	58	32	90
Sea Hornet Mk 20 strike fighters	…	9	…	9
Sea Hornet Mk21 night fighters	8	30	…	38
Sea Hornet Mk 22 P.R. aircraft	…	9	…	9
Attacker jet fighters	…	8	…	8
Wyvern Mk 2 torpedo strike	1	…	…	1
Non-combat types –				
Sea Fury as dual trainers	…	17	…	17
Meteor T.7 dual trainers	…	6	…	6
Anson Mk 21 as radio flying classroom	…	8	…	8
Light helicopters S.51	3	6	…	9
Sturgeon target towers for AA practices	8	…	…	8
	20 (c)	254	64	338
	274			
Emergency order –				
Firefly Mk 5 fighter/anti-submarine		66		

ITEM 5

WEAPONS AND THEIR EQUIPMENT

The provision proposed is for the purpose of replacing obsolete equipments, in ships coming in for refit and repair, with the latest available types of gun mountings and fire control now in production and to cover equipment for training purposes … The biggest item of expenditure on guns themselves is for Naval Aviation, mostly for new aircraft.

ITEM 6

ARMAMENT STORES

The reason for the increased provision under this head is the need for making a start on replenishing depleted stocks and for replacing, urgently, ammunition which is over-age and unsatisfactory …

Torpedo assembly and conversion will continue at the same rate as last year, thereby assisting to maintain some production at the RNTF. The production of mines and depth charges will he resumed on a small scale.

[1] Hawker Sea Hawk.

ITEM 7

TELECOMMUNICATIONS AND SIGNAL EQUIPMENT

The provision is largely for the continuation of existing orders and the start on long-term proposals to re-equip the Fleet with modern radio and radar has had to be substantially curtailed. Ships coming in hand for large repairs and refits can be fitted with present radio equipment such as can be supplied from stock, involving the continued use of American and other obsolescent equipment …

151. *Ship Design Policy Committee Memorandum*

[ADM 116/5632] 20 January 1949

SDPC(49)7 RETENTION OF OVER-AGE CRUISERS

Memorandum by DofP

The 1957 Fleet, on which the Controller's Nine-Year Plan is based, includes 23 cruisers which is the assessed requirement (COS(47)263(O)) on the outbreak of war, exclusive of the Dominions contributions. BELLONA and BLACK PRINCE, on loan to New Zealand, are included in the Dominions contribution which brings the total RN cruisers to be retained to 25.

2. We have at present 31 cruisers, including BELLONA and BLACK PRINCE, with three building. It is therefore necessary to decide which nine of our present cruisers should, if necessary, be disposed of by 1957 and what order of priority.

3. Views of Admiralty Divisions and Departments have been sought … and the pros and cons for each class of ship have been tabulated in Annex I. A list of the ships of each class, with completion dates is at Annex II …

4. [The] advantage of one ship compared with another from the hull and machinery points of view could only be determined by comprehensive surveys, which could not be undertaken for all cruisers without completely disrupting the normal programme of Fleet refits. [However,] some of the reports rendered … have given general indications of the conditions of ships about to pay off into Reserve …

5. Dof P recommends that this paper be considered by the Ship Design Policy Committee with a view to discussing the pros and cons of our cruisers by type and determining what action should be taken.

6. Dof P favours the retention of the Southamptons as a class in the 1957 Fleet in view of their larger size and endurance and their peacetime construction, subject to the condition of the individual ships.

ANNEX I

8-inch Cruisers

Pro	Con
Suitable in hot climates	Eight years older than other cruisers
Good endurance	Due to service in war years, machinery may be expected to give constant trouble
Good flagship	Lack of speed
Heavier armament	

There is general agreement that the 8-inch should be the first to go:– Those with AIO (NORFOLK and SUSSEX) to be the last.

Southamptons

Pro	Con
Suitable in hot climates	Ten years old
Large endurance	
Good flagships	
Present A/A armament could be improved	
Full AIO can be fitted	
Better stability, larger ships, more heavily built and armoured	
Built in peacetime	

Fijis and Ugandas

Pro	Con
Good endurance	Unsuitable in hot climates
Fairly modern	Cramped crew spaces
Can be modernised but only fitted with 1 control system	Poor flagship
Full AIO can be fitted	

Didos

Pro	Con
Very hardy and economical in fuel	Unsuitable in hot climates
Offer a big short-term advantage as stop-gap in that they can be modernised easily but turrets will be out of date by 1956	Bad flagship
	Cramped crew space
	Slightly less efficient than others due to small size
	Limited AIO

ANNEX II

Class	Name	Completed	
8″ Cruisers	CUMBERLAND	1928	Earmarked for Trials Cruiser
	LONDON	1929	
	SUSSEX	1929	
	DEVONSHIRE	1929	Training Cruiser
	NORFOLK	1930	
Southamptons	NEWCASTLE	1937	
	SHEFFIELD	1937	
	GLASGOW	1937	
	BIRMINGHAM	1937	
	LIVERPOOL	1938	
	BELFAST	1939	
Fijis	NIGERIA	1940	
	KENYA	1940	
	MAURITIUS	1941	
	JAMAICA	1942	

	GAMBIA	1942	
	BERMUDA	1942	
Ugandas	NEWFOUNDLAND	1943	
	CEYLON	1943	
Didos	DIDO	1940	
	PHOEBE	1940	
	EURYALUS	1941	
	SIRIUS	1942	
	CLEOPATRA	1941	
	ARGONAUT	1942	
	ROYALIST	1943	
	BELLONA	1943	On loan to RNZN
	BLACK PRINCE	1943	On loan to RNZN
	DIADEM	1944	
Swiftsures	SWIFTSURE	1944	
	SUPERB	1945	

152. *Plans Division Memorandum*

[ADM 116/5632] 25 January 1949

PD.R51/75 CRUISER DESIGN[1]

DofP is of the opinion that the cruisers to be laid down in 1954 should have the following characteristics:–

Armament	6 medium calibre dual-purpose guns in 3 twin turrets
	8 3″/70 guns in 4 twin turrets
	2 DA close-range weapons
	No torpedo armament
Radar	Type 960 and 992
Protection	Full damage control arrangements but no side belt. Box protection for machinery spaces, magazines, TS, Bridge, steering gear
Speed	31 knots deep clean
Endurance	7,500 miles at 20 knots deep, clean, temperate conditions
Special Features	(i) All-round training for gun turrets

[1] This memorandum was written in response to a much fuller study conducted by the Ship Design Policy Committee SDPC(49)2 dated 11 Jan 1949 (also in ADM 116/5632) which produced several possible outline designs. A good discussion of the many abortive post-war cruiser designs is in David Brown & George Moore, *Rebuilding the Royal Navy: Warship design since 1945* (London, 2003), pp. 26–35.

(ii) No allowance for Seaslug unless this can be incorporated without hurting design
(iii) Twin funnels
(iv) Closed bridge
(v) Especially good sea-keeping qualities

It is hoped that a cruiser with these characteristics might be produced for a deep displacement of from 14,000 to 15,000 tons.

153. *Minute by Director of Manning*

[ADM 1/21473] 7 February 1949

CD 1234/48

…

2. … VICTORIOUS plus either VANGUARD or one KING GEORGE V class battleship will be able to meet the future commitment of trainees in the Training Squadron except that it would limit the training of specially selected Stoker Mechanics … and reduce the sea billets for Midshipmen.

3. If, however, it is required to retain one KING GEORGE V Class battleship as standby for VANGUARD in the event of a Royal Tour, this ship could be employed in the Training Squadron to accommodate the NS Seamen doing Part I training and relieve the Barracks of this commitment.

4. The following shows the present numbers borne for the duties in which ships are now employed and proposed (approx.) complements:–

	Borne	In Training Squadron	Immobilised & Refitting	Reducing to Reserve	In Reserve
VANGUARD	1311	700	–	–	–
DUKE OF YORK	1189	–	500	660	150
ANSON	626 (as Flag)	590	500	660	150
KING GEORGE V	615	570	500	660	150
HOWE (refit)	319	570	500	660	150
VICTORIOUS	572	523	–	–	–

5. It will therefore be seen that there is little difference between the complement required in the case of a KING GEORGE V Class battleship immobilised and of that allowed in the Training Squadron – and a ship employed in the Training Squadron would undoubtably be kept in a better condition than if immobilised …

6. It is estimated that, with a complement of 660 a battleship would take 8 to 10 months to reduce to Reserve.

7. The following alternative proposals are suggested assuming that DUKE OF YORK is to become Flagship of FOCRF and reduce to Reserve (approved in principle only).

A. Training squadron to consist of VANGUARD and VICTORIOUS only – with no standby ship to allow for a Royal Tour or for long refit. ANSON and KING GEORGE V to be relieved in Training Squadron by VANGUARD in September and be built up to 660 each for reducing to Reserve. HOWE to commence reducing to Reserve forthwith and be built up by ratings ex VANGUARD in September.

B. Training squadron to consist of VANGUARD and VICTORIOUS with one KING GEORGE V Class battleship immobilised and/ or refitting as replacement for VANGUARD. Remainder Reduce to Reserve.

C. Training squadron to consist of VANGUARD, VICTORIOUS and one KING GEORGE V Class with no standby ship for a Royal Tour or for long refit. Remainder Reduce to Reserve.

D. Training squadron to consist of VANGUARD, VICTORIOUS and one KING GEORGE V Class with one KING GEORGE V Class immobilised refitting to act as replacement.

8. If C or D are adopted – the additional Battleship in the squadron could be employed to accommodate all NS Seamen now undergoing Part I training in Barracks. If C were adopted the NS candidates would have to be re-accommodated in Barracks in the event of a Royal Tour or long refit.

9. If B is adopted it would be preferred to retain ANSON in the Squadron (or as stand by) to maintain the balance between the Home Ports as VANGUARD and VICTORIOUS are both Devonport manned.

10. If D is adopted it would be preferred to retain ANSON and HOWE in the Squadron and as stand by and for KING GEORGE V to reduce so that the balance from KING GEORGE V could be available for INDOMITABLE in mid 1950.[1]

154. *Naval Assistant to First Lord of the Admiralty*

[ADM 1/21473] 25 February 1949

State of the Reserve Fleet

The following figures show what would be our state of readiness to meet the first three months of an emergency in April 1949, from ships in reserve.

Ships required in Category A		% Refitted within the last year
Destroyers	24	37%
Frigates (including ex-destroyers)	57	72%

[1]A handwritten note by the Director of Training dated 8 Feb recommended course C, allowing National Service training to be moved into the Training Squadron.

M/S	Ocean	32	100%
	Coastal	38	92%

These figures refer only to the Category A ships, ie. Those required in the first three months after mobilisation. Similar types are required for the later build-up – these are the Category B and C ships.

155. *Board Minutes*

[ADM 167/132] 21 March 1949

Conversion of HMS 'Cumberland' to Trials Cruiser

4277. The Board approved the conversion of HMS 'Cumberland' to a trials cruiser for testing new weapons and other equipment under seagoing condition. The cost of the first three stages of conversion was estimated at approximately £750,000.

Conversion of Pre-T Destroyers to Convoy A/S Escorts (Prototype)

4278. The Board approved the drawings and legend of particulars for the conversion of the Destroyers 'Rocket' and 'Relentless' to Convoy A/S Escorts.

Simplified Conversion of Destroyers to Convoy A/A Escorts (1949 Programme)

4279. The Board approved the drawings and legend of particulars for the simplified conversion of Fleet Destroyers to Convoy A/S Escorts. They agreed to discuss at a later meeting the possibility of increasing the rate of conversion of destroyers to A/S Escorts.

'T' Class Submarine Conversion

4280. The Board approved the drawings and legend of particulars for the conversion of two 'T' Class Submarines to prototype operational battery driven fast submarines.

156. *Paper by ACNS*[1]

[ADM 205/83] 13 April 1949

SHIPS OF THE FUTURE NAVY

I find myself exceedingly perplexed when asked to formulate recommendations on the shape and size of the ships of our future Navy; I have attempted in this paper to try to clear my own mind and stimulate argument and discussion amongst the Naval Staff.

[1] RA Ralph Edwards. This paper went to the First Sea Lord, VCNS and Controller a week later. Note in ADM 205/84.

2. Today we are busy considering in particular the cruiser and the destroyer and I find that the standard destroyer, if she is to fulfil all her old functions, is approaching more and more the shape and size of the small cruiser. I am reasonably confident, moreover, that if we were also considering the battleship, we should find the upper limit of the cruiser impinging on it.

3. It seems possible therefore that we are mistaken in confining our considerations to the types of ships we have known over the last half century …

4. In order to achieve this objective, it will be necessary to consider first:–

(a) The threats with which we are likely to be faced.
(b) The functions for which our ships are required.
(c) The weapons with which they may expect to be armed.

ASSUMPTIONS

5. Before considering these points it is necessary to make certain assumption. These are:–

(a) In the foreseeable future there is no maritime power other than Russia with whom we are likely to go to war.
(b) We will not go to war with Russia unless America is on our side from the outset.
(c) The size of the fleet which this country will be able to support in the future will be severely restricted by economic factors.
(d) The main task for our Navy in war … are the defence of sea communications, the defence of the UK and the defence of the Middle East.

POLICY

6. Arising from these assumptions, there are two factors affecting the composition of the future Navy which are not easy to reconcile. On the one hand we have a number of operational tasks to perform and cannot afford to do them all as well as we should like; on the other hand it is politically impossible for this country, whose very life depends on secure sea communications, to accept a situation in which some part of its essential sea security is surrendered wholly to the safe keeping of another power, however friendly. Such a step would mean accepting complete domination of our policy in peace and war by another country. We cannot, therefore, leave entirely to the Americans any one branch of sea warfare. This means we must have a balanced fleet. But in deciding its composition, financial stringency will force us to accord priority to those tasks which are most vital to our security and to accept less insurance in other directions.

THE THREAT WITH WHICH WE MUST EXPECT TO BE FACED

7. The threats with which we are faced should, I suggest, be placed in the following order of importance:–

(a) Mining of our ports and shipping channels – by air, S/M or surface ships.
(b) S/M attack on our ships and convoys.
(c) Air attack on our ships and convoys.
(d) Surface attack.
(e) Attack by Atomic, Biological or Chemical weapons.

FUNCTIONS FOR WHICH OUR SHIPS MAY BE REQUIRED

8. (a) In war
(i) To counter the mine threat.
(ii) To protect our long line of sea communications primarily against submarine and air attack but also to a much less extent against surface attack.
(iii) To harass the enemy's sea communications.
(iv) To support the other Services in combined operations.

(b) In peace
(i) Overseas policy duties, calls for which, in a Cold War type of peace, may be expected to increase rather than diminish.
(ii) Showing the flag.

TACTICAL TASKS

9. Tactically, the wartime functions can be expressed as a number of tasks:–

(a) Prevention of enemy minelayers (ships and aircraft) from reaching their objective. This involves:–
   (i) Air defence of our ports and coastal shipping lanes. Mainly an AA Command and RAF task.
   (ii) Anti-submarine defence of our parts and coastal shipping lanes.
   (iii) Defensive minelaying.
   (iv) Surface cover.
(b) Minesweeping, mine location and destruction. This involves:–
   (i) Mine watching and reporting.
   (ii) Minesweeping.
   (iii) Mine locating.
   (iv) Protection of minesweeping operations against air and surface attack.
(c) Protection of convoys against S/M attack. This involves:–
   (i) Provision of A/S escort (both ships and aircraft).
   (ii) Provision of A/S patrols (both ships and aircraft).
   (iii) Offensive and defensive A/S mining.

(iv) Attack at source.
(v) Offensive S/M patrols off enemy bases.

(d) Protection of convoys against air attack. This involves:–
(i) A/A gun protection.
(ii) Fighter cover.
(iii) Air direction.

(e) Protection of shipping against surface attack. This involves:–
(i) Surface cover to neutralise the surface forces available to Russia.
(ii) Air strike.

(f) Harassing the enemy's sea communications. This involves:–
(i) S/M attack on enemy shipping.
(ii) Air attack on enemy shipping.
(iii) Surface attack on enemy shipping.
(iv) Offensive mine-laying.

(g) Neutralisation of the enemy ports and bases. This involves:–
(i) Heavy bombing. Mainly an RAF task.
(ii) Minelaying.

(h) Support for other Services in combined operations. This involves:–
(i) Bombardment by air and surface ship.
(ii) Special landing operations.

SHIPS NEEDED TO CARRY OUT THESE TASKS

10. The main threats with which we shall be faced at sea in a war against Russia are the mining, submarine and air threats. The first call on our limited resources must therefore be to provide the ships necessary to counter these three threats. That is to say we should, from our own resources, be able to provide the bulk of the ships required to fulfil the tasks set out in paragraphs 8(a) to (d) above. These can be summarised as:–

(a) *To counter the mine threat* (Paragraphs 8(a) and (b))	Minesweeping ships Special mine location craft Coastal A/S and Seaward Defence craft Light surface cover
(b) *To counter the S/M threat* (Paragraph 8(c))	Small A/S escorts in large numbers for convoy protection Aircraft carriers for convoy escort Ships & aircraft for offensive minelaying Submarines, both for minelaying and Offensive A/S patrols
(c) *To counter the air threat*	Aircraft carriers (as above)

(Paragraph 8(d))	Small A/A escorts in large numbers Convoy protection A/D escorts

11. The above … constitutes the first requirement for the composition of the British Fleet. Ships for other tasks are important but financial straits will … compel us to restrict them to the following:–

(a) The protection of shipping against surface attack (Paragraph 8(e))	Fast ships of the cruiser/destroyer type capable of mounting guns of about 5-inch calibre and carrying anti-ship torpedoes (see paragraphs 19 and 20 below) Aircraft carriers MTBs and MGBs
(b) (i) *Air protection for important convoys against heavy air attack*	Large aircraft carriers capable of operating the best fighters and strike aircraft and carrying a good A/A gun armament
(ii) *Offensive minelaying, anti-shipping air strikes and offensive bombing of shore targets*	
(c) *The provision of A/A gun and A/S protection for aircraft carrier groups*	Fast ships with good A/A gun armament and 'hand-off' A/S capacity (See paragraphs 19 and 20 below)
(d) *Harassing the enemy's sea comm ications and offensive action against the Russian fleet or bases* (Paragraph 8(f))	Submarines Aircraft carriers Cruiser/destroyers as in (i) above
(e) *Supporting other Services* (Paragraph 8(h)	Cruiser/destroyers as in (i) above Aircraft carriers Special Combined Operations ships and craft

CHARACTERISTICS OF SHIPS

13. … there is general agreement concerning the characteristics of:–

Minesweepers
Submarines
MTB/MGBs
Mine location craft
Coastal A/S and Seaward Defence craft

14. Controversy starts when the anti-submarine and A/A escorts and the small cruiser/destroyer types of ship are discussed. It is important to remember here that the exacting performance requirements for modern equipment cannot be met without a great increase in size, weight and complexity. This applies equally to A/S, radar and gunnery equipment. For example, the double Limbo outfit complete will weigh some 90 tons. The best fighter interception equipment has an aerial weighing 9 tons and needs a large space between decks for plots and intercept positions. Modern fire control with its associated radar and high-performance gun mountings makes heavy demands on weight and space – and to postulate 'simple fire control' serves no purposes since it is valueless against modern aircraft. Thus, it will be seen that modern equipment makes ever increasing demands of the ship designer.
15. In the past it has always been our endeavour to avoid the specialised ship. But now to provide the modern equipment of the old all-round destroyer type with high speed, good dual-purpose guns, the best available A/S quality, torpedoes and the necessary radar would need a ship of some 3,500 to 4,000 tons standard displacement. Clearly, financial and manpower economy alone rule out the use of such ships in large numbers for escort purposes. We must recognise, therefore, that since we cannot provide these all-purpose vessels, we must accept specialisation in our escorts. In other words, we are according to the weapon the domination of the small ship.
CONVOY ESCORTS
16. Having accepted the principle of specialisation we must, for reasons of economy, aim at building the smallest hull which has good sea-keeping qualities and will carry the armament needed for the ship to fulfil her purpose. Convoy escort vessels are required to fulfil three functions:– anti-submarine defence, A/A gun defence and air direction. It would be ideal if a standard convoy escort hull could be produced to be fitted out as required. Unfortunately, however, whereas a speed of about 25 knots, which can be achieved with a diesel type of engine, can be accepted for the two air defence types of escort, the A/S escort needs at least 27 knots if she is to compete adequately with the fast submarine and this means she must be engined with high powered turbines. It may be possible in the future to evolve a common hull which can carry either type of machinery, but for the present we are compelled to sub-divide our convoy escorts into two main categories, anti-submarine and air defence.
17. The air defence escort requirements are two-fold:– to provide a gun platform for A/A fire and a base upon which interception radar can be carried. To combine these two requirements in one ship would once again force up the tonnage. Furthermore, few of the Air Direction escorts are

needed but the demand for the A/A gun type will undoubtably be large. Thus, though a common hull may well be practicable for these two slower types of escort, each must be equipped with the emphasis on its own particular function.

18. Our convoy escort requirements can therefore be summed up as a demand for three types of vessel, each with the emphasis on one principle function to the needs of which other weapons and equipment must be subordinated:–

(a) *A/S Escorts*	To carry the best possible A/S armament, eg best Asdics, Limbo And A/S torpedoes – and have a speed of at least 27 knots. Gun armament is relatively unimportant but one medium range A/A Gun with adequate control is necessary.
(b) *A/A Escorts*	To carry a good A/A gun armament with the necessary gunnery Radar (eg 3″/70 equipment) A/S is less important but they should also carry Asdics and the best A/S weapon possible for hand-off A/S tactics.
(c) *A/D Escorts*	To carry the best Air Warning and Air Interception equipment practicable in a small ship and one medium range A/A gun mounting with adequate control for self-protection.

CRUISER/DESTROYERS

19. The next tasks we have to consider are the protection of shipping, particularly our coastal convoys, against surface attack and the provision of A/A gun and A/S protection for aircraft carrier groups. Hitherto these tasks have been fulfilled by destroyers with good surface action and A/S characteristics and cruisers with good dual-purpose guns. But I believe that the developments of modern equipment, which are forcing up the tonnage of destroyers, and the reduction in the surface threat will enable the destroyer and the cruiser types to be merged. What we require is a ship whose primary role is anti-aircraft but which should have good surface action and anti-submarine capabilities as well. Such a ship would need armament of the following order:–

4 x 5″ Dual purpose guns (2 twin or 4 single)
Close range AA
Good Asdics
Single Limbo
A/S / Anti-Surface torpedoes.

Such an armament coupled to qualities of good endurance, high speed and good radar would probably require a ship of about 5,000 tons standard displacement. These ships would need to hand-off enemy submarines rather than hunt them but, with the advent of the homing A/S torpedo together with a mortar with all-round training, the disadvantages of a large ship for A/S purposes are greatly reduced. Furthermore, the fact that these ships are of considerable size should enable them to keep up and fulfil their functions with a carrier force in foul weather.

20. It seems to me that this type of ship in addition to meeting efficiently its primary tasks would fulfil many other roles, such as the anti-aircraft protection of vital convoys or independent operations against the enemy and at the same time provide a useful deterrent against surface attack even from KIROV Class cruisers. In a war against Russia, I feel that they would achieve at least as much as a very much more extravagant force of cruisers and convention destroyers. The advantages claimed for them are:–

(a) Their ability to combine a powerful punch against air or surface targets with sufficient A/S capabilities to escort fast aircraft carrier groups or to operate independently themselves.
(b) They would be excellent ships for a variety of offensive operations.
(c) While more than able to deal with the Russian destroyers they would be a strong deterrent to surface attack by anything less than a capital ship.
(d) They would effect a great saving in expense and manpower as compared with large cruisers and their destroyer escorts.

eg	TIGERS	DARINGS	Proposed Cruiser/destroyer
Cost	£5.2 million	£1.75 million	About £3 million
Complement	800	300	About 350 to 400

(e) In peace-time they would be excellent and economical ships for police work and showing the flag – small enough to go to most ports and large enough to command respect (cf the old 'C' Class cruisers that did so much foreign service in the past). Their small complements and much reduced running costs, in comparison with large cruisers, would be of enormous advantage in peace-time.

21. I visualise that a wartime fleet of some 50 of these ships, which I suggest should be known as 'Light Cruisers' would meet our needs and to the work for which at present we plan to have 23 heavy cruisers and 58 large fleet destroyers. Perhaps 30 of these light cruisers would meet our peace-time needs …

22. With regard to the protection of our shipping against attack by heavy surface ships … a balanced force of carriers and the light cruisers I have described would provide us with adequate cover against them.

AIRCRAFT CARRIERS

23. … there are two main functions required of these ships:–

(a) The protection of our convoys and shipping against:–
   (i) Submarine attack.
   (ii) Air attack.

(b) To form the backbone of the Task Force which will:–
   (i) Protect our shipping against surface attack.
   (ii) Provide our share of the offensive war against the enemy's ships and bases.

24. These ships must be able to operate their aircraft in all but the most inclement weather. To [operate] modern aircraft, they must provide a reasonably steady platform and have a good turn of speed. Many of our present light fleet carriers do no fulfil these requirements.

25. It seems to me that we are left, therefore, with two alternatives. Either we must build all our carriers large enough to enable them to operate these modern aircraft in all weathers or we must modify our ideas about some of our aircraft. Since I cannot see that our financial position now, nor the combined US/British production in war, is likely to enable more than a few large aircraft carriers to be built, I believe it would be wise now to accept this governing factor and develop some of our aircraft for operation from the 'Woolworth' type of carrier.

26. The need for aircraft on the Atlantic trade routes is mainly to fight the submarine and to drive off the reconnaissance aircraft with which it may be co-operating. I suggest that we should investigate whether, for these purposes, it would not be possible to have aircraft of reduced performance which, while capable of fulfilling their functions, are yet able to operate from small carriers in weathers normally to be expected over the oceans.

27. We shall, however, need modern aircraft of the highest quality to strike at enemy warships and merchant shipping and for other offensive purposes and we shall need the fastest fighters to provide air protection for our carrier groups and for any convoys that may be subjected to heavy air attack. For this we must have large aircraft carriers capable of operating large, fast and heavy aircraft and of carrying a good AA gun armament; but the number of these large carriers needed will be much smaller than that of the Atlantic convoy escort type.

GUIDED WEAPON SHIPS

28. Guided weapons … development is still in a very fluid state. It is, however, fairly safe to predict that the long-range A/A guided weapon of the 'Seaslug' type will need to be carried and launched from a special

Guided Weapon Ship … Guided weapons as an operational reality are, however, still a long way off.

BATTLESHIPS

29. … I think it can be assumed that we shall never be able to afford the luxury of battleships for any task other than to neutralise those of the enemy. Our prospective enemy has no modern battleships though there are two in Europe, RICHELIEU and JEAN BART, which might conceivably go communist and come under Russian control. The battleship threat cannot, therefore, be regarded as serious … in our present financial straits we should [not] expend money providing against a threat which does not at the moment exist.

30. I suggest, therefore, that our battleships should be placed in 'cold storage' and no more money be spent on them. The five which we possess give us a more than sufficient lead over the Russians …

CONCLUSIONS

31. To summarise therefore:–

(a) The main task of the Royal Navy will be to control the sea communications in the Atlantic and in the waters around the UK and to safeguard the Middle East supply line.

(b) In order to achieve this objective, we must first be able to defend our shipping against mine, submarine and air attack since these are the most serious threats. For this purpose, we must have:–
Ocean, coastal and inshore minesweepers and mine location craft.
Coastal A/S and Seaward Defence craft
Submarines
Minelayers
Convoy escorts consisting of:–
A/S escorts (at least 27 knots)
A/A escorts (small ships with common hull)
A/D escorts
MTBs and MGBs
Aircraft carriers
(Guided Weapon escorts later on)

(c) Many of the above ships will also be employed in offensive roles against the enemy.

(d) The A/A escorts and MGBs will provide defence against E-boat attack.

(e) This predominantly small ship navy will need to be backed by:–
Large aircraft carriers
Fast all-purpose light cruisers
Which will have the following roles:–

(i) To provide air and A/A gun protection for vital convoys.
(ii) For offensive bombing, minelaying and anti-shipping air attacks.
(iii) For protection of shipping against surface attack by cruisers and destroyers.
(iv) For offensive operations against Russian shipping and the Russian fleet.
(v) For support of other Services.

32. These conclusions mean that it is proposed to omit from the navy of the future the cruiser of the order of 12,000 tons and the old 'maid-of-all-work' destroyer. In their place it is proposed to provide a fast, well-equipped light cruiser, comparable in tonnage to the old light cruisers of the 1914 war. This change … would effect a very great saving in expense and manpower.

RECOMMENDATIONS

33. If the principles of this paper are accepted it remains to see what steps can be taken towards achieving the type of fleet, we shall require in ten to fifteen years' time. It is obviously impracticable to suggest a large building programme in the near future, but I suggest we should examine very carefully whether we are wise to embark on a large and expensive programme of modernising certain classes of old ships which may not be suitable in the future. If we continue to spend so much or our available resources pouring new wine into old bottles and assuming that in peacetime we can never expect to get more money than we are getting at the moment, I cannot see how we are ever to break away from the pattern of a fleet which is not really suited to our future needs and certainly not to our future purse.

34. I suggest, therefore, that we should examine carefully our modernisation and new construction programmes for cruisers and Fleet destroyers and see whether it would not be more profitable, and less expensive in the long run, to start building up a force of modern light cruisers to take their place. As a first step I would make the following recommendations, which take into account the need to provide some short-term safeguards. We should:–

(a) Place our battleships in category 'D' reserve but prepare, and keep up to date, plans for modernising their A/A armament.
(b) Defer any consideration of modernising our large cruisers and refit only those which we require for our peace-time police duties.
(c) Modernise our DIDO class cruisers by providing them with a modern fire control system and giving them some modicum of anti-submarine armament.

(d) Consider providing the TRAFALGAR and ARMADA class destroyers with a modern fire control equipment.
(The measures recommended under (b) and (c) will go some way, as an interim measure, towards providing the light cruiser visualised in this paper.)

(e) Convert for A/S escort duties those of the old destroyers whose engines and hulls have a reasonable expectation of life.

(f) Press on with the production of prototypes for our three types of frigates and minesweepers …

(g) Investigate whether our anti-submarine aircraft policy requires reconsideration in view of the limitations imposed upon us by the capabilities of the small carrier; and examine in the same light the performance of fighters necessary for Atlantic convoy duties.

(h) Resolve that if it is decided that the high-performance fast aircraft are really essential over the oceans, all those carriers unsuitable for these duties in normal Atlantic weather should be discarded.

(i) Examine from a staff aspect whether light cruisers of the type proposed will meet our needs in the future, having regard to our likely economic position and, if so, how many will be needed in war and peace.

(j) Examine briefly the design of such a light cruiser with a view to determining the size of ship necessary to carry the armament and have the characteristics outlined in paragraph 19 of this paper.

ANNEX TO SHIPS OF THE FUTURE NAVY [*simplified*]

I MANNING

(a) In War

	Cruisers		Fleet Destroyers	Total Manpower
9 Year Plan Fleet	15 6″ Cruisers	8 5.25″ Cruisers	58	31,300
DofP's Restricted Fleet	10 6″ Cruisers	8 5.25″ Cruisers	58	27,300
Proposed Fleet	50 5″ Light Cruisers (paras 19 & 20)			17,500 to 20,000

(b) In Peace

	Interim peace complements	
Present Peacetime Fleet (Full Commission)	10 large cruisers 4 DIDOs 34 Fleet Destroyers	15,920
Proposed Peacetime Fleet	30 light cruisers	10,500

II BUILDING COST

TIGER	DARING	Modernisation of 6″ Cruiser	Proposed Light Cruiser
£5.2 m.	£1.75 m.	£1.6 m.	£3 m.?

III ARMAMENT

DARING	all-purpose Fleet Destroyer	destroyer smaller than (b) with future weapons	Proposed Light Cruiser
3 x 4.5″ twin	4 x 4.5″ twin	2 x 5″ DP single	4 x 5″ DP
Bofors	Close range A.A.	Close range A.A.	Close range AA
2 Pentad torp. tubes	2 Pentad torp. tubes	Up to 8 torpedoes	8 torpedoes
1 Squid	Single Limbo	Single Limbo	Single Limbo
2,600 tons	3,500–4,000 tons	2,700–2,900 tons	Good radar
			4,000–5,000 tons

157. *Report of Inter-Service Working Party on Size and Shape of the Armed Forces*[1]

[CAB 131/7] 28 February 1949

[The Harwood Report]

Misc/P(49)6

TERMS OF REFERENCE

1. We were appointed by the Chiefs of Staff Committee (COS(46) 166th Meeting, Item 6) to recommend the manner in which £2,100 million should be spent on the Armed Forces over the three years from April 1950 to March 1953, to give the best value for money in terms of security against foreseeable threats …

ANNEX VIII

THE ROYAL NAVY

Introduction

115. … we have concluded that the allocation of resources to the Royal Navy during the three years concerned should be as follows:–

	1950–51	*1951–52*	*1952–53*	*Total*
	£m	*£m*	*£m*	*£m*
Re-equipment and New Works	42.5	49.5	52.0	144.00
Pay and Maintenance	124.08	117.08	114.58	355.75
	166.58	166.58	166.58	499.75

116. There are four questions which need answering in designing a Navy. These are:–

(a) What is it required in war?
(b) What ships and aircraft are needed for this war-time function and how must they be equipped?
(c) What force can be supported in peace and is it adequate for training for war and fulfilling its peace role?
(d) Can the peace-time force be expanded sufficiently for war in the time available?

[1]Known as the Harwood Report, after Sir Edmund Harwood, Chairman of the Working Group. Also published as COS(49)113 & DO(49)47.

117. If these four main questions are to be answered satisfactorily within a given financial ceiling a series of approximations must be made. Desirable wartime roles and strengths may be defined only to discover that insufficient money remains to provide the peace-time force needed as a basis for expansion in war. The roles must then be cut and the whole picture redesigned again and again until a balance is finally struck which appears to give due weight to all four factors.

118. This was the process adopted and this paper sets out the results of our work …

119. It must constantly be remembered that no war is envisaged without the United States as Allies from the start. The United States has a very great preponderance of naval strength *vis-a-vis* possible enemies and everything which follows is coloured by the need for the British to build naval forces which, while still balanced, shall be complementary to rather than in competition with the United States Navy.

The Role of the Royal Navy at the Start of a War

120. *Home Waters –*

Seaward defence of ports and anchorages.

Protection of coastal shipping including cross-Channel convoys.

Protection of North Atlantic shipping to and from the United Kingdom including the Canadian, Gibraltar and Norwegian routes.

Mediterranean –

Seaward defence of Gibraltar, Malta and the Levant ports.

Protection of initial British troop convoys through the Mediterranean until the United States Navy takes over full responsibility for the Mediterranean.

Protection of local shipping in the Levant.

121. These immediate tasks must be supplemented by the following additional ones which may be required of the Royal Navy soon after the outbreak of war:–

Home Waters –

The disruption of enemy seaborne lines of communication round European coasts and offensive submarine action against enemy U-boats.

The mounting of small-scale raids against enemy held coasts.

Clandestine coastal operations.

Defence against seaborne invasion.

122. We have been forced to the conclusion that the above tasks, which we regard as essential British responsibilities, are about the most which the Royal Navy can undertake. In consequence the following tasks

(which have hitherto been regarded as to some extent a British Naval commitment) must be performed by Allied naval forces or not at all:–

Home Waters –

Cover against the small surface threat to Atlantic shipping.

This threat has been accepted in so far as it cannot be countered by carrier-borne fighter of A/S aircraft.

Mediterranean –

Protection of routine fast and slow convoys throughout the Mediterranean.

This task must be an American responsibility.

Persian Gulf –

Seaward defence of oil ports and the protection of shipping in the Persian Gulf and its approaches.

These tasks must be undertaken by American forces supplemented where possible by other Commonwealth naval forces.

Indian Ocean and Australasia –

The control of these sea communications must be regarded as a commitment of the RAN, RNZN and other Commonwealth forces.

Far East –

An American responsibility.

123. It should be noted that *no* plan makes any provision for the attack of the U-boat bases in the White Sea area by naval forces. Since this area is unlikely to be within reach of suitable shore-based British aircraft for several years to come, this omission is serious.

The Target Wartime Fleet

124. The naval forces provided under our plan for the carrying out of the above are shown in detail in Appendix A …

126. Certain major changes have been made in the proposed wartime fleet as compared with present Admiralty plans. These changes have been largely occasioned by the increased weight we have given to the Battle of the Coasts as compared with the Battle of the Atlantic. No battleships have been included. The modern carriers are cut from 14 to 12. Modernised cruisers are reduced from 23 to 12. On the other hand, the number of smaller ships has been substantially increased. Escorts have been increased from 230 to 249, ocean minesweepers and danlayers from 60 to 140, coastal minesweepers from 171 to 250, MTBs from 50 to 80, seaward defence MLs from 100 to 150 and 120 Boom Patrol craft have been added. The target strength in naval aircraft remains unchanged at 200 First Line by 1952 and 300 by 1957.

The Re-equipment Programme

127. A sum of £144 million has been set apart over the three years for new works, new construction, modernisation of ships and aircraft and the provision of seaward defence equipment …

Civilians and Shore Services

129. Today the Navy employs some 185,000 civilians at an annual cost of about £49.2 million. If the future Navy is to maintain any 'teeth' it is obviously imperative to start by pruning this civilian 'tail' … An outline of the economies allowed for in these calculations is given in Appendix B.

Uniformed Personnel

130. Even after making these drastic cuts in civilian and shore services, we do not believe that it is possible on our allocations to provide more than the following annual average uniformed strengths:–

Present Planned Target 31 March 1950	1950–51	1951–52	1952–53	Average
146,000	120,000	97,500	90,000	102,500

If the average uniformed strength during 1950–51 of 120,000 is to be attained, it will be imperative to start reducing as soon as possible. Delay in approving or implementing this Report may well render the above figures unattainable. Furthermore, the above *rate* of reduction cannot be attained unless commitments are cut as we propose without delay.

Our plan does not envisage the axeing of regular ratings. By a substantial reduction of intake, the figures for men can be made to fall as required by means of wastage. In other cases, gratuities will be necessary …

134. The Major cuts can broadly be summarised as follows:–

Overseas

Naval forces are withdrawn from the West Indies, the Cape, the East Indies and Far East except for a small force on the China coast based on Hong Kong.

The above-named Commands (except China) are also abolished, but an Australian Naval Command is substituted at Singapore.

Singapore and Trincomalee dockyards are abandoned. Bermuda and Simonstown yards are placed on care and maintenance.

Naval air stations at Malta are closed.

At Home

Naval Aviation:– The naval flying and ground training commands are integrated with their Royal Air Force counterparts. This allows certain Royal Naval air stations and Technical Training establishments to close but involves an increased annual grant in aid to the Royal Air Force (assessed at £1 million).

Combined Operations:– Role reduced. Headquarters closed.

Commands and Staffs:– Flag Officer Scotland and Northern Ireland and all Chatham and Sheerness commands are reduced or possibly abolished.

Dockyards, Bases, Training etc:– Sheerness and Portland dockyards are closed and – possibly – Chatham. All possible shore training is concentrated in Portsmouth and Devonport areas.

Reserve Fleet:– Personnel cut from 12,400 on 31 March 1950 to 10,000 despite an increase in the number of ships in reserve.

Personnel, Depots etc:– Abolish the Royal Marines, Abolish the WRNS, Close Chatham Depot.

135. We have tried throughout to keep as many ships and aircraft in commission as possible and to ensure that the cuts shall fall on the shore and supply services of the Navy rather than on the seagoing fleet. Even so, it is estimated that peace-time forces of the following order are the maximum which can be maintained. Details are given in Appendix D.

The minimum forces have been allocated to geographical areas, *eg* United Kingdom, Mediterranean, Persian Gulf and China, the remainder being concentrated into a peripatetic task force which must cover the North and South Atlantic and the Mediterranean. This organisation has, in any case, considerable merit. Visits to Latin American ports will now be made by a Fleet and not by a single cruiser, whilst travelling and overseas married quarters problems are reduced. This task force has been provided with a small fleet train.

Main Fleet (North and South Atlantic and Mediterranean)

Aircraft Carriers	3	
Cruiser	1	
Fast Minelayer	1	
Destroyers	16	
Frigates	8	
Minesweepers	4	
Aircraft Repair Ship	1	
Fast Tanker	1	
Fleet Train	As requisite	
A/S Training Squadron Based on United Kingdom		
Aircraft Carrier	1	(and for deck landing training)
Destroyers } Frigates }	16	
Submarines Based on United Kingdom		
Submarines	16	
Fast A/S Targets	2	
Miscellaneous Ships Based in United Kingdom		
Aircraft Carrier	1	(For trials and deck landing training)

Cruiser	1 (Cadet training)
Destroyers	16
Frigates	24
Minesweepers	24 (Ocean and Coastal)
Mediterranean Station and Persian Gulf	
Cruisers	3
Destroyers	8
Minesweepers	8
Submarines	12
Submarine Depot Ship	1
China and Japan, based on Hong Kong	
Cruisers	2
Minesweepers	4

All Commands and Stations other than those specified above must be relinquished.

Naval aircraft first-line strength will rise to 200 by 1952. Thereafter expansion to 300 is planned.

136. The Reserve Fleet will be larger than to-day and not more than 10,000 men can be spared for its maintenance …

137. The forces shown above are calculated to require about 43,000 men afloat. This represents some 47.5 per cent of the total uniformed strength. Today this percentage is about 44.5 per cent. The number of men directly or indirectly concerned with naval aviation is calculated as 28,500 or 31.5 per cent of the total. Today this figure is about 23 per cent.

Battleships

138. We do not foresee any need for the 4 KGV class and Vanguard except:–

(a) as possible platforms for new weapons …

(b) Royal tours.

If Russia started to build battleships, we believe that an increase in naval air strength would be the proper reply. To keep these ships in reserve must be a costly business … unless they are to be allowed to deteriorate to such an extent as soon to become useless …

Cruisers

139. Twelve modernised cruisers are required for the wartime fleet. Seven cruisers are planned to be in commission in peace. There are 29 cruisers in existence today and 3 building.

As an insurance against possible weapon development, 14 cruisers have been placed in reserve in peace and 8 (excluding those building) have been scheduled for disposal.

Naval Aviation

140. If the officers and men of the Navy are to retain their long-standing characteristics, as many as possible must be afloat. Today, largely due to the needs of naval aviation, the Navy has spread ashore and these characteristics are being lost. For this paramount reason, if for no others, the minimum possible number of men must be withdrawn from sea service to support naval air establishments, and it follows that the greatest possible use must be made by naval aviation of the shore facilities which the Royal Air Force must, in any case, provide for themselves. This matter is discussed in greater detail in Appendix F.

The WRNS

141. On the manpower strength available it seems, unfortunately, to be imperative to abolish the Women's Royal Naval Service in peacetime …

The Royal Marines

142. Cut to this extent, the Navy cannot afford to maintain the Marine Commandos who can only perform an Army role in peace … it might prove possible to retain the identity of the Corps by incorporating it as a regiment in the Army.

Combined Operations

143. A very high proportion of the peace-time expenditure on Combined Operations falls upon the Navy Vote. The future policy has been taken as follows:–

(a) To be prepared early in a war to mount small-scale raids against an enemy-held coast line (up to 300 men).
(b) To continue raiding in clandestine operations such as canoeists, frogmen, embarking and disembarking agents etc.
(c) To continue research and development into (a) and (b) above.
(d) To study the technique of larger operations …

144. If this reduced role is accepted it follows that a reduction of the present organisation can be effected …

The Indian Ocean and Singapore

145. Certain shore wireless stations, oil fuel storage tanks and boom defence depots in this area have been left open; otherwise the Royal Navy must withdraw completely and we propose that, in both peace and war, this area shall become the naval responsibility of Commonwealth Naval Forces …

146. We see no reason to keep the general facilities of Singapore dockyard in care and maintenance for another war, nor can we afford to do so …

The Maintenance of the Peacetime Fleet and its Bases

147. It has not been possible to get any clear idea of what economies are either feasible or desirable in dockyards at home or at Malta and Gibraltar. Admittedly, the re-equipment programme will throw added work on

some if not all, of these establishments but the task of maintaining the fleet in commission is reduced. On the other hand, we have not lessened the burden of maintaining the Reserve Fleet and there is today a heavy backlog of this work if ships in reserve are to be maintained fit for use … we would like to see Chatham and Sheerness dockyards closed. Their approaches are very restricted and mineable, and the area is in any future front line …

148. We calculate that the money we have allowed for 'maintenance' under Votes 8 and 9 is about £8 million annually less than is said to be needed … we are confident that there is room for pruning in this field …

Expansion for War

151. The numbers required to man the Wartime Fleet given in Appendix A have been estimated as 213,000. This calculation makes no allowance for manning armament in merchant ships nor for immediate expansion of naval aviation or other training facilities. The rapid reopening of Simonstown and Bermuda yards has also not been allowed for. It is, therefore, probable that a figure of some 230,000 is the more likely.

152. It is generally agreed that, on mobilisation, the Navy cannot accept a dilution greater than one reservist to one regular … a figure of about 200,000 can be accepted on mobilisation.

153. On the basis of 200,000 officers and men being available, we estimate that the whole of the Wartime Fleet could be fully manned on mobilisation except for 55 frigates. These could probably not be manned for 6 months …

Conclusions

154. The effects of our recommendations on the Navy will undoubtedly appear very drastic but it is as well to remember that these are not all caused by the financial cut which we have been forced to impose. It is quite clear that since 1945 the Navy has supported a peacetime force which could not possibly have been sustained if a proper programme of capital re-equipment and refitting had been put in hand. Moreover, there are still a large number of dispersed shore establishments which are legacies of the last war and which will never be abandoned unless and until a real contraction takes place.

155. Our recommendations therefore include many measures which would in any case have been necessary if the Navy is to be properly re-equipped, efficient and battleworthy for another war. Except for the danger of concentrating naval shore establishments once again in the Portsmouth and Devonport areas in an atomic age – a danger which we have been forced to accept – we believe that, to retain the quality of the Service, steps on the lines we have recommended – though possibly not so drastic – would in any case have been necessary – and necessary soon.

APPENDIX A TO ANNEX VIII

156. PROPOSED SHAPE AND SIZE OF NAVY ON OUTBREAK OF WAR (1956–57)

Type of Ship	
Battleships	Nil
Fleet Carriers (Modernised)	9
Light Fleet Carriers (Modernised)	3
Cruisers	12
Destroyers	62
Frigates (including ex-destroyers)	249
Minesweepers (Ocean)	140
Minesweepers (Coastal)	350 (including 100 Trawlers M/S)
Submarines	60
MTBs	80
Seaward Defence A/S Vessels	150
Boom Patrol Craft	120
Fast Minelayers	3
Aircraft Repair Ship	1
Submarine Depot Ships	4
Fleet Replenishment Ship	1
Radar Training Ships	1
Fleet Train	As required
CO Ships and craft	As required to support a lift of 300 men
Front Line Aircraft	300

APPENDIX D[1] TO ANNEX VIII

172. PROPOSED SIZE AND SHAPE OF PEACE-TIME FLEET (1950–53)

Type of Ship	Main Fleet	AS Trng Sqn and Home Misc.	Med	PG	Hong Kong	Reserve		
						A & B	C	Z
Battleships	...	...	...	...	...	...	...	5
Fleet Carriers	1	1	...	...	...	4	...	...
Light Fleet Carriers	2	1	...	...	...	3	...	...
Cruisers	1	1	2	1	2	9	5	8
Fast Minelayer	1	...	...	...	...	2	...	...
Destroyers	16	16	8	...	...	41	38	...
Frigates	8	24	...	...	...	66	78	...
Minesweepers (Ocean)	4	8	4	4	4	21	21	...
Minesweepers (Coastal)	...	16	...	...	...	45	...	...
Minesweepers ML	...	10	...	...	...	...	...	...
Danlayers	...	2	...	...	...	9	...	...
Submarines	...	16	12	...	...	33	...	...
Submarine Depot	...	1	1	...	...	1	1	1
Survey	...	3	1	1	...	...	3	...
Boom Vessels	...	9	2	2	2	2	...	...
Net Layers	...	...	...	...	...	2	...	...
Air Repair Ship	1	...	...	...	...	...	...	...
Fast Tanker	1	...	...	...	...	...	...	...
Fleet Train	A/R	...	...	...	...	...	...	...
MTB/MGB	...	24	...	...	...	12	...	...
Survey ML	...	6	...	...	...	...	...	...
ND Training Ship	...	1	...	...	...	...	...	...
Wreck Dispersal	...	6	...	...	...	...	...	6
Wreck Dispersal Store Carrier	...	1	...	...	...	...	...	1
Fleet Tugs	...	2	1	...	1	...	3	...
Salvage Vessel	...	1	...	...	...	...	1	...
HSTS	...	3	...	...	...	...	7	...
Miscellaneous Small Craft	...	16	...	...	...	...	14	...
Miscellaneous Small Craft (Air)	...	4	...	...	...	...	17	...
A/S Target (Fast)	...	1	1	...	...	...	...	...
Destroyer Depot Ship	...	...	...	...	...	...	2	...
Monitors	...	...	...	...	...	...	...	2
Repair Ships	...	...	...	...	...	1	2	2
Escort Maintenance Ships	...	...	...	...	...	1	2	...
Gunboats	...	...	...	...	...	...	...	1
Armament Maintenance Ship	...	...	...	...	...	...	...	1
Coastal Force Maintenance Ships	...	...	...	...	...	...	2	...
Harbour Craft Maintenance Ships	...	...	...	...	...	...	5	5
Aircraft Transport	...	...	...	...	...	...	1	...
Aircraft Maintenance Ships	...	...	...	...	...	...	2	...
Maintenance Ship (LS)	...	...	...	...	...	...	...	1
Maintenance Ship (LC)	...	...	...	...	...	...	...	2
Royal Yacht	...	...	...	...	...	...	1	...
AFD	...	...	...	...	...	...	...	...

[1] Appendices B and C are not reproduced. Appendix B deals with Administrative Services, and recommends, inter alia, the closing or rationalisation of victualling yards, hospitals, stores depots and armament depots. Appendix C is a bar chart of the proposed Naval Estimates.

APPENDIX E TO ANNEX VIII
NOTES ON NAVAL CUTS ENVISAGED TO REDUCE NAVY TO UNIFORMED MANPOWER OF 90,000

173. *Ships in Commission and reserve as shown in* Appendix D (paragraph 172).

174. *Naval Aviation* – 200 first line aircraft by 1952 thereafter rising to 300 by 1957.

(a) *Flying Training Command* integrated with RAF. Stations naval manned:–

Syerston
Lossiemouth/Milltown
Eglinton } *Ab initio* training of naval pupils

Culdrose — Special naval post-graduate courses

Other post-graduate flying courses to be lodged at RAF airfields.

(b) *Ground Training Command* integrated with RAF Following establishments naval manned:–

Arbroath
Yeovilton

… transfer pupils and 2/3 instructors for basic technical training to RAF establishments.

(c) *Staffs* – Abolish staff of FO Air Med, Lee on Solent staffs and depots cut 20 per cent …

(d) *Reserve aircraft and Repair* – … the ARY at Belfast has been assumed closed.

(e) *Miscellaneous* – Northern FRU abolished. Donibristle air station closed. Fearn not to open. AFEE abolished.

(f) *Overseas* – Naval air establishments at Malta closed.

Note – It is realised that expansion of naval air is planned. This expansion must be taken up by (a) further economies in maintenance organisations and (b) closer integration with the RAF eg first line CAGs will disembark to RAF stations for leave and practice camp.

175. *Combined Operations*

(a) Abolish COHQ.

(b) Amphibian School cut *pro rata.*

(c) Reserve major landing craft to be turned over to Ministry of Transport for use on beach supplies for United Kingdom in emergency.

(d) Replace Royal Marines by seamen.

176. *Commands and Staffs*

(a) Abolish Commands overseas other than those needed for new peace-time fleet.

(b) Abolish Flag Officer Scotland and Northern Ireland.
(c) Cut all staffs of Home Commands and Commanders-in-Chief and Flag Officers afloat by one-third.
(d) Reduce or possibly abolish Commands at Chatham.

177. *Dockyards, Base Ships and Depots*
(a) Abandon Singapore other than for oil fuel and certain ancilliary services. Abandon Trincomalee
(b) Place Bermuda and Simonstown on C&M.
(c) Reduce Malabar and Afrikander to C&M.
(d) Abolish Terror.
(e) Cut St Angelo 80 per cent.
(f) Cut Rooke and Tamar by one-third.
(g) Abolish Highflyer except for NLO.
(h) Cut Victory and Drake by one-third.
(i) Abolish Pembroke (Chatham Depot).
(j) Naval servicing craft to be cut 15 per cent and naval manned.

178. *Reserve Fleet* – Cut to a total of 10,000 personnel. On this manpower figure it may well be necessary to make further reductions in the ships retained in reserve.

179. *New Entry Training Establishments* – Abolish St Vincent, Royal Arthur, Ceres and Hawke. The functions of all these establishments, if retained, must be concentrated in the remaining barracks at Portsmouth and Devonport, remembering that intake will be much reduced forthwith.

180. *Technical Training Establishments*
(a) Excellent, Vernon and Mercury to absorb Chatham and Devonport Gunnery, Torpedo/AS and Signal Schools respectively.
(b) Close Cochrane.
(c) Fisgard and Raleigh to absorb all stokers and engineers technical training.
(d) Absorb POs' School into RN Barracks.
(e) Cut Stamshaw by one-third.
(f) Cut all Spare Part Distributing Centres.

181. *W/T Stations and Shore Signal Stations*
(a) Close Singapore and Bermuda W/T stations.
(b) Shore Signal Station commitment in United Kingdom to cease in 1952.

182. *Medical*
(a) Close Portland and Port Edgar hospitals and all RM infirmaries.
(b) Cut all miscellaneous medical staffs by one-third.
(c) Close Bermuda, Capetown and Trincomalee hospitals.

183. *Boom Defence Depots* – Cut by 15 per cent throughout.

184. *Royal Marines and WRNS* – Replace Royal Marines and WRNS where necessary by seamen. Close all special Royal Marine and WRNS establishments.

APPENDIX F TO ANNEX VIII
NAVAL AVIATION

185. … If the special qualities of the Navy are to be retained, it is essential that the highest possible proportion of naval officers and men must always be afloat in sea-going ships.

186. Of recent years, a large number of permanent shore establishments have grown up as the natural result of the Navy having taken over its own aviation … this tendency can be reduced or even reversed …

188. whenever and wherever possible the Navy should share shore facilities already provided by the Royal Air Force …

190. Similarly, in the technical training field, we consider that the naval aircraft artificer, for whom no Royal Air Force counterpart exists, must continue to be trained in a naval establishment … But where basic technical training in any particular trade is concerned, there appears no good reason for the existences of a naval school separate from its Air Force counterpart.

191. We therefore recommend that the present Naval Flying Training Command be integrated with the Royal Air Force Flying Training Command and that naval ground training be likewise fused with the Royal Air Force Technical Training Command.

192. We have in mind a truly *Combined* Command for each function, responsible to the Air
Ministry (as the major user) who, in turn, will be responsible for meeting the needs of the Admiralty. The Staffs of the Combined Commands would be *integrated*, not duplicated …

193. We are confident that an inter-Service agreement on these lines could be worked out and that considerable economy would result … This agreement should also provide for the present vessels manned by the Royal Air Force to be taken over by the Navy …

APPENDIX G TO ANNEX VIII

195. NEW CONSTRUCTION PROGRAMME [*simplified*]

		1950/1	1951/2	1952/3	1953/4	1954/5	1955/6	1956/7	1957/8	1958/9
	£m	£m	£m	£m	£m	£m	£m	£m	£m	£m
Existing Programme		13.48	14.83	10.23	4.56	2.50	0.53	...	...	...
Small craft		.25	.25	.25	.25	.25	.25	.25	.25	.25
Tanker Programme		.60	1.10	1.40	1.60	1.60	1.30	1.10	...	...
Further Programme										
6 Destroyers	...	...	...	...	...	...	...	...	0.50	1.50
27 Frigates	33.75	...	...	0.14	0.56	5.50	11.50	11.00	4.40	0,65
62 Ocean M/S	18.00	...	...	0.75	2.10	3.15	3.60	3.60	3.60	1.80
19 F.B.D.S S/Ms	13.00	...	...	0.95	2.50	3.70	3.20	2.00	0.80	0.15
1 FF Oiler	1.50	...	...	...	0.50	0.50	0.50	...	...	...
206 Coastal M/S	34.00	...	0.50	1.80	3.75	5.24	6.20	6.60	6.60	3.30
18 Inshore ML.		...	...	....	...	...	0.20	0.25	...	...
44 MTB/MGB	6.00	...	0.40	0.86	0.98	0.98	0.98	0.98	0.98	...
120 Boom Pat. Craft	3.00	...	0.125	0.25	0.50	0.50	0.50	0.50	0.625	...
50 Sea Def MLs	4.00	...	0.112	0.263	0.535	0.656	0.675	0.675	0.675	0.189
Totals		14.33	17.317	16.893	17.835	24.576	29.435	26.955	18.43	7.819
Abate R and D		1.605	1.099	.134	...	...	...	...	...	...
		12.725	16.218	16.759	17.835	24.576	29.435	26.955	18.43	7.819

158. *Chiefs of Staff Minutes*

[DEFE 4/20] 28 & 30 March 1949

COS(49) 48th Meeting MISC/P(49)6 [Harwood Report]

… The report … represented a real inter-Service view of how a strictly limited sum of money might be allocated …

The next step must be for the detailed proposals in the report to be examined by the Service Ministries … They should be asked:–

(i) to state whether the forces suggested by the Working Party could in fact be maintained on the proportions of the overall sum suggested …

(ii) to put forward any alternative solutions which, on the same money, might better implement our policy.

(iii) to assess the risks that would have to be accepted if the assumed financial ceiling was, in fact, imposed.

…

159. *Board Minute*

[ADM 167/132] 12 April 1949

Harwood Report

4283. The Board had before them a memorandum summarising the issues affecting the Royal Navy raised by the Report of an Inter-Service Working Party on the Size and Shape of the Armed Forces, which had been charged with the task of recommending how a defence budget of £700 million would best be apportioned between the fighting services in each of the next three financial years.

… the First Lord said that the report of the Working Party raised matters of the greatest importance not only for the Service Departments, and the Admiralty in particular, but for HM Government, the Commonwealth and the countries associated with Western Union and the Atlantic Pact. The proposals made in the Report would have to be examined against the background of recent developments in planning an organisation for common defence among the Atlantic Powers, of the declared wish of the US Government to participate in a system of mutual aid for defence … He felt, however, that it would be right to accept at once the principle that the naval forces of the United Kingdom were not competitive with, but complementary to, those of the United States, and the Board agreed with this view.

In subsequent discussions, the Board agreed that the fundamental issues in the Report were:–

(a) the adequacy of the naval forces proposed in peace;
(b) the adequacy of the forces proposed on the outbreak of war;
(c) the acceptability of the proposals affecting naval personnel;
(d) the soundness of the recommendations regarding re-equipment policy.

These were then considered in turn, and the Board's views were as follows:–

(a) the naval forces recommended by the Working Party for retention in peace were not properly balanced, and were not adequate either to meet the commitments which would fall upon the Royal Navy in supporting the foreign and colonial policy of HM Government or to allow satisfactory training for war;
(b) the forces recommended by the Working Party to be available on the outbreak of war were broadly sufficient to meet the tasks which would be expected to fall upon the Royal Navy. They were, however, not properly balanced, the relation between the numbers of aircraft carriers and cruisers in particular being unsound. The omission of battleships was also not acceptable. Naval forces of the size postulated could, however, not be available on the outbreak of war unless there were a sharp rise in the financial provision from 1953 onwards. This was recognised in the report;
(c) if the general recommendations of the Working Party regarding naval personnel were accepted, a manpower strength of 90,000 would be adequate to man and support a peacetime fleet of the size postulated in the Report. It would, however, not be possible to reduce to this figure within three years without completely unbalancing naval manpower. Moreover, once the present resources of recently demobilised officers and men had been dissipated by the passage of time, on so small a manpower strength there would be a serious shortage of reserves to man the fleet on the outbreak of war. If the Navy were to take no National Servicemen the voluntary reserves would have to be built up to a strength much greater than had ever previously been contemplated. The Board agreed that the Working Party's proposal to transfer the Royal Marines to the Army could not be accepted, in view of the great traditions of the Corps and their important contribution to the discipline and morale of the naval service, and their value as a striking force. The abolition of the Women's Royal Naval Service would be politically very difficult, in view of the recent announcement that the service was to become a permanent feature of naval organisation; it would also have the

effect of increasing the proportion of men serving ashore, which would be entirely contrary to current policy;

(d) the proposal that a definite proportion of the total money provision for the Navy should be earmarked for re-equipment was sound in principle, and given the size of forces recommended in the Report, the figures suggested for the next three financial years were not unreasonable. The Board felt that provision for re-equipment could properly be regarded as a capital charge to be financed outside the Estimates, though the annual allocations towards it would have to be brought within the total defence budget. Money provided for re-equipment should, if necessary, be capable of being carried forward from one financial year to another.

The Board agreed that in the further examination of the Report which was shortly to be undertaken by the Chiefs of Staff, the First Sea Lord should be guided by the above views …

160. *Chiefs of Staff Memorandum*

[DEFE 5/14] 23 April 1949

COS(49)143 HARWOOD REPORT

Memorandum by First Sea Lord

PART I – ACCURACY OF THE REPORT

MANPOWER

1. Taken as a whole (ie assuming that the Navy takes no National Servicemen, that the Royal Marines are transferred to the Army and that the WRNS is abolished) and subject to the qualifications below, a manpower strength of 90,000 would be adequate to man and support in peace naval forces of the size proposed in the Harwood Report, but

(a) It would not be possible to cut down to a manpower strength of 90,000 in three years, as the Report suggests, without reducing intakes for several years below the annual figure which would be subsequently required to maintain a strength of 90,000 …..

(b) A manpower strength of 90,000 in peace would be insufficient to provide for the manning of the naval forces which the Report recommends should be available at the outbreak of war … The Admiralty estimates that the number of men required to man this fleet would be 230,000, ie 17,000 more than the figure of 213,000 mentioned in the Report. On a peacetime strength of

90,000 it would be unwise to expect an expansion on mobilisation to more than 180,000…

(c) The allowance of 10,000 men for the reserve fleet appears to be inadequate for the number of ships …

FINANCE

2. The Admiralty considers that the money provision of £500M for the next three years which the Report recommends is deficient by at least £25M. The Report admits … that the money allowed for maintenance is about £8M a year less than the figures given by the Admiralty … With extreme optimism the Working Party says that the necessary saving could be achieved by the "goodwill and ingenuity of all concerned" …

3. The provision recommended for re-equipment over the three year period can be regarded as adequate only if it accepted that there will be a very sharp increase from 1953 onwards …

PART II – COMMENTS ON THE POLICY RECOMMENDATIONS AS REGARDS NAVAL FORCES

GENERAL

5. The Report recommends a reduction of 40% in present naval … manpower. If this is achieved, the tasks at present carried out in peace … will have to be drastically curtailed. The naval forces allowed on the outbreak of war will be capable of playing only a modest and restricted part in naval warfare …

PEACETIME FORCES

8. The peacetime fleet recommended in the Report is regarded by the Admiralty as unbalanced. The peripatetic task force would be of little value for training purposes, naval aviation being the most obvious sufferer. It would also be likely to be split up to meet recurrent local emergencies and would in the end find itself permanently disintegrated … The forces suggested for foreign stations are also ill-balanced and inadequate.

9. The severe reduction in the Mediterranean would be regarded as … the abandonment … of the Middle East …

10. The withdrawal of the American and West Indies Squadron would mean that there were no naval forces in the Caribbean to be called upon in emergency …

11. The withdrawal of British naval forces from Simonstown would have serious political effects in the Union of South Africa …

12. The reductions proposed in the Far East and abolition of the East Indies Squadron would leave a void in South East Asia and the Indian Ocean …

13. Chatham dockyard could not be closed as it is needed for the maintenance of the fleet in peace and would be indispensable in war. The closing

of Portland and Sheerness could not be accepted without further investigation …

WARTIME FORCES

14. The total strength recommended in the Report to be available on the outbreak of war can, broadly speaking, be accepted as just about adequate provided that the present planned strength of the US Fleet is maintained. The forces are, however, not properly balanced; in particular the proportion of cruisers to carriers is too low. The entire omission of battleships could not be accepted. The numbers of frigates and minesweepers … falls far short of the base minimum requirement.

MANPOWER

15. … a peacetime manpower strength of 90,000 would be insufficient to provide for the manning of the fleet on the outbreak of war …

RE-EQUIPMENT

18. The Admiralty supports the policy advocated in the Report that a definite proportion of the total financial provision should be earmarked for re-equipment, but suggests that re-equipment should be regarded as a capital charge … capable of being carried forward to subsequent years …

ADMINISTRATIVE OVERHEADS

20. … The Admiralty cannot agree that the scope for economy … is anything like so great as that suggested in the Report …

161. *Chiefs of Staff Minutes*

[DEFE 4/22] 25 May 1949

COS(49) 77th Meeting SIZE AND SHAPE OF THE ARMED FORCES

… Lord Fraser said that he thought any further examination of the finances [of the Harwood Report] would be a waste of time … Everyone knew that many of the proposals in the Harwood Report were unacceptable; all that was necessary was to submit it to Ministers in proof that present government policy could not be executed on £700 million for defence. The Chiefs of Staff should then submit their own proposals for the defence forces necessary to execute the present government policy. The Admiralty would be ready to put in their own plan for the next seven years in a week's time … individual Service plans should then … finally [be] submitted to Ministers as a collective plan.

… it was agreed that ultimately it would be necessary for the Chiefs of Staff to make their own proposals on the lines of the First Sea Lord's suggestion …

162. *Defence Committee Memorandum*

[CAB 131/7] 21 June 1949

DO(49)48

THE SIZE AND SHAPE OF THE ARMED FORCES:– THE HARWOOD REPORT

The attached summary of the Harwood Report has been prepared to assist Ministers …

Introduction

The Harwood Working Party was set up by the Chiefs of Staff at the beginning of December 1948 to submit proposals on an inter-Service basis which would assist the Chiefs of Staff in their task of placing before Ministers recommendations for armed forces costing no more than £700 million annually in the three years from April 1950. The forces recommended were required to give the greatest practicable measure of security against foreseeable threats and the Working Party took as their basis the Chiefs of Staff agreed assumptions as to the relative seriousness of different threats to our security. In particular, as directed in their terms of reference they based their work upon three essentials of our defence policy.

These were –

(i) the need to meet current occupational and garrison commitments and to wage the cold war effectively;

(ii) that provision must be made against the possibility of becoming involved in unpremeditated war in the near future;

(iii) that during the three years under review a foundation must be laid for a rearmament programme aimed at preparing the forces against premeditated war by 1957.

2. The Working Party consisted of an independent civilian chairman and a senior military representative from each of the three Service Departments. Its report, which was unanimous, was made at the end of February 1949. The Working Party make it clear that their approach to the problem disregarded both the traditional and present roles of the individual services. They also point out that, both of necessity and because they believed it to be the right approach, they made no attempt to go into detail in their report, but confined it to broad essentials. Moreover, they do not pretend that the forces which they recommend are sufficient for our needs, but merely that the apportionment of the £700 million annually which they recommend between re-equipment and current maintenance of the forces and between the three Services would give the best value for money. They make it abundantly clear that, if no more than £700 million annually is spent on defence, the risks involved will be serious and they

doubt whether the aggregate forces which can be provided would be adequate to support our position in the world. They state their belief that their recommendations are capable of achievement while insisting that they should be considered as a whole, since major alterations in any of the main proposals or a failure to proceed speedily with the recommended reshaping of the Forces would upset the financial and strategic calculations upon which the whole report is based and would destroy the unanimity which they have achieved.

3. It should be noted that the financial calculations in the Report … were not officially costed.

(NOTE – Departmental views which have since been obtained are that the Working Party have considerably under-estimated the cost of the reduced forces which they recommend …)

Approach and Basic Principles

4. The way in which the problem was presented to the Working Party enabled them to make an unconventional approach to it. They did not start by assessing threats to security, framing the roles of the Services in meeting these threats and then estimate the size and shape of the forces necessary to perform the resultant tasks. The only firm factor in their calculations was the annual defence budget of £700 million and their approach was therefore to assess the threats and then to see how far the available resources would go towards meeting them.

5. After considering the various threats to our security the Working Party decided that they must devote the resources available for defence towards fulfilling three main tasks. These were:–

(1) the maintenance of sufficient strength to support resistance to cold war tactics;
(2) the provision of *limited* insurance against the less likely and less severe risk of an unpremeditated war in the near future;
(3) the provision of the *maximum* insurance against the more likely and more severe premeditated war in 1957 or thereafter.

The Report makes it clear that the Working Party realised that within a defence budget of £700 million they could not provide forces which would perform all three of these tasks satisfactorily, and that in spreading the available resources to the best advantage they would have to accept serious risks to security both in the present and in the near and more distant future.

6. Their preliminary consideration of how best to allocate the slender resources at their disposal led the Working Party to decide that, before considering the size and shape of the forces which could be produced, certain sums of money must be put aside to meet vital needs … The following were the results:–

(a) *Intelligence* – The fact that our defence forces would be very small makes it the more essential that our intelligence organisation should be as good as possible …
(b) *Research and Development* – Success is research and development could go far towards compensating for the small forces which can afford by improving their fighting power …
(c) *Re-equipment and New Works* – … insufficient funds are at present being devoted to the re-equipment of the forces …

… It was thought essential to the build-up of the Royal Navy that an early start should be made on a re-equipment programme directed to producing forces for the control of sea communications in the approaches to the United Kingdom and the seaward defence of ports …

Size and Shape of the Forces Recommended

9. In the light of all the above factors the Working Party recommended the following size and shape of forces over the three years as the largest that could be supported on a money allocation of £700 million annually.

(a) *Royal Navy* – The uniformed strength should fall from 146,000 at present to 90,000 by 1952–53 with an average of no more than 102,000 over the three years. There would be no national servicemen in the Navy. Aside from small forces in the Mediterranean and Persian Gulf and on the China Station, an anti-submarine training squadron and other training ships in home waters, the main fleet would consist of a mobile carrier task force. The front-line air strength of the Royal Navy would rise to 200 aircraft by 1952. No naval forces would be maintained permanently in the West Indies, the Cape or the East Indies except on the China coast. The Royal Marines would be abolished unless as the Working Party hope, they could be accepted as a regiment in the Army. The WRNS would disappear. No battleships would be retained, and the numbers of cruisers would be considerably reduced. Combined Operations would be retained but on a much-reduced scale; certain Naval commands would be abolished; Singapore and Trincomalee dockyards would be abandoned by the Royal Navy and Bermuda and Simonstown placed on a care and maintenance basis. Sheerness and Portland dockyards and possibly Chatham would be closed.

The Working Party recommend[s] that re-equipment funds should be devoted towards the build-up of a carrier and small ship Navy, whose main wartime task would be the protection of the United Kingdom, and of its approaches and sea communications with North America against submarine attack …

163. *Defence Committee Memorandum*

[CAB 131/7 & DEFE 7/592] 22 June 1949

DO(49)50 SIZE AND SHAPE OF THE ARMED FORCES 1950–52[1]

Report by the Chiefs of Staff

We were asked to submit, for consideration by Ministers, joint proposals for armed forces which, including defence research and development, would cost no more than an average of £700 million a year during each of the three years from April 1950 onwards, and which would, *within the limitations of this figure*, give the greatest possible measure of security against foreseeable threats.

2. We appointed a Working Party in December 1948 to study this problem and make proposals to us … In accordance with our instructions the Working Party in their Report (hereinafter referred to as the Harwood Report) related the development of our defence policy to the following factors:–

- *(a)* The Present:– *ie* current occupational and garrison commitments and the necessity to wage the "Cold War" effectively.
- *(b)* The Near Future:– *ie* the possibility of becoming involved in an unpremeditated war in the near future.
- *(c)* The More Distant Future:– *ie* the necessity for a foundation for a rearmament programme designed to enable us to meet a premeditated aggression effectively by 1957.

3. The Harwood Working Party state (paragraphs 2 to 3 of their Report) that they have approached the problem by calculating, in relation to the various risks, the shape and size of the forces which could be provided for the given sum of money, and by estimating the policy and strategy which such forces might be able to support. We agree generally with their approach to the problem.

4. We also consider that, taking into account the three requirements mentioned in paragraph 2 above, there is no way of producing larger forces from this money …

5. It is stated in the Report itself (paragraph 55) that the given sum of money is clearly insufficient to provide against the three dangers – the present cold war, the risk of accidental war in the near future and the threat of premeditated war in eight to ten years' time. We consider that the Harwood forces fail to provide against any of these dangers.

6. The Harwood proposals confirm our previous opinion that the forces obtainable on £700 million per year would be seriously inadequate to

[1] Previously COS(49)214, 16 June 1949. DEFE 5/14 & DEFE 7/592.

carry out our foreign and colonial policy in peace and the requirements of strategy in war …

8. … we consider that the balance proposed between sea, land and air forces is generally correct …

Support for our Policy in Areas Overseas

12. The Harwood Report proposes that the main peacetime fleet, called the Peripatetic Task Force, should be able to proceed round the world supporting our policies as and when required. We consider that this force would almost inevitably be split up to meet recurrent local emergencies and would thus ultimately find itself permanently disintegrated into small detachments, leaving no fleet to continue training for war …

15. The abolition of the East Indies Squadron would create a void in South-East Asia and the Indian Ocean …

16. The Naval forces allowed in peace to the China Sea would be inadequate to support our policy in normal times, quite apart from the growing Chinese Communist threat …

…

19. The withdrawal of British Naval forces from Simonstown would have political effects in the Union of South Africa, where the presence of these forces is the only tangible sign of the benefits which South Africa receives in the defence field from remaining a member of the Commonwealth.

20. It would be virtually impossible to retain our title to the Simonstown base if it were to lie reduced to a care and maintenance basis.

21. Moreover, there would be no British Naval forces available to deal with any emergency which may arise in our West African possessions.

22. The withdrawal of the America and West Indies Squadron would mean that there would be no British Naval forces in the Caribbean area to be called on in an emergency, particularly in the event of further trouble in British Honduras and the Falkland Isles Dependencies …

Inadequacies of the Forces Proposed

34. The wartime fleet proposed in the Report could not be achieved even if there were no financial limitation, since the building and modernisation programme required after 1952 would be too great for the shipbuilding capacity to undertake in the five years before 1957.

35. Even if this fleet could be achieved it would still suffer from the following weaknesses:–

(a) There would be a shortage of carriers for trade protection.

(b) There would be a shortage of minesweepers and mine location craft.

(c) Escort groups for the convoys would be composed of seven ships instead of ten and there would be no reserve escort groups.

(*d*) There would be no patrol groups (*ie* offensive anti-submarine hunter/killer groups).
(*e*) There would be a shortage of cruisers.
(*f*) There would be no offensive task force for operations against the enemy's sea communications (*eg* against an enemy amphibious assault on Norway) …

Re-equipment after 1953

40. If we are to have a reasonable chance of surviving the early stages of premeditated war in or after 1957, there must, as pointed out in paragraph 49 of the Harwood Report, be a *steep increase in the provision for re-equipment after* 1952–53 …

General Comments

54. The peacetime fleet recommended in the Harwood Report is regarded by the Admiralty as unbalanced …

Conclusion

60. The Harwood Report is a valuable analysis of the position, but we cannot recommend the Defence Committee to accept it as it stands. Although many of its proposals are acceptable, or would be acceptable with some modification, the forces it describes are inadequate to carry out the Government's policy.

61. We are not at present in a position to submit alternative proposals because we do not know the extent to which Ministers are prepared to accept the implications and risks to which we have drawn attention, or if Ministers are not prepared to accept them, what additional sums of money could be made available over the next few years …

164. *Standing Committee of Service Ministers Minutes*

[DEFE 7/592] 22 June 1949

SM/M(49)18 SIZE AND SHAPE OF THE ARMED FORCES

The Committee considered a report by the Chiefs of Staff[1] on the Harwood Report.

…

The First Lord of the Admiralty said that the effect in this country, the Commonwealth and the United States of accepting the forces suggested in the Harwood Report must be considered particularly as in the case of the Navy, the whole size and shape of the force recommended was based on immediate American intervention on our side if war broke out and on considerable assistance at sea from the Commonwealth. As far as the

[1]COS(49)214, not reproduced.

Admiralty was concerned, the recommendations in the Harwood Report were quite unacceptable, both as regards peacetime and wartime fleets. The proposed peacetime fleet was out of the question politically, both in its size and dispositions. We could not accept the proposed closing of, for instance, the West India station, Simonstown, Trincomalee or dockyards at home.

…

165. *Board Memorandum*

[ADM 167/133] 21 April 1949

B.589 Naval New Construction Programme 1949/50

It will be necessary to secure the approval of the Cabinet to the New Construction Programme 1949/50. Provision has been made in the 1949/50 Estimates for such a programme to the extent of £140,000 out of a total expenditure in that year and the years to follow of £3,612,000.

2. Details of the New Construction Programme with an indication of the stage reached in the earlier New Construction Programme already approved by the Cabinet are contained in the draft paper attached which the First Lord proposes to place before the Defence Committee …

3. The proposals made in this paper were formulated before receipt of the report of the Harwood Committee on the Shape and Size of the Forces, and the Board will need to consider to what extent the proposals contained in that report, or in the related Plans Division memorandum on a restricted Fleet, point to modification of the 1949/50 New Construction Programme.[1]

166. *Memorandum by Director of Plans*

[ADM 205/83] 4 May 1949

PDR 51/107 RESTRICTED FLEET – PD.011/49

The Sea Lords at their meetings on 2 & 3 May considered Plans Division Memorandum PD.011/49 – Restricted Fleet.[2]

[1] A slightly revised programme was finally submitted to the Defence Committee on 8 Dec as DO(49)81, reproduced as Doc. No. 183. The April draft attached to this Memorandum is not reproduced.

[2] The original PD.011/49 does not appear to have survived, though the essentials of the Restricted Fleet became the basis of the Revised Restricted Fleet. A later version of PD.011/49 is an enclosure to the First Sea Lord's memorandum for the Chiefs of Staff, reproduced as Doc. No. 170.

2. The Sea Lords approved the minimum acceptable fleet for war as that shown in Annex I Column 1:– the Sea Lords considered that, with the present tasks of the Navy in peace, the minimum acceptable fleet in commission in peace to be as shown in Annex I Columns 2 and 3. Consequently the Reserve Fleet in peace and the ships to be placed on the disposal list are as shown in Annex I Columns 4, 5, 6 and 7.[1]
3. Various amendments were made to the New Construction Programme (PD.011/49 Appendix IV) and the modernization programme (Appendix V)…
4. The distribution of the Fleet in peace given in PD.011/49 Appendix VII was considered and … amendments decided upon …
5. It was decided in the light of these decisions, that the Second Sea Lord should assess the minimum naval manpower required in peace on the assumption that the Navy takes no National Servicemen. It was decided that the Secretary should be invited to give a rough cost of the amended fleet over the period of the next eight years. For the purpose of assessing this cost, the general assumptions given in PD.011/49 should be accepted; in particular, that it would be impossible to provide all the money required to build up stocks of stores and equipment.
6. The general administrative economies were not discussed in detail, but the following decisions were made in principle:–

(a) The East Indies Station should remain with its own Commander-in-Chief but he should conduct the Station from his flagship with no shore component of his staff; Captain-in-Charge Ceylon should however remain.
(b) Commander-in-Chief Far East Station should conduct his station from his flagship (provided Ministerial approval could be obtained); FOMA should represent the Commander-in-Chief Far East on the Commanders-in-Chief Committee at Singapore; Flag Officer Second-in-Command FES should be withdrawn.
(c) Sheerness Dockyard and Naval establishments at Sheerness should be closed (subject to confirmation by Controller).
(d) In the present state of affairs in China, it would not be possible to dispose of Singapore Dockyard.
(e) The Royal Marines should be reduced to a strength of some 8,700 …

[1] Annex I appears, virtually unchanged, in Board Memorandum B.590 which is reproduced as Doc. No. 168.

167. *Director of Plans to First Sea Lord & VCNS*

[ADM 205/84] 21 May 1949

PDR.51/110 A COMPARISON BETWEEN
THE PRESENT PLANNED FLEETS (PD.06/48)[1]
AND THE REVISED RESTRICTED FLEET

As directed, I have prepared a statement, attached, giving a brief comparison between the fleet in 1954/55 as shown in PD.06/48 and the Revised Restricted Fleet.

2. 1954/55 is chosen as the main part of the carrier programme would be completed in each plan by that date.

1. Strength of Fleets

The following is a comparison of the Fleets in 1954 between the Planned Fleet (P.D.06/48) and the Revised Restricted Fleet (PD.011/49 amended by PDR.51/107)

	Planned Fleet	Revised Restricted Fleet
Battleships	5	1 + 4
Fleet Carriers	8 †	6 ‡
Light Fleet Carriers	12 ±	4 ø
Cruisers	23 +	18
Disarmed Cruisers (Trials and Training)	2	2
Fast Minelayers	2	3
Destroyers	62	62
Frigates	230	182
Submarines	65	53
Ocean M/S	60	61
Coastal and Inshore M/S	75	185
Minelocation Craft	–	16
Fleet A/D Escorts	1	–
Midget S/M	4	2
Seaward Defence A/S Craft	14	10
MTB/MGB	38	50
Front Line Aircraft	300 (in 1957)	250 (in 1957)

† 4 not modernised
‡ 2 not modernised
± 3 not modernised (excludes 3 for Dominions)

[1] PD.06/48, the basis of the 'nine-year plan', does not appear to have survived. It is adequately summarised in this paper.

ø All modernised

+ Another 4 cruisers are retained pending decisions as to their disposal

2. Financial Comparison

Financial Year	Planned Fleet PD.06/48	Revised Restricted Fleet
	£m	£m
1950/51	203	202.5
1951/52	234	209.9
1952/53	253	215.4
1953/54	285	216.0
1954/55	312	223.4
	1287	1067.2

Difference £m. 219.8

3. Comparison of Manpower

	Planned Fleet	Revised Restricted Fleet
Peacetime Vote A strength	145,000	121,500
Wartime Vote A strength	285,000	243,000

4. Comparison by Classes of Ship of items each plan during the period under consideration

	Planned Fleet	Revised Restricted Fleet
Battleships	Large repair of 3 ships by 1954/55	Large repair of 1 ship by 1957/58
Fleet Carriers	Completion of 2 building	Completion of 2 building
	Modernising of 2 existing ships	Modernising of 2 existing ships
	Retention of 4 unmodernised	Retention of 2 unmodernised
		Disposal of 2 unmodernised
Light Fleet Carriers	Completion of 2 MAJESTIC Class	Disposal of 2 MAJESTIC Class
	Completion of 4 HERMES Class	Completion of 4 HERMES Class
	Modernising of 3 existing ships	Disposal of 6 existing ships
	Retention of 3 unmodernised	
Note:–	*Light Fleets for the Dominions have been omitted from this comparison*	
Cruisers	Completion of 3 cruisers	Completion of 3 cruisers
	Retention of a total of 23 cruisers	Retention of a total of 21 cruisers
	Allows for retention of 4 cruisers pending disposal	Disposal of 9 existing ships
Fast Minelayers	Retention of 2 Fast Minelayers	Retention of 3 Fast Minelayers
	Conversion of 1 Fast Minelayer to FADE	
Destroyers	Modernising 54 by 1957	Modernising 54 by 1957
	Completion of 8 building	Completion of 8 building
Frigates	2 ex Destroyers full conversion to Frigate	15 ex Destroyers full conversion to Frigate
	57 ex Destroyers conversion to Frigates	44 unconverted Destroyers retained
	Build 4 frigates	Build 5 frigates
	Retain a total of 230 frigates	Retain a total of 182 frigates
Submarines	Retain a total of 65 submarines	Retain a total of 53 submarines
	Convert 8 T Class to FBD	Convert 4 T Class to FBD
	Build 10 new design submarines	Build 2 new design submarines

Ocean Minesweepers	Retain a total of 60 ships No new construction	Retain a total of 61 ships Build 1 new ship
Coastal and Inshore M/S	Retain a total of 75 No new construction	Retain a total of 185 Build 70 new design
Minelocation Craft	None included	Build 16
Midget Submarines	Build 4	Build 2
Seaward Defence	Build 12	Build 10
A/S Craft	Retain 2 existing conversions	Retain 2 existing conversions
MTB/MGB	Retain 36 existing craft Build 2	Retain 36 existing craft Build 14
Front Line Aircraft	300 allowed for in 1957	250 allowed for in 1957

168. *Board Memorandum*

[ADM 205/84 & ADM 167/133] 23 May 1949

B.590 REVISED RESTRICTED FLEET

1. Consideration by the Board of the recommendations concerning the Navy in the Harwood Report, the results of which have been communicated to the Chiefs of Staff by First Sea Lord, has shown that they are not such as the Board could recommend to the Government as an acceptable solution of the long term policy for the size and shape of the Fleet. Accordingly, it was considered that the Admiralty would have to put forward their own proposals to this end, as an alternative to the Harwood proposals …

Restricted Fleet PD011/49

2. The Director of Plans had meanwhile been instructed to prepare a paper to show the Shape and Size of the Fleet over the period 1950–1958; on the assumption that not more than an annual average of £200m would be available over this period. This plan was issued as PD011/49 (hereafter also referred to as the Restricted Fleet).

3. When this paper was considered by the naval members of the Board, there was a general consensus of opinion that though it was far preferable to the Harwood Plan it would require modification in a number of respects before it could be laid before the Board as an acceptable alternative to Harwood. Moreover, the costing, which was carried out hurriedly, was considered to need revision. By now it was becoming apparent that the task of designing a Fleet capable of meeting the requirements of both peace and war at the desired level of efficiency was not possible within the financial limits previously laid down.

4. Accordingly, the naval members of the Board concluded that the above approach should be abandoned and that the problem should be approached on a fresh basis:–

(a) that the Fleet should be capable of carrying out the Foreign and Colonial policy of HM Government in time of peace;

(b) that its essential structure should at the same time be maintained in a form capable of
  (i) 'fighting with what we have got' in an unpremeditated war between now and 1957;
  (ii) meeting the immediate requirements of a premeditated war in 1957 and serving as a nucleus for expansion after outbreak of war. The necessary provision for re-equipment would therefore have to be included in the plan;

(c) subject to the above objects, the financial cost should be reduced to the bare minimum necessary, but without any preordained financial limit.

5. A revised plan was prepared and has been endorsed by the naval members of the Board. This is hereafter referred to as the Revised Restricted Fleet.

6. Details are shown in Annexes attached, as follows:–
  (a) Annex I. Part 1 shows the Fleet required in war (Col.1), the Fleet to be maintained in Commission and in Reserve in peace (Cols 2–6) and the ships to be placed on the disposal list (Col.7). Part 2 illustrates (in the same tabular form as Part 1) where the Revised Restricted Fleet varies from the proposals in the Harwood Report.
  (b) Annex II shows the Revised Restricted Fleet New Construction Programme.
  (c) Annex III shows the Revised Restricted Fleet Modernisation and Conversion Programme.
  (d) Annex IV shows the proposed distribution of the Fleet in peace.

7. Cost in Money and Manpower

The manpower provision has been assessed on the assumption that no National Servicemen will be taken … it has been accepted that it will be impossible to provide all the money required to build up stocks of stores and equipment …

9. Administrative Economies

The various recommendations made in the Harwood and PD.011/49 have not been examined in detail but the naval members of the Board have made the following recommendations:–
  (a) No war reserves of stores should be maintained east of Ceylon.
  (b) The East Indies Station should remain with its own Commander-in-Chief, but he should conduct the Station from his Flagship with no shore component of his staff; Captain-in-Charge Ceylon should however remain.
  (c) Commander-in-Chief Far East Station should conduct his station from his flagship; FOMA should represent the Commander-in-Chief, Far East on the Commanders-in-Chief Committee at

Singapore; Flag Officer Second-in-Command FES, should be withdrawn.

(d) Sheerness Dockyard and Naval Establishments at Sheerness should be closed.

(e) It would not be possible to dispose of Singapore Dockyard, because of the continuing need for it in peace and the necessity to maintain its docking and repair facilities in war.

(f) The Royal Marines should be reduced to a strength of some 8,700. This should result in the closing of all Royal Marine Establishments in the Chatham Command, except the Royal Marine Depot Deal and also in the closing down of the Royal Marine Camp, Browndown.

ANNEX I – PART 1
REVISED RESTRICTED FLEET

CATEGORY OF SHIP	1 WAR FLEET 1957	2 PEACE FLEET	3	4 RESERVE FLEET CATEGORY	5	6	7 FOR DISPOSAL	REMARKS
		FULL COMMISSION	TRAINING	A	B	C		
Battleships	1 + 4	–	1	–	–	4	–	Battleships not to be modernised until Guided Weapons are in supply
Fleet Carriers	6	2	1	1*	2	–	–	Two carriers to be disposed of when EAGLES join Fleet * Employed on harbour training
Light Fleet Carriers	4	3	1	–	–	2	–	Consideration to be given to disposal of 6 Light Fleet Carriers when HERMES class join Fleet
Cruisers	18	13	–	2	2	1	9	3 8″ cruisers for disposal now 3 6″ or 5.25″ to be disposed when large repairs necessary 3 further 6″ cruisers to be disposed when TIGERs join the Fleet
Disarmed Cruisers	–	–	2	–	–	–	–	DEVONSHIRE and CUMBERLAND
Fast Minelayers	3	2	–	1	–	–	–	
Destroyers	62	38	2	6	8	–	–	8 DARING class building
Frigates	182	32	33	23	40	54	18	18 frigates to be disposed of when uneconomical to repair 21 frigates to be disposed of when new frigates join fleet
A/S Experimental Ship (HELMSDALE)	1	–	1	–	–	–	–	

Submarines	53	20	20	13	–	–	12	12 submarines to be disposed of when uneconomical to repair 6 more to be disposed of when new submarines join fleet
Ocean Minesweepers	61	16	7	16	16	6	–	5 Ocean M/S to be disposed of when new ships join fleet
Danlayers	12	4	–	4	4	–	–	
Coastal & Inshore Minesweepers	250	20	–	95	–	–	–	
Coastal Forces (MTB/MGB)	50	–	12	24	–	–	–	16 MTB/MGB to be disposed of on replacement by new construction
Seaward Defence A/S Craft	18	–	2*	–	–	–	–	
Minelocation Craft	36	–	–	–	–	–	–	* Not operational
Midget Submarines	2	–	2	–	–	–	–	
Fleet Replenishment Ship	1	–	–	–	1	–	1	
Submarine Dept Ships	4	2	–	1	–	–	1*	*WOLFE

CATEGORY OF SHIP	1 WAR FLEET 1957	2 PEACE FLEET	3	4 RESERVE FLEET CATEGORY	5	6	7 FOR DISPOSAL	REMARKS
		FULL COMMISSION	TRAINING	A	B	C		
Destroyer Dept Ships	2	1	–	1	–	–	–	
Coastal Force Maint. Ship	–	–	–	–	–	–	1	
Escort Maintenance Ship	3	–	–	1	1	1	–	
Aircraft Maintenance Ship	2	–	–	1	–	1	1	
Aircraft Transport Ship	1	3	–	–	1	–	–	
Repair Ships	3	–	–	–	2	1	2	
N.S.C. Maintenance Ships	2	–	–	–	2	–	–	
Maintenance Craft	6	–	–	6	–	–	6	
Survey Ships	7	–	4	–	–	–	2	
Survey M/Ls	6	–	6	–	–	–	–	
N.D. Training Ship	1	–	1	–	–	–	–	
Rescue M/Ls	6	–	6	–	–	–	–	
Monitors	2	–	–	–	–	2	–	Not to be modernised

Gunboats	–	–	–	–	–	–	1	
Fleet Tugs	As requisite	5	–	As	Req.	Civ.	Manned	
Boom Working Vessels	80	———	———	Civ.	Man.	or	C and M.	
Salvage Vessels	As requisite	———	———	Civ.	Man.	or	C and M.	
High Speed Targets	6	–	6	–	–	–	–	
Coastal Minelayers	1	–	1	–	–	–	–	
Controlled Minelayers	11	–	5	3	3	–	–	
Deep Diving Vessel	1	–	1	–	–	–	–	Note:– The Far East Squadron will be augmented until normal conditions are restored in the Far East
Experimental Mine Location Craft	2	–	2	–	–	–	–	
Combined Operations Ships & Craft	Brigade Lift	1/3 Brigade	Lift for Trg.	–	–	2/3 Bde.L.	–	
Aircraft (F.A.E.)	250	250	–	RNVR	Sqn.	60	–	

ANNEX I – PART 2
REVISED RESTRICTED FLEET
A COMPARISON BETWEEN THE REVISED RESTRICTED FLEET AND THE HARWOOD FLEET

CATEGORY OF SHIP	1 WAR FLEET 1957	2 PEACE FLEET	3	4 RESERVE FLEET CATEGORY	5	6 FOR DISPOSAL	REMARKS
		FULL COMMISSION	TRAINING	A & B	C		
Battleships	+1 (+4)	Same	+1	same	+4		
Fleet Carriers	same	+1	same	–1	same	–5	Two carriers to be disposed of when EAGLES join Fleet
Light Fleet Carriers	–2	+1	same	–3	same	same	Consideration to be given to disposal of 6 Light Fleet Carriers when HERMES class join Fleet
Cruisers } Disarmed Cruisers }	–1	+7	+1	–5	–4	+6	3 6″ cruisers to be disposed when TIGERs join the Fleet
Fast Minelayers	same	+1	–	–1	same	+1	
Destroyers } Frigates }	–39	+38	–4	–22	–51	same	8 DARING class building
Submarines	–10	+3	+7	–20	same	+39	2 submarines on loan to Dutch excluded
Ocean Minesweepers	–5	same	–1	+11	–15	+10	
Danlayers	same	+4	–3	–1	same	+5	

Coastal & Inshore Minesweepers	+179	+20	–26	+185	same	same	135 Coastal & Inshore M/S to be built included
Coastal Forces (MTB/MGB)	+14	same	–12	+36	same	same	14 MTB/MGB to be built included
Fleet Replenishment Ship	same	same	same	same	same	same	
Submarine Dept Ships	same	+1	same	same	–1	same	
Destroyer Depot Ships	same	+1	–	+1	–2	same	
Coastal Forces Maintenance Ship	same	same	same	same	same	same	
Escort Maintenance Ships	same	same	same	+1	–1	same	
Aircraft Maintenance Ships	same	same	same	+1	–1	same	
Repair Ships	same	same	same	+1	–1	same	
Survey Ships	same	+1	+1	same	–2	same	
Aircraft F.A.E.	–50	–	–	–	–	–	

ANNEX II
REVISED RESTRICTED FLEET
New Construction Programme

Ship:–	1950/51	1951/52	1952/53	1953/54	1954/55	1955/56	1956/57	1957/58
2 Fleet Carriers								
EAGLE	---/ (Nov 1950)							
ARK ROYAL	--/ (End 1952)							
4 Light Fleet Carriers	-----2 ships----------------/ (End 1951)							
4 HERMES	----------------2 ships----------------------/ (End 1952)							
4 Cruisers								
3 TIGERs			/-----3 ships----------/					
1 New Ship								/--1 ship----
12 Destroyers	-5 ships--/							
8 DARINGS	---------3 ships-----------/							
4 New Ships								/--4 ships---
21 Frigates								
4 A/D	/------------1 ship------------------/			/-------------------1 ship--------------------/				/--1 ship---
						/------------------------1 ship---------------/		
4 A/A	/----------------1 ship----------------/		/---------------2 ships----------------/				/------------2 ships----------------	
	----------1 ship-----------/			/------------------2 ships----------------/		/---------------2 ships-------------/		/-5 ships-
12 A/S					/-----------------1 ship-----------------/		/----------1 ship-------	
6 Submarines	/-------------1 ship-------------/			/------------1 ship-----------/		/-------------1 ship-------------/		
			/---------1 ship---------/		/-----------1 ship---------/		/------------1 ship-------------	
5 Ocean Minesweepers				/----1 ship----/	/----1 ship----/	/----2 ships---/	/----1 ship----/	

73 Coastal Minesweepers	-----2-----/ /------5------/ /------11------/ /------11------/ /------11------/ /------11------/ /------11------/ /------11-------/
62 Inshore Minesweepers	---2---/ /------6------/ /------8------/ /------8------/ /------8------/ /------8------/ /------8------/ /------7-------/ /-----7----
36 Mine Location Craft	/-------1-------/ /-------5-------/ /-------5------/ /------5-------/ /-------5-------/ /-------5-------/ /-------5------/ /-----5------
18 Seaward Defence A/S Craft	/--------2--------/ /--------4-------/ /--------4-------/ /--------4-------/ /--------4-------/
30 M.T.B./M.G.B.	/--------2-------/ /------4-------/ /------4-------/ /-------4-------/ /------4------/ /-------4-------/ /-------4-------/ /-----4-
2 Midget Submarines	/---------2--------/
Combined Operations L.S.T.(4) Amphibs	-------2------/ /---------1----------/

ANNEX III
REVISED RESTRICTED FLEET
Modernisation and Conversion Programme

Ship:–	1950/51	1951/52	1952/53	1953/54	1954/55	1955/56	1956/57	1957/58
4 Fleet Carriers	--------------------1 ship--------------------/							
		/--------------------------1 ship-----------------------------/						
				/---------------------------1 ship------------------------------/				
					/------------------1 ship------------------/ for DLT only			
5 Cruisers			/------------1-----------/					
				/------------1-----------/				
					/-----------2-----------/			
						/------------1-----------/		
54 Destroyers (to be modernised)								
27 Destroyers	-----2------/	/-----------3--------------/		/-----------4--------------/		/-----------4--------------/		
Full Conversions to fast frigate	/-----------2--------------/		/-----------4--------------/		/-----------4--------------/		/-----------3--------------/	
6 Submarines	----1----/ ----1----/	/-------------1-------------/		/-------------1-------------/		/-------------1-------------/		/------1- ----
3 L.S.T.(3) to L.S.T.(A)	----1----/	/-------------1-------------/		/-------------1-------------/				
1 L.C.T.(8)	----1----/							

ANNEX IV
DISTRIBUTION OF THE FLEET IN PEACE

1. HOME FLEET

(i) The Active Fleet at Interim Peace Complement

2 Fleet Carriers	(1 Flagship CinC HF, 1 Flagship FO 3rd ACS)	
1 Light Fleet Carrier		
3 Cruisers		(C.S.1)
1 Fast Minelayer		(Commodore(D) HF)
18 Destroyers	6 BATTLES	(D4)
	8 CAs	(D5)
	4 WEAPONS	(D6)
8 Frigates	4 BAYS	(SO)
	4 CASTLES	
8 Ocean Minesweepers	(ALGERINES)	
2 Danlayers		
8 Coastal Minesweepers		
12 Inshore Minesweepers		
3 Fleet Tugs		

(ii) Training Ships at Special Complement (operationally coordinated by CinC HF)

2 Frigates ex destroyers	(Joint A/S School)	
5 Frigates	1 S/M Target (WOODBRIDGE HAVEN)	
	4 Joint A/S School (LOCH Class)	
10 Submarines	9 A. or T.	for Joint A/S School
	1 S. (Fast A/S Target)	
1 Submarine Depot Ship		

(iii) Summary of Home Fleet

Type	FC	Sp.	Total
Fleet Carriers	2	–	2
Light Fleet Carriers	1	–	1
Cruisers	3	–	3
Fast Minelayers	1	–	1
Destroyers	18	–	18
Frigates ex destroyers	–	2	2
Frigates	8	5	13
Submarines	–	10	10
S/M Depot Ship	–	1	1
Ocean M/S	8	–	8
Danlayers	2	–	2
Coastal M/S	8	–	8
Inshore M/S	12	–	12
Fleet Tugs	3	–	3

2. MEDITERRANEAN FLEET

(i) The Active Fleet at Interim Peace Complement

2 Light Fleet Carriers	(FO Air Med)	
4 Cruisers	(CS1)	
1 Fast Minelayer		
16 Destroyers	8 CH. Class	(D1)
	8 BATTLES	(D3)
8 Frigates	4 BLACK SWAN	
	3 LOCHs	
	1 BAY Class Despatch Vessel	
8 Ocean Minesweepers	8 ALGERINES	
2 Danlayers		

10 Submarines	4A 4T 2S	2 to be stationed in Australia (Fast A/S Targets)
1 Submarine Depot Ship		
1 Destroyer Depot Ship		(FOD)
2 Survey Ships		
2 Fleet Tugs		

(ii) <u>At Special Complement</u>

3 High Speed Targets (2 crews)
2 Rescue M/Ls

3. EAST INDIES SQUADRON (Including Persian Gulf)

<u>At Interim Peace Complement</u>

2 Cruisers	(CinC EI)
5 Frigates	1 BAY 4 LOCHs

4. AMERICA AND WEST INDIES SQUADRON

<u>At Interim Peace Complement</u>

1 Cruiser	(CinC AWI)
3 Frigates	LOCHs

5. SOUTH ATLANTIC SQUADRON

<u>At Interim Peace Complement</u>

1 Cruiser	(CinC SA)
2 Frigates	BAYS

6. FAR EAST SQUADRON

<u>At Interim Peace Complement</u>

2 Cruisers	
4 Destroyers	
6 Frigates	2 BLACK SWAN 4 LOCHs
1 Survey Ship	

Note:– In view of the present unsettled conditions in the Far East the composition of the Far East Squadron has been temporarily increased by 1 cruiser and 1 destroyer.

7. BASED IN UNITED KINGDOM (Training, Trials etc)

(i) <u>At Special Complement</u>

<u>Employed on New Entry and Cadets Training</u>

1 Battleship, VANGUARD 1 Fleet Carrier, VICTORIOUS	Harbour Training
1 Cruiser, DEVONSHIRE	(Cadets Training)
4 Frigates, HUNT Class	(Boys Training)

Note:– The possibility of continuing Boys Training with TAS training at Portland is being investigated.

<u>Employed on TSS and Submarine Training</u>

4 Frigates ex destroyer	(TAS Training)
5 Frigates, CASTLE Class	(" ")
19 Submarines, A or T Class	(S/M and A/S)
1 Submarine Depot Ship	(" ")
1 Submarine Fast A/S Target	(A/S Training)
2 Frigates ex destroyer	(S/M Training Targets)
2 Seaward Defence A/S Craft	(1 crew)
2 Midget Submarines	
2 Large Controlled Minelayers	(attached VERNON)
3 Controlled Minelayers	(" ")
1 Coastal Minelayer	(" ")
1 Deep Diving Vessel	(" Diving School)

Employed on M/S Training
2 Ocean Minesweepers
Employed on 'N' Training
1 N/D Training Ship
2 Frigates (BLACK SWAN Class)
Employed on Air Training
1 Fleet Carrier (Trials)
1 Light Fleet Carrier (Training)
4 Frigates ex destroyer
4 Rescue MLs
1 Air Target (ORSAY)
Employed on Coastal Forces Training
12 MTB/MGB (6 large, 6 small, 10 crews only)
Employed on Gunnery Training
1 Destroyer (Gunnery Firing Ship)
3 High Speed Targets (2 crews)
Employed as local Flotillas and 'E' Training
1 Destroyer (E. Training and Plymouth local Flotilla)
2 Frigates (1 HUNT & 1 BAY) (local Flotilla Nore and Plymouth)
Employed on Surveying at Home
4 Survey Ships
6 Survey MLs
Employed on Fishery Protection
1 Frigate (BLACK SWAN Class)
5 Ocean Minesweepers
Employed on Research and Trials
1 Cruiser (CUMBERLAND)
1 Frigate ex destroyer (M/S Trials)
1 Frigate A/S Experimental (River Class)
1 Frigate Radio Trials (FLEETWOOD)
2 ex German M/S Experimental Vessels
2 Trawlers Minelocation Experimental
2 MTB for A/S Development

(ii) Summary of Ships employed on Training, Trials etc

Battleship	1		
Fleet Carrier	2	Survey MLs	6
Light Fleet Carrier	1	Rescue MLs	4
Cruisers	2	Air Target	1
Destroyers	2	MTB/MGB	12
Frigates ex destroyers	11	Seaward Defence A/S Craft	2
Frigate A/S Experimental	1	Coastal Minelayer	1
Frigates	15	Controlled Minelayers	5
Submarines	20	Deep Diving Vessel	1
Submarine Depot Ship	2	High Speed Targets	3
Ocean M/S	7	Ex German M/S Vessels	2
Midget S/Ms	2	Minelocation Vessels	2
ND Training Ship	1	A/S Development MTB	2
Survey Ships	4		

8. RESERVE FLEET

The Reserve Fleet is as shown in Annex I, part 1.[1]

[1] Not reproduced.

169. *Board Minutes*

[ADM 167/132] 26 & 30 May 1949

Revised Restricted Fleet

4285. The Board had before them a memorandum on a Revised Restricted Fleet, which represented the conclusions of the naval members of the Board as to the naval forces which the Board of Admiralty should recommend as the minimum required to meet the commitments laid upon the Royal Navy by the present policy of HM Government.

It was explained that though the proposals embodied in the memorandum had been framed with the closest regard for economy and took full account of the financial situation of the country, no arbitrary assumption had been made as to the maximum financial provision which HM Government could be expected to make for the Royal Navy during the next few years. Some members of the Board took the view that it would have been a more realistic approach if such an assumption had been made and if the naval forces had then been calculated so as to make the best use of the funds available within the assumed financial limit. The more general view was, however, that the method adopted in the memorandum was sounder and that it would be for HM Government to say whether the commitments of the naval forces would have to be reduced in order to bring expenditure within the amount which it would be possible to provide.

In assessing the size of the Fleet which would be needed in war full weight had been given to the contribution to the naval war effort which the United States could be expected to make. The strength of the forces would be governed as much by the requirements of convoy escorting, minesweeping and similar tasks as by the necessity for dealing effectively with the opposing naval forces.

In determining the size and composition of Vote A care had been taken to preserve the basic structure and balance of the naval service. The Royal Marines and Women's Royal Naval Service would be retained, though at reduced strengths, and recruitment for the Royal Navy would be maintained at a level sufficient to avoid serious lack of balance in the various rates in the latter years of the programme. In order to reduce training commitments and to eliminate the need for employing relatively inefficient men in complement billets, no National Service men could be accepted; this would make the problem of providing reserves for mobilisation still more difficult.

In the course of a detailed examination of the memorandum and its annexes, the following were the main points which emerged:–

(a) The proposed front-line air strength of 250 was the minimum necessary for manning the carriers in the peacetime fleet and for providing a nucleus for expansion in war.
(b) The number of frigates included in the war fleet, though considerably less than that recommended by the Harwood working party, should be adequate, and was the maximum that could be provided if the Fleet was to be properly balanced. Many of the existing frigates would probably be too slow to deal with the enemy submarine threat as it could be expected to develop in the next few years. Specific authority would be sought on each occasion before any ships were scrapped.
(c) The number of cruisers was extremely low. The retention of the King George V Class Battleships in reserve would be in some measure a compensation for the reduction in cruiser strength. First Lord indicated that he would be prepared to consider circulating a paper to the Defence Committee concerning the future of the remaining 8-in. cruisers.
(d) The simplified form of conversion of destroyers to fast Escort Vessels had been abandoned in favour of the full-scale conversion of a smaller number of ships.
(e) It was not clear whether capacity could in fact be found for the whole of the proposed New Construction Programme and this would require further study.
(f) The recommendations regarding administrative economies contained in paragraph 9 of the covering memorandum were endorsed in principle, subject to closer investigation of the financial effect of certain of them, which would be the subject of a further submission to the Board.

The Board agreed that the naval forces proposed in the memorandum and its annexes represented the minimum which it would be necessary to maintain in order to meet the peace and war commitments of the Royal Navy, and agreed that they should be submitted to HM Government at the appropriate stage in the forthcoming discussions on the size and shape of the forces.

New Construction Programme 1949/50.

4287. The Board had before them a memorandum on the New Construction Programme 1949/50. The Board approved the proposed New Construction Programme, and the First Lord undertook to make the necessary submission to the Defence Committee.

170. *Chiefs of Staff Memorandum*

[ADM 1/21547 & DEFE 5/15] 14 July 1949

COS(49)236 THE FUTURE SHAPE AND SIZE OF THE NAVY

Memorandum by the First Sea Lord

In accordance with the Chiefs of Staff decision in COS(49) 77th Meeting, Item 2,[1] the Admiralty proposals for the future shape and size of the Navy are shown in the Enclosure to this paper.

2. It may be of help if I summarise briefly the reductions and modifications in the structure of the Navy which are proposed.

WARTIME FLEET

3. The wartime Fleet now proposed is less than the Fleet tabled in COS(48)212(O)[2] (in which I reported the state of the Navy as at September 1948) by the following number of ships:–

8 Light Fleet Aircraft Carriers
3 Cruisers
8 Fleet Air Direction Escorts
48 Frigates
12 Submarines

4. These reductions are made possible by relying on the American Navy for the provision of half the Naval Forces required for the control of the sea communications in the North Atlantic and the Mediterranean, and for all the forces required for the control of sea communications in the South Atlantic and Pacific. For the control of sea communications in the Indian Ocean reliance has similarly been placed upon the Australian and New Zealand Navies to provide the forces required.

PEACETIME FLEET

5. The proposed peacetime Fleet in commission is approximately the same as that we now maintain since the peacetime commitments of the Navy have not been reduced.

6. Great economies are, however, proposed in training and administration … by which it is hoped to save some 20,000 men. This saving will only be possible if the Navy ceases to take a National Service entry except for a small number entered through the RNVR.

With the money likely to be available a number of existing ships are considered to be uneconomical to maintain and repair, and the Admiralty proposals will include placing the following on the disposal list, resulting in a further saving of money and manpower:–

[1] Reproduced as Doc. No. 161.

[2] Reproduced as Doc. No. 139.

9 Cruisers
39 Frigates
12 Submarines
And a considerable number of ancillary vessels.

Other ships will be placed on the disposal list when replaced by new construction, notably 2 'Colossus' Class Light Fleet Carriers.

NEW CONSTRUCTION AND MODERNISATION

7. The new construction and modernisation programme has been drastically reduced from that tabled in JWPS(48)54, and the replacement of worn-out ships will have to be spread over a longer period than was previously planned.

COMPARISON WITH HARWOOD FLEETS

8. As an illustration of the differences proposed it may be interesting to make a comparison in some respects with the recommendations of the Harwood Report as follows:–

Battleships	The present proposal is that these ships should be retained in Reserve instead of being scrapped. No one can say what heavy ships the enemy may have built by 1957 and the Battleships must be regarded as an essential insurance.
Cruisers	There is an increase over Harwood from 12 to 18 necessary to carry out our peacetime commitments and meet our war requirements.
Frigates and	There is a considerable reduction in the number of small craft on
Similar Light	Harwood recommendations as there is neither the money nor the
Craft	manpower available to build and maintain them. Should war tension increase such ships can more easily be built than larger ships.

SUMMARY

9. In the aggregate all these economies reduce the Naval expenditure over the next 8 years from an average of £300,000,000 per year to £225,000,000 per year; whilst the average manpower bearing of the Navy will be reduced from 150,000 to 124,000 …

ENCLOSURE TO FIRST SEA LORD'S MEMORANDUM OF 14 JULY 1949

PD.011/49/3 FUTURE SHAPE AND SIZE OF THE NAVY (1949)

THE ROLE OF THE NAVY IN WAR

The tasks of the Navy in war, which can only be achieved by operating in the closest cooperation with the RAF, are:–

(a) To control sea communications in order to ensure:–

(i) that the United Kingdom can remain a main support area and become an offensive base. This necessitates complete control of the Atlantic sea communications and, in conjunction with the Commonwealth and Allied Forces, or worldwide sea communications.

(ii) that the Middle East Base and its supply lines are safeguarded. This in particular necessitates control of the Mediterranean sea routes.

(iii) the movement and maintenance of the Army and Air Force overseas in accordance with our strategy and if required their withdrawal. This role includes the requirement for seaborne assault and seaborne flank support when necessary.

(b) To deny the enemy the use of the sea so that:–

(i) the United Kingdom and the Commonwealth are defended against seaborne invasion.

(ii) the enemy are unable to use the sea for the deployment or maintenance of their Armies and Air Forces.

(c) To provide seaborne tactical air support when shore-based air support is not available or adequate.

(d) To assist the RAF with a strategic air offensive if so required.

THE ROLE OF THE NAVY IN PEACE

2. The tasks of the Navy in peace are:–

(a) To support British foreign and colonial policy, and to uphold British prestige throughout the world.

(b) To prepare for war.

3. PLANNED FLEETS

The plan which is set out in detail in the attached appendices provides for [the] following naval forces to undertake these tasks.

(a) War

(i) The minimum naval forces required for control of United Kingdom coastal waters and the defence of the United Kingdom ports.

(ii) Approximately half the naval forces required for the control of the North Atlantic sea communications.

(iii) Approximately half the naval forces required for the control of Mediterranean/Middle East sea communications.
(iv) The minimum naval forces required for the defence of the Eastern Mediterranean ports.
(v) The minimum naval forces required for the defence of colonial ports (in part these forces will be provided by colonial naval forces).
(vi) The agreed contribution towards the naval forces required for the support of the Western European campaign.
(vii) Amphibious forces sufficient for a brigade group lift.
(viii) A training organisation to enable the naval forces to be expanded during the first two years of war to go over to the offensive.
(ix) Defence of Merchant Shipping on a modified scale.

(b) Peace
(i) The Mediterranean Fleet for support of our Mediterranean Middle East policy. This fleet will also provide higher training for war.
(ii) The Home Fleet as strategical reserve. The Home Fleet will also have the task of individual ship and squadron training. It will also provide detachments required for the support of our foreign and colonial policy in America and the West Indies.
(iii) A small squadron in the Far East for the support of our foreign and colonial policy.
(iv) A small squadron in the East Indies for the support of our foreign and colonial policy.
(v) A token force in South Africa for the support of our foreign and colonial policy in South and West Africa.
(vi) A reserve fleet equal to the difference between our peacetime and wartime fleets, divided into three categories:–

Category A Ships required for service within three months of mobilisation; the majority of ships to be at 30 days' notice for service.

Category B Ships at three months' notice for service.

Category C Ships required for service in war, but at longer notice than three months.

Note:– Category Z Reserve includes all ships on the Disposal List which are no longer required for service.

(vii) A training squadron and ships attached to training schools in the United Kingdom.
(viii) A minimum number of ships required for research and development.

(ix) A training organisation ashore capable of meeting the training commitments for supporting some 120,000 men and women on regular or short service and for training the reserves.

(x) Survey ships throughout the world and wre3ck dispersal ships in United Kingdom waters. The latter to be civilian manned.

(xi) A small Fishery Protection Squadron for the North East Atlantic Fisheries.

(xii) A nucleus for the seaward defences of UK ports and the colonial ports required to be defended during the first six months of war.

(xiii) Training facilities for Commonwealth, Colonial and Allied officers and men (on repayment).

4. LOGISTIC SUPPORT

The plan also provides logistic support for the Fleet as follows:–

War

(i) Store holding on a 'two theatre' basis in support of forces deployed and subsidiary store holding in support of forces operating outside the main theatres.

(ii) Nucleus floating support, emergency repair facilities and major repair facilities.

Peace

(i) Store holding on a worldwide basis in support of forces deployed.

(ii) Stockpiling of strategic reserves.

(iii) Dockyard facilities for maintenance of peacetime and reserve fleets.

5. ASSUMPTIONS

This plan has been drawn up upon the following assumptions:–

(a) The economic and financial state of the country make it impossible to maintain a British Fleet capable of carrying out all the tasks given in paragraph 1.

(b) Our Allies will provide:–

(i) Approximately half the naval forces required for the control of the North Atlantic sea communications.

(ii) Approximately half the naval forces required for the control of Mediterranean sea communications.

(iii) All the naval forces required for the control of sea communications in the South Atlantic, the Pacific and the Western Indian Ocean.

(iv) The naval forces required for the control of their own coastal waters and ports.
(v) The agreed contribution to the Naval Forces required for the support of the campaign in Western Europe.

(c) Commonwealth countries will provide:–
(i) The naval forces required for the control of sea communications in South East Asia and the Eastern Indian Ocean.
(ii) Naval forces required for the control of their own waters and defence of their ports.

(d) Approximately 25% of the conjectural naval estimates must be set aside for new construction, modernisation and re-equipment of the Fleet and Establishments.

(e) Approximately 5% of the conjectural naval estimates must be set aside for research and development.

(f) The Fleet must be as nearly as possible ready for war in 1957.

(g) There will be no national service component of the Navy in peace apart from a small number of men who are either earmarked for the Naval Reserves or have done their training voluntarily in the Reserves.

(h) It will not be possible to provide for
(i) Full modernisation of the Ships of the Fleet.
(ii) The full build-up of reserves of stores and equipment required for mobilisation.
(iii) The standard of amenities and the scale of quarters (including married quarters) previously planned.

6. Details of the Plan are given in the following Annexes:-[1]

Annex I Planned Fleet
Annex II New Construction Programme for the Years 1950/51 to 1957/58
Annex III Modernisation and Conversion Programme for the Years 1950/51 to 1957/58 together with notes on the degree of modernisation and conversion.
Annex IV Distribution of the Fleet in Peace
Annex V Conjectural Naval Estimates for the Years 1950/51 to 1957/58 Shown by Votes including estimates of the manpower to be borne on Vote A together with explanatory notes
Annex VI Reductions under Consideration at the Admiralty

[1] Annexes I–V are attached to Board Memorandum B.590, reproduced as Doc. No. 168.

171. *Board Memorandum*

[ADM 167/133] 14 June 1949

B.595 Manning Difficulties

On 13 April, Second Sea Lord circulated to all members of the Board a memorandum (copy attached) on the difficulties with which he was faced in manning the present fleet and associated naval commitments, due primarily to

(a) unwillingness of men to accept higher rating (both substantive and non-substantive).

(b) reluctance of ratings to re-engage to complete time for pension.

The First Lord agreed to the establishment of a working party to examine the causes of these difficulties and to make recommendations to overcome them …

Second Sea Lord is anxious that all members of the Board should be fully apprised of the seriousness of the situation and First Lord has accordingly agreed to the matter being tabled for discussion at the Board Meeting.

For some time, it has been evident that we were about to face a period of great manning difficulty, owing to a shortage of experienced and qualified men in most, if not all, branches of the Navy.

2. Ever since the war the number of men re-engaging to complete time for pension has fallen far below the figures we want for a balanced Fleet, so that the qualification and experience of those promoted to Petty Officer will drop until, there being a minimum below which we cannot go, the supply of available material will run dry.

3. We had hoped that this was a temporary phenomenon, and that with the passing of the inevitable postwar weariness the re-engagement figures would improve. Our hopes have not been realised; and the re-engagement figures have shown a noticeable decline since last summer. It is now clear that, unless we take some immediate and drastic steps to arrest and reverse the process, we shall be faced within the next two years not with manning difficulties but with a first-class breakdown.

4. Various suggestions have been made during the past few months for creating inducements to men to remain in the Service. Commonly these have arisen sectionally, as one branch after another has begun to feel the draught; but some are of more general application. One of the latter is now before the Board, in a proposal to pay a cash bonus to men who re-engage. In spite of the difficulties of carrying out this idea, I am most anxious that it should be considered for immediate adoption …

5. I know that this proposal, and indeed any which improves prospects and offers incentives to senior men, must cost money for which we have

not budgeted, and that the Treasury have firmly set their face against any supplementary estimates during the current year. I do not think this fact should deter us from making such proposals as we think to be necessary. It is not merely our right but our duty to tell the Government, if such appears to us to be the position, that for want of some extra money much of that already voted will be ineffective; or, at the worst, that their choice lies between a supplementary estimate plus a Navy, or neither.

6. The problem is one that affects the whole Navy, and should be regarded as a general one. That we should be driven to take action sectionally, stopping each worst gap in turn, cannot be right or economical or in the long run effective. At the same time, it is our business to assure ourselves that any remedies which we propose cost no more and last no longer than necessary to put the position right. We should, I suggest, take such measures as are immediately necessary to enable the Fleet to carry on over the next two or three years and, simultaneously, [examine] the problem of the unpopularity of the Service with men of the middle age groups … I therefore propose:–

(a) That the scheme for a re-engagement bonus now before you should be approved for consultation with the other Services and the Treasury, to meet temporary need.

(b) That a working party should be set up at once to:–

  (i) look into the causes for the present unwillingness of men to re-engage and qualify for positions of higher rank and responsibility.

  (ii) propose such permanent changes in the remuneration and conditions of the Lower Deck as will provide adequate incentives for men to remain and progress in the Navy and make it their career.

172. *Board Memorandum*

[ADM 167/133] 29 July 1949

B.602 MANPOWER POLICY IN 1949/50 AND THE RESTRICTED FLEET[1]

I should like to draw your attention to the manpower position which will arise in the course of this financial year unless immediate steps are taken to adjust it.

[1] Actually, the Revised Restricted Fleet. This memorandum, by the Deputy Chief of Naval Personnel, was distributed to the Board on 19 Aug.

2. In conformity with the White Paper on Defence, the Navy Estimates for 1949/50 provided for a manpower ceiling strength of approximately 145,000 at the beginning of the financial year …
3. A recent appreciation has shown that on present trends the strength at the end of this financial year may exceed the manpower ceiling quoted above. I am therefore taking measures to ensure that the strength at the end of the financial year does not exceed 145,000 on the manpower ceiling basis …
4. These measures will of course be virtually useless as steps towards implementing the 'Restricted Fleet' plan. It will be recalled that in the Board Memorandum B.590, which was considered by the Board on the 26 and 30 May 1949, a run down to a Vote A strength of approximately 135,200 by 31 March 1950 was contemplated. This was to be achieved by a cessation of national service entries and a substantial curtailment of regular recruiting from the 1 July last. However, since no decision has yet been given on the 'Restricted Fleet', both national service entries and regular recruiting are continuing on the former basis. Moreover, neither a cessation of the national service entry nor a drop in regular entries can be implemented at once, and even an immediate decision would probably not be effective until about 1 October 1949. If, therefore, the steps previously contemplated are decided on forthwith, the delay will have produced at 31 March 1950 a Vote A strength some 5,000 higher than the 'Restricted Fleet' figure of 135,200. In my view it would be impracticable at this stage to attempt to reach the letter strength by the end of this financial year. For instance, if it were to be attempted by a further cut in entries, it would entail a virtual cessation of regular recruiting from which it would be difficult for the service to recover. The only other – and almost as unacceptable – alternative would be to release prematurely substantial numbers of national service men …
5. Furthermore, I wish to emphasise strongly that any action to reduce manpower at 31 March 1950 below the strengths formerly contemplated ie about 145,000 on the manpower ceiling basis, is only acceptable provided that services are cut at the same time … This fall in strength of trained manpower will call for continued reductions in naval commitments … I conclude that action to cut services must begin almost simultaneously with that on entries.
6. It is also important to point out that practically all the cuts in services which are involved in the 'Restricted Fleet' will have to be complete by April 1951 since the run-down of manpower will entail a very substantial drop in strength, especially in the national service portion of the Navy during 1950/51. I have considered the possibility of maintaining a higher effective strength during 1950/51 than has hitherto been discussed, and

of accepting a correspondingly steeper fell in 1951/52 end 1952/53, but this turns out on examination to be impracticable. To attempt it through a higher entry of regulars would cause the regular component in 1950/51 to grow beyond its present size end thus to exceed that which will ultimately be required in a Vote A of about 124,000 – with obviously unacceptable results. It could therefore only be realised by continuing a substantial entry of national service men. This measure would, however, in no way assist in manning foreign commitments and would accentuate the acute shortage of petty officers and other experienced ratings, on the supply of which the successful meeting of manning commitments essentially depends.

7. If it can now be regarded as certain that the ultimate Vote A from, say, 1953 onwards will be in the neighbourhood of 124,000, or that the money available under Vote 1 is to be substantially less in 1950/51 than this year, early action to diminish national service and regular entries is essential – even though it is now no longer practicable to reduce strength by 31 March next to the full extent formerly envisaged. With regard to the national service entry, Board Memo B.590 contemplated that this should cease immediately. Such a measure may, however, be politically impossible at present … I therefore conclude that for the present it would be inadvisable to reduce the national service intake into the Navy below 2,000 a year.

8. As regards regular recruiting, Board Memo B.590 envisaged … that the strength of regular RN ratings would be held level throughout the whole period of the run-down, the ultimate requirement being almost identical with the strength expected at 31 March 1950. The maintenance of this level bearing would however require an entry fluctuating between some 10,000 and 12,000 a year, compared with the present intake of about 17,500 regular ratings. On further consideration, I suggest that it would be advantageous to maintain a fixed rate of entry throughout the period and to accept the ensuing minor fluctuations in bearings. The fluctuation in the bearing of regulars could, as it happens, be counterbalanced by a continued national service entry at the rate of 2,000 per year for the next two years or so …

12. To summarise, I consider that the Board should urgently consider the following points:–

(i) whether fleet services should be reduced, starting in the immediate future, to permit of a reduced Vote A strength at 1 April 1950.

(ii) if so, whether the Vote A to be aimed at on that date should be 141,000 (to be achieved on the lines discussed in paras 6 and 7 above), or a higher figure intermediate between that and the present planned strength of about 150,000. Any figure lower than 141,000 is undesirable and anything below 140,000 impracticable.

(iii) if such a reduced figure is to be accepted

(a) whether an approach should be made to the Minister of Defence, and presumably the Cabinet, with a view to a drastic reduction in the numbers of national service men accepted for the Navy and

(b) whether action should be taken to reduce regular recruiting from 1 October 1949.

…

173. *Joint Planning Staff Memorandum*

[DEFE 6/9] 29 July 1949

JP(49)63(S)(Final) FORCES REQUIRED TO IMPLEMENT ALLIED STRATEGY – 1957

The broad outline of the probable Allied strategy in 1957 is contained in the paper "Overall Strategic Concept for War in 1957"[1] …

APPENDIX A

NAVAL FORCES REQUIRED

The estimate of forces given below is that which we consider would enable the Allies to control sea communications in the face of the probable threat. We have not been tied by the present plans for naval forces in 1957.

ATTACK AT SOURCE – WORLDWIDE

Task Force 'A'

Heavy Carrier Task Force. The primary role of [this] will be strategic bombing.[2] It may, however … be diverted to operate in support of the control of sea communications in the role of Attack at Source. Units composing the Task Force are therefore listed below as being required for the control of sea communications. The force will operate in the Arctic, Indian Ocean or Sea of Japan as required.

Task Force 'A' should be of the following order:–

(i) Operational

2 Heavy Carriers – 10 aircraft each – 20 aircraft.
6 Fleet Carriers – 60 aircraft each … (fighter and A/S defence …)
2 Heavy Cruisers or Battleships }
12 Cruisers (including FADEs) } 1 Heavy or 2 Light Cruisers for each carrier as A/A protection.
32 Destroyers (complete screen for forces operated as one unit).

[1] JP(48)59, not reproduced.

[2] In Nov 1949 the Chiefs of Staff decided that all further study into the use of aircraft carriers for the strategic air offensive should be suspended. COS(49) 164th Meeting, 4 Nov 1949, DEFE 4/26.

(ii) Reserve or Refitting

1 Heavy Carrier (50%)
2 Fleet Carriers (33.3%)
95 Naval aircraft (Disembarked air groups from operational carriers) (25%)
3 Cruisers (25%)
8 Destroyers (25%)

ATLANTIC AND HOME WATERS

(a) Attack at Source

(i) Task Force 'B' (might be used in support of the Mediterranean Carrier Task Force if req'd).

8 Fleet Carriers – 60 aircraft each … Offensive ops, fighter & A/S protection).
2 Heavy Cruisers or Battleships } 1 Heavy or 3 Light Cruisers for each carrier
12 Cruisers (including FADEs) } as A/A protection.
32 Destroyers (complete screen for forces operated as one unit).

(b) Offensive Contro

(i) Patrol Groups 'A', 'B', 'C' and 'D' (Atlantic)

8 Light Fleet Carriers – 30 aircraft each – 240 aircraft.
48 Frigates A/S (6 for each carrier).

(ii) Patrol Groups 'E' and 'F' (Channel)

24 Frigates A/S and A/D

(iii) Other Forces Required

4 Cruisers (for Ocean patrols)
4 Fast Minelayers
50 Submarines (for minelaying and A/S operations allowing 2/3 operational)
192 MGBs (1 flotilla of 12 at each of 16 bases on East and South coasts of UK).

(c) Defensive Control

(i) Escort Forces

Close Escort of Atlantic Convoys:
10 Escort Carriers – 20 aircraft each … (1 with each convoy east of 30°W).
224 Frigates A/S
34 Frigates A/A
Close Escort of UK Coastal Convoys: 56 Frigates A/S, 28 Frigates A/A
Close Escort of US Coastal Convoys: 85 Frigates A/S
Close Escort of Continental Convoys: 16 Frigates A/S, 8 Frigates A/A and A/D

(ii) Minesweepers

Home Waters and Iceland: 88 Ocean, 416 Coastal
UK Continental Waters: 16 Ocean, 12 Coastal
West African Ports: 64 Coastal
USA Eastern Seaboard: 96 Coastal

(iii) Minelayers (anti-submarine)

5 Coastal Minelayers

(d) Reserve and Refitting

2 Fleet Carriers (25%)
2 Light Fleet Carriers (25%)
2 Escort Carriers (20%)
230 Naval aircraft (Disembarked air groups from operational carriers) (25%)
4 Cruisers (25%)
8 Destroyers (25%)
1 Fast Minelayer (20%)
47 Frigates A/S (10%)
7 Frigates A/A (10%)

20 Submarines (40%)
48 MGBs (25%)
1 Coastal Minelayer (20%)

MIDDLE EAST

(a) Attack at Source

(i) Task Force 'C' (may be supported by Task Force 'B').

8 Fleet Carriers – 60 aircraft each – 480 aircraft. Offensive ops, fighter & A/S protection).
2 Heavy Cruisers or Battleships } 1 Heavy or 3 Light Cruisers for each carrier
12 Cruisers (including FADEs) } as A/A protection.
32 Destroyers (complete screen for forces operated as one unit).

(b) Offensive Control

(i) Patrol Groups 'G' and 'H'

24 Frigates A/S and A/D.

(ii) Other Forces Required

2 Cruisers (for Ocean patrol in Indian Ocean)
2 Fast Minelayers
40 Submarines (for minelaying and A/S operations allowing 2/3 operational)
48 MGBs (1 flotilla of 12 at each of 16 bases on East and South coasts of UK).

(c) Defensive Control

(i) Escort Forces

Close Escort of Mediterranean Convoys:	69 Frigates A/S, 46 Frigates A/A
Close Escort of Italian Sections:	6 Frigates A/S, 4 Frigates A/A
Close Escort of Red Sea – Persian Gulf Convoys	40 Frigates A/A

(ii) Minesweepers

Mediterranean and Levant	40 Ocean, 256 Coastal
Persian Gulf and Red Sea	72 Ocean, 216 Coastal

(d) Reserve and Refitting

2 Fleet Carriers (25%)
120 Naval aircraft (Disembarked air groups from operational carriers) (25%)
2 Cruisers (15%)
8 Destroyers (25%)
1 Minelayer (50%)
10 Frigates A/S (10%)
9 Frigates A/A (10%)
16 Submarines (40%)
12 MGBs (25%)

PACIFIC AND FAR EAST

(a) Attack at Source

(i) Task Force 'D'

8 Fleet Carriers – 60 aircraft each … Offensive ops, fighter & A/S protection).
2 Heavy Cruisers or Battleships } 1 Heavy or 3 Light Cruisers for each carrier
12 Cruisers (including FADEs) } as A/A protection.
48 Destroyers (complete screen for forces operated as one unit plus additional 16 in view of number of Russian destroyers deployed in this area).

(b) Offensive Control

(ii) Patrol Groups 'E' and 'F'

4 Light Fleet Carriers – 30 aircraft each – 120 aircraft
24 Frigates A/S (6 for each carrier)

(iii) Other Forces Required

2 Cruisers (for Ocean patrols)
50 Submarines

(c) Defensive Control

(i) Escort Forces

Close Escort of Pacific Convoys:	133 Frigates A/S
Close Escort of Far East Troop Convoys:	20 Frigates A/S

(ii) Minesweepers

Japan and Formosa	16 Ocean, 72 Coastal
South East Asia, Australia and New Zealand	48 Ocean, 146 Coastal

(d) Reserve and Refitting

2 Fleet Carriers (25%)
1 Light Fleet Carrier (25%)
150 Naval aircraft (Disembarked air groups from operational carriers) (25%)
2 Cruisers (15%)
16 Destroyers (33%)
18 Frigates A/S (10%)
20 Submarines (40%)

SUMMARY OF ALL MAIN NAVAL FORCES REQUIRED FOR THE CONTROL OF SEA COMMUNICATIONS

	Heavy Carriers	Fleet Carriers	Small Carriers	Escort Carriers	Naval Aircraft	Heavy Cruisers or Battleships	Light Cruisers	Destroyers	Fast Minelayers	Frigates A/S	Frigates A/A	Submarines	MGBs	Ocean Minesweepers	Coastal Minesweepers	Coastal Minelayers
ATTACK AT SOURCE																
World-wide	2	6	–	–	380	2	12	32	–	–	–	–	–	–	–	–
Atlantic	–	8	–	–	480	2	12	32	–	–	–	–	–	–	–	–
Middle East	–	8	–	–	480	2	12	32	–	–	–	–	–	–	–	–
Pacific/Far East	–	8	–	–	480	2	12	48	–	–	–	–	–	–	–	–
OFFENSIVE CONTROL																
Atlantic	–	–	8	–	240	–	4	–	4	72	–	50	192	–	–	–
Middle East	–	–	–	–	–	–	2	–	2	24	–	40	48	–	–	–
Pacific/Far East	–	–	4	–	120	–	2	–	–	24	–	50	–	–	–	–
DEFENSIVE CONTROL																
Atlantic	–	–	–	10	200	–	–	–	–	397	74	–	–	104	588	5
Middle East	–	–	–	–	–	–	–	–	–	75	90	–	–	112	472	–
Pacific/Far East	–	–	–	–	–	–	–	–	–	153	–	–	–	64	218	–
RESERVE																
Heavy Carrier TF	1	2	–	–	95	–	3	8	–	–	–	–	–	–	–	–
Atlantic	–	2	2	2	230	–	4	8	1	47	7	20	48	–	–	1
Middle East	–	2	–	–	120	–	2	8	1	10	9	16	12	–	–	–
Pacific/Far East	–	2	1	1	150	–	2	16	–	18	–	20	–	–	–	–
TOTALS	3	38	15	12	2975	8	67	184	8	820	180	196	300	280	1278	6

174. *First Sea Lord to Air Marshal Sir William Elliot*[1]

[DEFE 7/610] 6 September 1949

Naval Estimates

… I do not think it can be entirely appreciated that … we have already reached bedrock strength to carry out our peacetime tasks and war requirements.

2. A brief resume will show you the situation:–

(i) We have put all our battleships in a low reserve category, except the 'Vanguard' which we are using for training so that an expensive shore establishment can be closed down in lieu.

(ii) Cruisers … we are proposing to scrap 9 leaving us with 18 – the very minimum to maintain 12 or 13 in commission for peacetime duties and I think the smallest number acceptable for war; the Russians we know are building modern ones. We are building none at present and our cruisers in service are getting worn out.

(iii) Destroyers. We have 8 new ones completing – no more building – and these are only a small replacement for the over age ships.

(iv) Carriers. We have 2 Fleet Carriers nearing completion and 4 Light Fleet Carriers reaching that stage. When complete, obsolete carriers will be scrapped. I know that CAS would like us to give up Naval Aviation but I can see no other method of providing fighter cover for the Fleet or ships at a distance from bases, or for the A/S war …

(v) Any other new construction that we are proposing to put in hand is all connected with anti-submarine or mining warfare.

(vi) Modifications to ships mostly consist in enabling their guns to compete as far as possible with modern aircraft.

(vii) We are reducing our personnel by one-seventh, from 145,000 to 124,000.

(viii) Even if we continue at £203 million, the Fleet will gradually reduce as ships get older until in 1963 we will have only half what we have got now.

3. In these circumstances there is no doubt that the Navy is taking great risks which are only justified by the fact that we are relying upon a 50 per cent contribution from the Americans.

…

8. In fact there is nothing further we can do to reduce Naval Estimates unless we cut down on anti-submarine, anti-air, or minesweeping. I hope this makes the position clear.

[1]Chief Staff Officer to the Minister of Defence.

175. *Report by Inter-Departmental Committee on Defence Estimate*

[CAB 131/7] 19 September 1949

DE/P(49)17

The Committee was set up to prepare for the consideration of Ministers a coordinated Defence Budget for three years from April 1950 to March 1953. Our terms of reference placed a limit of £810 million annually on defence expenditure over this three-year period and laid down that the uniformed manpower strength of the Forces should be reduced to 700,000 by 31 March 1951, and to 650,000 by 1952–53.

2. In submitting its preliminary report on 15 August, the Committee drew attention to the fact that, after all possible savings had been made, departmental estimates of the minimum expenditure necessary to provide for present planned forces so far exceeded £810 million annually, particularly towards the end of the three-year period, that no agreed allocation of money among departments could then be put forward. Further progress depended upon strategic guidance from the Chiefs of Staff, which would indicate in which Services and in what proportions cuts should be made and risks taken …

3. Subsequent discussions by the Chiefs of Staff and in the Committee have resulted in agreement as to where the necessary reductions can best be made so far as expenditure by the Service Departments themselves is concerned. The resultant allocation of resources would give an average annual defence budget of £810 million over the next three years provided that it proves possible to ensure that there is no more than a moderate rise in the defence element of Ministry of Supply expenditure … On this assumption the allocation of money to departments, together with the uniformed manpower strength … over the next three years, would be:–

(a) Money (£ million)

	1949–50	1950–51	1951–52	1952–53	*Totals*
Royal Navy	(189.25)	201	201	201	603

(b) Manpower

	1 April 1949	1 April 1950	1 April 1951	1 April 1952	1 April 1953
Royal Navy	(145,000)	140,000	127,500	124,800	123,000

The National Service intakes estimated to be necessary on the basis of these manpower figures are:–

	1950–51	1951–52	1952–53
Royal Navy	2,000	1,000	Nil

…

4. It has been necessary, in order not to exceed the annual total of £810 million, to keep expenditure on equipment well below a level which would ensure our ability to expand production quickly in an emergency …
5. The acceptance of the above allocations of money and men involves serious risks in regard to the adequacy of the Forces and in the field of research and development. Details of the proposed Forces during the next three years, of the commitments which they will be able to undertake and of the risks which will have to be accepted are given in a parallel report by the Chiefs of Staff Committee.
6. It should be noted that the recent reduction in the exchange value of sterling against the dollar will result in considerable increases in Service Department expenditure …

176. *Chiefs of Staff Committee Memorandum*

[CAB 131/7] 27 September 1949

COS(49)313(Final) THE SIZE AND SHAPE OF THE ARMED FORCES OVER THE NEXT THREE YEARS[1]

We have considered, as instructed by the Minister of Defence, the question of the security of this country in relation to an annual allocation of funds for Defence purposes amounting to an average of £810 million over the next three years. We have first considered the nature of the threat which we must be ready to meet.
2. We have two enemies – Communism and Russia. We are already at war with Soviet Communism, but not yet with Russia. If Communism wins the Cold War which it is now waging, the Western powers will have been defeated without Russia having to resort to force at all. If the Western powers win the Cold War, Russia may start a shooting war in desperation or, quite possibly, find us so strong that she dare not attack. Our first political and strategic object, therefore, is to win the Cold War; our second is to make ourselves as strong as possible to meet the possibility of a shooting war with Russia.

The Cold War

3. All three services must play their part in the Cold War by:–
   (a) Holding our present possessions and influence against attacks, internal or external, which fall short of Major War.
   (b) Encouraging other nations to resist Communism …

…

[1] Issued to the Defence Committee as an enclosure to DO(49)65.

5. Fortunately, neither in the Navy nor in the Royal Air Force is there, to the same extent [as in the Army] this direct conflict between the needs of the Cold War and a Major War. Where conflict does occur in these Services, we consider that the requirements for a Major War should take precedence.
6. For the Cold War, the highest scale of equipment is not so vitally necessary as for a Major War. It follows that the Army will incline more to trained manpower at the expense of equipment, while the other two Services will have, to some extent, to sacrifice manpower to equipment.

A Major War

7. In war, our strategy has three main pillars – the United Kingdom, our sea communications and our position in the Middle East. The Defence services should therefore he organised in peace to cover the requirements of the Cold War and, in co-operation with our allies in war, to secure these three pillars.
8. The Russians, besides subsidiary offensives elsewhere, are likely to direct their main efforts to:–
   (a) A land and air offensive into Western Europe.
   (b) An air attack on the United Kingdom.
   (c) An extensive mining campaign against our ports and harbour approaches.
   (d) A combined submarine and air attack on our sea communications.
   (e) A land and air offensive in the Middle East.
9. The odds against the Western Powers and the risk of defeat are greatest on land and least at sea, but the risks of defeat to this country are most immediate in the air, less sudden on sea and longest delayed on land. If our air strength was inadequate, we could lose the air war in a very short time and, having lost it, no other operation on sea or land in our defence could succeed. If we avoid defeat in the air, but are unable to maintain our sea communications, we should be denied vital supplies which could lead to our defeat in a few months. If, however, we avoid defeat in the air war and preserve our vital sea communications, the loss of Western Europe and the Middle East would not necessarily be decisive. These factors must be taken into account when considering our preparations for a major war.

Priorities

10. On this basis, we can place our requirements functionally in the following order of urgency:–
   (a) Success in the Cold War.
   (b) The defence of the United Kingdom against air attack.

(c) The security of sea communications vital to the United Kingdom and of the approaches to our ports and harbours against mining attack.
(d) The retention of the Middle East.
(e) The provision of forces for Western Europe.
(f) The general build-up for an ultimate offensive.

Air Defence of Great Britain

11. … *must be our first priority in preparation for war.*

Security of Sea Communications

12. … The forces required to combat the threat of the submarine, the mine and the aeroplane against sea communications should have equal preference. Full advantage should be taken of American Naval and Air assistance in dealing with the submarine and air attack on the high seas …

Effect of these Proposals

18. This allocation of money[1] will enable the Services to maintain the forces and to carry out the tasks shown in the Appendices to this paper …

Conclusion

21. Any substantial reduction in the suggested annual allocation of £810 million can only result in unacceptable defence risks, or in our inability to meet some of our present commitments with the political consequences that this would entail. There are no appreciable savings to be made by marginal economies.

22. We are unanimously agreed that:–

(a) The plan evolved is the best that can be made on the basis of the financial restrictions imposed and represents a great advance on the proposals contained in the Harwood Report.
(b) The sum of £810 million a year for the next three years is, in our opinion, not sufficient to ensure the security of this country either against surprise attack or if American aid were to be delayed or limited.

…

(f) Readiness for war in the long term will depend on increased budgets in future years.

[1]Not reproduced here – stated above in DE/P(49)17 as Doc. No. 175.

APPENDIX I – NAVY
STRENGTH OF THE ROYAL NAVY ON ANNUAL NAVY ESTIMATES OF £201 MILLION FOR 1950–51 TO 1952–53

Manpower

It is intended to reduce the man-power bearing (Vote A) to 124,000 by 1953, the run-down to this figure being as follows:–

1 April 1950	141,100
1 April 1951	128,300
1 April 1952	124,800
1 April 1953	124,000

2. These numbers will enable approximately the same number of ships as at present to remain in commission, permit the necessary sea training to be carried out, and provide the nucleus on which to expand in the event of war.

3. The National Service intake into the Royal Navy is being reduced to 2,000 a year from 1 October 1949. It will remain at this level for about two years, after which it will cease altogether, except for a small number of men to be trained as pilots and observers …

Peacetime Fleet

4. On £201 million it will be possible to maintain the same Fleet in commission as at present for the next three years …

5. The Navy will therefore maintain the same support to our Foreign and Colonial Policy as now, continue to play its present part in the Cold War and carry out training as a preparation for war.

6. The peace-time disposition of the Fleet at the present time is given in Table I.

Wartime Fleet

7. In the following table is set out the strength of the Fleet in 1950, giving ships in commission and in reserve. In the column headed 1957 is given the minimum war Fleet that the Admiralty consider essential for the control of sea communications, it is based on the United States Navy providing half the Naval Forces required in the North Atlantic and Mediterranean/Middle East area, which is the most they can promise:–

Type	*1950*			*1957*
	In Commission	*In Reserve*	*Total*	
Battleships	1	4*	1 + 4*	1 + 4*
Fleet Carriers	3	3	6	5 + 1⁺
Light Fleet Carriers	4	2	6	4
Aircraft Repair Ships	1	0	1	1
Cruisers	15	12	27	18
Fast Minelayers	0	3	3	3

Destroyers	39	15	54	62
Frigates	60	165	225	182
Submarines	33	30	63	53
Ocean Minesweepers	15	46	61	61
Coastal or Inshore M/S	10	72	82	250
Mine-location Craft	0	0	0	36
Front-Line Aircraft	150		150	250

* Not to be modernised until guided weapons are in supply.

[+] Modernised for deck landing training only.

8. Comparing the strength of the Fleet in 1950 with that required for war in 1957, it will be seen that in some types there is a shortage of ships while in others there is an excess; the latter the Admiralty proposes to dispose of. To make good the shortages new construction is required and the proposed programme for the next three years is given in paragraph 11. It will, however, be necessary to increase greatly the building programme after 1952–53 if the shortages are to be made good and over-age ships replaced by 1957.

9. Although the numerical strength of the wartime Fleet for the next three years is not below the Admiralty's minimum figure, except for shortages referred to above, an average sum of £201 million during this period has a serious effect in later years, as many of our ships are obsolescent and their re-equipment will be deferred. Also, the speed at which the Fleet can be mobilised will be slow owing to lack of stockpile of stores and equipment for mobilisation.

10. After 1957 the rate at which ships become obsolete is such that there will be a steady decline of numerical strength of the Navy from then onwards. This remains true even if the rate of new construction from 1952–53 onwards, referred to in paragraph 8 above, were continued.

New Construction

11. Below is set out the new construction which the Admiralty proposes to put in hand during the next three years; two Fleet Carriers, four Light Fleet Carriers and eight Destroyers, at present under construction, are not shown in the table.

NEW CONSTRUCTION

	1950–51	*1951–52*	*1952–53*	*Total*
Frigates	3	0	3	5
Submarines	0	2	0	2
Coastal Minesweepers	5	11	8	24
Inshore Minesweepers	5	8	8	21
Mine Location Craft	6	0	8	14
Coastal Forces MTB/MGB	1	4	4	9
Seaward Defence A/S Craft	2	0	4	6

12. The above new construction programme is larger than that proposed in the Harwood Report but smaller than that which the Admiralty hold to be the minimum necessary …

Modernisation and Conversion of Ships

13. As many of our ships are rapidly becoming obsolescent … it is necessary to re-equip and modernise them if they are to carry out their tasks; the conversion of a number of our older Fleet Destroyers to fast A/S frigate is required in order to control the fast submarine.

14. The Admiralty propose to put in hand the following modernisation and conversions during the next three years:–

Modernisation of Fleet Carriers	1
Modernisation of Cruisers	1
Modernisation of Destroyers	12
Modernisation of Frigates	9
Convert old Fleet Destroyers to A/S Frigates	10
Convert 'T' Class Submarines to fast battery drive	2

15. The rate of conversion and modernisation is much slower than that which the Admiralty hold to be the minimum necessary; the above programme does make a start in re-equipping the Fleet to meet submarine and air attack, but it only modernises about one-eighth of the force.

Naval Aviation

16. A front-line strength of 250 aircraft is considered to be the minimum which will enable Naval Aviation to carry out its prescribed roles in wartime. It was planned to reach this strength through gradual expansion by 1957.

17. The reduction of the Naval Vote to £201 million will, however, entail holding the front line at its existing level of 150 aircraft during the next three years with a reduced reserve backing.

18. During the next three years it is planned that a few squadrons of more modern aircraft will replace some of the existing types now in service; this can be provided for to a limited extent within the £201 million estimates.

War Reserves of Stores

19. The Admiralty have planned to allocate some £6.2 million for stock-piling of war reserves of stores for the next three years; this figure has been cut by a third …

Administrative Economies

20. The Admiralty have already proposed the most drastic economies in administrative and shore establishments. It is the intention to press on firmly with these measures, but it is clear that, due to the variety of the interests involved, there will be difficulty in achieving the financial savings planned as early as expected.

TABLE I

THE PRESENT PEACETIME FLEET

Station	*Class of Ship*	*Number*
Home	Fleet Carrier	1
	Light Fleet Carriers	2
	Cruisers	3
	Destroyers	16
Mediterranean	Light Fleet Carriers	1
	Cruisers	4
	Destroyers	11
	Frigates	7
	Submarines	8
	Ocean, Coastal and Inshore Minesweepers	9
East Indies	Cruisers	2
	Frigates	5
America and West Indies	Cruisers	1
	Frigates	3
South Atlantic	Cruisers	1
	Frigates	2
Far East	Light Fleet Carrier	1
	Aircraft Repair Ship	1
	Cruisers	3
	Destroyers	7
	Frigates	10
Trials and Training	Battleships	1
	Fleet Carriers	2
	Cruisers	1
	Destroyers	5
	Frigates	33
	Submarines	25
	Ocean, Coastal and Inshore Minesweepers	11
Summary	Battleships	1
	Fleet Carriers	3
	Light Fleet Carriers	4
	Aircraft Repair Ship	1
	Cruisers	15
	Destroyers	39
	Frigates	60
	Submarines	33
	Ocean, Coastal and Inshore Minesweepers	20

177. *Defence Committee Memorandum*

[CAB 131/7] 18 October 1949

DO(49)66 THE REQUIREMENTS OF NATIONAL DEFENCE:– SIZE AND SHAPE OF THE ARMED FORCES 1950 – 1953

Memorandum by the Minister of Defence

Introductory

My colleagues will be aware that, ever since the institution of the Ministry of Defence in January 1947, an unremitting effort has been made with the advice of the Chiefs of Staff to elaborate for the approval of Ministers a comprehensive long-term plan for the three Services to which current expenditure could be related. I now present to my colleagues a tri-Service scheme covering the three years 1950–51, 1951–52 and 1952–53 – the full details of which will be found in the Reports circulated as DO(49)65 … Expenditure on the scale of £810m per annum in our present financial state may seem a lot of money to spend on defence and I must therefore at the outset explain some of the main reasons which lead me to propose such a sum, not merely as reasonable, but as the inescapable minimum consistent with the maintenance of our world position.

Basic Considerations – the Objective

2. Armed Forces are not an end in themselves. They represent the power, actual and potential, which a nation thinks it prudent and necessary to maintain to support its policies …

3. From the desire to achieve these ends derives the level and structure of the Armed Forces which have had to be maintained. I remind the Committee of how the Services have had over the past four years to conform to the shifts and changes of policy as it has developed … The pressure on each of the three Services created by these unstable conditions … made it virtually impossible to reach any co-ordinated long-term plan for all three Services …

History of Recent Discussions

5. For the year 1948–49 my colleagues will recall that the Defence Budget was fixed in the Spring of 1948 at £693m, including £60m of terminal expenditure. We decided, when the Berlin situation became acute, to institute a modest re-equipment programme and to retain additional men with the Colours. The effect of those decisions matured in 1949–50 when a Budget of £760m including about £14m terminals was agreed. This will now be exceeded due to the special measures in connection with Hong Kong and the additional Western Union production programme. It was in the course of the discussions last autumn that the Chancellor of the Exchequer pressed me strongly to have prepared a long-term defence plan

designed to keep our annual financial provision under this head down to £700m. To enable this to be done and with my approval the Chiefs of Staff set up an inter-Service Committee with a civilian chairman to draw up a plan showing what forces should and could be maintained on this figure over the three years 1950–53. This body was the Harwood Committee whose report was submitted to the Chiefs of Staff in March last. In June, after careful examination, the Chiefs of Staff reported that they agreed generally with the Committee's line of approach to the problem remitted to them and that it would be impossible on £700m to maintain larger forces than the Committee proposed. Indeed, subsequent Departmental scrutiny had already revealed that the Harwood proposals would in fact cost over £750m. The Chiefs of Staff took the view that the implications of the proposals were so grave and involved the taking of such risks and the abandonment of so many hitherto unchallenged commitments that they had no alternative but to seek Ministerial guidance as to which of the risks could be accepted politically.

6. The following is a brief statement of the consequences which would have resulted from acceptance of the Harwood proposals:-[1]

...

(d) a visible reduction of striking forces of all arms at the very time when the Atlantic Pact Organisation is being developed and the United States are preparing to contribute heavily in money and equipment for the strengthening of the democratic powers;

(e) ... reliance on the United States Navy for the control of sea communications in the Mediterranean – a policy which subsequent developments have shown to be based on false assumptions as to American strategic conceptions ...

(g) withdrawal of all United Kingdom forces in peace from the West Indies, South America, South Africa and the Indian Ocean;

(h) a proposal to hand over to Australia and New Zealand responsibility for Naval forces in South-East Asia and the Indian Ocean – a responsibility which they were in no position to accept and which would certainly have led to serious political difficulties;

(j) ... a reduction of Naval forces overseas on which we have always relied for the rapid reinforcement of threatened points; and

(k) at Home, the abandonment of defence installations, including dockyards at Portland, Sheerness and possibly Chatham and the disbandment of ... the Royal Marines.

[1]Elements not relating to the Navy have been omitted.

7. … no acceptable plan could be devised on the basis of a money allocation of £700m … The defence budget approved for 1949–50 is £760m to which must be added commitments which we have incurred under the Western Union arrangements and obligations which we have already assumed in regard to the defence of Hong Kong. Moreover, the findings of the Harwood Committee and the investigations which followed it made it very plain that, at the present level of expenditure, we are failing to make even the minimum provision for re-equipment necessary to avoid a progressive decline in the fighting quality of our forces. Considering the problem as a whole I felt it to be unrealistic to suppose that any acceptable solution could be sought on a level of less than £800m. In those circumstance I considered it necessary to initiate a fresh study on different assumptions, the main features of which were:–

(i) A limit on the annual estimates of £800m plus a margin of £10m for contingencies;
(ii) A higher priority to the requirements of the Cold War, even if this involved spreading our re-equipment programme over a somewhat longer period than up to 1957; and
(iii) Service manpower to be reduced to 700,000 by 31/3/51 and to 650,000 by 31/3/53 …

<u>Conclusion</u>

17. The proposals now before the Committee in the Reports of the Working Party and of the Chiefs of Staff represent the culmination of many months of intensive work. They are the outcome of a thorough-going attempt to evolve a balanced three Service plan and represent an integrated defence scheme which will take us over the next three years. The forces we shall have, if the plan is approved, are not as large as those which the Chiefs of Staff consider necessary on purely military grounds, but equally they are not so small as to lead to the frustration, if not abandonment, of some of the major objectives of our foreign policy such as would have been entailed by the Harwood proposals. Risks – considerable risks – will still have to be taken …

18. … the essence of the matter is this. Only by avoiding war can we hope to realise our economic strength; if war should come, we shall surely lose all that we have planned and struggled for in the last few years. To avoid war our best hope lies in the provision of adequate defence services which afford clear evidence to the world of our strength, determination and resolve.

19. <u>Recommendation</u>

I accordingly invite the Committee:–

(a) to endorse the proposal that a sum of £810m (with any upward adjustment rendered necessary by the devaluation of the £) be allocated to defence in each of the three financial years 1950/51, 1951/52, 1952/53;

(b) to approve the underlying strategic conceptions on which it is based as set out by the Chiefs of Staff; and

(c) to seek the approval of the Cabinet to the proposals outlined in the two reports.

178. *Defence Committee Memorandum*

[CAB 131/8] 19 October 1949

DO(49) 19th Meeting

1. Size and Shape of the Armed Forces, 1950–53

The Committee had before them:–

A memorandum by the Minister of Defence (DO(49)66) inviting the Committee to endorse a proposal that a sum of £810 million … should be allocated to defence in each of the three financial years 1950–51, 1951–52 and 1952–53.

General

The Minister of Defence reminded the Committee that the Chancellor of the Exchequer, when he agreed to the figure of £760 million for the 1949–50 Defence Budget, had asked that an enquiry should be made into the possibility of reducing the annual cost of Defence to £700 million. In response to this request the Chiefs of Staff had set up the Harwood Committee under an independent Chairman who had made a thorough study of the subject. The Forces which they found it possible to recommend within the figure of £700 million – the cost of which was subsequently found to be nearer £750 million than £700 million – were quite inadequate to support current foreign policy. The reductions proposed would have meant extensive withdrawal of our Armed Forces from various parts of the world and would have relegated the United Kingdom to the position of a second-class Power. These proposals were in his view clearly unacceptable.

At the time, the Emergency Programme which had been launched in the autumn of 1948, the promises we had made to increase production on behalf of Western Union and the extra expenditure which flowed from the decision to prosecute the Cold War in Malaya and Hong Kong, all pointed to the need for a Budget of something like £830 million to £840 million – a figure which he well realised might be out of the question. He thought however that a solution might be found round the figure of £810 million and he had accordingly initiated a further enquiry to discover whether a satisfactory system of defence could be devised within this amount. It was the result of this enquiry which he now brought before the Committee.

He asked the Committee to note that for the first time since the war the Defence Committee had before them a properly coordinated inter-Service plan. The size of the Forces which would be found within this figure of £810 million was not by any means what the Chiefs of Staff regarded as adequate – they would, of course, be quite inadequate in the event of war – but in all the circumstances he himself felt that the adoption of the plan now put forward would place the defences of the country on a reasonably satisfactory basis. He did not see how any scheme could be devised with less money. The reduction of the Budget to the figure of £760 million for 1950–51, as proposed by the Chancellor of the Exchequer … would mean that we should be forced, as under the Harwood proposals, to abandon our overseas commitments on an extensive scale – a process which would relegate the United Kingdom to the position of a second-class Power.

The Chief of the Air Staff[1] said that the plan before the Committee was the result of nine months' careful study by the Chiefs of Staff in Committee. In the opinion of the Chiefs of Staff it represented the best that could be done on the basis of the figure of £810 million which had been laid down by the Minister of Defence and it was certainly a great advance on the proposals put forward by the Harwood Committee. As the Minister of Defence pointed out in paragraph 12 of DO(49)66, however, the adoption of the plan would involve the acceptance of serious risks which, from the military point of view, were most unpalatable. It was of course for Ministers to say whether those risks should or should not be accepted …

179. *Defence Committee Memorandum*

[CAB 131/8] 15 November 1949

DO(49) 20th Meeting
Size and Shape of the Armed Forces, 1950–53.

The Committee resumed their discussion of the Minister of Defence's Budget proposals for the years 1950–53 …

The Minister of Defence explained that some … economies had already been, or would be, carried out whether or not his Budget proposals were accepted. Others of a more far-reaching character and with serious political or other implications were awaiting the formal decision of the Defence Committee on his proposals as a whole …

[1] Lord Tedder, who was Chairman of the Chiefs of Staff Committee.

The Prime Minister asked why, if all these reductions and economies were to be made, it was still necessary for the Defence Budget to rise from £760 million in 1949–50 to £810 million in 1950–51.

The broad answer given to this question was that … the point had now been reached when stocks and reserves of almost all kinds were exhausted and it was impossible for the three Services to go on living on their 'fat' …

The Minister of Defence and *The Chiefs of Staff* pointed out that the proposals now before the Committee had been the subject of intense study for many months and the forces recommended in them were in fact the minimum with which the present responsibilities of the Services could be discharged. Unless those responsibilities were reduced, in their opinion no further review would be likely to disclose means of affecting any additional substantial economy …

The Chief of the Air Staff said that the Chiefs of Staff had now been studying the problem of the size and shape of the Armed Forces for four years and throughout this period they had scrupulously tried to avoid asking for more money or men or material than they had thought absolutely necessary, even though this meant taking grave risks …

The Chief of the Air Staff then gave the Committee a description of the responsibilities which fell on the Armed Forces. Broadly, and on a geographical basis, they fell into four main areas[1] …

180. *Defence Committee Minutes*

[CAB 131/8] 21 November 1949

DO(49) 21st Meeting

…

2. Size and Shape of the Armed Forces, 1950–53.

The Committee resumed their discussion of the Minister of Defence's Budget proposals for the years 1950–53 …

The Prime Minister suggested that discussions should in the first place be concentrated on the extent to which new production entered into the Minister of Defence's budget proposals …

The position might roughly be summarised by saying that half of the expenditure on re-equipment was in respect of the Royal Air Force, a quarter in respect of the Army and a quarter in respect of the Navy.

Expenditure on *naval construction* in 1950–51 would be confined to the provision of frigates, minesweepers, mine-location craft and certain smaller units, with a certain amount of modernisation of existing

[1] The UK, the Far East, the Middle East and Western Europe.

ships. The programme involved the scrapping of all but 18 cruisers and a reduction of the Fleet Air Arm below the level recommended by the Harwood Committee.

In discussion of the naval programme the following points were raised:–

(a) Would it not be practicable to reduce still further the number of cruisers? This country might have to leave to the United States, to a greater extent than had hitherto been contemplated, the provision of an adequate cruiser force to meet any Russian threat. In reply it was pointed out that a force of 18 cruisers meant that only 13 vessels would be in commission at any one time and this strength was required to meet possible emergencies which might arise from time to time in connection with the Cold War. In the event of war, a cruiser force of this size would be inadequate since the indications were that the Russians would have a considerable fleet of heavy cruisers by 1957.

(b) Some concern was expressed lest the Fleet Air Arm were being reduced too much, but it was pointed out in reply that the provision of aircraft carriers was very costly and it was better to make a severe cut here than to reduce still further the cruiser strength …

The Chancellor of the Exchequer said that … expenditure on defence per head was higher in this country than in other West European countries …

181. *Defence Committee Minutes*

[CAB 131/8] 25 November 1949

DO(49) 22nd Meeting
Size and Shape of the Armed Forces, 1950–53.

The Committee resumed their discussion of the Minister of Defence's Budget proposals for the years 1950–53 …

The Provision for Naval Equipment

The Prime Minister said that in the matter of equipment it was clear that first priority should be given to the Royal Air Force and to radar and the air raid warning system. Other re-equipment programmes would have to be scrutinised more closely and in particular he wondered whether the imminence of the naval threat had not been over-estimated and there was no room for some further reduction in the provision proposed for naval equipment.

The First Lord of the Admiralty said that the naval construction programme was primarily directed against the under-water menace. It would be wasteful to stop at this stage the construction of two aircraft carriers and six destroyers and it was impossible to contemplate a cruiser strength of less than the eighteen proposed. The Navy were undertaking a drastic reduction of manpower, including a reduction of 8,000 in the number of regular seamen.

In subsequent discussion, the question was raised whether it was safe to rely on United States assistance being available in the Atlantic or the Mediterranean. The general view was that it was out of the question to consider that this country could meet any Russian threat without full United States assistance …

The Minister of Defence said that the re-equipment programme would be seriously prejudiced by the Chancellor's unwillingness to undertake any provisional commitment for years later than 1950–51. So far as that year was concerned, a figure of £760 or £770 million was quite inadequate. The Chancellor had failed to give full credit to the extent to which additional expenditure was necessarily incurred because the Services had exhausted their war-time stocks and this accounted for about £20 million in the estimate of £810 million which he had put before the committee. It would also be difficult, if not impossible, for the Service Departments to meet the additional cost due to devaluation, amounting possibly to £20 million a year, without cuts which would affect the ability of the Services to fulfil their existing responsibilities … As proof of the validity of his approach to the problem, as distinct from the Chancellor's approach, he pointed out that the Harwood Committee proposals in their full form had been calculated to cost £750 million, plus the cost of devaluation, and it had been universally agreed that it was not practicable to accept the drastic reduction of commitments (including the abandonment of Singapore) which would have been involved in the acceptance of the Harwood Committee's scheme …

The Prime Minister said that, in his view, the case had been made for some increase in defence expenditure over £760 million …

The Committee:–

agreed that the provision for defence in the 1950–51 Estimates should amount to £780 million, on the understanding that if this amount was shown to be insufficient to meet the expenditure on essential equipment which the Defence Committee might hereafter agree to be necessary for the Services, the necessary balance should be made by way of supplementary estimates …

182. *Note by Director of Plans*

[ADM 1/21305] [undated: 1949]

Proposed UK Naval Shipbuilding on the Outbreak of War

In order to ascertain the naval shipbuilding programme required on the outbreak of war in 1950, it is first necessary to assess the numbers and types of warships the Royal Navy will be short of on the outbreak of war.

It is considered that apart from Harbour Defence craft, the Navy's greatest shortage will be:–

(i) Coastal and Inshore minesweepers,
(ii) Mine location craft,
and to a lesser extent
(iii) Frigates of all types,
(iv) Small escorts and
(v) MGB/MTBs …

Appendix A gives the total of:–

(a) Our shortages on the outbreak of war and
(b) Our expected losses during the first 18 months of war.

If, between now and 1 January 1950 no aircraft carriers or cruisers other than 8-inch are scrapped and those under construction are completed, it is considered that the Navy would have sufficient ships of these types to stand the expected losses. D of P therefore proposes not to include any aircraft carriers or cruisers in his Forecast of Naval Building Programme to be started on the outbreak of war, which can be summarized as:–

7 Destroyers
43 A/S Frigates
25 A/A Frigates
8 A/D Frigates
11 Submarines
18 Ocean Minesweepers
400 Coastal or Inshore Minesweepers
100 Mine Location Craft
127 MTB/MGBs
166 Small Escorts
5 Minelayers

APPENDIX A

	SHORTAGES ON THE OUTBREAK OF WAR	EXPECTED LOSSES DURING THE FIRST 18 MONTHS OF WAR[1]	TOTAL
Aircraft Carriers		1	1
Cruisers		5	5
Destroyers		7	7
A/S Frigates	28	15	43
A/A Frigates	15	10	25
A/D Frigates	8		8
Submarines		11	11
Ocean Minesweepers		18	18
Coastal Minesweepers	300	101	401
Mine Location Craft	100		100
MTB/MGBs	100	27	127
Small Escorts	50	116	166
Minelayers		5	5

183. *Defence Committee Memorandum*

[CAB 131/7] 8 December 1949

DO(49)81 NAVAL NEW CONSTRUCTION PROGRAMME 1949–50

Memorandum by the First Lord of the Admiralty[2]

For reasons of economy, only two small New Construction Programmes have been put forward since the conclusion of the Second World War; a revised Programme for 1945–46 (CP(45)291 of 22 November 1945) and a Programme for 1947–48 (DO(47)52 of 12 July 1947). These were Programmes of minor essential requirements for training and operational purposes.

New Construction Programme 1949–50

2. My Programme of further New Construction for 1949–50 is again a small one, limited to the most important items, which are as follows:–

1 prototype Anti-Submarine Frigate

2 prototype Coastal Minesweepers

Together with 4 dockyard tugs and a minor programme of miscellaneous small craft.

3. It is necessary to develop an A/S Frigate capable of combating the developments of the modern submarine. Orders for the engines have been placed in anticipation of approval, but the construction of the hull will not start until 1951.

[1] Estimated losses were based on a detailed analysis of WWII losses, also in ADM 1/21305.

[2] An earlier draft (Board Memorandum B.589, reproduced as Doc. No. 165) had been submitted to the Admiralty Board in April.

4. If the prototype proves satisfactory on trial, I shall propose further construction to replace older and slower ships. As an interim measure it is intended to convert a number of fleet destroyers to A/S frigates before 1957. Treasury sanction has already been obtained for the expenditure necessary for the first two conversions and these are now in hand. This has already been announced in Parliament.
5. I have included in the Programme two prototype Coastal Minesweepers because new minesweeping methods and equipment are being developed to counter the development of mine warfare and new design ships are required for this equipment. More vessels of the same type will have to be included in future Programmes.
6. The estimated cost of the further New Construction Programme including the dockyard tugs and miscellaneous small craft is £2,483,000 and the probable spread of expenditure is shown in Table I. The sum of £140,000 has been provided in the Navy Estimates for 1949–50 for the start of the Programme.

Previous Programmes

7. Details of the ships remaining to be completed from previous Programmes are shown in Table II. Work is proceeding on some of these ships, namely 2 Fleet Carriers, 4 Light Fleet Carriers and 8 destroyers, bit work has been suspended on 4 Light Fleet Carriers and 3 Cruisers. One of these 'suspended' Carriers (*Majestic*) is to be sold to the Royal Australian Navy and work will be resumed shortly.
8. Progress is being, or will be, made in this financial year on the following further vessels approved in earlier Programmes:–

1 prototype Aircraft Direction Frigate.
1 prototype Anti-Aircraft Frigate.
2 prototype Submarines (high test peroxide driven).
2 prototype Convertible MTB/MGBs.
1 Surveying Ship.
1 prototype Landing Craft, Personnel.
1 development Build-up Amphibian.

9. As regards the Frigates the construction of one Anti-Aircraft and one Anti-Submarine Frigate was included in the 1945–46 Programme. In DO(47)52 (New Construction Programme 1947–48) the design of the Anti-Submarines Frigate was changed and it was decided that it should be completed as an Aircraft Direction Frigate. The provision in the 1945–46 Programme therefore became one Anti-Aircraft Frigate and one Aircraft Direction Frigate. The machinery was ordered in 1948 and the work on the construction of the ships will commence in 1951. If these vessels prove satisfactory on trial, I shall propose in later Programmes further construction to replace existing ships …

10. The new design Submarines were to be equipped with HTP (high test peroxide) machinery and although they have been ordered, construction is suspended temporarily until engine development is more advanced. Pending the availability of new construction, it is planned to convert a number of 'T' class submarines to fast battery driven operational submarines before 1957. The Treasury have sanctioned the first two such conversions and work has commenced.

11. The contracts for the two prototype convertible MTB/MGBs have been placed.

12. Surveying Ships have generally been provided by the conversion of other types of ships. This is never completely satisfactory and in the 1945 Programme it was approved that two ships designed for surveying should be built. The ships were not laid down and although it was hoped that a start could be made in 1947–48 this was not possible owing to delays in completion of the design and financial considerations. The design has, however, now been settled and although the first ships has not yet been laid down, preparatory work has commenced. The other ship is still required but financial considerations preclude start of work on it for the time being.

13. Owing to delays in design and production, work has not yet been started on the prototype Landing Craft, Personnel. The construction of the vessel will, however, be started this financial year.

14. One of the two Build-up Amphibians is being progressed this year. The second craft has been cancelled except that work on the Track Suspension Unit will be completed to enable comparative trials with that fitted on the first craft to be carried out.

15. Table III shows the vessels outstanding from earlier Programmes which are now regarded as cancelled.

Summary

16. To sum up, I intend that progress, as outlined in the immediately preceding paragraphs, should be made on vessels approved in earlier Programmes and I seek approval to the following new Programme for 1949–50:–

1 prototype Anti-Submarine Frigate
2 prototype Coastal Minesweepers
4 twin screw dockyard tugs
Miscellaneous small craft

At the estimated cost of £2,483,000 and with the probable spread of expenditure as shown in Table I.

Table IV shows the expenditure likely to be incurred in each year for all Programmes which would be in hand.

TABLE I – 1949–50 NEW CONSTRUCTION PROGRAMME

Estimate of Expenditure by Financial Year

Vessels	1949–50	1950–51	1951–52	1952–53	1953–54	Total
	£	£	£	£	£	£
1 – A/S Frigate	1,000	98,000	411,000	415,800	96,000	1,021,800
2 – Prototype Coastal M/S	8,000	175,700	194,000	17,900	–	395,600
3–3,000 HP Dockyard Tug	66,000	335,300	357,000	1,300	–	759,600
1–2,000 HP Dockyard Tug	1,000	72,000	100,000	9,000	–	182,000
Small Craft & Motor Boats	64,000	59,000	1,000	–	–	124,000
	140,000	740,000	1,063,000	444,000	96,000	2,483,000

TABLE II – STATEMENT OF SHIPS REMAINING TO BE COMPLETED FROM APPROVED PROGRAMMES

(Excluding Harbour Service Craft and Motor Boats)

Pro-gramme Year	Class of Ship	Name	Date of Laying Down	Date of Launch	Date of Completion as at present foreseen	Remarks
1935	Magnetic Survey Vessel	*Research*	9.9.37	4.4.39	Uncertain	Work suspended
1940	Fleet Carrier	*Ark Royal*	3.5.43	3.5.50	End of 1952	
1941	Cruisers "Tiger Class"	*Tiger*	1.10.41	25.10.45		Work suspended
1942		*Defence*	24.6.42	2.9.44		Work suspended
1943	Fleet Carriers	*Eagle*	24.10.42	19.3.46	March 1951	
1944	"Ark Royal Class"					
1945	Light Fleet Carriers	*Hercules*	14.10.43	22.9.45		Work suspended
1947–48		*Leviathan*	18.10.43	7.6.45		Work suspended
		Majestic	15.4.43	28.2.45	End 1952	To be completed For RAN
		Powerful	27.11.43	27.2.45		Work suspended
	Cruiser "Tiger Class"	*Blake*	17.8.42	20.12.45		Work suspended
	Light Fleet Carriers	*Albion*	23.3.44	6.5.47	End of 1951	
	"Hermes Class"	*Centaur*	30.5.44	22.4.47	End of 1951	
		Hermes	21.6.44	Uncertain	1953	
		Bulwark	10.5.45	22.6.48	Mid 1952	
	Destroyers "Daring Class"	Eight	Between Sept. 1945 & Mar. 1949	Between Mar 1949 & Jul 1950	Between Mar 1951 & Jun 1952	
				22.4.48		
	MTB	One	10.9.46			
	Prototype Submarine	One	Not yet			
	Surveying Ships	Two	Not yet			One not to be proceeded with for the present
	Frigates	Two	Not yet			One A/D, one A/A
	Prototype Submarine	One	Not yet	24.9.45	May 1950	
	Surveying Ships	*Cook*	30.11.44		Oct. 1950	Laid down as "Bay Class' frigate …
	Build-up Amphibians	Two	E.1			One (E.2) cancelled except track suspension unit
	Convertible MTB/MGB	Two	Not yet			
	Landing Craft Pers.	One	Not yet			
	Prototype Distant Controlled Target	One	Not yet			

TABLE III

Vessels outstanding from approved programmes which it is now proposed to regard as cancelled:–

1 Landing Ship Dock

1 Assault Amphibian

These two vessels were approved as part of the 1947–48 Programme, in which the cost was estimated at £890,000 for the Landing Ship Dock and £88,300 for the Assault Amphibian. The urgency of the Landing Ship Dock has receded, while progress with the Assault Amphibian cannot be made until the Build-up Amphibians (see paragraph 11 of Narrative) have been built and tried out. It is not proposed, therefore, to start work on either vessel in 1950–51 and it would make for convenience if they were regarded as formally cancelled from the 1947–48 Programme. Provision will be made for them in future programmes as may appear necessary.

TABLE IV – NAVY ESTIMATES 1949–50

Estimated Expenditure on New Construction (all Programmes)

	1949–50	1950–51	1951–52	1953–53	1954–55 and later
	£	£	£	£	£
1945 and earlier programme	8,844,000	10,752,000	9,616,000	8,350,000	7,157,000
1945–46 programme	889,000	1,213,000	1,416,000	746,000	267,000
1947–48 programme	906,000	263,000	218,000	40,000	—
1949–50 programme	140,000	740,000	1,063,000	444,000	96,000
Total	10,779,000	12,968,000	12,313,000	9,580,000	7,520,000

184. *Defence Committee Minutes*

[CAB 131/8] 15 December 1949

DO(49) 24th Meeting

. . .[1]

6. Naval New Construction Programme 1949–50

The Committee had before them a memorandum by the First Lord of the Admiralty (DO(49)81) containing the Naval new construction programme for 1949–50.

The First Lord of the Admiralty said that the programme was a modest one which would entail an expenditure of some £2 million spread over four to five years. The amount of money to be allocated in any particular year would be determined annually by the allocations made within the total vote for the Navy. The amount of money to be allocated to the

[1] The Defence Committee also approved the closure of the Dockyard in Bermuda (Item 4).

programme in 1950–51 for instance had been included in the Admiralty share of the Defence Budget for that year which had just been approved by the Cabinet.

The Committee:– Took note of DO(49)81.

185. *Defence Committee Memorandum*

[CAB 131/7] 30 December 1949

DO(49)89 DEFENCE BURDENS AND THE COMMONWEALTH
Memorandum By The Secretary Of State For Commonwealth Relations

Recent discussions in the Defence Committee regarding the size and shape of the United Kingdom's Armed Forces have raised the question of the contributions which are being or could be made by the other members of the Commonwealth to the common purpose of defence. There have also been suggestions in the press that some Commonwealth countries are not bearing an adequate share of this burden …

2. The Minister of Defence has made some comments on this subject (DO(49)66):– "It is often tempting to think, when an effort is called for, that 'the other fellow' is not pulling his weight. So it is with the Dominions. We have given them, and shall continue to give them, every encouragement to develop their forces … But while we can encourage the free countries of the Commonwealth to develop their defence forces, we cannot command them".

Present Defence Position in Other Commonwealth Countries[1]

3. The following statement shows the main facts in each other Commonwealth country:–

CANADA

Pre-War	*Present*
6 Destroyers	1 Aircraft Carrier
5 Minesweepers	1 Cruiser (+ 1 in reserve)
	5 Destroyers (+ 6 in reserve)
	2 Frigates (+ 2 in reserve)
	1 Minesweeper (+8 in reserve)

AUSTRALIA

Pre-War	*Present*
4 Cruisers (+ 2 in reserve)	1 Aircraft Carrier
3 Destroyers (+ 2 in reserve)	1 Cruiser (+ 2 in reserve)
2 Escort Vessels	5 Destroyers (+ 3 in reserve)
1 Survey Ship	4 Frigates (+ 7 in reserve)

[1]Only details of naval forces are reproduced.

	2 Survey Ships
	2 Minesweepers (+30 reserve)

NEW ZEALAND

Pre-War	*Present*
2 Cruisers	1 Cruiser (+ 1 in reserve)
	6 Frigates
	1 Survey Vessel

SOUTH AFRICA

Pre-War	*Present*
Nil	3 Frigates
	2 Minesweepers
	1 Surveying Ship

INDIAN SUB-CONTINENT

(a) The Naval and Air Forces of undivided India were negligible.

(b) India

1 Cruiser
3 Destroyers
7 Frigates
12 Minesweepers

(c) Pakistan

2 Destroyers (with prospect of one additional)
4 Frigates
4 Minesweepers

186. *Joint War Production Staff Memorandum*

[CAB 131/7] 21 December 1949

REPORT BY THE JOINT WAR PRODUCTION STAFF
TO THE MINISTER OF DEFENCE

JWPS(49)98(Final) SERVICE PRODUCTION PROGRAMMES 1950–51

Cost of 1950–51 Programmes and Comparison with Previous Year

The production programmes of the three Services for 1950–51, expressed in terms of money, compare as follows with the programmes planned for 1949–50:–

	1949–50	*1950–51*
	£'000	*£'000*
Admiralty	65,542	78,287
War Office	69,472	70,699
Air Ministry	79,003	92,670

Ministry of Supply	1,920	4,090
Total	215,937	245,746

The above figures, as explained in Section 6, do not include production for Commonwealth or foreign countries, but include such of the additional production under the Western Union programme as will be supplied to United Kingdom forces. The figures are necessarily approximate. Broadly speaking they represent, in the case of stores procured by the Ministry of Supply, the cost of items to be delivered to the Service Departments during the financial year. The Admiralty, however, is its own Supply Department and it total also includes disbursement on ships and other items which take a long time to build and which may have been delivered before the financial year begins, or will not be delivered until after it has ended. For this reason, the totals for each Service are not strictly comparable …

Analysis of the Programmes

The aim of the programmes for 1950–51 is to:–

(a) provide as far as possible for the replacement of the normal wastage of stores and equipment due to current consumption;

(b) continue with the work of reconditioning and, where necessary, with the conversion or modernisation of existing equipments;

(c) proceed, on a limited scale, with the more urgent of the re-equipment plans.

It should be emphasised that there is no possibility, within the limits of the projected financial provision, of making more than a modest contribution towards re-equipment and modernisation.

Because of the depletion of war stocks, much more expenditure is now necessary on the normal replacement of stores and equipment currently expended or worn out by the Forces. In general, the new provision is restricted to the quantities required to maintain stocks at the approved working level.

Large sums are still being spent on the repair and reconditioning of existing equipment and on the conversion or modernisation of this equipment, where feasible, as a less expensive and speedier alternative to entirely new production …

Main Features of each Programme

ADMIRALTY

Repairs and Conversions

The programme provides for the maintenance of the active Fleet and for the continuation of work on the conversion of two submarines to fast battery drive and two destroyers to escort vessels. Provision is also made for continuing large repair work on two aircraft carriers and one cruiser and for starting large repairs on three cruisers, the modernisation of one aircraft carrier and the conversion of two further submarines and five destroyers. It is also planned to modernise four fleet destroyers, but expenditure in 1950–51 will be confined to the production of equipment which must be ordered in advance of the actual work on the ships. Provision has also been made for further progress to be made with the reconditioning of ships of the Reserve Fleet.

The capacity of the Royal Dockyards will continue to be fully occupied with the repair, conversion and modernisation of His Majesty's Ships. A relatively small amount of work, chiefly the refit of ships of the Reserve Fleet, will be carried out by contract in the private ship repair yards; but for the first time for many years the refit of submarines will not be carried out in private yards.

New Construction

The increase in financial provision for new construction is almost entirely on account of continuing work. Because of the economic importance of making good the war losses of the Mercantile Marine, work on new naval ships has been allowed to take second place to merchant new construction and frequently to be regarded as a stand-by job. The rate of new naval construction has in consequence been very slow and therefore uneconomic. The work on the two fleet carriers has at last reached an advanced stage where a rising expenditure on fitting out is essential if serious dislocation in the shipyards is not be caused and unnecessary expenditure incurred. Also, merchant work over a large part of the shipbuilding industry is beginning to ease and in order to maintain an appropriate balance of work and trades and to avoid dislocation in the shipyards, a more normal tempo of work on His Majesty's Ships is now possible and desirable. Continuance of the present slow rate of construction would add to the unemployment problem in the shipyard areas and also inevitably to the final cost of the ships.

The programme provides for work to proceed on the small 1949–50 new construction programme and for a modest beginning to be made on the construction of minesweepers and inshore craft under the Western Union additional production programme.

Naval Aircraft

The programme for all types of naval aircraft has been arranged with the Ministry of Supply to ensure a smooth flow of aircraft delivery and the most economical arrangement for changing over to new types on the production line in the near future.

Future requirements for Sea Furies are approximately 150. On the advice of the Ministry of Supply production of 100 has been arranged for 1950–51, to be followed by the balance in 1951–52. This ensures balanced and economical production in the aircraft firm concerned since the re-equipment plan provides for the introduction into the firm's production line of Sea Hawks in 1951–52.

Twenty of the Firefly aircraft are ordered because of the requirement for a retrospective modification programme during the whole of next year of Firefly Mark 5 to Firefly Mark 6 to enable them to operate Sonobuoys. This will immobilise at least 20 of the Navy's stock at any one time throughout the year …

Stores and Equipment

The programme provides for the inception of a long-term plan for providing for immediate mobilisation requirements of essential stores, clothing and equipment, but not of guns and ammunition. Some initial provision is included for certain essential defence services which must be in operation at the outbreak of war. In certain of these fields (such as Fixed Defences and Degaussing equipment) full emergency requirements would, on the basis of the present rate of provision, take 10–12 years to build up …

187. *Defence Committee Memorandum*

[CAB 131/9] 16 February 1950

DO(50)9 SERVICE PRODUCTION PROGRAMMES 1950–51

Memorandum By The Minister Of Defence

1. When the Service Production Programmes for 1950–51 were discussed by the Defence Committee on 9th January (DO(50) 1st Meeting)[1] I explained that it would probably not be possible to implement them in full within a total Defence Vote of £780 million. Supplementary estimates of about £15 million to £20 million might have proved to be necessary, depending on the amount of shortfall in production and on the savings, which could be achieved in other parts of the Defence Estimates as the result of investigations then proceeding.

2. The Defence Committee were unwilling to approve the production programmes on a basis which assumed the need for supplementary estimates. They invited me to arrange for the adjustment of the programmes so as to bring the estimated expenditure within the approved total of £780 million.

3. This has now been done. I have reviewed the whole field of Defence expenditure in consultation with my Service colleagues and the Chiefs of Staff. Savings have been made over the Votes as a whole. We have agreed that various provisions should be deleted from Votes other than the

[1]Not reproduced.

production Votes in order to reduce to the minimum the serious slowing down of re-equipment which would ensue if the cuts were confined to the production Votes. After allowing for the savings resulting from these steps and for adjustments which were found to be justified on various matters of detail it was found necessary to reduce the provision for production by £11.82 million.

4. As a result of the review, the total Defence estimates have been reduced to £780.82 million, made up as follows:–

	£M
Admiralty	193.00
War Office	299.00
Air Ministry	223.00
Ministry of Supply	65.00
Ministry of Defence	0.82
Total	780.82

5. The cut of £11.82 million falling on the production Votes is made up as follows:–

	£M
Admiralty	4.00
War Office	3.50
Air Ministry	3.02
Ministry of Supply	1.30
Total	11.82

6. It would not be desirable, nor is it necessary, to provide for the whole of these reductions by cutting out complete projects from the production programmes, although some such cuts have had to be made.

7. Over a very wide field the production of the items shown in the programmes previously submitted to the Defence Committee will be continued. In these cases, the necessary savings will be achieved by slowing down the rate of production during the year, to the extent necessary to keep the expenditure within the sums now provided. The extent of this slowing down will depend on the degree of shortfall in deliveries as compared with the published programme. In the case of certain types of aircraft, it may not be necessary in any case to slow down the rate of production. If (for financial reasons) deliveries under the programme prove to be greater than the capacity of the Air Force to absorb them, the possibility of releasing extra aircraft to overseas customers will be considered, as an alternative to reducing the production rate.

8. *Royal Navy*

Two inshore minesweepers and two mine-location craft have been deleted from proposed new construction, the naval aircraft programme

has been cut by over £1/2 million and large cuts have been made in the provision for mobilisation needs of clothing and general stores …
9. The general effect of these cuts is to delay the build-up of our preparedness for war and, so far as the RAF and the Royal Naval Air Service [*sic*] are concerned, by the smaller provision of reserves of aircraft, etc to reduce our ability to withstand the increased rate of wastage which must inevitably follow the outbreak of war …

188. *Board Minute*

[ADM 167/135] 10 February 1950

Limited Conversion of Fleet Destroyer to A/S Frigate.
4335. The Board considered a memorandum on limited conversion of a Fleet Destroyer to A/S Frigate. The Board were advised that since their decision, recorded in Board Minute 4290, the situation had changed in two respects. First, it had become clear that the financial provision for the Royal Navy during the next few years was likely to be even more restricted than had seemed probable earlier. Secondly, the Naval Staff had now modified its previous views in favour of a policy of combining 'first rate' A/S vessels with 'second rates'. It had also been found possible to improve the design of the limited conversion so as to increase its fighting power and yet to reduce its cost.

The Board agreed that provision should be made in the 1950/51 modernisation programme for the conversion of the destroyer HMS 'Tenacious' to second rate A/S frigate as proposed in the memorandum. This conversion should be regarded as a prototype, and a decision whether further limited conversions should be undertaken should be deferred until the Board had considered the Naval Staff views mentioned above and it was known how successful the conversion of HMS 'Tenacious' proved to be.[1]

189. *CNS*[2] *to First Sea Lord*

[ADM 205/74] 24 March 1950

I have had a very careful analysis made by DTASW of:–

(a) the number of escorts and modernisation programme we expect to carry out in 1952, 1954 and 1957.

[1] A total of 10 former destroyers received the 'limited' conversion (Type 16) between 1951 and 1956.

[2] RA Ralph Edwards.

(b) the details of the anti-submarine material which should be in escorts in the years 1952, 1954 and 1957.

(c) the number of minesweepers we should have to meet our minimum requirements, the number of minesweepers which are planned and the consequent shortages which can be expected in the years 1952, 1954 and 1957.

2. This statement indicates that should any additional financial provision be made, first, consideration should be given to the escorts and minesweeping forces and, conversely, if further cuts have to be made it is imperative that shall not fall upon these forces.

TRADE PROTECTION

STATEMENT OF NUMBER OF ESCORTS AND MODERNISATION PROGRAMME
NUMBER OF ESCORTS

The difference for the years 1952, 1954, 1957 between the number of Escorts allowed in "Future Fighting Ships" PD.06/49 and the number previously planned in PD.035/39 taken in conjunction with PDM.205 are shown in RED [*italics*]

	Requirement On D + 6	Planned in 1952	Difference in 1954	Planned in 1957	Difference	Planned	Difference
A.S Frigates	248	106	226 *22*	106	216 *32*	107	215 *33*
A.A Frigates		71		61		59	
A.D. Frigates		16		16		16	
Commercial Trawler A/S Conversions		33		33		33	

STATE OF A/S MATERIAL IN ESCORTS

Estimated progress of the fitting of up-to-date A/S weapons and equipment to Escorts of the Revised Restricted Fleet. Figures in [*italics*] show numbers still to be fitted

	1952					1954					1957				
	Limbo	Squid		Total Fitted	Not Fitted	Limbo	Squid		Total Fitted	Not Fitted	Limbo	Squid		Total Fitted	Not Fitted
	Fitted					Fitted					Fitted				
A.S Frigates	7	44	=	51	*(56)*	13	52	=	67	*(40)*	33	63	=	96	*(11)*
A.A Frigates		3	=	3	*(56)*		16	=	16	*(43)*		37	=	37	*(22)*
A.D. Frigates		2	=	2	*(14)*		7	=	7	*(9)*		15	=	15	*(1)*
Commercial Trawler A/S Conversions	A/S Equipment is available for 25 Coastal Trawlers														
TOTALS	7	49	=	56	*(126)*	15	75	=	90	*(92)*	33	115	=	148	*(34)*

STATEMENT OF NUMBER OF MINESWEEPERS AND NEW PROGRAMME

The deficiencies between the Minimum Emergency Requirements and the Minesweepers allowed in "Future Fighting Ships" PD.06/49 are shown in [*italics*]

	Minimum Emergency Requirements	Planned in 1952	Difference	Planned in 1954	Difference	Planned in 1957	Difference
Ocean	68	61	*7*	61	*7*	61	*7* (see Note 1)
Coastal	244	95	*149*	117	*127*	150	*94* (see Note 1)
Inshore	106	58	*48*	74	*32*	100	*6*
Danlayers	37	12	*25*	12	*25*	12	*25* (see Note 2)

Notes:–
1. 92 Trawlers are planned to be taken up for minesweeping. Of those only 68 can be used on Coastal Minesweeping due to 'Safe Depth' limitations, leaving a net deficit of 26 in 1957. 1957 deficiency in Ocean Minesweepers will be made up by the remaining trawlers.
2. 46 Trawlers and MFVs to be taken up for conversion to danlayers to meet this deficit and give a surplus.

STATE OF MINESWEEPING GEAR

1950	1951 (and onwards)
Mine Countermeasures Working Party investigating position and submitting report in March.	All new construction Minesweepers will be fitted to use existing sweeps and those now under development.

Existing sweepers will require modification of the Control Gear of the Magnetic Sweep to enable them to use gear now under development.

190. *Board Memorandum*

[ADM 167/135] 20 March 1950

B.626 CRUISER PROGRAMME

The Sea Lords have had under consideration the various opinions expressed on the policy to be adopted for modernisation of cruisers …

Numerical Strength of Cruisers

2. Omitting the 8″ cruisers and those on loan to New Zealand there are at present 16 6″ and 8 5.25″ cruisers in the Navy. The planned cruiser strength in the Future Shape and Size of the Navy (1949) is 18 in 1957. As three of these will be Tigers, 15 of our present cruisers will be retained and the remaining 9 disposed of. Of these nine, three will be disposed of when the Tigers come into service (1955–56)[1] and the others are available for disposal when large repairs become necessary.

3. It is planned that 13 of our cruisers are required to be in full commission in peacetime, with two in category 'A' reserve; this leaves three available at any one time for large repairs or modernisation.

Age of 6″ and 5.25″ Cruisers

4. On the assumption that a cruiser requires large repairs after about 10 years of her life, and that no large repairs have yet been carried out, 13 cruisers will be due for large repairs in 1950 and all 24 in 1955. It will, therefore, be necessary to carry out large repairs during the next eight years on 15 ships if our cruiser strength of 18 is to be maintained. This, of course, assumes that no new construction, other than the three Tigers, is completed by 1957. (But see paragraph 23 below).

Factors affecting Modernisation

5. Considerable thought has been devoted to and many papers written on what we should do to improve the fighting efficiency of our cruisers by fitting them with new weapons and control systems. It is fair to say that this problem has only during the last year been studied with a background of readiness for war in 1957, availability of new equipment and severe financial restrictions. It is therefore necessary to discuss these three points now as they will inevitably tie down a policy of modernisation to what is possible as opposed to what is desirable.

Readiness for War

6. The main policy behind the re-equipment programme in the Future Shape and Size of the Navy (1949), is to be prepared for war in 1957. Any programme for modernisation of cruisers should therefore go as far as 1957 but it is not considered necessary at this stage to take it any further.

[1] The three *Tigers* did not enter service until 1959–61.

Availability of New Weapons and Equipment

7. The following are the facts concerning the availability of new weapons and equipment:–

(a) 6″ Cruisers

(i) A new dual-purpose gun and mounting, 6″ or 5″, could probably be made available in 1955/56.

(ii) The 3″/70 mounting to replace the secondary armament could probably be available in 1955.

(iii) The fire control system MRS3 which is required for fitting with the 3″/70 mountings and which is suitable to fit to the present 4-inch secondary armament, will not be available before 1954. A suitable alternative (flyplane type) could probably be available by 1952 ...

(iv) The director to carry type 932 gunnery equipment (splash spotting) to improve the surface gunnery of the main armament will not be available until 1952.

(b) 5.25″ Cruisers

Gunnery equipment, apart from directors to carry type 932 radar, can be provided early 1952.

(c) General

The provision of equipment such as electric generators, which would be required for modernisation of either type of ship, may take up to two years to deliver from the date of ordering.

8. Taking into consideration paragraphs 3 and 7 (a), (b) and (c) and assuming modernisation would take two years, equipment should be available to modernise some 9 cruisers by the end of 1957. This does not of course take financial considerations into account.

Financial Considerations

9. In the Future Shape and Size of the Navy (1949), financial provision was made for modernising three 6″ Cruisers and two 5.25″. The conjectural Navy Estimates for the eight years to 1957/58 was considered the minimum on which the Navy could prepare for a war in 1957 and carry out its normal peacetime functions. Indications are that the Navy will not be voted the money required by the plan during the next three years and therefore it is unlikely to get in full the increased sums required in later years. Under these circumstances it will be exceedingly difficult to find any additional money for an increased programme of cruiser modernisation without drastically curtailing expenditure on some other equally important requirement.

10. The proposals for modernisation and large repair of the Cruisers in this paper vary from those in the Revised Restricted Fleet as shown in the following table:–

Present Scheme	RRF
By 1954	By 1954
Complete Large Repair Four 6″	Complete Large Repair Three 6″
Complete Modernisation Three 5.25″	Complete Large Repair Two 5.25″
In Hand Modernisation Two 6″	Complete Modernisation Two 5.25″
In Hand Modernisation One 5.25″	In Hand Modernisation Two 6″

Modernisation Policy for 6″ Cruisers

11. The Air Defence Working Party of the Ship Design Policy Committee stated in May 1948 that major changes to the armament for AA defence were essential and recommended mounting 6″ DP guns, also that the 3″/70 mounting should as far as possible replace the 4″ secondary armament, but as a minimum the 4″ control should be modernised.

12. DofP therefore included in the Restricted Fleet, which was the forerunner of the Future Shape and Size of the Navy (1949) three 6″ cruisers to be fully modernised.

13. Doubt has since been expressed on the wisdom of modernising the main armament of 6″ cruisers in view of the vast expense and the age of the ships. It is however generally agreed that the secondary armament is the greater weakness and should be improved as far as possible. It is open to question whether it is worthwhile fitting the 3″/70 twin to these cruisers as the mounting is expensive and involves extensive reconstruction. The single 3″/70 might replace the 4″ twins at present fitted without much difficulty but if the guns in either case are controlled by MRS3, the single 3″/70 would be only slightly the better.

14. As regards surface gunnery, it is essential to improve the efficiency of all cruisers by fitting the latest radar sets available.

Modernisation Policy for 5.25″ Cruisers

15. The 5.25″, already being a dual-purpose gun, is suitable for modernisation and from the gunnery point of view these ships can be made satisfactory dual-purpose cruisers for relatively little cost. Two ships have been included in the Future Shape and Size of the Navy, but … more of these ships should be modernised for reasons given above.

Conclusions on Modernisation

16 … (a) The fitting of 6″ dual purpose guns in any of our existing 6″ cruisers is too expensive to be justified in view of the age of the ships and financial limitations.

(b) A new fire control system only should be fitted to the secondary armament of as many 6″ cruisers as funds will permit.

(c) A number of 5.25″ inch cruisers should be put in hand for modernisation as soon as equipment is available.

Proposals for Modernisation

17 … (a) Modernise four 5.25″ cruisers. Ships to be taken in hand up to a maximum of three at any one time, from 1952 onwards.

(b) Fit Flyplane predictors to the secondary armament of thee 6″ cruisers.

(c) Fit the latest surface gunnery radar sets as soon as available to all cruisers as they are taken in hand for large repairs or modernisation.

18. The number of ships under (a) and (b) above is dependent on the cost of modernisation, but the number of 5.25″ Cruiser modernisations may be reduced if the programme suggested in paragraph 23 below is approved.

Numbers of Cruisers of each type to be retained

19. Of the 16 6″ cruisers and 8 5.25″, 15 ships are to be retained. The Sea Lords propose that six of these ships should be 5.25″ leaving 9 6″ to be retained and 7 available for disposal (three on completion of TIGERS and the remainder when large repairs are necessary).

20. It is proposed that nine 6″ Cruisers to be retained should be made up of five Town Class, BELFAST, SWIFTSURE, SUPERB and NEWFOUNDLAND. The Town Class have been suggested for retention in preference to Colony Class as, although they are older, they are likely to give better service in view of their more robust pre-war construction. They are also larger and therefore more suitable for modernisation to increase their fighting efficiency and habitability.

Cruiser Programme

21. … During the next year or two the choice of ships for large repair is largely governed by their present or planned employment … in view of financial considerations the Sea Lords consider that no latitude can be permitted in the first two to four years of the proposed programme. On the other hand, it is considered that the later stages of the proposed programme should be regarded as flexible. It might be possible, for instance, to modernise the last four cruisers due to be taken in hand (SWFTSURE, SUPERB and two DIDOS) although these ships are at present scheduled only for large repairs.

22. No new construction other than the TIGERs has been included in the programme but this is discussed below.

New Construction

23. In the Future Shape and Size of the Navy, it is planned to start the construction of a large cruiser in 1957. No staff requirement for this cruiser have as yet been formulated and it is considered that no action need be taken at present until it is more firmly established what type of cruiser is required.

24. It has been suggested that we should start building a small cruiser, mounting 5″ DP guns, in 1955. (Staff requirements and a preliminary sketch design for this new type of Cruiser/Destroyer are at present under preparation). As this ship would not be ready in 1957 the Sea Lords consider that it is necessary to start construction earlier and therefore propose that one Cruiser/Destroyer should be laid down late in 1953 to be followed by 3 others at yearly intervals up to 1956. Money would be available in part for this programme from the resultant cancellation of repairs to two 5.25″ Cruisers, which could then be disposed of. The earliest date for completion of this first new 'Cruiser/Destroyer' is late 1956…

The following 6″ Cruisers are those nominated for eventual disposal (paragraph 20 refers).[1] No proposals have accordingly been made for large repairs or modernisation …

Instructions have been issued that the following ships[2] are to be surveyed in order that their future may be decided. The one in the best condition will be taken in hand for modernisation early in 1952… The other two will be available for eventual disposal l …

191. *Board Minutes*

[ADM 167/135] 30 March & 6 April 1950

HTP Submarines E.14 and E.15.

4344. … the Board considered a further memorandum[3] proposing that both submarines should carry out full sea trials, including acceptance trials, and that the total complement allowed for the two ships together should be such as to enable one to be kept running … This would mean allowing a one-third crew for the second ship, which … would be taken to sea for short periods with a full crew. Provided that any HTP fuel used for this purpose by the second ship was debited to the quota of fuel allowed for the one HTP submarine in full commission, there would be no significant extra cost in comparison with paying for the second ship to be put into reserve with a reduced complement.

The Board approved these proposals …

[1] *Ceylon, Gambia, Bermuda, Jamaica, Mauritius, Nigeria & Kenya.*

[2] *Phoebe, Argonaut & Dido.*

[3] Board Memorandum B.620 (not reproduced). The paper assumed that a single submarine would consume 3,000 tons of HTP per year, at a cost of £250 per ton – an annual cost, in fuel alone, of £750,000.

Cruiser Conversion Programme

4345. The Board had before them a memorandum on the policy to be adopted for the modernisation of cruisers.[1] The First Lord explained that all it was necessary to determine at the present meeting was which cruisers should be provisionally selected for modernisation, and that he proposed to bring before the Board at a later date the policy to be adopted in scrapping cruisers.

The Board agreed that HM Ships *Glasgow*, *Liverpool*, *Belfast*, *Sirius*, *Royalist* and *Diadem* should be provisionally selected for modernisation or large repairs in accordance with the programme indicated …

192. *Board Memorandum*

[ADM 167/135] 27 April 1950

B.631 DISPOSAL OF SHIPS

At meetings held on the 26th May and 30th May 1949 the Board had before them a Memorandum on the Revised Restricted Fleet. Annex 1 of that paper showed the planned Fleet which the Naval members of the Board recommended as the minimum necessary to meet commitments under the policy of HM Government. The Board agreed to submit the proposals to HM Government on this basis (Board Minute 4285) and they were subsequently circulated …

2. Adoption of this planned Fleet involves the disposal of 3 cruisers, 39 frigates, 12 submarines, 5 ocean minesweepers and various Depot and Maintenance ships with further disposals in the various categories as new ships join the Fleet. To implement this disposal programme, various proposals have been put forward to the Board and these are summarised in Appendix A to this paper. The financial and manning commitments shown as involved in the retention of surplus vessels in Category C Reserve must be taken as rough approximations only, as the complements vary considerably according to the berthing position etc. …[2]

193. *Board Memorandum*

[ADM 167/135] 16 May 1950

B.640 DISPOSAL OF SHIPS

Since the war the Board has considered, at intervals, plans for the required strength of the Navy for a future war. At first these plans were

[1] B.626, reproduced as Doc. No. 190.

[2] Details of ships for disposal are contained in B.640 (Doc No. 193).

based on what was "strategically essential" but when it became apparent there would never be sufficient money to maintain these fleets in times of peace, plans were based on what was "economically possible". The last two plans – those that became known as the "Restricted Fleet" and the "Revised Restricted Fleet" – were based upon this premise.

2. At meetings held on 26 May and 30 May 1949, the Board considered and approved the plan known as the "Revised Restricted Fleet" (now termed the Future Shape and Size of the Navy (1949)). The implementation of this plan, which is designed to produce a balanced fleet for war in 1957, entails broadly as far as ships are concerned:–

(a) The construction of certain new vessels as replacements or additions to those classes in which there is a deficiency on the planned strength (eg A/D frigates, minesweepers).

(b) The modernisation of a proportion of all classes of ships in the fleet except battleships.

(c) The disposal of certain ships of various classes to provide, to some extent, the money or the manpower for (a) or (b) above. These vessels comprise 9 cruisers, 39 frigates, 12 submarines, 5 ocean minesweepers and various depot and maintenance ships. Some of these disposals are planned to take place now and others when ships pass beyond the stage of economical repair; these ships are considered in greater detail below.

3. Cruisers. The cruiser strength of the planned fleet is to be 18 ships. Following consideration by the Board of the cruiser programme, which nominated 18 for retention, it is proposed that 3 ships be disposed of on completion of the TIGER Class and six ships when large repairs become necessary. Nominations for this disposal programme are shown in the Appendix. In addition, India has asked for a second cruiser and has been offered either JAMAICA or NIGERIA; it has also been proposed to offer 3 to Australia for modernisation as replacements for her existing 3 cruisers. In the absence of the[se] sales … or any others which may arise, there will be no alternative but to get rid of them by scrapping.

4. Frigates. The planned frigate strength of the Fleet is 182 ships, comprising 107 A/S frigates, 59 A/A frigates and 16 A/D frigates. Present day strength is 220 frigates comprising 68 A/S frigates, 95 A/A frigates and 57 M-Z class destroyers earmarked for conversion to A/S or A/D frigates. There is therefore at present an excess of 38 vessels to the planned strength, with an overbearing of A/A frigates. It is proposed that the disposal programme for these classes of ships should consist of:–

(a) 17 Type I HUNT Class A/A frigates to be disposed of now.

(b) 12 Type II HUNT Class A/A frigates and 9 RIVER Class A/A frigates to be disposed of when no longer economical to repair. Detailed nominations are in the Appendix to B.631 …

5. HUNT Class frigates were designed as A/A escorts. Types I and II … are unsuitable as ocean escorts owing to a small endurance … are obsolete and of little value … None has been refitted since 1946.

6. The RIVER Class … are obsolete ships of insufficient speed … of the nine ships nominated for disposal … none has been refitted since the war, with the exception of TEST …

…

8. Submarines. In addition to the five submarines it was approved should be scrapped at the Board meeting on 11 May 1950, 1 'T' Class and 3 'S' Class remain for disposal …

9. Factors affecting the selection of ships for disposal. In proposing the above disposal programme, the Naval Staff have taken the following factors into consideration:–

(a) Large numbers of ships, when paid off at the end of the war, were never placed in a proper state of preservation owing to lack of manpower caused by rapid demobilisation. In consequence these ships have deteriorated rapidly. This is particularly applicable to frigates.

(b) If the 38 frigates selected for disposal had been refitted … and properly maintained … the Naval Staff would not ask for their disposal …

(c) It is extremely difficult to find sufficient money within the Naval Estimates for the maintenance and modernisation of the Fleet without the added burden of the ships now under discussion for disposal.

(d) The naval manpower required to man and maintain these ships can only be found at the expense of some existing commitment …

(e) On mobilisation in war the manpower available is just adequate to man the ships which it is planned to retain … it is doubtful whether we should ever be in a position to man these additional ships.

10. Conclusions. Present Admiralty policy and plans are to produce a balanced Fleet for war in 1957, fitted with modern armament and equipment. The size of this Fleet is based on what is "economically possible". Money and manpower are not available to retain and man all the existing ships and modernise the Fleet at the same time. It is therefore necessary to dispose of some ships …

194. *Board Minute*

[ADM 167/135] 11 May 1950

A/S Frigate (Second Rate) Sketch Design.

4361. The Board considered a memorandum concerning the Sketch Design and Legend of Particulars of the Anti-Submarine Frigate (Second Rate) of the 1951 Programme.[1]

This ship would have the same submarine detection gear as the new First-Rate Frigate, but would have less group control and communications equipment and less anti-aircraft and anti-submarine armament. Ships of this type would be used as members of groups of which the First-Rate Frigates would be the leaders. The endurance of the ships would be sufficient to enable them to perform convoy escort duties the whole way across the Atlantic without the necessity to refuel. The full war complement as a private ship would be 143 and the total accommodation provided in the design was for 165 officers and men.

No accurate estimate of the cost of this new type had yet been made. The present tentative estimate was approximately £650,000, assuming that the prototype was built by contract, but a firm figure would be submitted to the Board at a later date.

The Board approved the Sketch Design and Legend of Particulars and decided that alternative titles for this class of ship and for the First-Rate Frigate should be submitted for approval as soon as possible …

195. *Brief for Minister of Defence*

[DEFE 7/593] 11 May 1950

SECURITY OF SEA COMMUNICATIONS

…

On the agenda for your Staff Conference with the Chiefs of Staff on Thursday 11 May, you have included the following item:–

> "The security of sea communications against the most modern submarines must be the primary task. Is it clear that the Navy are concentrating on this or are they still maintaining, for traditional reasons, vessels and establishments that have outlived their usefulness?"

…

For your discussion with the Chiefs of Staff you may like to have before you the following table showing the ships in commission and

[1] The Type 14 *Blackwood* class, 12 of which were commissioned between 1955 and 1958.

reserve in 1950 and, taking into account the United States contribution, the minimum force considered to be required in 1957.

Type	1950 In Commission	1950 In Reserve	1950 Total	1957
Battleships	1	4+	1 + 4+	1 + 4+
Fleet Carriers	3	3	6	5 + 1*
Light Fleet Carriers	4	2	6	4
Aircraft Repair Ships	1	0	1	1
Cruisers	15	12	27	18
Fast Minelayers	0	3	3	3
Destroyers	39	15	54	62
Frigates	60	165	225	182
Submarines	33	30	63	53
Ocean Minesweepers	15	46	61	61
Coastal or Inshore M/S	10	72	82	250
Mine-location Craft	0	0	0	36
Front-line Aircraft	150		150	250

+ Not to be modernised until guided weapons in supply.

* Modernised for deck landing training only.

. . .

The fact that the Navy are concentrating on resources to combat the submarine and mine menace can be seen from the following two tables showing the programme over the next three years.

New Construction

	1950–51	1951–52	1952–53	Total
Frigates	3	0	2	5
Submarines	0	2	0	2
Coastal Minesweepers	5	11	8	24
Inshore Minesweepers	5	8	8	21
Mine Location Craft	6	0	8	14
Coastal Forces MTB/MGB	1	4	4	9
Seaward Defence A/S Craft	2	0	4	6

Modernisation and Conversion

Modernisation of Fleet Carriers	1
Modernisation of Cruisers	1
Modernisation of Destroyers	12
Modernisation of Frigates	9
Convert old Fleet Destroyers to A/S Frigates	10
Convert 'T' Class Submarines to fast battery drive	2

. . .

196. *Defence Committee Memorandum*

[CAB 131/9] 1 May 1950

DO(50)34[1] DEFENCE POLICY AND GLOBAL STRATEGY[2]

Report by the Chiefs of Staff

1. Since our last review in 1947 of the strategic situation many changes have taken place, notably the formation of the Western alliances under the Brussels and North Atlantic treaties and the discovery by Russia of the atomic bomb. We now submit for the Defence Committee a fresh review of Defence Policy and Global Strategy written in the light of these changes and from the joint point of view of a partner in a Western Alliance and a member of the British Commonwealth.

2. The British Commonwealth and the Continental Powers, whether individually or collectively, cannot fight Russia except in alliance with the United States:– nor could the United States fight Russia without the help of the British Commonwealth. Today it makes no sense to think in terms of British strategy or Western European strategy as something individual and independent …

5. Allied defence policy cannot be divided into …'cold' and 'hot' strategy. The former is largely conditioned by our ability in the last resort to defend our interests against armed aggression; while our readiness to fight defensively is inevitably affected by the demands of the cold war …

The Aim in the Cold War

8. This aim, which must be achieved if possible without real hostilities, involves first a stabilisation of the anti-communist front in the present free world and then, as the Western Powers become militarily less weak, the intensification of 'cold' offensive measures aimed at weakening the Russian grip on the satellite states …

The Aim in the Hot War

9. If real hostilities are forced upon the Western Allies the aim will remain broadly the same. Our first preoccupation must be to ensure survival in the face of the initial onslaught. Our ultimate military aim must be to bring the war to the speediest possible conclusion, without Western Europe being overrun, by bringing about the destruction of Russian military power and the collapse of the present regime …

Defence Research

14. … the Allies should not devote too much of their substance to existing means of defence. We must strike the difficult balance between trying

[1] Also COS(50)139, 1 May 1950. DEFE 5/20.

[2] Approved by the Prime Minister and re-issued as DO(50)45(Final) on 20 June.

to be ready too soon with weapons that will be obsolete if and when the attack comes, and being ready too late in the search for the perfect weapons. We must specially beware of preparing for the last war …

General considerations affecting Allied strategy in hot war

18. … We believe that the ability to achieve our aims without active hostilities depends largely upon the threat of the atomic weapon. We consider that weapon to be of decisive importance also in the event of a shooting war …

The Three Main Theatres of War – and the Sea

20. … the war, cold and hot, is indivisible and world-wide. But there are three main theatres in which Allied interests are threatened – Western Europe, the Middle East and East Asia. Against the contingency of shooting war, the Allies have also to provide for the protection of those sea communications which are really vital to survival and to our prospects of ever being able to bring to bear upon the enemy that offensive pressure which alone holds out hope of reasonably early victory …

Western Europe

22. … the defence of Europe – including the United Kingdom – must have top priority …

The Implementation of plans

28. … The rate of progress in transforming paper plans into practical reality now depends in the main on finding the necessary money and industrial capacity to arm and equip the existing manpower. We are convinced that the North Atlantic system of security can become a reality but only on the basis … that the North Atlantic military establishment should be regarded as an integrated balanced force to which the individual powers should contribute those forces to which they are best suited …

The Mediterranean

32. It is obviously important to retain the use of the short sea route to the Middle East as long as this can possible be done without serious prejudice to other interests which are vital … We believe that during the earlier stages of a Russian attack on the Middle East, at least for some years from now, a powerful carrier task-force with its own strong fighter and AA defence could operate in the Eastern Mediterranean and we attach great importance to making one available …

The Far East

36. There is still one very serious gap in our global cold war front. In the West we have the ramparts of the Atlantic Treaty and the European Recovery Programme. In Asia there is no such solidarity. South-East Asia, in hot as well as in cold war, is a secondary but none the less immensely important fron t …

37. The key to the problem in the Far East is China …

Sea Communications

43. The other pillar of Allied strategy remains the security of sea communications vital to the Allies. The British alone cannot afford, as they have done in the past, to protect all the important Allied sea communications. The defence of some must be left to the United States or to other Commonwealth countries; of some the British must take a greater or lesser share in the defence; some must be left unguarded.

One area is really vital, in the sense that if it is not secured the Allies lose the war. That is the North Atlantic and the home waters of the Allied Powers through which run what are literally their life lines. Their peoples cannot feed, their Air Forces cannot fly nor their Armies fight without a reasonably uninterrupted flow of seaborne traffic across the Atlantic. This therefore must be classed as the highest priority. The protection of other sea routes, however important, must not be allowed fatally to compromise the defence of the Atlantic and Allied home waters, or any other first priority commitment such as the air defences of the United Kingdom against atomic attack.

Defence Priorities

44. First Things First

(a) a secure base – which includes –

(i) the air defence of the United Kingdom,

(ii) the defence of our only really vital life lines, those between North America and Europe, and the home waters of the Allied Powers,

(iii) the defence of the front in Europe.

(b) adequate strategic striking power … and the bases from which it can reach its objective.

(c) the base minimum land, air and sea strength to hold our positions in the cold war – which includes the necessary occupation forces and garrisons in Europe, the Middle and Far East and the Pacific.

(d) the minimum forces to hold the Egyptian base …

197. *Pink List [summary]*

[ADM 187/56] 6 June 1950

HOME FLEET

Third Aircraft Carrier Squadron

Implacable	(C-in-C HF)
Theseus	
Vengeance	(AC3)

Fourth Destroyer Flotilla

Agincourt	(D4)
Aisne	
Corunna	
Jutland	

Training Squadron
Vanguard (FOTS)

Second Cruiser Squadron
Superb (CS2)
Cleopatra
Swiftsure

Frigate
Loch Alvie

Fifth Destroyer Flotilla
Solebay (D5)
Cadiz
Gabbard
St. James
St. Kitts
Sluys

Sixth Destroyer Flotilla
Battleaxe (D6)
Crossbow
Scorpion
Broadsword

FISHERY PROTECTION FLOTILLA

Frigates
Cygnet (SOFPS)

Minesweepers
Wave
Romola
Truelove
Mariner
Welcome

SUBMARINE COMMAND

Second Submarine Flotilla
Depot Ship
Maidstone (Capt SM2)
Alaric
Alliance
Aurochs
Scorcher
Sea Devil
Tiptoe
Totem
Tradewind

Third Submarine Flotilla
Depot Ship
Montclare (Capt SM3)
Submarine Target Ships
Woodbridge Haven
Tenacious

Alcide
Amphion
Anchorite
Andrew
Scotsman
Tireless
Trenchant
Truncheon
Tudor

Fourth Submarine Flotilla
(Based on Sydney, Australia)
Tactician
Thorough
Telemachus

Fifth Submarine Flotilla
(Capt SM5 in HMS Dolphin)
Affray
Alderney
Trespasser
Ambush
Artemis
XE7
XE8

On loan to RCN
Astute

ROSYTH COMMAND*

Accommodation Ships
Dodman Point
Girdle Ness
Protector

Fourth Training Flotilla
Wakeful
Whirlwind
Wilton
Wrangler
Heavy Repair Ship
Artifex

Third Training Flotilla
Destroyers
Crispin
Creole
Rapid

Frigates
Loch Fada
Loch Arkaig
Loch Tralaig
Loch Veyatie
Aircraft Maintenance Ship
Perseus

NORE COMMAND*

Destroyers
Bleasdale

Frigates
Hotham
Loch Scavaig

PORTSMOUTH COMMAND*

Aircraft Carriers
Victorious
Cruiser
Birmingham
Destroyers
Finisterre
Opportune
Contest
Minesweepers
Pluto Welfare
Minelayer
Plover

Second Training Flotilla
Zephyr Zest
Myngs Zodiac
Frigates
Helmsdale Leeds Castle
Fleetwood Hedingham Castle
Redpole Tintagel Castle
Starling Flint Castle
Deep Diving Vessel
Reclaim
Royal Yacht
Victoria and Albert

PLYMOUTH COMMAND*

Aircraft Carriers
Illustrious Ocean
Cruisers
Newfoundland
Cadets' Training Cruiser
Devonshire
Heavy Repair Ship
Alaunia

Destroyers
Ulster
Frigates
Burghead Bay
Minesweeper
Pyrrhus

* Excluding ships listed below as under repair or refit.

FRONT LINE NAVAL AIRCRAFT

HOME STATION

Ship	Squadron	Aircraft
Implacable	801	13 Sea Hornet
	813	12 Firebrand
	815	12 Barracuda
Vengeance	802	13 Sea Fury
	814	12 Firefly
	809	8 Sea Hornet
Theseus	702	8 Vampire
	807	13 Sea Fury
	810	12 Firefly

RNVR Squadrons

1830	9 Firefly
1831	9 Seafire
1832	14 Seafire
1833	9 Seafire

MEDITERRANEAN STATION

Ship	Squadron	Aircraft
Glory	804	13 Sea Fury
	812	13 Firefly

FAR EAST STATION

Ship	Squadron	Aircraft
Triumph	800	12 Seafire
	827	13 Firefly

SHIPS UNDER REPAIR AND REFITTING IN UNITED KINGDOM

Aircraft Carriers
Indefatigable
Indomitable
Cruisers
Bermuda Cumberland
Newcastle Sheffield
Frigates
Amethyst Loch Dunvegan
Erne Oakham Castle
Bigbury Bay Falmouth
Destroyer Depot Ship
Tyne

Destroyers
Cadiz Whirlwind
Onslaught Wizard
Relentless Zambesi
Rocket Zephyr
Roebuck Zest
Savage
Minesweepers
Truelove Wave
MFV
Watchful

MEDITERRANEAN FLEET

Despatch Vessel
Surprise
Second Aircraft Carrier Squadron
Glory (FO(Air Med)
First Cruiser Squadron
Gambia (CinC Med)
Phoebe (CS1)
Euryalus Liverpool
First Destroyer Flotilla
Chequers (D1)
Cheviot Chevron
Chieftain Chivalrous
Second Frigate Flotilla
Magpie Pelican
Veryan Bay Mermaid
St Austell Bay Peacock
Loch Scavaig

Destroyer/Submarine Depot Ship
Forth (FO(D) & Capt SM1)
Third Destroyer Flotilla
Gravelines Armada
Saintes (D3) Vigo

First Submarine Squadron
Solent Trump
Sturdy Tabbard
Talent Teredo
Token
Second Minesweeping Flotilla
Fierce (MS2) Rifleman
Chameleon Plucky

SOUTH ATLANTIC STATION

Sixth Cruiser Squadron
Nigeria

Frigates
Actaeon Nereide

AMERICA AND WEST INDIES STATION

Eighth Cruiser Squadron
Glasgow (CinC AWI)

Frigates
Sparrow Snipe

EAST INDIES STATION

Fourth Cruiser Squadron
Ceylon
Mauritius (CinC EI)
Frigates
Loch Glendhu Loch Quoich

PERSIAN GULF DIVISION
Frigates
Wild Goose Flamingo
Wren

FAR EAST STATION

First Aircraft Carrier Squadron
Triumph
Repair Ship
Unicorn
Fifth Cruiser Squadron
Belfast (5CS & FO2 FES)
Jamaica
Kenya
Eighth Destroyer Flotilla
Cossack (D8)
Comus Charity
Consort Cockade
Constance Concord

Third Frigate Flotilla
Black Swan (F3)
Alacrity Hart

Fourth Frigate Flotilla
Mounts Bay (F4)
Cardigan Bay Whitesand Bay
Morecambe Bay St Brides Bay
Despatch Vessel
Alert
Minesweeper
Jaseur
Hospital Ship
Maine

RESERVE SUMMARY

Category 'A"	Category "B'	Category "C"
	Battleships	
		Anson
		Duke of York
		Howe
		King George V
	Aircraft Carriers	
	Warrior	Formidable
	Cruisers	
Diadem	Dido	Argonaut
		Defence
		Newfoundland
		Royalist
		Sirius
	Fast Minelayers	
Apollo		
Ariadne		
Manxman		
	Destroyers	
Teazer	Obdurate	Marne
Troubridge	Obedient	Matchless
Tumult	Termagant	Meteor
Ulysses	Terpsichore	Milne
Undaunted	Tuscan	Musketeer
Undine	Tyrian	Napier
Urania	Grenville	Nizam
Urchin	Vigilant	Noble
Ursa		Norman
Kempenfelt		Orwell
Wager		Paladin
Whelp		Petard
Zealous		Venus
Zebra		Verulam
Zenith		Virago
Alamein		Volage
Barrosa		
Dunkirk		
Matapan		
Barfleur		
Camperdown		
Hogue		
Lagos		
Trafalgar		
Caesar		
Cambrian		
Caprice		
Carron		
Carysfort		
Cassandra		
Cavalier		
Cavendish		
Chaplet		
Childers		
Comet		

Category 'A"	Category "B'	Category "C"
	Frigates Hunts	
[10]	[8]	[20]
	Black Swan	
[6]		
	Bittern	
[1]		
	Bays	
[9]	[1]	
	Lochs	
[10]		
	Rivers	
		[25]
	Castles	
[6]	[13]	
	Flowers	
		[2]
	LSH(S)	
Meon		
	M/S HQ Ship	
Niger		
	Minesweepers Algerines	
[33]	[16]	[2]
	Danlayers	
[9]	[2]	
	Destroyer Depot Ship	
Woolwich		
	Heavy Repair Ships	
Alaunia		Artifex
Rampura	**Escort**	Ausonia
	Maint. Ships	Resource
	Berry Head	
	Duncansby Head	
	Rame Head	
	Fleet Replenish. Ship	
	Bulawayo	
	Monitors	
		Abercrombie
		Roberts

Submarines

Group M	**Group P**	**Group S**
Sanguine	Sea Scout	Spirit
Seneschal	Selene	Springer
Seraph	Sleuth	Subtle
Statesman		Thermopylae
	Group G	Thule
Group F	(refit)	
(refit)	Artful	**Group H**
Acheron	Auriga	(refit)
Aeneas	Scythian	Sirdar
Tally Ho	XE9	Taciturn
Tantalus	XE12	Turpin
	Group J	
	(refit)	
	Sentinel	
	Sidon	
	Truculent	

SHIPS BUILDING IN UK

Name	Where Building	Contractor's Sea Trials Begin	Final Sea Trials	Remarks
		Aircraft Carriers Ark Royal Class		
Eagle	Belfast (Harland & Wolff)	End October	* March 1951	–
Ark Royal	Birkenhead (Cammel Laird)	–	* End 1952	–
		Light Fleet Carriers Majestic Class		
Majestic	Barrow (Vickers)	* July 1952	–	For transfer to RAN
Hercules	–	–	–	Contract cancelled Laid up at Faslane
Leviathan	–	–	–	Contract cancelled Laid up at Portsm'h
Powerful	–	–	–	Contract cancelled Laid up at Belfast
		Hermes Class		
Albion	Tyne (Swan Hunter)	October 1951	* April 1952	Rosyth Docking Complete end June
Centaur	Belfast (Harland & Wolff)	–	* End 1951	
Bulwark	Belfast (Harland & Wolff)	–	* Mid 1952	
Hermes	Barrow (Vickers)	–	* 1953	
		Cruisers Tiger Class		
Blake	Clyde (Fairfield)	–	–	Work suspended Laid up Greenock
Tiger	Clyde (John Brown)	–	–	Work suspended Laid up Dalmuir
Defence	–	–	–	Laid up Gareloch

		Destroyers Daring Class		
Daring	Tyne (Swan Hunter)	* November 1950	* March 1951	–
Dainty	Cowes (J.S. White)	* February 1951	* June/July 1951	–
Diamond	Clyde (John Brown)	* March 1951	* End June 1951	–
Defender (ex Dogstar)	Clyde (Stephen)	April 1951	* Aug/Sept 1951	–
Delight (ex Disdain)	Clyde (Fairfield)	* June 1951	* October 1951	–
Duchess	Southampton (Thornycroft)	* July 1951	* November 1951	–
Decoy (ex Dragon)	Glasgow (Yarrow)	* August 1951	* December 1951	–
Diana (ex Druid)	Glasgow (Yarrow)	* February 1952	* June 1952	–
		Survey Vessels		
Cook (ex Pegwell Bay)	Devonport	15 June	11 July	–
Research	Dartmouth (Philip)	–	–	Magnetic survey vessel. Suspended
Vidal	Chatham	* June 1952	* End July 1952	–

* Tentative date

SOURCES AND DOCUMENTS

Archives

The National Archives (NA)

ADM 1	Admiralty: Correspondence and Papers
ADM 116	Admiralty: Record Office: Cases
ADM 167	Board of Admiralty: Minutes and Memoranda
ADM 187	Admiralty: Naval Staff, Operations Division: Pink Lists
ADM 205	Admiralty: First Sea Lord: Correspondence and Papers
ADM 211	Admiralty: Office Memoranda
ADM 229	Admiralty: Director of Naval Construction: Director's Papers
CAB 65	War Cabinet and Cabinet: Memoranda (WM and CM Series)
CAB 66	War Cabinet and Cabinet: Memoranda (WP and CP Series)
CAB 69	War Cabinet and Cabinet: Defence Committee (Operations) Minutes and Papers (DO Series)
CAB 79	War Cabinet and Cabinet: Chiefs of Staff Committee: Minutes
CAB 80	War Cabinet and Cabinet: Chiefs of Staff Committee: Memoranda
CAB 81	War Cabinet and Cabinet: Chiefs of Staff Committee: Minutes and Papers
CAB 82	War Cabinet and Cabinet: Deputy Chiefs of Staff Committee: Minutes and Papers
CAB 84	War Cabinet and Cabinet: Joint Planning Committee later Joint Planning Staff: Minutes and Memoranda (JP Series)
CAB 119	War Cabinet and Cabinet: Joint Planning Staff: Correspondence and Papers
CAB 128	Cabinet: Minutes (CM and CC Series)
CAB 129	Cabinet: Memoranda (CP and C Series)
CAB 130	Cabinet: Miscellaneous Committees: Minutes and Papers (GEN, MISC and REF Series)

CAB 131	Cabinet: Defence Committee: Minutes and Papers (DO, D and DC Series)
CAB 141	War Cabinet and Cabinet Office: Central Statistical Office: Working Papers
CAB 158	Joint Intelligence Sub-Committee: Memoranda
DEFE 4	Ministry of Defence: Chiefs of Staff Committee: Minutes
DEFE 5	Ministry of Defence: Chiefs of Staff Committee: Memoranda
DEFE 6	Ministry of Defence: Chiefs of Staff Committee: Reports of the Joint Planning Staff
DEFE 7	Ministry of Defence prior to 1964: Registered Files (General Series)
DEFE 9	Ministry of Defence: Papers of Sir Henry Tizard, Chairman of Defence Research Policy Committee
DEFE 10	Ministry of Defence: Major Committees and Working Parties: Minutes and Papers

Naval Historical Branch (NHB)

Blue Lists	Admiralty: Naval Staff, Operations Division: Lists of Ships Building
Undated study	'Future Composition of the Navy and the Relevant Estimates'

Published Works

Bew, John, *Citizen Clem: A Biography of Attlee* (London, 2016).

Brown, David, *Nelson to Vanguard: Warship Development 1923–1945* (London, 2000).

Brown, David & George Moore, *Rebuilding the Royal Navy: Warship Design Since 1945* (London, 2003).

Friedman, Norman, *The Postwar Naval Revolution* (London, 1986).

———, *British Destroyers & Frigates: The Second World War and After* (London, 2006).

Grove, Eric, *Vanguard to Trident: British Naval Policy since World War II* (London, 1987).

Harding, Richard (ed.), *The Royal Navy 1930–2000: Innovation and Defence* (London, 2012).

Hobbs, David, *British Aircraft Carriers: Design, Development and Service Histories* (Barnsley, 2013).

———, *The British Carrier Strike Fleet After 1945* (Barnsley, 2015)

Hore, Peter (ed.), *Dreadnought to Daring: 100 Years of Comment, Controversy and Debate in the Naval Review* (Barnsley, 2012).

Jackson, Bill & Edwin Bramall, *The Chiefs: The Story of the United Kingdom Chiefs of Staff* (London, 1992).
Lewis, Julian, *Changing Direction: British Military Planning for Post-war Strategic Defence, 1942–47* (London, 1988).
Moore, George, *Building for Victory: The Warship Building Programmes of the Royal Navy 1939–1945* (Gravesend, 2003).
Wettern, Desmond, *The Decline of British Seapower* (London, 1982).

Numerical List of Documents
(all The National Archives unless otherwise stated)

Part I: Wartime Planning for the Postwar Fleet, January 1944–August 1945

1	Blue List, 7 Jan 44	11 Jan 1944	NHB
2	Memorandum by DofP for FBC	undated [Dec 1943 or Jan 1944]	ADM 205/36
3	Minutes of First Sea Lord's Meeting	13 Jan 1944	ADM 205/36
4	DofP to First Sea Lord	27 Jan 1944	ADM 205/36
5	Plans Division Memorandum for FBC	19 Feb 1944	ADM 1/17036
6	FBC Memorandum FB(44)14	21 Mar 1944	ADM 116/5151
7	War Cabinet Memorandum WP(44)245	1 May 1944	CAB 66/49
8	War Cabinet Conclusions, 65th Meeting	18 May 1944	ADM 229/34
9	Board Memorandum B.374	15 May 1944	ADM 205/41
10	Board Minute 3954	19 May 1944	ADM 167/120
11	Memorandum by Controller	9 June 1944	ADM 116/5052
12	Plans Division Memorandum PD.0154/1944	11 Sept 1944	ADM 116/5052
13	COS Memorandum COS(44)597(O) Annex I	7 July 1944	CAB 80/85
14	JPS Memorandum JP(44)226(O)	25 Aug 1944	CAB 84/65
15	FBC Memorandum FBC(44)17 Revised	28 Aug 1944	ADM 205/36
16	FBC Minutes, 10th Meeting	29 Aug 1944	ADM 205/36
17	Board Minute 3983	22 Nov 1944	ADM 167/120
18	DACR to Fifth Sea Lord	4 Dec 1944	ADM 1/17395
19	Minutes of Fifth Sea Lord's Meeting	13 Dec 1944	ADM 1/17395
20	Minute by Head of Air Branch	5 Feb 1945	ADM 1/17395
21	Minutes of Sea Lords' Meeting	28 Feb 1945	ADM 205/51
22	JPS Memorandum JP(44)226(Final)	3 Jan 1945	CAB 84/65
23	Board Memorandum B.403	19 Feb 1945	ADM 167/125
24	Memorandum by DofP, PD/OL.046/45	5 Mar 1945	ADM 205/53
25	Minute by DofP	23 April 1945	ADM 1/18659
26	Report by Battleship Committee	1 May 1945	ADM 1/17251

27	Note by First Sea Lord	24 April 1945	ADM 205/51
28	Plans Division Memorandum PD/OL.0133/45	29 May 1945	ADM 167/125
29	Treasury Letter to all Departments	14 May 1945	ADM 167/125
30	War Cabinet Memorandum WP(45)307	16 May 1945	ADM 167/125
31	COS Memorandum COS(45)373(O)	5 June 1945	ADM 116/5658
32	COS Memorandum COS(45)484(O)	22 July 1945	CAB 80/96
33	Second Sea Lord to First Lord's Office	9 Aug 1945	ADM 116/5658
34	COS Memorandum COS(45)402(O)	16 June 1945	CAB 80/94
35	Cabinet Memorandum CP(45)54	29 June 1945	CAB 66/67
36	Admiral (Submarines) to Secretary of Admiralty	21 June 1945	ADM 1/19610
37	Minute by Head of Military Branch	19 July 1945	ADM 1/19610

Part II: Postwar Retrenchment, August 1945–March 1947

38	Notes on Controller's Monthly Meeting	22 Aug 1945	ADM 116/5342
39	Minutes of Fifth Sea Lord's Meeting	24 Aug 1945	ADM 1/17477
40	Mottershead to First Lord	28 Aug 1945	ADM 116/5342
41	Note for First Lord	29 Aug 1945	ADM 116/5658
42	Minute by DofP	2 Sept 1945	ADM 1/19610
43	Plans Division Memorandum PD 0139/45	5 Sept 1945	ADM 205/50
44	COS Memorandum COS(45)565(O)	6 Sept 1945	CAB 80/97
45	Cabinet Memorandum CP(45)170	14 Sept 1945	CAB 129/2
46	Cabinet Memorandum CP(45)161	8 Sept 1945	CAB 129/2
47	Defence Committee Minutes, 7th Meeting	5 Oct 1945	CAB 69/7
48	Plans Division Memorandum PD.0140/45	12 Sept 1945	ADM 1/17300
49	DNC Memorandum 10852/45	10 Oct 1945	ADM 1/19096
50	PAS, Admiralty to US (London)	22 Oct 1945	ADM 1/17300
51	Loose Minute by First Lord	26 Oct 1945	ADM 1/17300
52	DNC Memorandum 10873/45	16 Oct 1945	ADM 1/19096
53	Defence Committee Memorandum DO(45)22	24 Oct 1945	CAB 69/7
54	COS Minutes, 264th Meeting	1 Nov 1945	CAB 79/41
55	Defence Committee Memorandum DO(45)28	5 Nov 1945	CAB 69/7
56	Defence Committee Minutes, 13th Meeting	8 Nov 1945	CAB 69/7
57	Board Memorandum B.434	5 Nov 1945	ADM 167/124
58	Anonymous Loose Minute	23 Nov 1945	ADM 1/17797
59	Cabinet Conclusions, 56th Meeting	27 Nov 1945	CAB 128/7
60	Admiral (Submarines) to Secretary of Admiralty	4 Dec 1945	ADM 1/18578

61	Minutes of VCNS Meeting	28 Dec 1945	ADM 1/19301
62	Mottershead to First Lord	13 Dec 1945	ADM 1/19096
63	Mottershead to First Lord	15 Dec 1945	ADM 1/19096
64	Note by Mottershead	23 Dec 1945	ADM 1/19096
65	JPS Memorandum JP(45)277(Final)	7 Jan 1946	CAB 84/76
66	COS Memorandum COS(46)5(O)	8 Jan 1946	CAB 80/99
67	Defence Committee Minutes, 1st Meeting	11 Jan 1946	CAB 131/1
68	COS Memorandum COS(46)9(O) (Revise)	15 Jan 1946	CAB 80/99
69	Defence Committee Memorandum DO(46)7	17 Jan 1946	CAB 131/2
70	Defence Committee Minutes, 3rd Meeting	21 Jan 1946	CAB 131/1
71	DofP to VCNS	23 Jan 1946	ADM 205/65
72	COS Memorandum COS(46)39(O)	10 Feb 1946	CAB 80/99
73	Defence Committee Memorandum DO(46)20	13 Feb 1946	CAB 131/1
74	Defence Committee Minutes, 5th Meeting	15 Feb 1946	CAB 131/1
75	JPS Memorandum JP(45)259(Final)	26 Jan 1946	CAB 84/75
76	Defence Committee Memorandum DO(46)12	6 Feb 1946	CAB 131/2
77	Defence Committee Minutes, 4th Meeting	8 Feb 1946	CAB 131/1
78	Defence Committee Memorandum DO(46)18	12 Feb 1946	CAB 131/2
79	Board Memorandum B.446	13 Feb 1946	ADM 167/127
80	Board Minute 4065	14 Feb 1946	ADM 167/126
81	JTWC Memorandum TWC(46)12	21 Mar 1946	CAB 81/74
82	Blue List, 31 Mar 1946	3 April 1946	NHB
83	Admiral (Submarines) to VCNS	5 April 1946	ADM 1/19428
84	COS Memorandum COS(46)131(O)	2 May 1946	CAB 80/101
85	VCNS to First Sea Lord	4 May 1946	ADM 205/65
86	Minutes of First Sea Lord's Meeting	5 June 1946	ADM 167/127
87	Board Memorandum B.469	8 July 1946	ADM 167/127
88	Defence Committee Memorandum DO(46)97	26 July 1946	CAB 131/3
89	Plans Division Memorandum PD/OL.0204/45	12 Sept 1946	ADM 1/20906
90	Defence Committee Memorandum DO(46)117	9 Oct 1946	CAB 131/3
91	Defence Committee Minutes, 27th Meeting	17 Oct 1946	CAB 131/1
92	Defence Committee Memorandum DO(46)135	8 Nov 1946	CAB 131/3
93	COS Minutes, 176th Meeting	3 Dec 1946	CAB 79/54
94	COS Minutes, 187th Meeting	23 Dec 1946	CAB 79/54
95	Defence Committee Memorandum DO(47)3	7 Jan 1947	CAB 131/4

96	Lang to Wilson Smith	18 Dec 1946	ADM 1/20417
97	Defence Committee Minutes, 2nd Meeting	14 Jan 1947	CAB 131/5
98	Plans Division Memorandum PD.012/47	26 Feb 1947	ADM 1/20906
99	Report by Principal Personnel Officers' Committee	19 Mar 1947	DEFE 5/1

Part III: The Nine-Year Plan, March 1947–November 1948

100	JPS Memorandum JP(46)164(Final) Section IX	31 Mar 1947	CAB 84/84
101	JPS Memorandum JP(47)67(Final)	19 May 1947	DEFE 4/4
102	Defence Committee Memorandum DO(47)44	22 May 1947	DEFE 5/4
103	COS Minutes, 74th Meeting	11 June 1957	DEFE 4/4
104	Board Memorandum B.513	22 May 1947	ADM 167/129
105	Defence Committee Memorandum DO(47)52	12 July 1947	CAB 131/4
106	Defence Committee Minutes, 16th Meeting	17 July 1947	CAB 131/5
107	JPS Memorandum JP(47)97(Final)	8 July 1947	DEFE 6/3
108	COS Minutes, 98th Meeting	31 July 1947	DEFE 4/6
109	JIC Memorandum JIC(47)7/2 Final	6 Aug 1947	CAB 158/1
110	Board Memorandum B.520	26 July 1947	ADM 167/129
111	Board Minute 4171	31 July 1947	ADM 167/128
112	Memorandum by DofP	1 Aug 1947	ADM 1/20667
113	COS Minutes, 106th Meeting	20 Aug 1947	DEFE 4/6
114	Board Memorandum B.526	28 Aug 1947	ADM 167/129
115	Board Minute 4175	29 Aug 1947	ADM 167/128
116	COS Minutes, 112th Meeting	30 Aug 1947	DEFE 4/6
117	COS Memorandum COS(47)184(O)	1 Sept 1947	DEFE 5/5
118	Defence Committee Memorandum COS(47)68	15 Sept 1947	CAB 131/4
119	Defence Committee Minutes, 20th Meeting	18 Sept 1947	CAB 131/5
120	Defence Committee Memorandum DO(47)74	25 Sept 1947	CAB 131/4
121	Defence Committee Minutes, 22nd Meeting	29 Sept 1947	CAB 131/5
122	JPS Memorandum JP(47)129(Final)	11 Nov 1947	DEFE 6/3
123	COS Minutes, 148th Meeting	27 Nov 1947	DEFE 4/9
124	Board Memorandum B.533	17 Nov 1947	ADM 167/129
125	Defence Committee Memorandum DO(47)96	15 Dec 1947	CAB 131/4
126	Defence Committee Minutes, 27th Meeting	19 Dec 1947	CAB 131/5
127	Defence Committee Memorandum DO(48)3	5 Jan 1948	CAB 131/6
128	DofP to Head of Military Branch	22 Jan 1948	ADM 116/5966

129	DofP to VCNS	1 Mar 1948	ADM 1/21473
130	JPS Memorandum JP(48)11(Final)	8 April 1948	DEFE 4/12
131	Board Memorandum B.556	18 June 1948	ADM 167/131
132	JIC Memorandum JIC(48)42(O) (Final)	12 June 1948	CAB 158/1
133	DofP to VCNS	20 July 1948	ADM 205/69
134	Special Military Branch Acquaint 3358	23 July 1948	ADM 116/5966
135	Defence Committee Memorandum DO(48)45	20 July 1948	CAB 131/6
136	Defence Committee Memorandum DO(48)46	26 July 1948	CAB 131/6
137	Defence Committee Minutes, 13th Meeting	27 July 1948	CAB 131/5
138	Defence Committee Memorandum DO(48)53	11 Aug 1948	CAB 131/6
139	COS Memorandum COS(48)212(O)	21 Sept 1948	DEFE 5/12
140	COS Minutes, 136th Meeting	24 Sept 1948	DEFE 4/16
141	PPO Memorandum PPO/P(48)27	28 Sept 1948	DEFE 4/16
142	COS Memorandum COS(48)227(O) Annex I	2 Oct 1948	DEFE 5/12
143	COS Memorandum COS(48)148	2 Nov 1948	DEFE 5/8

Part IV: The Revised Restricted Fleet, December 1948–June 1950

144	Defence Committee Memorandum DO(48)83	6 Dec 1948	CAB 131/6
145	Defence Committee Minutes, 23rd Meeting	8 Dec 1948	CAB 131/5
146	JPS Memorandum JP(48)123(Final)	8 Dec 1948	DEFE 6/7
147	Board Memorandum B.577	1 Jan 1949	ADM 167/133
148	Board Memorandum B.579	27 Jan 1949	ADM 167/133
149	Board Minutes 4270–4271	1 Feb 1949	ADM 167/132
150	DPC Memorandum DPC(49)1	18 Feb 1949	CAB 131/7
151	SDPC Memorandum SDPC(49)7	20 Jan 1949	ADM 116/5632
152	Plans Division Memorandum PD.R51/75	25 Jan 1947	ADM 116/5632
153	Minute by Director of Manning	7 Feb 1949	ADM 1/21473
154	Naval Assistant to First Lord	25 Feb 1949	ADM 1/21473
155	Board Minutes 4277–4280	21 Mar 1949	ADM 167/132
156	Paper by ACNS	13 April 1949	ADM 205/83
157	Harwood Report	28 Feb 1949	CAB 131/7
158	COS Minutes, 48th Meeting	28 & 30 Mar 1949	DEFE 4/20
159	Board Minute 4283	12 April 1949	ADM 167/132
160	COS Memorandum COS(49)143	23 April 1949	DEFE 5/14
161	COS Minutes, 77th Meeting	25 May 1949	DEFE 4/22
162	Defence Committee Memorandum DO(49)48	21 June 1949	CAB 131/7

163	Defence Committee Memorandum DO(49)50	22 June 1949	CAB 131/7 & DEFE 7/592
164	Standing Committee of Service Ministers Minutes	22 June 1949	DEFE 7/592
165	Board Memorandum B.589	21 April 1949	ADM 167/133
166	Memorandum by DofP, PDR 51/107	4 May 1949	ADM 205/83
167	DofP to First Sea Lord & VCNS	21 May 1949	ADM 205/84
168	Board Memorandum B.590	23 May 1949	ADM 205/84 & ADM 167/133
169	Board Minutes 4285 & 4287	26 & 30 May 1949	ADM 167/132
170	COS Memorandum COS(49)236	14 July 1949	ADM 1/21547 & DEFE 5/15
171	Board Memorandum B.595	14 June 1949	ADM 167/133
172	Board Memorandum B.602	29 July 1949	ADM 167/133
173	JPS Memorandum JP(49)63(S) (Final)	29 July 1949	DEFE 6/9
174	First Sea Lord to Air Marshal Sir William Elliot	6 Sept 1949	DEFE 7/610
175	Report by Inter-Departmental Committee on Defence Estimates	19 Sept 1949	CAB 131/7
176	COS Memorandum COS(49)313(Final)	27 Sept 1949	CAB 131/7
177	Defence Committee Memorandum DO(49)66	18 Oct 1949	CAB 131/7
178	Defence Committee Minutes, 19th Meeting	19 Oct 1949	CAB 131/8
179	Defence Committee Minutes, 20th Meeting	16 Nov 1949	CAB 131/8
180	Defence Committee Minutes, 21st Meeting	21 Nov 1949	CAB 131/8
181	Defence Committee Minutes, 22nd Meeting	29 Nov 1949	CAB 131/8
182	Note by DofP	undated [1949]	ADM 1/21305
183	Defence Committee Memorandum DO(49)81	8 Dec 1949	CAB 131/7
184	Defence Committee Minutes, 24th Meeting	15 Dec 1949	CAB 131/8
185	Defence Committee Memorandum DO(49)89	30 Dec 1949	CAB 131/7
186	JWPS Memorandum JWPS(49)98(Final)	21 Dec 1949	CAB 131/7
187	Defence Committee Memorandum DO(50)9	16 Feb 1950	CAB 131/9
188	Board Minute 4335	10 Feb 1950	ADM 167/135
189	ACNS to First Sea Lord	24 Mar 1950	ADM 205/74
190	Board Memorandum B.626	20 Mar 1950	ADM 167/135
191	Board Minutes 4344–4345	30 Mar 1950 & 6 April 1950	ADM 167/135
192	Board Memorandum B.631	27 April 1950	ADM 167/135

193	Board Memorandum B.640	16 May 1950	ADM 167/135
194	Board Minute 4361	11 May 1950	ADM 167/135
195	Brief for Minister of Defence	11 May 1950	DEFE 7/593
196	Defence Committee Memorandum DO(50)34	1 May 1950	CAB 131/9
197	Pink List	6 June 1950	ADM 187/56

INDEX

NAVY RECORDS SOCIETY – LIST OF VOLUMES
(as at 1 July 2023)

1. *State Papers relating to the Defeat of the Spanish Armada, 1588.* Vol. I. Ed. Professor J.K. Laughton.
2. *State Papers relating to the Defeat of the Spanish Armada, 1588.* Vol. II. Ed. Professor J.K. Laughton.
3. *Letters of Lord Hood, 1781–1783*. Ed. D. Hannay.
4. *Index to James's Naval History*, *1886*, by C.G. Toogood. Ed. Hon. T.A. Brassey.
5. *Life of Captain Stephen Martin, 1666–1740*. Ed. Sir Clements R. Markham.
6. *Journal of Rear Admiral Bartholomew James*, *1752–1828*. Eds. Professor J.K. Laughton & Cdr. J.Y.F. Sullivan.
7. *Hollond's Discourses of the Navy, 1638 and 1659 and Slyngesbie's Discourse on the Navy, 1660*. Ed. J.R. Tanner.
8. *Naval Accounts and Inventories of the Reign of Henry VII, 1485–1488 and 1495–1497*. Ed. M. Oppenheim.
9. *The Journal of Sir George Rooke, 1700–1702*. Ed. O. Browning.
10. *Letters and Papers relating to the War with France, 1512–1513*. Ed. A. Spont.
11. *Papers relating to the Navy during The Spanish War, 1585–1587*. Ed. J.S. Corbett.
12. *Letters and Papers of Admiral of the Fleet Sir Thomas Byam Martin, 1733–1854*, Vol. II (see Vol. 24). Ed. Admiral Sir Richard Vesey Hamilton.
13. *Letters and Papers relating to the First Dutch War, 1652–1654*, Vol. I. Ed. S.R. Gardiner.
14. *Dispatches and Letters relating to the Blockade of Brest, 1803–1805*, Vol. I. Ed. J. Leyland.
15. *History of the Russian Fleet during the reign of Peter The Great, by a Contemporary Englishman, 1724.* Ed. Vice-Admiral Sir Cyprian A.G. Bridge.
16. *Logs of the Great Sea Fights, 1794–1805*, Vol. I. Ed. Rear Admiral Sir T. Sturges Jackson.

17. *Letters and Papers relating to the First Dutch War, 1652–1654*, Vol. II. Ed. S.R. Gardiner.
18. *Logs of the Great Sea Fights, 1794–1805*, Vol. II. Ed. Rear Admiral Sir T. Sturges Jackson.
19. *Letters and Papers of Admiral of the Fleet Sir Thomas Byam Martin, 1773–1854*, Vol. III (see Vol. 24). Ed. Admiral Sir R. Vesey Hamilton.
20. *The Naval Miscellany*, Vol. I. Ed. Professor J.K. Laughton.
21. *Dispatches and Letters relating to the Blockade of Brest, 1803–1805.* Vol. II. Ed. J. Leyland.
22. *The Naval Tracts of Sir William Monson*, Vol. I. Ed. M. Oppenheim.
23. *The Naval Tracts of Sir William Monson*, Vol. II. Ed. M. Oppenheim.
24. *Letters and Papers of Admiral of the Fleet Sir Thomas Byam Martin, 1773–1854*, Vol. I. Ed. Admiral Sir R. Vesey Hamilton.
25. *Nelson and the Neapolitan Jacobins*. Ed. H.G. Gutteridge.
26. *A Descriptive Catalogue of the Naval Mss. in the Pepysian Library*, Vol. I. Ed. J.R. Tanner.
27. *A Descriptive Catalogue of the Naval Mss. in the Pepysian Library*, Vol. II. Ed. J.R. Tanner.
28. *The Correspondence of Admiral John Markham, 1801–1807*. Ed. Sir Clements R. Markham.
29. *Fighting Instructions, 1530–1816*. Ed. J.S. Corbett.
30. *Letters and Papers relating to the First Dutch War, 1652–1654*, Vol. III. Eds. S.R. Gardiner and C.T. Atkinson.
31. *The Recollections of James Anthony Gardner, 1775–1814*. Ed. Admiral Sir R. Vesey Hamilton and Professor J.K. Laughton.
32. *Letters and Papers of Charles, Lord Barham, 1758–1813*, Vol. I. Ed. Professor Sir J.K. Laughton.
33. *Naval Songs and Ballads*. Ed. Professor C.H. Firth.
34. *Views of the Battles of the Third Dutch War.* Ed. J.S. Corbett.
35. *Signals and Instructions, 1776–1794*. Ed. J.S. Corbett.
36. *A Descriptive Catalogue of the Naval Mss. in the Pepysian Library*, Vol. III. Ed. J.R. Tanner.
37. *Letters and Papers relating to the First Dutch War, 1652–1654*, Vol. IV. Ed. C.T. Atkinson.
38. *Letters and Papers of Charles, Lord Barham, 1758–1813*, Vol. II. Ed. Professor Sir J.K. Laughton.
39. *Letters and Papers of Charles, Lord Barham, 1758–1813*, Vol. III. Ed. Professor Sir J.K. Laughton.
40. *The Naval Miscellany*, Vol. II. Ed. Professor Sir J.K. Laughton.
41. *Letters and Papers relating to the First Dutch War, 1652–1654.* Vol. V. Ed. C.T. Atkinson.

42. *Papers relating to the Loss of Minorca, 1756*. Ed. Captain. H.W. Richmond.
43. *The Naval Tracts of Sir William Monson*, Vol. III. Ed. M. Oppenheim.
44. *The Old Scots Navy, 1689–1710*. Ed. J. Grant.
45. *The Naval Tracts of Sir William Monson*, Vol. IV. Ed. M. Oppenheim.
46. *Private Papers of George, 2nd Earl Spencer, 1794–1801*, Vol. I. Ed. J.S Corbett.
47. *The Naval Tracts of Sir William Monson*, Vol. V. Ed. M. Oppenheim.
48. *Private Papers of George, 2nd Earl Spencer, 1794–1801*, Vol. II. Ed. J.S. Corbett.
49. *Documents relating to the Law and Custom of the Sea*, Vol. I, *1205–1648*. Ed. R.G. Marsden.
50. *Documents relating to the Law and Custom of the Sea*, Vol. II, *1649–1767*. Ed. R.G. Marsden.
51. *The Autobiography of Phineas Pett*. Ed. W.G. Perrin.
52. *The Life of Admiral Sir John Leake*, Vol. I. Ed. G.A.R. Callender.
53. *The Life of Admiral Sir John Leake*, Vol. II. Ed. G.A.R. Callender.
54. *The Life and Works of Sir Henry Mainwaring*, Vol. I. Ed. G.E. Manwaring.
55. *The Letters of Lord St. Vincent, 1801–1804*, Vol. I. Ed. D. Bonner-Smith.
56. *The Life and Works of Sir Henry Mainwaring*, Vol. II. Eds. G.E. Manwaring and W.G. Perrin.
57. *A Descriptive Catalogue of the Naval Mss. in the Pepysian Library*, Vol. IV. Ed. J.R. Tanner.
58. *Private Papers of George, 2nd Earl Spencer, 1794–1801*, Vol. III. Ed. Rear Admiral H.W. Richmond.
59. *Private Papers of George, 2nd Earl Spencer, 1794–1801*, Vol. IV. Ed. Rear Admiral H.W. Richmond.
60. *Samuel Pepys's Naval Minutes*. Ed. Dr. J.R. Tanner.
61. *The Letters of Earl St. Vincent, 1801–1804*, Vol. II. Ed. D. Bonner-Smith.
62. *The Letters and Papers of Admiral Viscount Keith*, Vol. I. Ed. W.G. Perrin.
63. *The Naval Miscellany*, Vol. III. Ed. W.G. Perrin.
64. *The Journal of the 1st Earl of Sandwich, 1659–1665*. Ed. R.C. Anderson.
65. *Boteler's Dialogues*. Ed. W.G. Perrin.
66. *Letters and Papers relating to the First Dutch War, 1652–1654*, Vol. VI (& index). Ed. C.T. Atkinson.
67. *The Byng Papers*, Vol. I. Ed. W.C.B. Tunstall.
68. *The Byng Papers*, Vol. II. Ed. W.C.B. Tunstall.

69. *The Private Papers of John, Earl Sandwich, 1771–1782*. Vol. I, *1770–1778*. Eds. G.R. Barnes & J.H. Owen.
70. *The Byng Papers*, Vol. III. Ed. W.C.B. Tunstall.
71. *The Private Papers of John, Earl Sandwich, 1771–1782*, Vol. II, *1778–1779*. Eds. G.R. Barnes & J.H. Owen.
72. *Piracy in the Levant, 1827–1828*. Ed. Lt. Cdr. C.G. Pitcairn Jones R.N.
73. *The Tangier Papers of Samuel Pepys*. Ed. E. Chappell.
74. *The Tomlinson Papers*. Ed. J.G. Bullocke.
75. *The Private Papers of John, Earl Sandwich, 1771–1782*, Vol. III, 1779–1780. Eds. G.R.T. Barnes & Cdr. J.H. Owen.
76. *The Letters of Robert Blake*. Ed. Rev. J.R. Powell.
77. *Letters and Papers of Admiral the Hon. Samuel Barrington*, Vol. I. Ed. D. Bonner-Smith.
78. *Private Papers of John, Earl Sandwich*, Vol. IV. Eds. G.R.T. Barnes & Cdr. J.H. Owen.
79. *The Journals of Sir Thomas Allin, 1660–1678*, Vol. I, *1660–1666*. Ed. R.C. Anderson.
80. *The Journals of Sir Thomas Allin, 1660–1678*, Vol. II, *1667–1678*. Ed. R.C. Anderson
81. *Letters and Papers of Admiral the Hon. Samuel Barrington*, Vol. II. Ed. D. Bonner-Smith.
82. *Captain Boteler's Recollections, 1808–1830*. Ed. D. Bonner-Smith.
83. *The Russian War, 1854: Baltic and Black Sea*. Eds. D. Bonner-Smith & Capt. A.C. Dewar R.N.
84. *The Russian War, 1855: Baltic*. Ed. D. Bonner-Smith.
85. *The Russian War, 1855: Black Sea*. Ed. Capt. A.C. Dewar.
86. *Journals and Narratives of the Third Dutch War*. Ed. R.C. Anderson.
87. *The Naval Brigades of the Indian Mutiny, 1857–1858*. Ed. Cdr. W.B. Rowbotham.
88. *Patee Byng's Journal, 1718–1720*. Ed. J.L. Cranmer-Byng.
89. *The Sergison Papers, 1688–1702*. Ed. Cdr. R.D. Merriman.
90. *The Keith Papers*, Vol. II. Ed. C. Lloyd.
91. *Five Naval Journals, 1789–1817*. Ed. Rear Admiral H.G. Thursfield.
92. *The Naval Miscellany*, Vol. IV. Ed. C. Lloyd.
93. *Sir William Dillon's Narrative of Professional Adventures, 1790–1839*, Vol. I, *1790–1802*. Ed. Professor M. Lewis.
94. *The Walker Expedition to Quebec, 1711*. Ed. Professor G.S. Graham.
95. *The Second China War, 1856–1860*. Eds. D. Bonner-Smith & E.W.R. Lumby.
96. *The Keith Papers*, Vol. III. Ed. C.C. Lloyd.

97. *Sir William Dillon's Narrative of Professional Adventures, 1790–1839*, Vol. II, *1802–1839*. Ed. Professor M. Lewis.
98. *The Private Correspondence of Admiral Lord Collingwood*. Ed. Professor E. Hughes.
99. *The Vernon Papers, 1739–1745*. Ed. B.McL. Ranft.
100. *Nelson's Letters to his Wife and Other Documents, 1785–1831*. Ed. G.P.B. Naish.
101. *A Memoir of James Trevenen, 1760–1790*. Ed. Professor C.C. Lloyd.
102. *The Papers of Admiral Sir John Fisher*, Vol. I. Ed. Lt. Cdr. P.K. Kemp R.N.
103. *Queen Anne's Navy*. Ed. Cdr. R.D. Merriman R.I.N.
104. *The Navy and South America, 1807–1823*. Eds. Professor G.S. Graham & Professor R.A. Humphreys.
105. *Documents relating to the Civil War*. Eds. Rev. J.R. Powell & E.K. Timings.
106. *The Papers of Admiral Sir John Fisher*, Vol. II. Ed. Lt. Cdr. P.K. Kemp R.N.
107. *The Health of Seamen*. Ed. Professor C.C. Lloyd.
108. *The Jellicoe Papers*, Vol. I, *1893–1916*. Ed. A Temple Patterson.
109. *Documents relating to Anson's Voyage Round the World, 1740–1744*. Ed. Dr. G. Williams.
110. *The Saumarez Papers: The Baltic 1808–1812*. Ed. A.N. Ryan.
111. *The Jellicoe Papers*, Vol. II, *1916–1935*. Ed. A Temple Patterson.
112. *The Rupert and Monk Letterbook, 1666*. Eds. Rev. J.R. Powell & E.K. Timings.
113. *Documents relating to the Royal Naval Air Service*, Vol. I, *1908–1918*. Ed. Capt. S.W. Roskill.
114. *The Siege and Capture of Havana, 1762*. Ed. Professor D. Syrett.
115. *Policy and Operations in the Mediterranean, 1912–1914*. Ed. E.W.R. Lumby.
116. *The Jacobean Commissions of Enquiry, 1608 and 1618*. Ed. A.P. McGowan.
117. *The Keyes Papers*, Vol. I, *1914–1918*. Ed. Professor P.G. Halpern.
118. *The Royal Navy and North America: The Warren Papers, 1736–1752*. Ed. Dr. J. Gwyn.
119. *The Manning of the Royal Navy: Selected Public Pamphlets, 1693–1873*. Ed. Professor J.S. Bromley.
120. *Naval Administration, 1715–1750*. Ed. Professor D.A. Baugh.
121. *The Keyes Papers*, Vol. II, *1919–1938*. Ed. Professor P.G. Halpern.
122. *The Keyes Papers*, Vol. III, *1939–1945*. Ed. Professor P.G. Halpern.

123. *The Navy of the Lancastrian Kings: Accounts and Inventories of William Soper, Keeper of the King's Ships, 1422–1427*. Ed. Dr. S. Rose.
124. *The Pollen Papers: The Privately Circulated Printed Works of Arthur Hungerford Pollen, 1901–1916*. Ed. Dr. J.T. Sumida.
125. *The Naval Miscellany*, Vol. V. Ed. N.A.M. Rodger.
126. *The Royal Navy in the Mediterranean, 1915–1918*. Ed. Professor P.G. Halpern.
127. *The Expedition of Sir John Norris and Sir Francis Drake to Spain and Portugal, 1589*. Ed. Professor R.B. Wernhan.
128. *The Beatty Papers*, Vol. I. *1902–1918*. Ed. Professor B.McL. Ranft.
129. *The Hawke Papers, A Selection: 1743–1771*. Ed. Dr. R.F. Mackay.
130. *Anglo-American Naval Relations, 1917–1919*. Ed. M. Simpson.
131. *British Naval Documents 1204–1960*. Eds. Professor J.B. Hattendorf, Dr. R.J.B. Knight, A.W.H. Pearsall, Dr. N.A.M. Rodger & Professor G. Till.
132. *The Beatty Papers*, Vol. II, *1916–1927*. Ed. Professor B.McL. Ranft.
133. *Samuel Pepys and the Second Dutch War*. Ed. R. Latham.
134. *The Somerville Papers*. Ed. M. Simpson with assistance from J. Somerville.
135. *The Royal Navy in the River Plate, 1806–1807*. Ed. J.D. Grainger.
136. *The Collective Naval Defence of the Empire, 1900–1940*. Ed. Professor N. Tracy.
137. *The Defeat of the Enemy Attack on Shipping, 1939–1945*. Ed. Dr. E.J. Grove.
138. *Shipboard Life and Organisation, 1731–1815*. Ed. B. Lavery.
139. *The Battle of the Atlantic and Signals Intelligence: U-boat Situations and Trends, 1941–1945*. Ed. Professor D. Syrett.
140. *The Cunningham Papers*, Vol. I: *The Mediterranean Fleet, 1939–1942*. Ed. M. Simpson.
141. *The Channel Fleet and the Blockade of Brest, 1793–1801*. Ed. Dr. R. Morriss.
142. *The Submarine Service, 1900–1918*. Ed. N.A. Lambert.
143. *Letters and Papers of Professor Sir John Knox Laughton, 1830–1915*. Ed. Professor A.D. Lambert.
144. *The Battle of the Atlantic and Signals Intelligence: U-boat Tracking Papers, 1941–1947*. Ed. Professor D. Syrett.
145. *The Maritime Blockade of Germany in the Great War: The Northern Patrol, 1914–1918*. Ed. J.D. Grainger.
146. *The Naval Miscellany*, Vol. VI. Ed. Dr. M. Duffy.
147. *The Milne Papers. Papers of Admiral of the Fleet Sir Alexander Milne 1806–1896*, Vol. I, *1820–1859*. Ed. Professor J. Beeler.

148. *The Rodney Papers*, Vol. I, *1742–1763*. Ed. Professor D. Syrett.
149. *Sea Power and the Control of Trade: Belligerent Rights from the Russian War to the Beira Patrol, 1854–1970*. Ed. N. Tracy.
150. *The Cunningham Papers*, Vol. II: *The Triumph of Allied Sea Power, 1942–1946*. Ed. M. Simpson.
151. *The Rodney Papers*, Vol. II, *1763–1780*. Ed. Professor D. Syrett.
152. *Naval Intelligence from Germany: The Reports of the British Naval Attachés in Berlin, 1906–1914*, Ed. Dr. M.S. Seligmann.
153. *The Naval Miscellany*, Vol. VII. Ed. Dr. S. Rose.
154. *Chatham Dockyard, 1815–1865. The Industrial Transformation*. Ed. P. MacDougall.
155. *Naval Courts Martial, 1793–1815*. Ed. Dr. J. Byrn.
156. *Anglo-American Naval Relations, 1919–1939*. Ed. M. Simpson.
157. *The Navy of Edward VI and Mary*. Eds. Professor D.M Loades and Dr. C.S. Knighton.
158. *The Royal Navy and the Mediterranean, 1919–1929*. Ed. Professor P. Halpern.
159. *The Fleet Air Arm in the Second World War*, Vol. I, *1939–1941*. Ed. Dr. B. Jones.
160. *Elizabethan Naval Administration*. Eds. Professor D.M. Loades and Dr. C.S. Knighton.
161. *The Naval Route to the Abyss: The Anglo-German Naval Race, 1895–1914*. Eds. Dr M.S. Seligmann, Dr F. Nägler and Professor M. Epkenhans.
162. *The Milne Papers. Papers of Admiral of the Fleet Sir Alexander Milne 1806–1896*, Vol. II, *1860–1862*. Ed. Professor J. Beeler.
163. *The Mediterranean Fleet, 1930–1939*. Ed. Professor P. Halpern.
164. *The Naval Miscellany*, Vol. VIII. Ed. Mr B. Vale.
165. *The Fleet Air Arm in the Second World War*, Vol. II, *1942–1943*. Ed. Dr B. Jones.
166. *The Durham Papers*. Ed. Dr H.L. Rubinstein.
167. *Nelson's Letters to Lady Hamilton and Related Documents*. Ed. Dr M.R.E. Czisnik.
168. *Anglo-American-Canadian Naval Relations, 1943–1945*. Ed. M. Simpson.
169. *Papers and Correspondence of Admiral Sir John Thomas Duckworth*, Vol 1: *The French Revolutionary War, 1793–1802*. Ed. J.D. Grainger.
170. *The Milne Papers. Papers of Admiral of the Fleet Sir Alexander Milne 1806–1896*, Vol. 3, *1862–1864*. Ed. Professor J. Beeler.

OCCASIONAL PUBLICATIONS.

O.P. 1 *The Commissioned Sea Officers of the Royal Navy, 1660–1815.* Eds. Professor D. Syrett & Professor R.L. DiNardo.

O.P. 2 *The Anthony Roll of Henry VIII's Navy*. Eds. Dr. C.S. Knighton & Professor D.M. Loades.